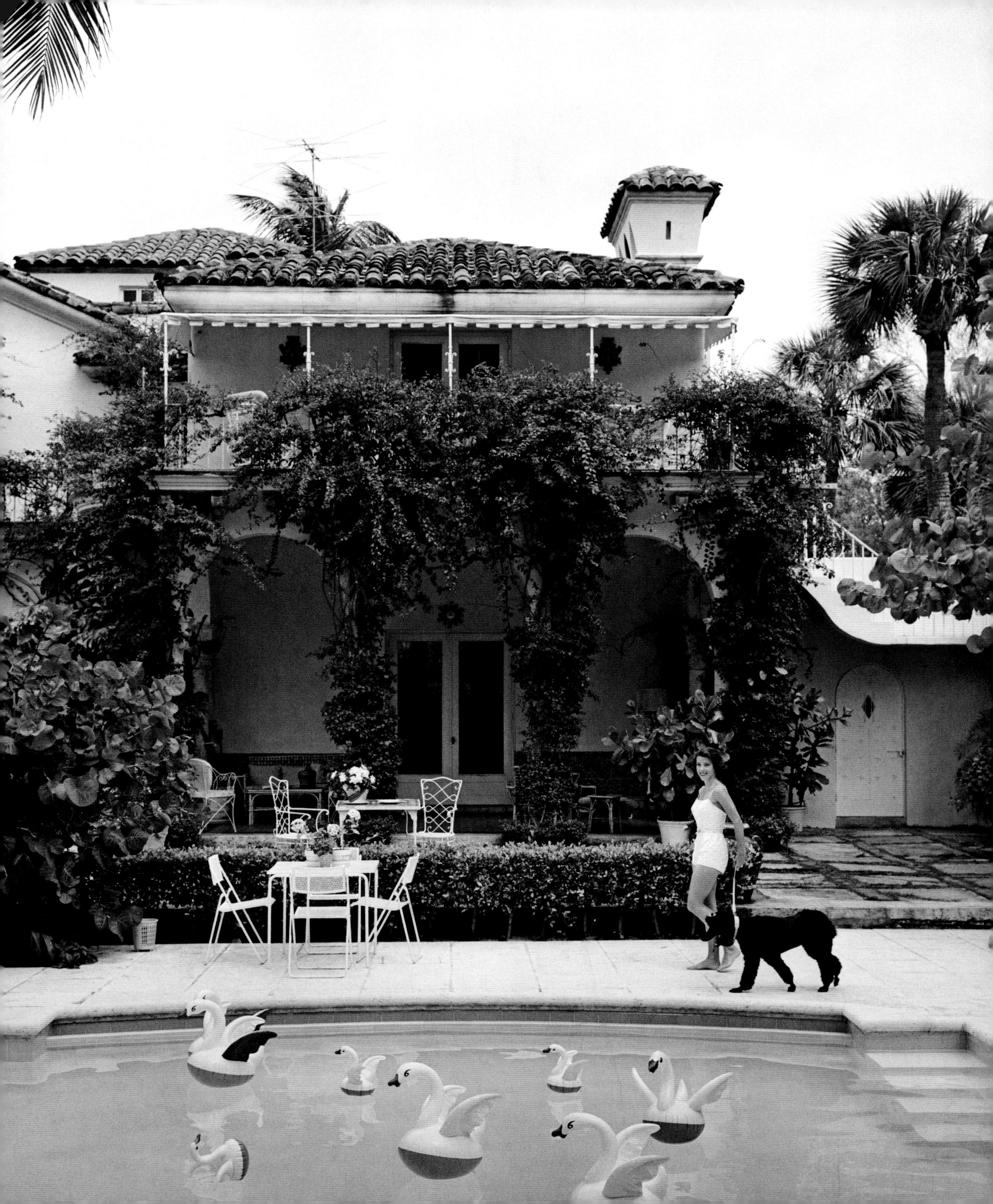

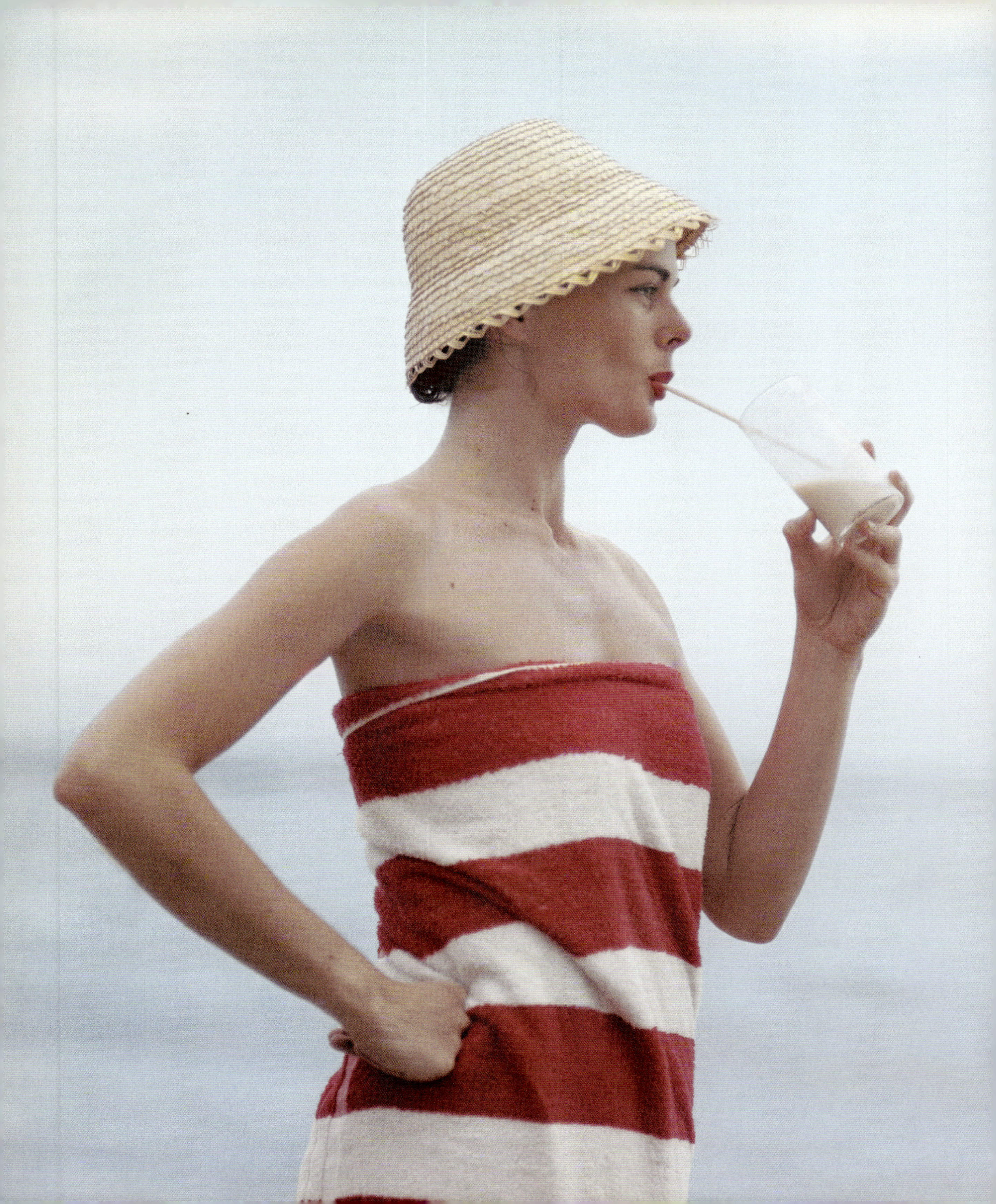

SLIM AARONS
WOMEN

PHOTOGRAPHS BY SLIM AARONS

WRITTEN & EDITED BY LAURA HAWK

GETTY IMAGES   ABRAMS, NEW YORK

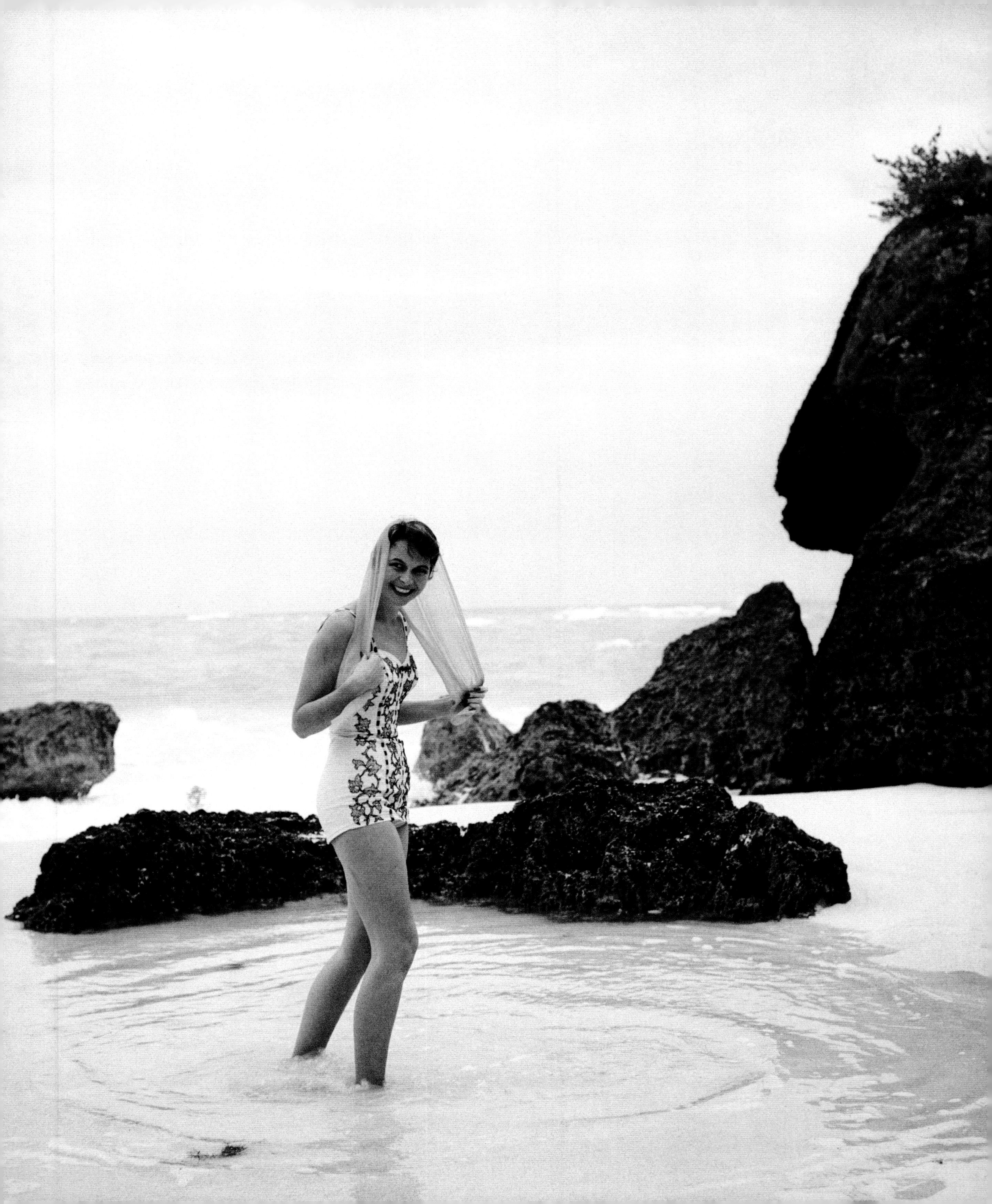

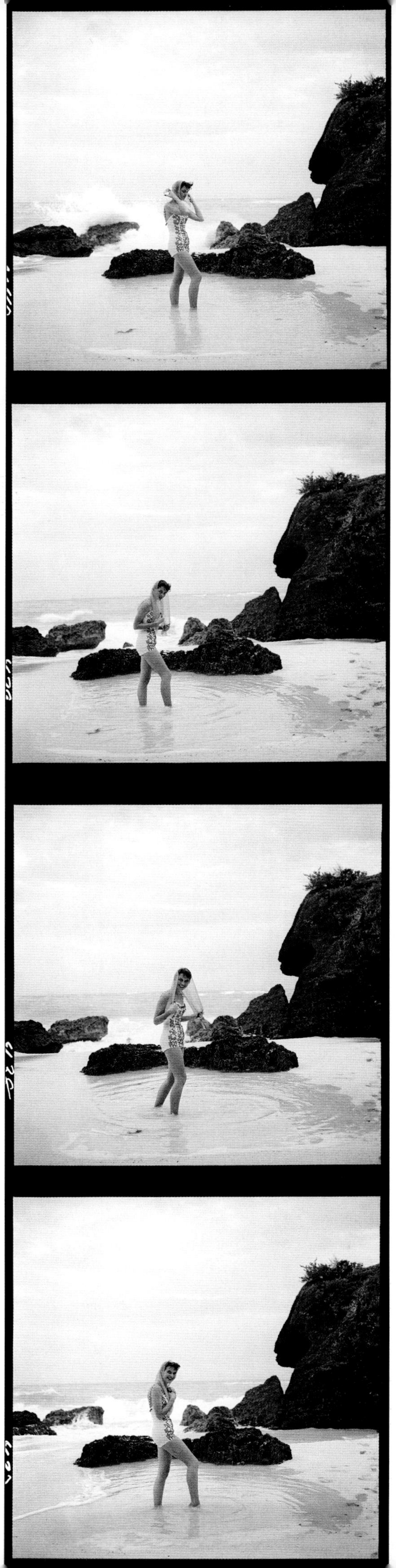

CONTENTS

INTRODUCTION

6

. . . ATTRACTIVE PEOPLE . . .

25

. . . DOING ATTRACTIVE THINGS . . .

83

. . . IN ATTRACTIVE PLACES . . .

171

page 1 Mrs. A. Atwater Kent Jr. (the former Hope Hewlett Parkhurst) at H. Loy Anderson's pool, Palm Beach, circa 1955. A. Atwater Kent, her father-in-law, was the inventor who pioneered the home radio.

page 2 Actress Dee Hartford, Jamaica, 1958. See also pages 28 and 50.

opposite and left Anne Bindon, model and competitive swimmer, stretches her legs at Long Bay Beach, Bermuda, 1955.

INTRODUCTION

"You're Going to Love Me and You're Going to Hate Me"

IN THE SUMMER OF 1977 the celebrated photographer Slim Aarons was lunching at the magnificent Goldener Hirsch Hotel in Salzburg with Princess Grace of Monaco and her daughter Caroline. At one point, as he later told the story time and again, Grace was struck by what she thought was a wonderful idea: "Oh, Slim, why not hire Caroline to work with you? You two could travel around the world together!" Caroline excitedly nodded her approval. As Slim recounted the story his chest puffed ever so slightly, his posture corrected, and a devilish smile crept across his face. "Why, what a wonderful idea, Grace," he replied, making it clear he was on a first-name basis with the princess and fully in command. "But there's just one question," he said. He already knew the answer, but he strung it along, luxuriating in it. "Caroline," he asked, leveling his gaze at her, "can you get up in the mornings . . . early? *Every* morning?" They both looked at him, perplexed, so the story went, and shortly thereafter the subject changed.

When it came to his work ethic, Slim Aarons made no concessions—not even to princesses. Several years later I would learn this firsthand, after meeting Slim when he stopped by my mother's Park Avenue apartment for an informal interview. He was looking for a new sidekick; I was considering a job change.

Slim was exactly as I will always remember him: upbeat, self-satisfied, and wearing a boyish grin that was one part Tom Sawyer, one part Huck Finn. We exchanged a bit of small talk as Slim gulped down a ginger ale—his drink of choice no matter where in the world he was. And never one to equivocate, he began a deluge of questions that had to be answered immediately. "Can you be ready to leave with little advance notice? Is your passport in order? Can you stand the sun? Can you write? Can you walk up hills at high altitudes? Do you speak any languages? Can you get up in the morning, early? *Every* morning?" *Um, yes,* I stammered, taken aback (though intrigued, of course). I will confess at this point: I'd never heard of Slim Aarons. I'd been working on a cattle ranch in Oklahoma since graduating from college and had no clue about the famed, longtime Roving Editor of *Town & Country* magazine, who was by then in his early fifties.

I thought he was finished, but then came his list of rules: "No heavy suitcases, no tennis rackets, no hairdresser appointments, no minibar tabs, no shopping, no dry cleaning, no days off, no boyfriends, no sightseeing, and for God's sake—no cameras." *Not a problem,* I said as I shook my head.

My unqualified assent to his list of demands must have been convincing for, after a bit more small talk, he finally stood up to leave, signaling the end of the interview. At the door, as we shook hands, he looked me squarely in the eyes and told me in so many words that I'd gotten the job: "You're going to love me and you're going to hate me."

So began a working relationship that would span more than ten years, by the end of which I would move with my young family not far from Slim's home in Katonah, New York. He would become a surrogate grandfather to my two daughters and remain a great friend until his death in 2006. By the end of that decade, Slim and I had logged upwards of four hundred thousand miles of travel, exploring some of the most dazzling enclaves of exclusivity in the world and reporting on the people who frequented them.

ABOUT THIS BOOK

Slim's visual narratives give us an intimate glimpse into the world of the upper classes and their rituals in the pursuit of leisure. That his half century of work continues to captivate successive generations of admirers—and that this is the fifth book published on his photography—reveals not only a yearning for an irretrievable time gone by but also a universal fascination with the seemingly forbidden worlds of wealth and privilege.

opposite Slim's uncompromising tenacity in "getting the shot" was legendary; here he is perched atop an extension ladder to photograph starlet Mara Lane (see pages 32 and 33) by the Sands Hotel pool, Las Vegas, 1954.

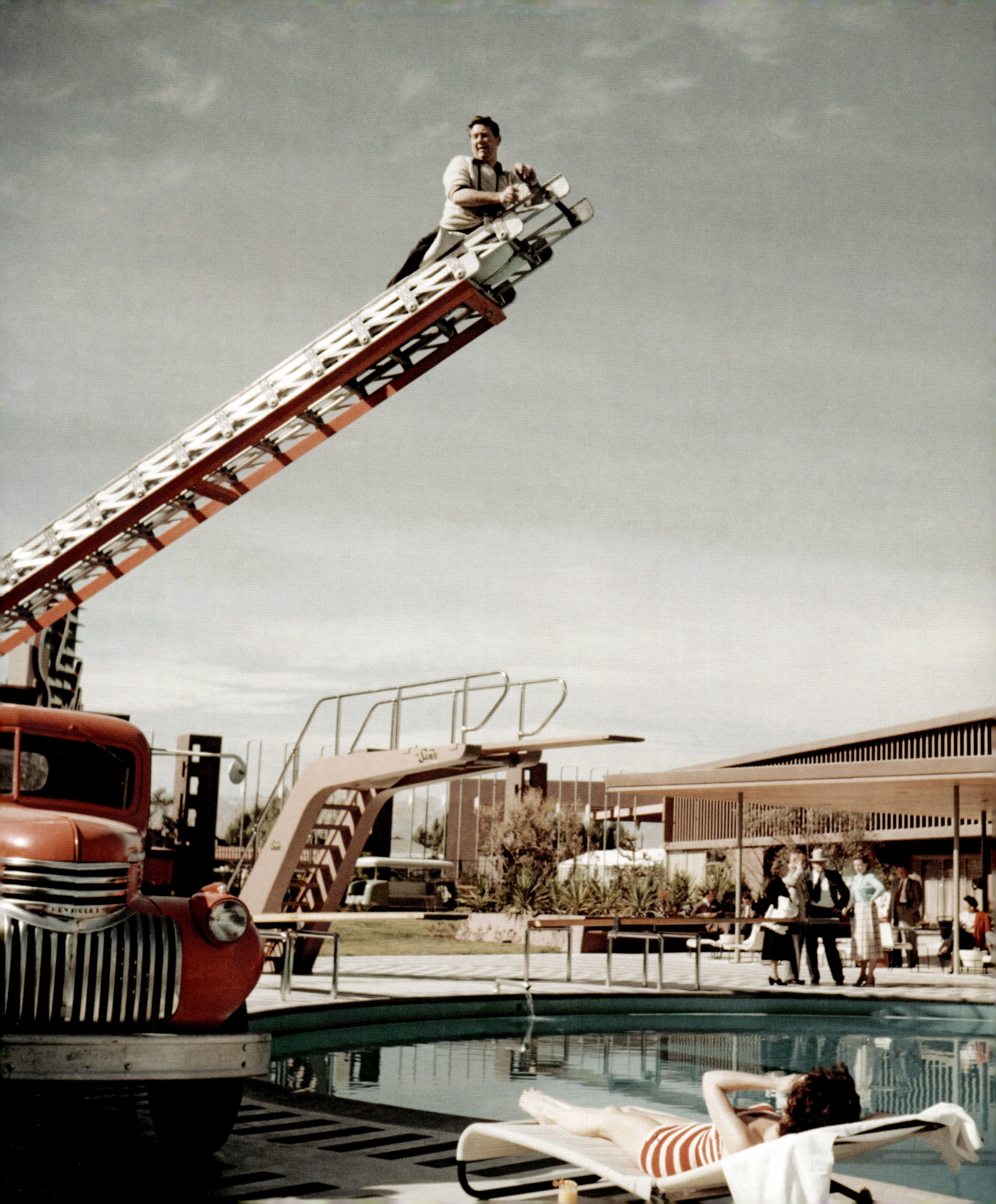

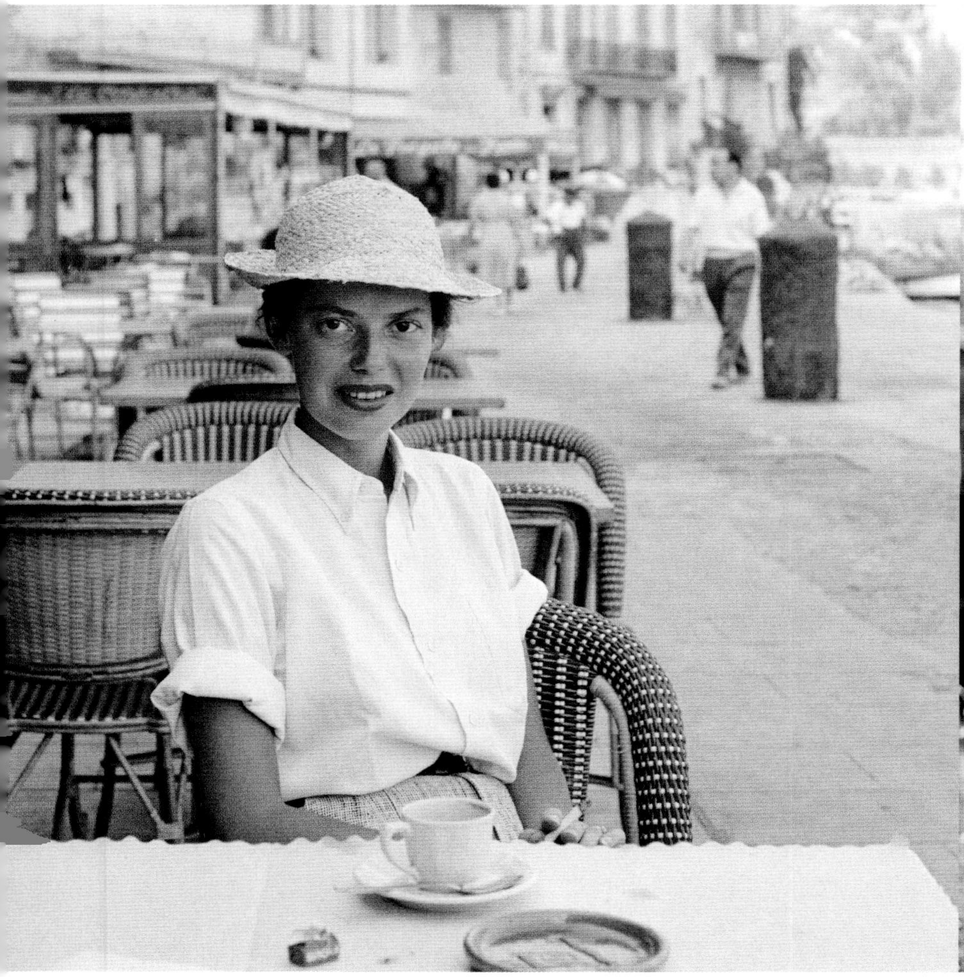

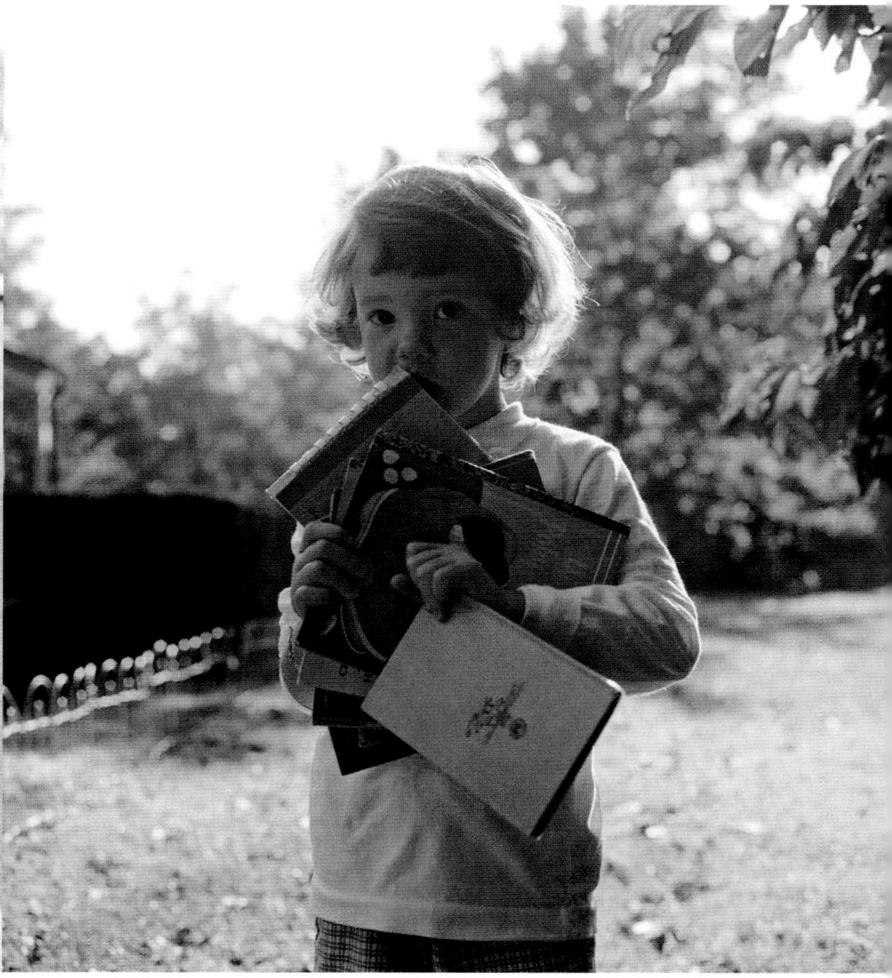

The collection showcased in this book has been culled from Slim's vast body of work with the goal of examining his photography of women, the principal subjects of his work. Another objective of this collection is to feature little-known material never before published in book form. Many of these previously unpublished images provide fresh representations of Slim's vision and allow the viewer to observe his attention to detail.

In this book you will find a host of extraordinary women—among them, the women who shared Slim's life and work: his daughter, Mary Aarons (above right); his wife, Rita Dewart Aarons (above left, 58, and 59); the society decorator Lady Anne Orr-Lewis (page 122); the Austrian princess and socialite Manni Wittgenstein (page 188); the Avon heiress Baroness Terry von Pantz (page 202); and the Roman photographer Elisabetta Catalano (pages 45 and 49).

Featuring a broad sampling of Slim's work, the book spans every decade in which he photographed, with pictures that were taken in North America, South America, Europe (including Eastern Europe), Asia, and parts beyond. Of course, any book on the women Slim photographed throughout his career must include his most iconic images of renowned figures, such as Babe Paley (pages 36 and 150), Marilyn Monroe (page 60), Ursula Andress (pages 68 and 69), Eva Gabor (page 63), Marlene Dietrich (page 151), Jackie Kennedy (page 155), C. Z. Guest (pages 14, 54, and 201), and the Duchess of Windsor (pages 160 and 161). In many cases these famous images are paired with several outtakes from the original photo shoot, offering an unprecedented insider's look into how Slim worked (for example, see pages 34, 72, and 161).

In this collection of photographs, the exclusive realm that Slim so deftly navigated is once again revealed, but with a tight focus on the women who inhabited this world. In addition to these images, to give further context and insight, I've recounted in many of the captions, where relevant, my observations gleaned from working with him for more than a decade.

above Two of the extraordinary women who shared Slim's life were his wife Rita and his daughter Mary. Rita is shown in Monaco, 1956 (left), and Mary is pictured in Bedford, New York, in 1960 (right).

SLIM'S EARLY YEARS

It's dizzying to think of the precipice upon which young Slim Aarons stood when he started out in the late 1940s, camera in hand, ready to take on the world. His half century of work would witness societal shifts that were monumental: the dawn of photojournalism, the rise of commercial air travel and birth of the "jet set," the global sweep of television, civil rights, the women's movement, the pill, AIDS, color photography, and the invention of the Internet. Equally astonishing were the changes in the way society viewed women. At the start of his career, Slim's female subjects were primarily society ladies and movie stars. His 1955 photograph of socialite C. Z. Guest poolside in Palm Beach (see page 14) would capture the imagination of a generation and become the archetype for Slim's female subjects. By the end of his career in the early 1990s, however, he had photographed an array of women who played far more varied roles in society: ranchers, lawyers, poets, politicians, surgeons, historians, race car drivers, big game hunters, philanthropists, opera singers, designers, and royalty in their own right.

Slim certainly didn't set out to become "the preeminent chronicler of American and European society in the postwar period," as observed by photo editor Crary Pullen, Slim's longtime friend and colleague. What is indisputable is that George Allen Aarons was a born adventurer with a lifelong case of wanderlust, a childlike curiosity about life, and an independence so fierce that he often appeared brusque and condescending—even to those closest to him. He loved to tell the story of his classic New Hampshire childhood. Cared for by his grandparents after the death of his parents, "little Georgie Aarons," as he fondly remembered being called, was mischievous from the start. His tales revealed a wild boy, largely unsupervised, who took great delight in creating mayhem. His favorite one entailed dipping a girl's pigtails in an inkwell at school, then evading punishment by jumping out the window and hiding in the woods until dark. It was straight out of Mark Twain, whose books Slim often tucked into his suitcase while circumnavigating the world. Whatever was real or imagined about his stories, what is readily apparent is that Slim's refusal to play by the rules was a part of his character from a very young age.

When Slim's grandmother put a camera in his hands during an unsettled period in his teenage years, it would prove serendipitous. He enlisted in the army just after high school, and when World War II broke out shortly thereafter, he was hired as a military newspaper photographer. His stories of his experiences as a combat photographer tell of a young rabble-rouser aching for action. He wasn't above using unconventional methods to get a scoop, which resulted in his receiving more than one busting of rank—though his demotions were always reversed once his photographs were developed. He not only joined the invasion of Anzio, Italy, without proper accreditation, but also illegally commandeered a jeep in order to get there. When a bomb landed within steps of the press corps encampment in Anzio, Slim suffered a head wound. The Purple Heart he earned for bravery during this event was presumably the deciding stroke against his pending court-martial.

Although the war left him profoundly disillusioned and physically depleted, Slim returned to the United States with a career path in place and the determination to transform the way he looked at life. "What the hell did we fight in the war for if it wasn't to make the world a better place to live in and even occasionally enjoy," he explained once to old friend and legendary editor Frank Zachary. "I was honorably discharged with a Purple Heart and I'd had a bellyful of the horrors of war. From now on I'm going to walk on the sunny side of the street. I'm going to have fun photographing attractive people doing attractive things in attractive places, and maybe take some attractive photographs as well."

At first he worked as a stringer shooting New York and Los Angeles party stories. As Europe began to normalize and rebuild after the war, *Life* magazine opened a bureau in Rome and offered Slim a job. It was in Rome that his lifelong love affair with Italians was born and here that he began to establish his own distinctive brand of portraiture. As he loved to recount, "My beat in Rome was the movie stars, the gangsters, and the Vatican." He photographed the notorious gangster Lucky Luciano in Sicily, Louis Armstrong at the Colosseum, and Pope Pius XII at the Vatican. He hung around Cinecittà, the Roman studios that were the hub of Italian cinema, and photographed Lamberto Maggiorani on the set of Vittorio De Sica's *The Bicycle Thief*. He even took some time off for *un'avventura* with actress Joan Fontaine (see page 10), after photographing her on the set of her movie *September Affair*. When well into his eighties Slim still fondly described those years as some of the richest of his life, knocking around postwar Rome while residing in Room 648 at the fabled Excelsior Hotel, with a balcony overlooking Via Veneto, for 150 dollars a month. "The best part was that you could fill

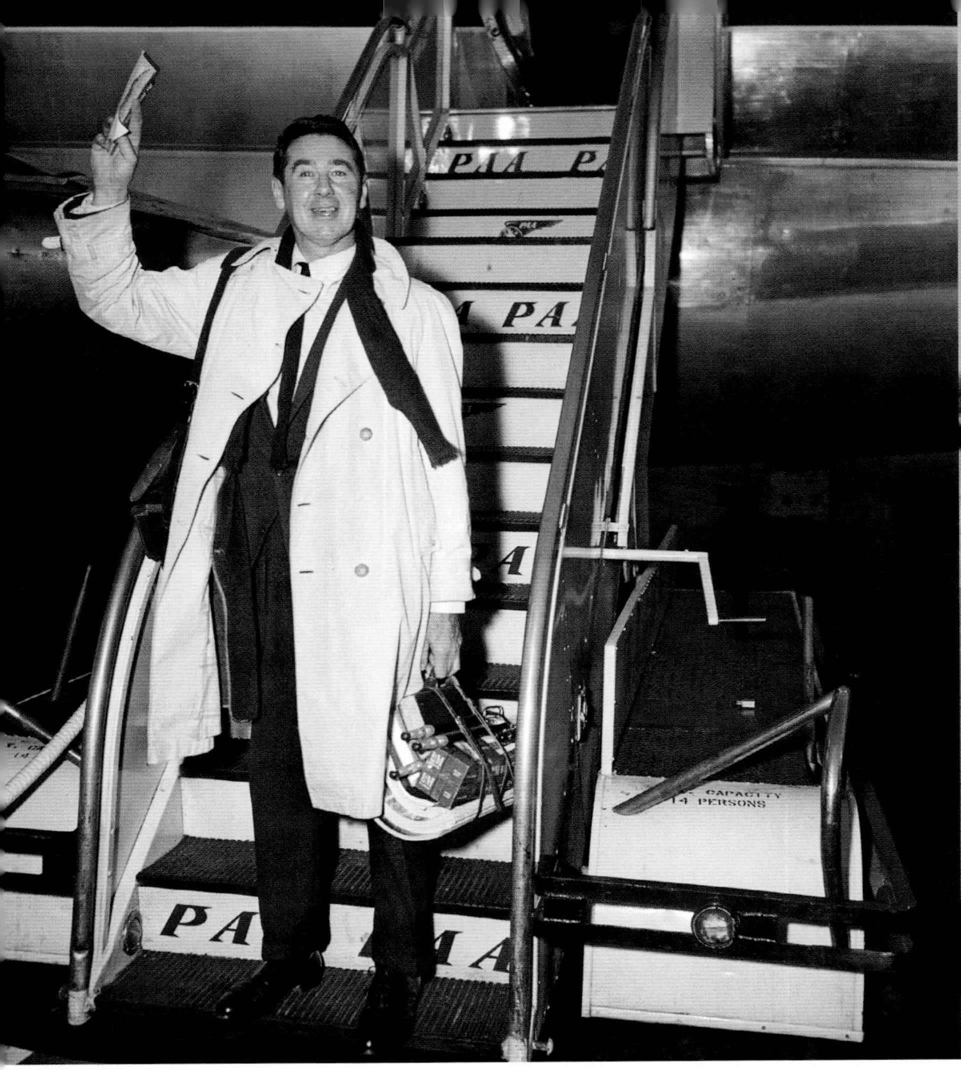

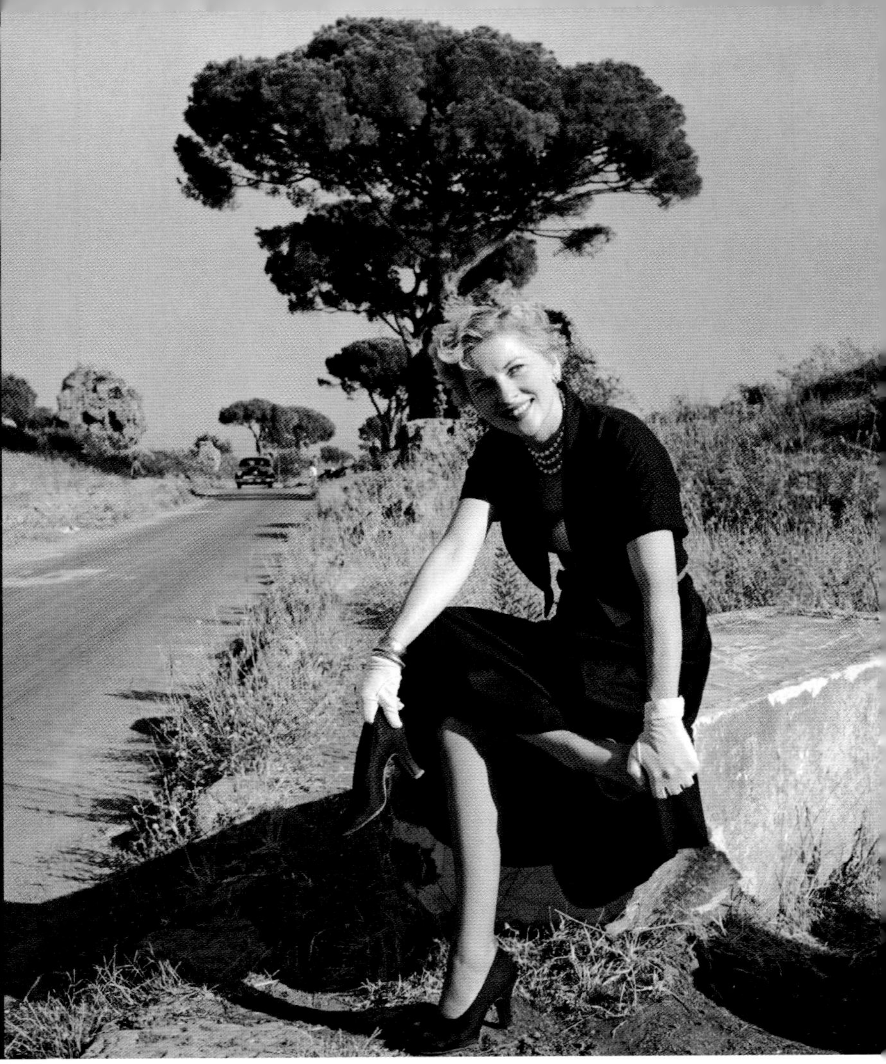

a girl's room with flowers for a hundred lire, fifty cents in those days!" he loved to retell.

When *Life* sent Slim to photograph a nineteen-year-old ingenue named Betsy von Furstenberg for a possible cover story, it may have been the break that set his remarkable career in motion. Von Furstenberg was a German baroness and a budding movie star. "I had to get her away from the Roman nightlife to get rid of the bags under her eyes," he explained. "So I took her up to a little hotel in Ravello on the Amalfi Coast and made her sleep and rest for two days. We took meals together and I kept calling her parents to reassure them that I wasn't taking advantage of their daughter." His portrait of von Furstenberg made the cover of *Life* in January 1951. Because *Life* was the first magazine to have a global reach, a cover photograph was a thrilling feat for a young photographer and ensured immediate entry into a fellowship of other esteemed *Life* photographers.

above Slim Aarons descends from plane, 1955 (left). Actress Joan Fontaine relaxes roadside on a day trip through the Italian countryside, while in Rome filming her movie, *September Affair*, 1949 (right). *opposite* Slim Aarons, Eva Gabor, and Philip Shell enjoy a moment of levity at a formal event, 1950s.

Many of them, including Carl Mydans, George Silk, Robert Capa, Gjon Mili, and David Douglas Duncan, became Slim's lifelong friends.

The black-and-white photograph of von Furstenberg was timeless, surprisingly stark yet full of intimacy and authenticity (see page 62). As Slim recounted the story time and again, there was no question that he saw this as an important turning point in his career. Whether it was a eureka moment or a gradual denouement, this experience helped him to fully realize his unique talent to describe, evoke, and control—all in the click of a shutter. His unparalleled flair for both observation and storytelling was born, and most important for an original like Slim, it was a role that gave him nearly sole authority to call the shots.

If the von Furstenberg experience was pivotal for Slim in terms of defining his professional path, it was so in part because it bolstered his confidence in how to arrange his subjects in their own environment. After all, it was under his direction alone that the von Furstenberg portrait succeeded. As his career flourished, he would photograph dozens of Betsy von Furstenbergs, and as each portrait appeared in print in *Holiday*, *Harper's Bazaar*,

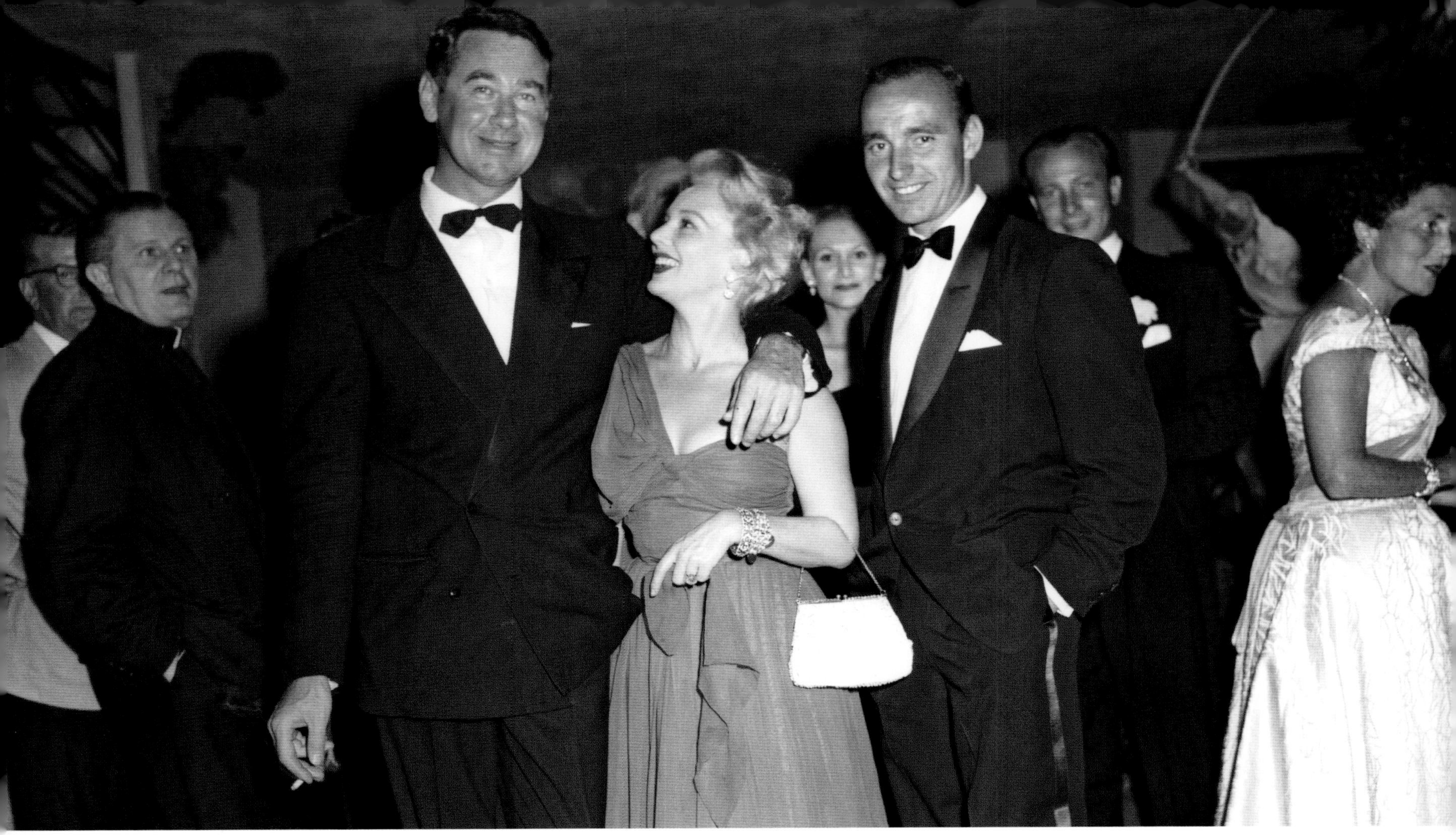

and *Town & Country*, it bolstered his growing reputation for photographing important people and for making beautiful people even more so. And as this recognition began to precede him, the consequent accumulation of trust ensured the one thing that would eventually set him apart from his peers: access to private worlds behind closed doors.

He was increasingly welcomed into majestic châteaus, cavernous palazzi, mountaintop chalets, private islands, and thousand-acre fincas. He gradually covered people and places few other photographers could get to and often breezed into the most exclusive resorts and old-guard clubs where the press was restricted, if not completely banned, such as the Eagle Club in Gstaad, the Corviglia Club in St. Moritz, the Caccia Club in Rome, Bailey's Beach Club in Newport, and the Bath and Tennis Club in Palm Beach. His honorary membership into the world of high society was cinched, and as the years went by his access reached even into successive generations of the same venerable families.

Slim's longtime friend Michele Mazzola, wife of editor Tony Mazzola, observes, "Slim's long and distinguished run with *Town & Country* magazine lasted for almost fifty years. He has one of the longest collaborations in magazine history with *Town & Country* under Tony Mazzola and Frank Zachary. The magazine gave him unfettered access to European and American society and Slim gave the magazine images that chronicled an era."

SLIM'S WORKING STYLE

Wendy Vanderbilt Lehman (see page 224) knew Slim nearly her entire life. When she was a teenager, she recalls, Slim frequently stopped by her parents' home in Palm Beach whenever he was in town doing a story. He typically took a few photographs of her mother, Manuela Hudson, and stayed for lunch.

Now a painter and sculptor, with grown children of her own, Wendy remembers Slim well: "He was always around Palm Beach, Newport, Lyford, and the DR. He'd pop up everywhere. He used to come for lunch with Mummy and Neddy when he was in town doing a story, and we always called him 'Slimbo.' Everyone knew Slim—he was everywhere. He was fun and funny, very fatherly. He always arrived in a celebratory mood that made me feel that all was right in the world. He was the ultimate hail-fellow-well-met."

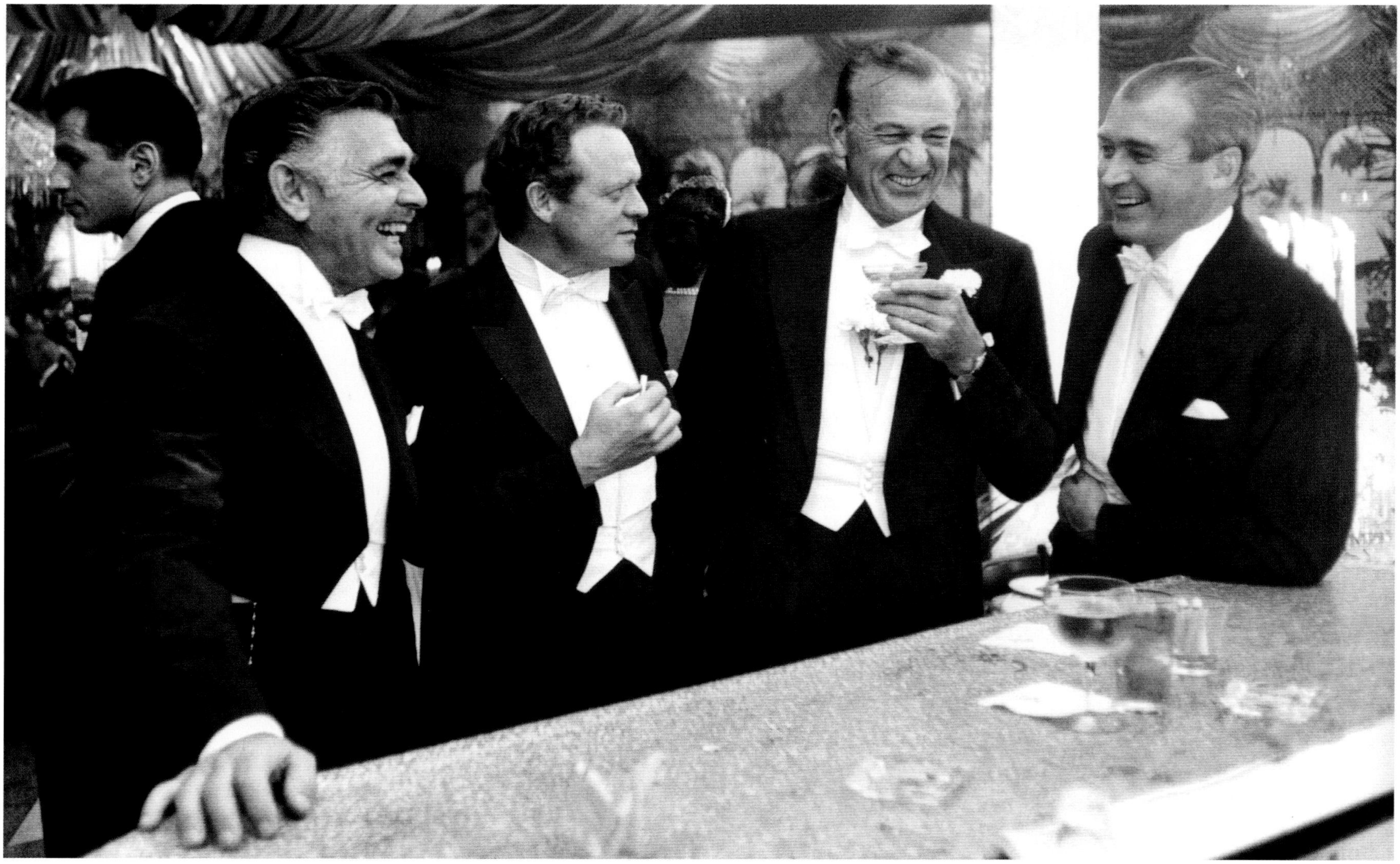

Maria Cooper Janis tells a similar story. Her famous father, the elegant actor Gary Cooper, was one of the four laughing "kings" in Slim's most famous photograph, *Kings of Hollywood* (see above). A fast friendship was formed between Cooper and Slim as a result of that photo. Maria remembers Slim's presence in their family life: "My parents always had lots of laughs with Slim and liked him a lot. He had a mixture of funny stories, gossip stories. Even the serious ones he narrated with an irony and kind of brushing off of anything too serious. He surely loved to capture people having fun and celebrating the good life. I think Slim was really interested in trying to show something else, something more, while photographing the surface trappings of these 'rich and famous' people he lived around." The "something more" that Maria Janis singles out in Slim's approach to photography reveals a basic truth about his attitude toward his subject matter and echoes his postwar pledge to himself, that he didn't take the subject of wealth and fame all that seriously—what moved him most was a desire to examine the pleasures and diversions of life.

In the unique professional niche he carved for himself, Slim was keenly aware that his rapport with people was an important key to his success. He was conveniently blessed with the gift of gab and was a natural raconteur who loved to entertain people with his curious mix of worldly travel stories and tales of meetings with famous people, topped off with a dash of homespun American-boy-made-good charm. His arch banter had a Rabelaisian flavor but was never coarse or aggressive. More often it was lighthearted, amusing—and it achieved exactly what it was meant to do: cajole and disarm, put people at ease while gaining their trust. I loved listening to him holding court with stuffy Europeans, regaling them with silly stories. One of his

above Slim's most beloved photograph, *Kings of Hollywood*, shows Clark Gable, Van Heflin, Gary Cooper, and James Stewart enjoying an inside joke at a New Year's party at Romanoff's, Beverly Hills, 1957. The joke, according to Slim's daughter Mary Aarons, was what a lousy actor Slim had been as an extra on the movie *It Started in Naples* with Clark Gable and Sophia Loren in 1959. The story became a part of the Aarons family lore, though, as Mary points out, the dates don't exactly line up.

favorite topics was their languages, many of which Slim spoke imperfectly but without a trace of inhibition. On a story in Florence in the 1980s we were lunching with several members of the venerable Antinori wine family. The Antinoris have been in the wine business for more than six centuries, and the head of their clan, Marchese Piero Antinori, is as formal in bearing as he is a formidable vintner. Yet with his customary pluck, Slim spun a yarn about having discovered the most romantic word in the Italian language, a word that would make every woman go weak in the knees and that every man should know. He strung the prank along skillfully until finally revealing the word in an elongated and exaggerated enunciation of every syllable, as if seducing a woman himself . . . *stuz-zi-ca-den-ti*. It ended with laughs all around when they realized the mystery word was *toothpick*! These moments of folly not only served to put people at ease; they also chipped away at the toughest veneers he encountered, those of aloof industrialists or the sometimes standoffish leaders of the patrician clans. He didn't care if he looked silly—he knew he had to sing for his supper.

While he loved holding court and telling stories, Slim was by no means a fawning court jester to the upper crust. He deferred to no one, and his outspokenness became legendary at a certain point—as did his lack of tolerance for parvenus and posers, whom he could sniff out like a bloodhound. At times, he even played the part of provocateur, with no hesitation whatsoever to call things out as he saw them—he famously told John D. Rockefeller III that his lawn looked a little shabby. In Mougins, France, upon entering the ancient stone farmhouse of the avant-garde art dealer Leo Castelli, Slim chided him for its entirely empty white walls. Castelli patiently explained that the lack of visual stimulation in his vacation home was what kept him sane in his line of work.

Slim had an acute prejudice against women wearing their hair parted down the middle; he claimed it made for better photographs if a woman's hair was parted on one side. And it mattered not at all whether it was a countess or a waitress with the offending hairdo—he made sure to let her know his views. He could also be a galling braggart—even among those who had plenty to gloat about themselves. And though he was a generous mentor to many younger people, his penchant for telling them how to do their jobs was well known. Not long after I started working with him, one *Town & Country* editor told me that Slim's habit of roaming their offices doling out unsolicited advice to the young editors and art directors had earned him the indelicate title of "Raving Editor," in place of his self-appointed title, "Roving Editor."

His confidence extended beyond his professional expertise to his own appearance. After circling the globe a time or two, Slim learned to put himself together with a greater sophistication than the country boy from New Hampshire had. By the time I met him, Slim likened his personal style to that of the classic English gentleman, the type epitomized by David Niven, whom he photographed in Monte Carlo in 1970. How he presented himself was certainly critical, and it helped that he looked the part—lanky and tall with a Waspy air of insouciance, though never a dandy. On one of the first occasions Slim and I worked together, we flew to Regensburg, Germany, to cover the christening of His Serene Highness Albert II, 12th Prince of Thurn und Taxis. Because of Slim's friendship with the baby's father, Prince Johannes, we were the only invited members of the American press. As we walked down to the abbey that morning—Slim in pressed khakis, smart English Oxfords, and a crisp navy blazer—he leveled his shoulders as he picked a piece of lint from his blazer and proudly mused, "You just can't come in looking like a photographer from the *Daily News*."

His transformation to English gent notwithstanding, Slim was New England frugal through and through—until his death in 2006, he still wore with great delight the same bespoke cotton button-downs, silk slacks, and navy blazers he'd had made inexpensively on a trip to Hong Kong in the 1950s. One day I noticed a monogram in Chinese characters under the pocket of one of his cotton shirts. Never having thought of him as a monogram type of guy, I asked him what it said. "No starch, please," he answered brightly, a twinkle in his eye. This dependable uniform, with a few brightly colored polo shirts thrown in, allowed him the luxury of focusing little energy on his clothes while ensuring that he'd fit in no matter where in the world he happened to be, and the formula failed him only occasionally. On a story on Ascot in the 1960s, Slim arrived without having arranged the proper formal attire. When he tried to enter the royal enclosure, he was barred by the guards. One version of the story describes Slim scuffling on the ground with a guard. Suddenly a voice boomed toward them, "Slim, is that you?" It was Prince Philip, who immediately gave him passage.

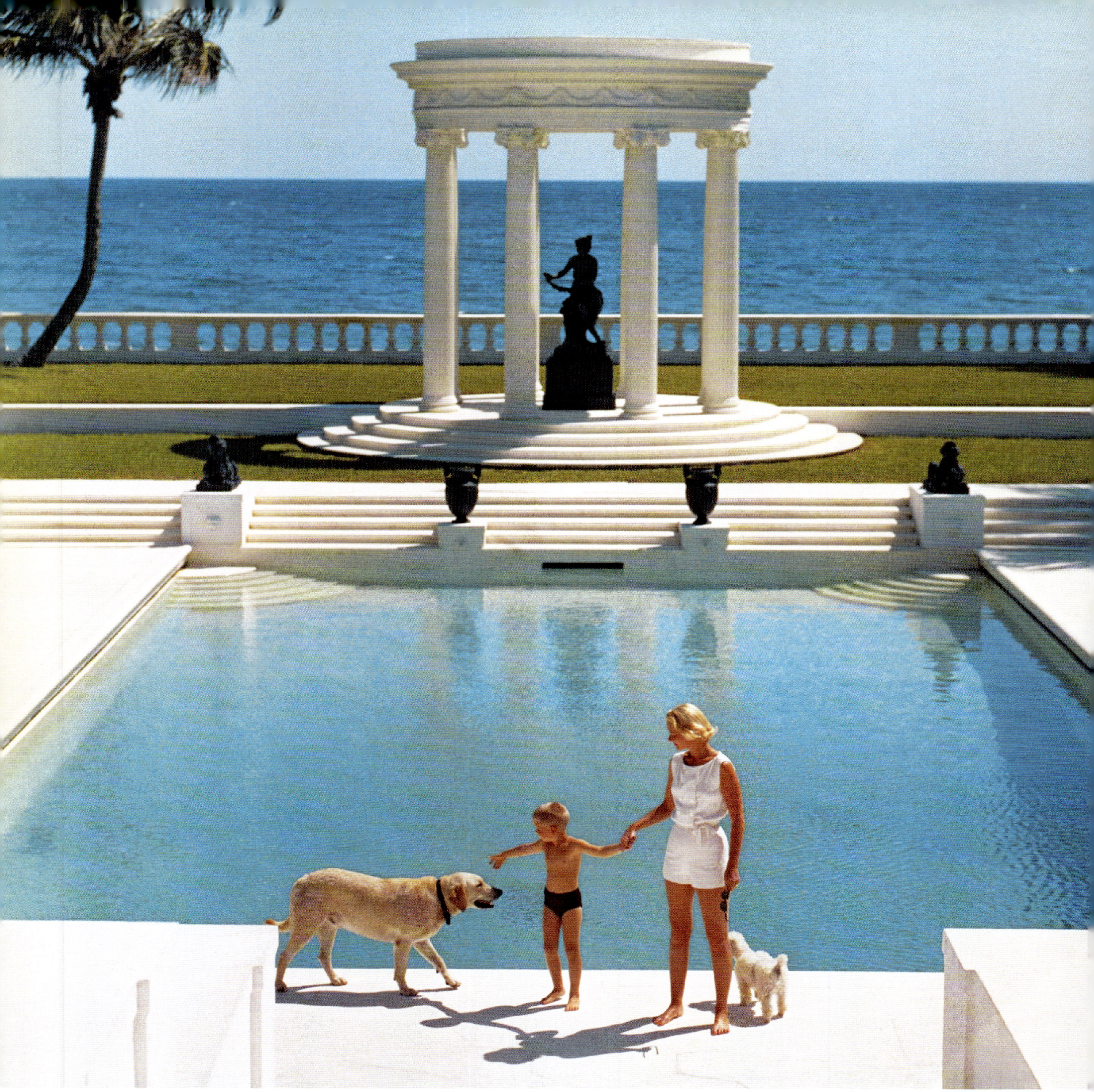

above C. Z. Guest, with her son Alexander Michael Douglas Dudley Guest, poolside at Villa Artemis, Palm Beach, 1955. This photograph captured the imagination of the postwar generation and became Slim's most admired photograph of a female subject.

WORKING WITH SLIM

At a certain point over the years, Slim further refined how he presented himself and worked, deciding that the industry norm of sending out crews of assistants, stylists, and editors on stories was not for him. Slim has been widely quoted for scoffing to his then editor, Tony Mazzola of *Harper's Bazaar*: "No assistants, no props, no stylists, no lights, no problems. That's how I work." He was clearly a one-man band by nature, but there was undoubtedly an element of calculation in his plan: He knew he'd have a better chance of being ushered into palatial homes and opulent estates if he wasn't trailing a throng of assistants carrying bags and equipment. His streamlined method of operation was to carry a stainless steel briefcase with one camera—at first a Leica, later a Nikon—plus a backup body, a couple of lenses, and a light meter. Nothing more. He measured out each day's allotment of Kodachrome film and carried it on his shoulder in a small, striped canvas bag (which he occasionally threw into a shot as a prop if some color was needed). He carried his own bags, loaded and unloaded his own film, and operated his own light meter. As for everything else that needed resolution on a shoot, he devised a formula of working with just one other resourceful person, whom he liked to call a *tuttofare*. The modern definition of the Italian word is a handyman—it literally means "do everything." The way he described it to me harkened back to his early days in Rome in the 1950s when all the needs of bustling postwar Italian households were taken care of by a diminutive widowed grandmother in black called a *tuttofare*.

As *tuttofare* I embraced any job that arose on location, from stylist to researcher, writer, muse, bouncer, extra, diplomat, and general problem solver. When a Florentine countess needed a specific undergarment for the dress Slim insisted she wear in her portrait, I accompanied her shopping and charged the cost to the magazine while Slim set up the shot. On a story in Palm Beach, Slim refused to photograph a woman who'd arrived for a cover try with her hair over-coiffed by a hairdresser. I hastily washed her hair in my hotel sink, she blew it dry, and the photo made the cover. I waded through a shallow pond in Palermo to arrange a shot of a woman reclining in a rowboat (see page 192) and donned water skis in the frigid, Alpine-fed waters of Lake Como for the background of a shot.

Sometimes the job was about dealing with the difficult people we needed to work with or work around. In Fuschl, Austria, it fell to me to smooth the ruffled feathers of a cantankerous count with whom we'd made an appointment for a portrait. Once we arrived at his schloss, it appeared he'd had a change of heart. When Slim excused himself to look around, I knew my job was to engage him in light conversation, and indeed he did come around. In 1985, on a story in Gstaad, we dropped by a luncheon at the home of Slim's great friends Baron and Baroness Hubert and Terry von Pantz hoping to make contact with several people for the story. At one point, a fifty-something French countess—who was hoping to be photographed—sidled over to us. I could feel the heat of her scrutiny as she looked me up and down, trying to size up whether I was obstacle or ally, while I tried to make small talk. Just as Slim's style of dress was of some consequence, mine was as well. On the Gstaad trip, my uniform included a luscious, knee-length silver fox (loaned from a *Town & Country* advertiser), yeti boots, a great haircut, and a good pair of one-carat diamond studs. I felt confident among the handsome, worldly crowd—certainly not on their level, but I held my own. Finally, as the small group was making its way into the dining room, the countess matched my stride for a moment and tipped her head toward mine. I thought perhaps she was going to give me a great quote about the inner circle of Gstaad. Instead she purred, "You know," as she glanced referentially at my earrings, "if you'd water those things, they might grow a little bit." I smiled thinly and found my place at the table, which thankfully wasn't next to hers. I didn't know why she felt the need to try to take me down a peg, but I did understand that in this case my role was to say nothing. To her great delight, Slim photographed her a few days later.

On location around the world, people occasionally pulled me aside to ask what it was like working with Slim. For years before devising his *tuttofare* formula, he'd been paired with a long list of writers, properly pedigreed editors, and society swans. A summa cum laude from Yale or a famous byline, however, couldn't prepare anyone for Slim's commanding personality or his particular brand of rigor. He was a consummate and tireless professional, an old-world newspaperman at heart, whose only goal was to bring home the story. But knotted quite intricately into Slim's cockeyed optimism and his unyielding work ethic were some darker threads—he could also be short-tempered, controlling, imperious, and at times inexplicably anxious about being usurped.

This fear was never more apparent than when people solicited his advice on photography. By his mid-forties, esteemed everywhere he went as an expert in photography, Slim was often asked by a variety of people about how to take pictures or what kind of camera to buy. He understandably felt competitive with other professional photographers, particularly those who worked for the same magazines he did. But it was an odd chink in his armor that he seemed to fear competition from amateurs as well, perhaps in part because continual technological advances had made photography increasingly accessible to the masses. To seekers of advice he made no mention of Nikons, Leicas, or Canons, the leading cameras of the day. Instead he always gave aspiring lensmen and women a more Machiavellian reply—he advised them to buy a "Brownie"—a simple, inexpensive camera made by Kodak that was used exclusively for taking snapshots.

Not surprisingly, it took a while for the two of us to iron out our working relationship. We bickered our way around the world for at least a year, against some of the most rarefied backdrops imaginable—along the Avenida Alvear in Buenos Aires, walking along a cobblestoned street in Patmos, Greece, and driving through the Mont Blanc Tunnel connecting France and Italy. Slim frequently reminded me that there were a dozen others waiting to take my place. Often, at the end of an assignment, as our plane touched down at Kennedy Airport, I thought to myself, "That's it. I can't do this anymore. I have to get a *real* job." Then a few weeks later the office would call with preliminary plans to go to Lamu, Bora Bora, or Brunei, and my resolve instantly evaporated. I believe that once Slim understood I didn't want to control him, I certainly didn't want to usurp him, and in many ways I was cut from a similar cloth to his, he gradually began to trust me. Although he never relaxed his "no camera" rule, I knew we'd passed a milestone when he started calling me "Old Bean," a nickname reserved for old friends and family. The real evidence of détente came after a long flight to Singapore, as we were about to disembark. I was gathering my things and chattering excitedly about the adventure ahead, never having been to that part of the world, when he looked at me and gave me his ultimate compliment: "You know, Old Bean, your good faults outweigh your bad faults."

By the time I met Slim in the 1980s, his story formula was set in stone, and I fell right into stride alongside him. He arrived at each location armed with his camera case, the force of his nature, and the wealth of his experience. No matter where in the world we landed, his approach to magazine assignments was always the same: Check in at the hotel, unpack, and rest up in our rooms for a couple of hours—but never more! Then wrench out of the sleep of the dead and hit the streets, embarking on Slim's first rule of on-location research, called "poking around." He never took his camera out of its case before the third day on the job. If God himself had been in Rougemont or Marrakech the day we arrived and agreed to be photographed, but was leaving the next day, I don't believe Slim would have opened his camera case.

Slim certainly had a reporter's nose for being in the right place at the right time—and I quickly learned how to recognize and capitalize on these moments. Somehow he knew which street to turn down or which restaurant to choose that would invariably lead to running into someone he knew or someone perfect for the story. En route to a story assignment in Tuscany in the 1980s, we flew to Milan, planning to rest up for one night at the storied Grand Hotel and head out the next day by car. It was late on a Sunday afternoon in the summer—all the shops were closed and aside from a few tourists here and there, the streets were empty. Walking off our jet lag, we set out on foot for the Duomo and were working our way back to the hotel. Slim, as always, took the lead and steered us this way and that from one piazza to another, through the winding cobblestoned streets. Sensing we'd overshot the hotel, I was just about to say something to him, when he abruptly decided to turn onto the narrow Via Rossari. There, walking along by himself window-shopping, seemingly deep in thought, was Ralph Lauren. Lauren had been an admirer of Slim's for years and had sought his counsel for a fragrance campaign. A warm exchange of pleasantries took place, a promise to meet up in New York, and we were on our way. On another story, in the Italian seaside town of Portofino, we'd been walking around the marina killing time before dinner. Slim insisted, to my great irritation, on finding the farthest dock and walking to the very end of it. As we neared the end, a Danish girl emerged from a small sailboat. She was lovely, angelic, without makeup, unassuming—she just had a certain something that caught both our eyes. We didn't break stride but looked at each other, and without a word he gave me *the nudge*. I circled around and introduced myself. He photographed her the next day, leaving a wide space at the top of the photo for the *Town & Country* magazine logo just in case she made the cover—and she did (see opposite).

Slim's uncanny sixth sense, paired with his uncompromising tenacity, was what made editors love him. He was known throughout the industry as the photographer who would always bring home the story. He waited four days in the village of Saint-Aubin-d'Écrosville—knowing full well that any delay would have squeezed his typically packed ten-day story schedule—to take his famous 1957 photo of the French noblewoman Laure de La Haye-Jousselin astride her horse in Normandy (see page 170). And he even got her two dogs to cooperate. In 1985 we were dispatched to Bandar Seri Begawan to do a story on the sultan of Brunei. After six days of waiting around in vain in the withering equatorial heat for the sultan to receive us, Slim switched the story idea and called the architect of the sultan's brand-new, 1.4-billion-dollar palace (in 1985 dollars). We brought home a pictorial essay of the new palace, and it ran in several spreads in *Town & Country* as an architectural piece, to great acclaim.

An unparalleled expert at running around the world and getting things done, Slim was a generous mentor to those he deemed worthy, proud to teach young journalists the ropes and pass along his tips. Janet Carlson, an associate editor at *Town & Country*, was assigned a number of stories with Slim in the 1980s and easily recalls his avuncular style and friendly counsel. She was once on a press trip in Monaco when she got a call to join Slim on a story in Milan. There was a dressy event to attend that evening, but she hadn't packed evening wear. Slim took her to Laura Biagiotti's showroom and got her outfitted, as she remembers it, "with the wave of his hand:"

> *I was in awe of that modus operandi of Slim's. I'd never seen it before. Slim had so many friends everywhere. It was as if Europe was his backyard, and he could call over the fence to a neighbor to borrow the charcoal starter. He could call Laura Biagiotti herself and set up this dress fitting for me at the drop of a hat. I learned his methods, as we all did. As I grew up in the world of magazine editorial, I then produced stories of my own by calling people and asking for entrée, making friends, and even borrowing a dress—as in, literally, for the Vienna Opera Ball years later, from Oscar [de la Renta], who else? That was a loaner. Though I still have the Laura Biagiotti number.*

Slim always carried with him a small, worn, black leather book, fastened with a rubber band, into which he had written the names and telephone numbers of his many acquaintances. Integral to every story recipe was the handful of contacts he reached out to immediately upon arrival—people he'd met on previous stories, the grandes dames he knew or their descendants, and locals with important titles or positions. Through these individuals he found the places and faces that would make up each story.

Finding the right women to photograph was always the primary focus, as the central visual theme of every magazine story he did was the local young beauty. "Whether it was the Italian Riviera, the Swiss Alps, or the Arizona desert, Slim captured the essence of a place through his photographs of the people who enjoyed its unique flavor. From the minute he arrived on location, he began to search for a handful of good-looking women or the latest pretty young trendsetter who could give his story a touch of fairy-tale romance," remembers Kathryn Livingston, a longtime Hearst executive editor who worked with Slim on a number of assignments.

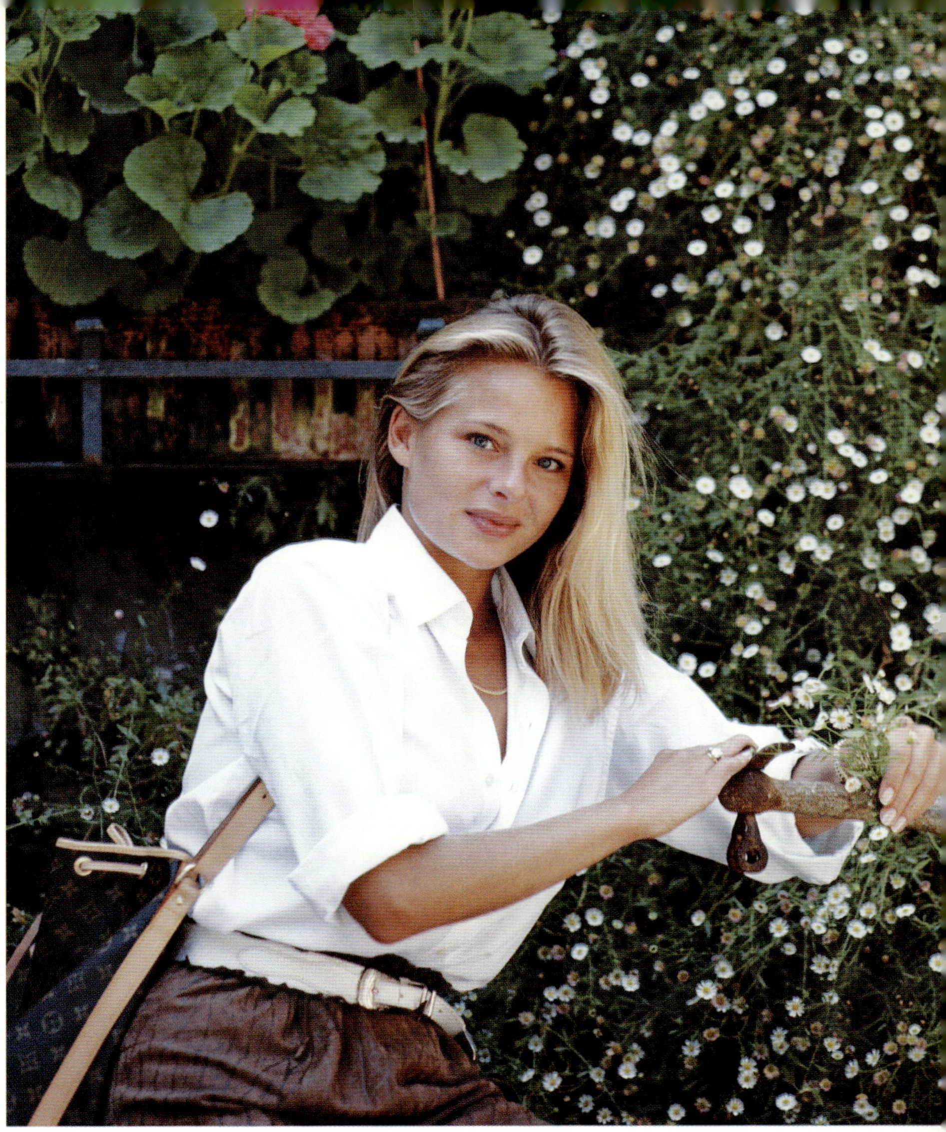

above Britta Mese, Portofino, Italy, 1985. A chance encounter with this young woman on a stroll before dinner landed Slim a *Town & Country* cover in 1986.

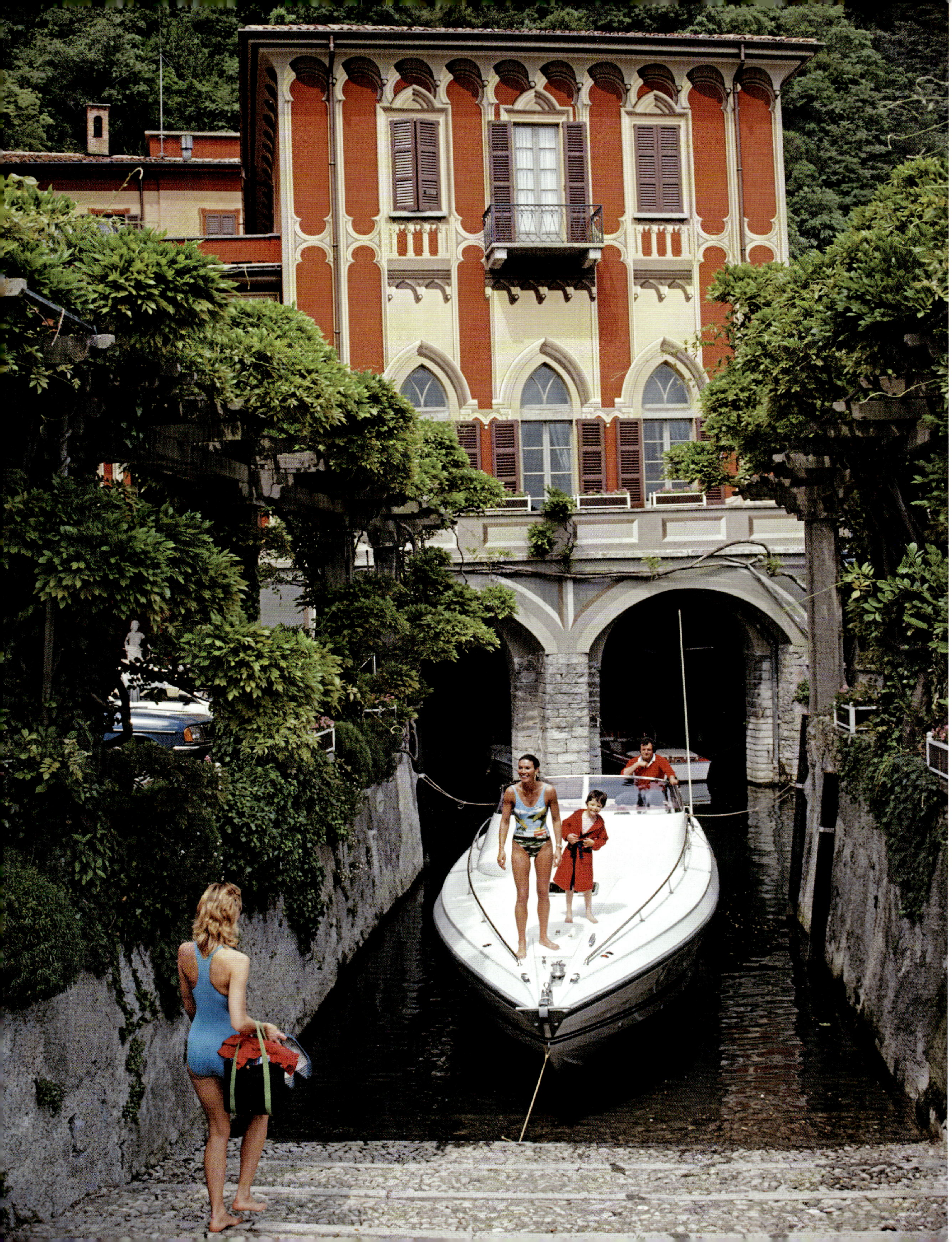

THE ENVIRONMENTAL PORTRAIT: SLIM AS STORYTELLER

Slim's body of work consists generally of three types of photographs: scenic shots, pickup shots taken at resorts or clubs, and portraits taken in people's homes. Although a variety of his photographs have reached "iconic" stature over time, such as *Kings of Hollywood,* Jackie Kennedy at the April in Paris Ball (page 155), and the Richard Neutra house in California (pages 84, 85, 86, and 87), it is his setup portraits of individuals in their homes that have led to his venerated status as a contributor to the development of the photographic genre called the "environmental portrait." In contrast to the artifice of studio photography, in which the subject, background, and accessories are predetermined, environmental portraiture is an on-the-spot matching of the subject to his or her own natural surroundings. An environmental portrait tells the story of the subject's life in part through the background against which it's taken, and the background is usually considered as significant as the subject.

When looking at an environmental portrait, it's often difficult to distinguish how much a photographer has inserted himself into the portrait. In Slim's environmental portraits, he decided not only who would be photographed but also where in their own milieu they would be positioned, how they would be arranged, and often how certain details of their surroundings would appear. My observation was that Slim had an almost childlike desire to idealize each mise-en-scène he encountered, to embellish the everyday scenarios he found with his idea—his fantasy—of what their world of leisure *should* look like. The portraits he created tell a story, and the arrangement of the visual details are the pieces of his fiction. His perfectionism in executing these portraits reached as far as noticing an errant brown leaf on a bougainvillea plant, a renegade wisp of hair, or a pant leg slightly shorter than its mate. Slim claimed it took him years to quit smoking because he used the ritual of lighting up and smoking a cigarette or two to steal a quiet moment in which to compose a photograph.

At the start of each new portrait, upon arriving at his subject's home, his first objective was to establish a setting—an exquisite drawing room, a sun-drenched garden, or an allée of hundred-year-old walnut trees.

The next decision was the subject's clothing and appearance. Most often he photographed his subjects in the clothing they appeared in. However, if he chose a ballroom with gilded paneling for the background, he asked the subject to bring out a choice of elegant clothing. He frowned upon women enhancing their hair or makeup, even for the dressier shots—he very much wanted his subjects to appear as they were in their everyday lives. "I don't do fashion. I take photos of people in their own clothes and that becomes fashion," he is now famous for boasting. There were three pieces of clothing he steadfastly refused to photograph and always asked his subjects to change out of: jeans, T-shirts, and running shoes.

The final decision was the arrangement of his subject in the setting. Once his idea was fixed, he sometimes spent hours orchestrating and executing the details. As for expression in his subjects, his only expectation was that they "give" or engage with the camera, most often advising them to think of nice things or to smile with their eyes. He contended that he was always looking for, but didn't often find, an "eighteenth-century smile." Because of the difficulty in garnering their cooperation, he often banished dogs and babies before the shoot started, only to usher them back in after the session was over for a few personal shots. It was his ardent belief that the challenge of working with real people who were not industry professionals made his job much more difficult than that of a fashion photographer, working with professional models in studios, with carefully sourced clothing and jewels and with hair and makeup artists.

Art historian and journalist Marie-Louise Mills (page 236) was photographed by Slim many times over the years, most memorably in a *Town & Country* spread on the curative waters of Montecatini, Italy, in 1980. She recalls what it was like having his camera pointed at her: "Watching Slim work was like reading a good novel, where character details and clues were handsomely placed to create a perfect picture. He was always sizing up and readjusting the scene before the final product—he made sure it worked for him before he clicked. What always amazed me about Slim was his total command of the vision he wanted to transmit. He was the author of great novels transmitted visually."

opposite Lake Como, Italy, 1983. During the years I worked with Slim, my contributions to his photos were principally behind the scenes. Occasionally I had a chance to style a photo, as in this case, where Tulio Abbate readies his boat for departure. Rather than leaving his wife and son seated next to him, I asked them to greet me as I approached, doubling as an extra for the scene.

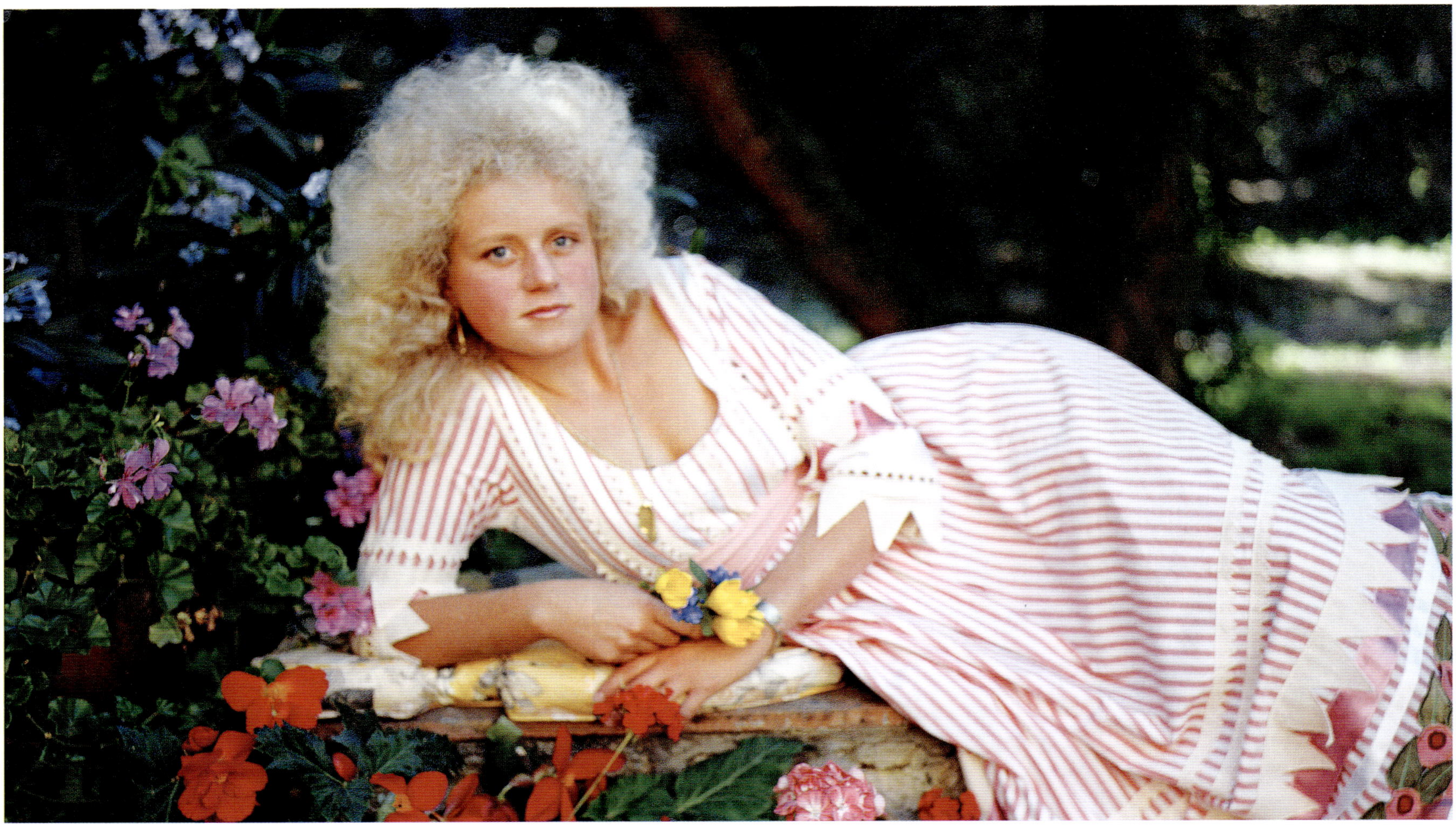

Another notable portrait sitting was that of Olimpia Gaetani in Tuscany in 1983 (see above), who has the unique distinction of having two ancestors invoked in Dante's *Inferno*. One was on her mother's side of the family: Count Ugolino della Gherardesca. The other was on her father's side: Pope Boniface VIII, born Benedetto Caetani. Slim arrived on her doorstep looking for her grandmother Countess Lea della Gherardesca for a story on Tuscan wine producers, but he ended up finding Olimpia instead, and she still remembers the unlikely circumstance of her photo being taken by Slim:

> *I didn't have anything to wear so we found this very nice dress that belonged to my mom, and he also combed my hair like it is in the picture—basically he did and decided everything. He was very creative and put me at ease. I think he got my essence. I don't know how to explain it—he got my interior strength. It looks like a romantic picture, and though it's not the best picture I have of me, for sure it is the most real. The photo was invented, maybe that's why I like it so much, and I think he liked it too because a few years after he took my picture he told a friend of mine that it was one of the pictures he liked the most.*

Despite being an autodidact with no education beyond high school, Slim had studied enough classical painting to appreciate the importance of compositions that were beautifully balanced. He often repeated the mantra "Form and design, form and design," particularly in the editing room when he was especially happy with how a shot had turned out. It's difficult to fathom that in those days one couldn't preview a photo on the back of a camera and art directors didn't have the luxury of digitally altering photographs. There was no way of knowing exactly what had been captured on film until it was professionally developed at home, which is why his portraits usually resulted in easily ten to twelve rolls of film per sitting, sometimes more. Once home, the editing process took place in a small studio on the second floor of his Katonah farmhouse. The edit from a ten-day shoot took three to four long days, which often entailed looking at dozens and dozens of images of the same subject in order to find the four or five that were perfect. Slim took great pride in never letting anything less than a perfect shot of someone leave his home studio. "Editing," he always professed, "is the art of elimination."

SLIM'S LEGACY: MAKING THE GOOD LIFE LOOK BETTER

Slim's long-distinguished career as a photographer earned him respect and sometimes envy, often from the unlikeliest sources. In 1984 on assignment in St. Moritz, we were having tea at the Palace Hotel with the famous owner brothers, Andrea and Hansjürg Badrutt, when in walked Gianni Agnelli, the elusive Fiat chairman and infamous playboy, known to his countrymen simply as "Il Re" (the king). Slim waved him over, and as they set up an appointment for a photograph later in the week, they bantered about where each had been and whom they had met there, playing a pleasant game of one-upmanship. More often than not, Slim knew more people and was better traveled than the people he was photographing. As Agnelli took leave, he gave Slim the greatest compliment possible in Slim's estimation when he offered, "Hey, Slim, I want *your* job!" Whenever he heard this—and he did frequently, mostly from men—he basked in it, and the more important the person, the better. It was his contention that many of the men he ran into on stories—royals, titans of industry, men of distinction who could have or buy anything they wanted—secretly envied him. In his thinking, they envied him because he had a reason to be there, a purpose. And while they may have felt ill at ease in their leisure, temporarily unhinged from the reliable comfort of being in charge, Slim relished his own unique brand of power: the power to make people look good.

Slim's skill at finding the world's most glamorous people, gaining unprecedented access to this extraordinary group of individuals, and making them look their best outside the studio with minimal equipment and support is without question his principal legacy. An important underpinning of this legacy is the essential story he told over and over again in every portrait, to some extent: his idealized vision of the good life. Quite often, at the end of one of Slim's shoots, with entire rooms having been upended and rearranged, and flowers brought in, as we walked to the door the subject would say, "You know, Slim, I like the way this looks—I think I'll leave it this way." This pleased him immensely, for his paramount desire was to make the subject and the scene better than he'd found them, to adorn their story with a bit of his own. For Slim this meant a continual retelling of his romanticized notion of life and leisure—and by extension, his notion of consummate feminine beauty.

The collection of images in this book presents a renewed look at the types of women Slim chose to photograph, revealing in some measure his vision of ideal feminine beauty. It was women, after all, who provided the indispensable inspiration for his work.

He traveled the world for decades searching for fascinating and beautiful women to photograph. Regardless of the type or look he admired, in so many of his photographs of women there is a consistent transcendent quality that endures. What is clear is that he favored as subjects of his photography, more than anything else, vibrant women with great personal style and an abundance of confidence. As has been said throughout time, the ultimate definition of beauty is ever changing and in the end exists only in the mind that contemplates it. In the final analysis, then, Slim's photographs of women tell us as much about him and his idealized vision of beauty as they do about the women he photographed.

In summary, this book is not only a celebration of Slim's work and the many memorable women upon whom he trained his lens; it is also a personal tribute to Slim and our many years as colleagues. There were certainly many instances of exasperation and isolation during my years of traveling and working with Slim, but when you glide for a moment in the slipstream of someone like him, it is exhilarating. He was an unfettered force of nature, an original who through his own drive and vision created a body of work that in today's world is still relevant and revelatory.

I've often reflected on the warning he gave me the day we met. Did I love him and hate him, as he predicted? I did. He knew it would be so and was quite comfortable being regarded this way. It was simply and irrevocably who he was, and there was nothing he could do about that. From time to time over the years, with an uncharacteristic dash of humility and wonder at his own success—and I'd like to think as a tacit mea culpa—he'd shrug his shoulders, call up that boyish grin, and sum it all up: "I'm just a guy with a Brownie."

• • •

opposite Olimpia Gaetani, Tuscany, 1983. This photograph was the result of another one of Slim's chance encounters. He was doing a story on the wine families of Tuscany when he ran into Olimpia at her grandmother's villa in Maremma.

following spread Villa Gli Arieti, the home of Lamberto Micangeli, is known for the striking view from its pool, Porto Ercole, Italy, 1986. His daughter Marina's sixteenth-century castle can be seen in the distance.

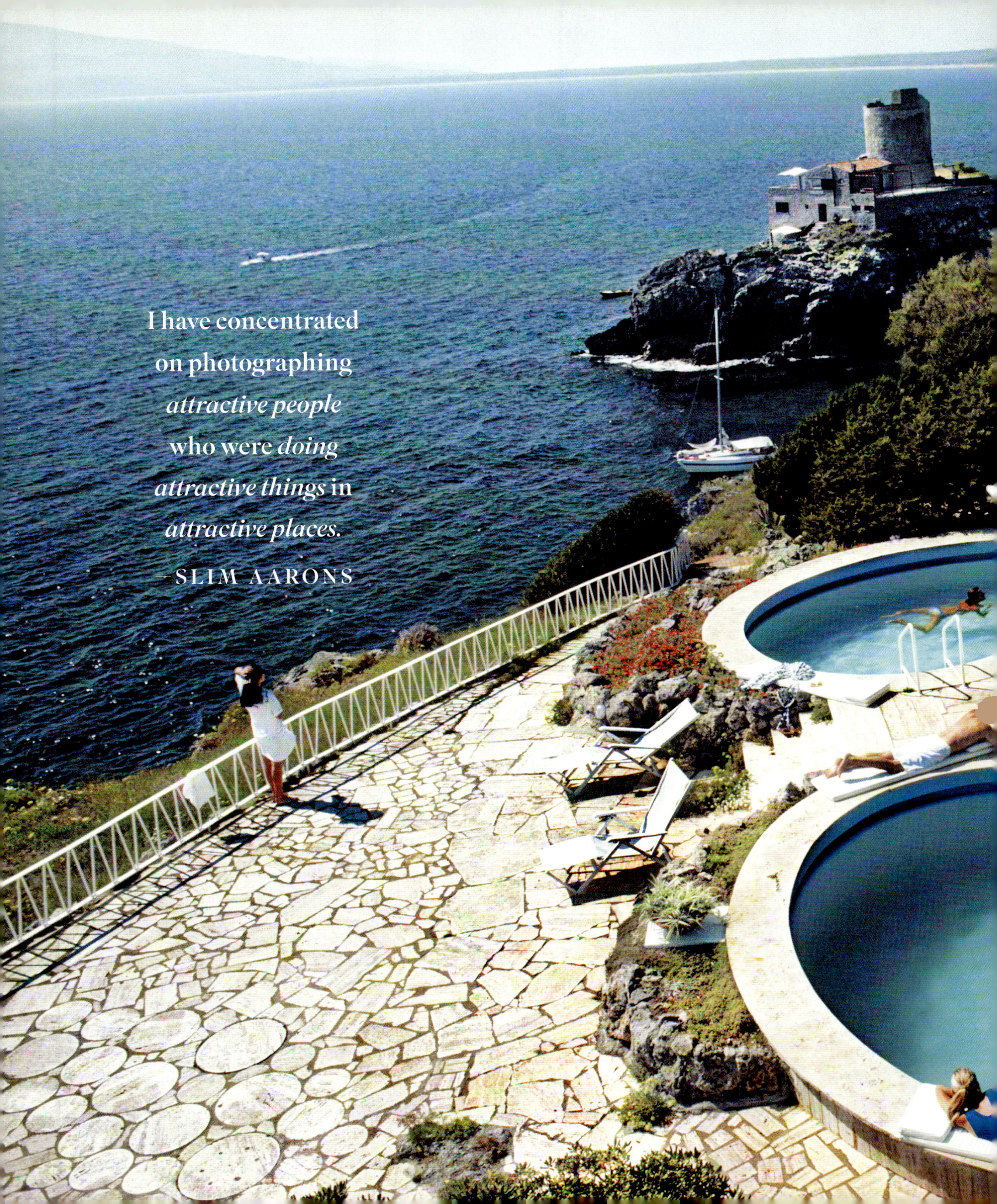

I have concentrated on photographing *attractive people* who were *doing attractive things* in *attractive places.*

—SLIM AARONS

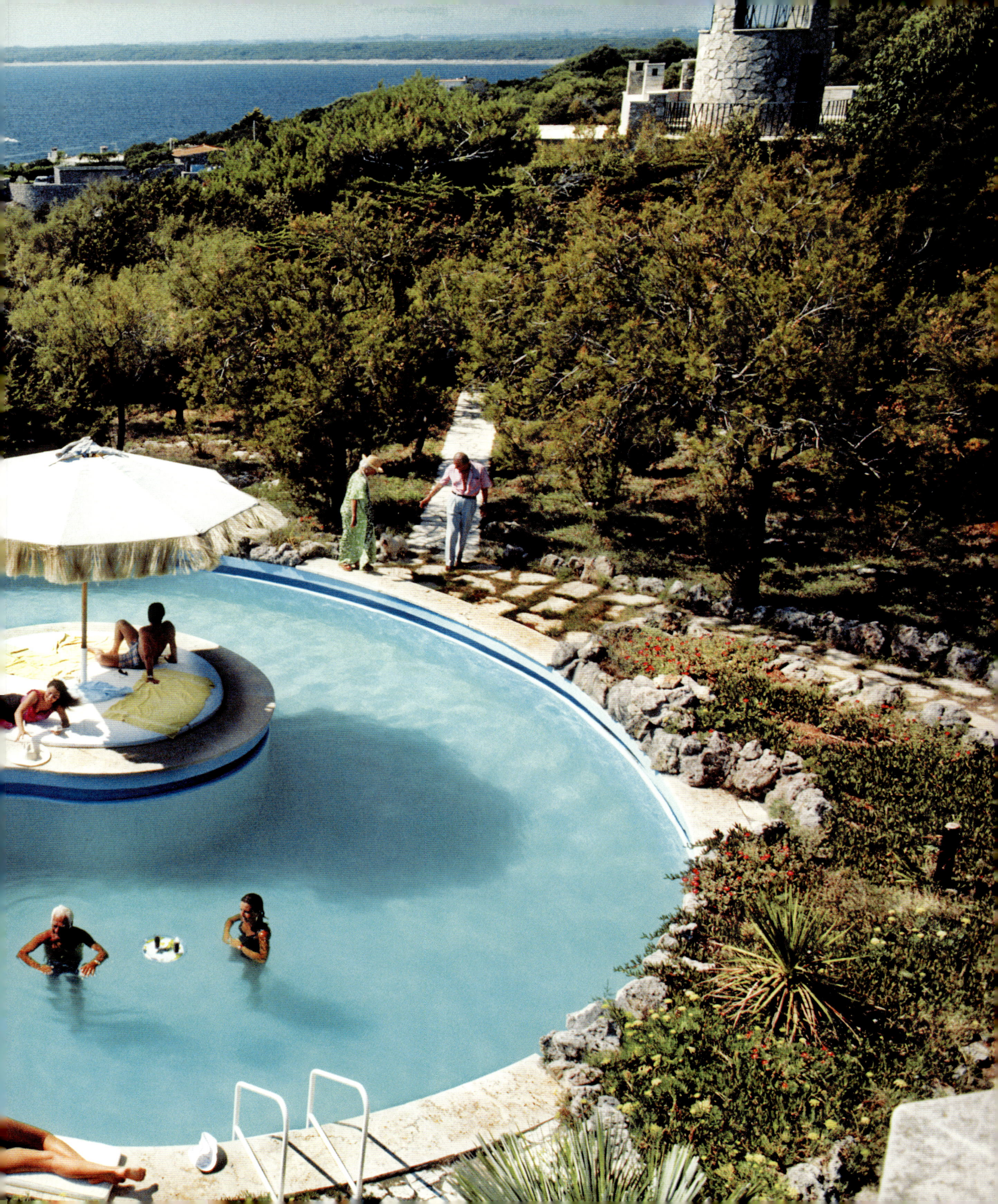

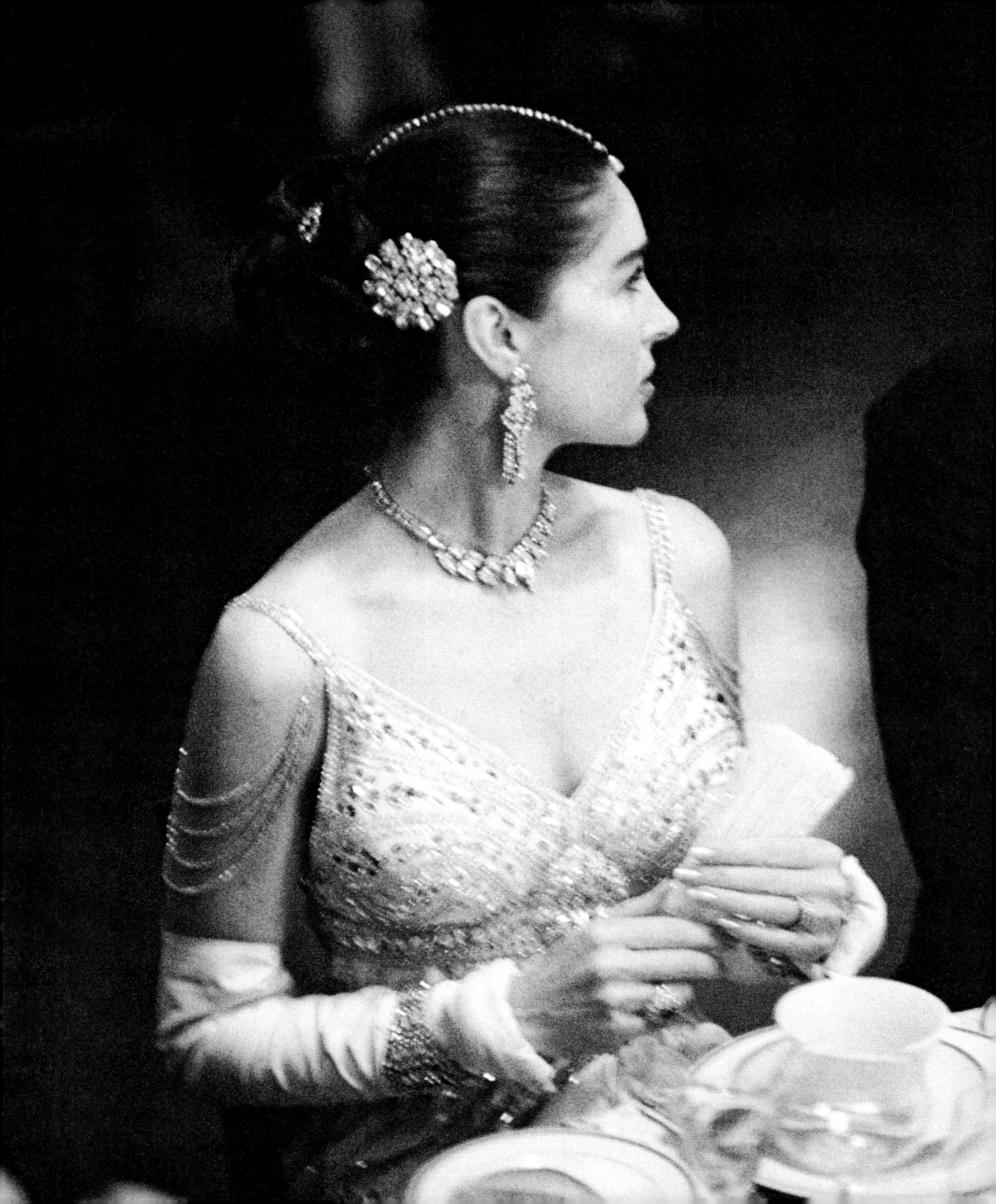

ATTRACTIVE *PEOPLE*

As he began his career in the late 1940s, Slim Aarons famously announced that, after the miseries of World War II, his overarching goal was to photograph "attractive people doing attractive things in attractive places." Over time he would create a highly original body of work, most of which was emblematic of this postwar declaration. The three chapters in this book present a selection of photography that underscores this theme, beginning here with the attractive people—the magnetic women who were the perennial focus of his photo stories. He chose some for their pedigrees; some were singled out for their striking looks. Still others were selected for their achievements. This chapter presents a sampling of the unforgettable women who were Slim's muses.

opposite An unknown guest at a New Year's Eve party held at Romanoff's in Hollywood, 1956. When the Lithuanian confidence man Hershel Geguzin arrived in Hollywood in the early 1940s, he had reinvented himself as Prince Michael Romanoff (see page 166). The restaurant he opened on Rodeo Drive became the ne plus ultra for the Hollywood elite to see and be seen throughout the 1940s and 1950s. Few actually believed he was titled nobility, but because he served the best French cuisine around, most went along with the ruse—after all, it was a town famous for reinvention. The "prince" could be seen nightly in his reserved spot, his bulldogs dining at the table with him. Slim photographed at Romanoff's many times during his Hollywood years. His most famous photo, *Kings of Hollywood*, was taken there, as were a number of others in this book.

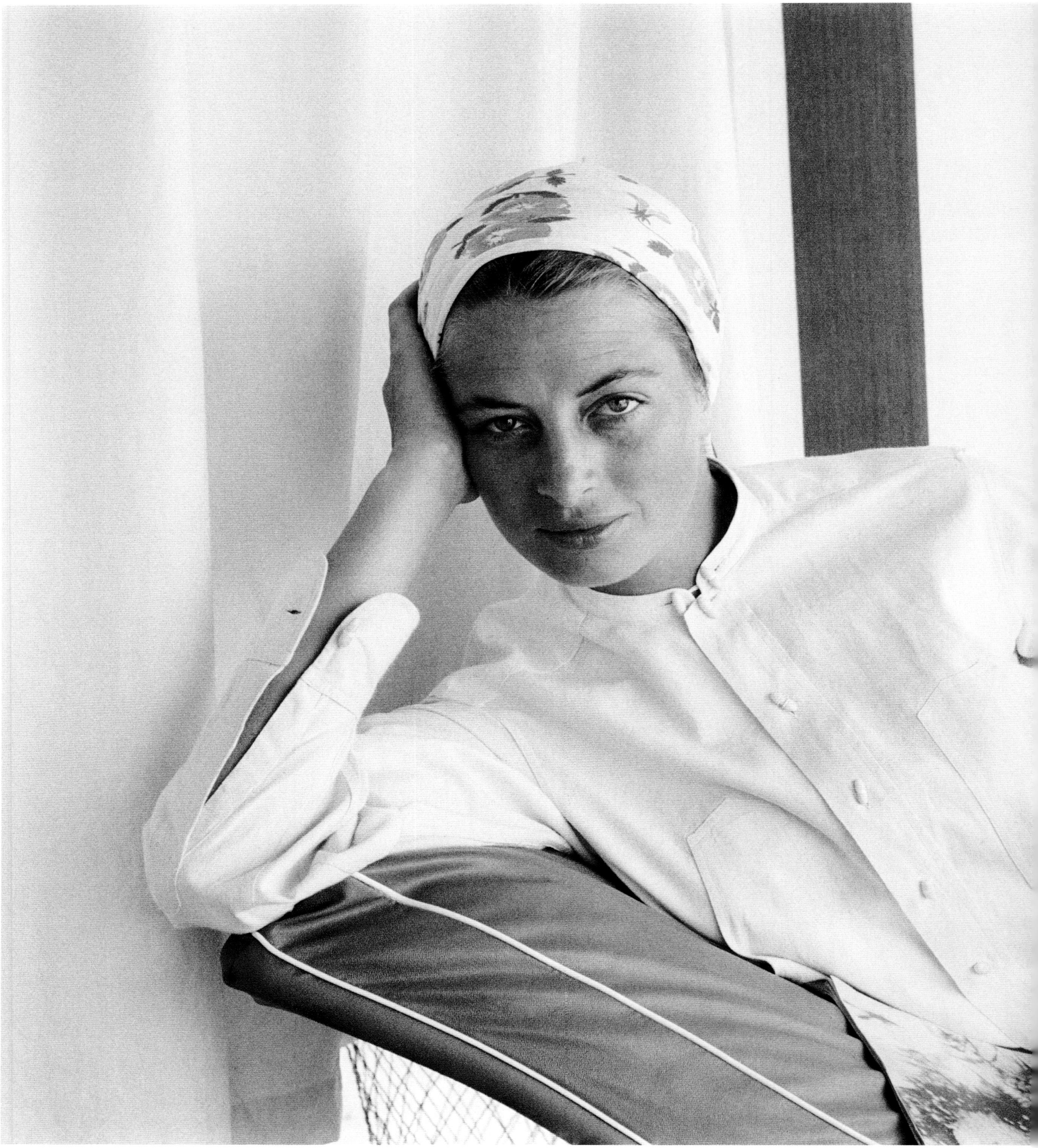

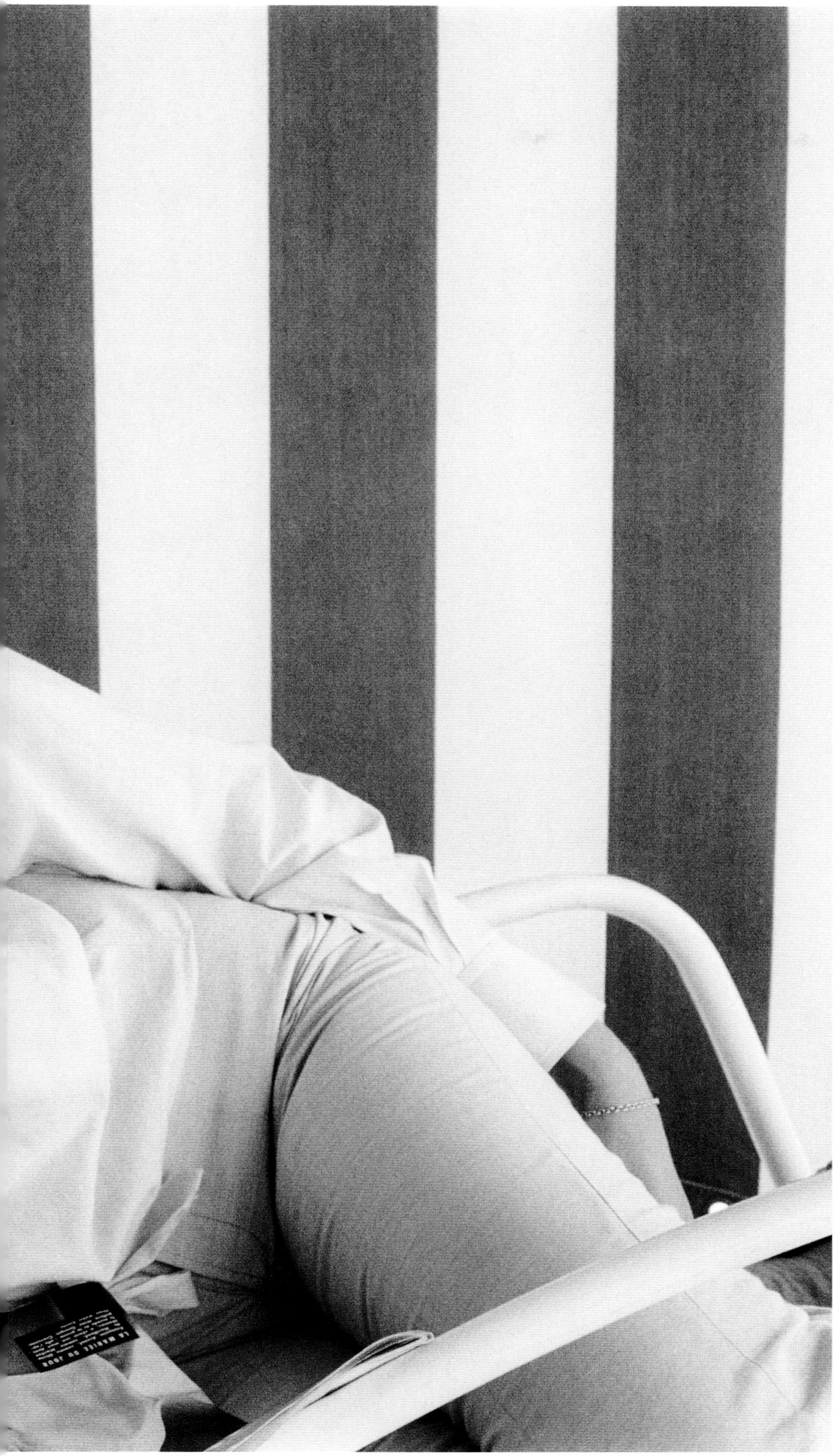

left The French model and actress Capucine, circa 1955. Born Germaine Lefebvre, she changed her name to Capucine, the French word for nasturtium. Discovered at age seventeen riding in a carriage in Paris, she became a top model for Christian Dior and Givenchy. At Givenchy she met Audrey Hepburn, who became a lifelong friend. Capucine (see also page 169) went on to costar in films such as *The Pink Panther* and *What's New Pussycat?*.

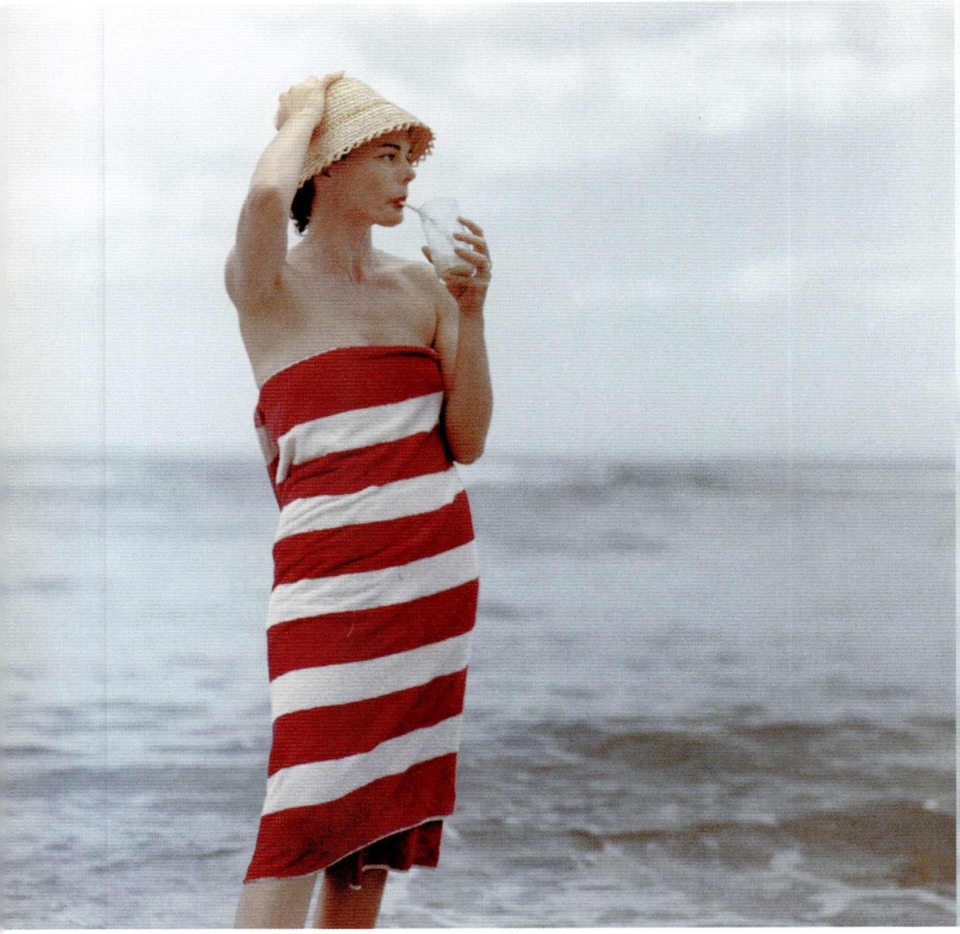

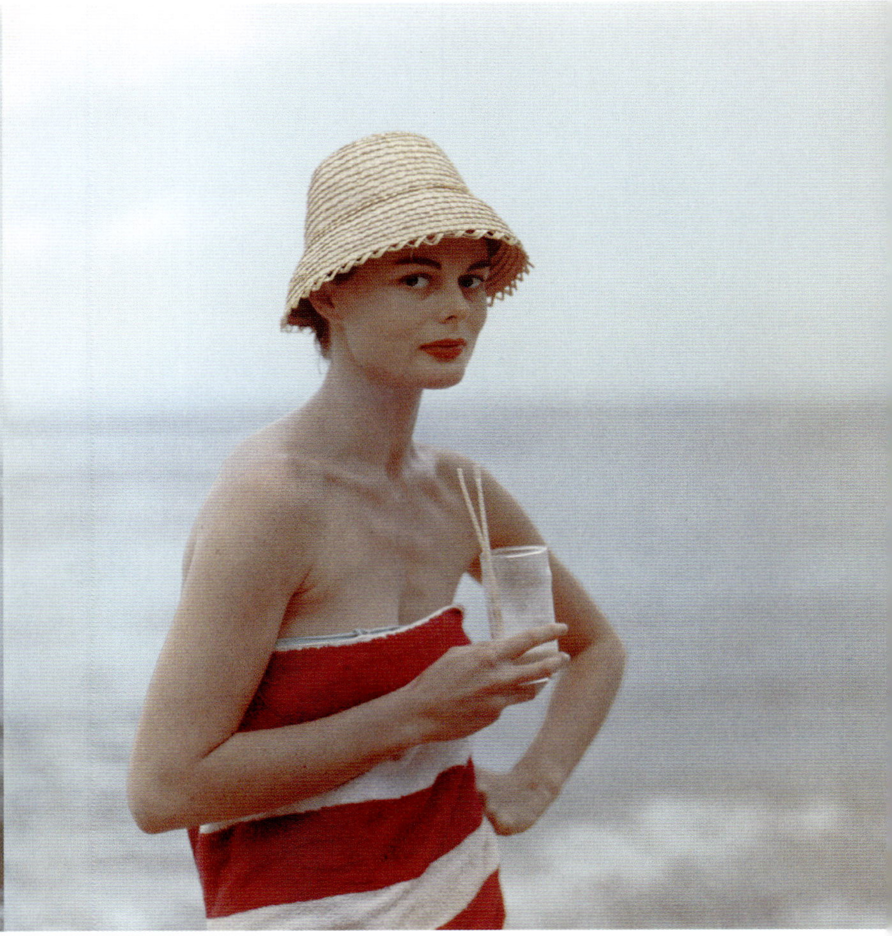

above Actress Dee Hartford sips a local drink called a Pussyfoot, Jamaica, 1958. A *Vogue* model turned actress, Hartford married the king of Hollywood directors at the time, Howard Hawks. She and her sister Eden, also an actress and married to Groucho Marx, quickened the pulse of Hollywood for a period with their great looks and gossip-column liaisons (see also pages 2 and 50).

opposite Inge Morath, Acapulco, 1961. Morath was an Austrian-born photographer who started her career in Paris in 1953. Some of her most notable work was of Marilyn Monroe, whom she photographed on the set of *The Misfits* in 1960. There she met Monroe's husband, playwright Arthur Miller. They later fell in love, and Morath became his third and last wife. Their daughter, Rebecca Miller, is a screenwriter and director. "Photography is a strange phenomenon," Morath once observed. "You trust your eye and cannot help but bare your soul."

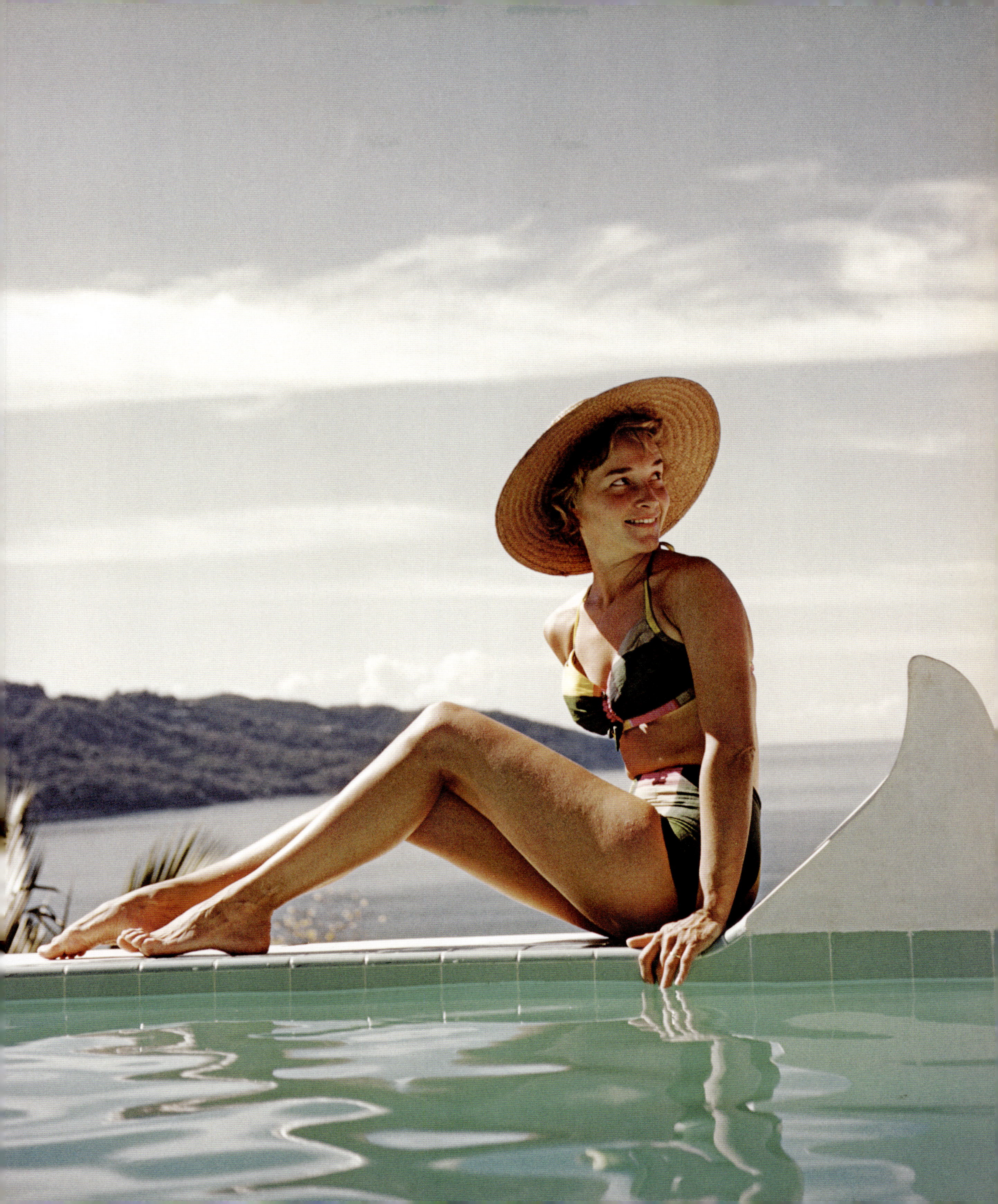

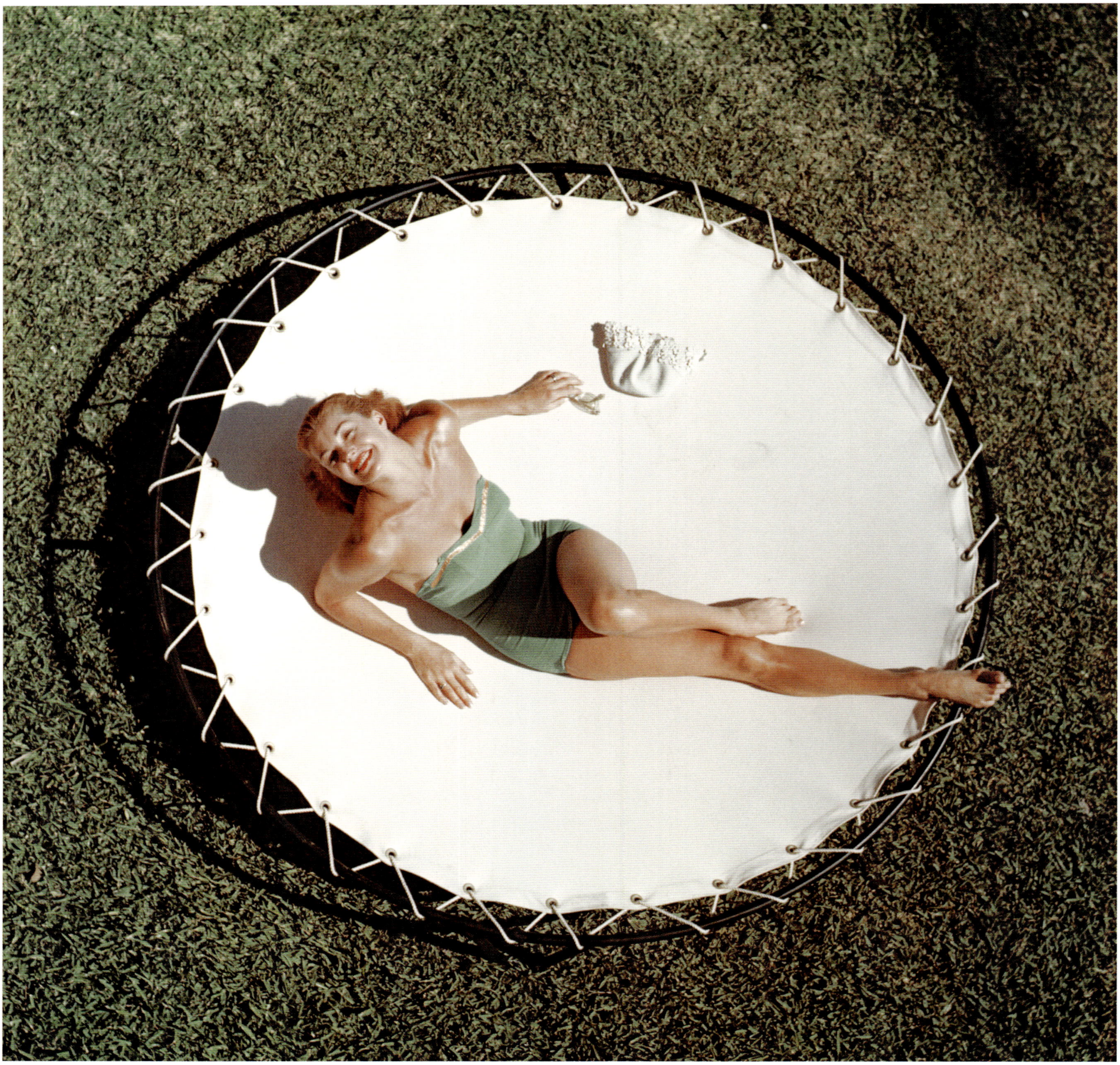

above and opposite The championship swimmer and movie star Esther Williams poolside in Florida, circa 1955. Williams was an American original, the darling of both the aquatic and the film worlds. Unable to compete in the 1940 Summer Olympic Games because they were canceled after World War II began, she joined Billy Rose's Aquacade in San Francisco, where she swam with *Tarzan* star Johnny Weissmuller—a five-time Olympic gold medalist in 1924 and 1928—and caught the attention of MGM scouts. At the pinnacle of her movie career, from 1945 to 1949, the actress dubbed "the Million Dollar Mermaid" had at least one film in the top twenty box office hits each year. After retiring, Williams invested in a variety of successful businesses—besides a line of swimwear and instructional swimming books and videos, she owned a metal products plant and a service station, traded in real estate, and was a commentator at the 1984 Summer Olympics.

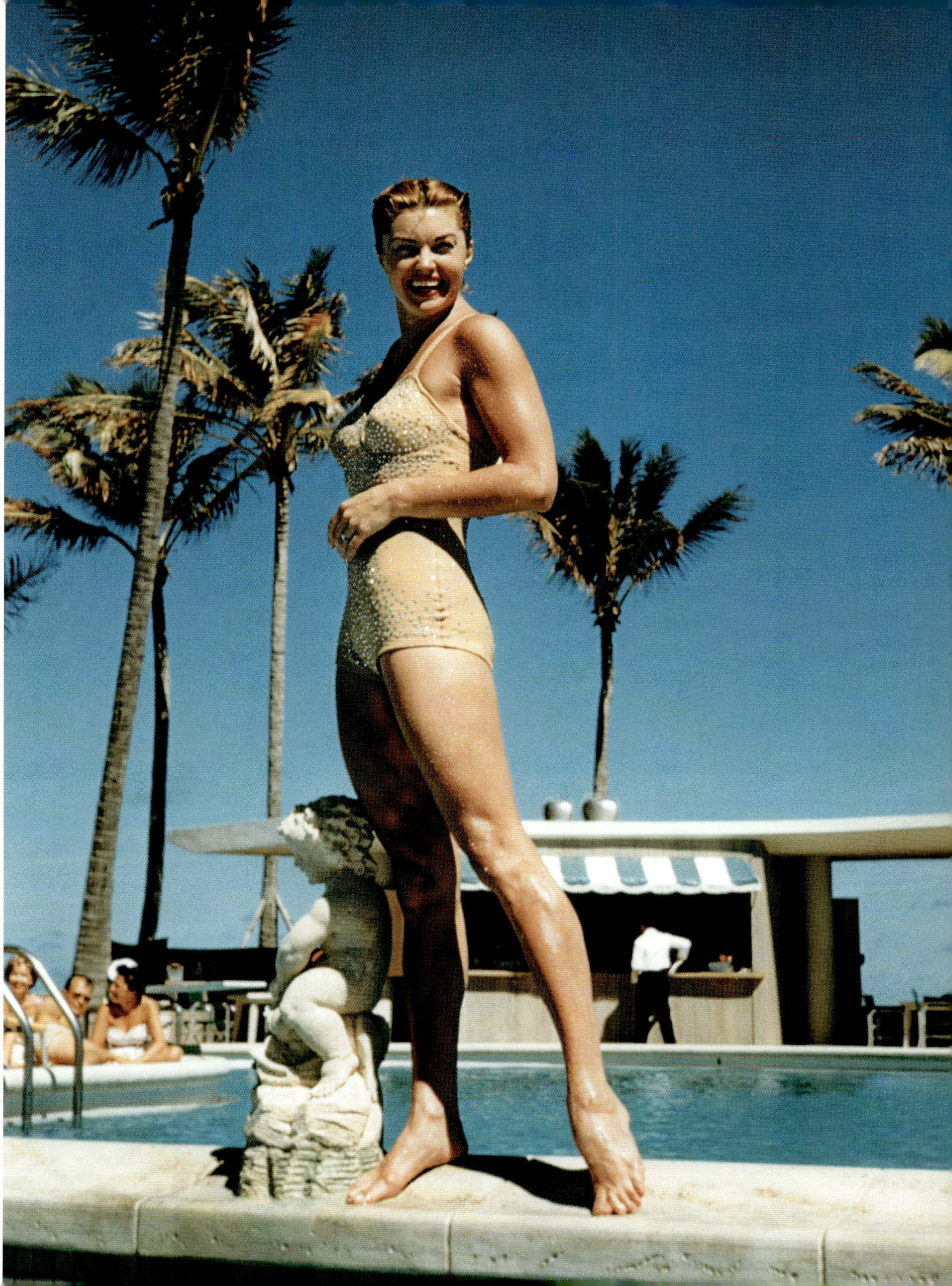

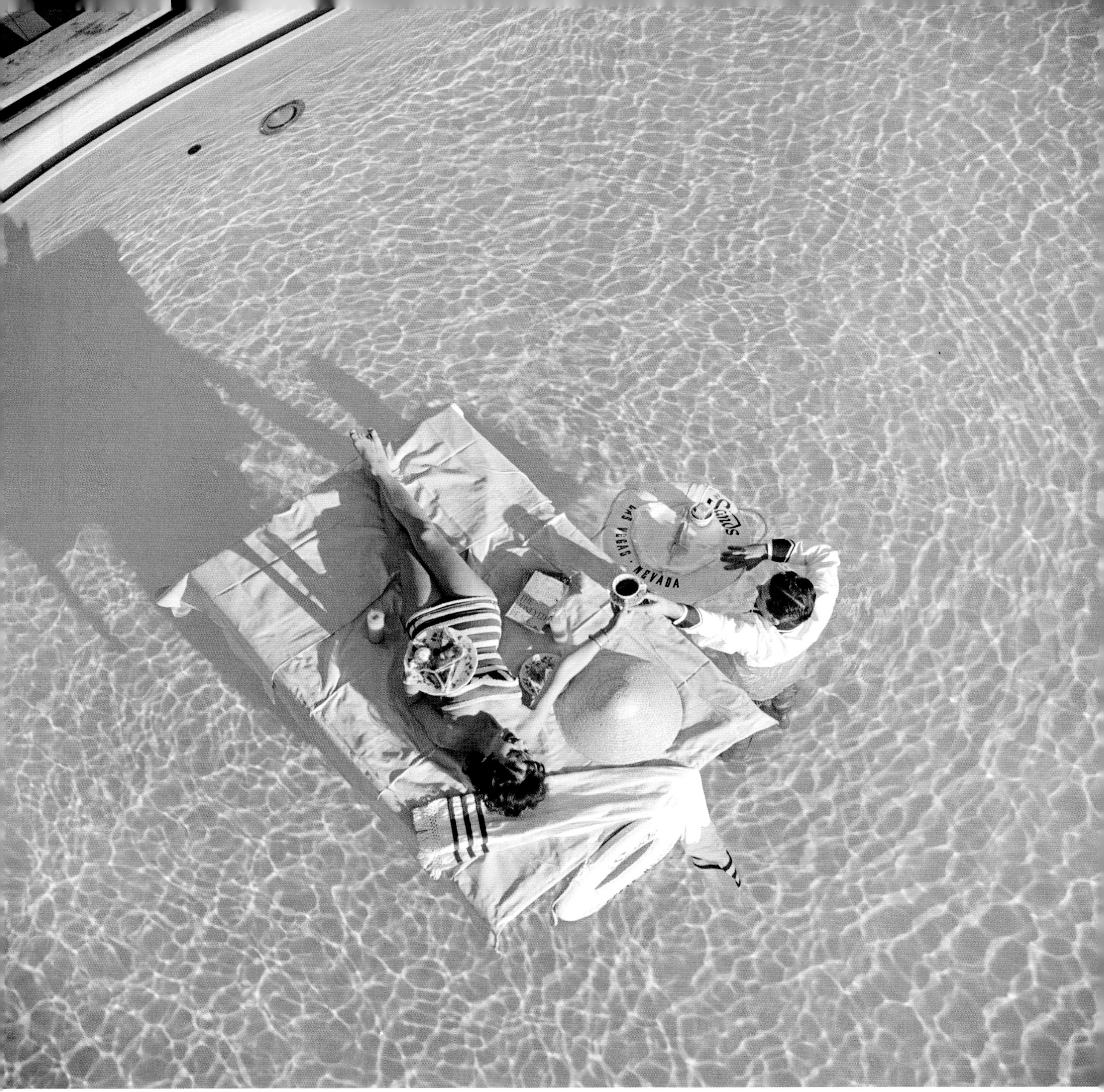

above and opposite The Austrian actress Mara Lane at the Sands Hotel, Las Vegas, 1954. Born Dorothy Bolton, Lane appeared in more than thirty films from 1951 to 1965. Slim took these photographs from the top of a Las Vegas ladder truck (see page 7). Slim was forever asking hotel managers and homeowners if he could see the view from a building's highest floor. If he had to arrange more than a few people from on high, he favored using a bullhorn, if available, and could never resist jovially booming to all down below, "This is the voice of God!" He also hired rowboats and motorboats, helicopters and hot-air balloons all over the world in pursuit of a fresh perspective.

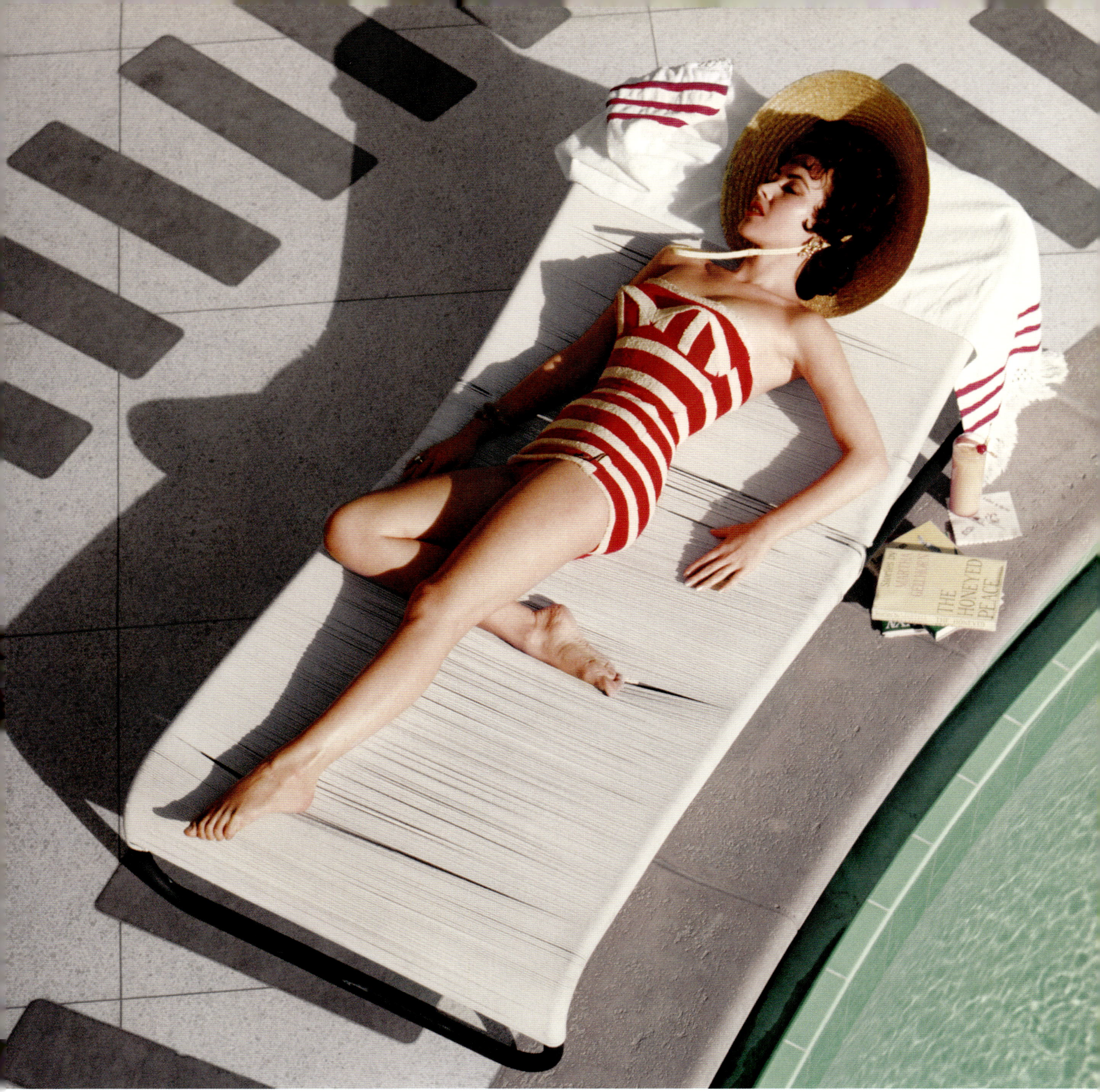

following spread Socialite Alice Topping, Palm Beach, 1959. The image (right) of Topping poolside has become one of Slim's most celebrated photographs. To the left are various outtakes from the same shoot. Topping was the type of female subject Slim most loved to photograph: great looking, unfussy, and splendidly self-confident. In 1992 he commented on the reaction when the poolside photo was first published in the late 1950s: "This innocent photo was considered risqué—people thought she was in her underwear."

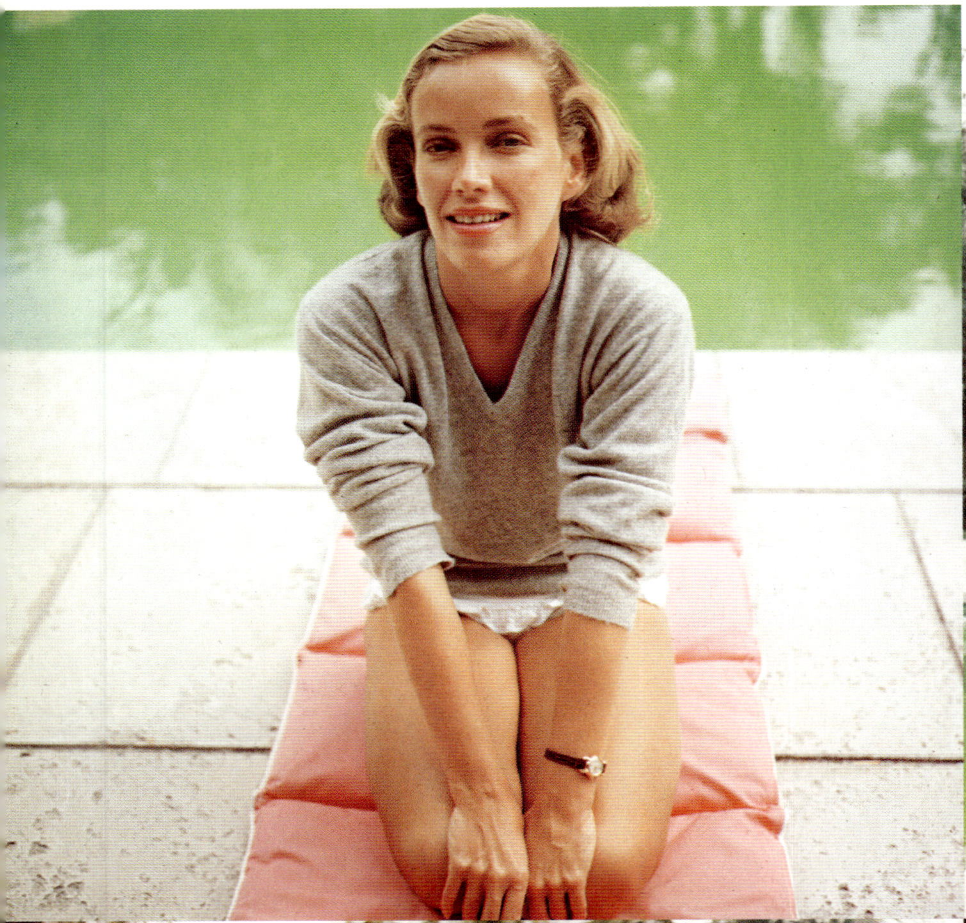

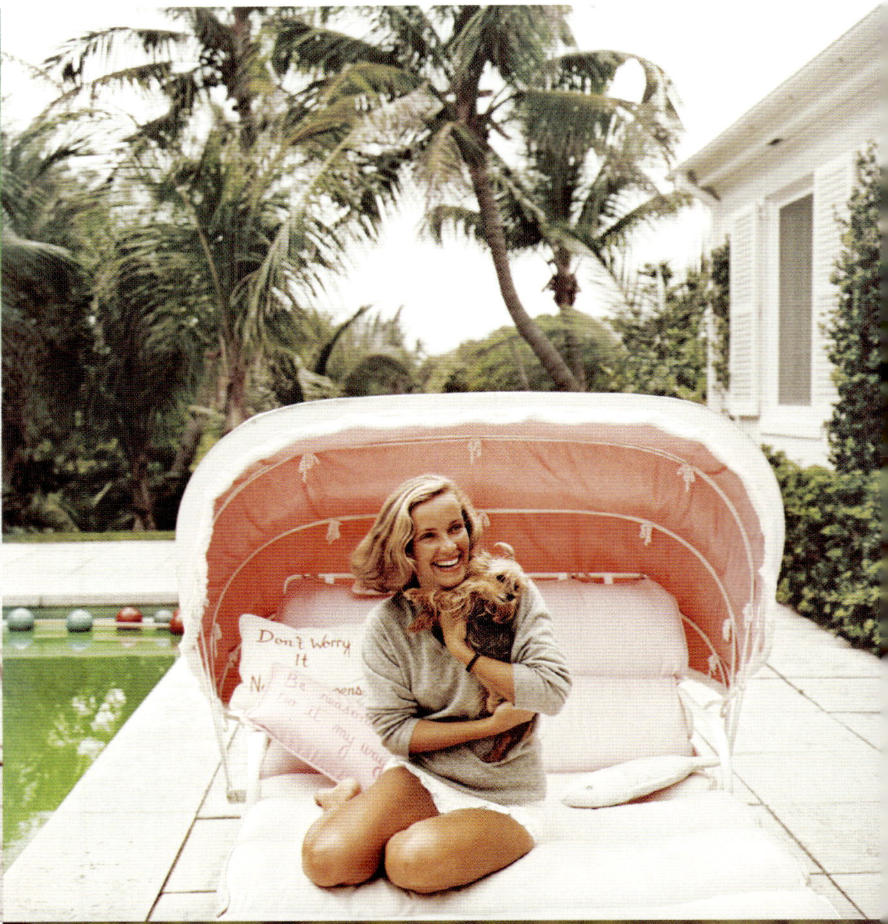
Don't Worry
It

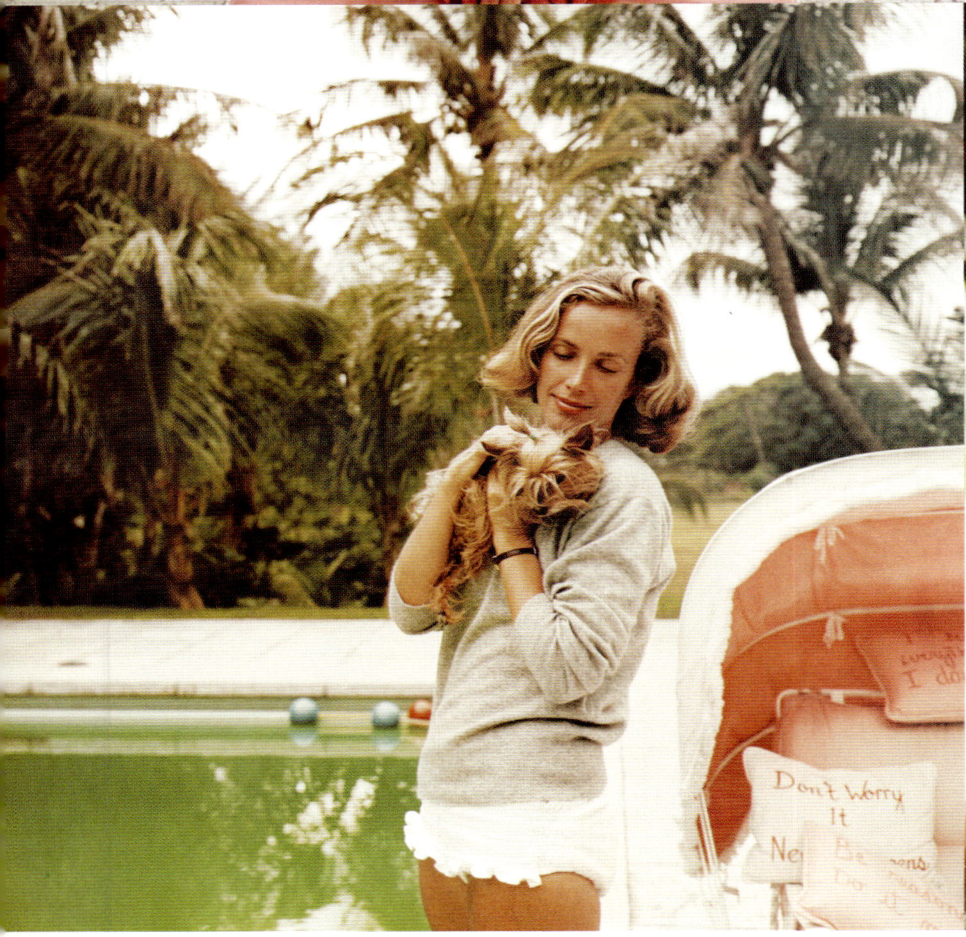
Don't Worry
It

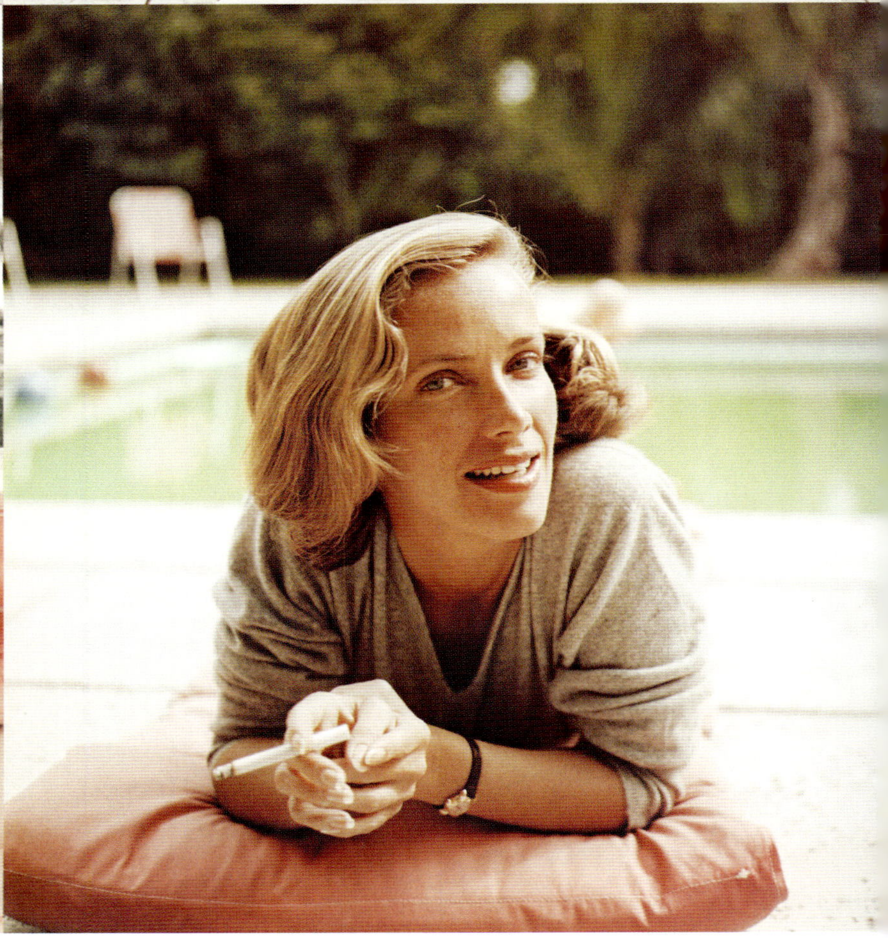

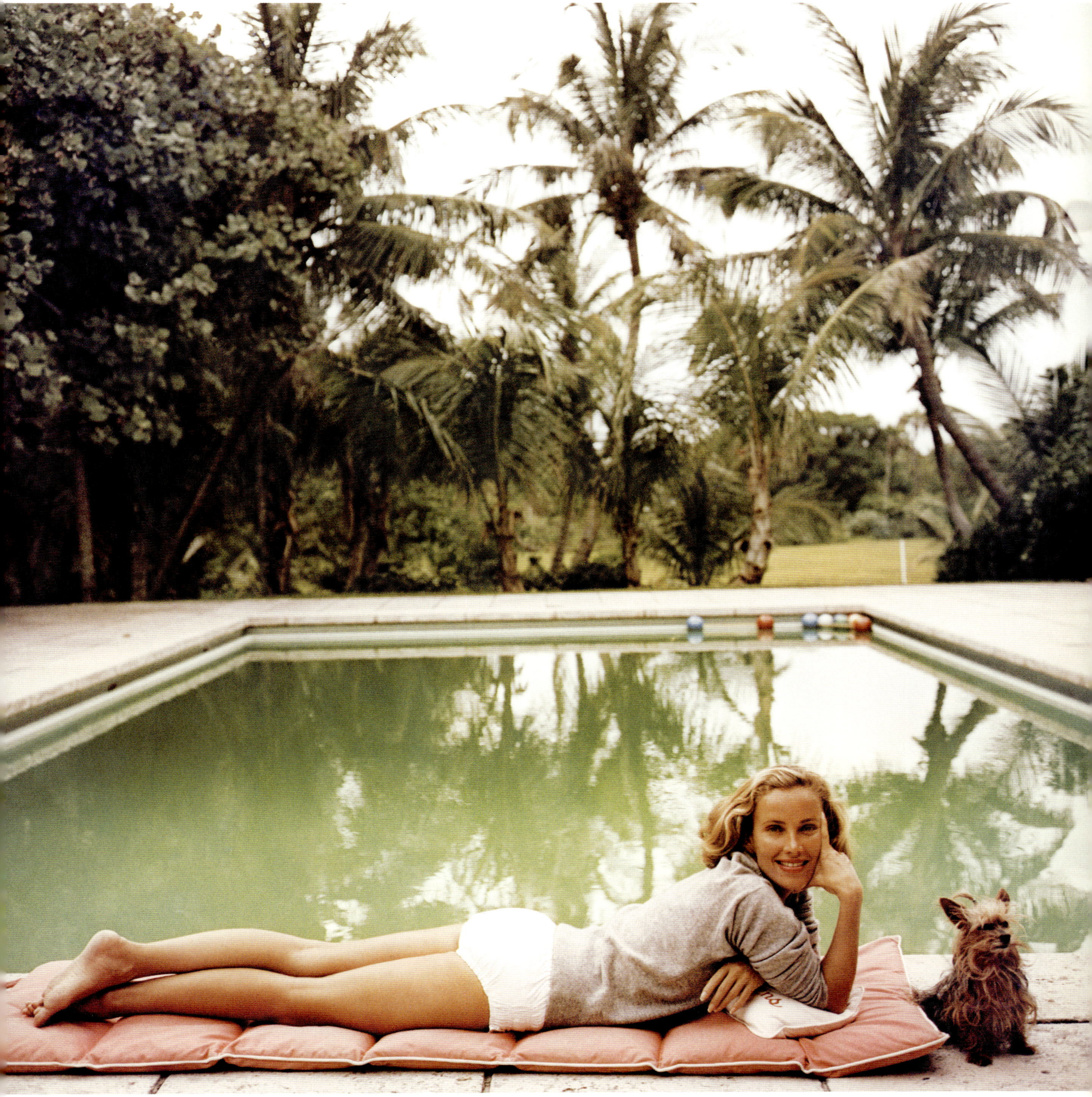

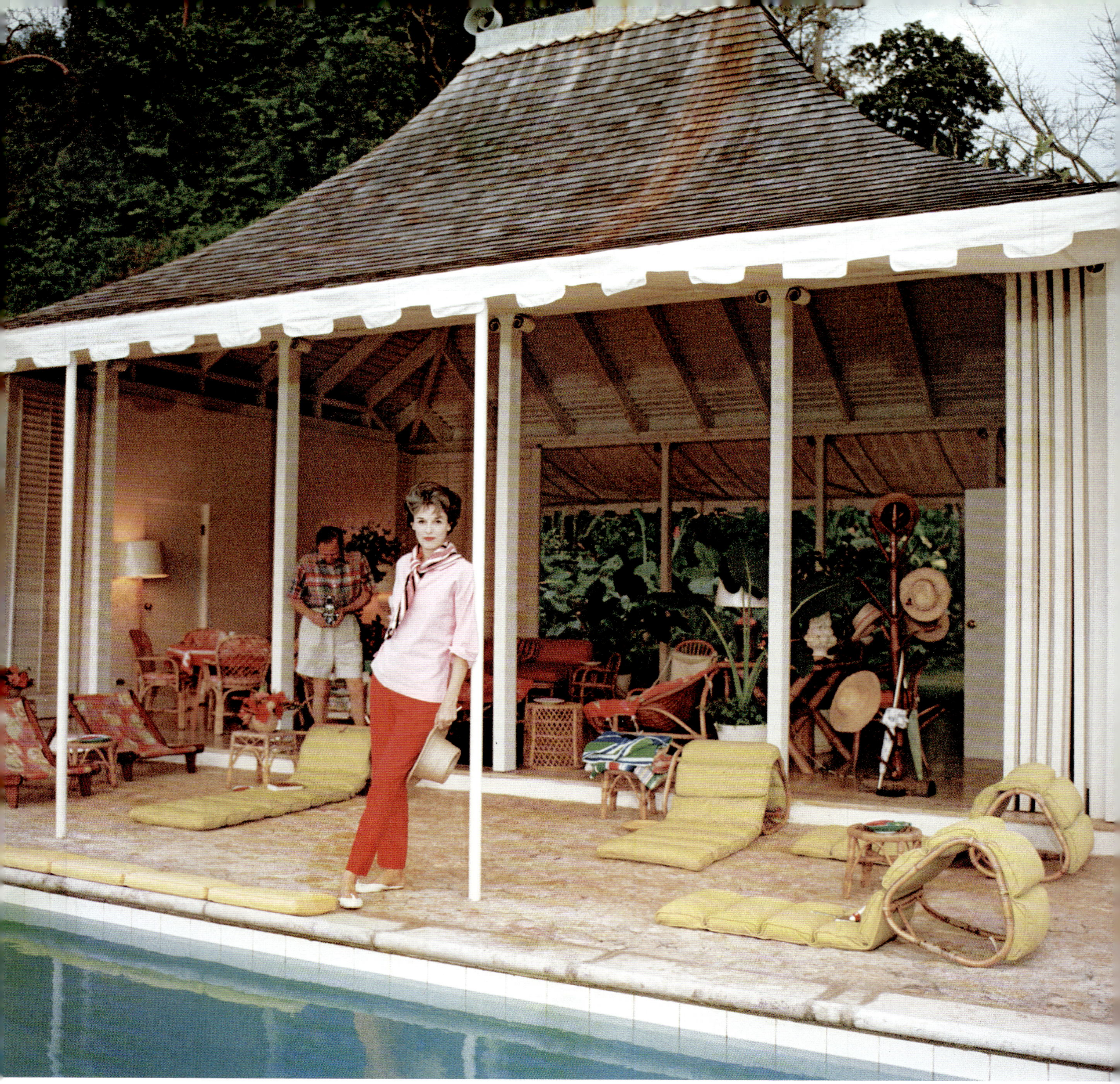

above Babe Paley by the pool at her cottage, Round Hill, Jamaica, 1959. More than thirty years after her death, Barbara "Babe" Cushing Mortimer Paley (see also page 150) remains one of the leading American style icons of all time. She and her husband William S. Paley, founder of CBS (and visible in this image taking a photo of Slim), were one of the great power couples of their era. Impeccably ancestored and a *Vogue* editor, she was known to possess a great wit and is widely credited with coining the line "You can never be too rich or too thin." Babe Paley was one of the three famous and beautiful Cushing sisters, who, along with Betsey Roosevelt Whitney and Minnie Astor Fosburgh, would entertain the world with their numerous marriages and escapades. Truman Capote said of Paley, "She had only one flaw: She was perfect. Other than that, she was perfect." And Bill Blass

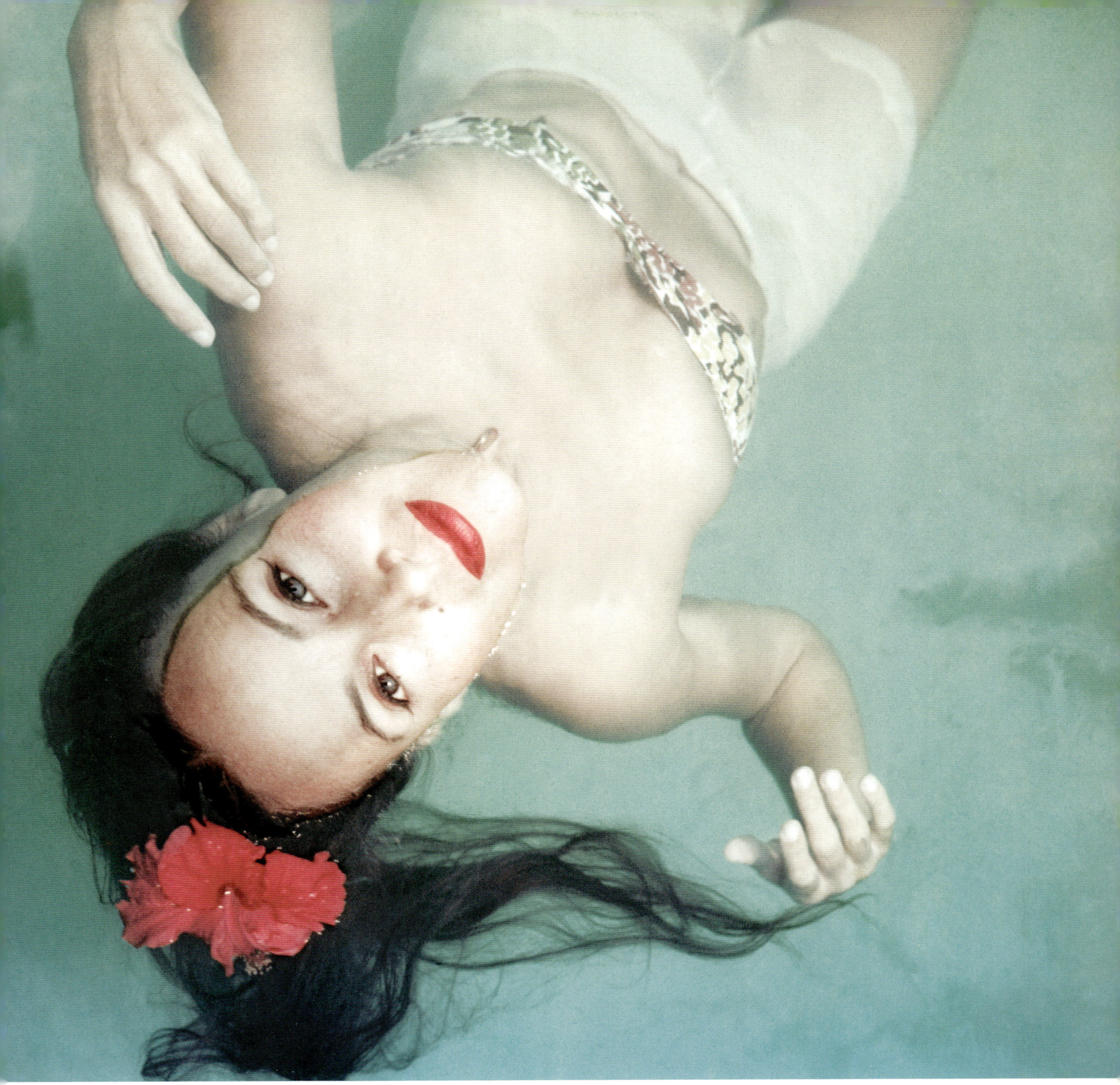

once observed, "I never saw her not grab anyone's attention, the hair, the makeup, the crispness. You were never conscious of what she was wearing; you noticed Babe and nothing else." Slim was proud of this photo and the accolades it has received—but most of all he was thrilled that a giant like Bill Paley was snapping *his* photo.

above The Mexican film star Dolores del Rio, Acapulco, 1952. In 1940s and 1950s Hollywood, del Rio was the first major Latina crossover star. In a time when the norm was to hide the ethnicity of actors, anglicize names, and follow the narrow directives of the studio formula, del Rio challenged Hollywood's prevailing views on race and gender.

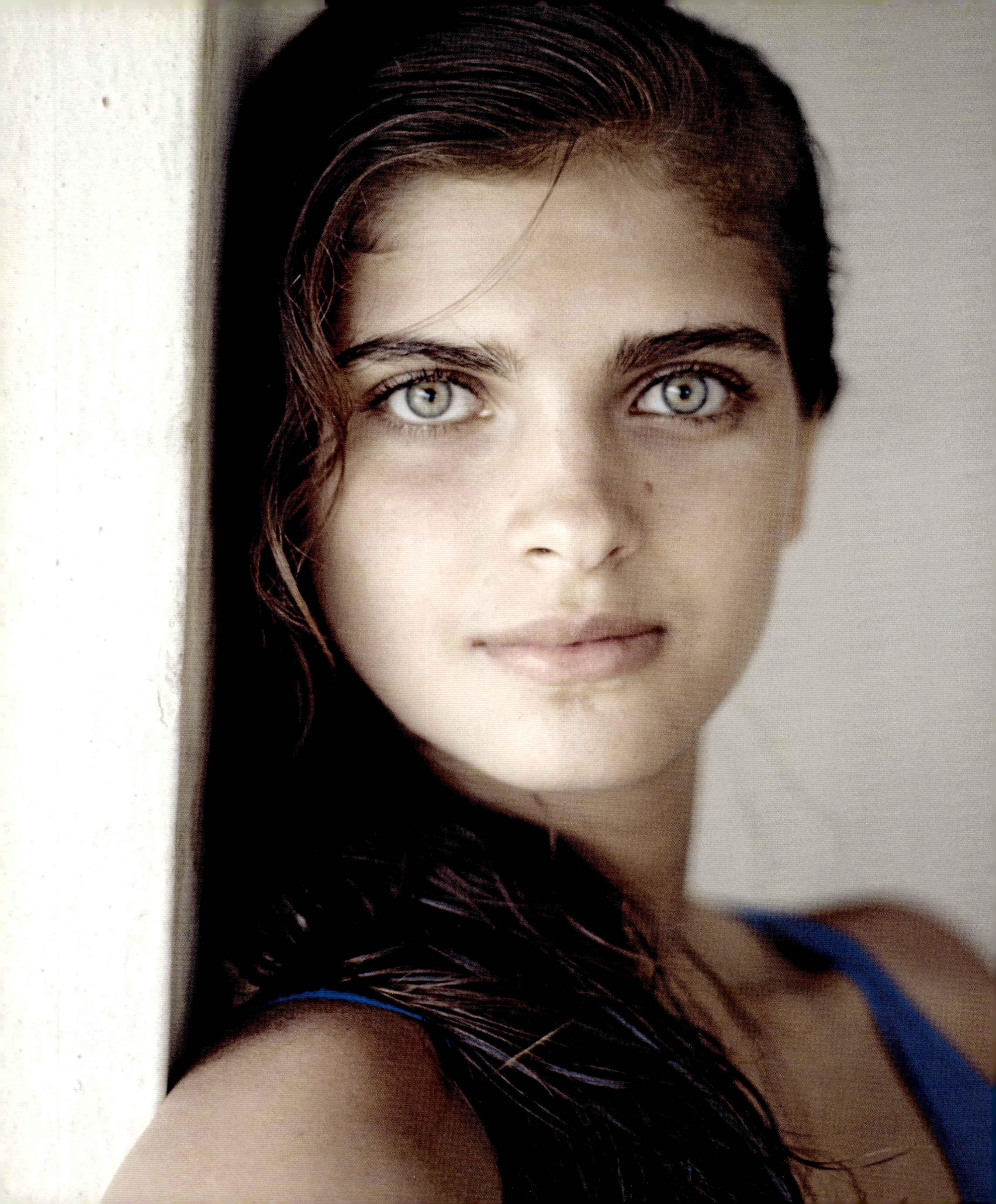

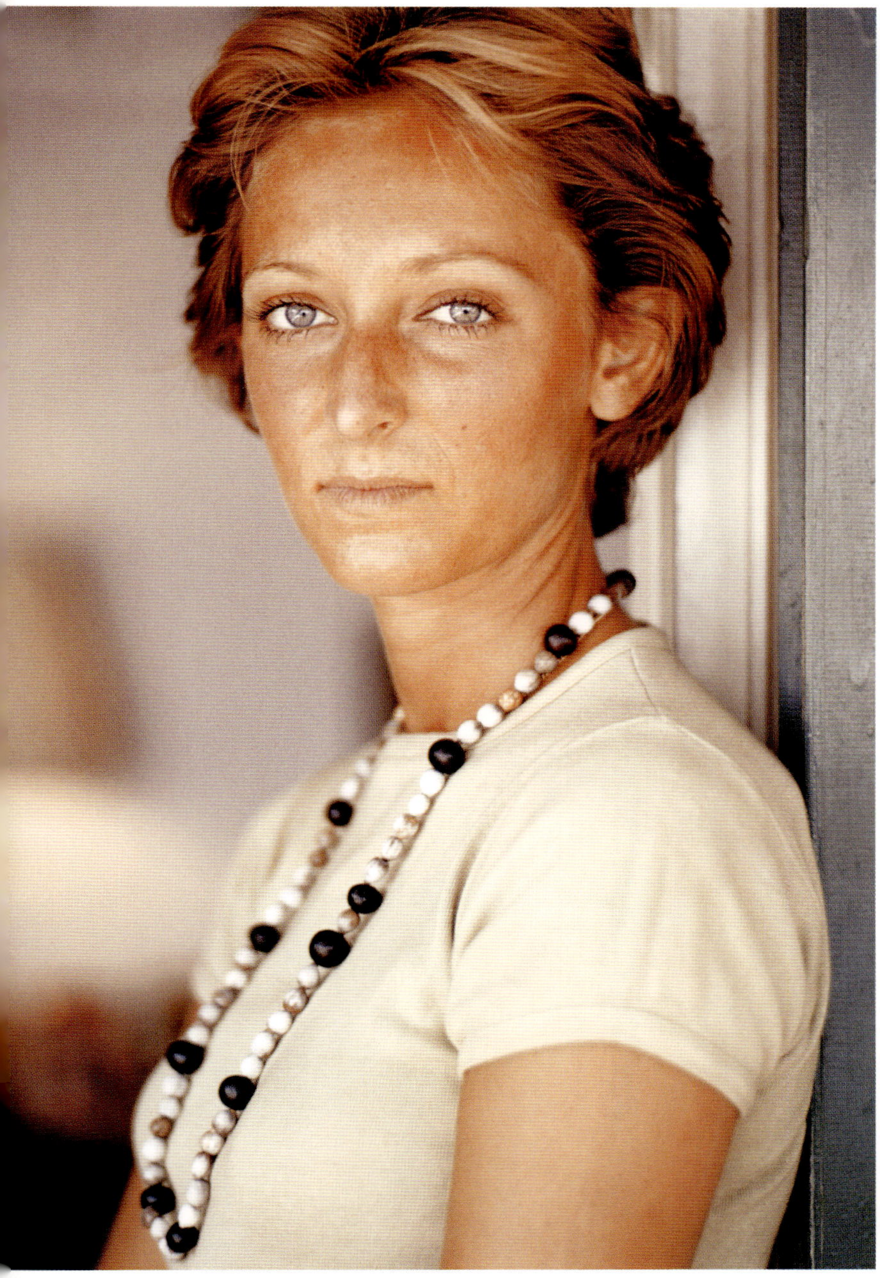

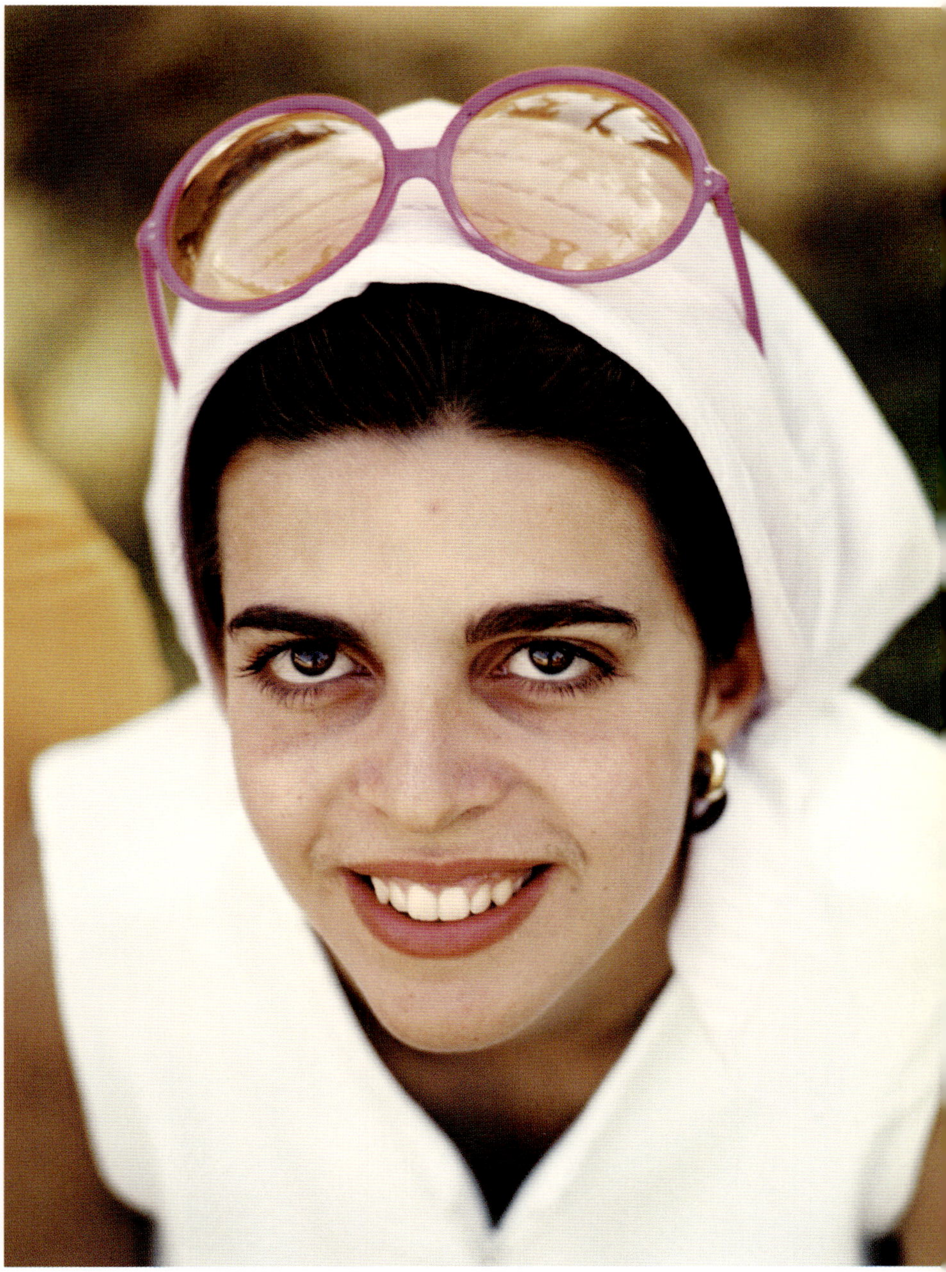

opposite Kristie Karbstein Gerep, Brazil, 1988. Shortly after Slim snapped this photo, an accident left her a quadriplegic. Her prognosis was so dire that one doctor told her she could not even sit up and was condemned to be bedridden for life. Nearly three decades later she is married (now Kristie Hanbury), the mother of five, Brazil's most celebrated female polo player, and widely credited with popularizing the sport there.

above left Countess Desideria Corsini, Porto Ercole, Italy, 1973.

above right Christina Onassis, daughter of the Greek shipping tycoon Aristotle Onassis, Palm Beach, 1968.

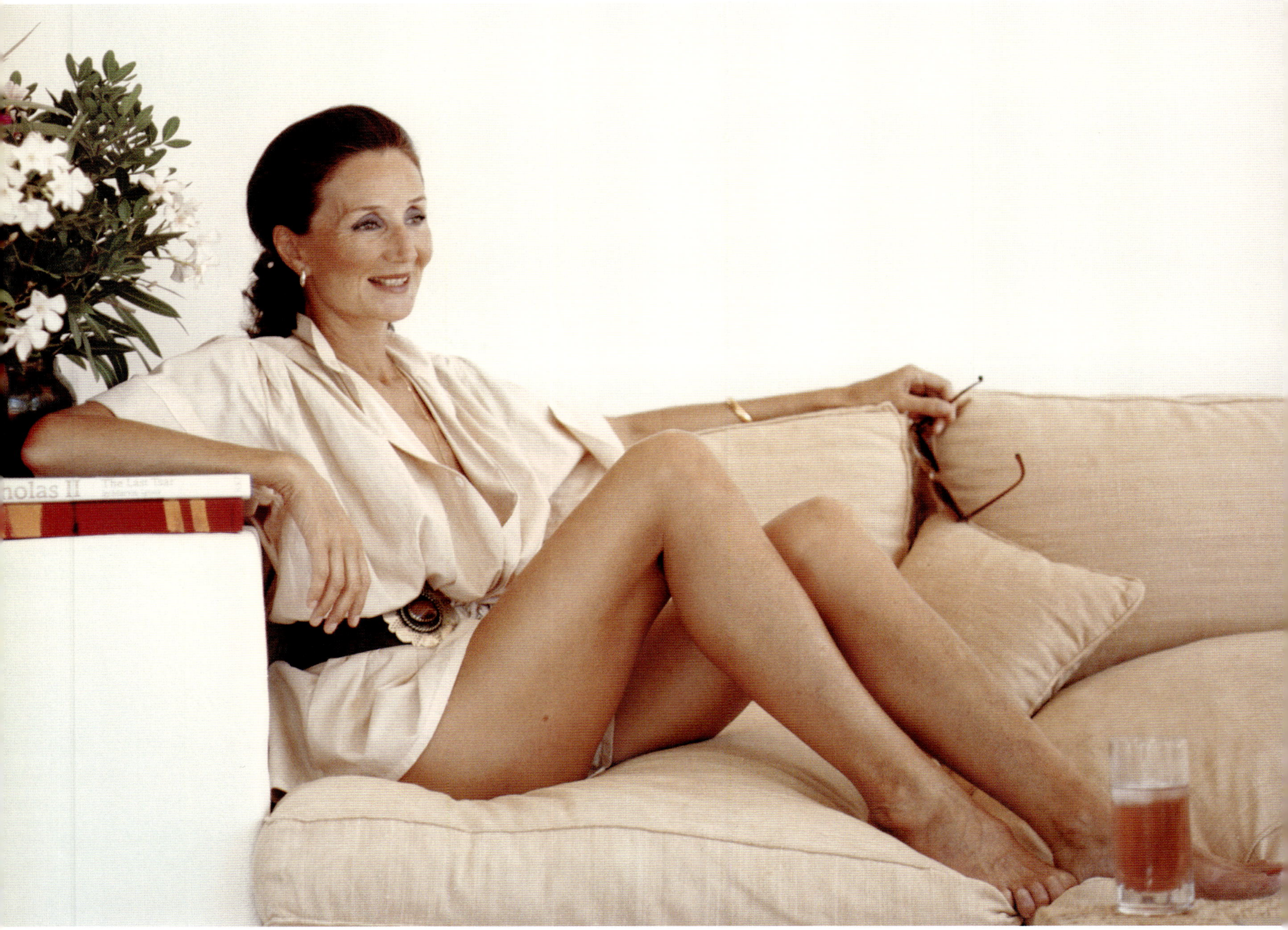

above and opposite French style icon Viscountess Jacqueline de Ribes relaxes on the terrace of her house in Ibiza, Spain, 1978. Once described as France's greatest fashion export, de Ribes comfortably reigned in her role as French socialite and unparalleled connoisseur of haute couture for years. Her sense of style and imagination were celebrated in particular for her tendency to tweak certain details of the designer clothing she wore, transforming them beyond their original look, often breaking long-established sartorial rules. In 1983 she turned to designing clothes herself. A conversation with her friend and agent Jody Donohue revealed an anecdote about this photo shoot that typified Slim and perhaps the viscountess as well. Slim loved wordplay and also loved to demonstrate to certain people that he was the one in charge. The photo shoot in Ibiza took a couple of hours to plan and execute, and during the time spent together Slim kept calling the viscountess, whom he'd met only briefly once or twice before, "Jackie." According to Ms. Donohue, de Ribes had never been called "Jackie" by anyone and typically would have been incensed to be referred to this way. But throughout the entire photo shoot she never said a word about it and did not correct him. They parted friends and over the years a mutual admiration and respect grew between them.

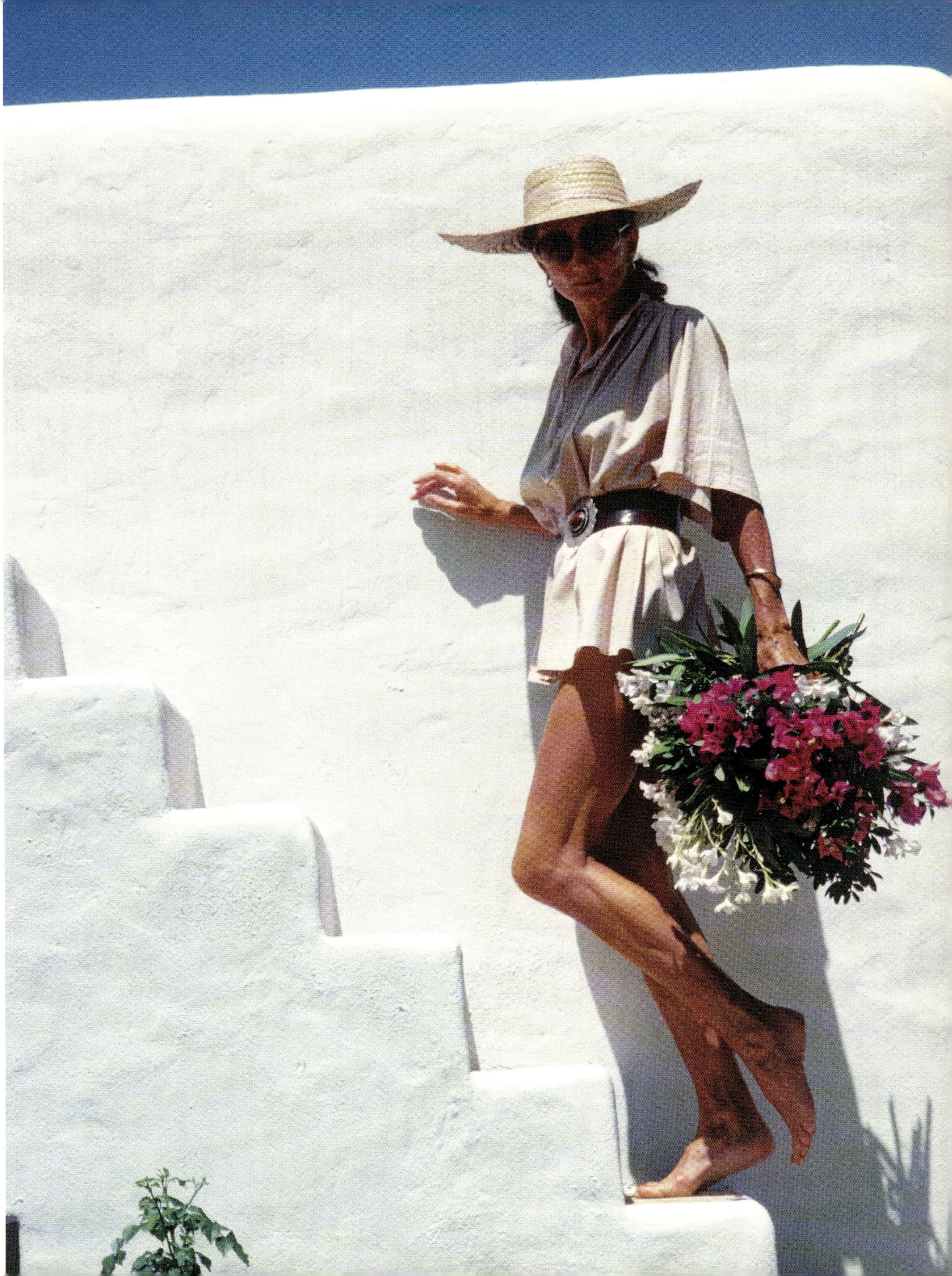

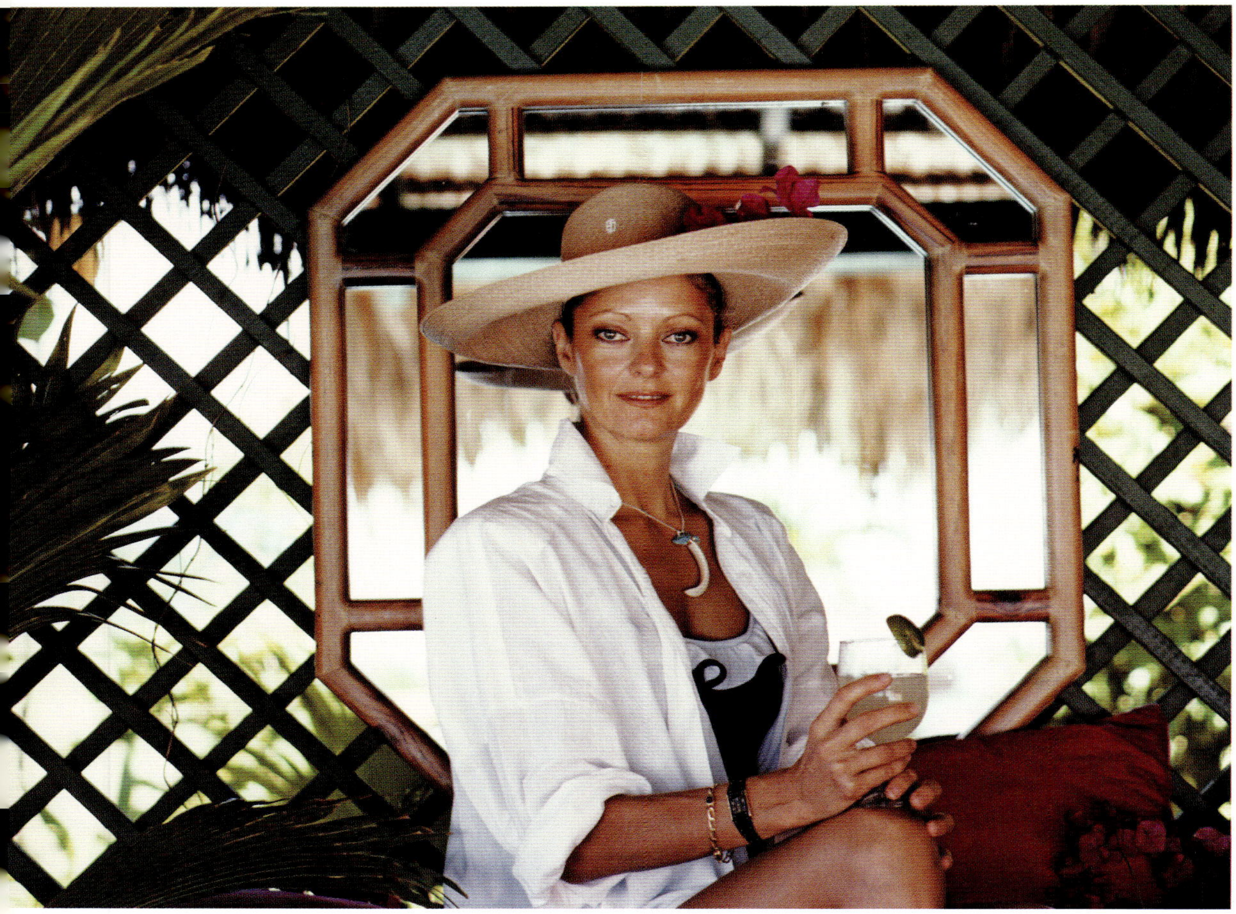

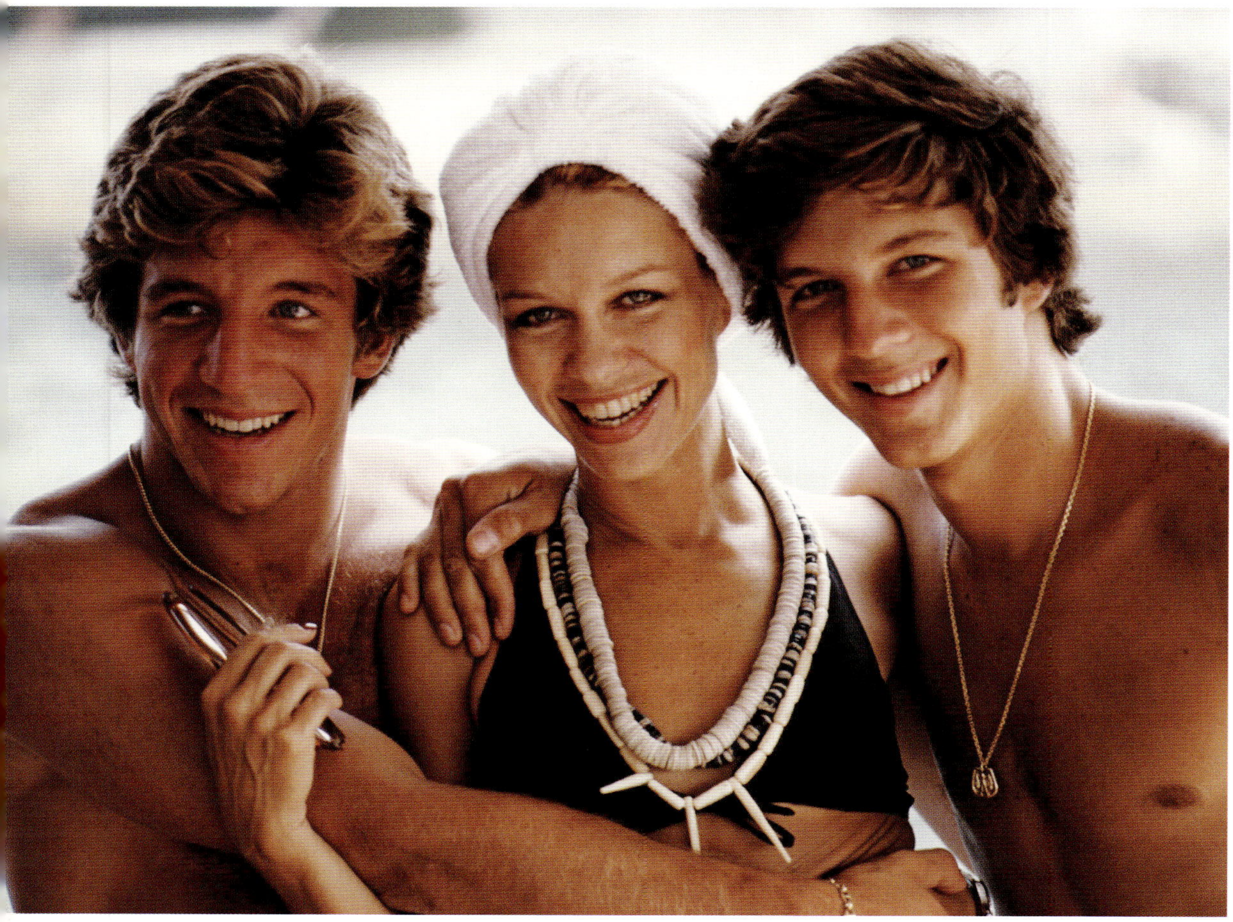

above left Countess Christina de Caraman Goldsmith, Casa de Campo, Dominican Republic, 1985. Born in Mexico to a French duke and English mother, de Caraman was first photographed by Slim on the slopes of Switzerland when she was a teenager. She had homes in many of the hot spots Slim frequented—Paris, Gstaad, and Monte Carlo—and every time he ran into her he arranged to take her photograph. They had an ease of affection with each other, which I believe is apparent in this image. Their relationship demonstrated the way he built trust with some of his more venerated subjects. In many cases he photographed them repeatedly over time and made certain never to let a less-than-perfect photo leave his studio, lest a magazine art director decide to run the questionable image. Thus his track record for making beautiful people even more so was unimpeachable.

below left Lynn Wyatt and her sons Steven (left) and Douglas (right), Monte Carlo, 1975. One of the great society ladies of her generation, she married the Texas oil legend Oscar Wyatt and they settled in Houston with their four sons. The petite blonde was well known for her love of the social whirl, flawless taste, and contagious laughter, all of which made her a fixture on the international party circuit. Her fried chicken dinners for Mick Jagger were legendary, as were her associations with Princess Grace, Prince Rainier, and Henry Kissinger. The Duchess of York once referred to the Wyatts as "walking wallets" for their lavish parties. Wyatt is reputed to have once flown in four thousand yellow roses for a party in Monaco. Slim photographed her all over the world and loved her simply because "you can't take a bad picture of Lynn."

opposite Tania Mallet, Eleuthera, Bahamas, 1961. An English model, Mallet made the leap to acting in the early 1960s, landing the role of Tilly Masterson in the James Bond film *Goldfinger*. She then turned down all other film offers and returned to modeling, citing a lack of freedom and abysmal pay—she claimed she could make in a day what the film industry was offering her for a week. Today, at age seventy-four, she is still modeling.

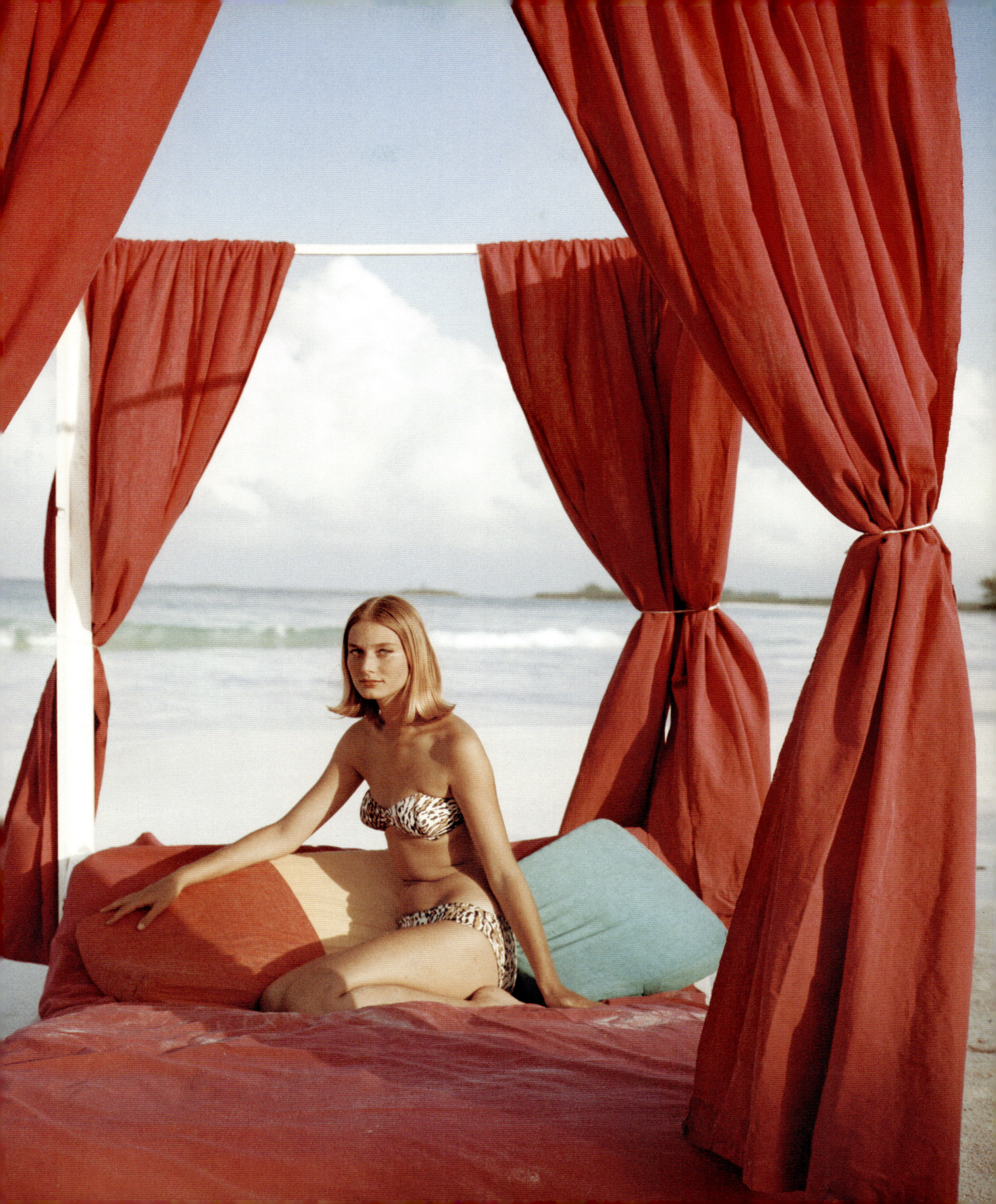

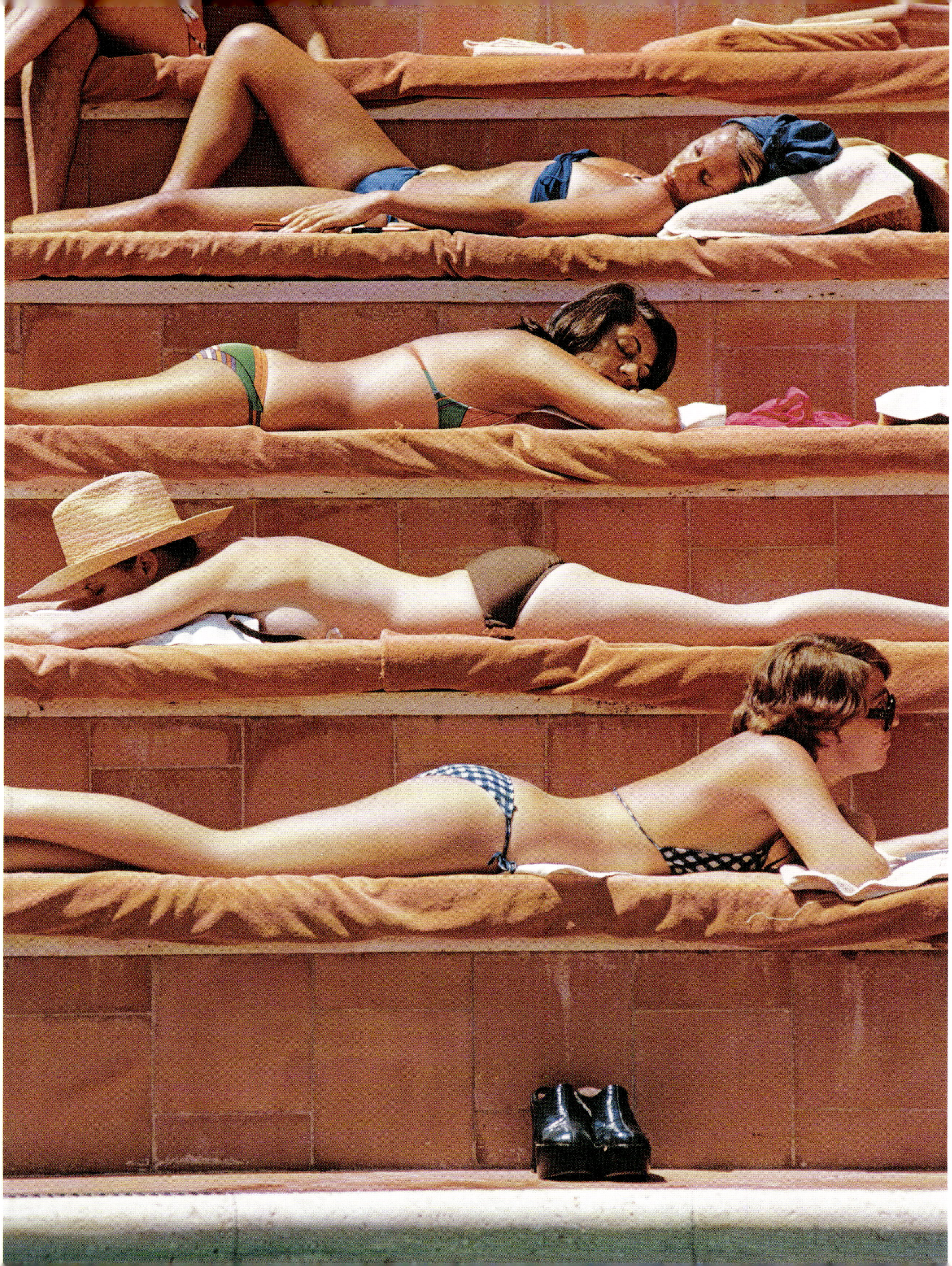

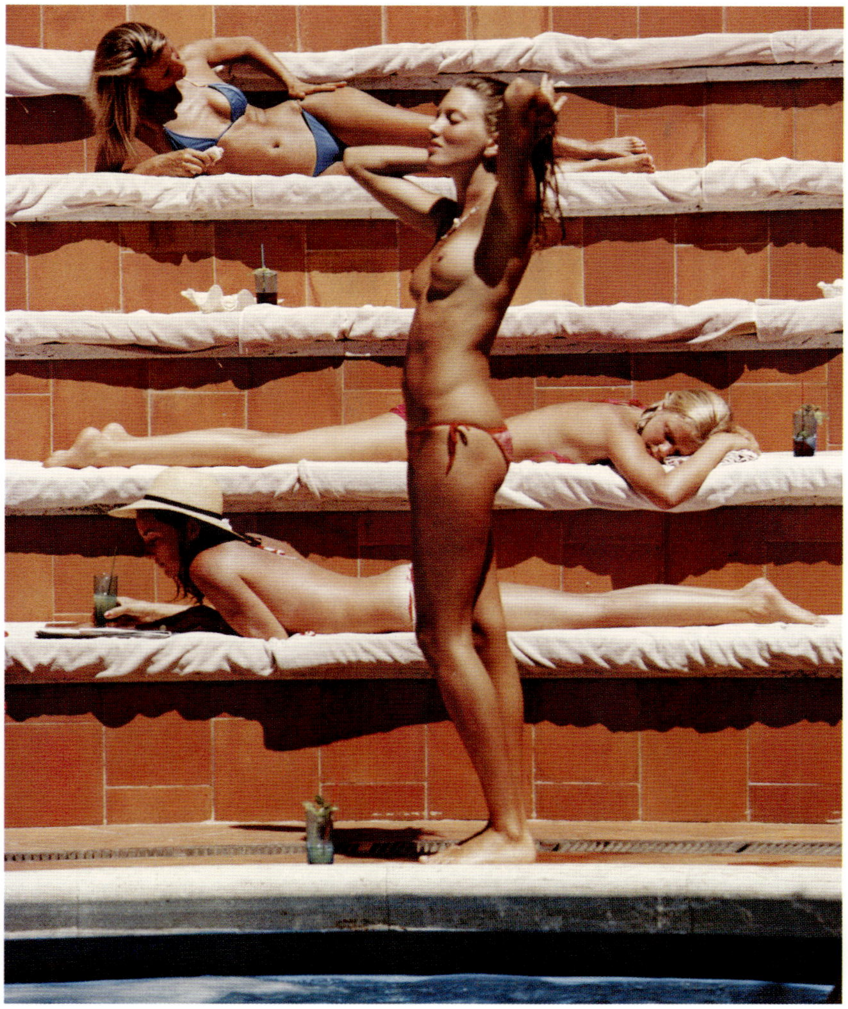
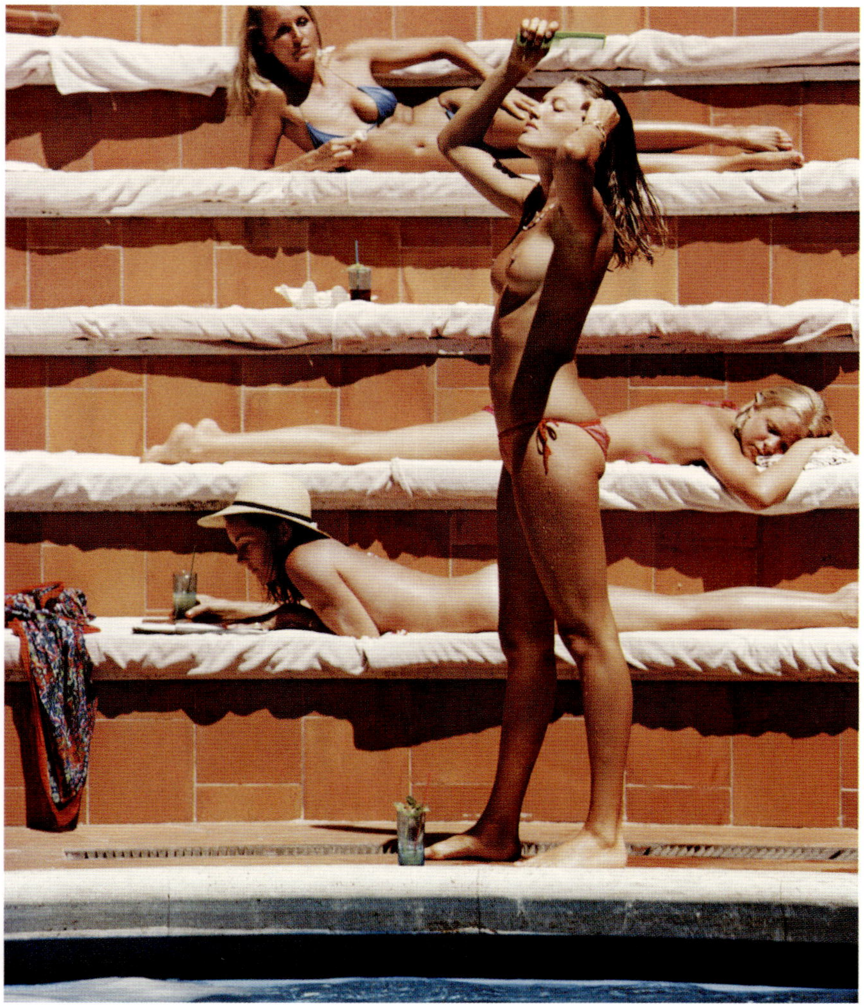
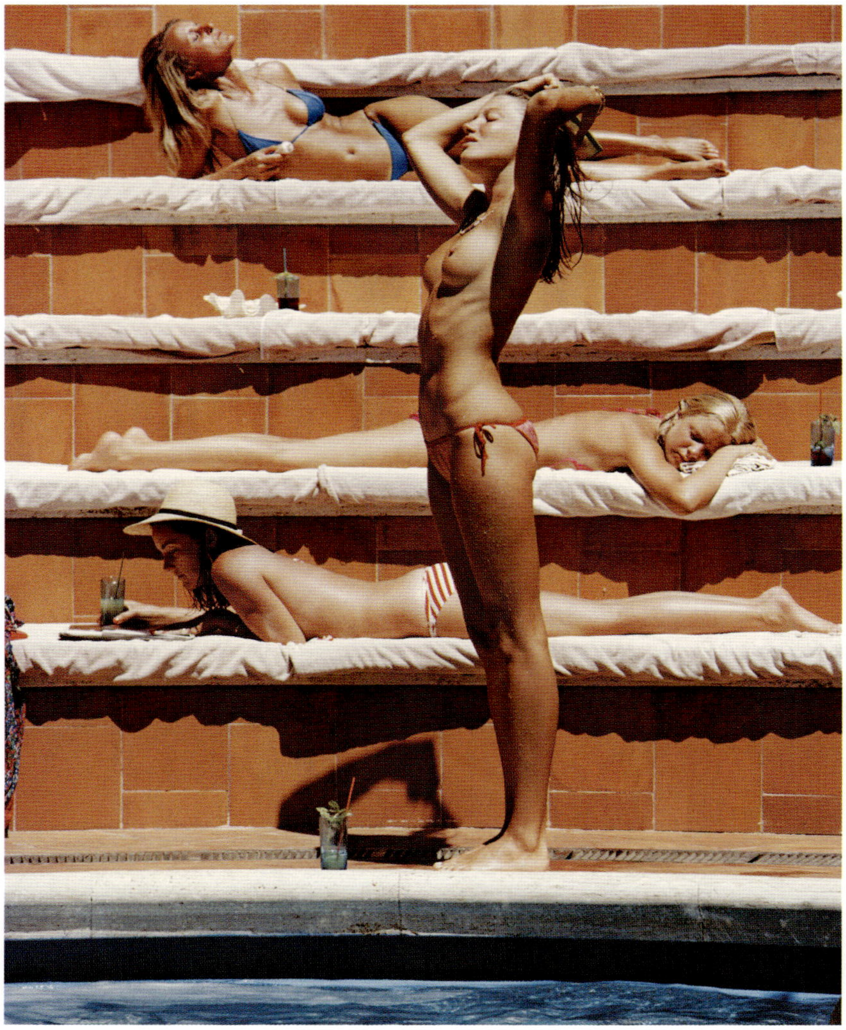
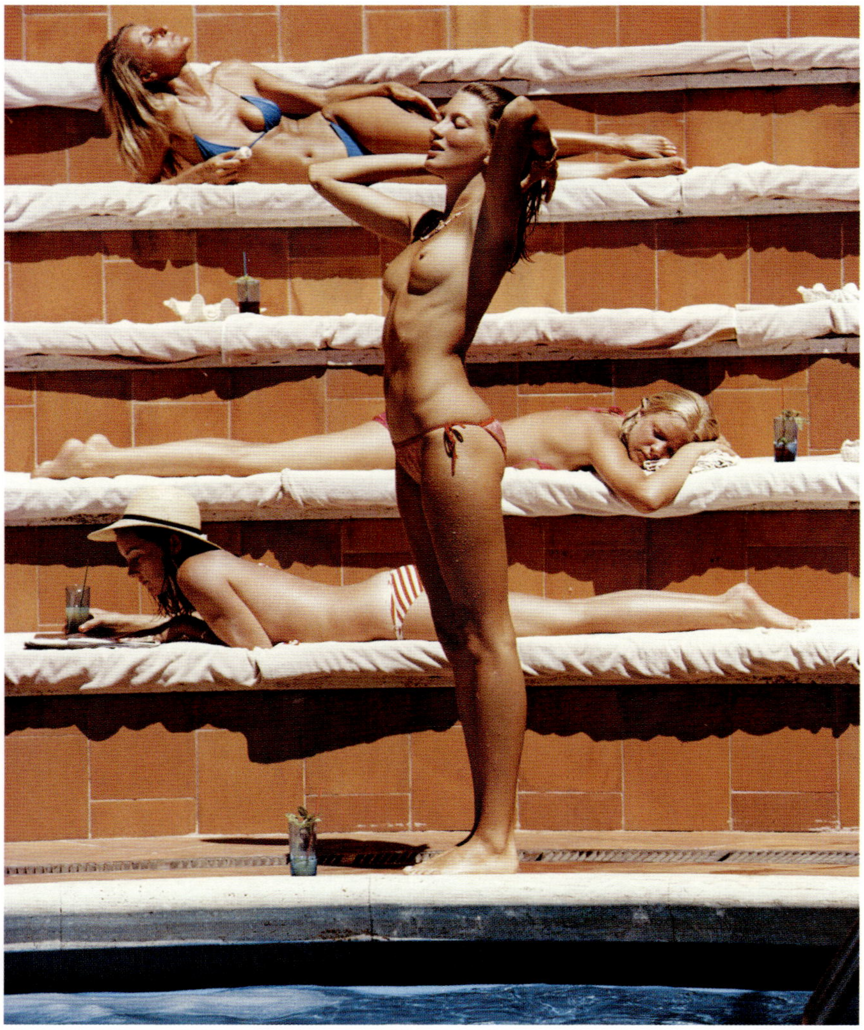

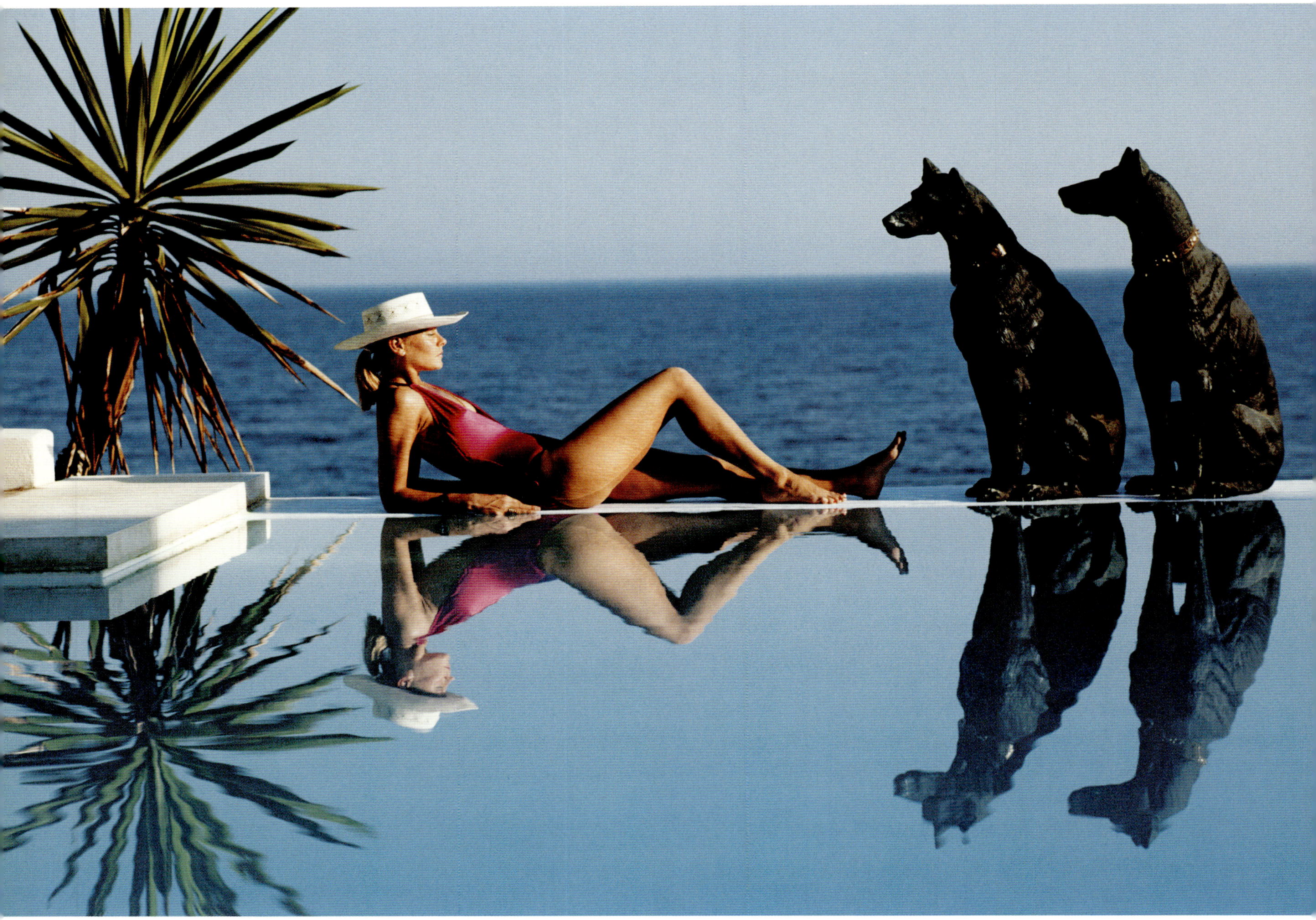

preceding spread Sunbathers, Capri, 1980. Slim set up this shoot at a little hotel in Italy and years later he still loved how it turned out—the tight composition, the sunbathing beauties, and his friend and fellow photographer Elisabetta Catalano as an extra in the blue bathing suit at the top. When model Catherine Wilke stepped into the shot, the resulting photograph (below right) became one of Slim's most lauded photographs. Included here are various images from the shoot, and in this case, the outtakes are nearly as alluring as the famous one. Also pictured are Charlotte Ticken and Pamela Grupas.

above Laura Hawk, Villa El Rincón, Marbella, Spain, 1985. Working with Slim entailed performing a wide variety of tasks, not the least of which was participating as an extra whenever needed. In this shot, I gladly filled in as a carefree guest luxuriating in the warmth of the Mediterranean sun.

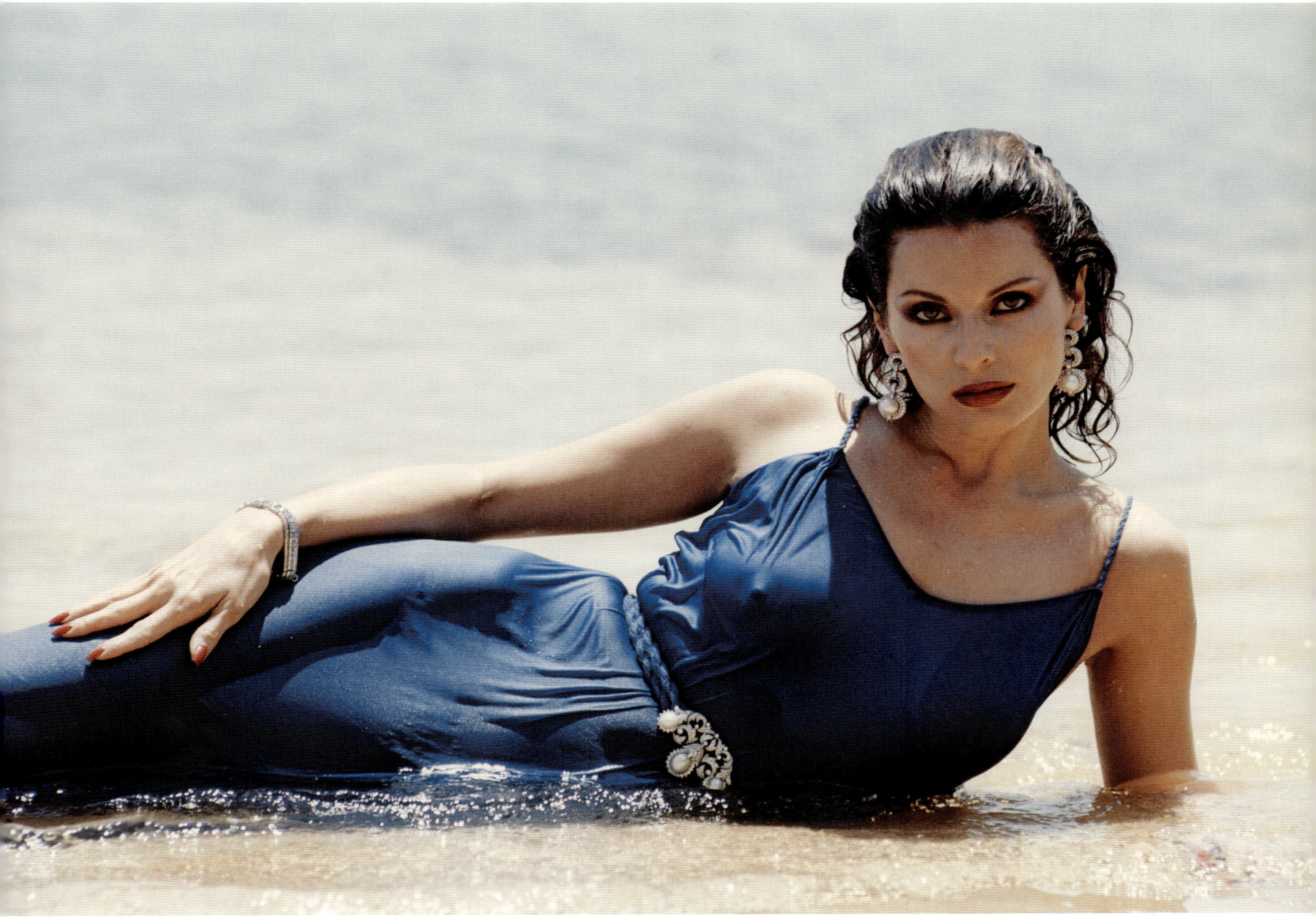

above Karen Kopseng Davis, Casa de Campo, Dominican Republic, 1977. The American singer (see also page 132) was on the cusp of making her operatic debut at La Scala in Milan. This photograph was one of the few from his nearly fifty-year career that Slim displayed in his home in Katonah, New York.

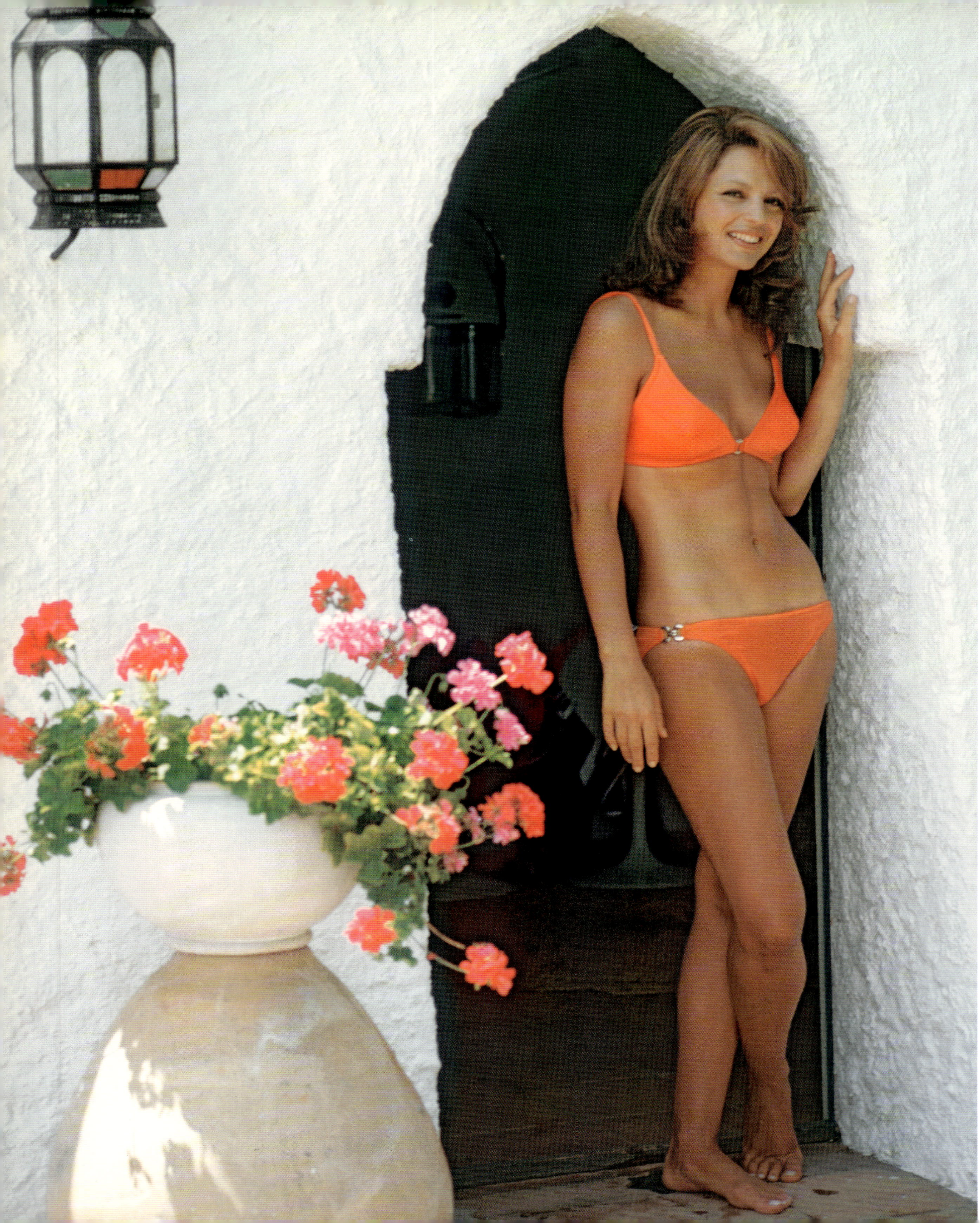

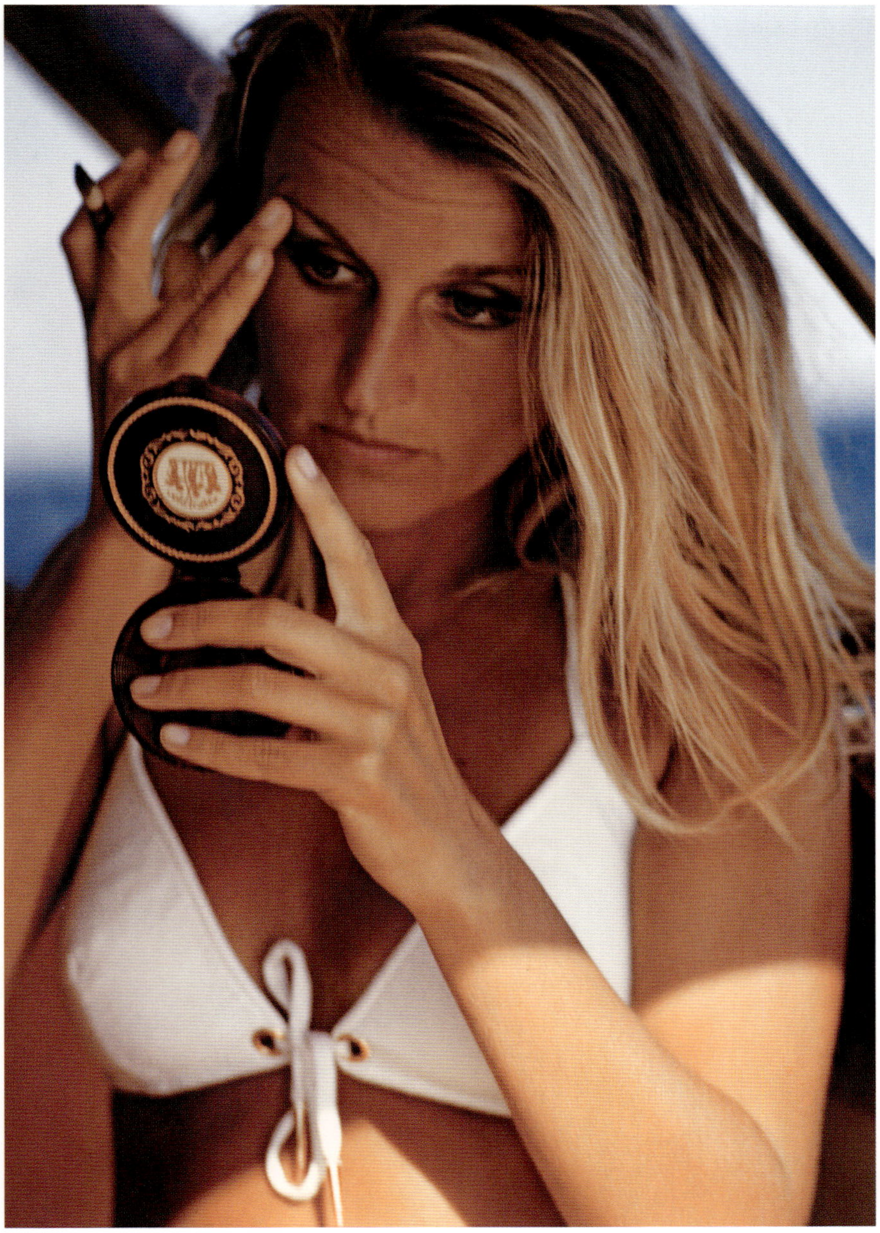

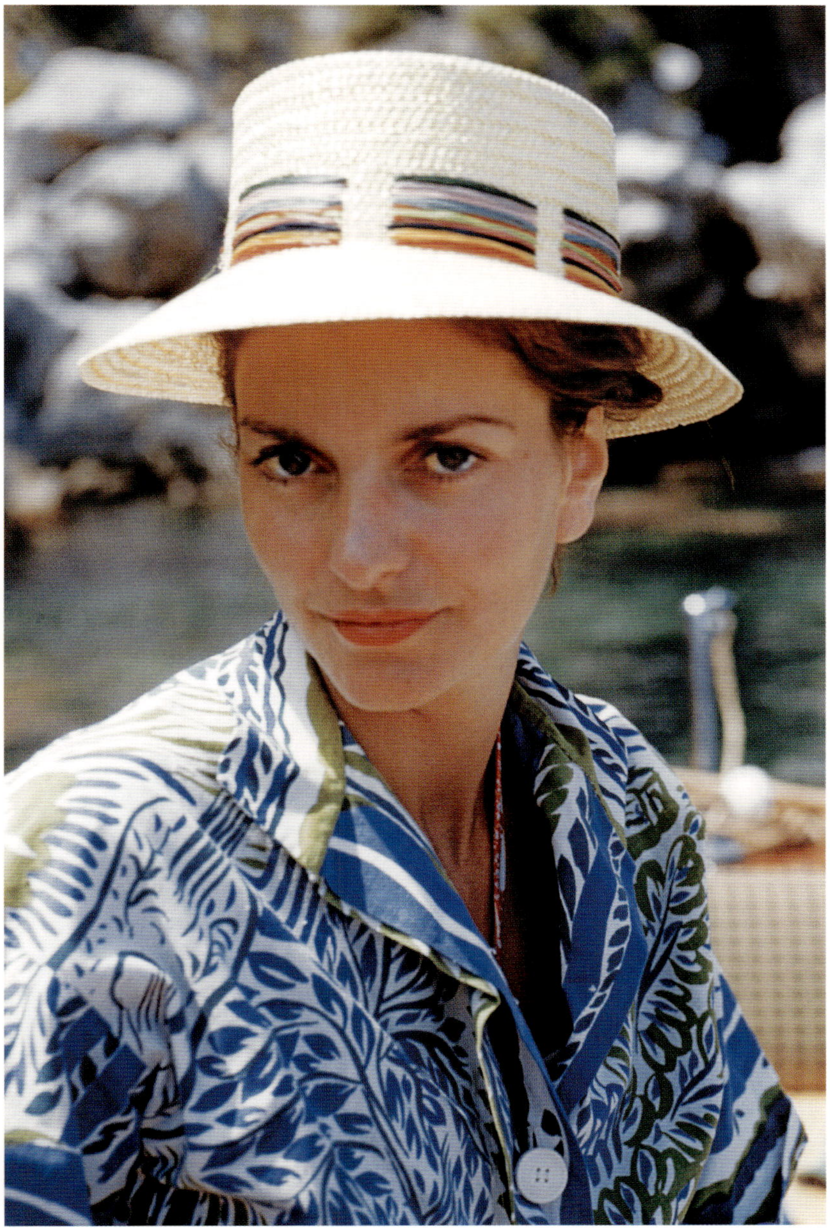

opposite Princess Ira von Furstenberg in Marbella, Spain, 1971. With a pedigree plucked from a fairy tale, the princess is the daughter of Prince Tassilo zu Furstenberg and his first wife, Clara Agnelli, the Fiat heiress. The elder of her two brothers was the fashion designer Egon von Furstenberg, and her former sister-in-law is the fashion designer Diane von Furstenberg. At age fifteen she was wed to Prince Alfonso of Hohenlohe-Langenburg, who was then thirty-one. The wedding procession through the canals of Venice was said to have included scarlet, black, and gold gondolas. Besides being a mother and a socialite, over the years she designed jewelry, acted in films, and was the public relations director to the fashion house of Valentino Garavani.

above left Elisabetta Catalano, Porto Ercole, Italy, 1969. See also page 45. A close friend and protégé of Slim, Catalano was a Roman autodidact photographer who began her career shooting for magazines such as *L'Espresso* and *Vogue Italia*, the Italian edition of the magazine. She also directed a film about the French painter J. H. Lartigue and appeared in Federico Fellini's film *8½*. She and Slim were fast friends and always met up to discuss the latest in cameras and lenses whenever work took him to Italy. In 1992 the Galleria Nazionale d'Arte Moderna in Rome held a retrospective of her work, which included large black-and-white portraits of such artists as Sandro Chia, Joseph Beuys, and Enrico Castellani. Her final exhibit was staged in 2014 at the MAXXI Museum in Rome.

above right Princess Colonna on the island of Capri, July 1958. With three popes in the long, rich Colonna family history, they are one of a handful of Roman families considered to be of the Black Aristocracy, which denotes a family with at least one pope or ties to the Vatican. One family member, Vittoria Colonna, was a friend and muse to Michelangelo Buonarroti—he even painted her in profile in his famous *Last Judgment*, behind the altar of the Sistine Chapel. Costanza Colonna befriended another artist, Caravaggio, and became his protector. In fact, it was at the Palazzo Colonna that the painter first sought refuge after he killed his opponent in a notorious duel and had to flee—an escape organized by Costanza and her brother Fabrizio.

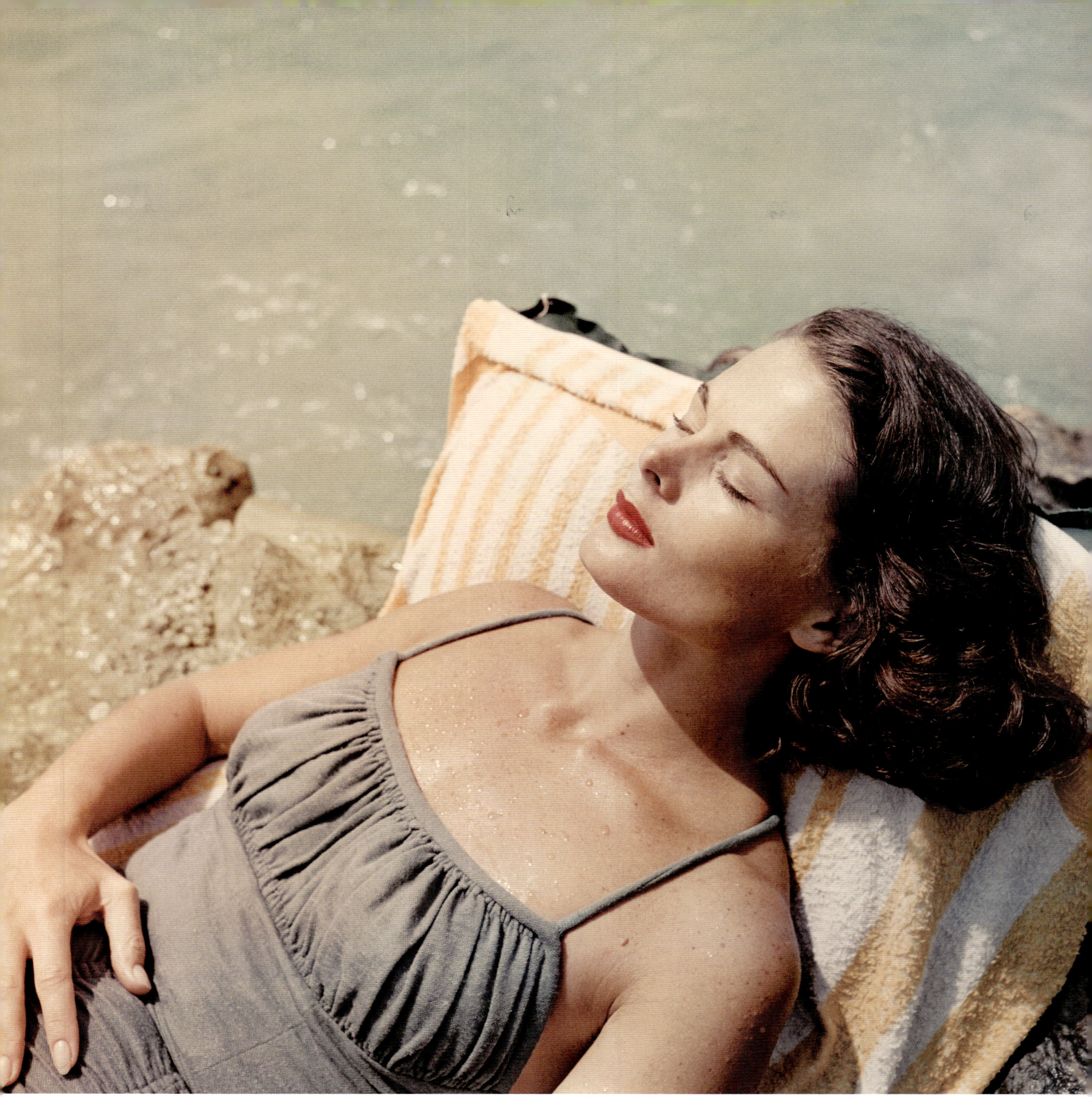

above Actress Dee Hartford, wife of film director Howard Hawks, Monaco, 1957. See also pages 2 and 28.

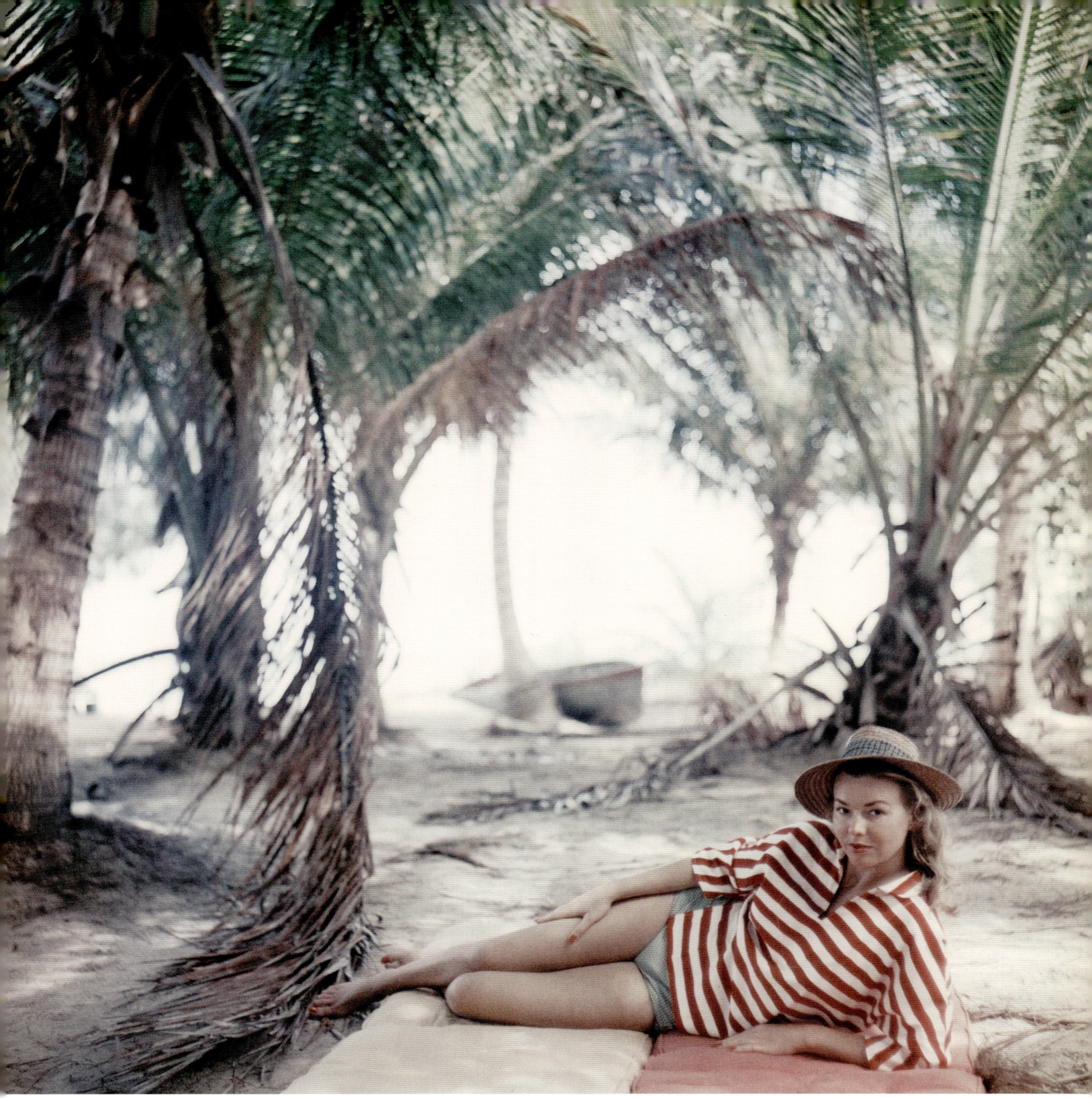

above The Paris-based artist Marsha Gayle on a deserted beach in Calabash Bay, Andros, Bahamas, 1957.

following spread Princess Laudomia Hercolani, known as "Daumiette" to friends, Capri, 1958.

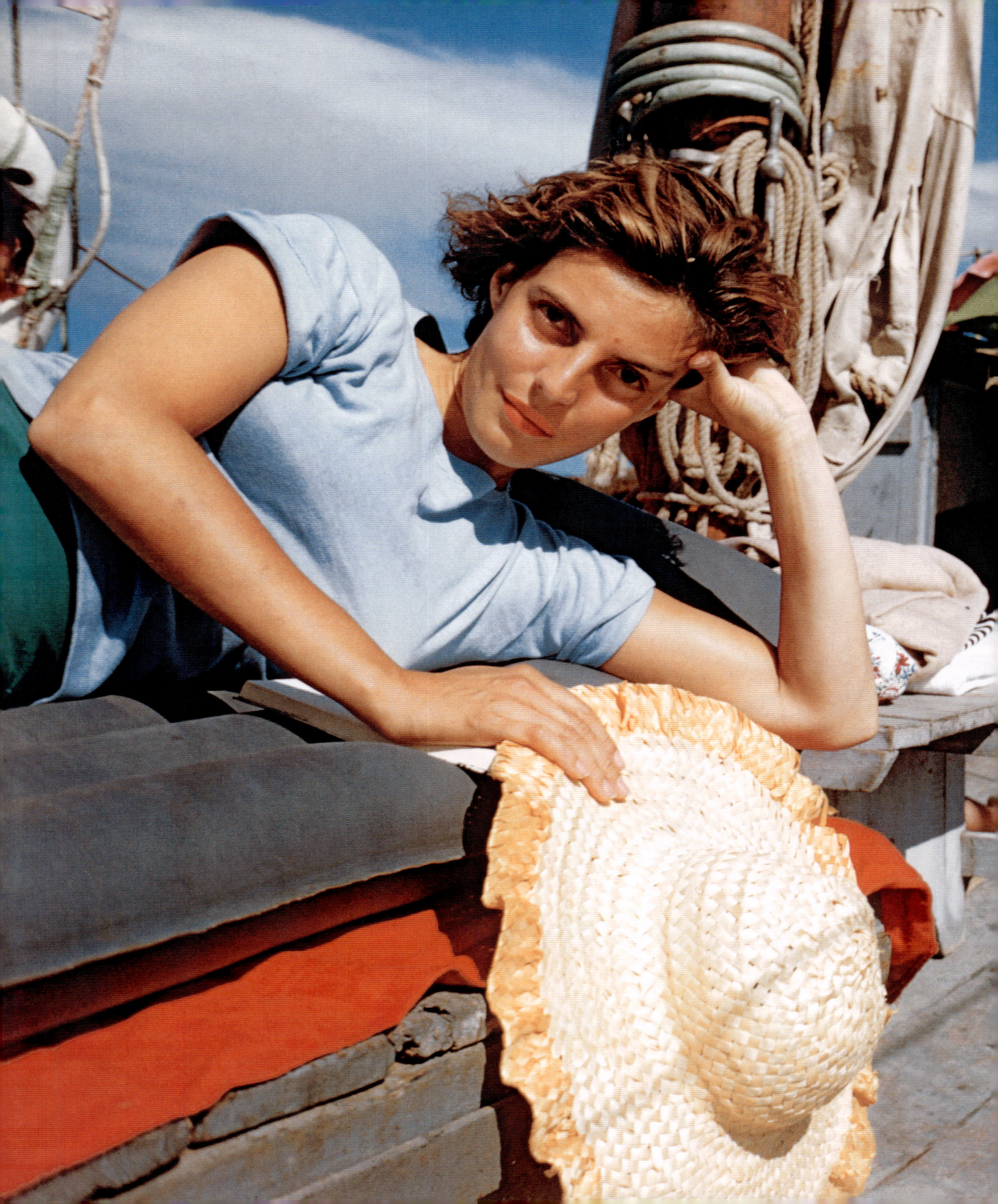

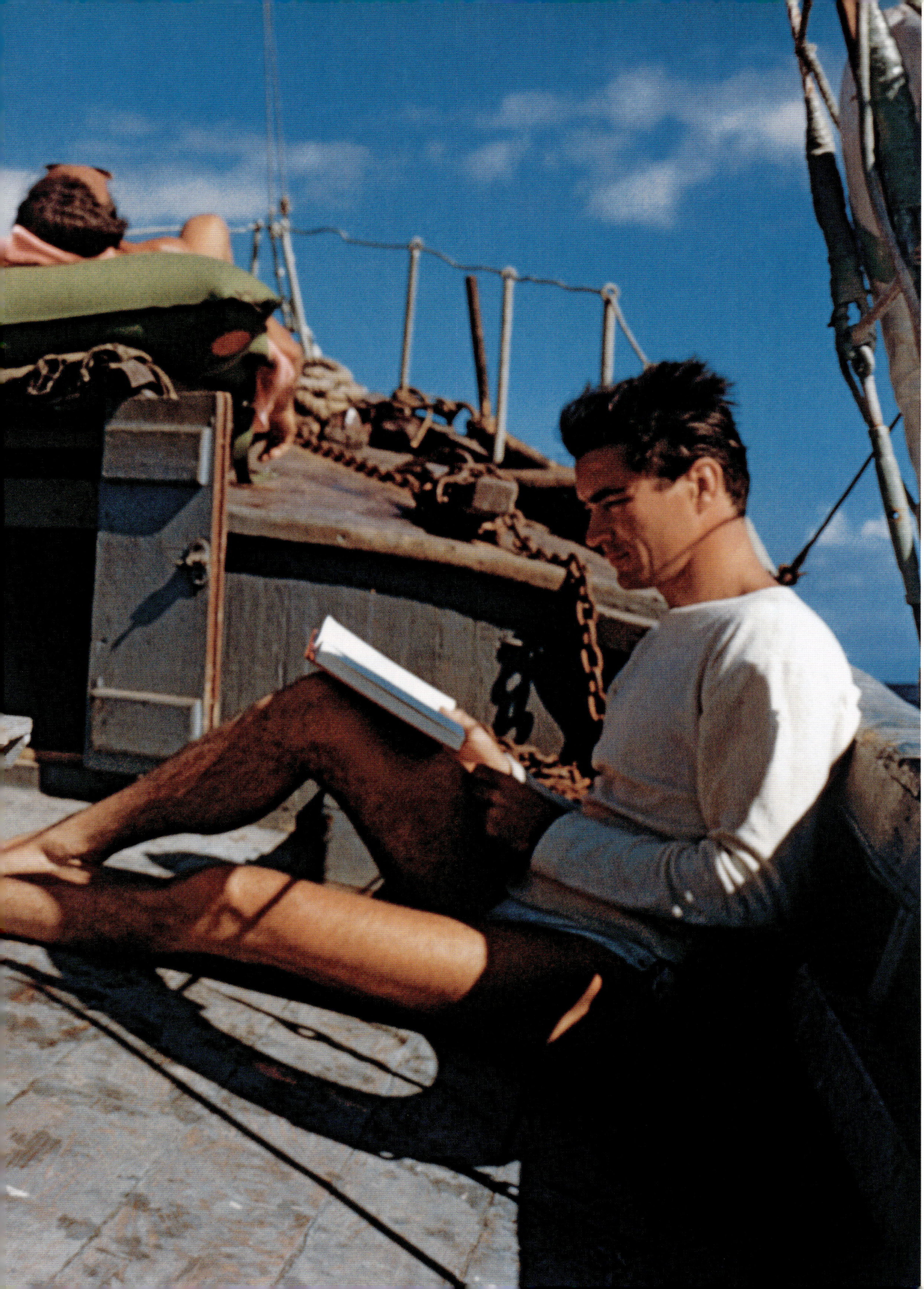

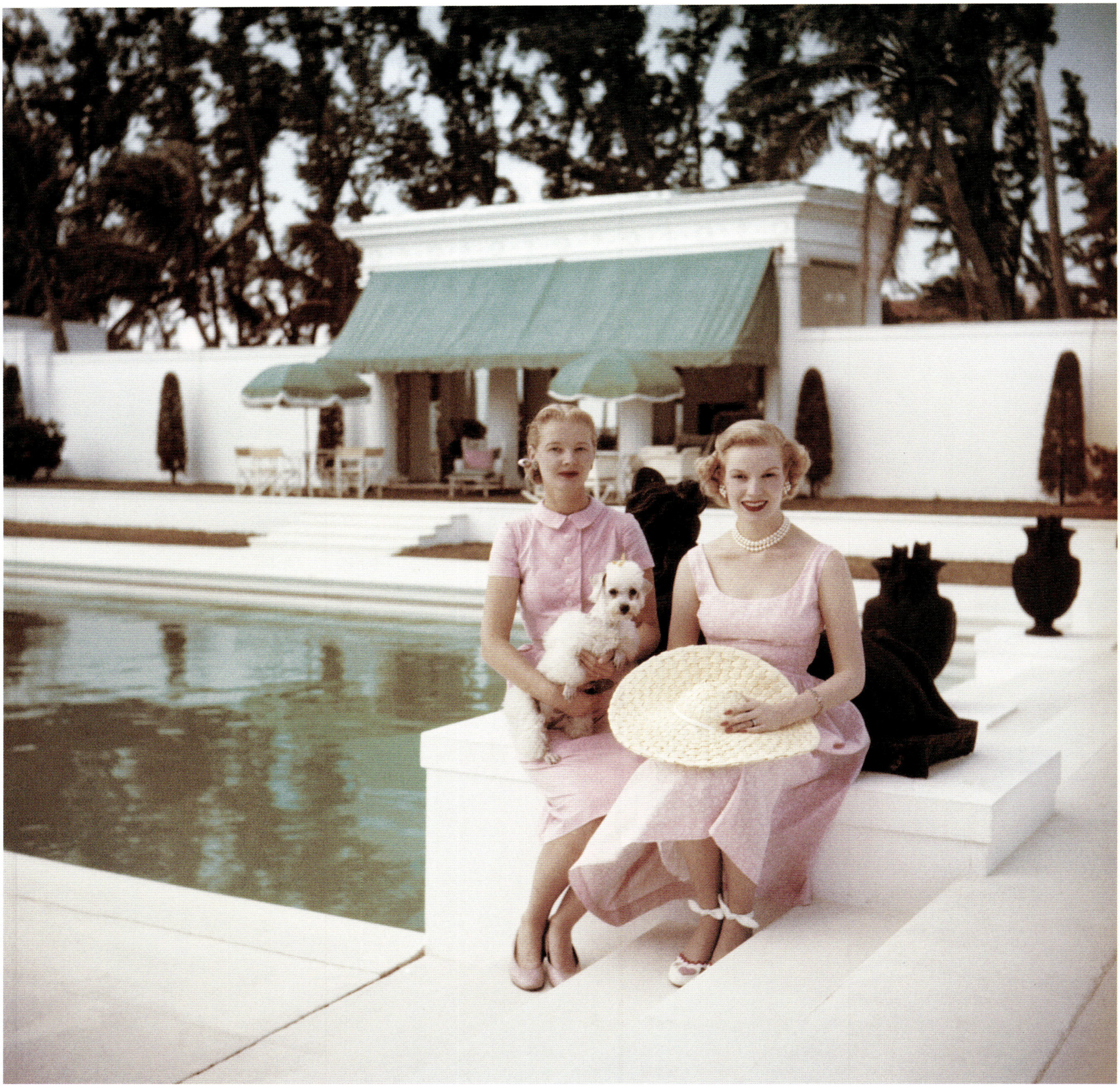

above C. Z. Guest (see also pages 14 and 201) and Joanne Connolly, Villa Artemis, Palm Beach, 1955.

opposite Viscountess Harriet de Rosière at Mougins, France, near Cannes, 1957. Many years later, Slim noted of this photograph, "She was everywhere. One of the great American beauties, who married a French nobleman." An Ohio native, Harriet Moeller was educated at Vassar College, where her friends included the future Selwa Roosevelt and the future Jacqueline Kennedy. When she married Viscount Paul de Rosière in 1955 and settled in France, her dinner parties became legendary among the most *raffiné* of Parisian society.

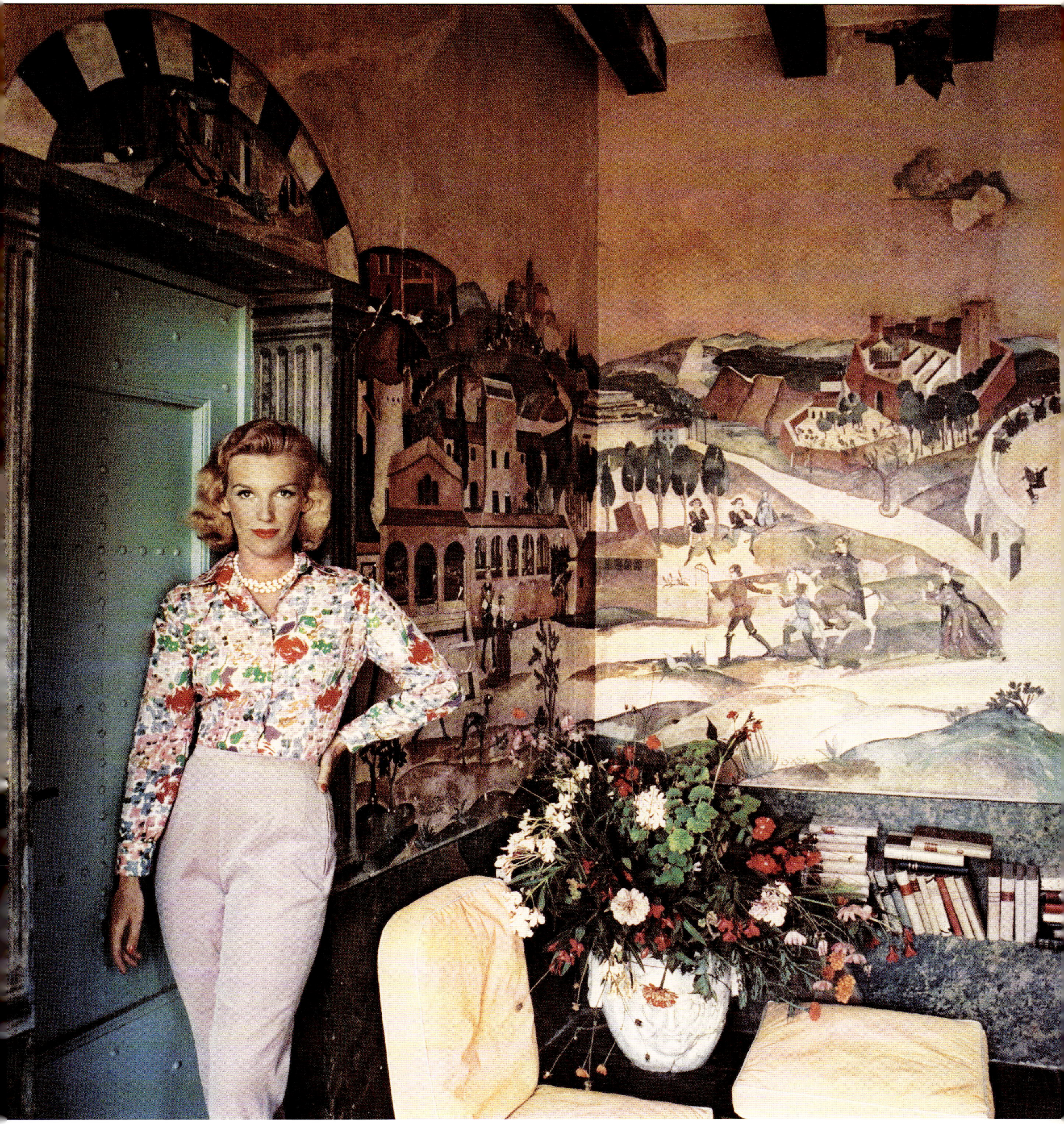

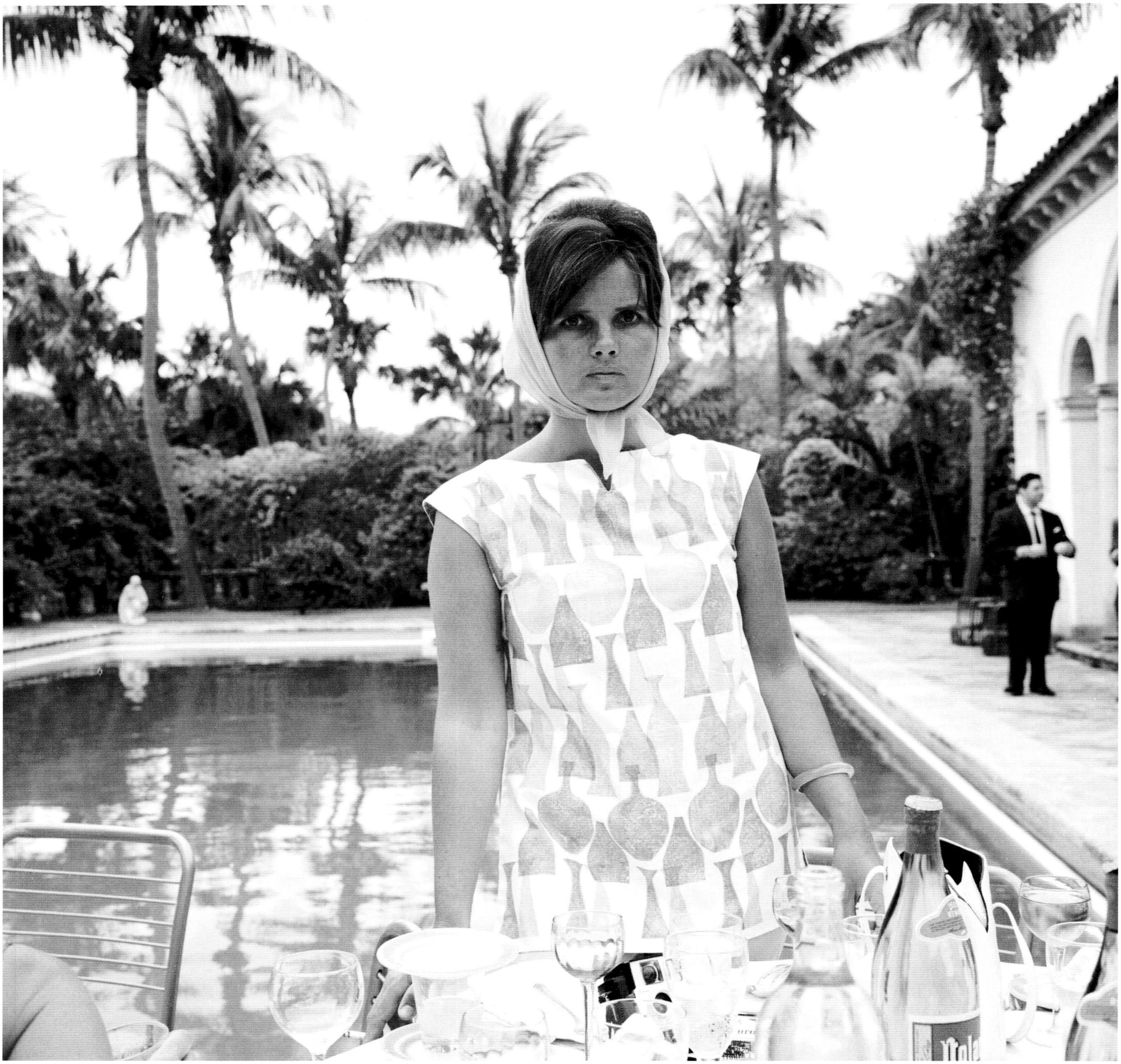

above Lilly Pulitzer, Palm Beach, circa 1955. "It's always summer somewhere," Pulitzer once quipped to garment trade professionals pushing her for a winter collection. Pulitzer was bohemian, artistic, and a highly pedigreed Palm Beach insider (the daughter of a Standard Oil heiress) who accidentally became a fashion leviathan. Due to a bout with depression after her third child was born, a doctor advised her to stay busy. She set up a stand and began selling pressed orange juice to friends on Worth Avenue, from husband Peter's orchards. As Pulitzer's biographer Kathryn Livingston relates, "She decided to design a work uniform for herself that wouldn't show the orange juice stains. So she picked up inexpensive fabrics at the five-and-dime that had orange, yellow, green, and pink in the color schemes, and asked a favorite family seamstress to make her a few dresses." Pulitzer's only directive was that she wanted "the easiest, coolest, most unencumbered shape imaginable." Slim and Lilly enjoyed a warm camaraderie born of

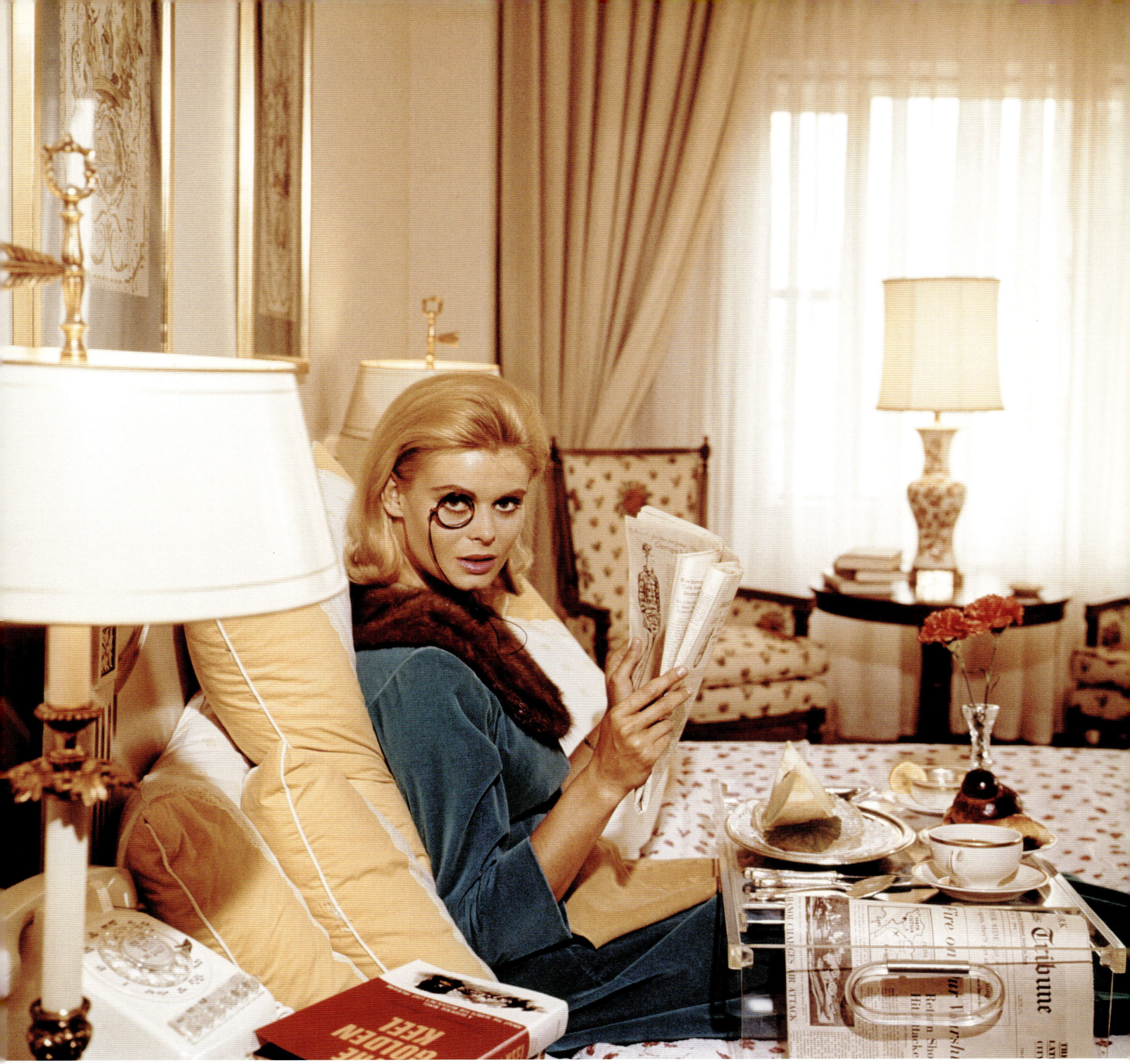

decades of friendship—during which he would photograph nearly every member of her extended family as well (see pages 76 and 121).

above Renata Boeck at the Regency Hotel in New York, 1964. When this German-born Eileen Ford model turned to acting and landed in Hollywood and Las Vegas, she was the talk of both towns. At one point, the famed Hollywood producer Robert Evans and singing legend Eddie Fisher were both in love with her at the same time. Evans and Fisher arranged a meeting on Fifth Avenue in New York at two o'clock in the morning to fight it out. Instead they agreed to send her to Europe, away from both of them and unclouded by pressure or fabulous presents, to let her decide. She chose Fisher (though they didn't marry). "The most beautiful of them all," he is reported to have said of her. Of this portrait Slim said, years later, "She was German, so I had her wear a monocle."

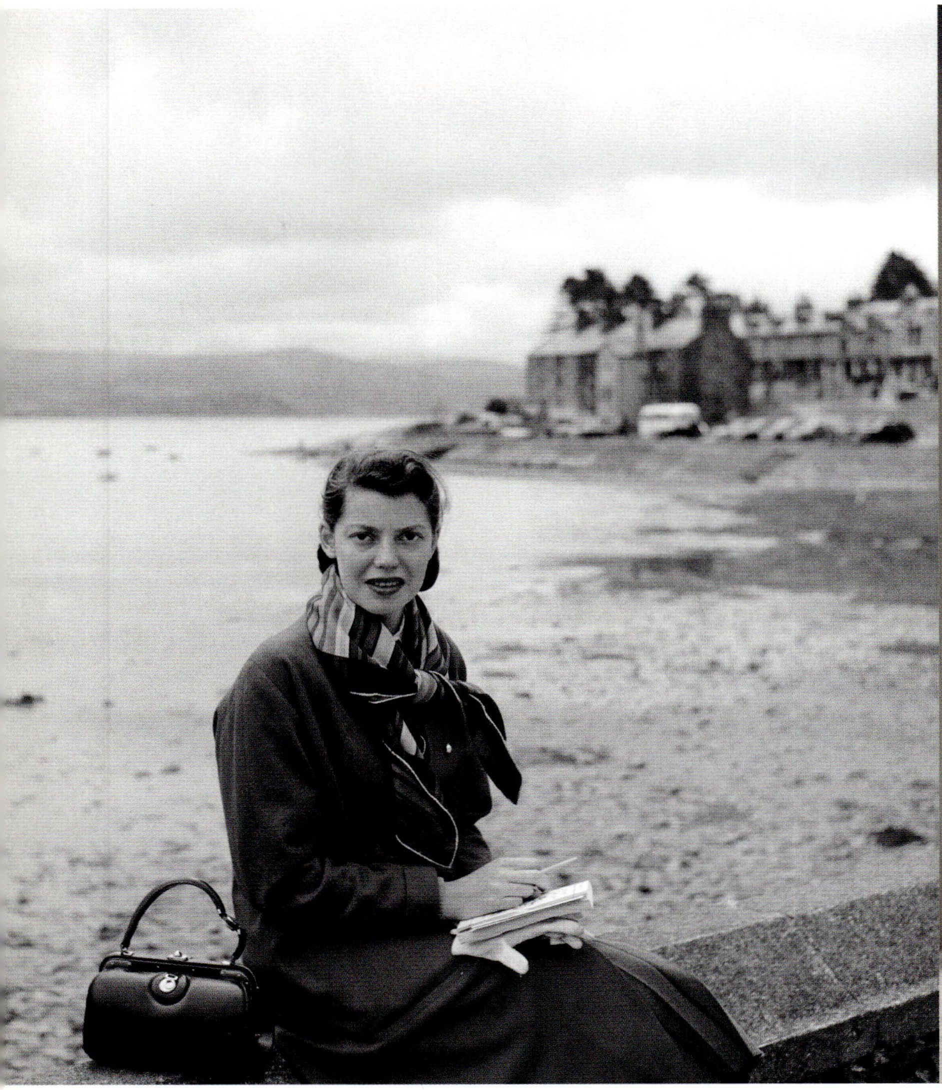

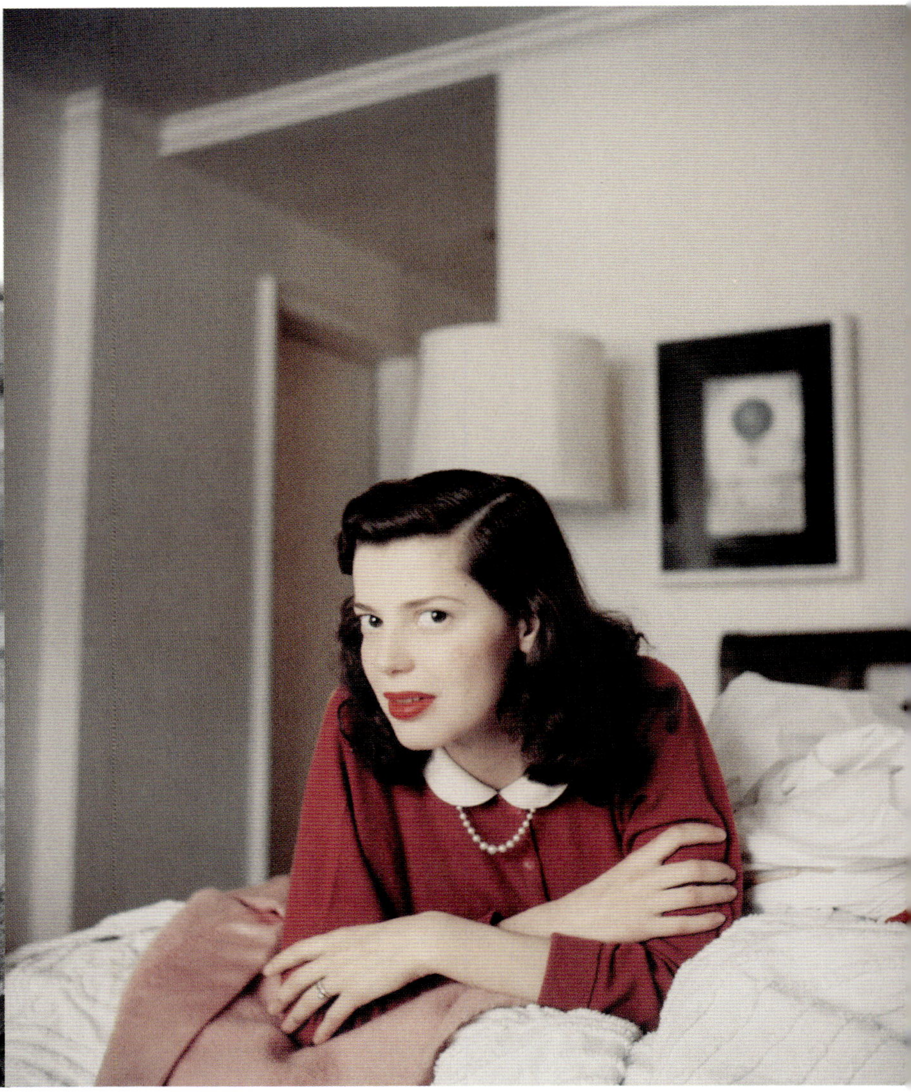

above and opposite Slim was a ranking *Life* magazine photographer when he met the lovely Rita (Lorita) Dewart at the *Life* offices in New York, where she worked as an assistant on the photo desk. He once wrote, "As a kid, I did not foresee that one day I would circle the world many times, using my camera as a passport to its many wonders. But there is no city in the world like Boston, and there is nobody quite like a Bostonian. I ought to know—I married one." From a venerated Boston family whose ancestors graced not only the pages of the Social Register but the pulpits of Boston churches as well, Rita was a cool, serene, and well-bred foil to Slim's indomitable and imperious vagabond. In 1951 Slim and Rita moved into a 1782 farmhouse in Katonah, New York, where they lived for four decades and had a daughter, Mary. They ran in a circle of writers, advertising executives, and publishing luminaries, sharing weekend dinners and afternoon swims in one another's pools. But there was no daily 7:55 commuter train into New York for Slim. Although in many ways he was most likely the quintessential absentee husband and father, Slim certainly wasn't boring. His half century of crisscrossing the globe seeking, befriending, and photographing jet-setters, patrician leaders, and the jeunesse dorée must have made for a colorful, if not exhausted, husband and father upon his return home from each trip. The dedication page of Slim's first book, *A Wonderful Time*, states simply, "To my wife and daughter, who have suffered through this peculiar life style of mine." She is pictured in Wales in 1957 (above left), Beverly Hills in 1952 (above right), and Hollywood, 1954 (opposite).

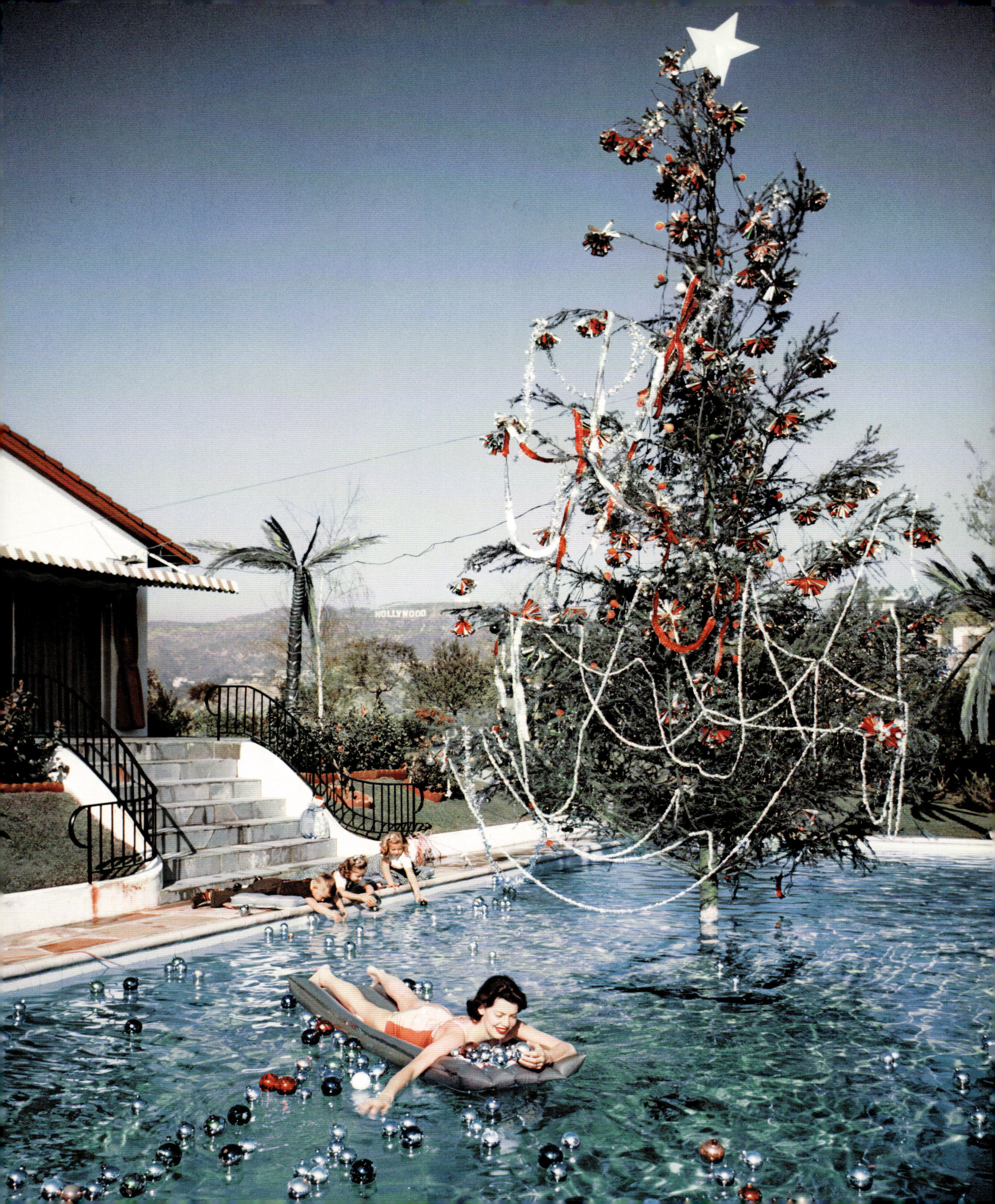
HOLLYWOOD

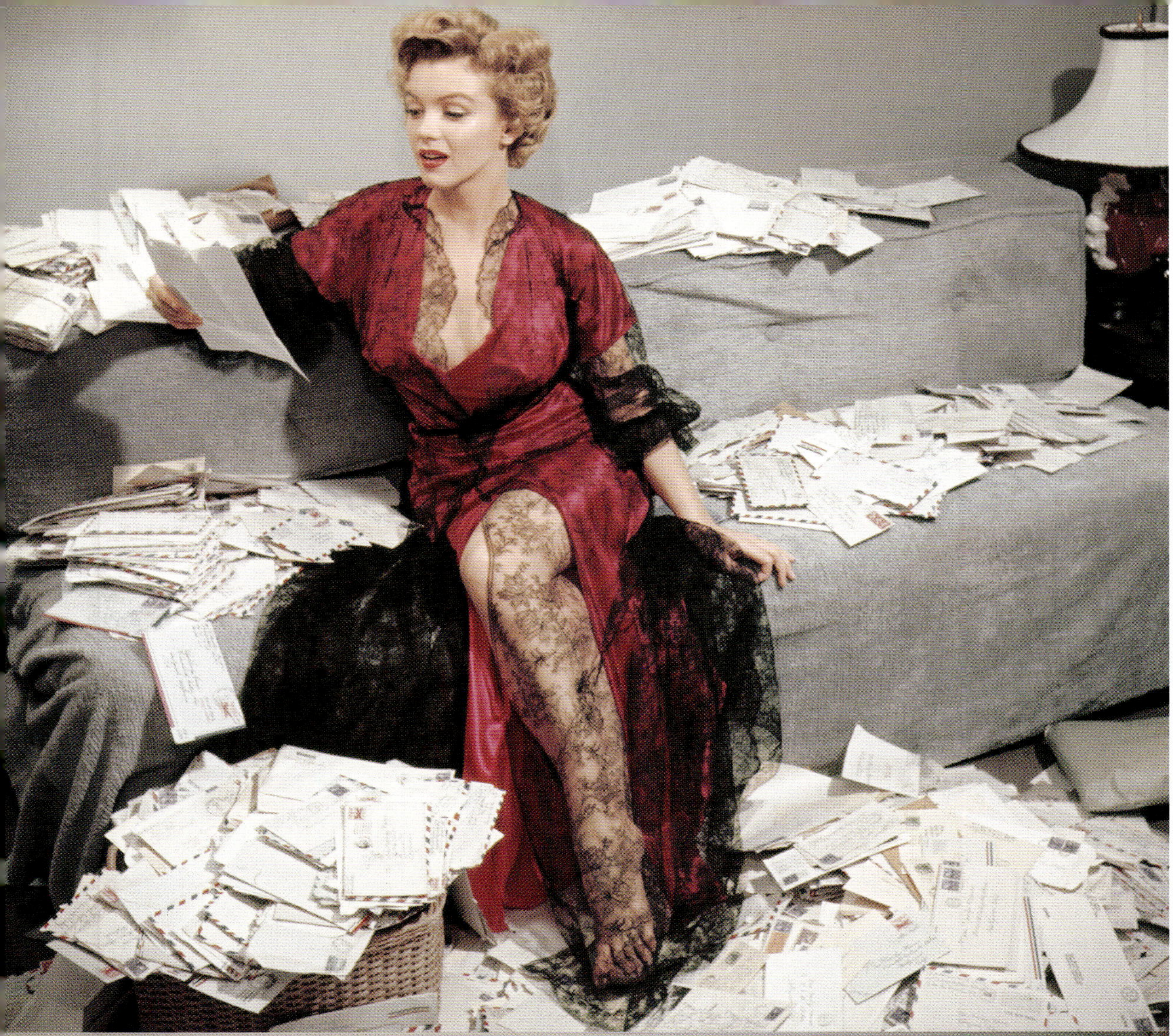

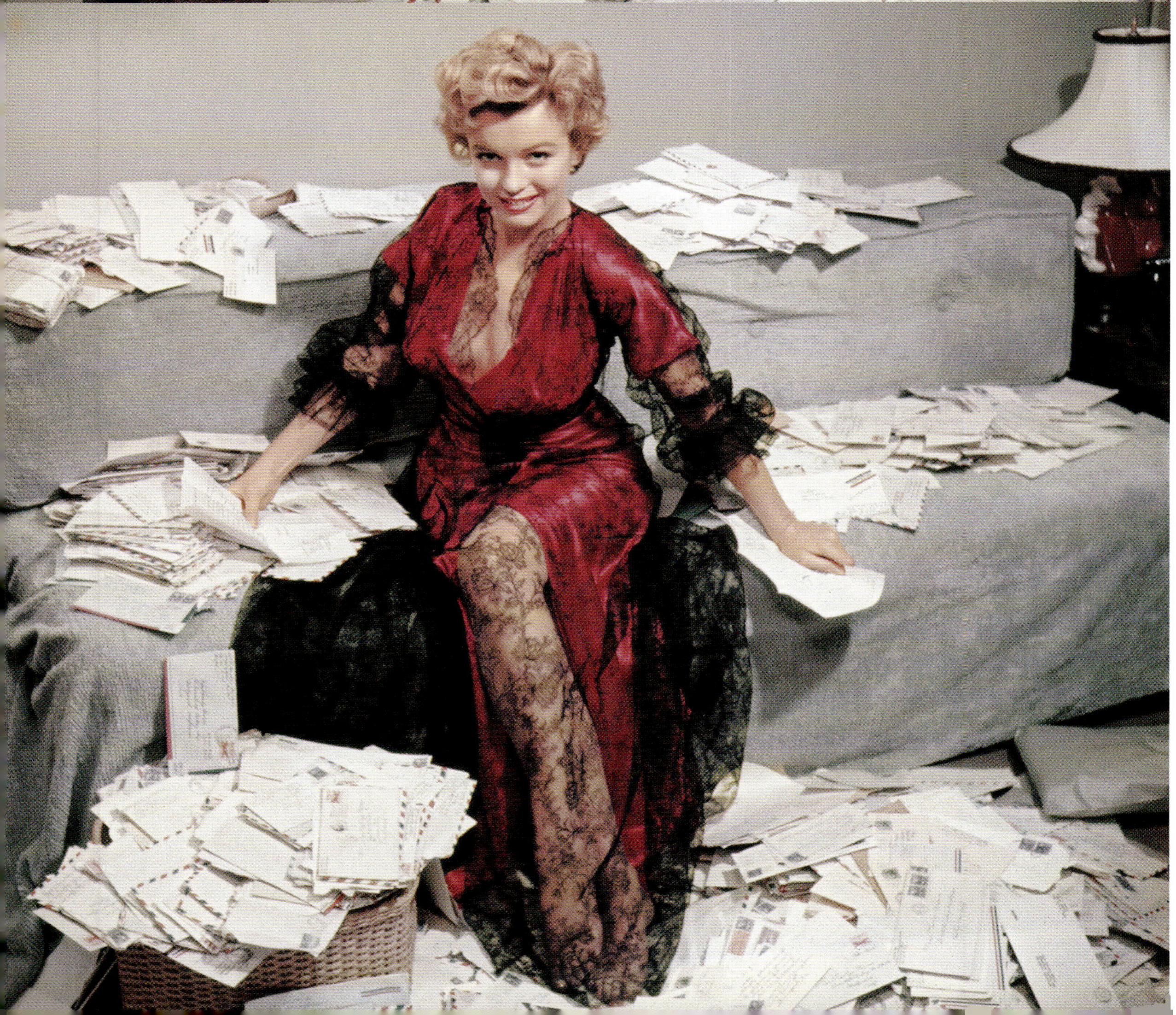

left Marilyn Monroe, Beverly Hills, 1950. Slim loved to tell the story of how this famous photo (bottom) came about. He was doing a story on Beverly Hills and heard about this great-looking young actress—but she had no association with Beverly Hills. Looking for a way to make a photo of her fit the concept of the story, he figured it would be legitimate to say that in order to be on time for an early studio call, she would have to spend the night at a motel on Olympic Boulevard in Beverly Hills. He photographed her there in a negligee, reading actual fan mail from GIs after the release of her movie *The Asphalt Jungle.* Slim explained, "She was very nervous about posing, and I reassured her by telling her that all you had to do was think about the nicest possible thing that could happen to you—but think about it with your eyes, and let the rest of your face do what it wanted. Years later, as her career was zooming, I had occasion to watch her on the set while she was making *The Seven Year Itch.* She happened to walk by me, and I, not wanting to bother her, said nothing. But she stopped before me, looked up, and said, 'You don't remember me, do you? I never forgot what you told me . . . think of the nicest thing possible.'"

opposite The Spanish actress and singer Carmen Sevilla, Spain, 1957.

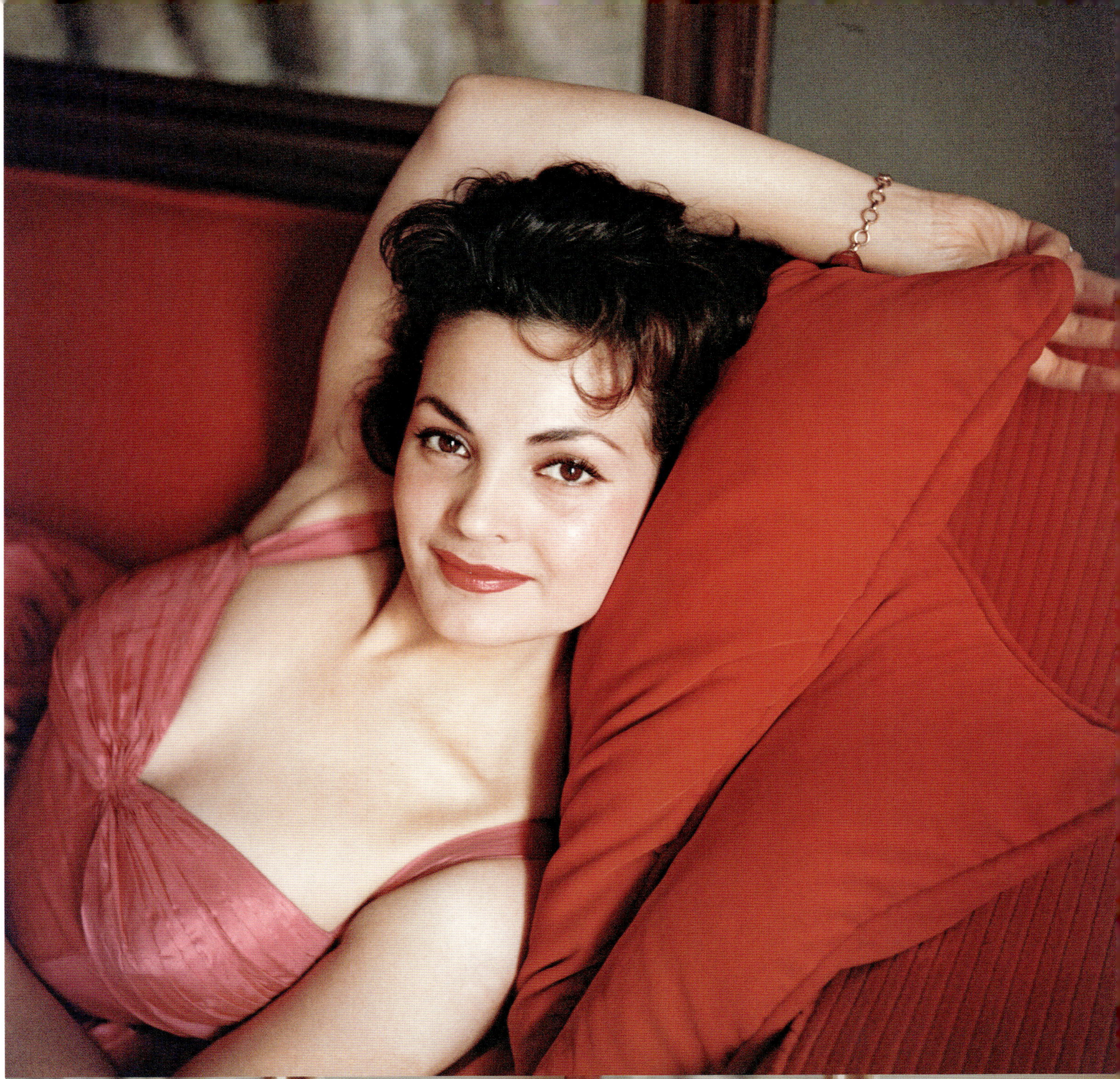

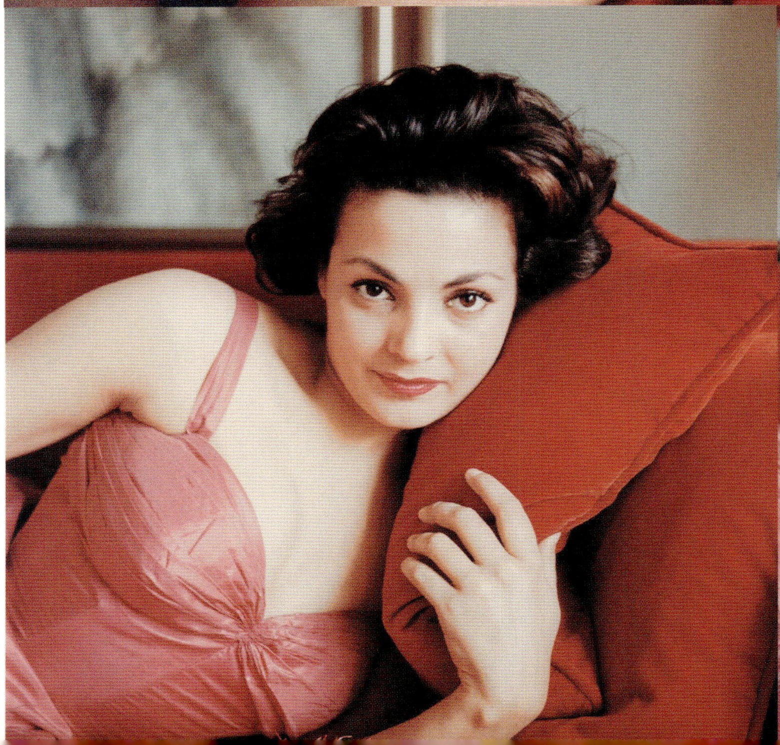

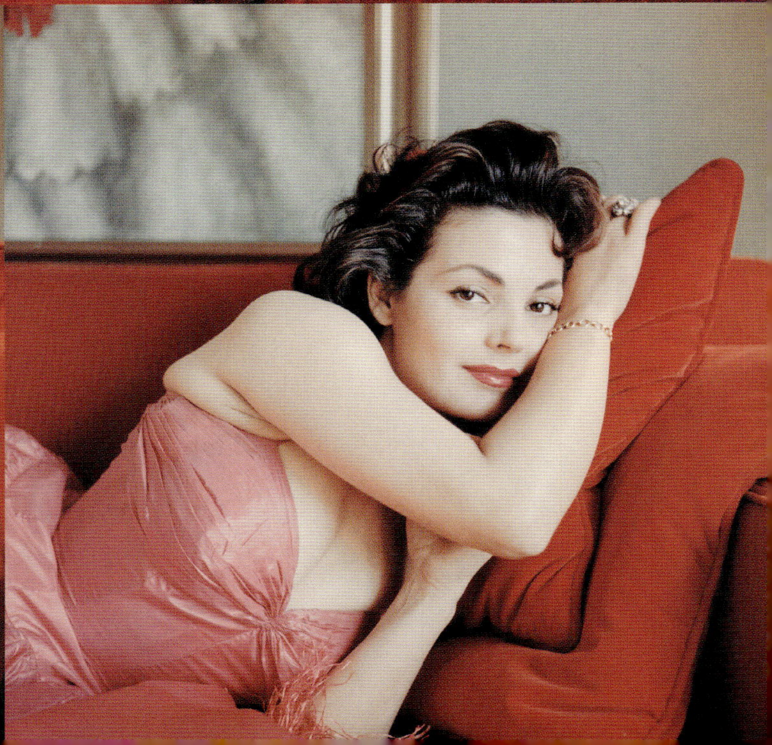

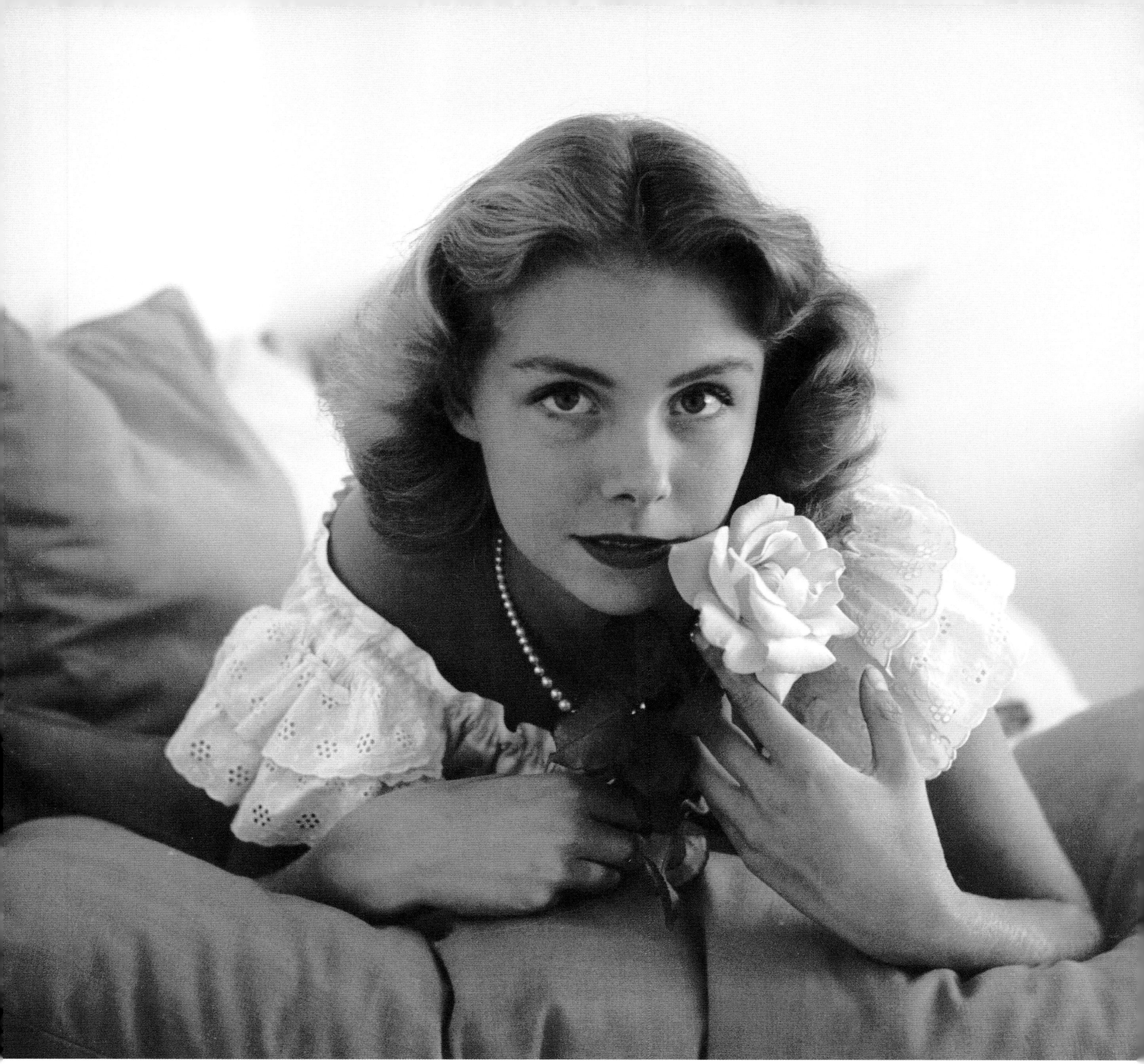

above Betsy von Furstenberg, Ravello, Italy, 1951. Born Elizabeth Caroline Maria Agatha Felicitas Therese, Baroness von Furstenberg-Herdringen, the stage and screen actress later became known simply as "Madcap Betsy." The American journalist Dorothy Kilgallen wrote in 1952: "Betsy von Furstenberg's much-publicized engagement to hotel heir Nicky Hilton hasn't depressed the New York swains to the point where they've given up. Current rehearsals of 'Dear Barbarians' at the John Golden Theatre are interrupted most often by the backstage telephone—it rings all day, and the voices on the other end all belong to optimistic young men trying to arrange dates with Betsy."

opposite Eva Gabor, Montego Bay, Jamaica, 1954. She was the youngest of the three Gabor sisters, also including Zsa Zsa and Magda, who arrived in the United States in the 1930s from Hungary. The stage and film careers

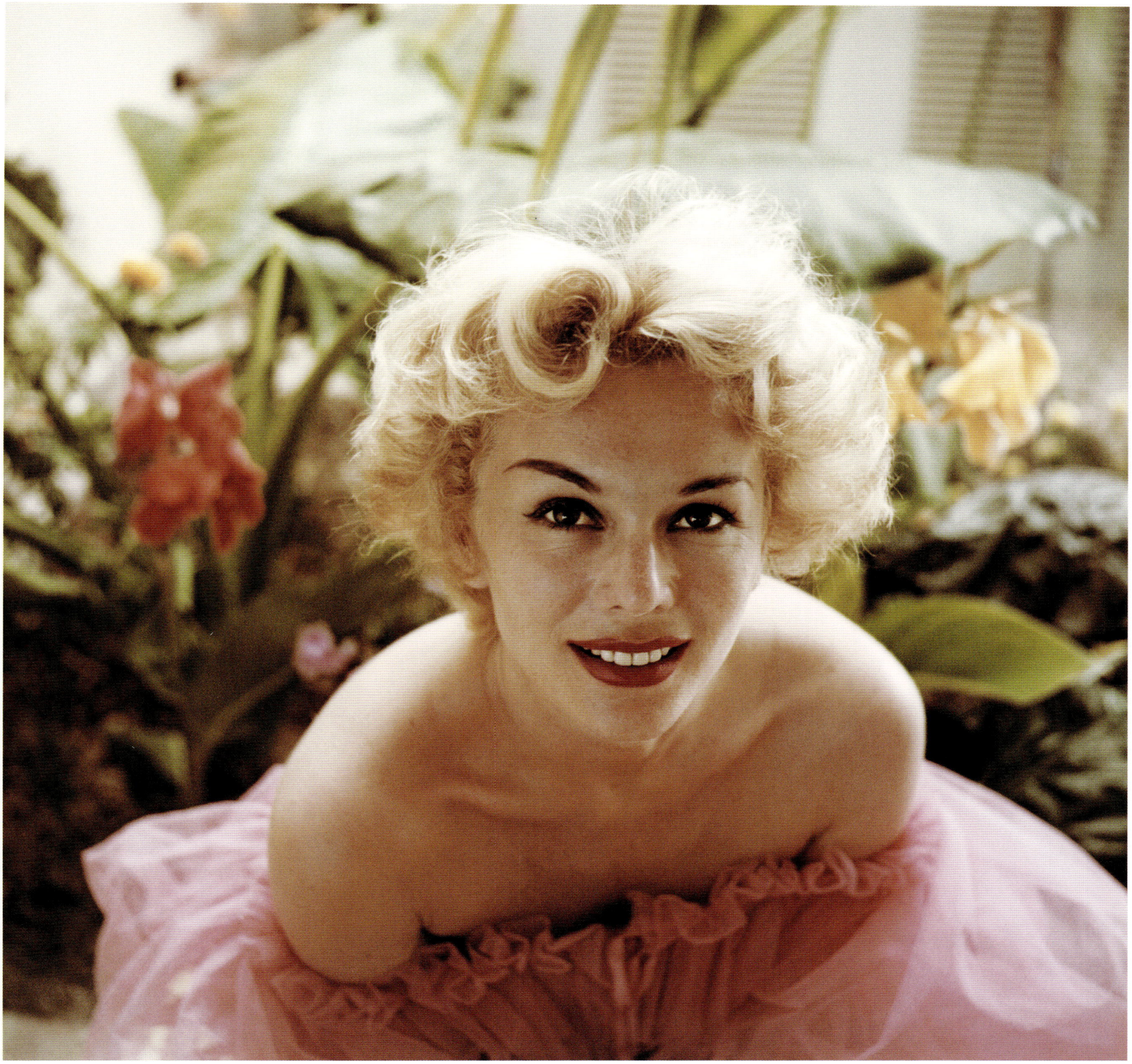

of all three daughters were famously directed by their mother, Jolie Gabor, and each one had a reputation for serial marriages—Zsa Zsa had eight, Magda had six, and Eva had five. In his first book, *A Wonderful Time*, Slim told the story of shooting this photo of Gabor: "The owner of a new hotel in Montego was anxious to get it mentioned in a story I was doing for *Holiday*. Eva was staying there and agreed to pose. The hotel wasn't finished yet, so early one morning I set the picture up in one of the unfinished units, which only had three bare walls. Bougainvillea was stuck to the walls with Scotch tape. Furniture and other items were brought in to make it look tropical—at least, like Jamaica. Then we woke Eva, who had overslept. No makeup—didn't need it, with that peaches-and-cream complexion. She *dahling*ed me and said she'd be ready in five minutes—and was!"

below Singer Julie London enjoying breakfast in bed at the Beverly Hills Hotel, 1957. Slim explained, "I did a story on the Beverly Hills Hotel, considered one of the world's finest. For it I decided to photograph one of the bedrooms in the most elaborate bungalow, and got Julie London to pose in one of the beds chaperoned by her boyfriend, who came along and held the light."

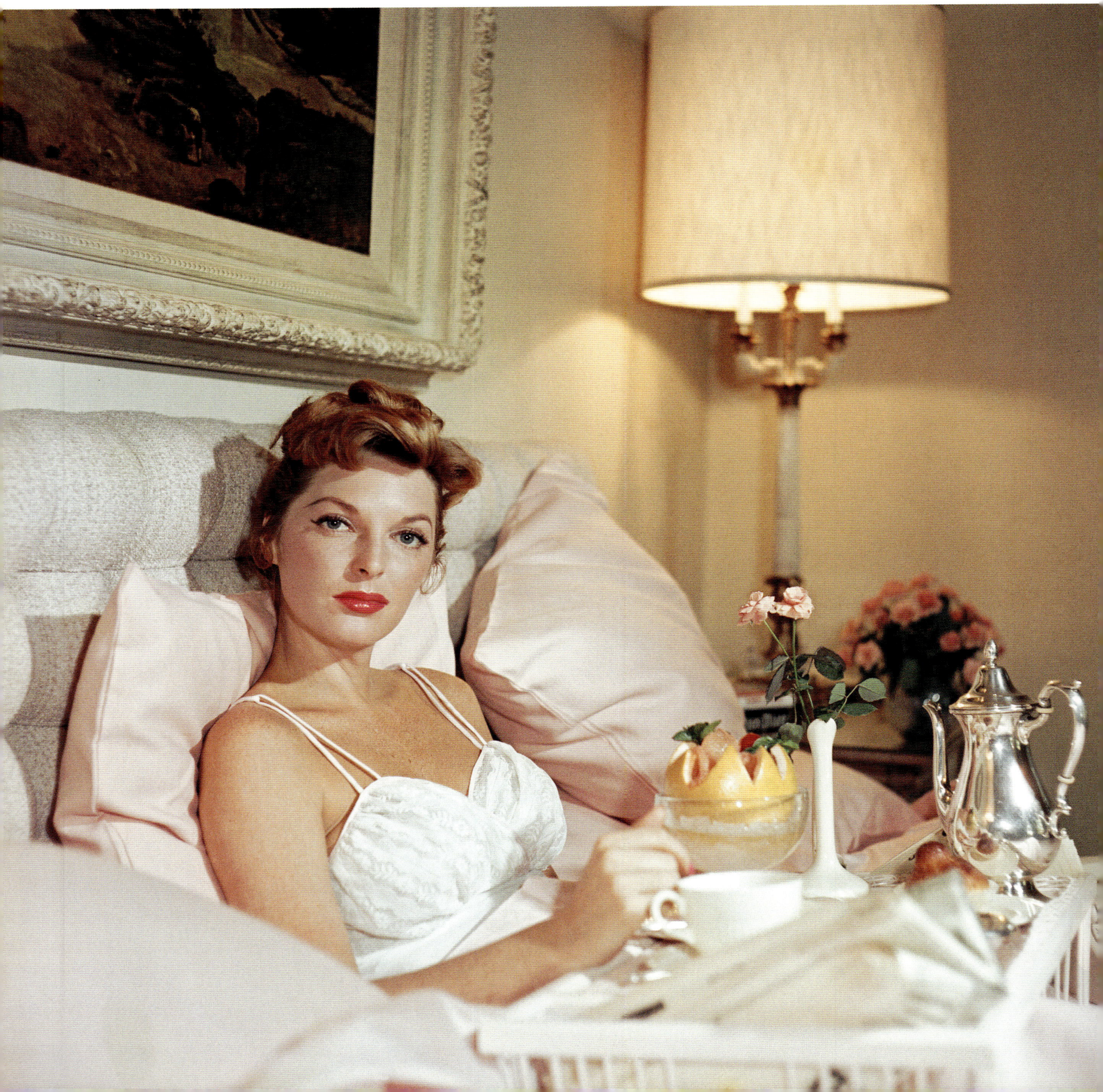

below The English film star and author Dame Joan Collins surrounds herself with all things pink, including her poodle, 1955. Joan Collins started her career in England mostly in B movies. After landing the role of the deliciously vengeful Alexis Carrington in the American daytime television soap opera *Dynasty*, she achieved cult status. Outspoken, tough, witty, and unfailingly glamorous, she epitomizes the old-style Hollywood star. Collins is famous for her numerous boyfriends and marriages, and when she married her fifth husband, Percy Gibson, an aristocratic Peruvian actor thirty-two years her junior, she teased with great panache, "If he dies, he dies."

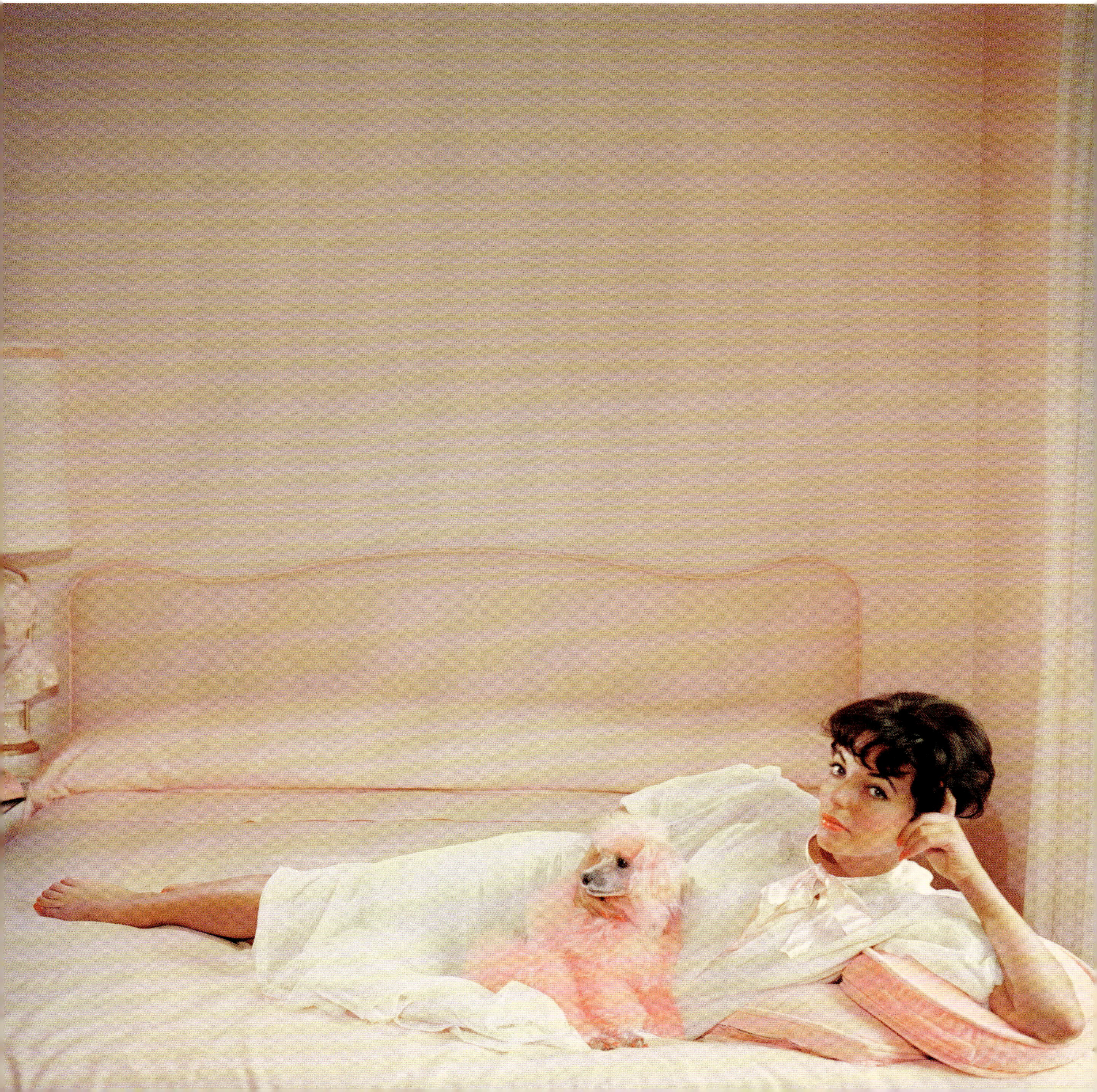

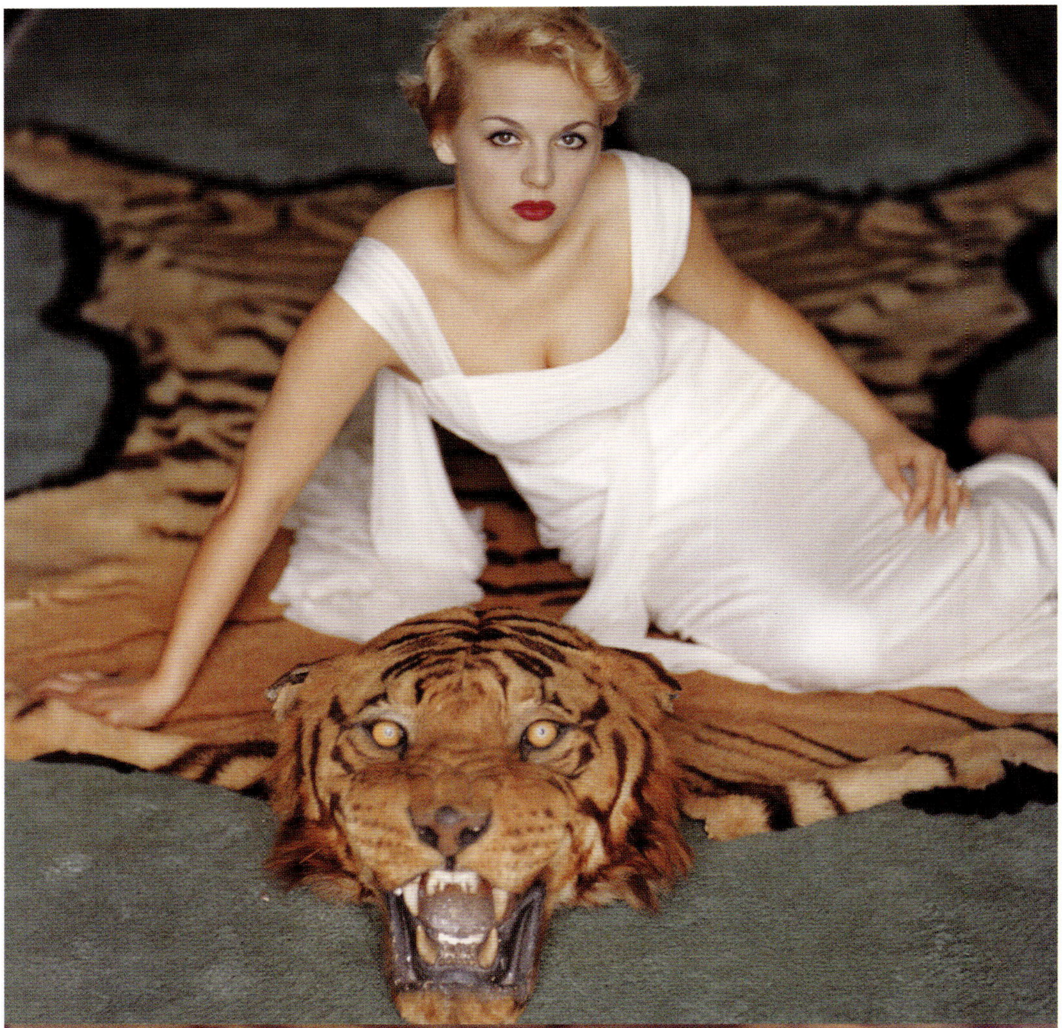

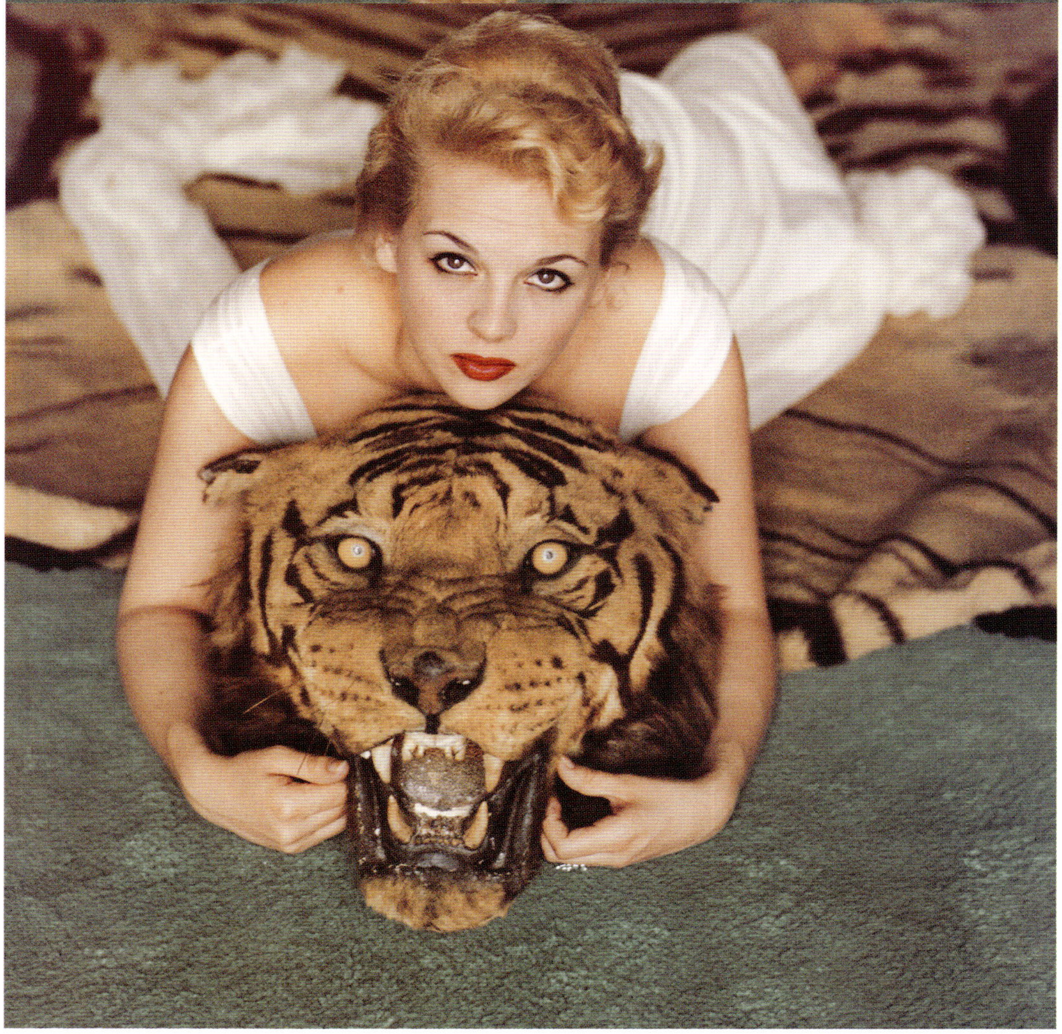

left and opposite Lady Daphne Cameron sits on a tiger pelt in the trophy room of Laddie Sanford's Palm Beach house, 1959. In 2003 Slim wrote of this photograph: "She was too much for ordinary people. There are so many beautiful girls in the world, then there's one that stands out; she had something you can't explain." In 1960, the socialite, polo player, and Palm Beach perennial Stephen "Laddie" Sanford wrote a song he called "Poor Little Palm Beach Baby" that could have been written about the mysterious and stunning woman on his tiger rug: "Poor little Palm Beach baby, / She leads a sad, sad life; / Nothing to wear but beautiful gowns, / Nothing to fear but millionaires' frowns; / She is the perfect lady, / Perfect as ladies go; / The season is short, / If she strikes it right, / She may become a queen overnight, / Married to millions—maybe, / Poor little Palm Beach baby."

following spread The Swiss actress Ursula Andress, Rome, circa 1955. Andress began her career as a model in Rome. Once she made the leap to Hollywood, she had a number of famous lovers, among them Marlon Brando, James Dean, and Ryan O'Neal. Andress was catapulted to fame for her role as the first Bond girl in the film *Dr. No*. She later said that she owed her career to the ivory-colored bikini she wore as the character Honey Ryder in the film: "This bikini made me into a success. As a result of starring in *Dr. No* as the first Bond girl, I was given the freedom to take my pick of future roles and to become financially independent." The famous bikini sold at auction for $59,755 in 2001.

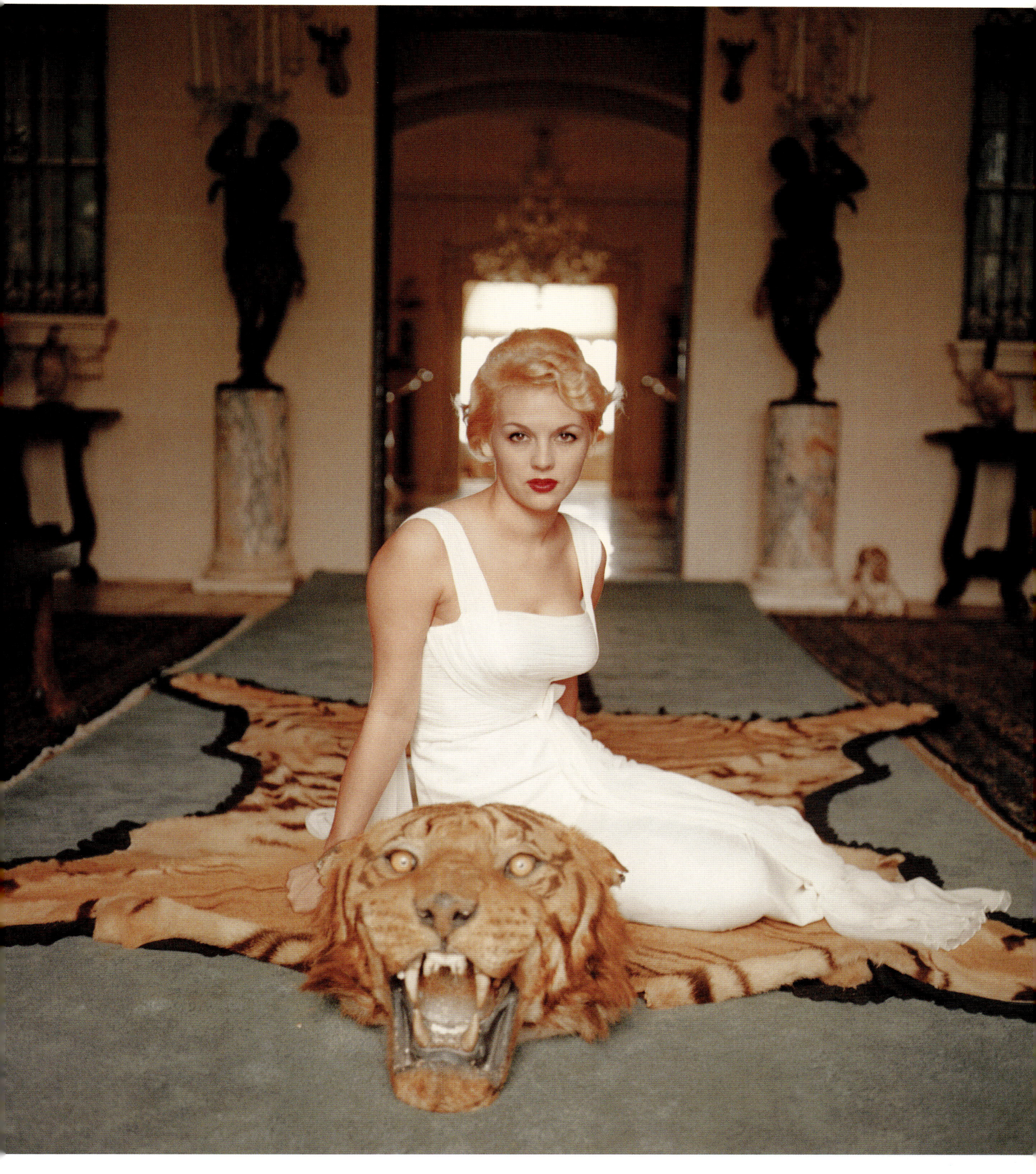

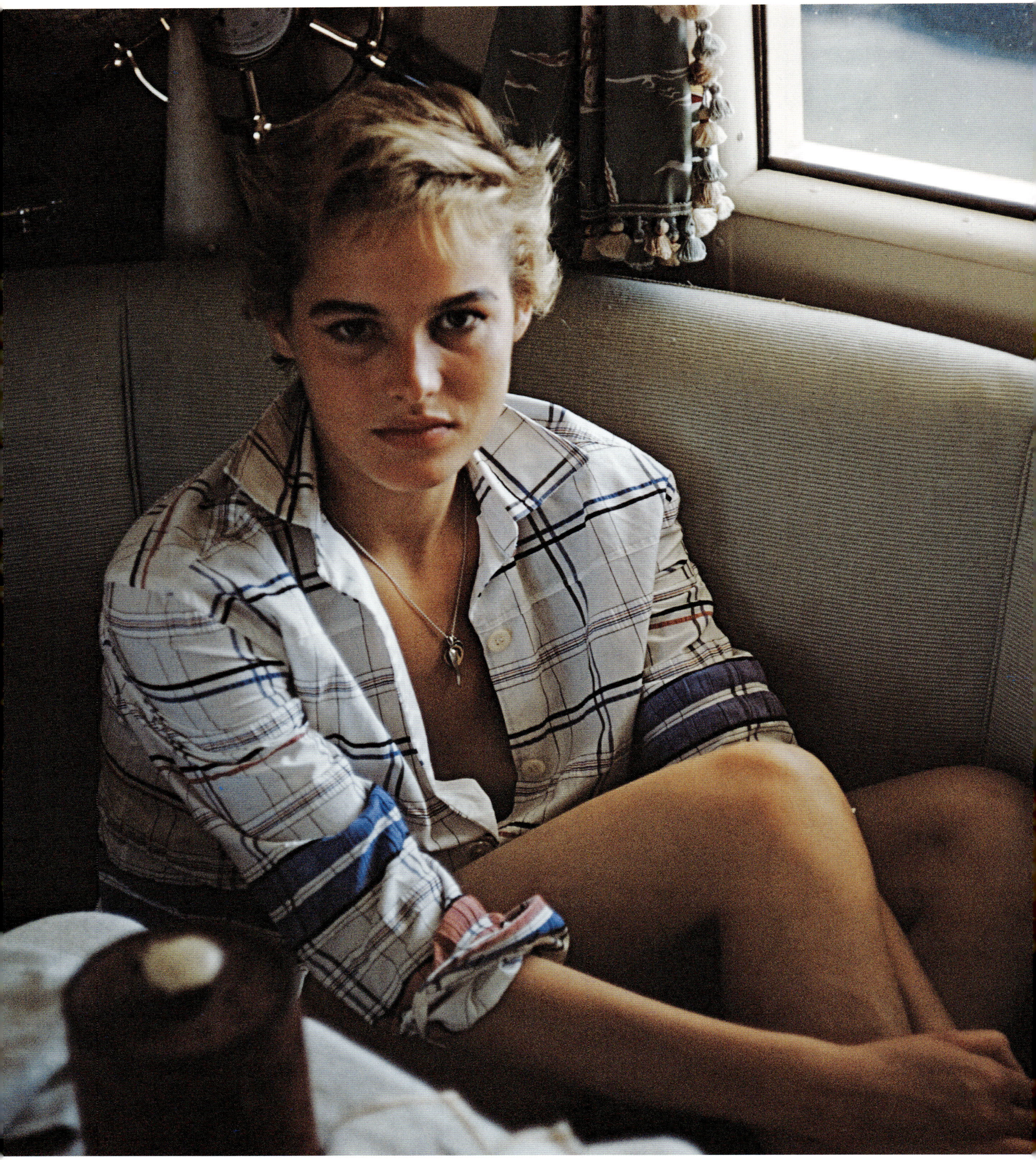

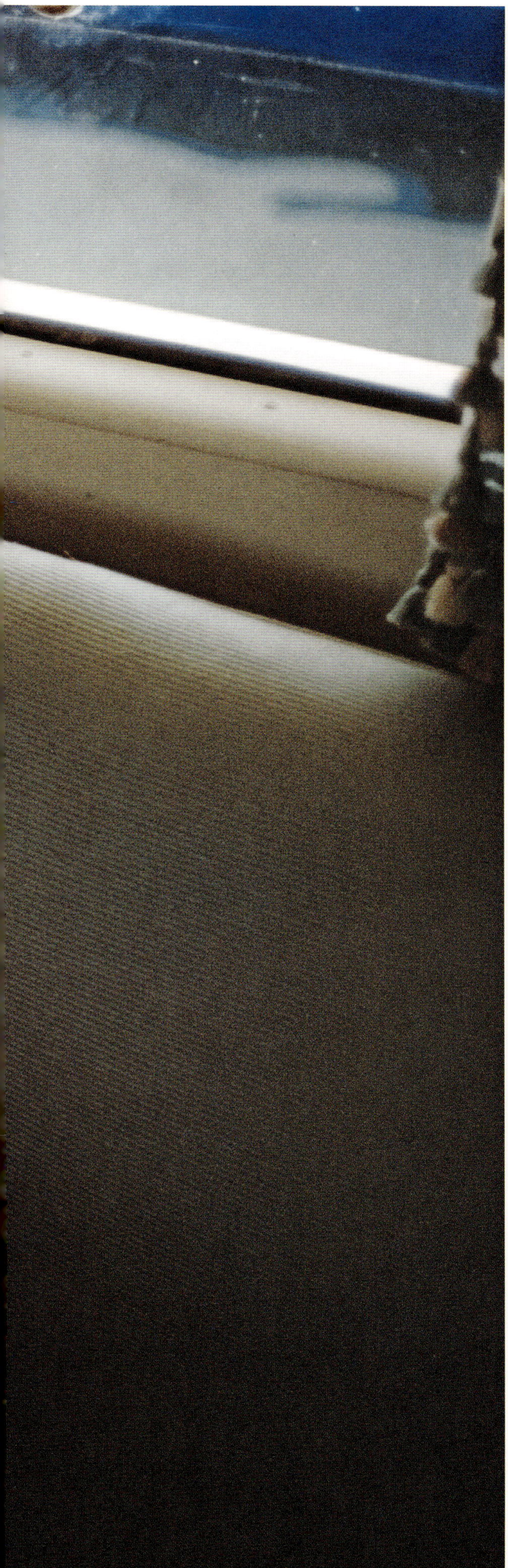

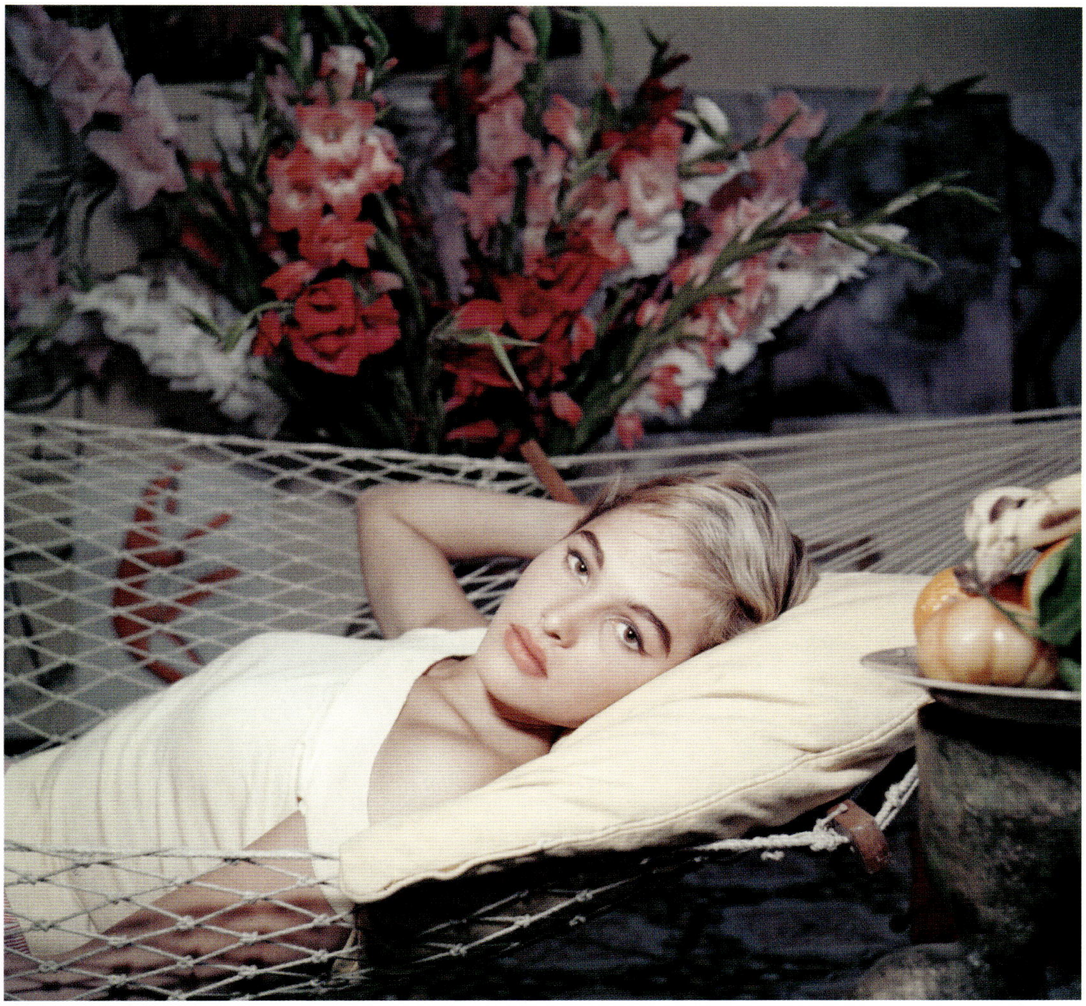

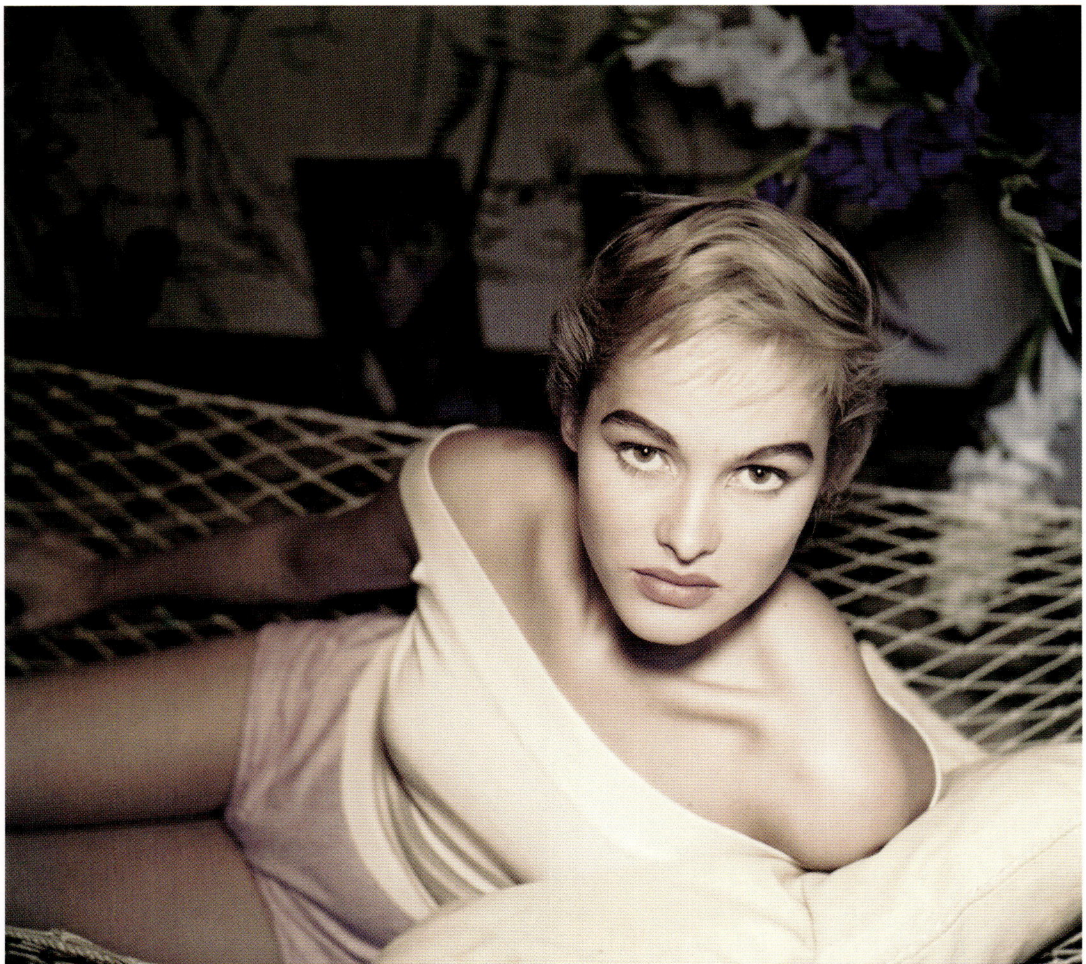

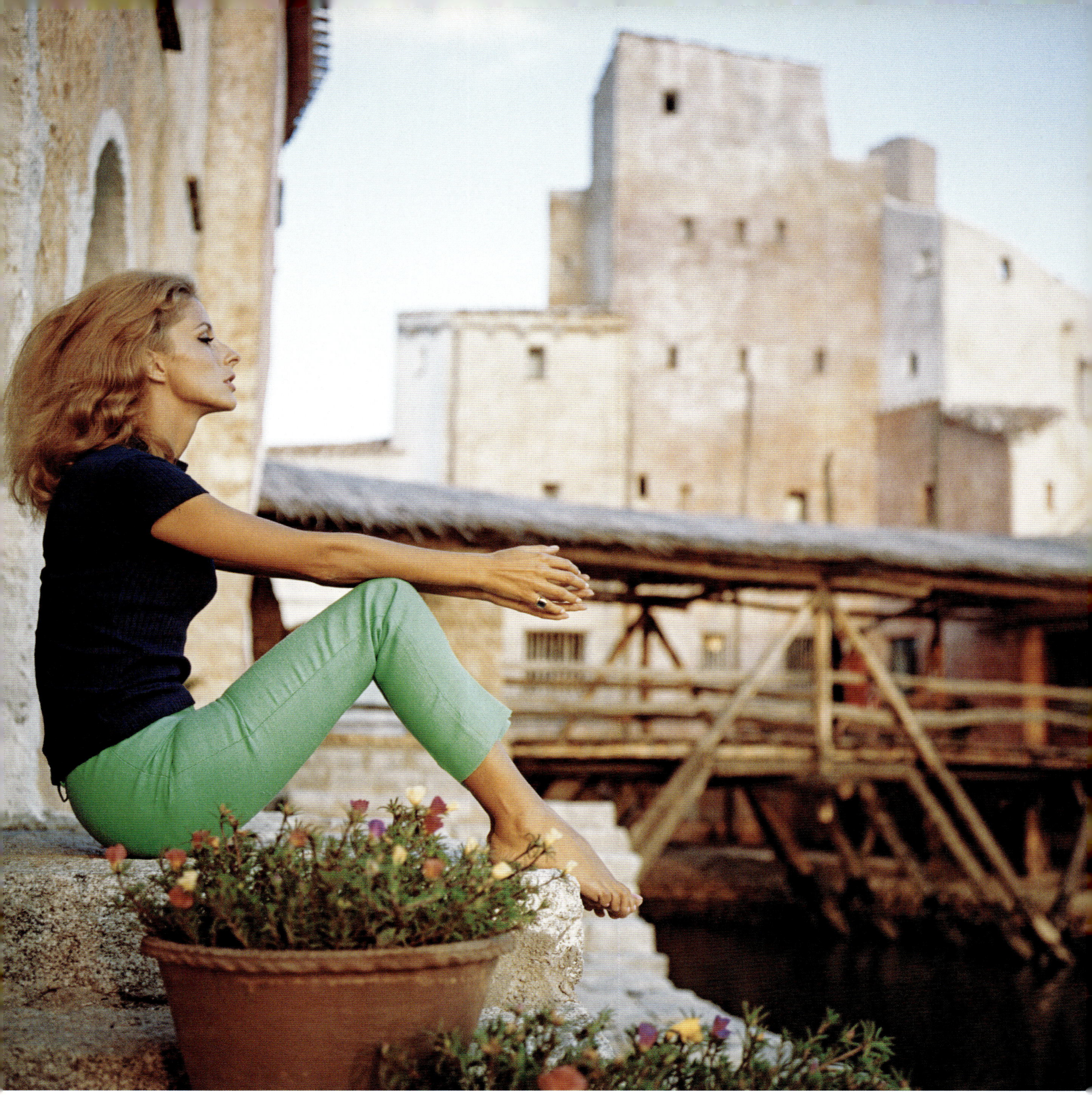

above and opposite Dolores von Furstenberg Guinness basks in the late-day sun outside the Hotel Cala di Volpe on the Costa Smeralda, Sardinia, 1965. The photo above has become one of Slim's most acclaimed images over the years. The outtakes from the original photo shoot show Slim's various attempts at capturing the essence of Guinness, a fashion and style icon like her mother, Gloria Guinness. Dolores was recently widowed when she fell in love with one of the world's most eligible bachelors, Prince Karim Aga Khan. Aga Khan developed the Costa Smeralda in 1962—a thirty-five-mile stretch

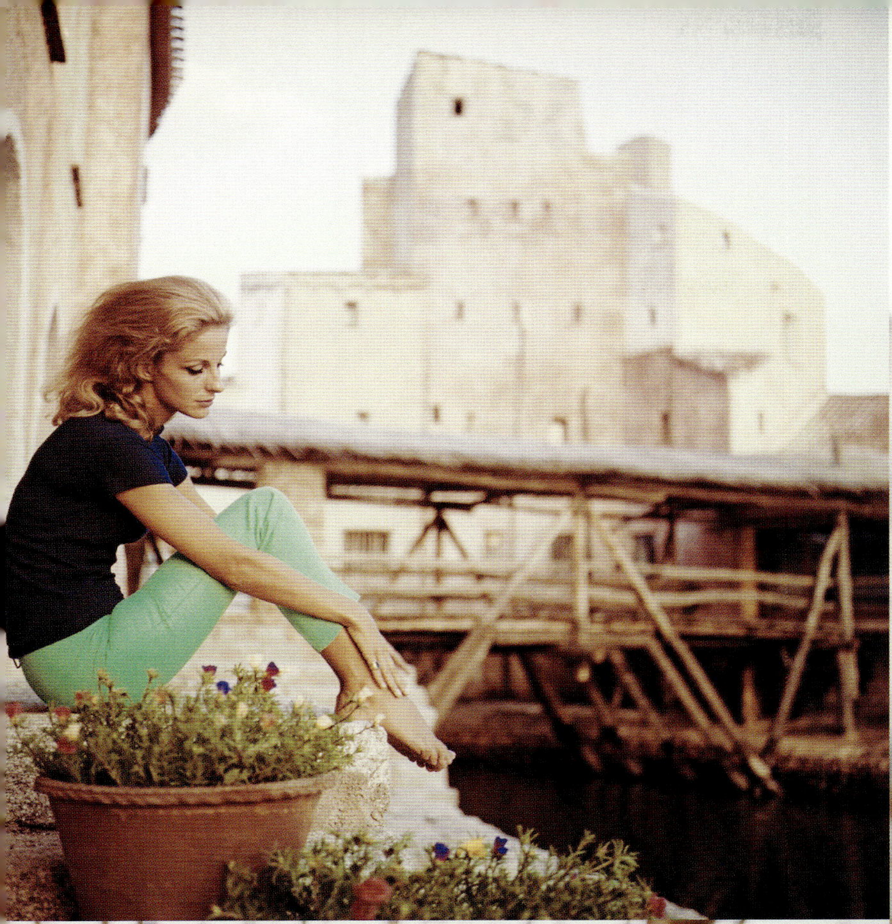
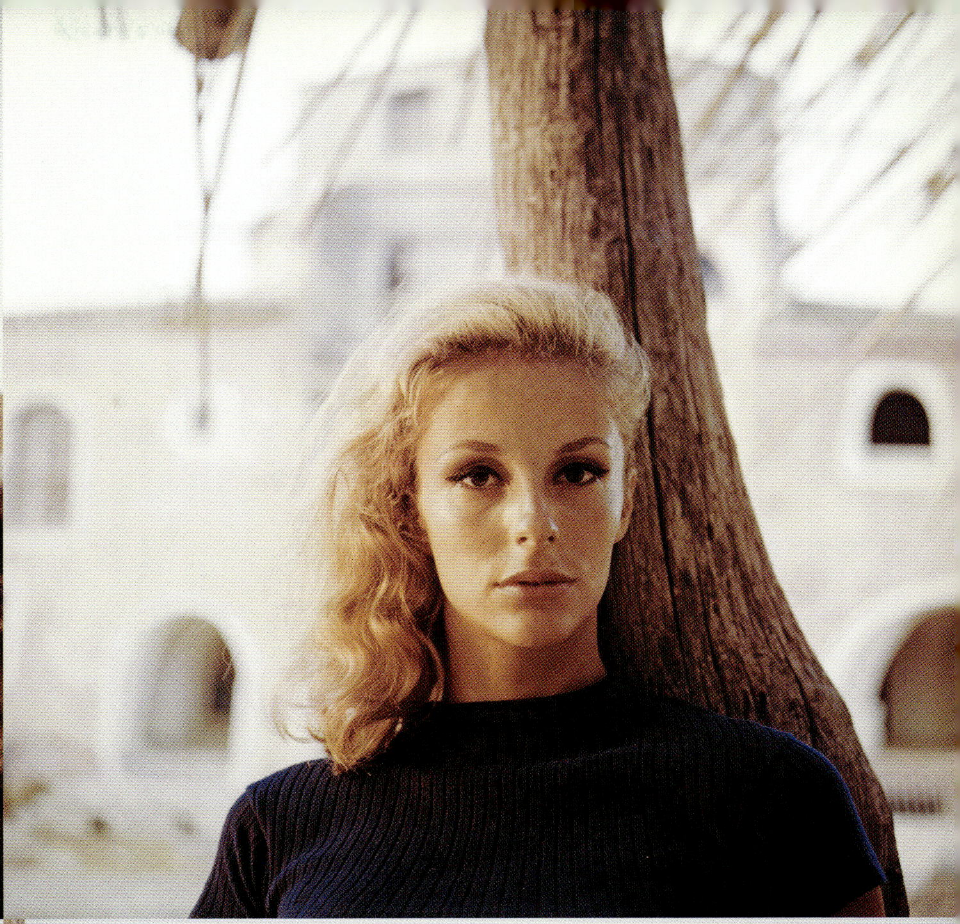
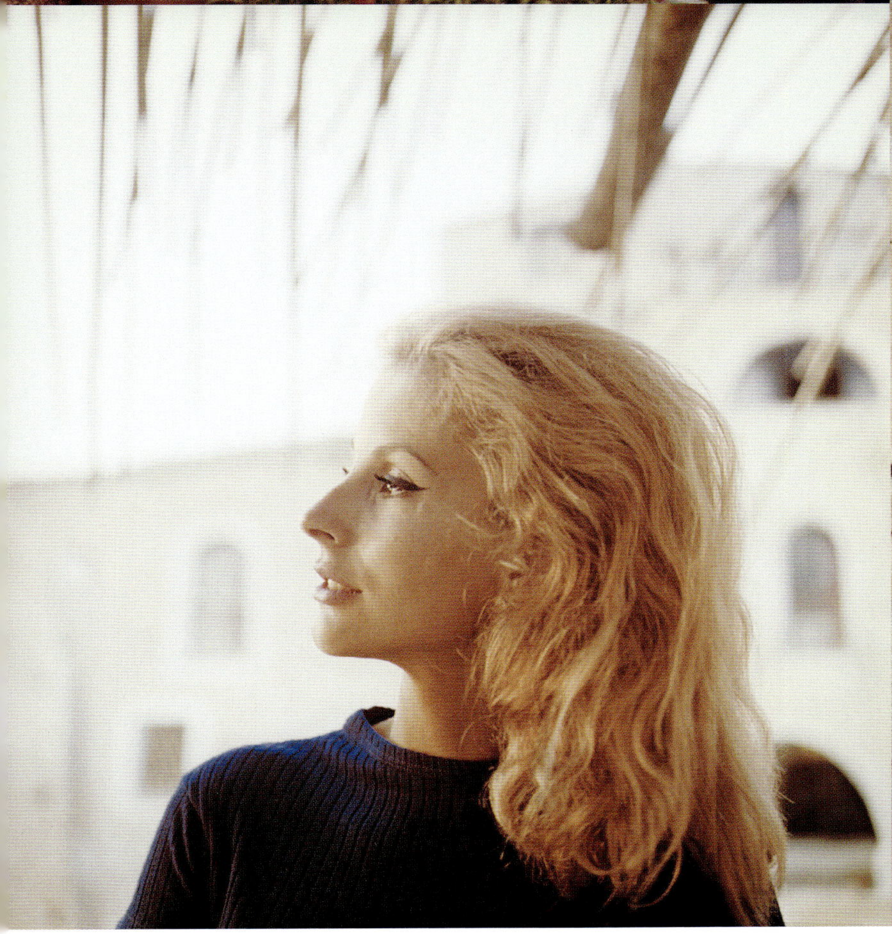
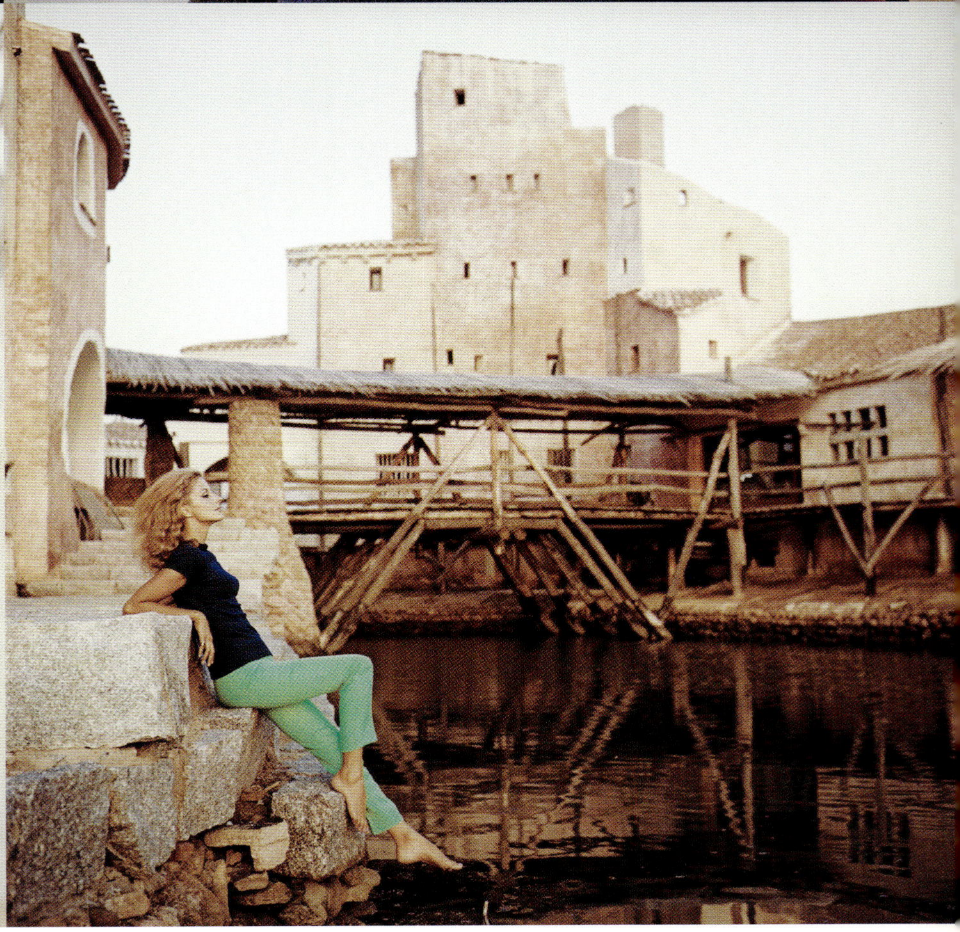

of untouched coastline, unchanged for centuries, on the island of Sardinia. The Ismaili prince, whose father was Prince Aly Khan, part of a long Persian dynasty and later a husband of Rita Hayworth, was considered to be a direct descendant of the Prophet Muhammad, but to his circle of wealthy friends, he was simply "Karim." He built the rustic Hotel Cala di Volpe and a handful of villas but otherwise did little to disturb the area's sun-soaked beaches, dusty lanes, and interior farmland. The area's nearly mythological fame in the 1950s was owed to its unparalleled blend of rusticity and sophistication.

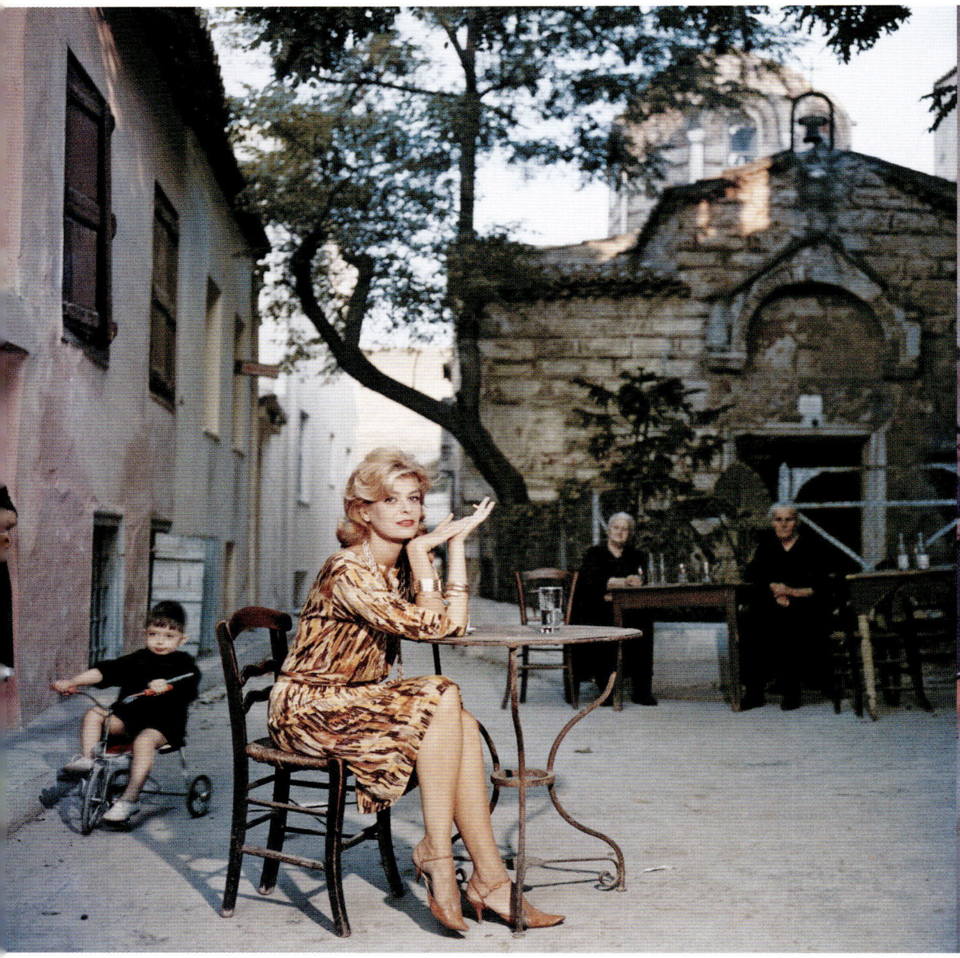

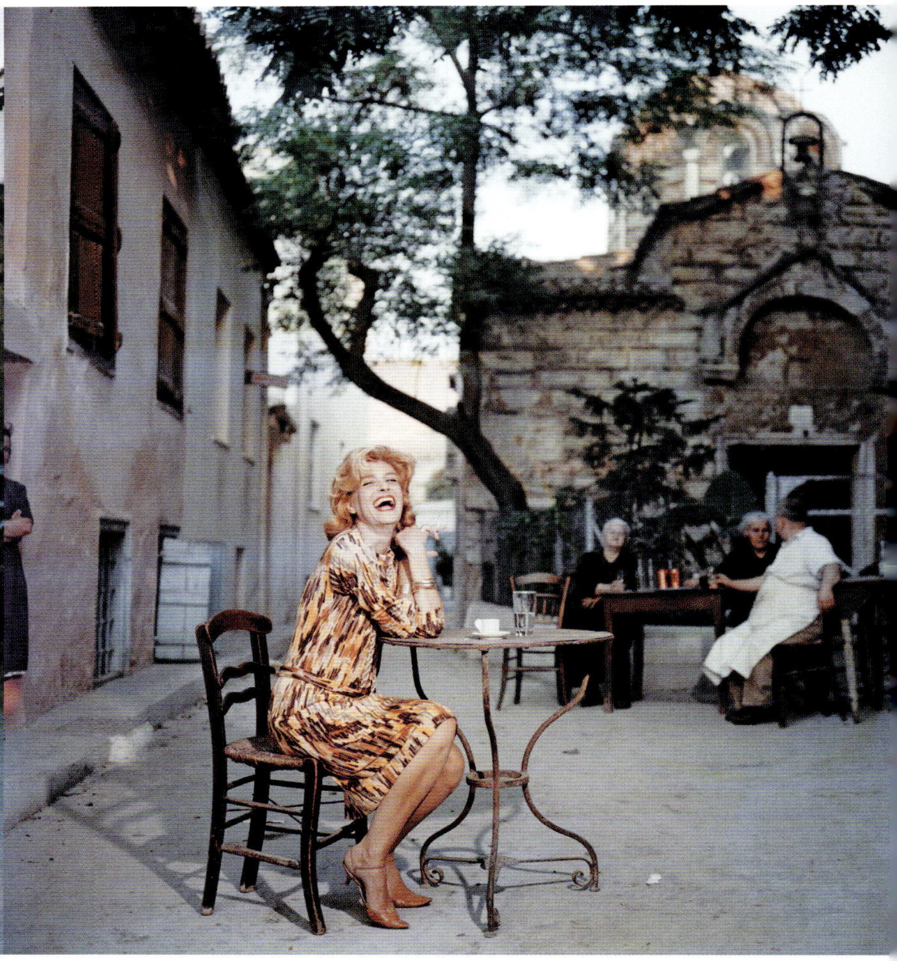

above and opposite The Greek actress Melina Mercouri, Athens, 1961. A spirited actress, singer, and politician, Mercouri was a late starter, making her first film at age thirty-five. Over the course of her career she received several BAFTA (British Academy of Film and Television Arts), Golden Globe, and Academy Award nominations. She won the Cannes Film Festival award for best actress in 1960. As her political awareness grew, she traveled the world speaking out against the Greek military dictatorship, which revoked her citizenship and confiscated her land. But even an assassination attempt did not silence her. After the dictatorship ended in 1974, she was elected to the Greek Parliament three years later and in 1981 became the first woman to hold the senior cabinet post of minister of culture. "Like any movie star, she was worried that the little boy would steal the shot," Slim would later recall about taking this series of photos.

following spread left The Italian actress Giovanna Ralli in Rome, circa 1960.

following spread right Poet Gwendolyn Brooks, Chicago, 1960. Slim took this photo of Brooks on a story for *Holiday* magazine on the city of Chicago. In her work Brooks was known for incorporating cameos of the people and personalities surrounding her in the urban setting, using conversational and syncopated rhythms. In 1945 Brooks wrote her first book of poetry, *A Street in Bronzeville*, named for the neighborhood where she lived on Chicago's South Side, and she is pictured here behind her apartment. Brooks was not only the first African American to win the Pulitzer Prize (for her book *Annie Allen*), she was the first African American woman to hold the position of poetry consultant to the Library of Congress and was the poet laureate of the state of Illinois.

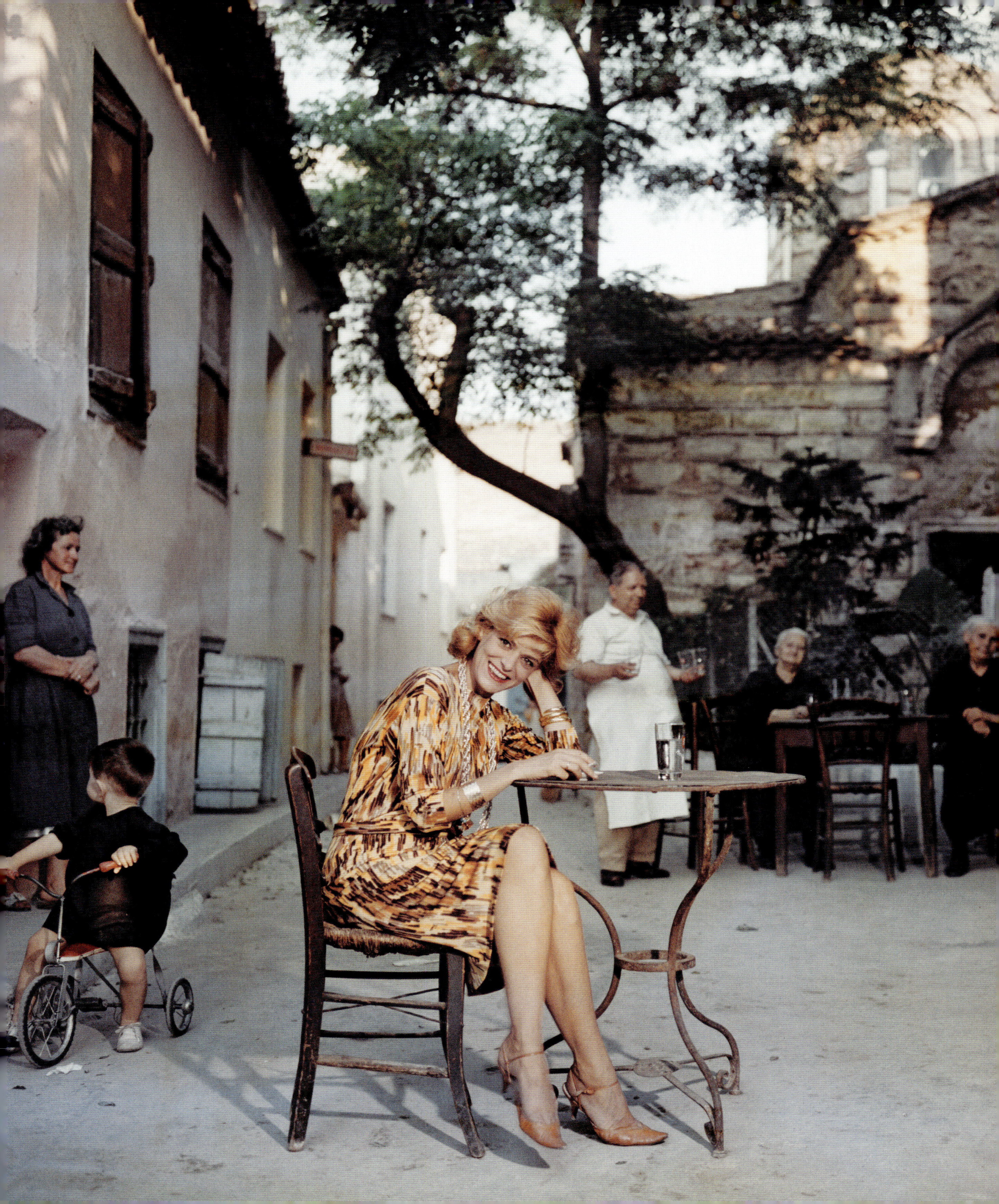

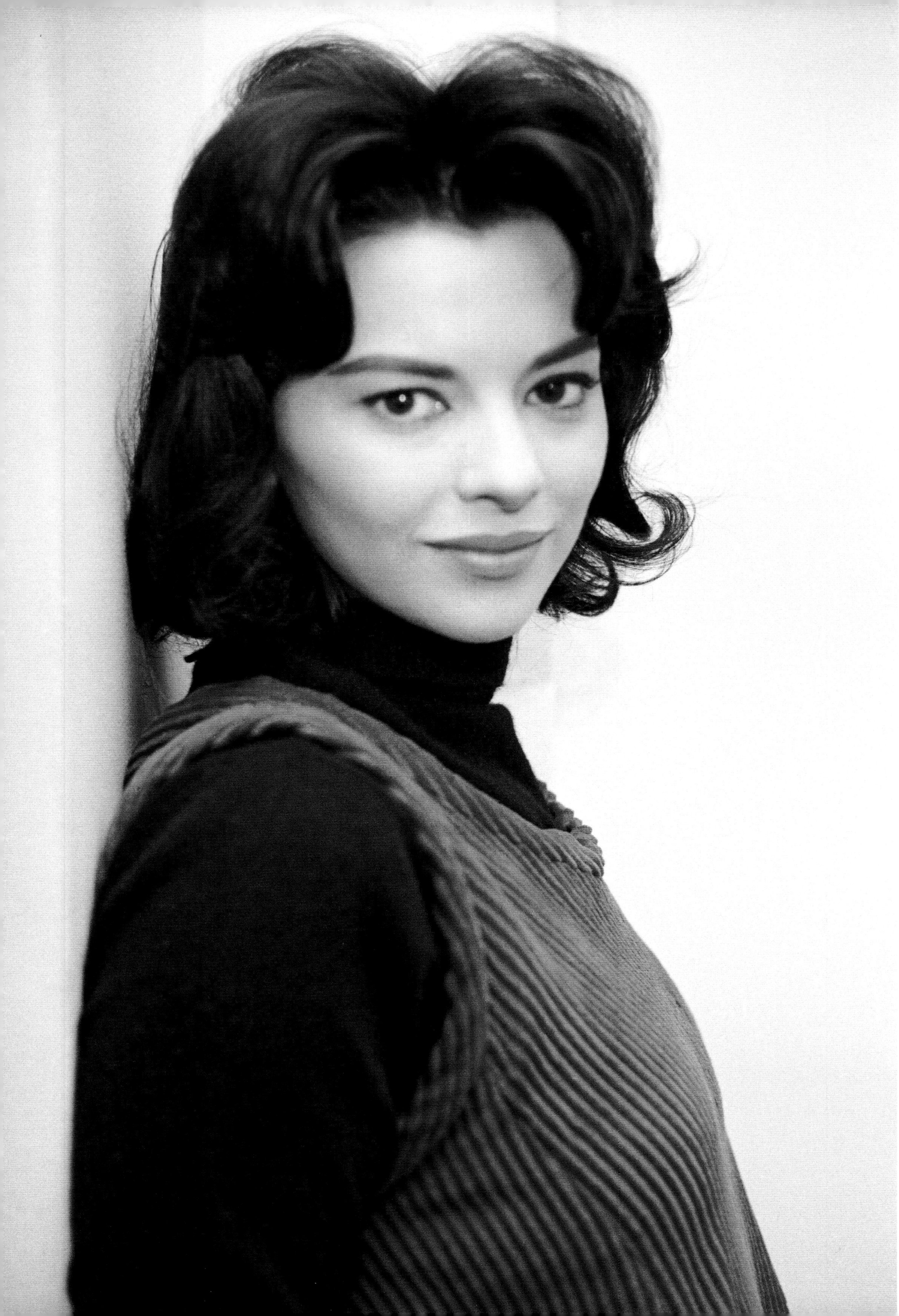

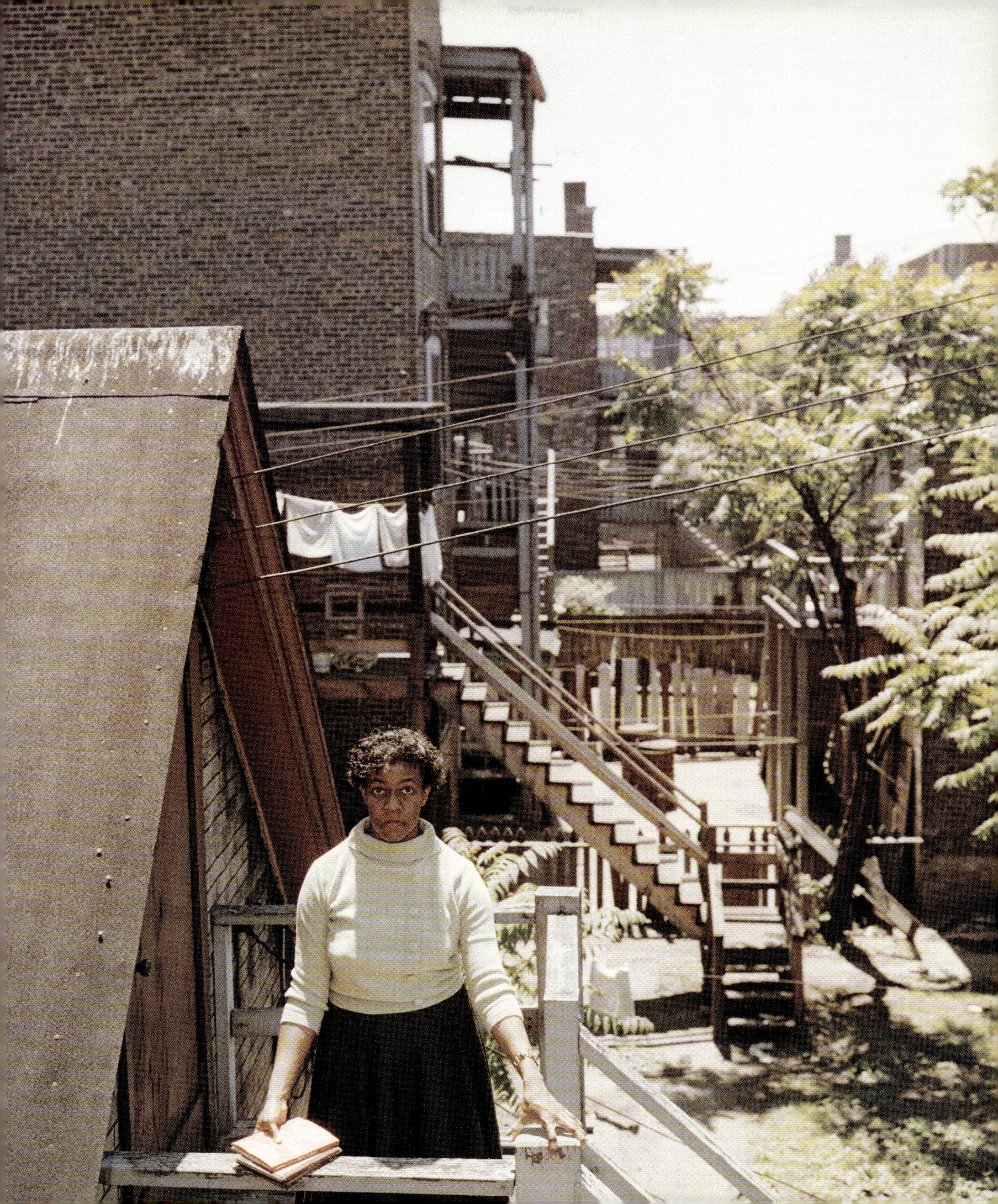

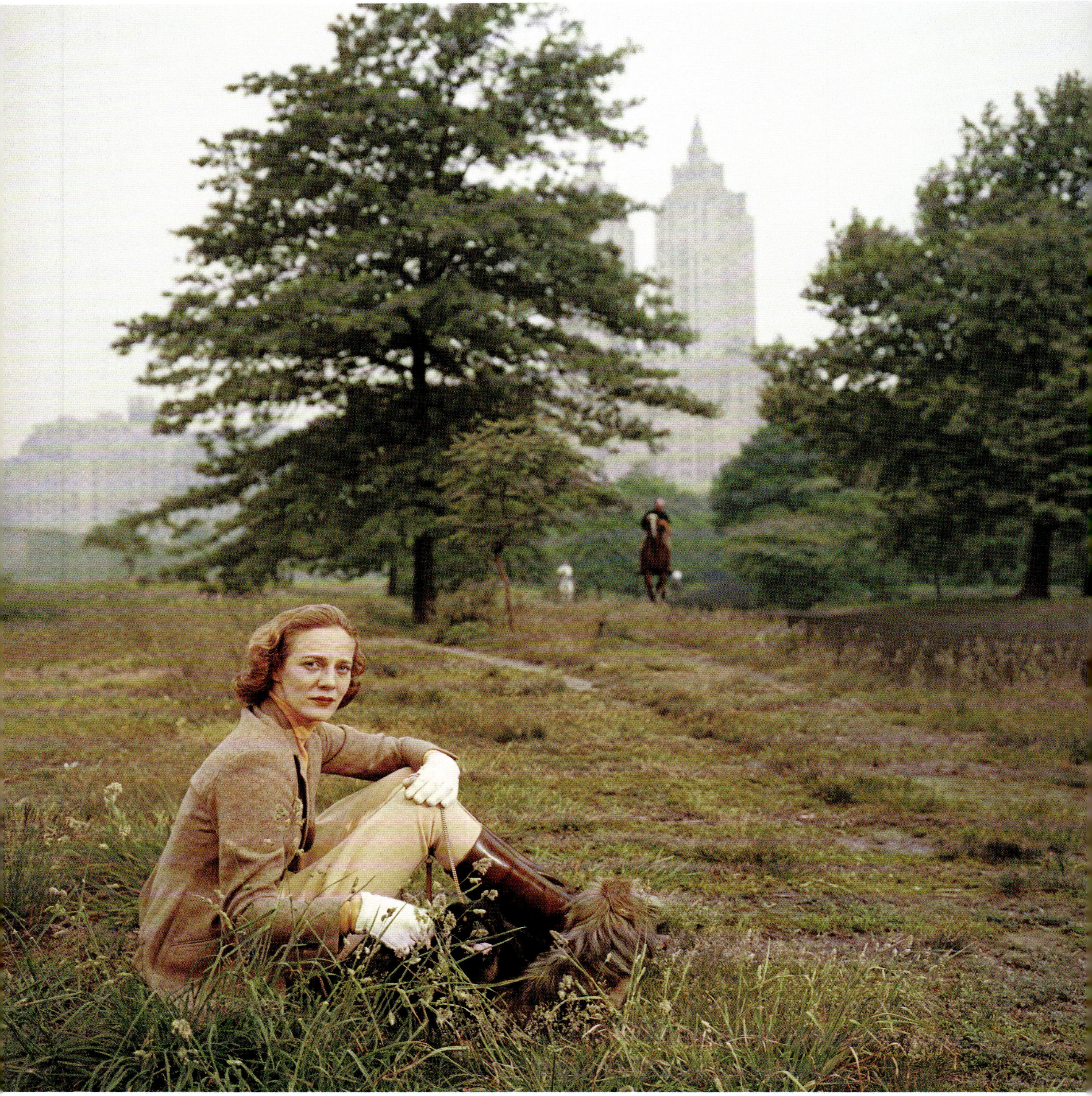

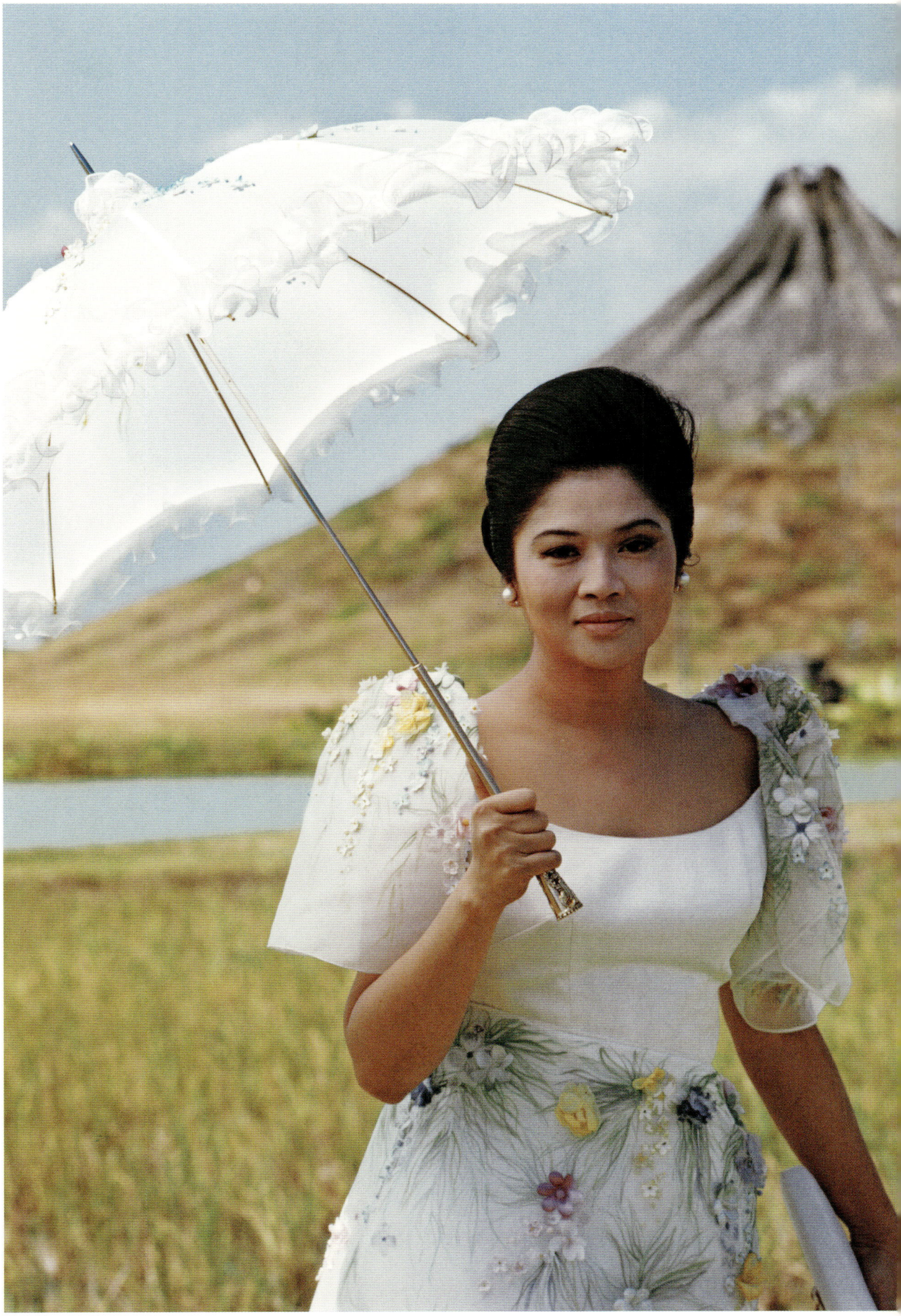

opposite Marie Maude McKim in Central Park, New York, 1959. McKim, known as "Memsie," was the eldest of the three daughters of Robert McKim and Lillian Bostwick. Her middle sister, Lilly Pulitzer, later became the legendary designer of preppy printed clothing (see page 56). And her youngest sister, Florence, nicknamed "Flossie," became Mrs. Nelson Doubleday, wife of the noted publisher. Riding to the hounds was a big part of their childhood on the North Shore of Long Island. Marie Maude's stepfather, Ogden Phipps, bred and raced some of the greatest equine champions of the twentieth century: Seabiscuit, Bold Ruler, and Secretariat, among others. Her mother's steeplechase horses won the coveted Grand National race in Liverpool a remarkable eight times.

right The first lady of the Philippines, Imelda Romuáldez Marcos, the wife of President Ferdinand Marcos, in Manila, 1972. This photo was taken for a story Slim did on Manila for *Travel & Leisure* magazine.

right Davina Marcia Herbert Ingrams, 18th Baroness Darcy de Knayth, at home in Bellasis House, Dorking, Surrey, 1957. De Knayth was a direct descendant of Lord Clive of India and was a peeress in her own right, not by marriage. At one time she was also the youngest baroness in England, after her father was killed in action during World War II. She married and had three children, but in 1964 an automobile accident took her husband's life and left her paralyzed from the neck down. Over time she regained some use of her upper body, learned table tennis and archery, and won gold medals at the Paralympic Games in swimming (1968) and table tennis (1972). One of the first sixteen hereditary peeresses admitted to the House of Lords, in 1963, she later spoke frequently on issues related to disabilities.

below left Ursula Pacelli, the Lido, Venice, 1957. Pacelli, grandniece of Pope Pius XII, belongs to the old-world Italian nobility that has long been at the heart of Venetian society.

below right Princess Lucy Ruspoli, Cortina d'Ampezzo, Italy, 1982. Ruspoli was one of Slim's favorite muses over the years (see also page 139). She had an intrinsic elegance and nearly regal bearing that he loved. In turn, she appreciated Slim's talent and, despite her innate formality, was always game for whatever photo idea Slim cooked up—and infinitely patient with his orchestration of those shots. She and her husband, Mario, crisscrossed the world with nearly the same frequency as Slim.

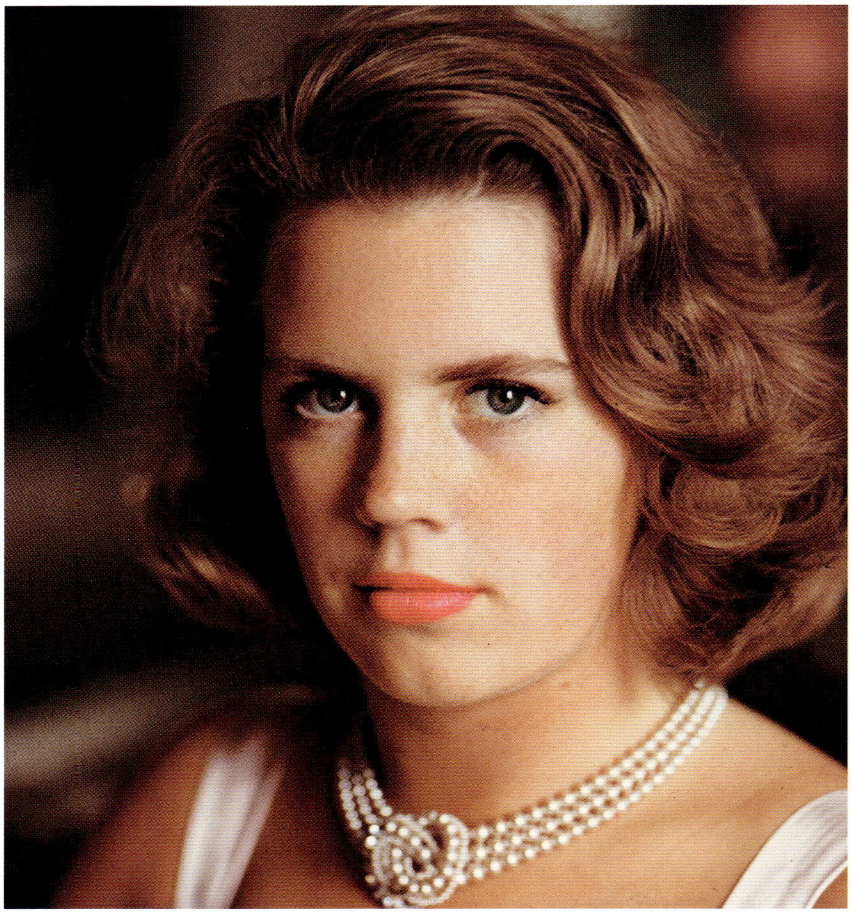

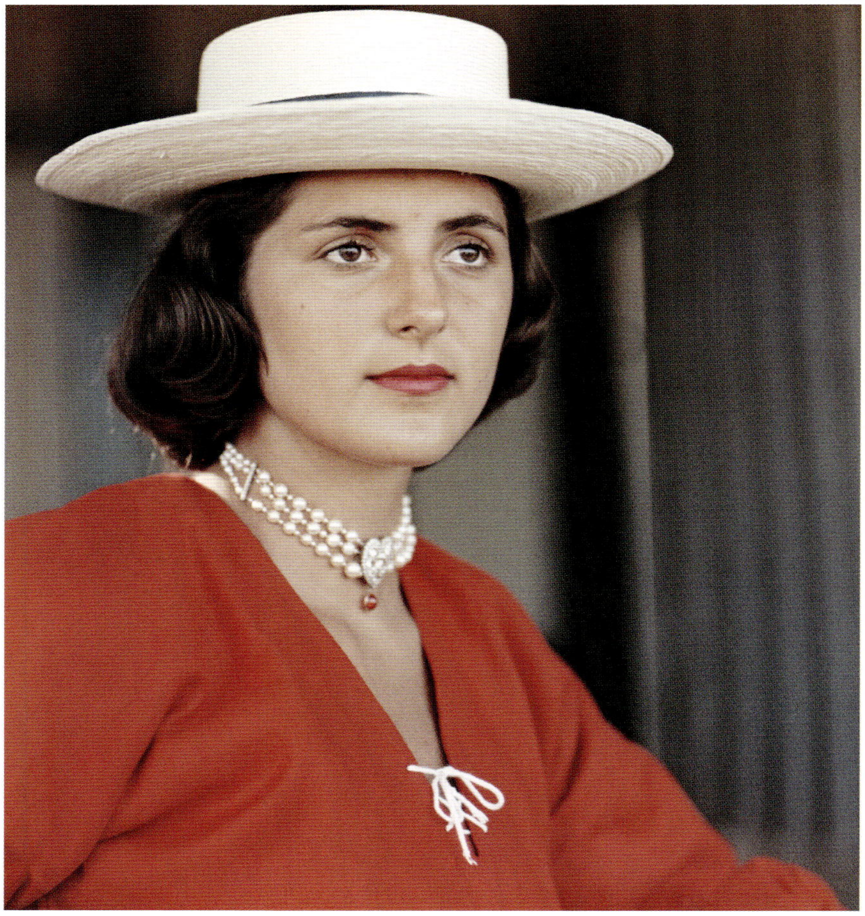

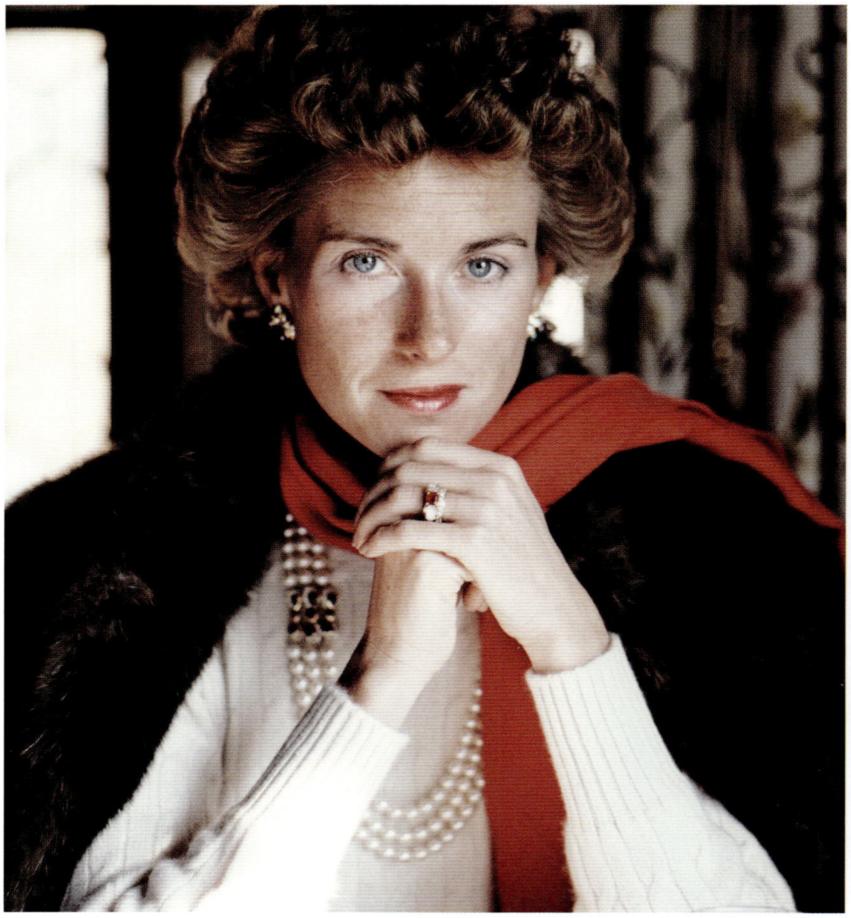

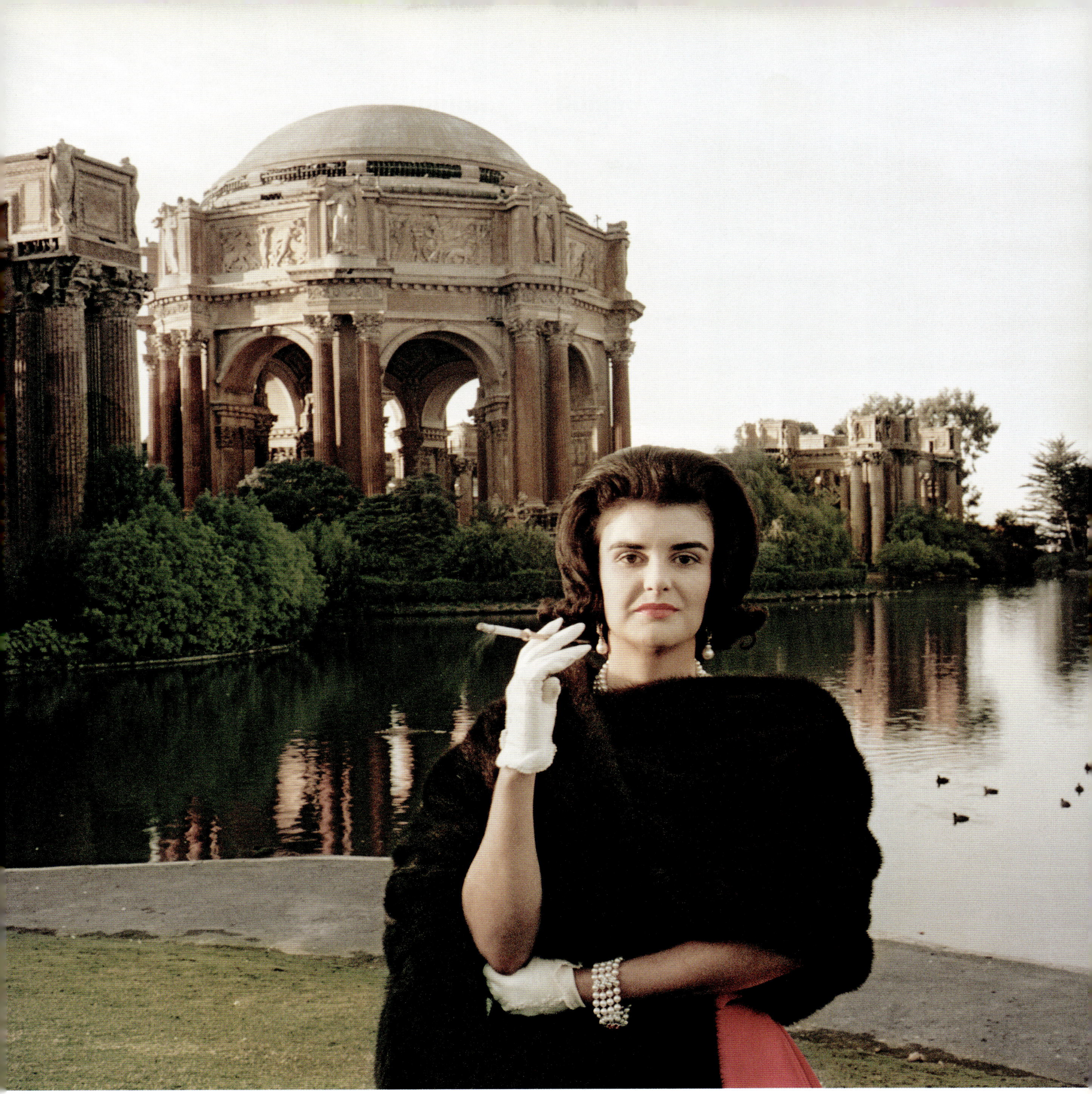

above Dolly Fritz by the lagoon-rimmed Palace of Fine Arts in San Francisco, 1961. Dorothy Fritz, better known as "Dolly," was a San Francisco heiress. While still a teenager Dolly inherited the Huntington Hotel, where she was reputed to have lived grandly in the style of the fictional character Eloise—one difference being that the spirited and vivacious Dolly owned the hotel. Slim wrote about her, "Another San Franciscan I enjoyed photographing is Dolly Fritz, a good friend whom I like to call 'the doll.' Dolly owns a large chunk of Nob Hill and is very active in managing her holdings."

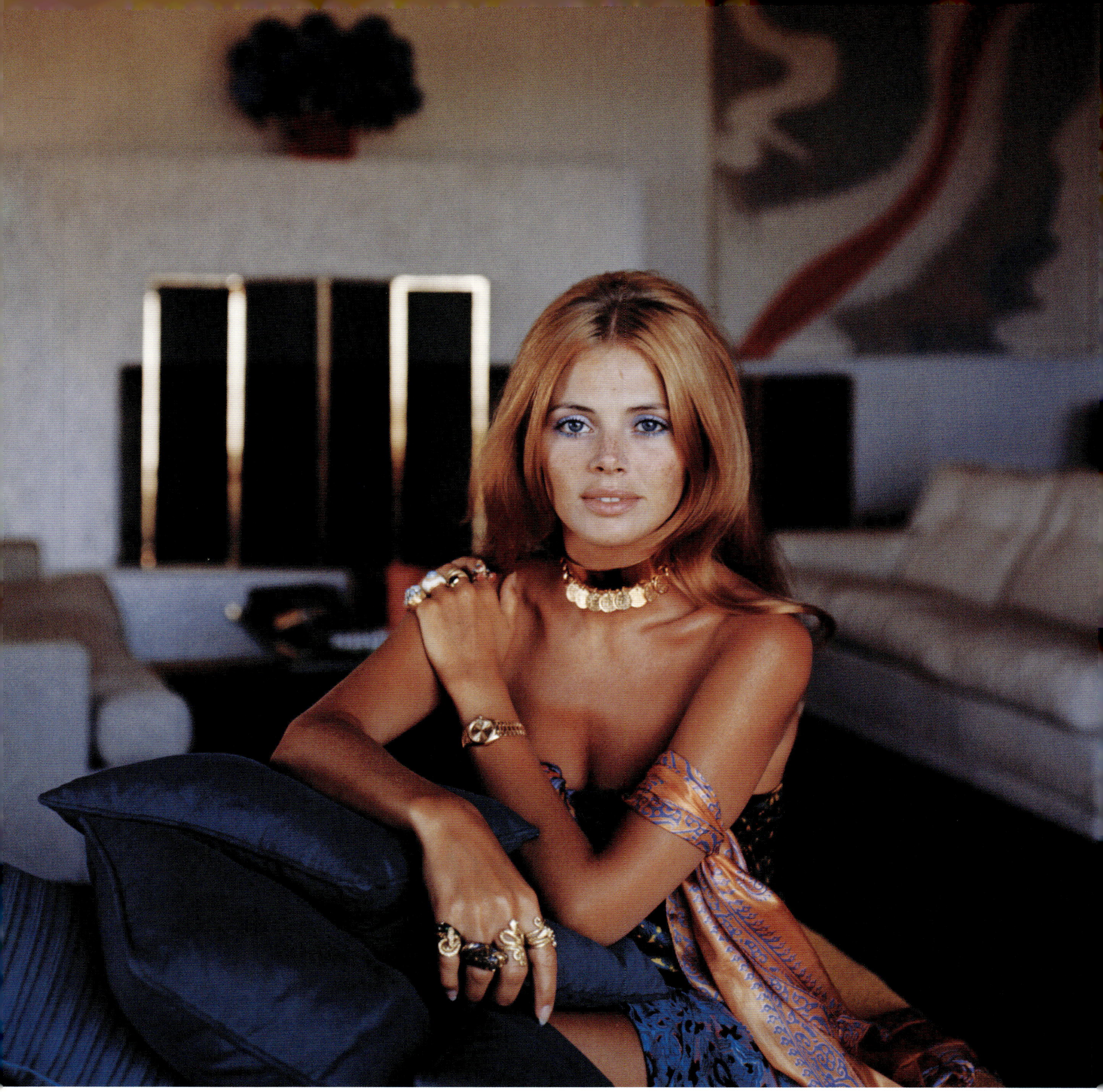

above The Swedish actress Britt Ekland, Porto Ercole, Italy, 1969. Slim commented on this portrait in 1992: "I never style my ladies. Those are all her rings. She showed up with them all on." He had a great eye for stylish women with original taste, even if they were unknowns, and sought them out as subjects all over the world. He rarely missed an opportunity, however, to trumpet the difficulties of photographing such individuals as opposed to professional models in studios.

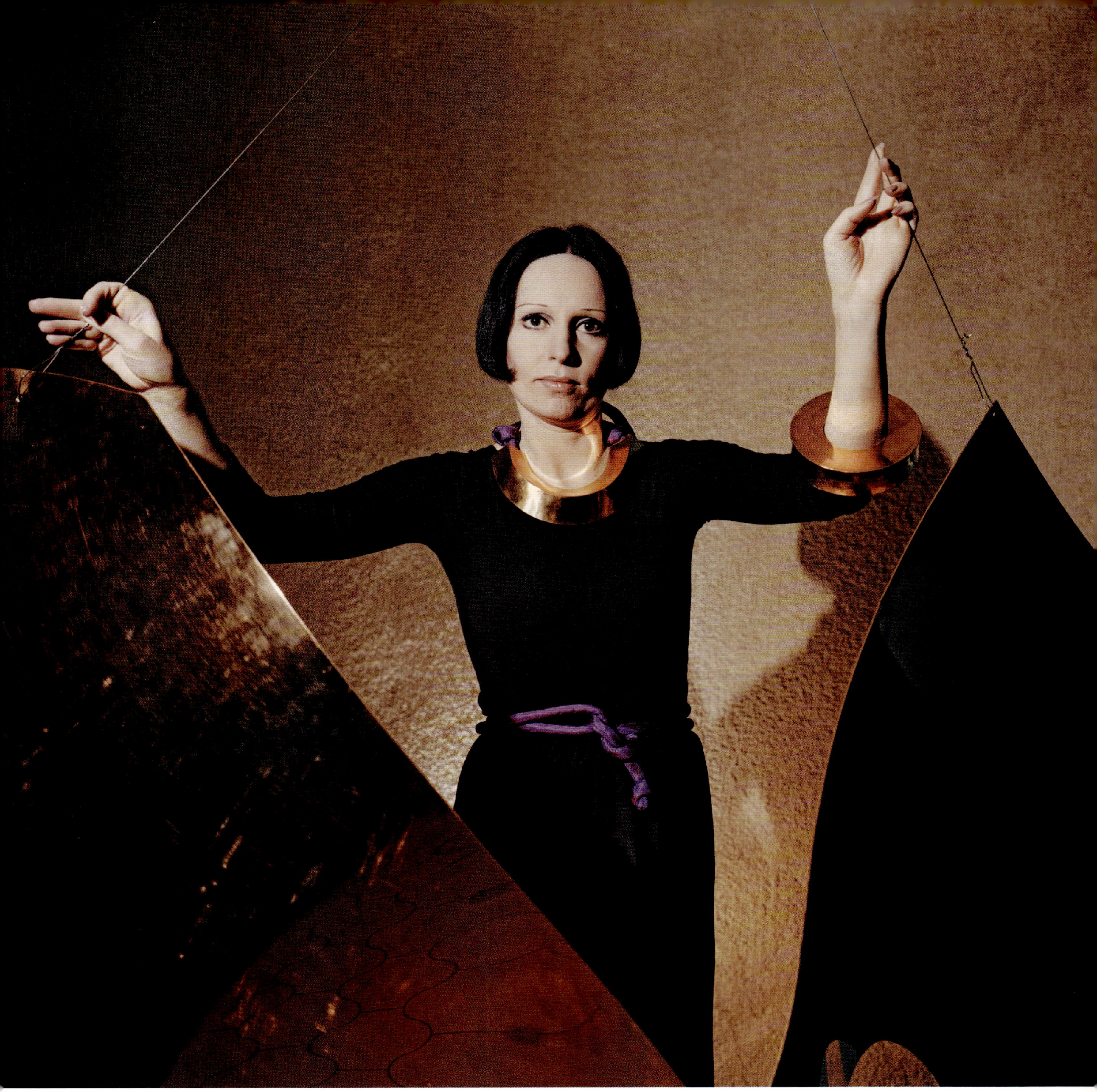

above The fashion original Mary McFadden, Palm Beach, 1976. When she began designing clothes in the early 1970s, McFadden created a sensation in the fashion world with her theatrical designs created from textiles gathered during her travels around the world. She featured hand-painted silks, embroidered jackets, and lots of pleats, inspired primarily by Greek and Roman statuary. She is the scion of two American aristocratic families: the Philadelphia McFaddens and the New York Cuttings.

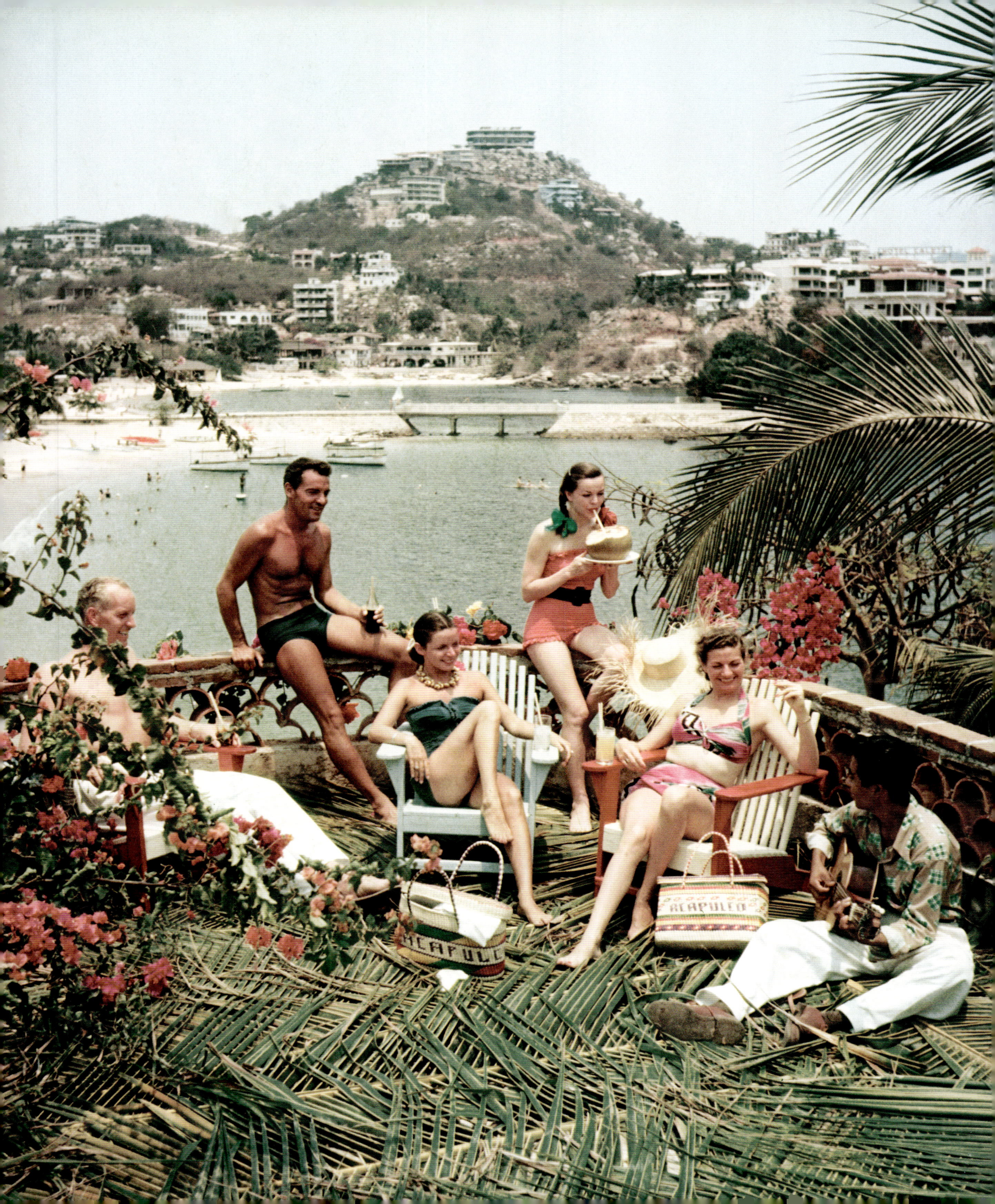
ACAPULCO

. . . *DOING* ATTRACTIVE *THINGS . . .*

Slim's visual narratives nourish a universal fascination with how the wealthy and privileged lived in the postwar era, in particular their rituals in the pursuit of leisure. The photographs in this chapter echo Slim's promise to himself as he began his career—to train his lens primarily upon life's pleasures and diversions. Whether in pearls, tweed jackets, or black stilettos, the women in the pages to follow are as inclined to find leisure on a yacht as on a thoroughbred, as apt to shoulder a skeet gun as to boat a black marlin.

opposite Bill Babb, Thomas Beecher, Jean Adams, Carolyn Phillips, and Mrs. Bill Babb enjoy a guitar serenade on a terrace in Acapulco, 1952. "It's hard to top Palm Springs or Newport or Jamaica as superb resorts. But from the standpoint of climate and spectacular scenery, there is nothing I have seen in the Western Hemisphere that equals Acapulco." This was Slim's description of the fabled resort town he was assigned to cover in the early 1950s. The Prince of Wales gave the sleepy Mexican fishing village its first famous nod on a trip there in 1920. Developed in the 1940s and 1950s, it became a sun-drenched sanctuary for millionaires and movie stars, its most exquisite homes built into mountainsides overlooking the majestic bay.

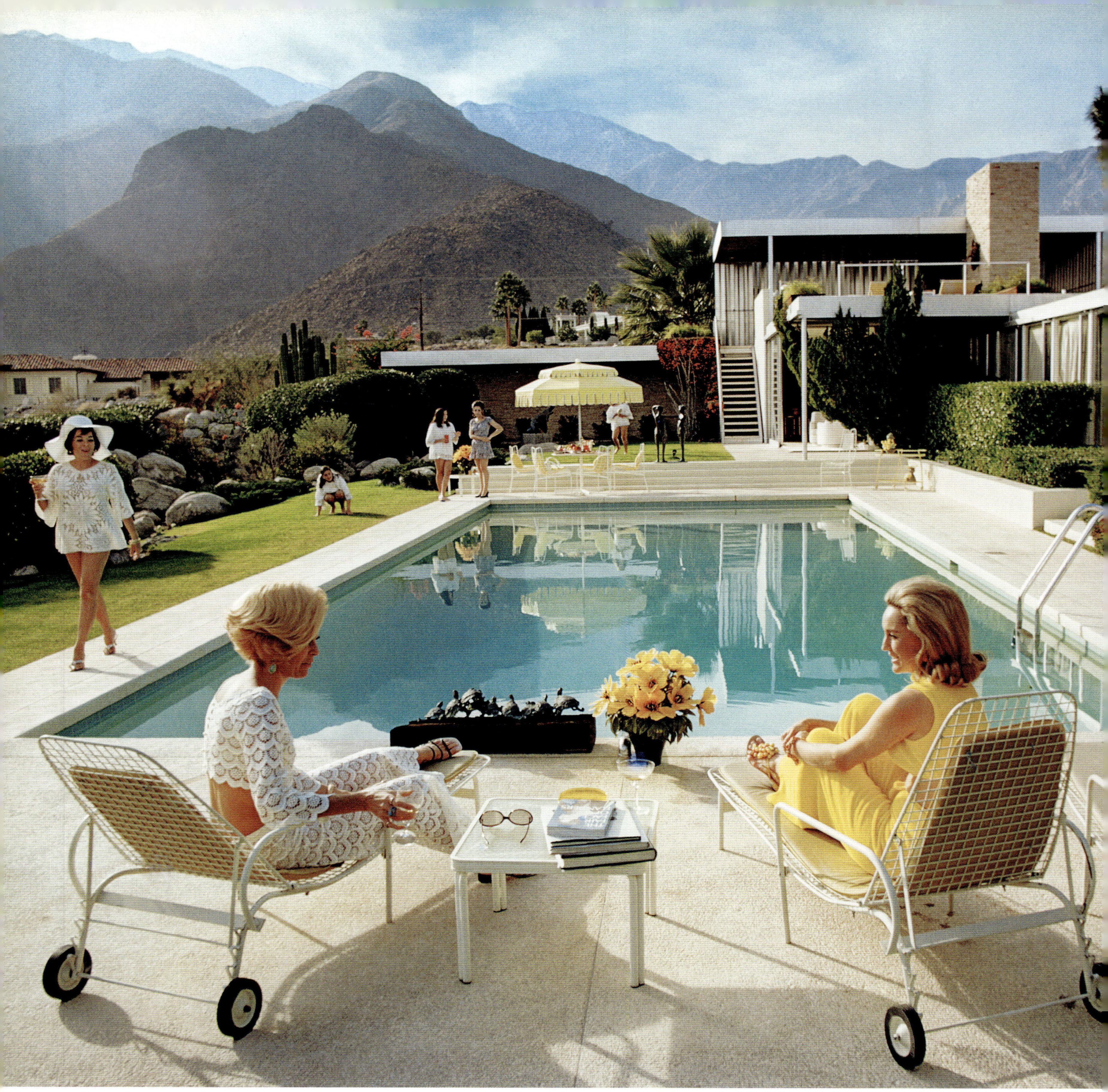

above and opposite A party at the Kaufmann Desert House, designed by Richard Neutra, Palm Springs, 1970. Many have speculated why the photograph above has become one of Slim's most iconic images. Was it the big hair and bare midriffs, the mod 1970s outfits, the dramatic view, or its "martini modern" aesthetic? The home's owner then, the Palm Springs socialite Nelda Linsk (in yellow), related years later that Slim had called and said, "I want to come over and do a pool shot. Call some friends over." His directive for what they should wear was simple: "Pull something out of your closet." Linsk was a Palm Springs real estate expert, and her husband, Joseph, was an art dealer. Outtakes from the famous photo shoot are opposite and on the following spread.

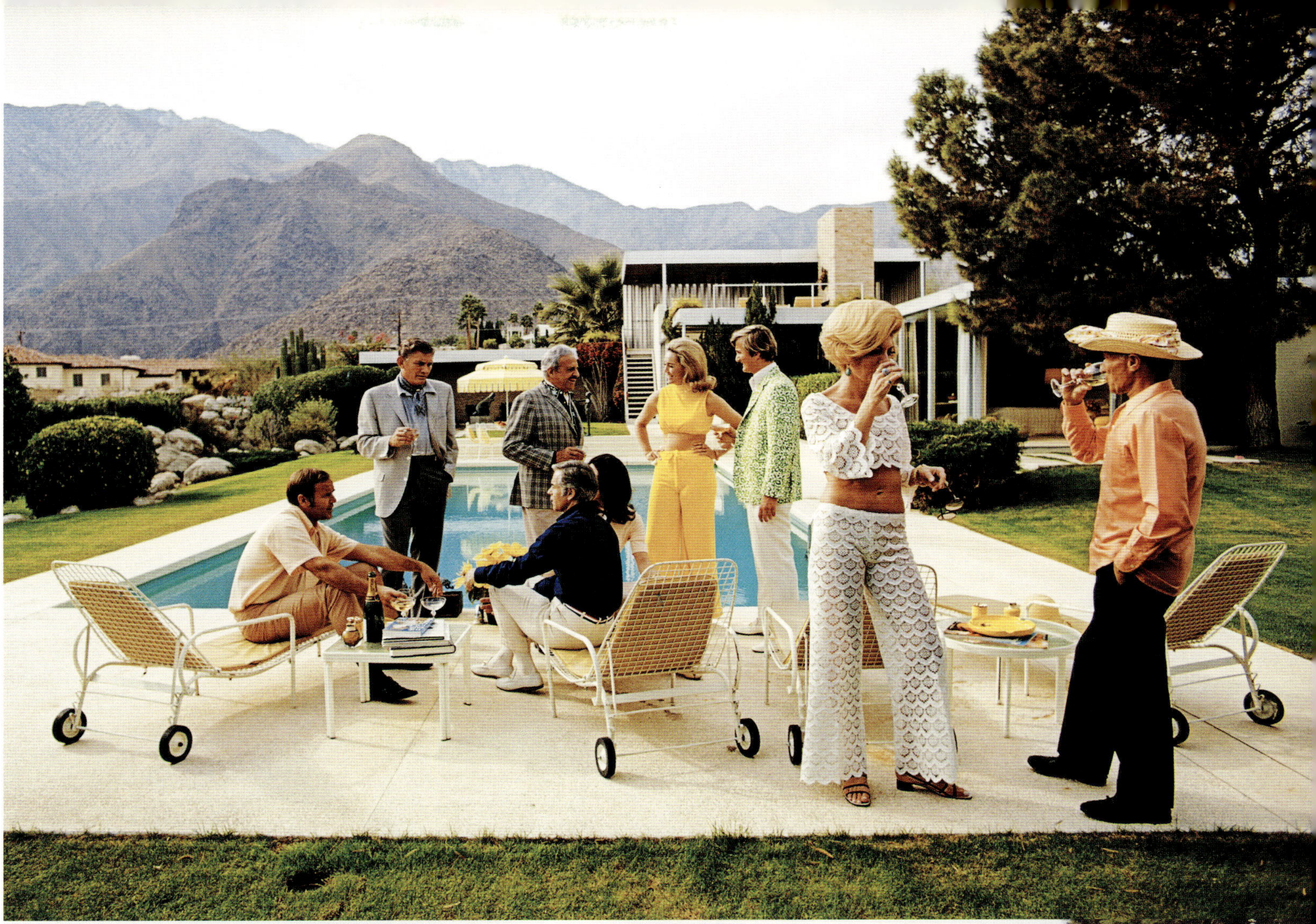

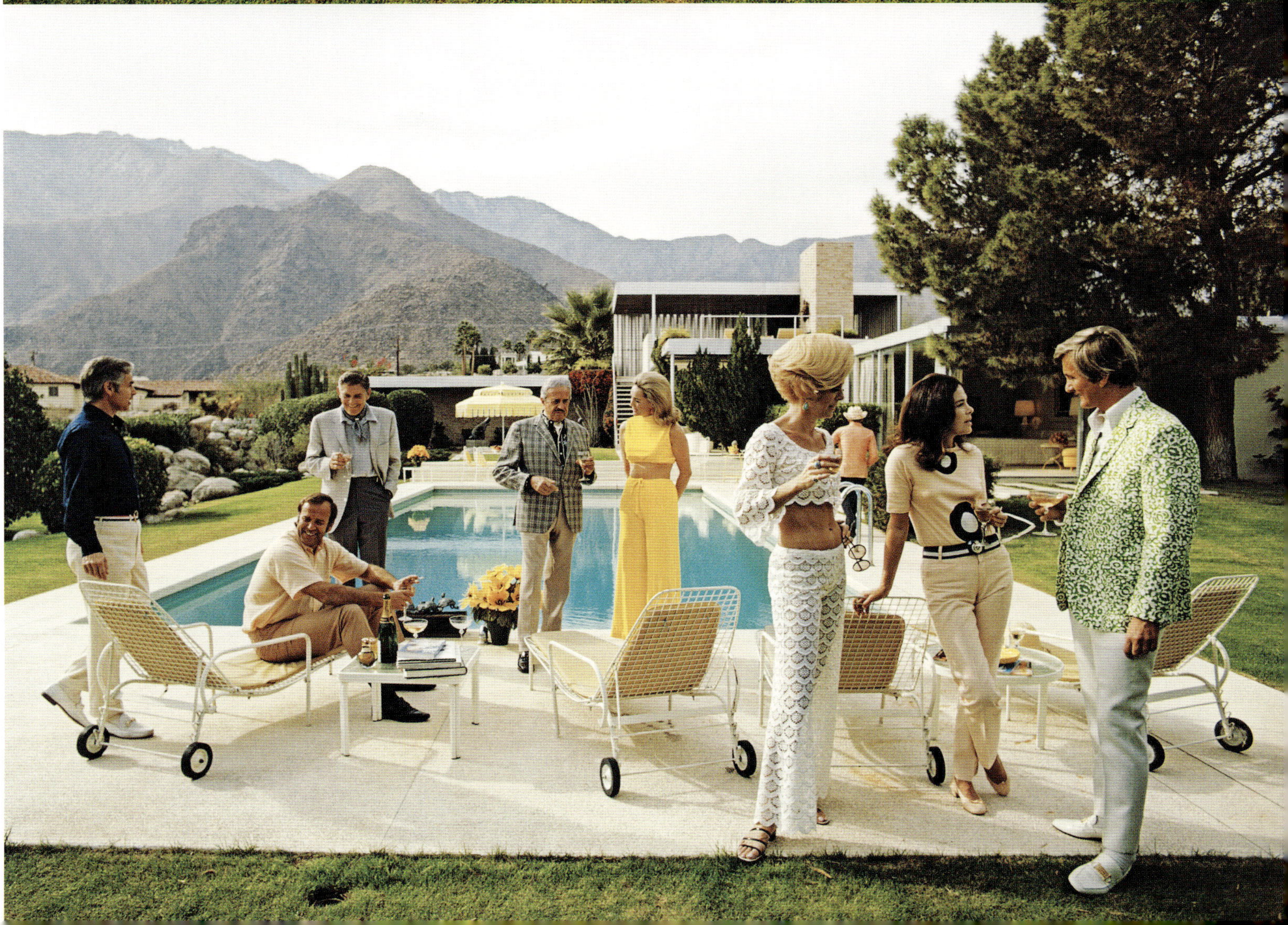

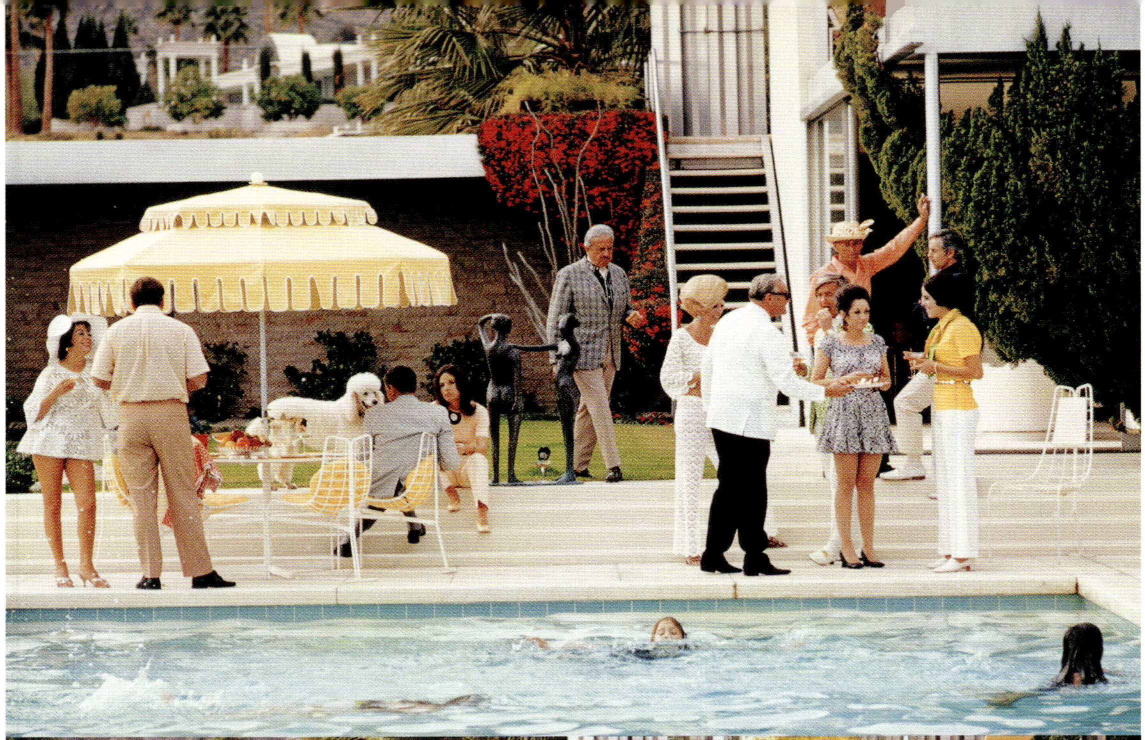

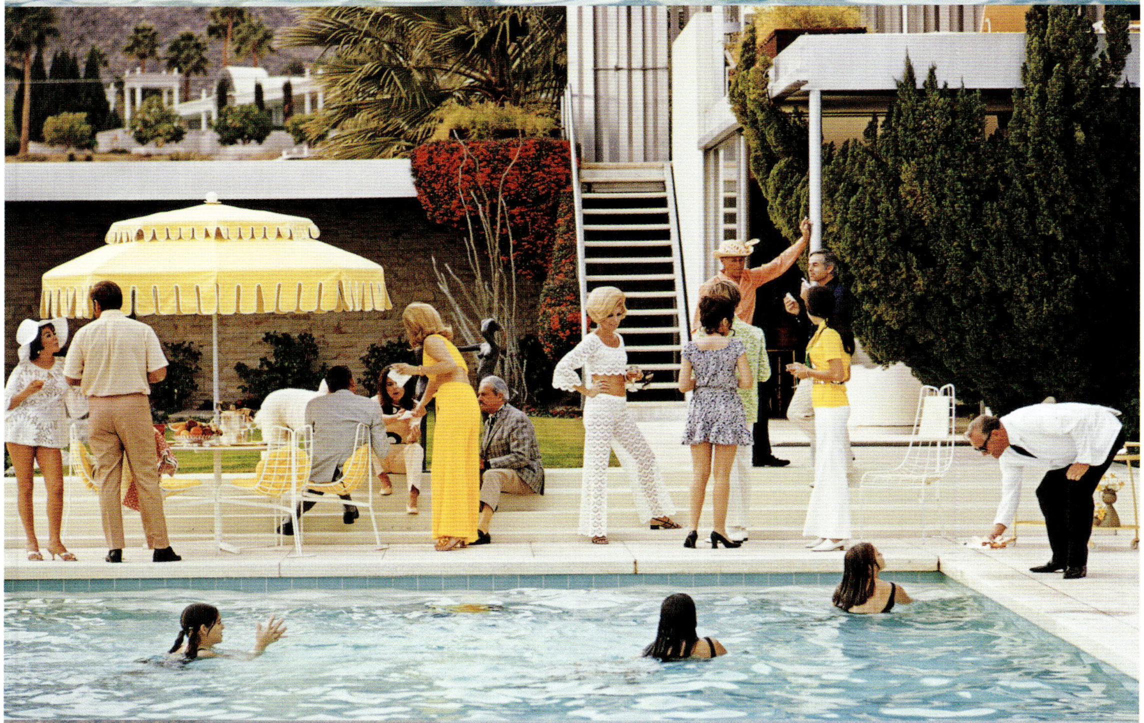

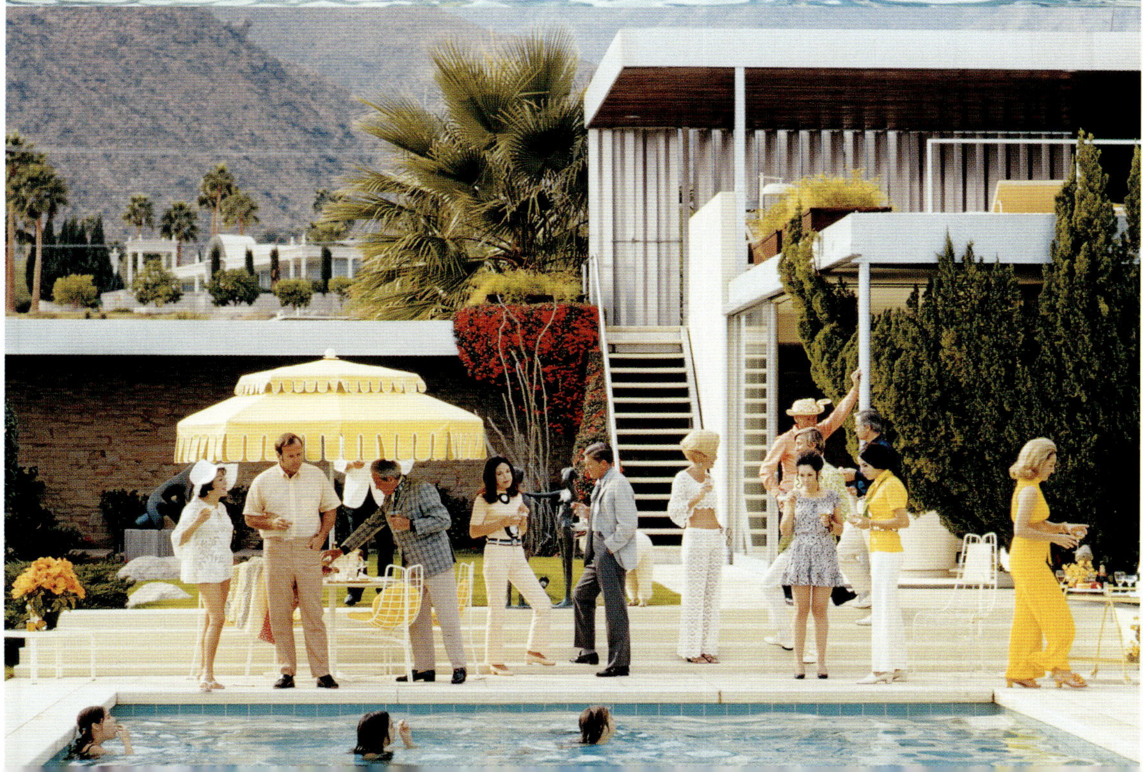

left and opposite The Neutra house has a notable history apart from Slim's memorable photoshoot taken there in 1970. It was commissioned in 1946 by Edgar Kaufmann, scion of the Pittsburgh department store family. A decade earlier Kaufmann had commissioned a house by Frank Lloyd Wright in Pennsylvania called Fallingwater. After many years of alterations and owners, including singer Barry Manilow, the Neutra house was listed for sale in 1993 just before the preservation movement of mid-century architecture was taking hold in Palm Springs. The listing agent labeled it a "tear-down" and added that "it could easily be made more stylish by converting it to a Spanish style." Within a decade, up for sale again, the final bid was fifteen million dollars. Today it has been designated a local landmark and is easily the most famous house in Palm Springs, with upwards of five hundred articles having been written about it. The architectural style of Desert Modernism is notable for its clean lines, ample use of glass and other natural and manufactured resources, and generous utilization of outdoor spaces.

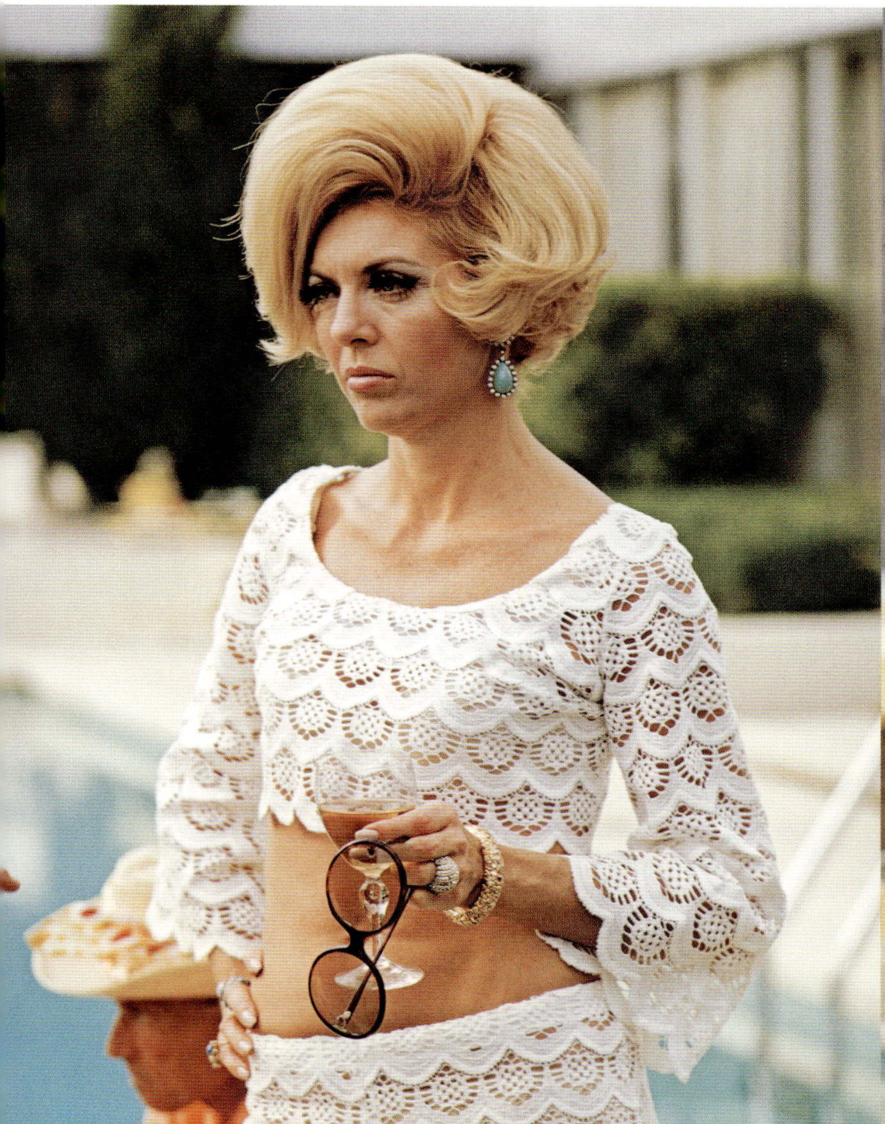

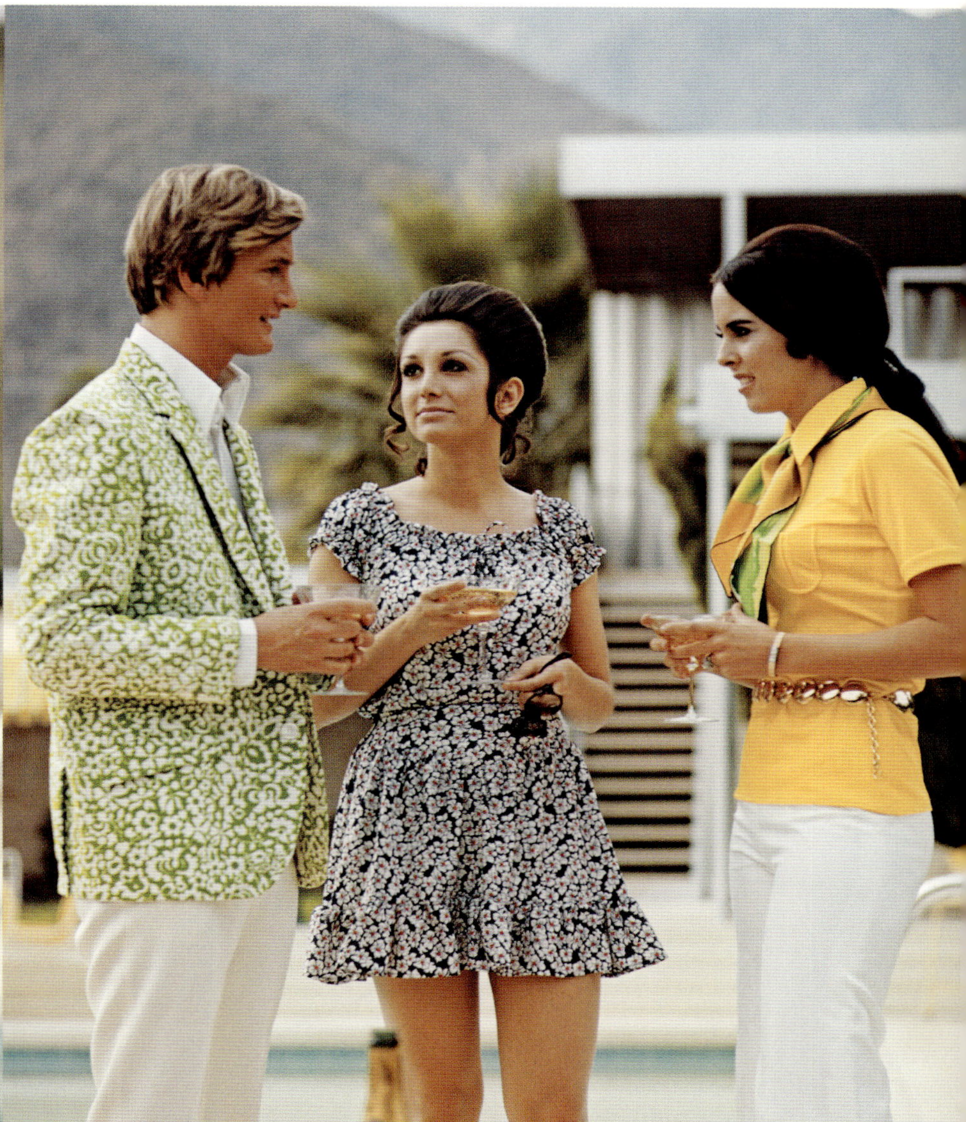

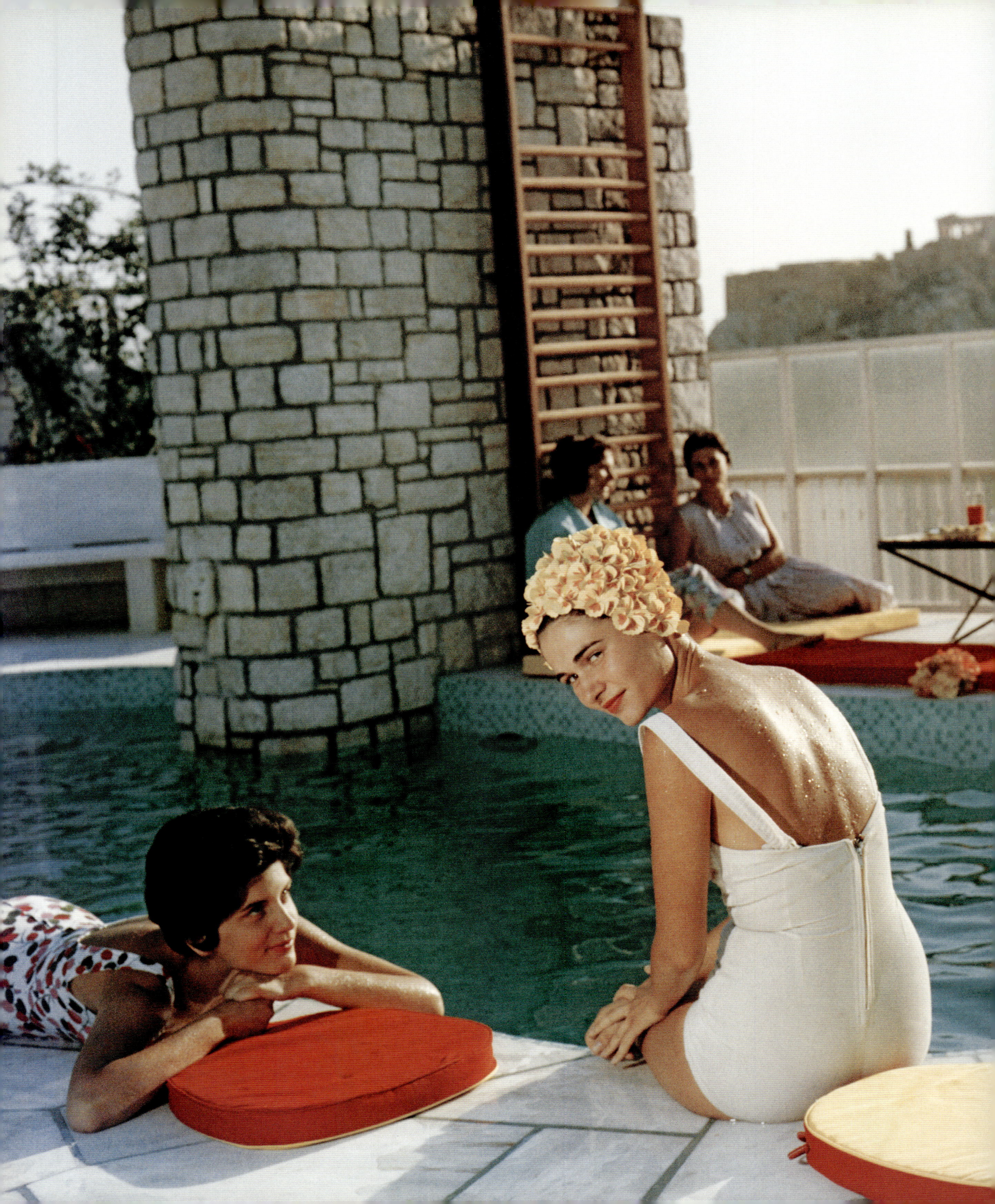

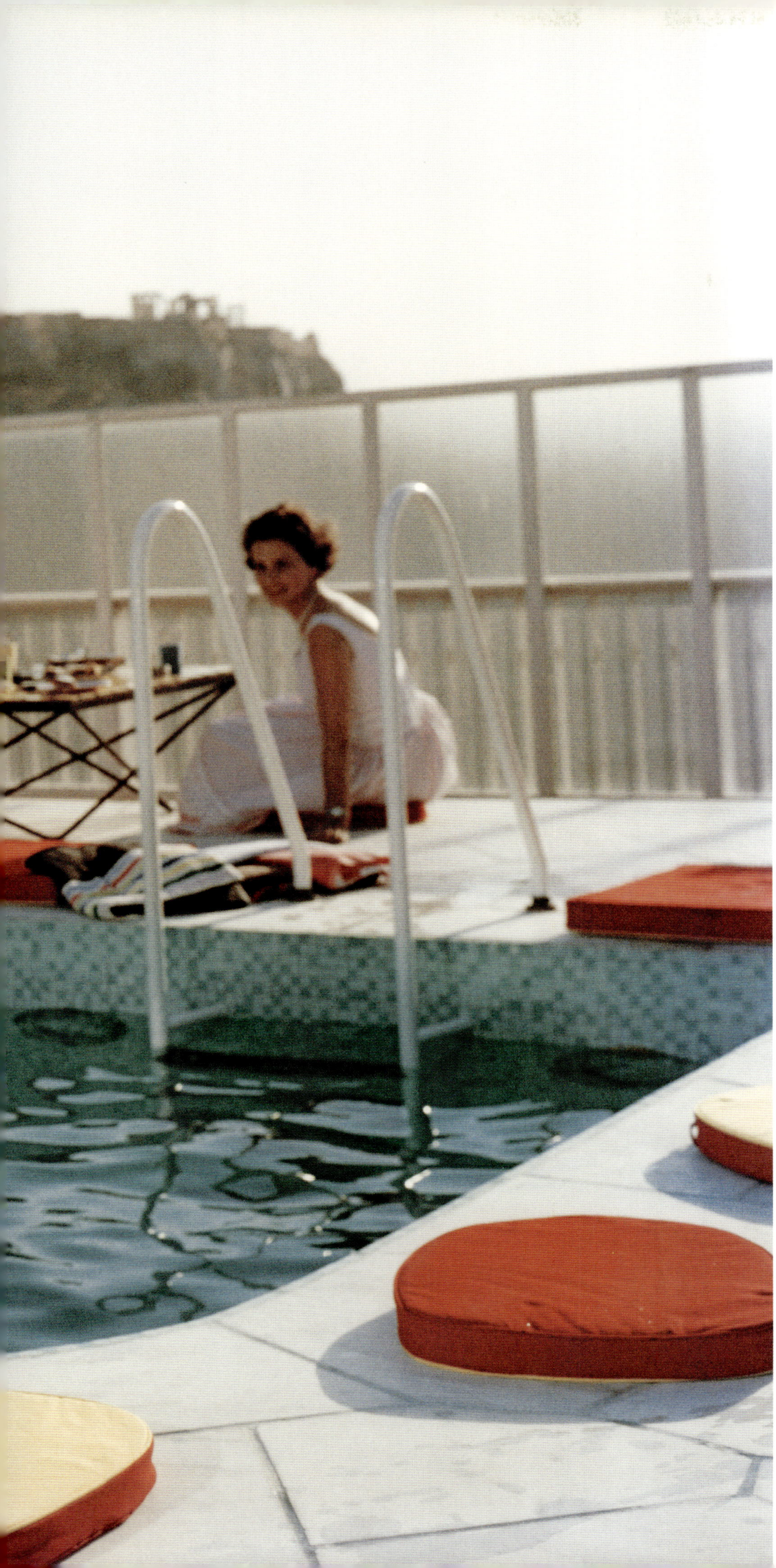

left Guests relax around the Canellopoulos penthouse pool, Athens, 1961.

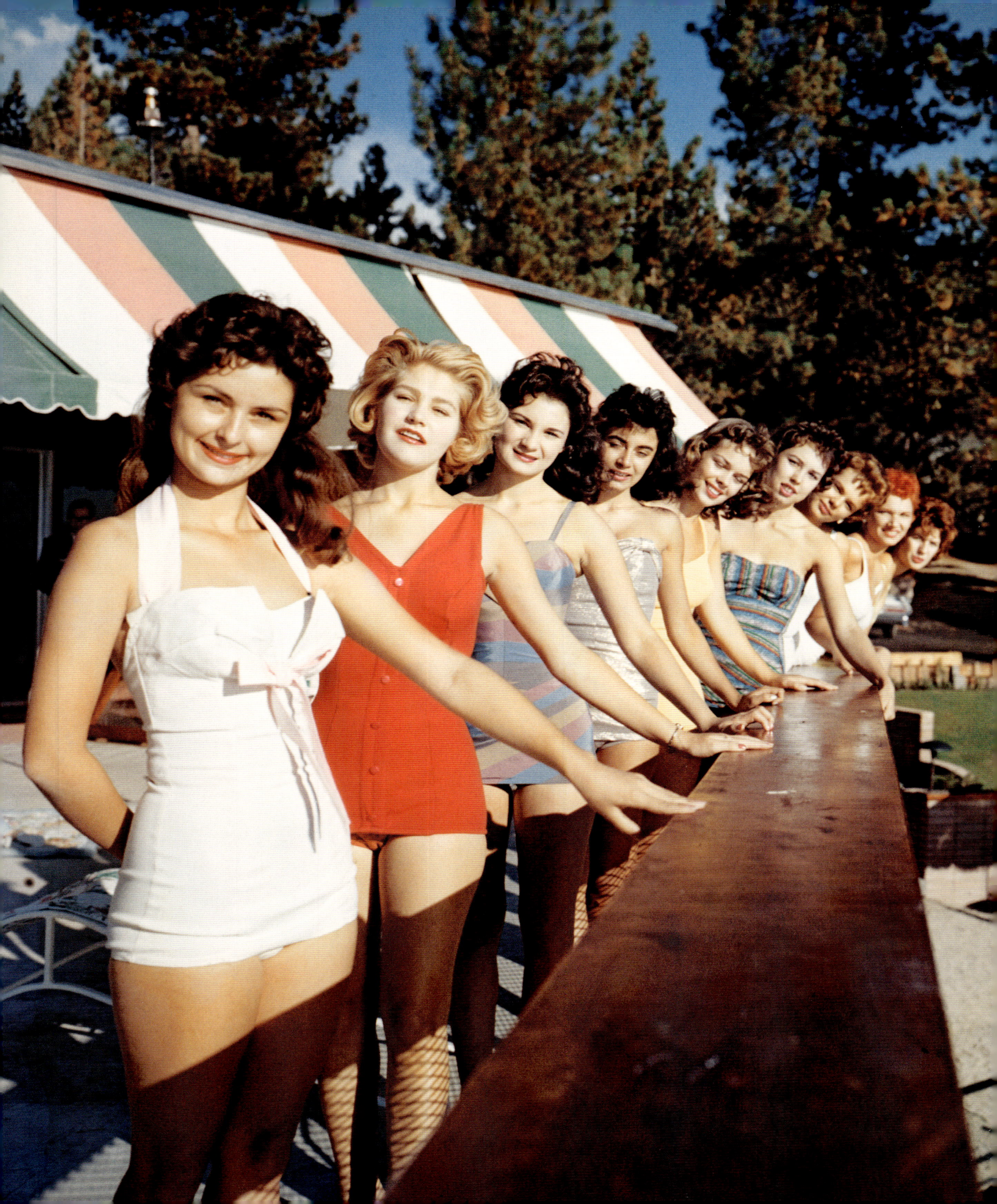

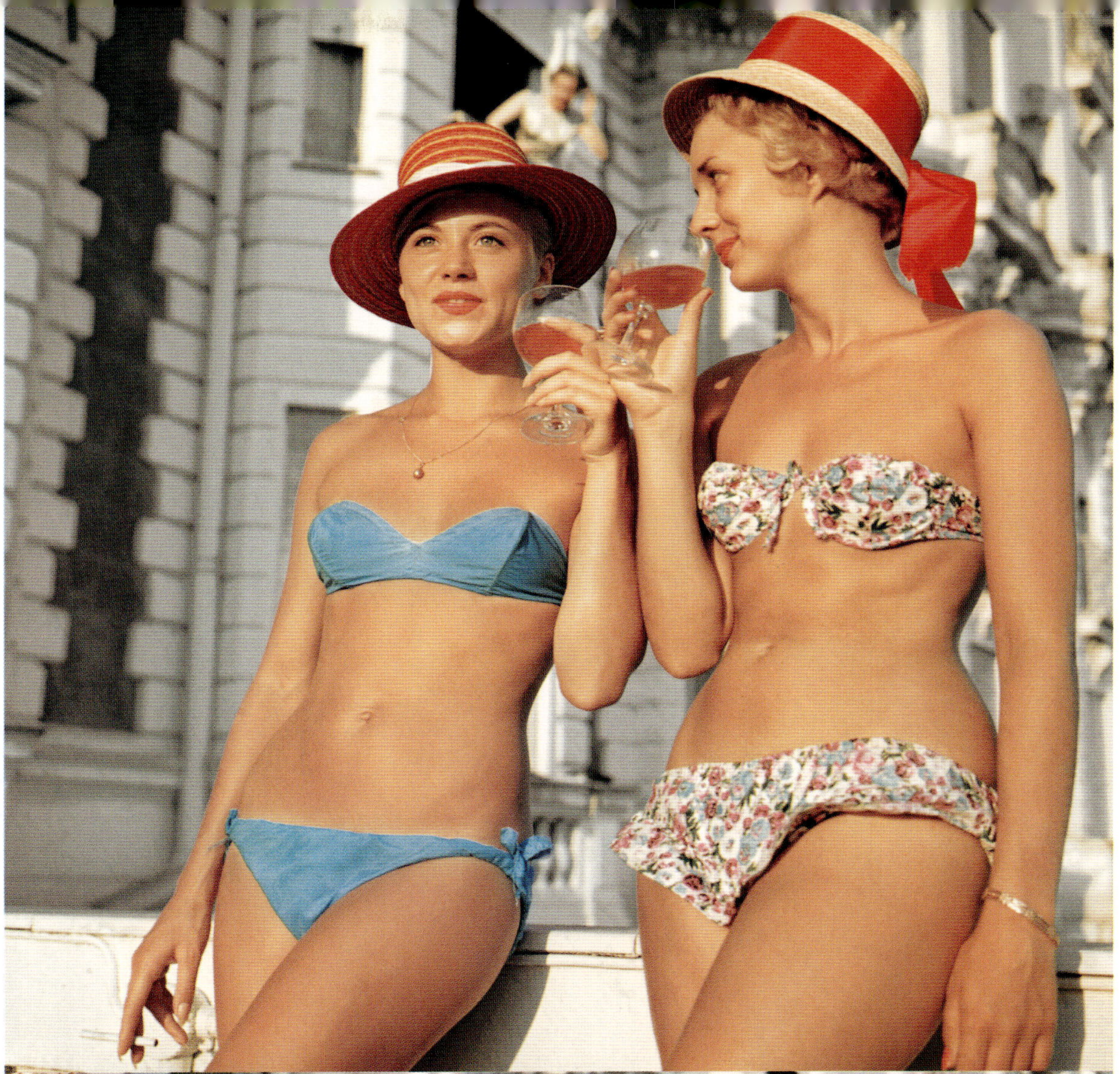

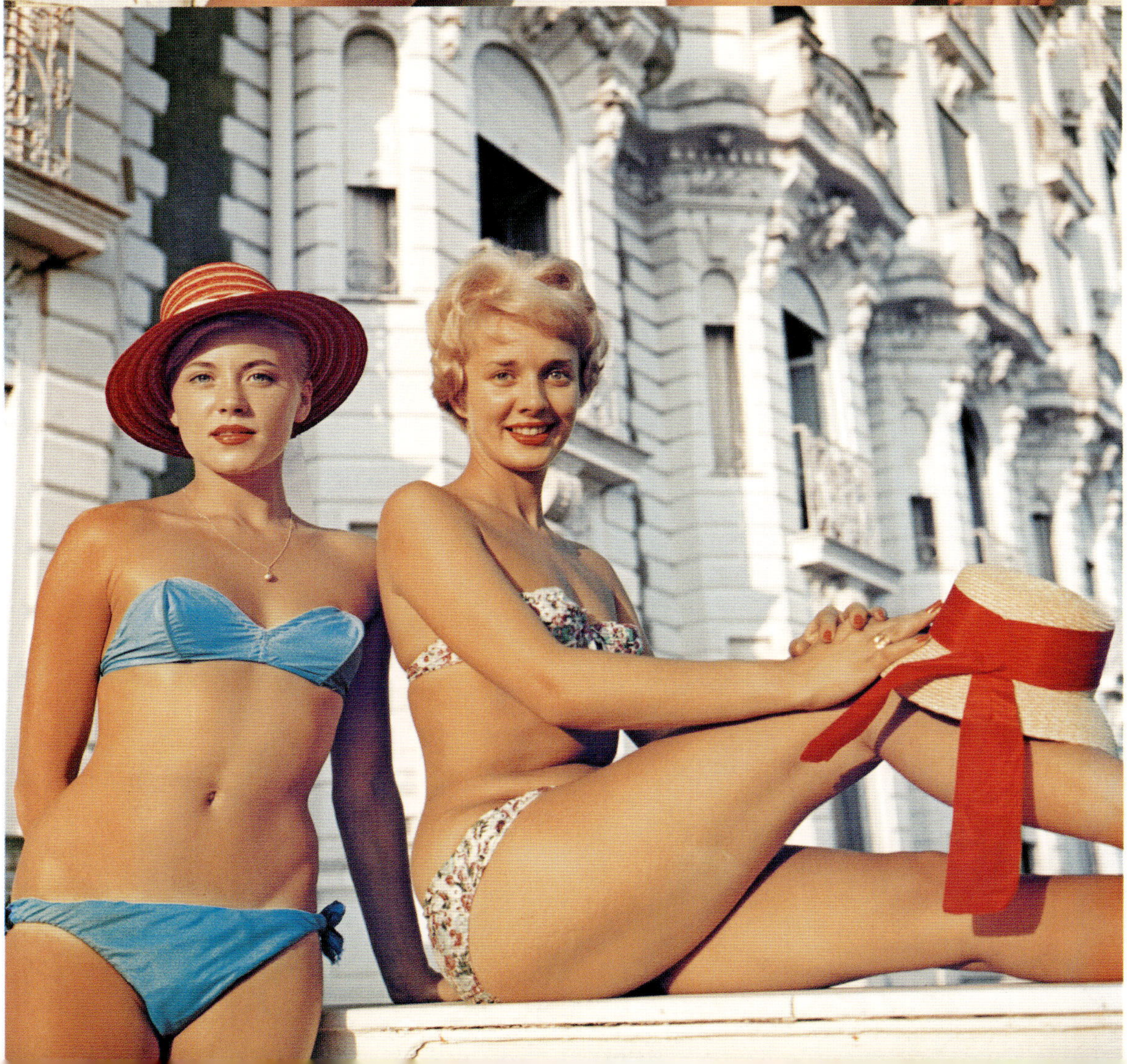

opposite Bathing beauties pose against the backdrop of Lake Tahoe, circa 1959. This desert oasis became well known for its cool Alpine waters.

right Sunbathers relishing the good life in the South of France, outside the Carlton Hotel, Cannes, 1958. Known for visits by Elizabeth Taylor with each of her seven husbands, for Faye Dunaway's goat milk baths, and for the world's biggest jewel heist, in 2013, the hotel has a storied past and still reigns as one of the French Riviera's *grandes(t) dames*.

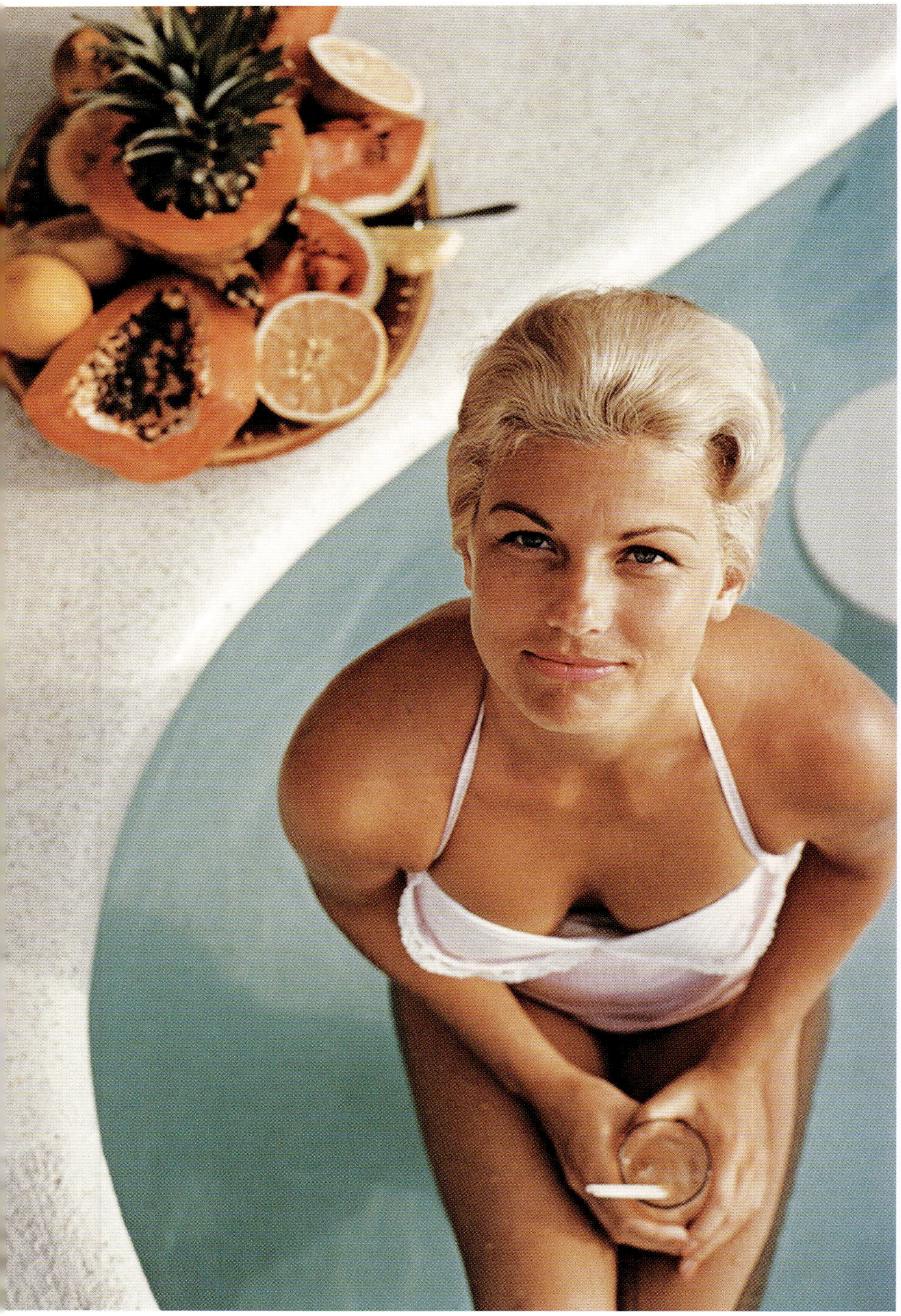

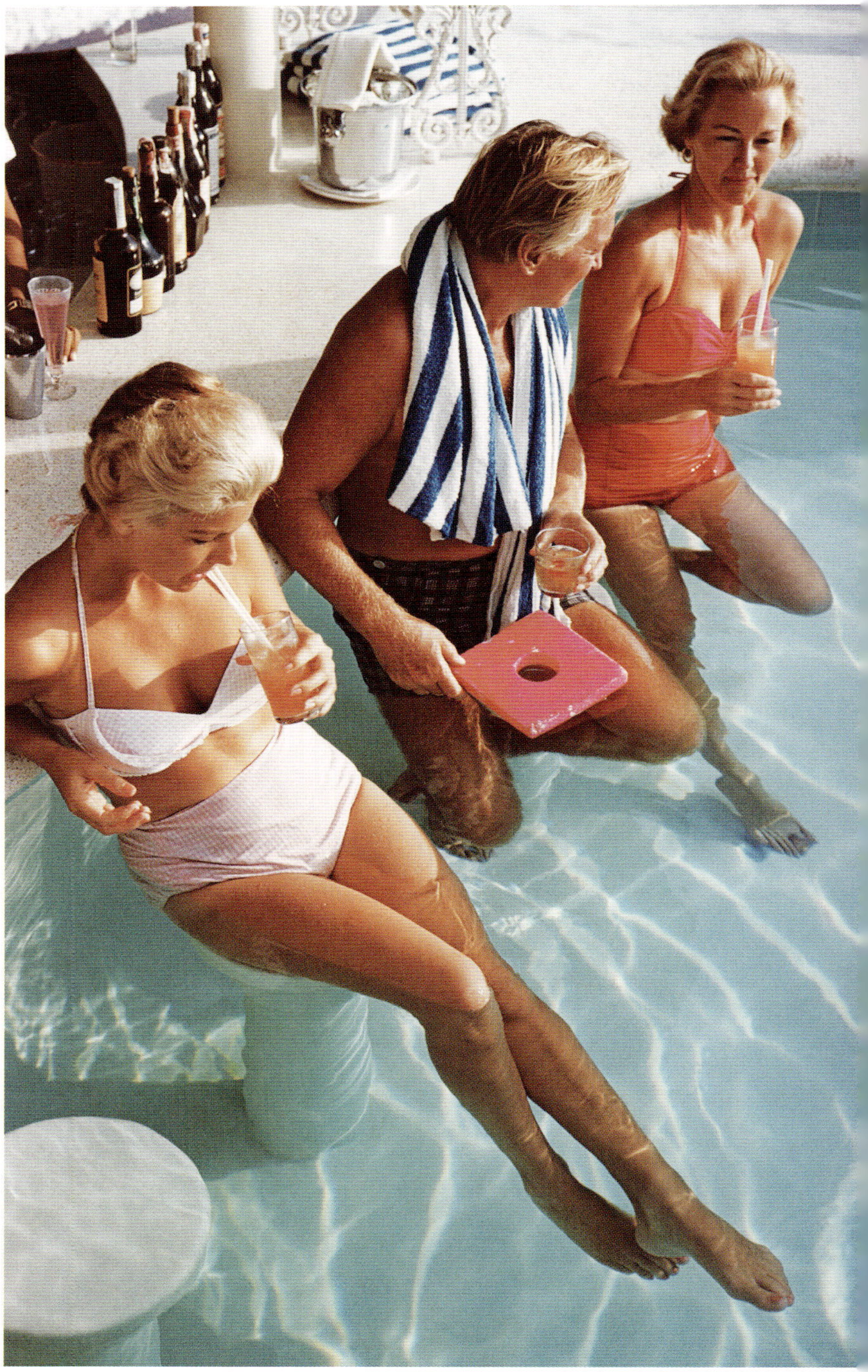

above and opposite The Villa Vera Hotel & Racquet Club pool bar, Acapulco, 1961. In the 1960s this was possibly one of the hottest spots in the world, attracting only those well-practiced in the serious business of international play. Nestled into the cliffs in a residential section of town, it became a legendary hideaway for the wealthy and well-known. Elizabeth Taylor and Mike Todd honeymooned here, and Elvis Presley, Yul Brynner, and Lana Turner were frequent guests. Against the backdrop of the Bay of Acapulco are Mrs. Charles Rogers (in white), Villa Vera manager Teddy Stauffer, also known as "Mr. Acapulco," and Dorothy Webb (in red).

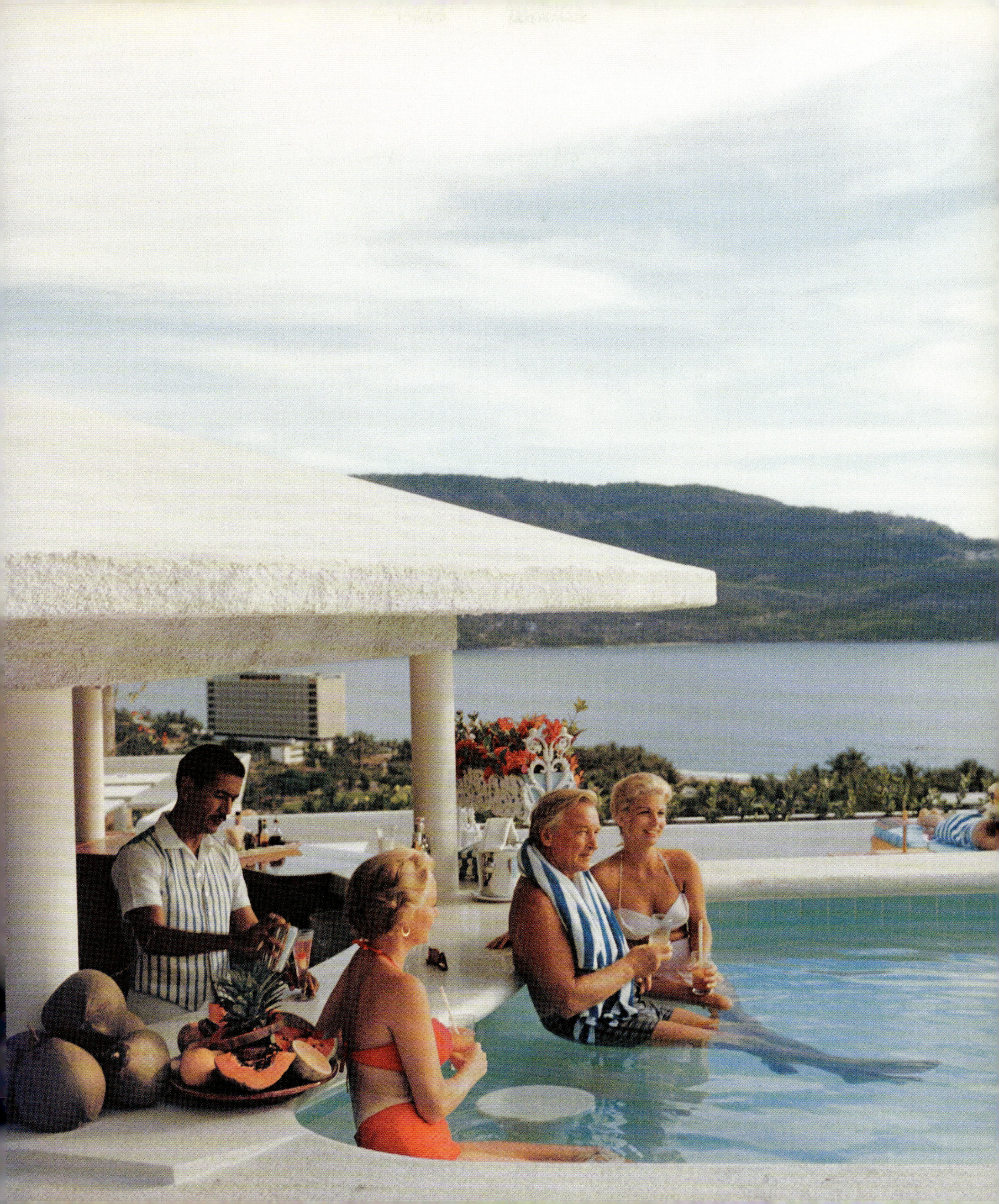

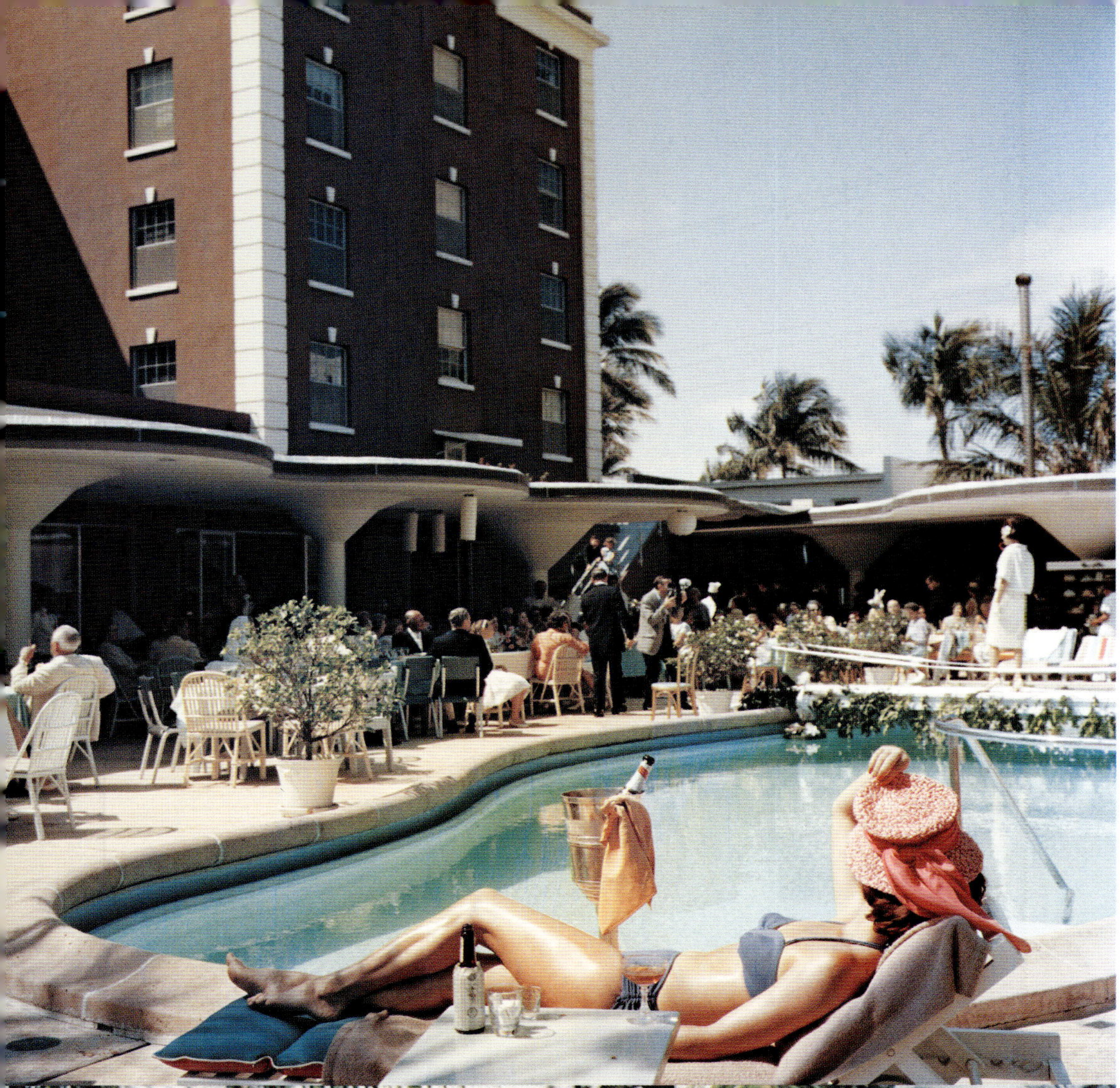

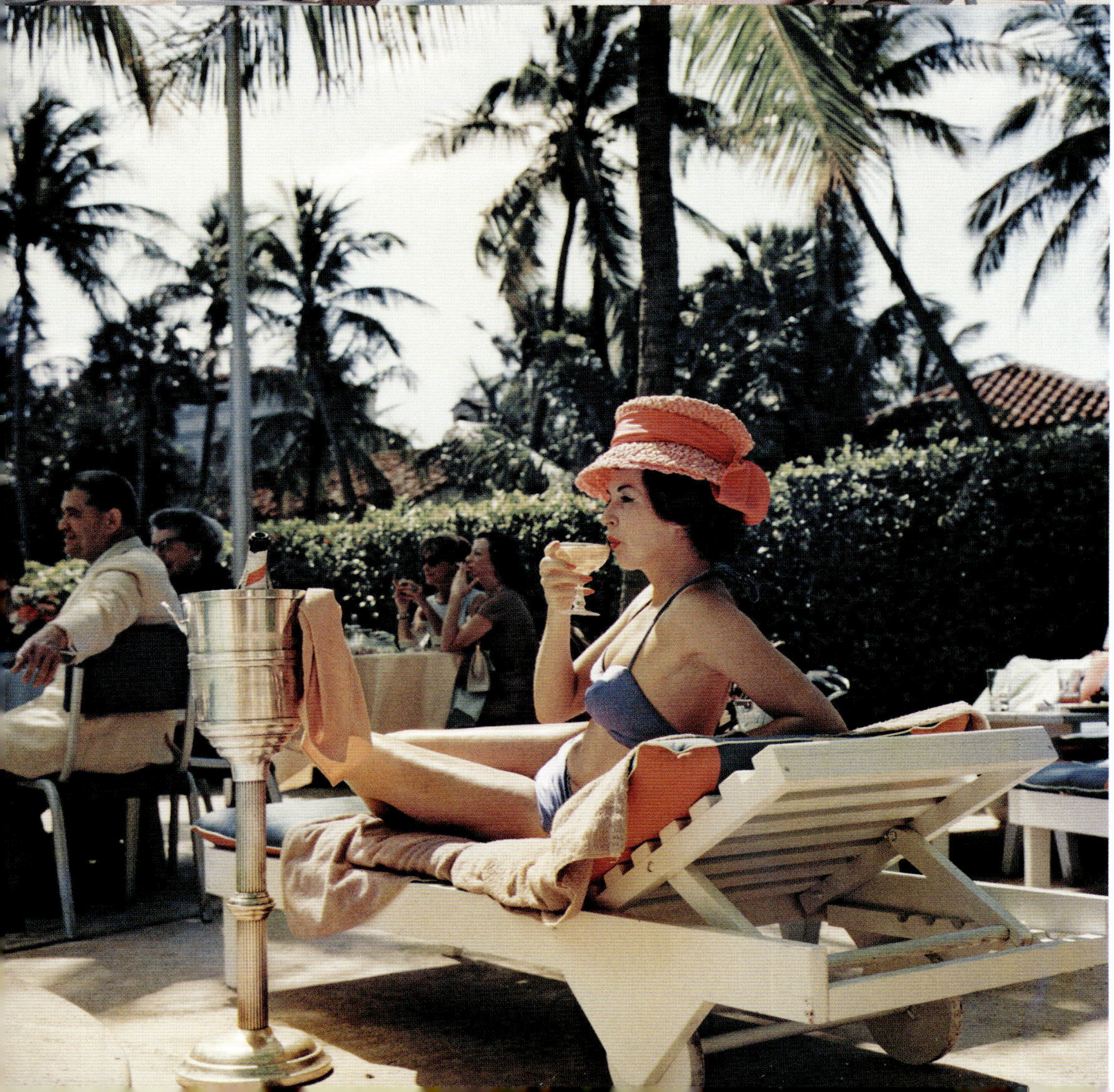

left and opposite A fashion show by the pool at the Colony Hotel, Palm Beach, 1962. Slim photographed more often in Palm Beach than perhaps in any other resort town. Each time he arrived, he checked in at each of the town's clubs and mainstays, one of which was the Colony Hotel, at the top of Worth Avenue. Known for its British Colonial architecture and Floridian decor, the historic hotel was built in 1947 and immediately became one of Palm Beach's hubs of sophisticated camaraderie, hosting the Duke and Duchess of Windsor and Frank Sinatra, among others.

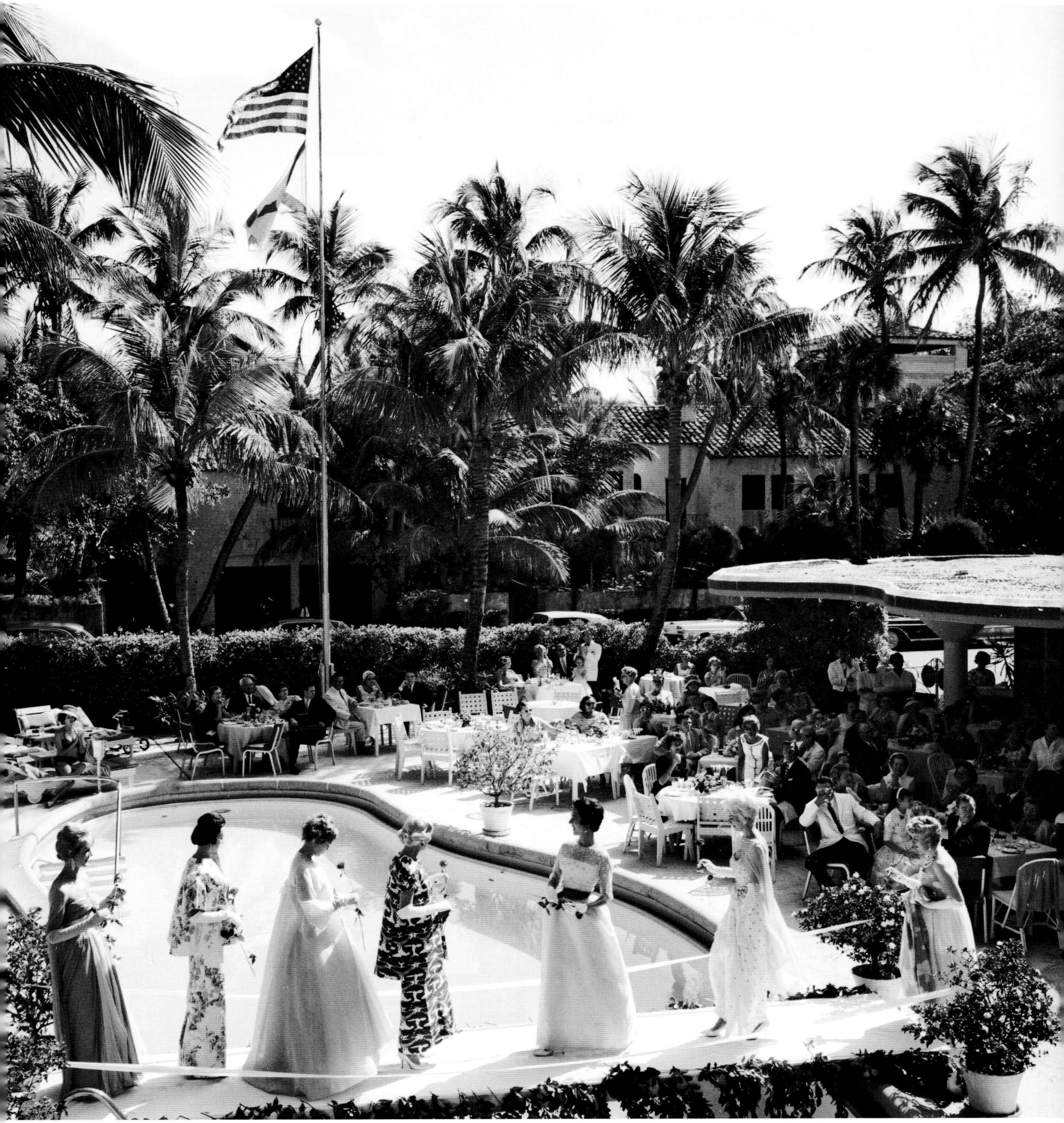

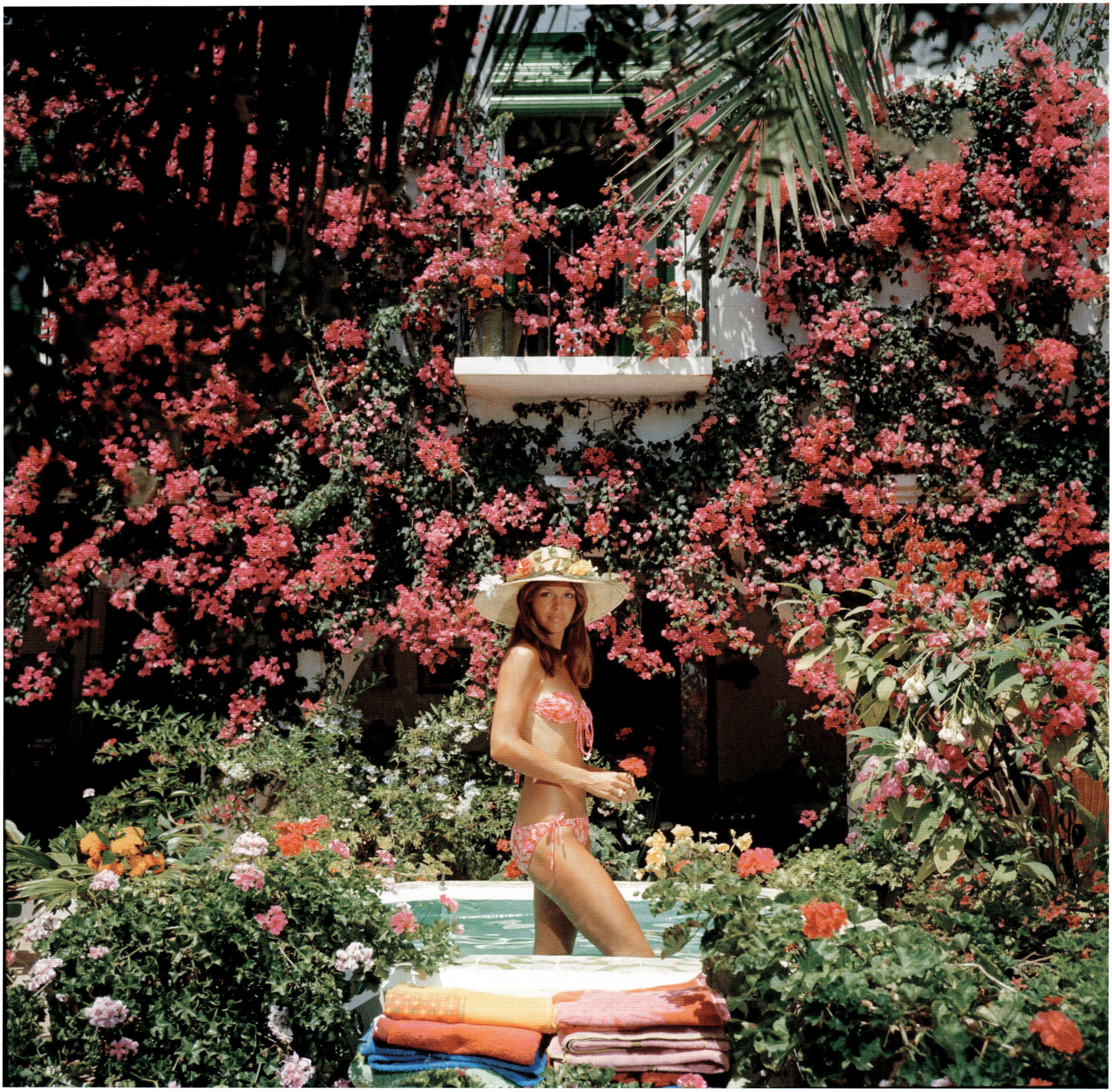

above Film producer Valerie Cates, Marbella, 1976. Descended from a decidedly theatrical family, Cates is the daughter of pioneering television and Broadway producer Joseph Cates, the niece of lauded film director Gilbert Cates, and the sister of actress Phoebe Cates.

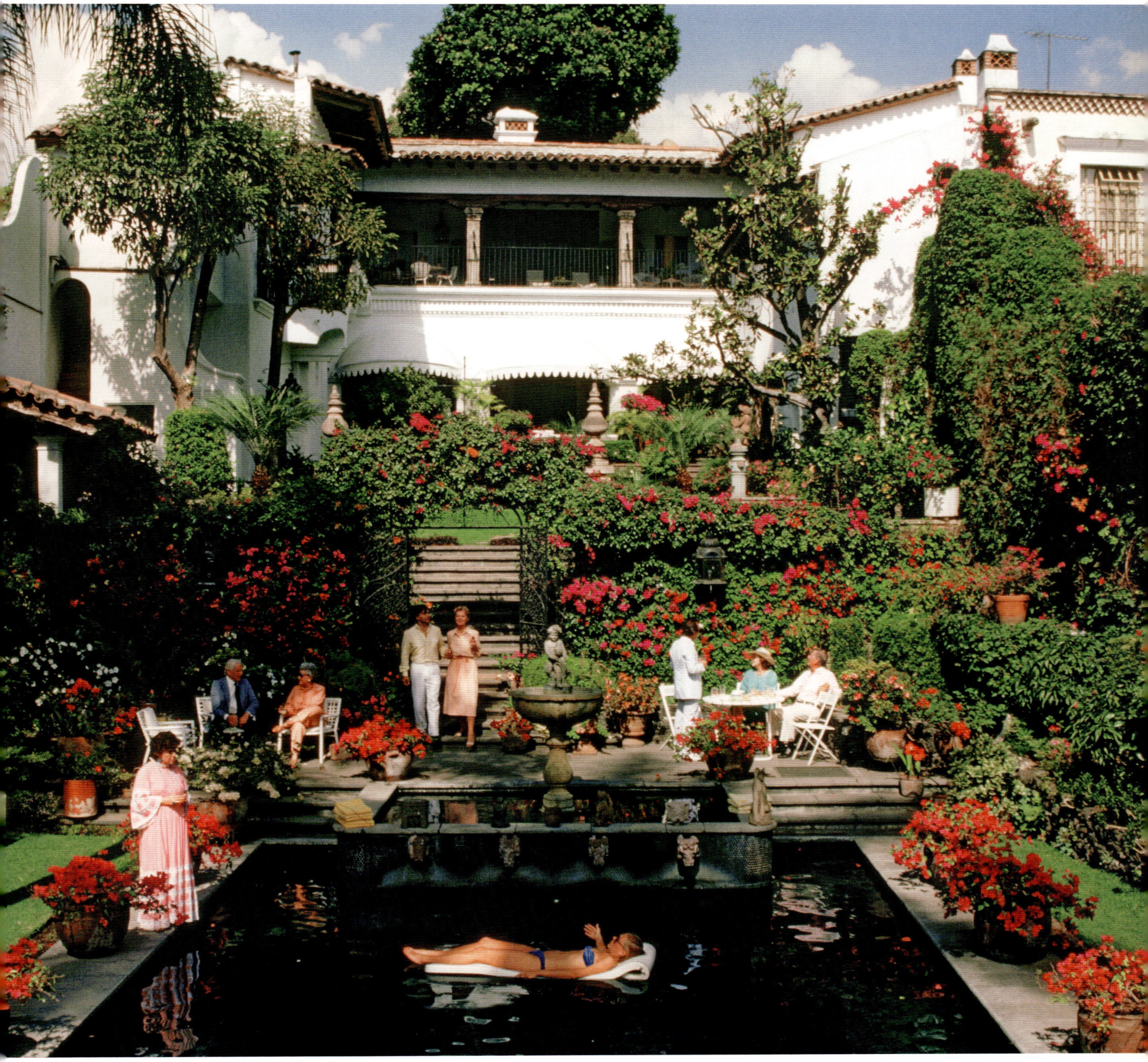

above A villa at the Cuernavaca Racquet Club, Cuernavaca, Mexico, 1985. This villa is typical of the exquisite homes in this lush, mountainous Mexican enclave. Set at 5,000 feet and known for its thermal springs and mineral waters, Cuernavaca is reputed to have the best weather in all of Mexico (spring-like throughout the year) and has long attracted innumerable luminaries and expats beginning with Aztec king Acamapichtli in the late 1300s.

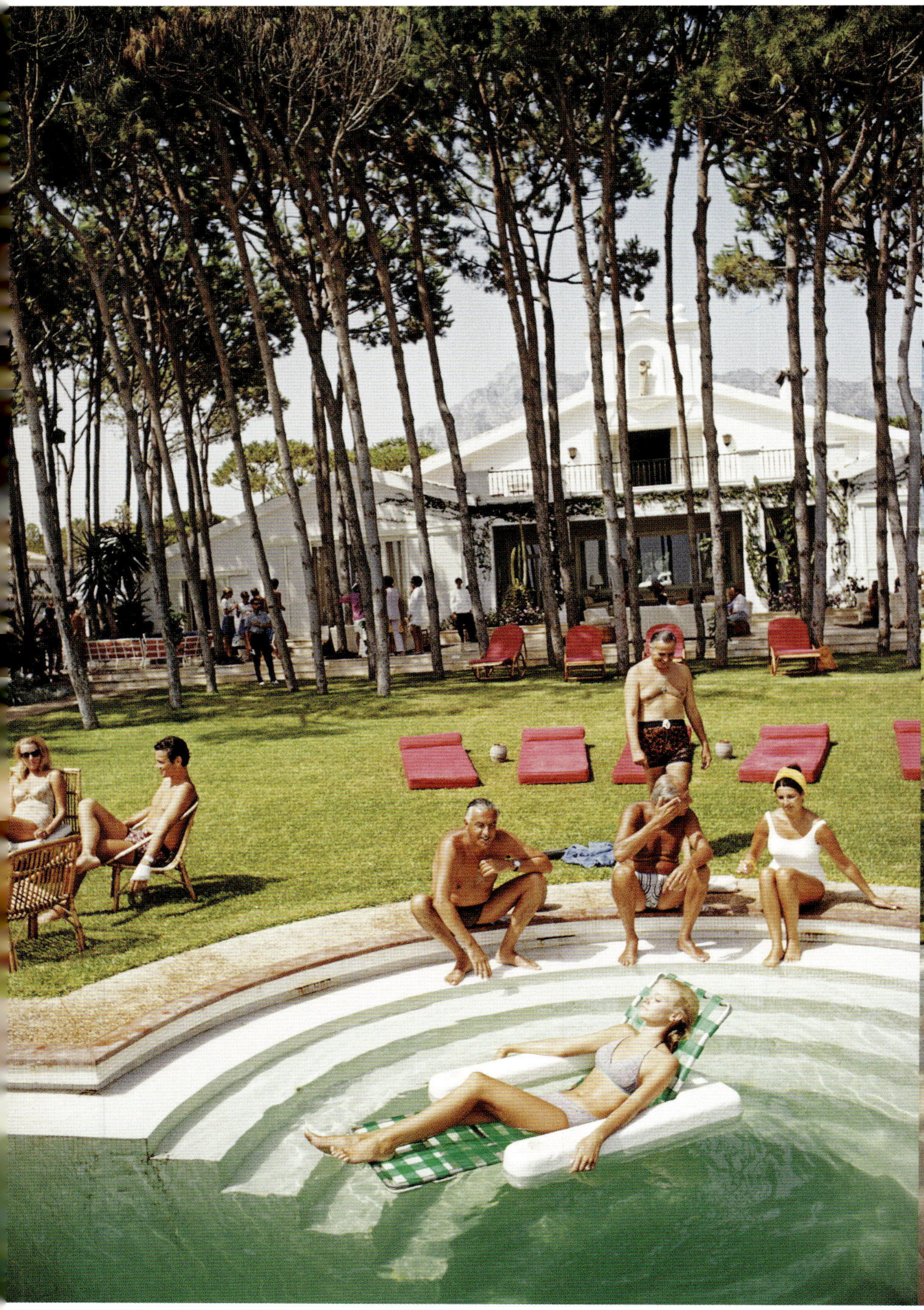

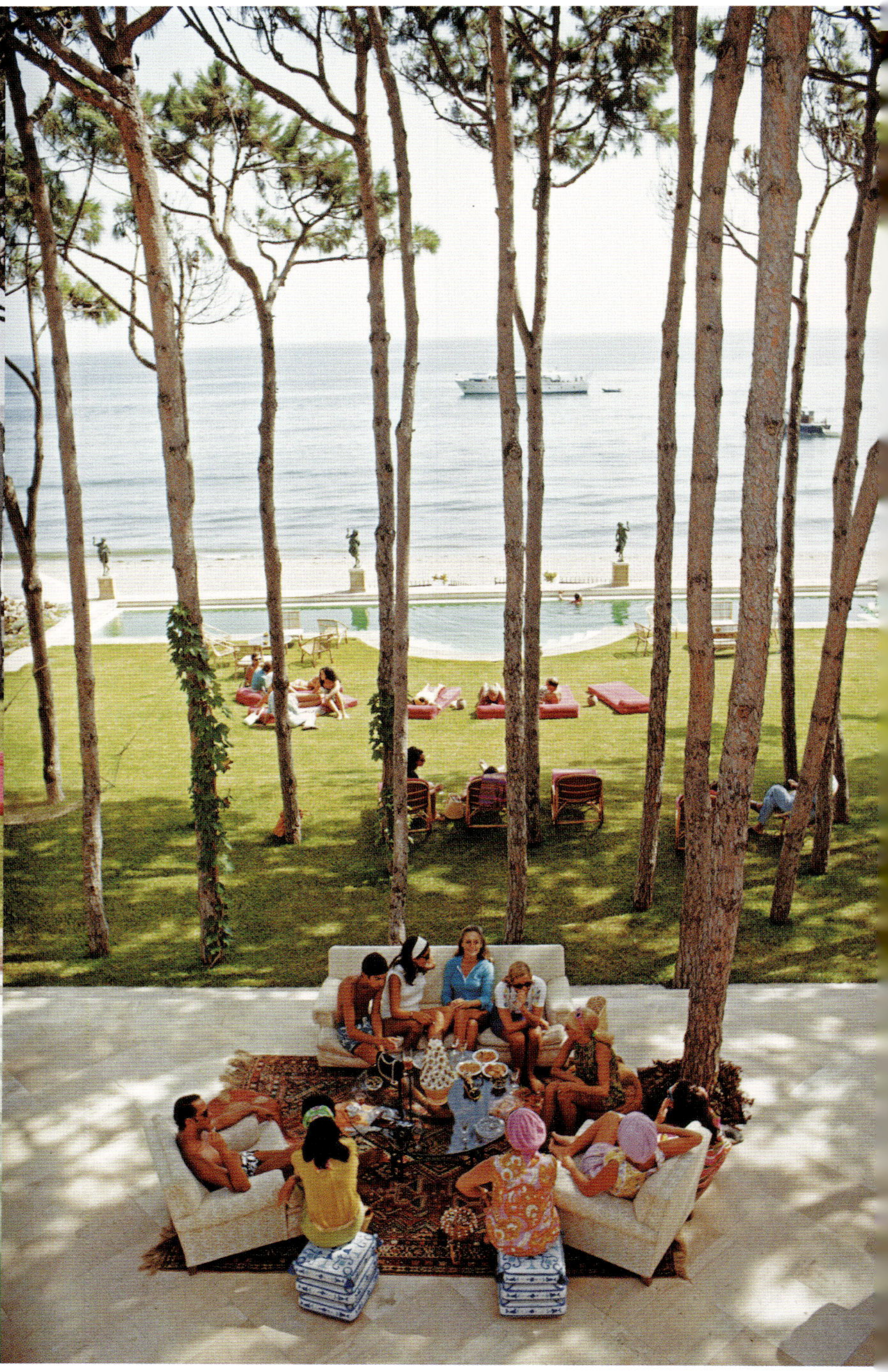

above Marbella, Spain, 1967. Reputed to have been the most luxurious at the Marbella Club, this villa belonged to Italian drug manufacturer Sebastiano Bergese and his wife Gudrun. In these two shots guests relax before luncheon, enjoying the distinctive bounty of the Costa del Sol. It has been said of the storied resort town, "Marbella is not in Spain—it is in another world."

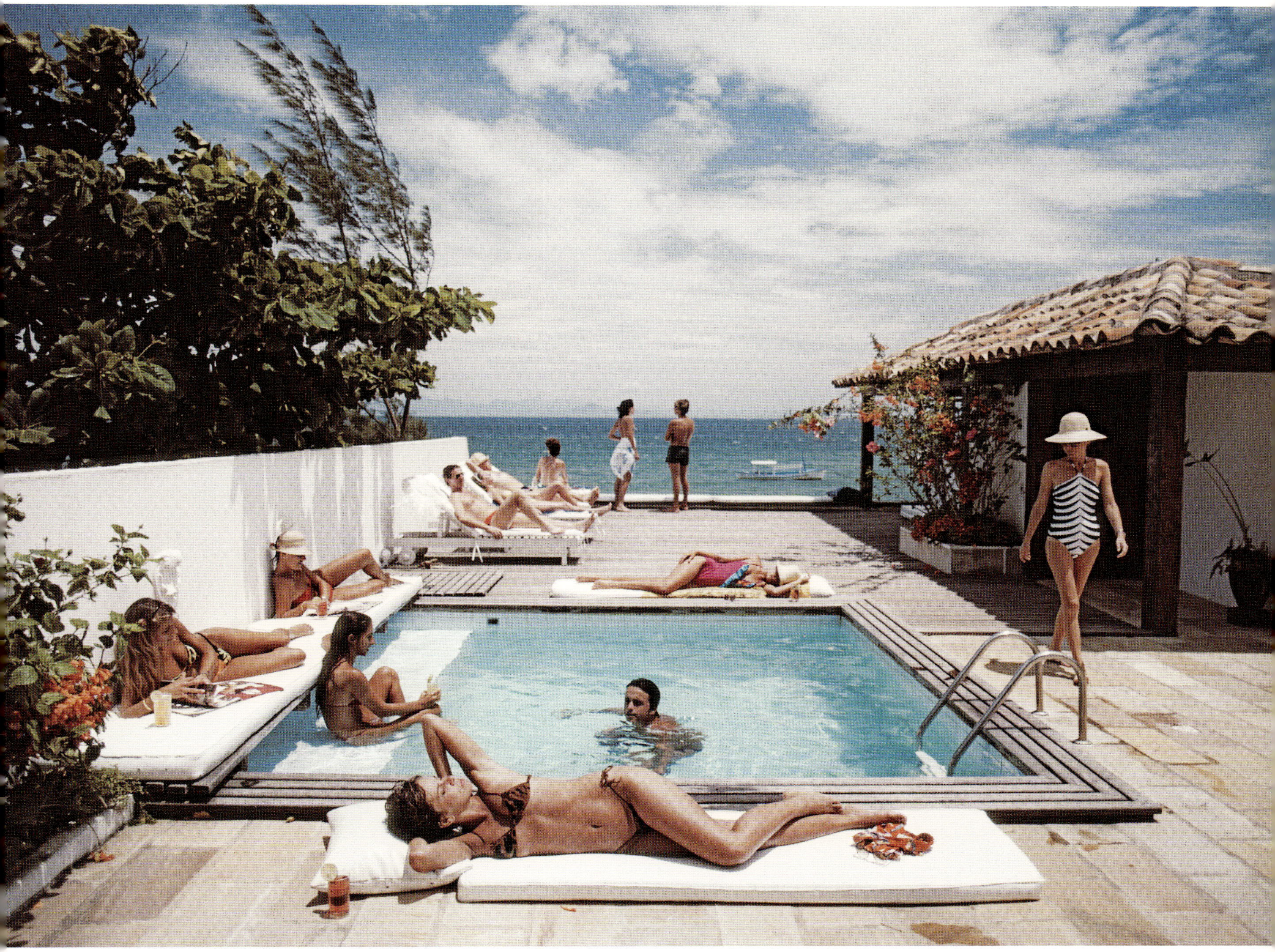

above Holidaymakers likely have little on their minds other than leisure in Armação dos Búzios, Brazil, 1983.

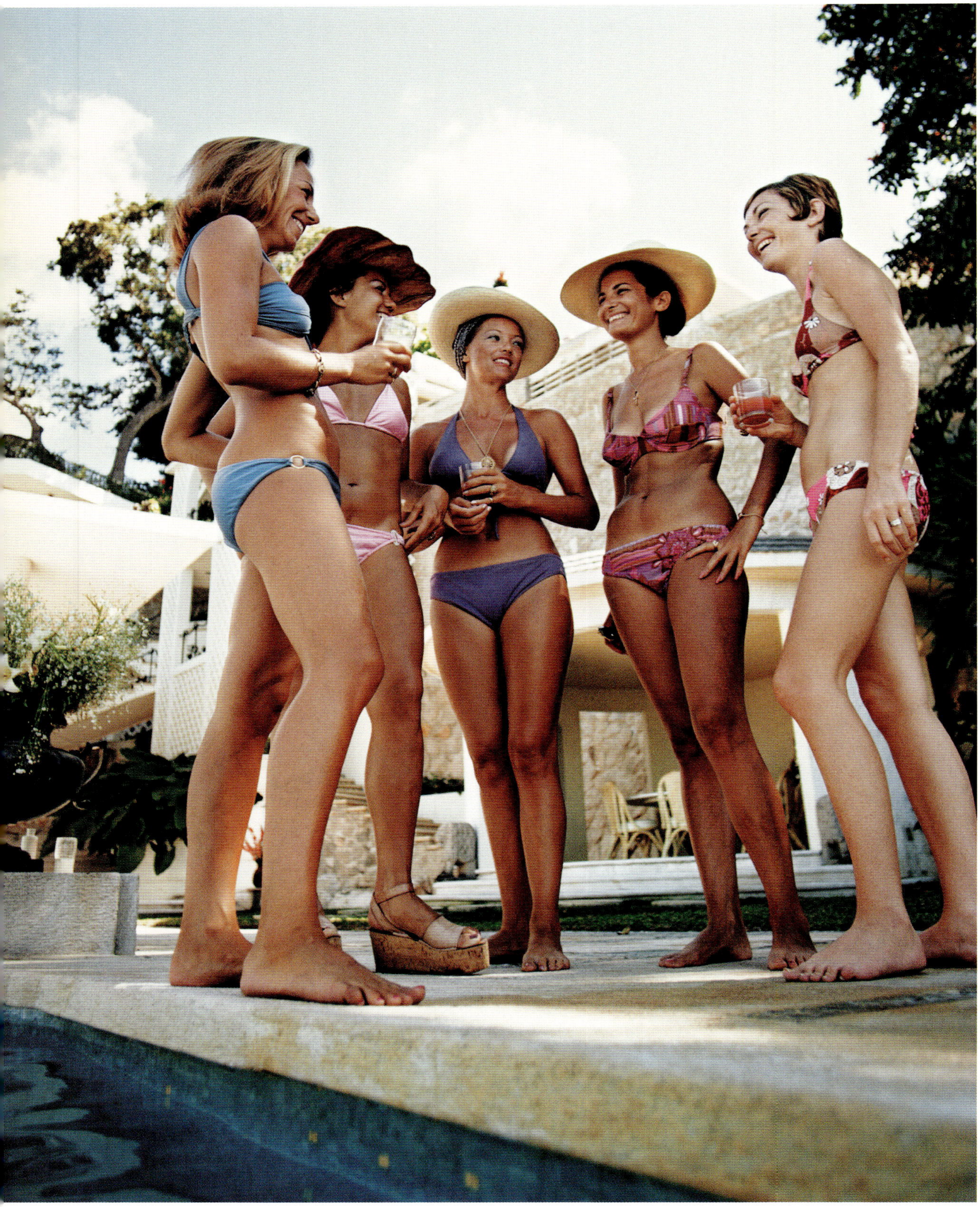

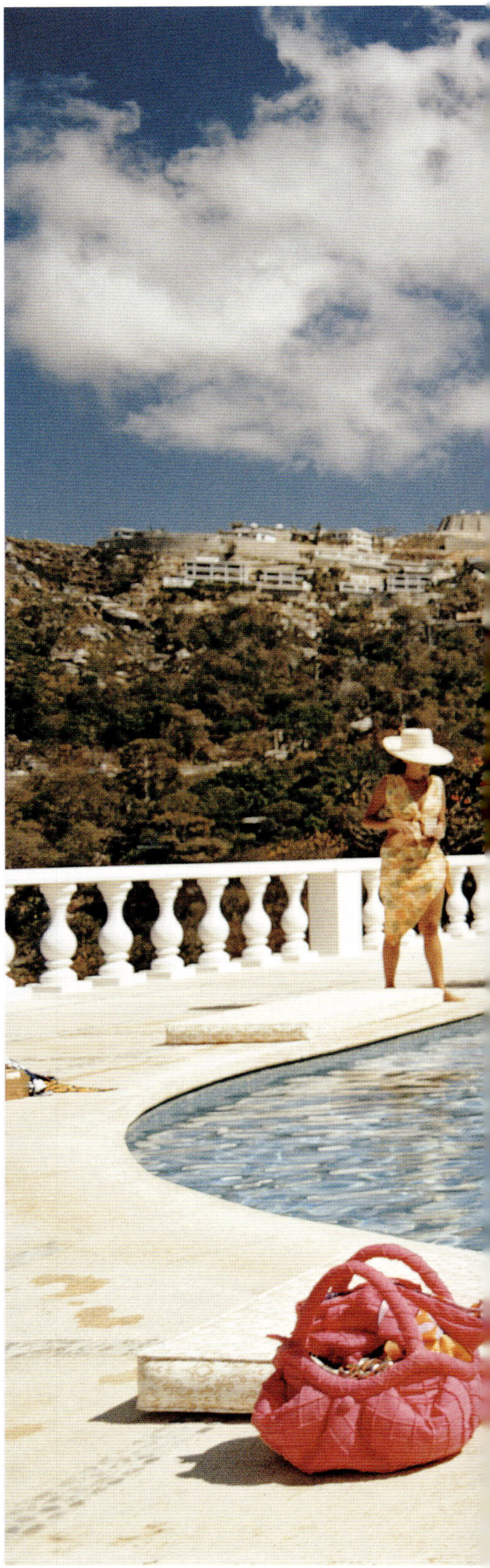

above Christina Chambonne, Elinor Hill, Clare Davidson, Suzy Naggia, and Carole Page prepare for a swim, Acapulco, 1972.

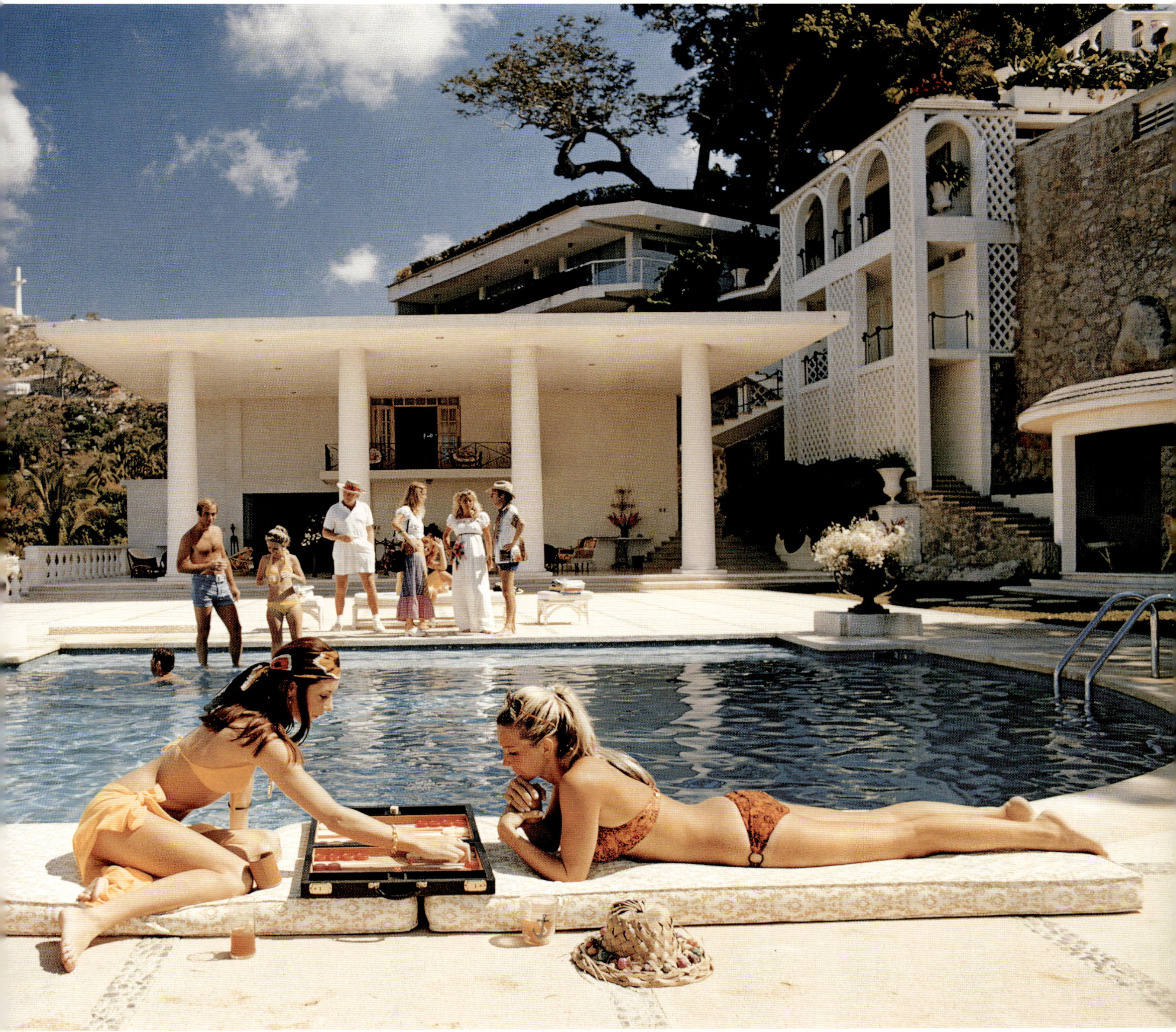

above Two young women enjoy a game of backgammon at Villa Nirvana, Acapulco, 1972. In the 1960s and 1970s, an invitation to Oscar Obregón's aptly named villa was the envy of any jet-setter making a stopover in Acapulco. Slim photographed at Villa Nirvana on numerous occasions on his many assignments to the resort town known as the "pearl of the Pacific." Another shot of this villa, with its cliffside Ionic columns standing sentry over the majestic sweep of Acapulco's bay, may be familiar to followers of Slim's work—it graced the cover of his first book, *A Wonderful Time,* and is one of Slim's most recognized photographs.

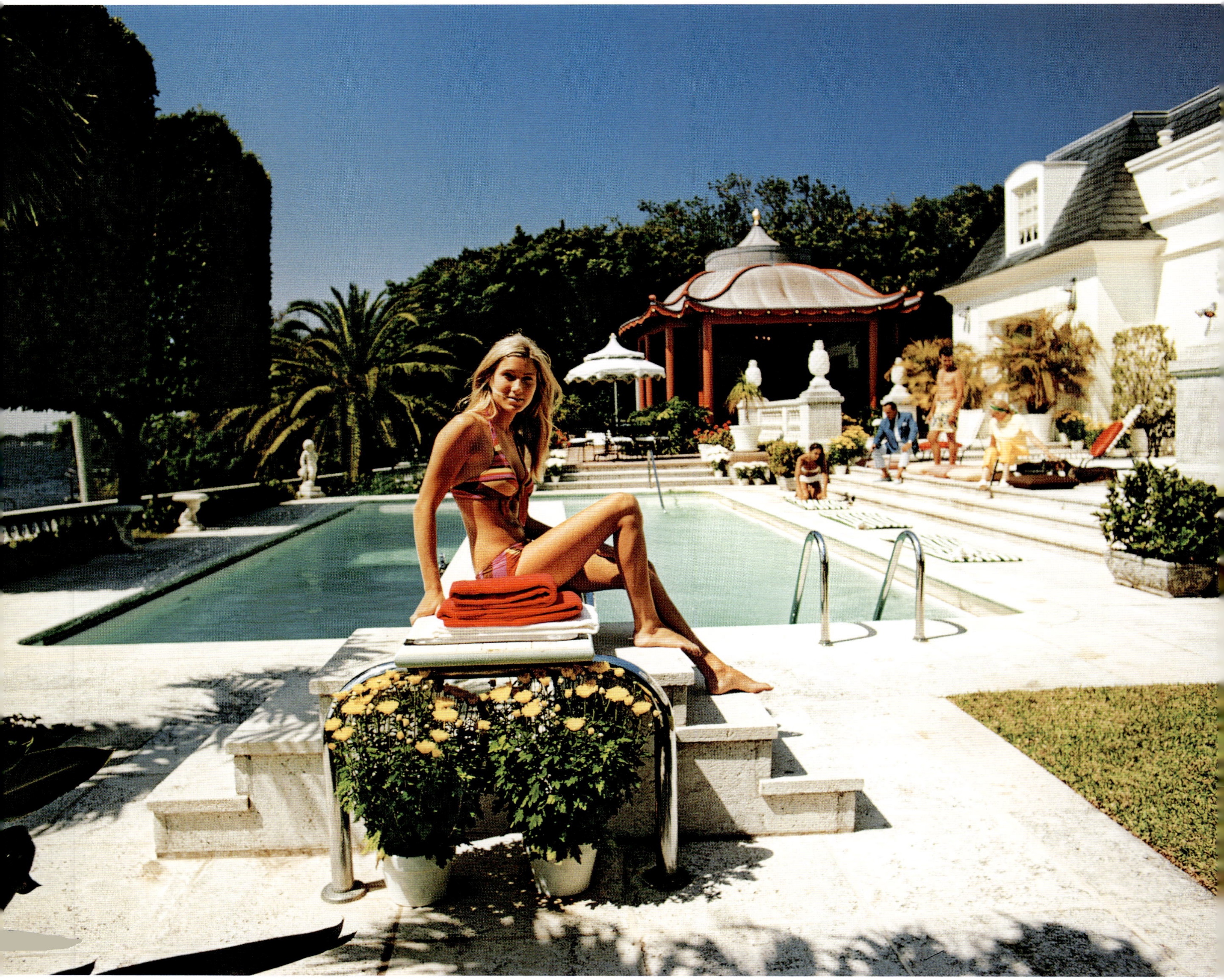

above Model Lillian Crawford, the wife of actor Lee Kinsolving, in Palm Beach, 1970.

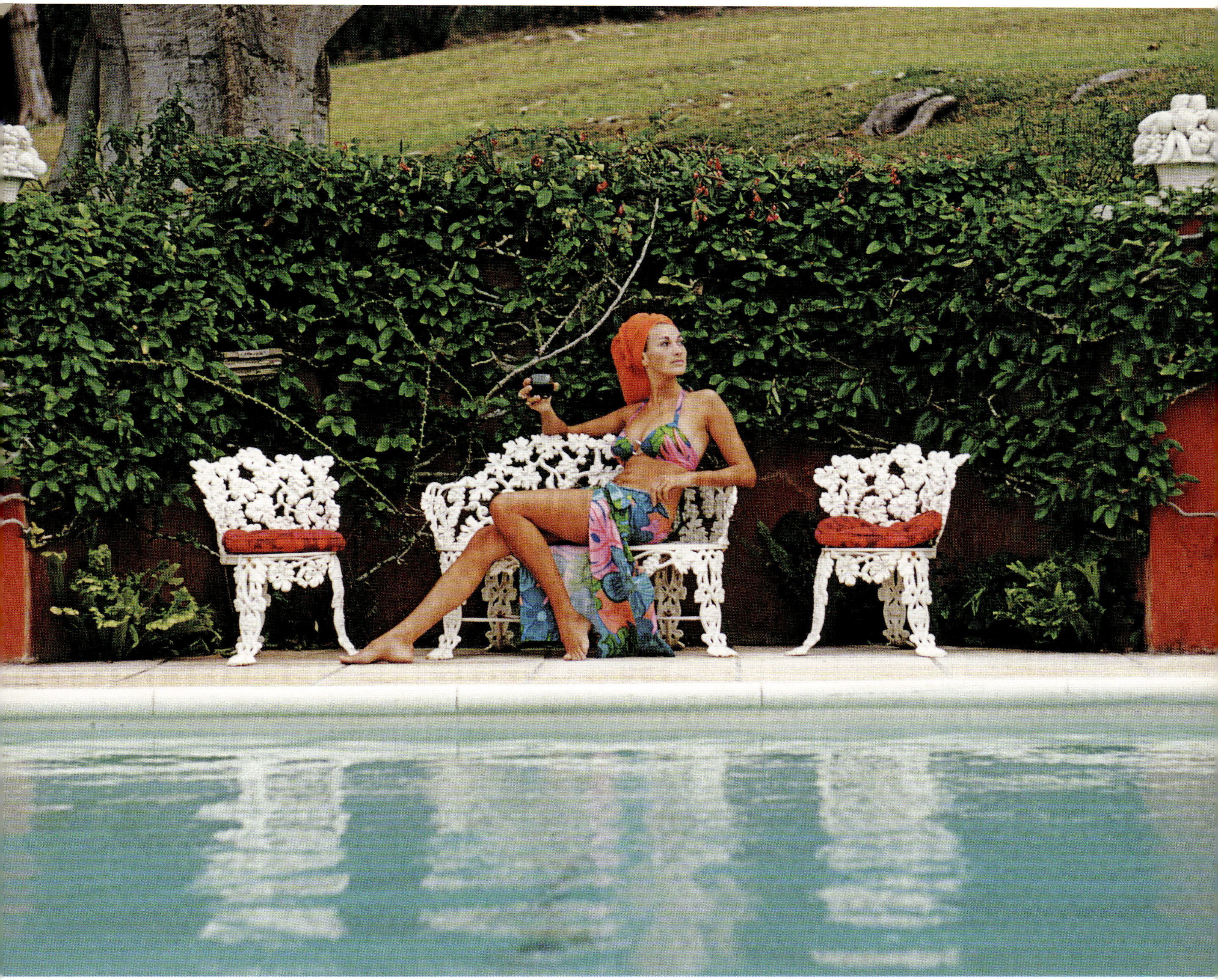

above Jill Council relaxes with a drink poolside, Bermuda, 1969.

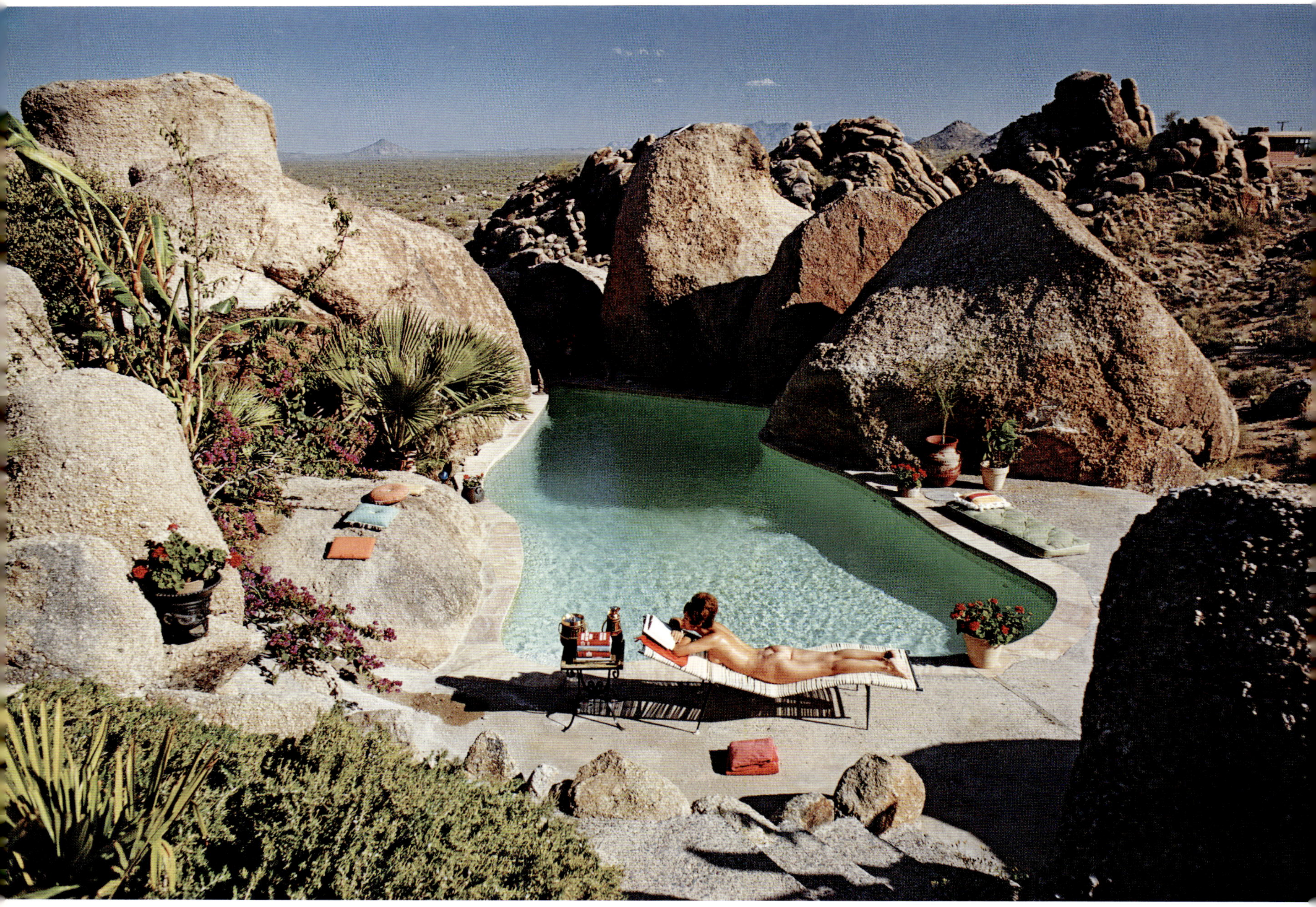

above A pristine pool hidden among the boulders allows for carefree sunbathing, Carefree, Arizona, 1967.

opposite A private cove tucked into the rocks gives sunbathers and swimmers an enviable spot from which to enjoy the dazzling waters of the Caribbean, Bermuda, 1967.

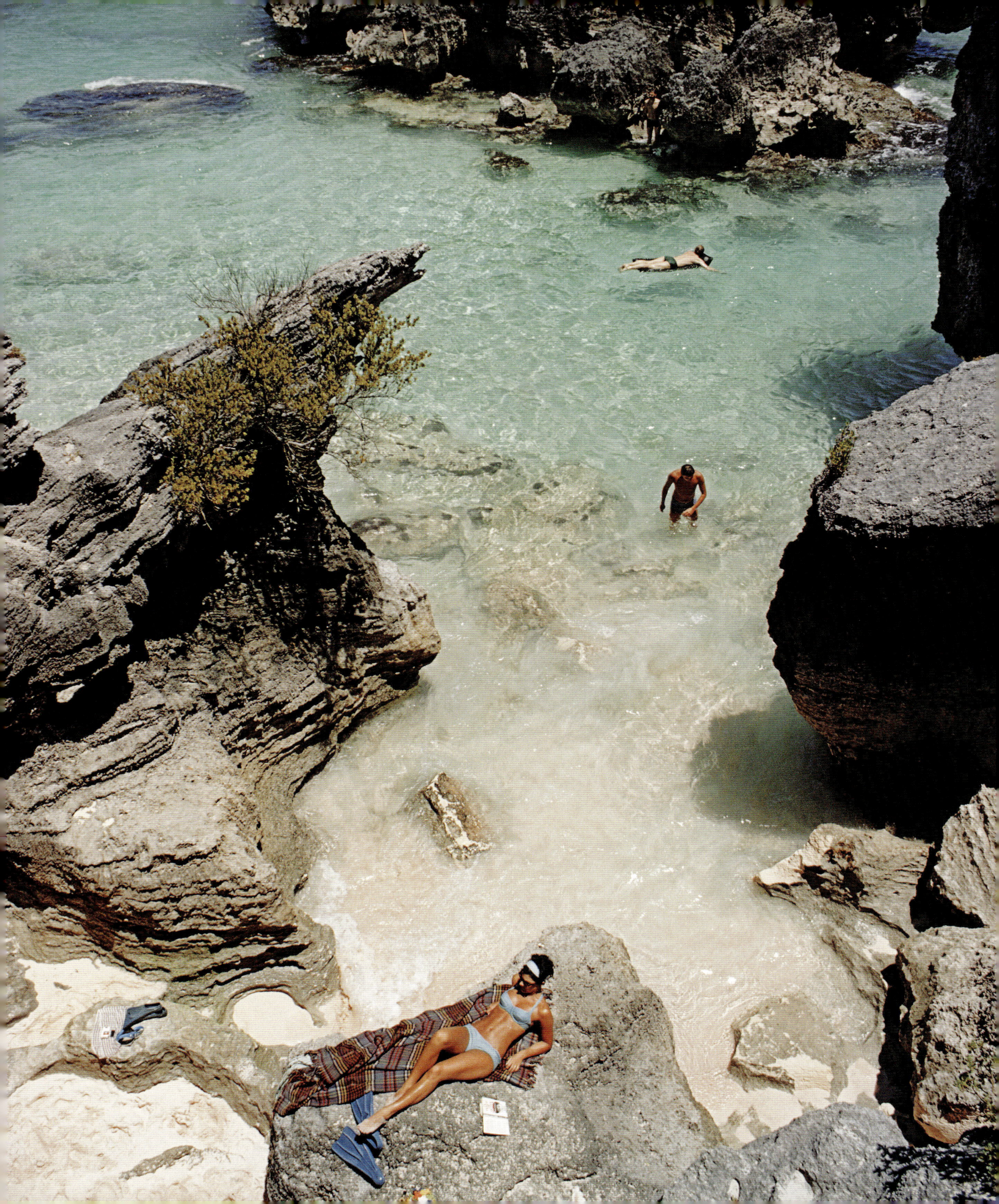

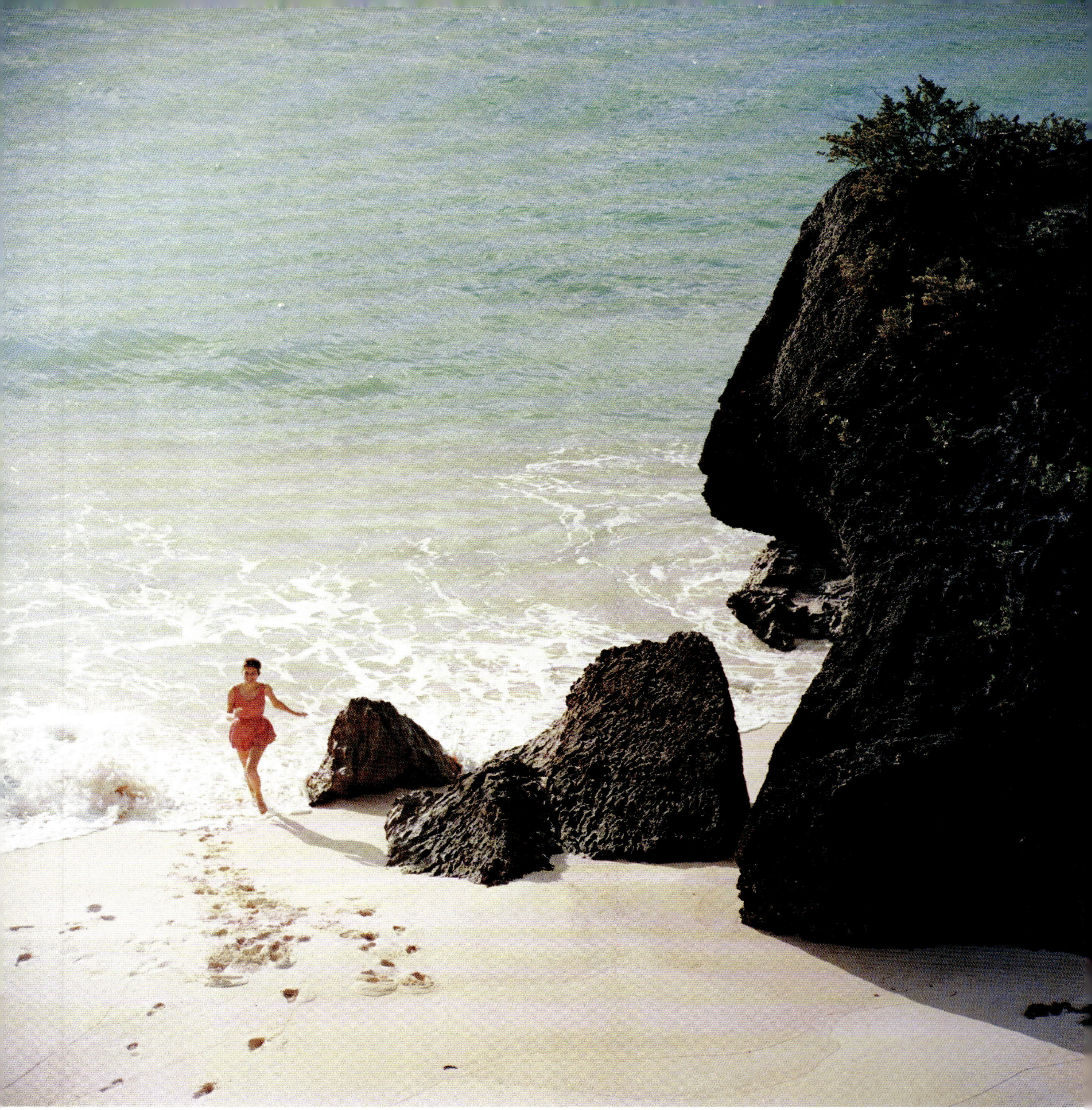

above A swimmer plays in the surf, Bermuda, 1957.

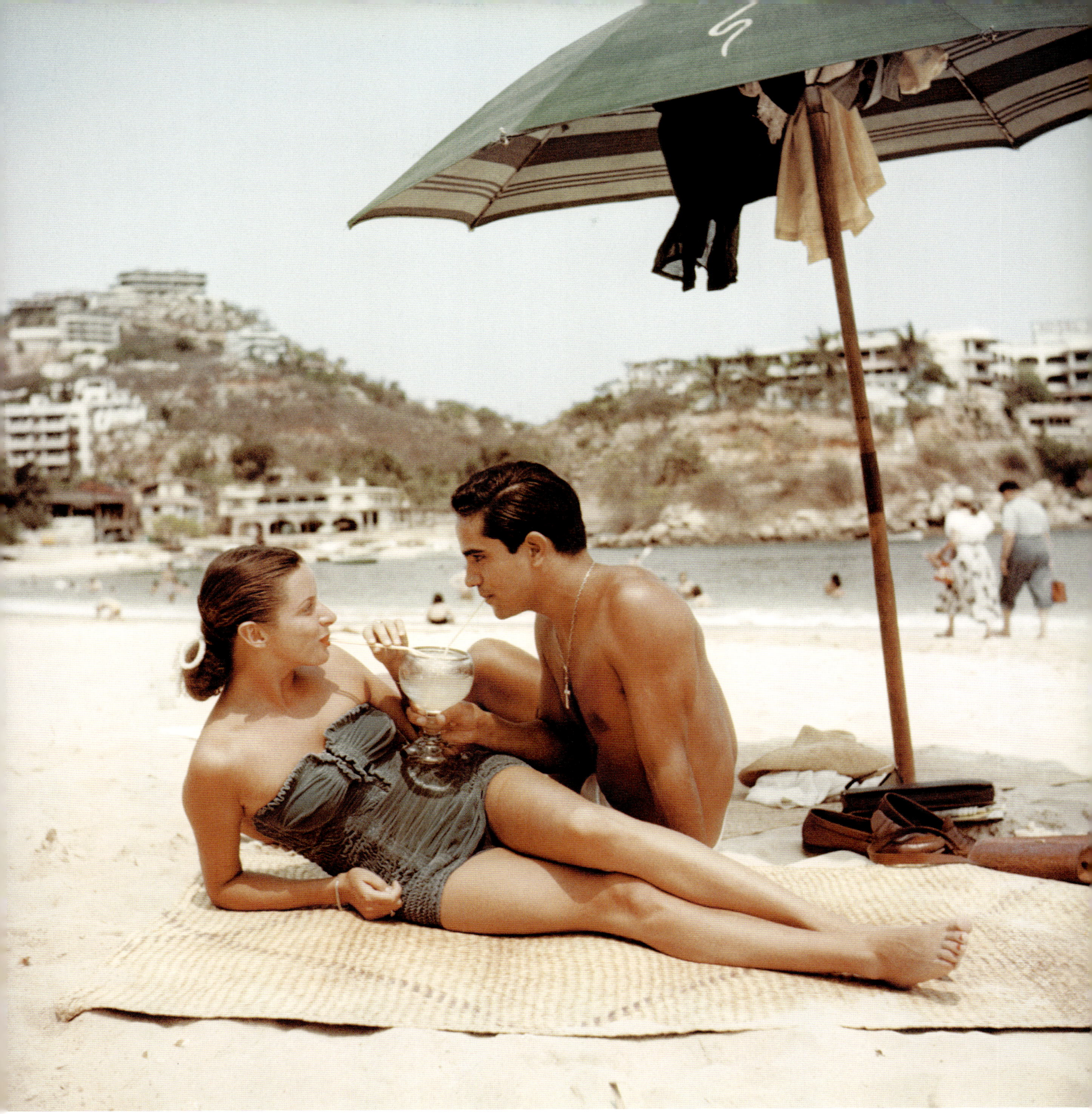

above The New York model Jean Adams and a friend on the beach in Acapulco, 1952.

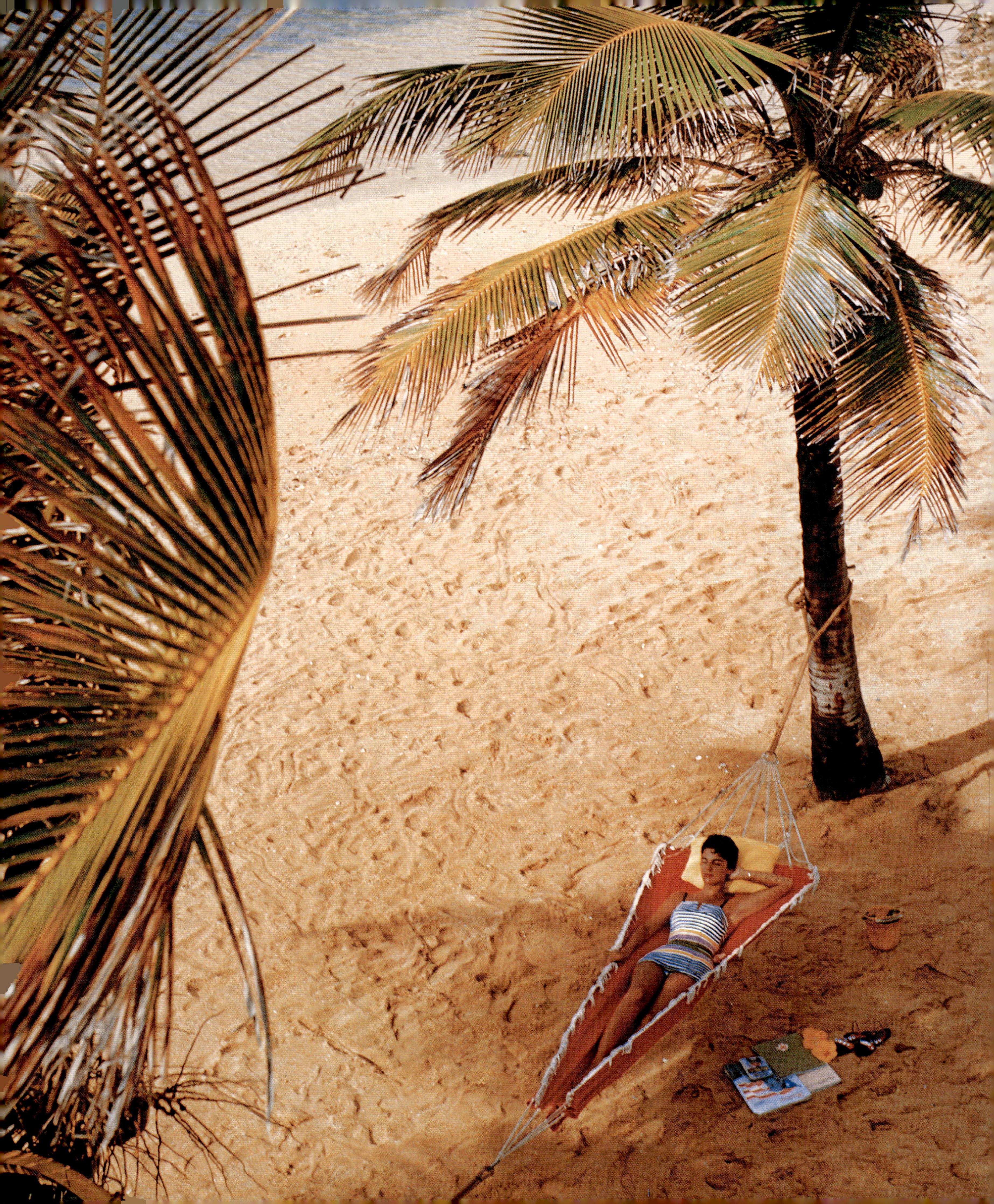

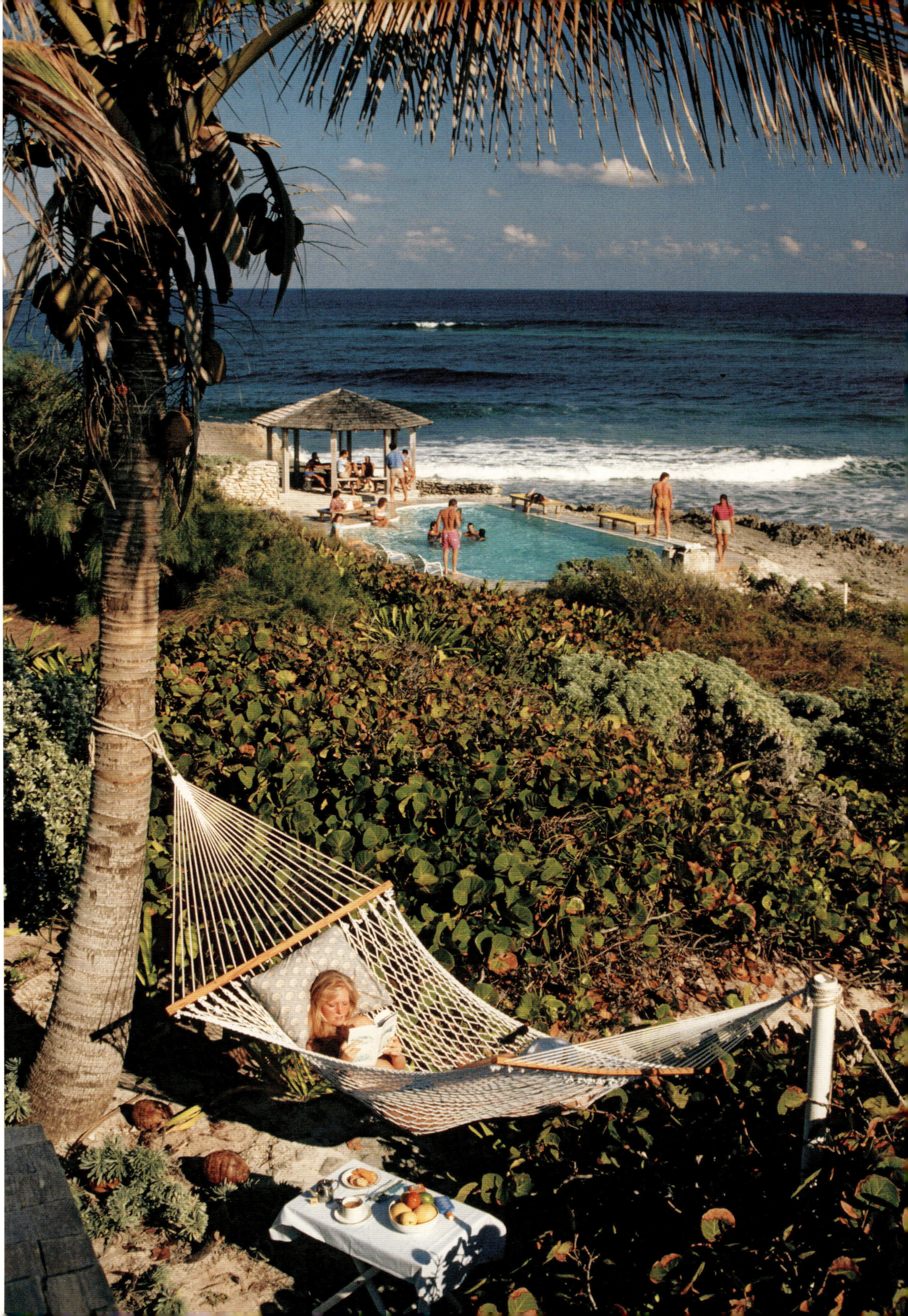

preceding spread left Paradise can be defined simply as a hammock hung between two palm trees on a beach, San Juan, 1956.

preceding spread right College student Jan Woods relaxes at the Abaco Inn on Elbow Cay, one of the Abaco Islands in the Bahamas, 1986.

below Mrs. Dauphinot, Marina Posson, Baroness Meriel de Posson, and a friend, Lyford Cay, New Providence Island, Bahamas, 1974.

opposite French model—and muse to designer Hubert de Givenchy—Bettina Graziani wades through the shallow waters of Costa Smeralda, Sardinia, 1964.

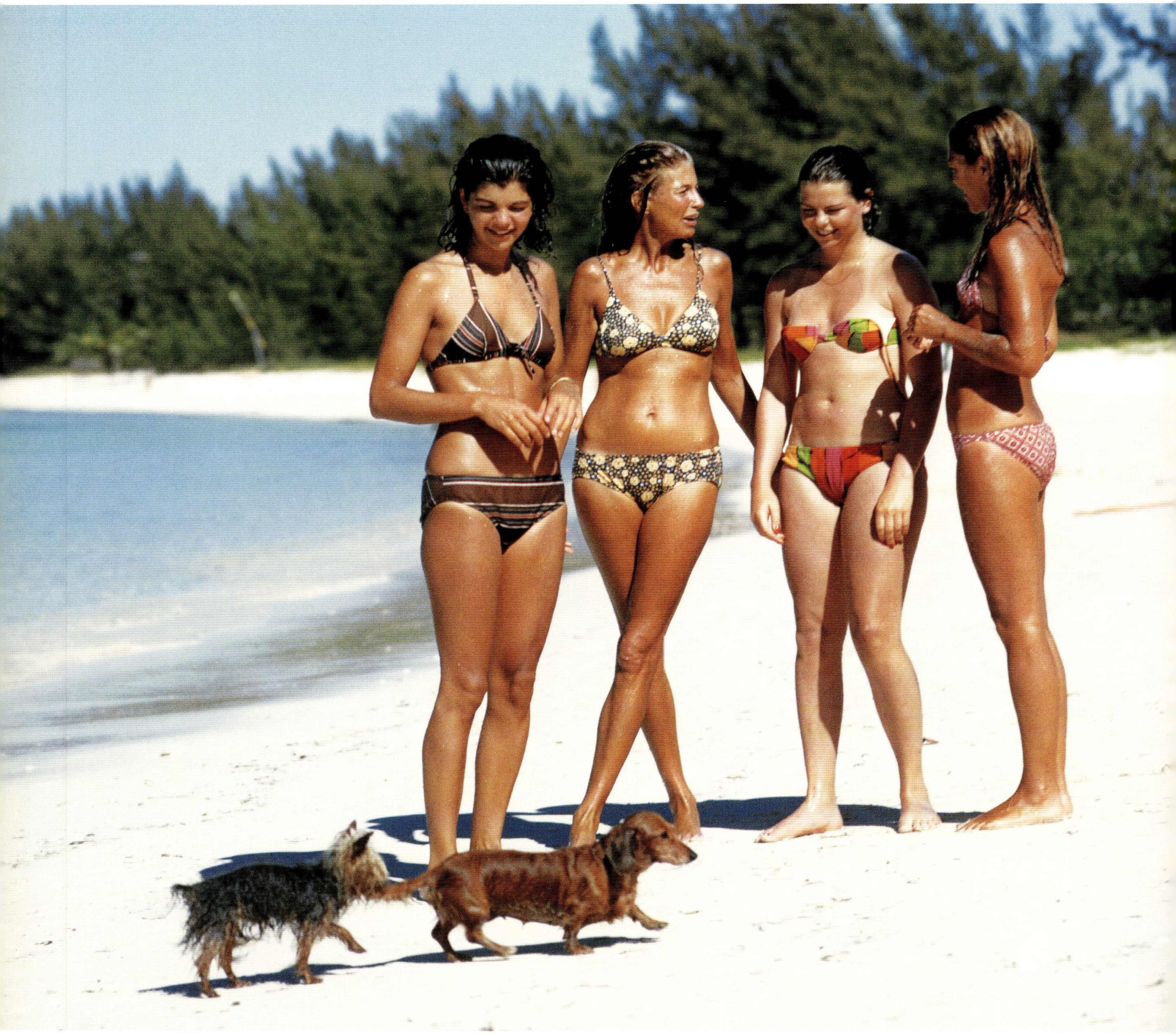

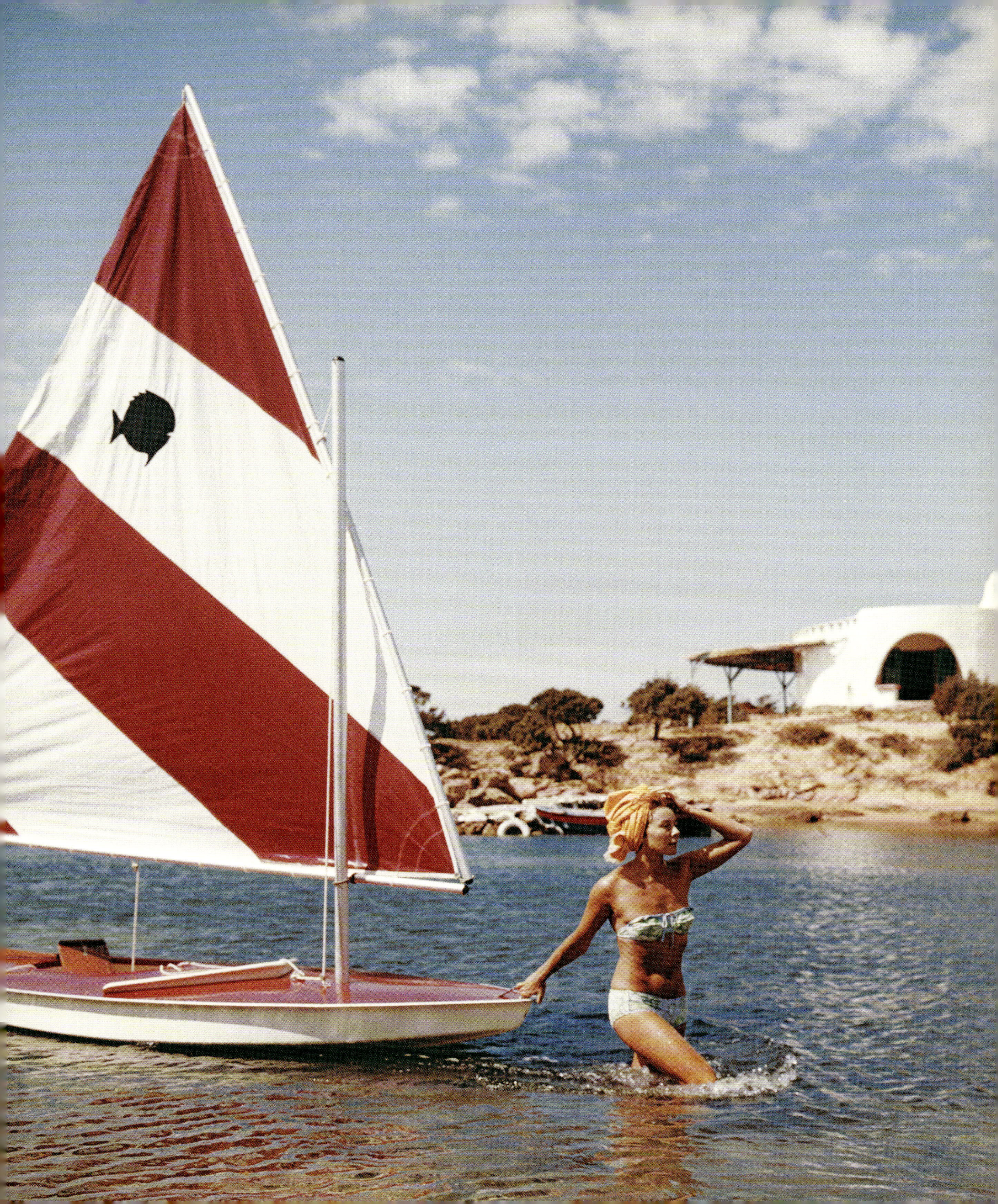

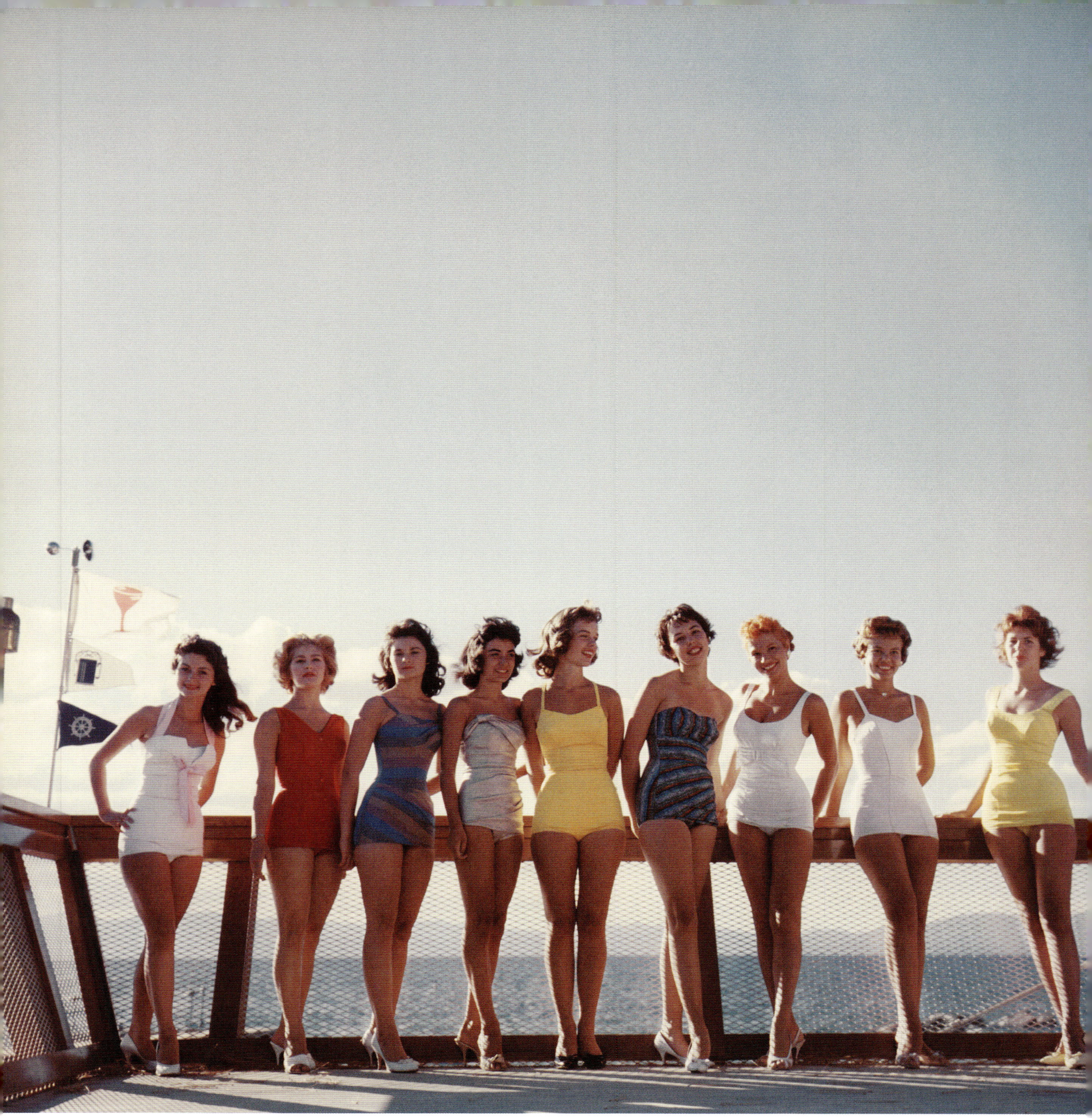

above Local ambience and playful camaraderie make for a relaxed reunion of friends, Lake Tahoe, 1959.

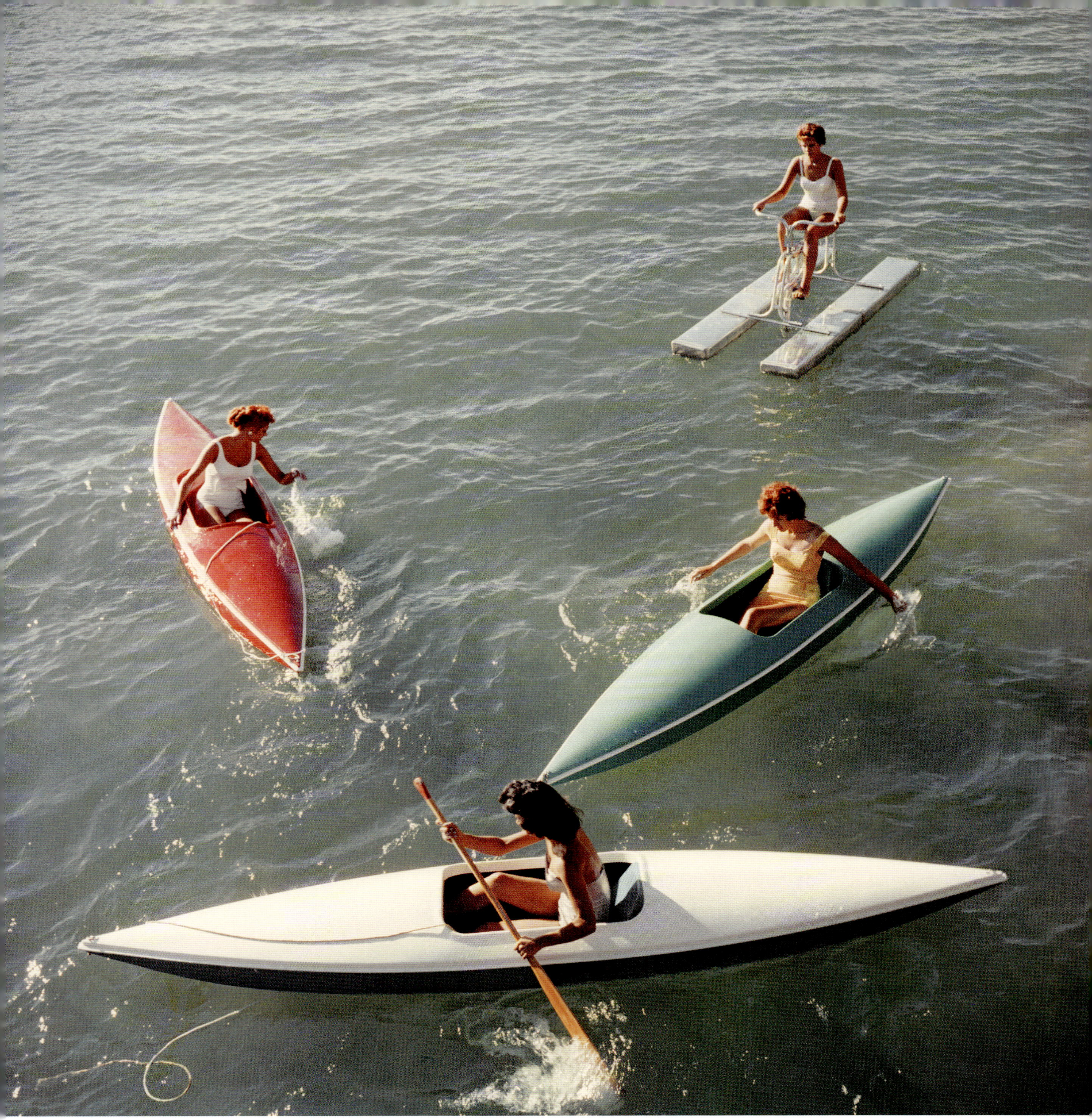

above Young women kayaking, Lake Tahoe, 1959.

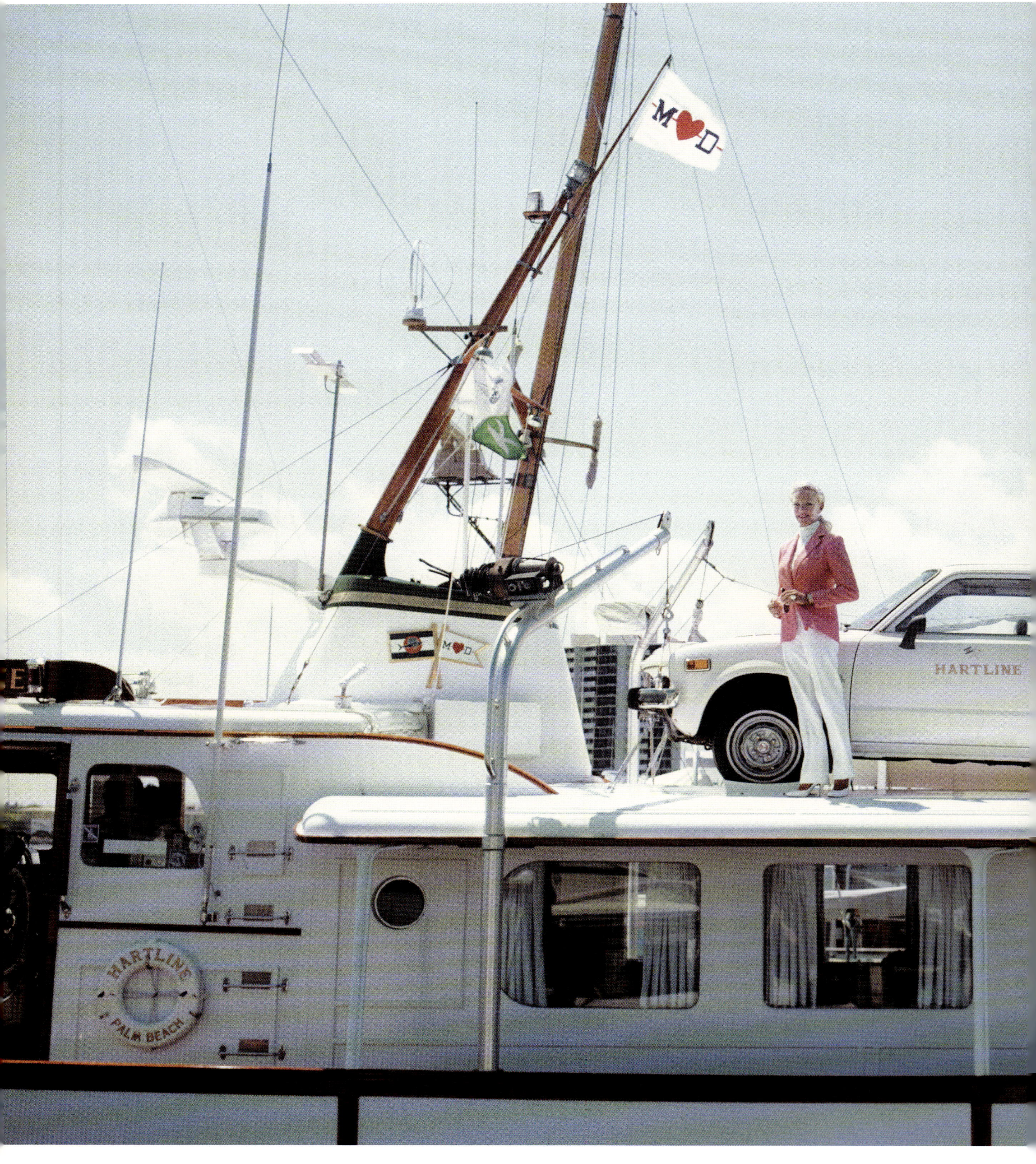
HARTLINE
HARTLINE
PALM BEACH

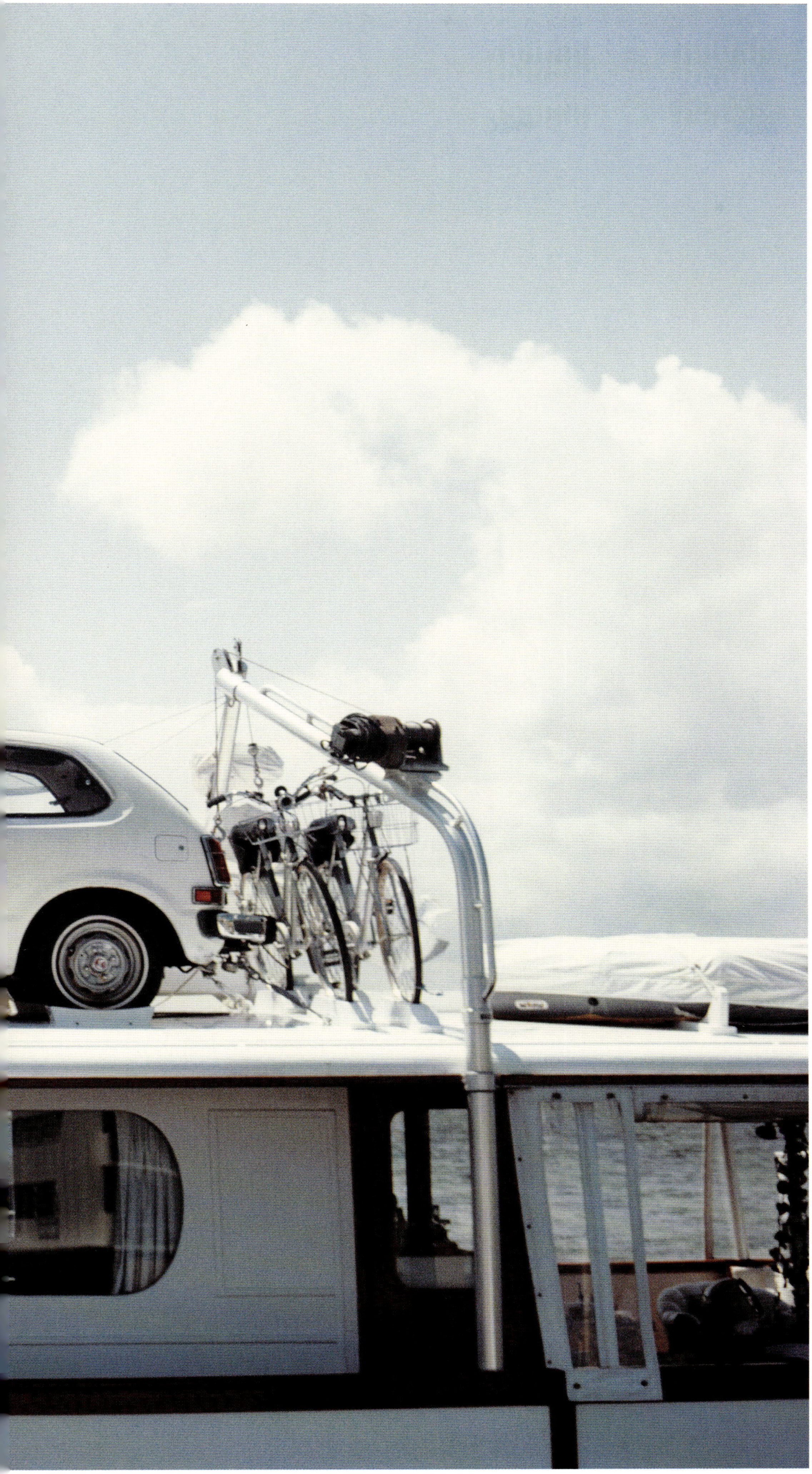

left Mary Woolworth Donahue on her well-appointed yacht, *Hartline*, Palm Beach, 1982. Named the "Queen of Love and Beauty" at her Hillsboro, Illinois, high school homecoming, Mary Hartline was a model, actress, and one of radio and television's earliest stars. She proved to be a marketing whiz as well, with her own line of more than three dozen different Mary Hartline products, including dolls, clothes, and boots. Her fourth (and final) husband was the F. W. Woolworth Company heir Woolworth Donahue. They became yachting enthusiasts and were fixtures on the Southampton and Palm Beach scenes.

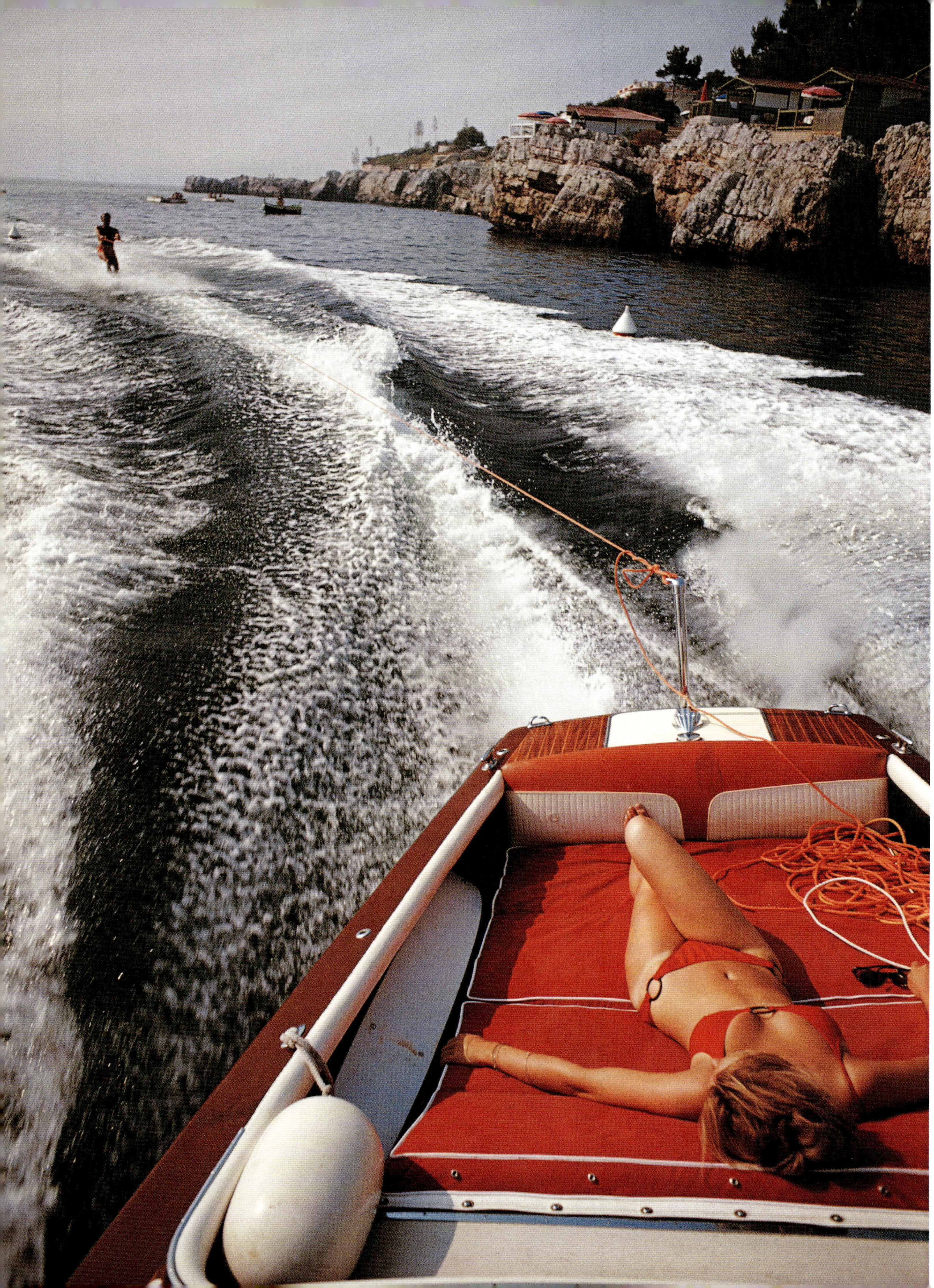

opposite The view of the Côte d'Azur from a motorboat cutting through the waters of the Mediterranean Sea, Antibes, 1969. One of the most famous coastlines in the world is this stretch just off the Hôtel du Cap-Eden-Roc.

right The French diva Lily Pons on the French Riviera, Cap Ferrat, 1957. Pons was a rare singer, a coloratura soprano—able to deftly perform runs, leaps, and trills at an elevated pitch. France's most illustrious opera star, she performed at the Metropolitan Opera in New York three hundred times between 1931 and 1960. One of the first celebrities who understood how to become a marketable icon, she was the face in advertising for Lockheed airplanes, Knox gelatin, and Libby's tomato juice, and she made numerous appearances on television, film, and radio. The remarkable longevity of her career was mirrored in her love life. When Howard L. Hunt—then the richest man in the world and never before known for any interest in the arts—suddenly began to pay attention to opera, it was suspected that he and Pons, then age fifty-six, were having an affair. "I admire her and we're just friends" was his only comment to the press.

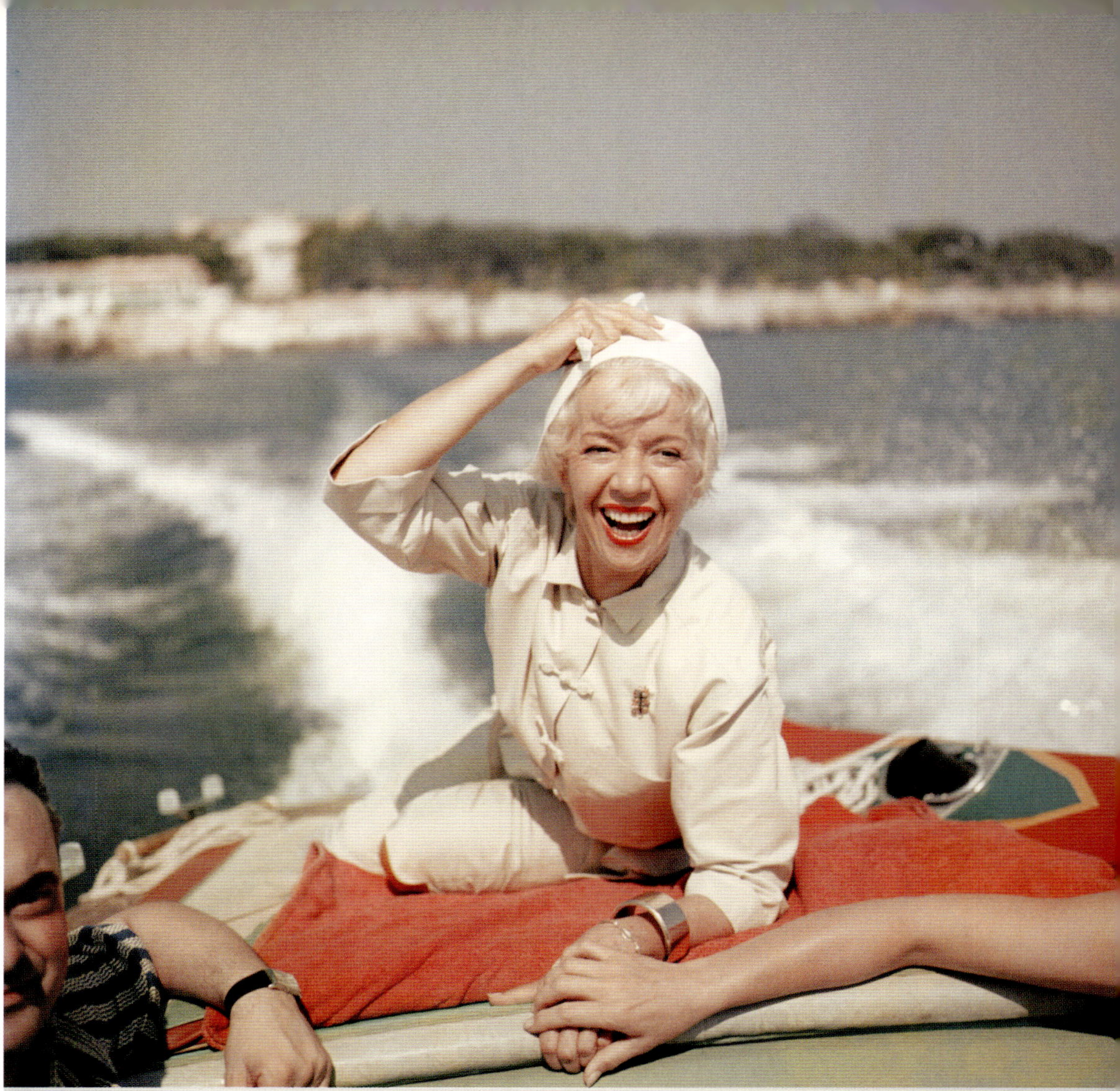

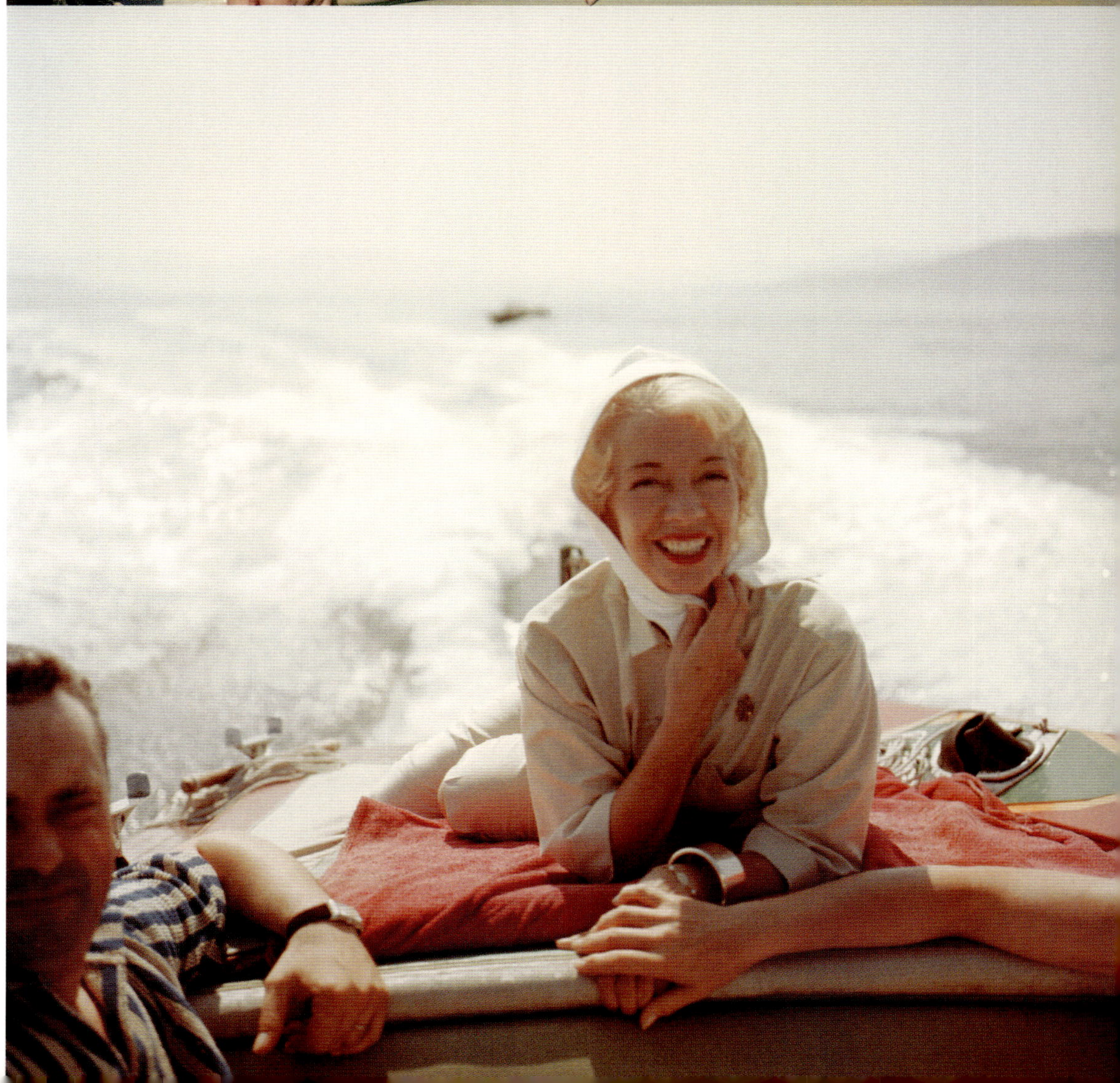

below The American society girl Minnie Cushing carries her surfboard at Spouting Rock Beach Club (informally known as Bailey's Beach Club), Newport, 1965. Slim wrote of this photo in 1971, "It was Minnie's father, Howard, who brought surfing to Bailey's Beach in the 1930s when he brought back a surfing board from Hawaii. No photographers are allowed inside the club, but an obliging member showed me a place to stand on the rocks bordering the beach." In later years, Slim would be allowed to bend that rule thanks to his venerated status as lensman to the upper class.

opposite High spirits precede a day of surfing in Laguna Beach, 1970.

following spread left A young holidaymaker prepares to paraglide over the breathtaking Acapulco Bay, Las Brisas Hotel, Acapulco, 1968.

following spread right Patsy Pulitzer, *Vogue* model and socialite, boards a seaplane at the Everglades Flying Service, Palm Beach, circa 1955. Pulitzer was one of her era's great "It Girls." She was the sister of the Palm Beach playboy Peter Pulitzer; the daughter of Herbert "Tony" Pulitzer, the rakish publisher of the *New York World*; and the granddaughter of Joseph Pulitzer, who made the *World* a hugely popular newspaper and left a bequest that led to the creation of the Pulitzer Prize. Patsy Pulitzer began modeling just as the trend of taking models out of the studios and putting them in more natural settings began to develop. She epitomized the desired look of the day, that of privileged and sporty girls who embraced the great outdoors. With her, it wasn't just a look—she was said to have once boated a 1,230-pound black marlin.

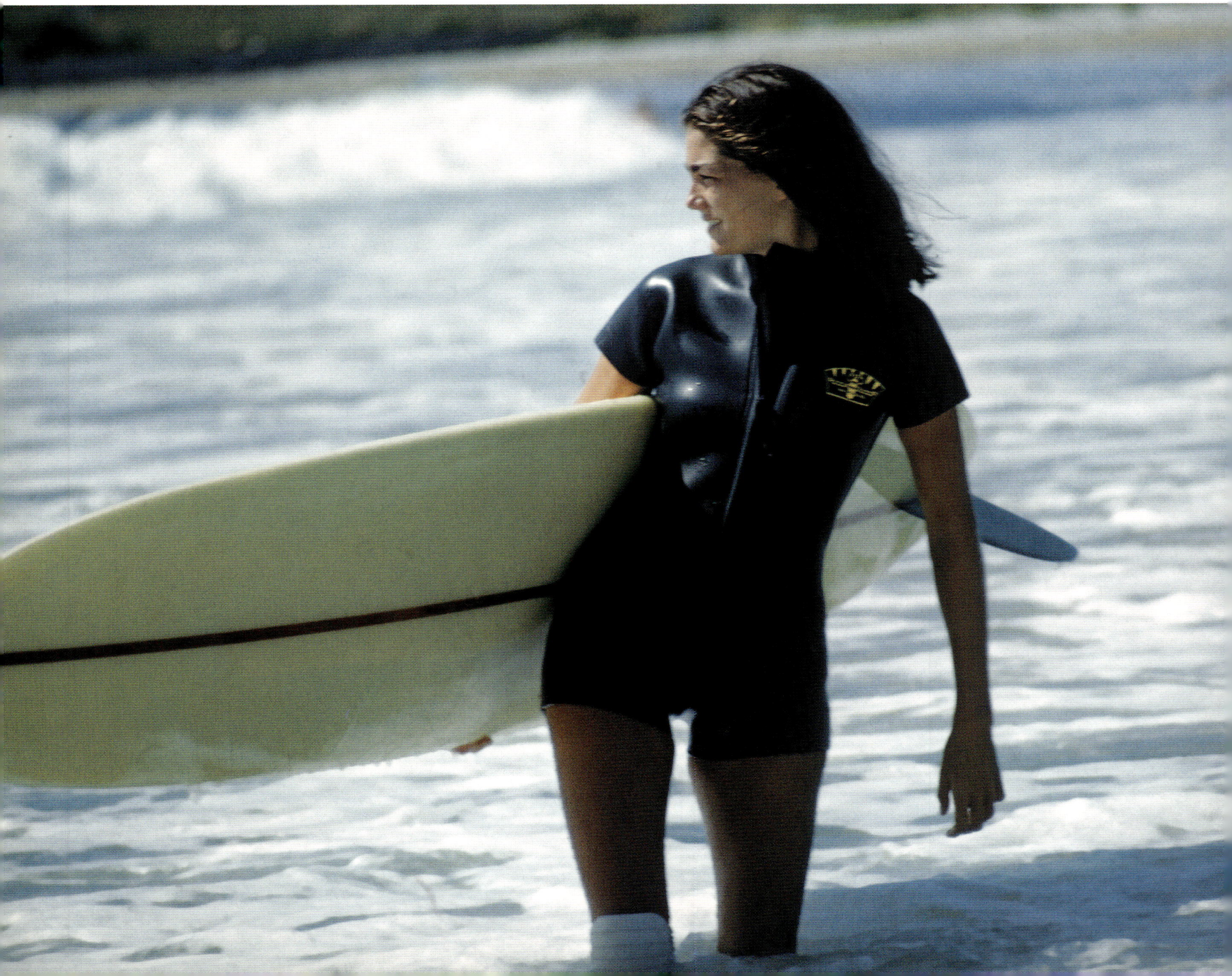

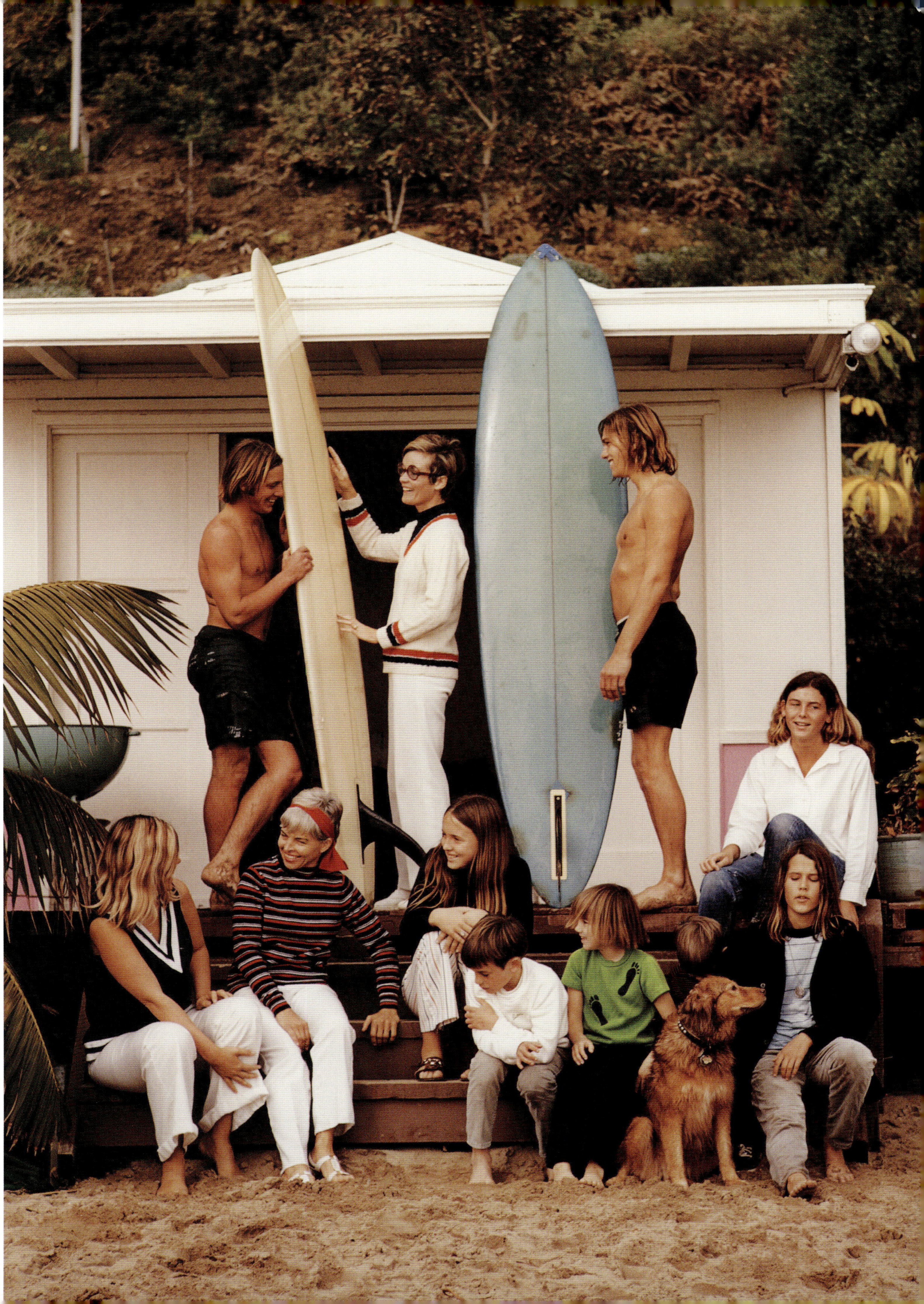

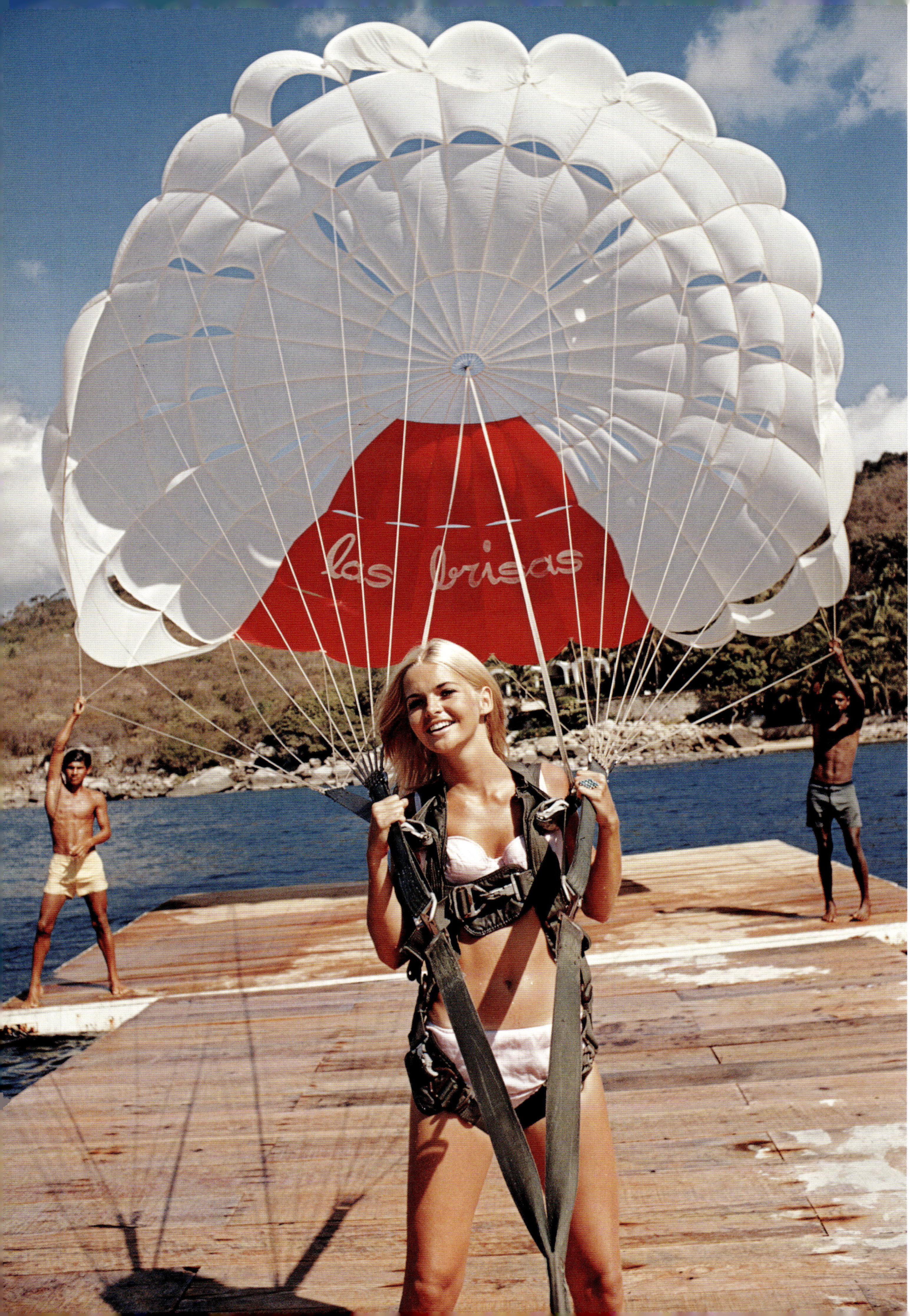
las brisas

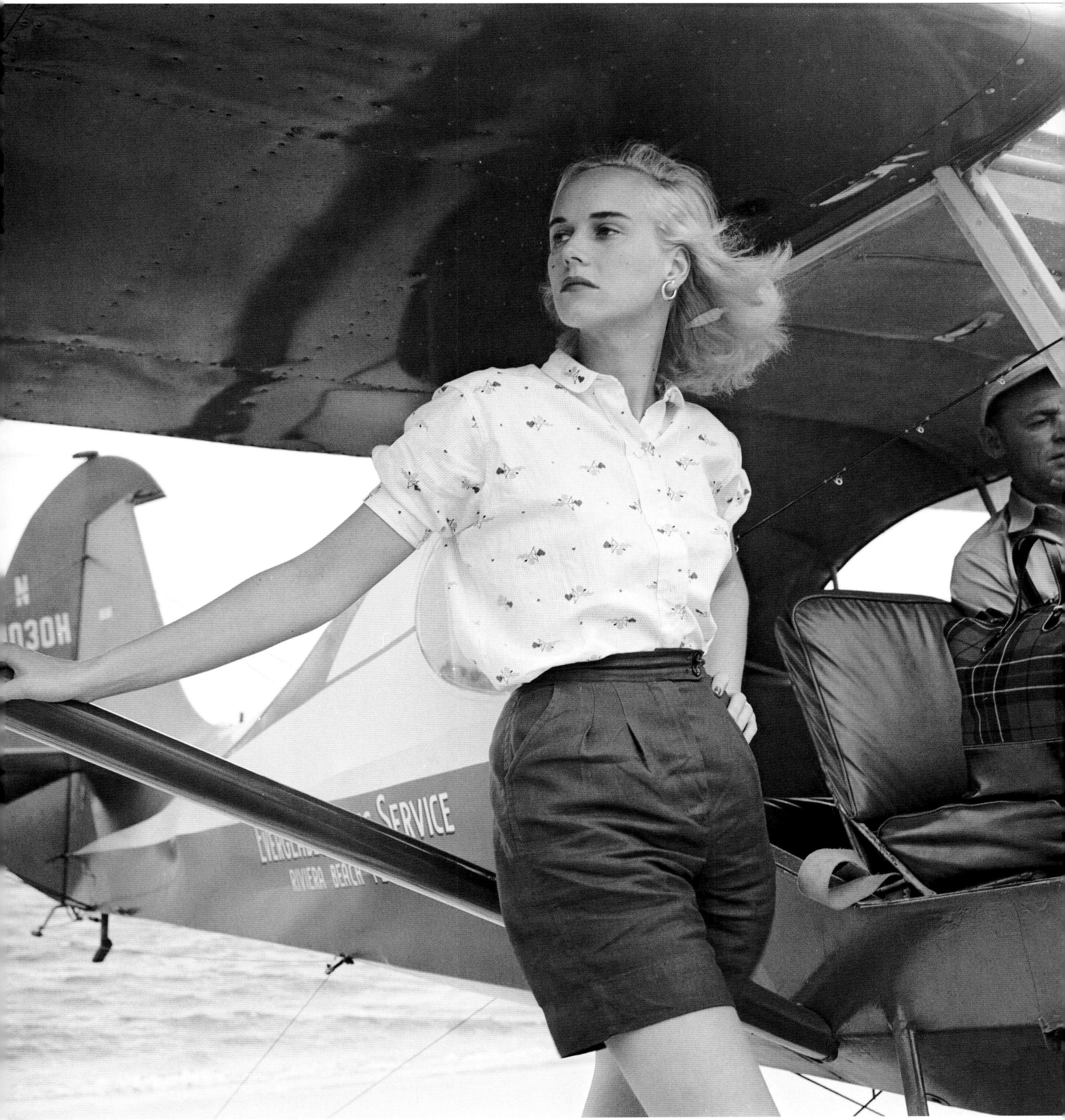
SERVICE
RIVIERA BEACH

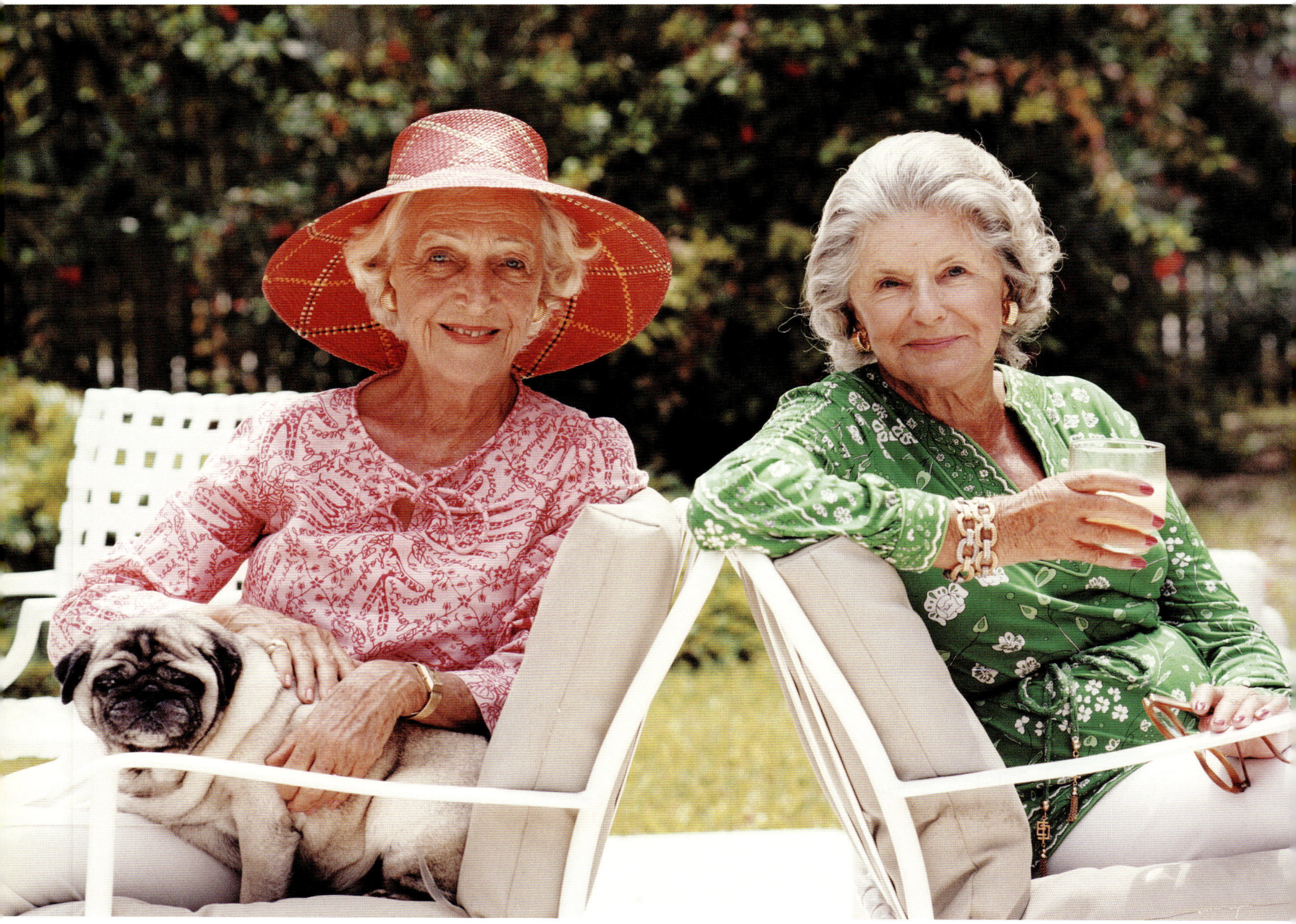

above Lady Virginia Christie (left) and Lady Anne Orr-Lewis at a luncheon in Lyford Cay, New Providence Island, Bahamas, 1983. Decorators to the stars, in their day this creative duo was responsible for the interior charms of most of the homes in Lyford Cay. "Annie Orr," as Slim called her, also directed new looks for the Windermere Island Club, the Lyford Cay Club, and the home of Prince Karim Aga Khan on the Costa Smeralda, Sardinia, among other places. She was one of Slim's favorite people, that type of formidable woman who possesses such an abundance of confidence, wit, and impeccable taste that she seems to have been cut from a more lavish cloth than most. She and Slim ran into each other all over the world; they had an instant rapport and a mutual wry sense of humor, and the cast of characters they each called friends were nearly the same group of people. Perhaps one aspect of their mutual admiration was that they were both roaming the world primarily for work.

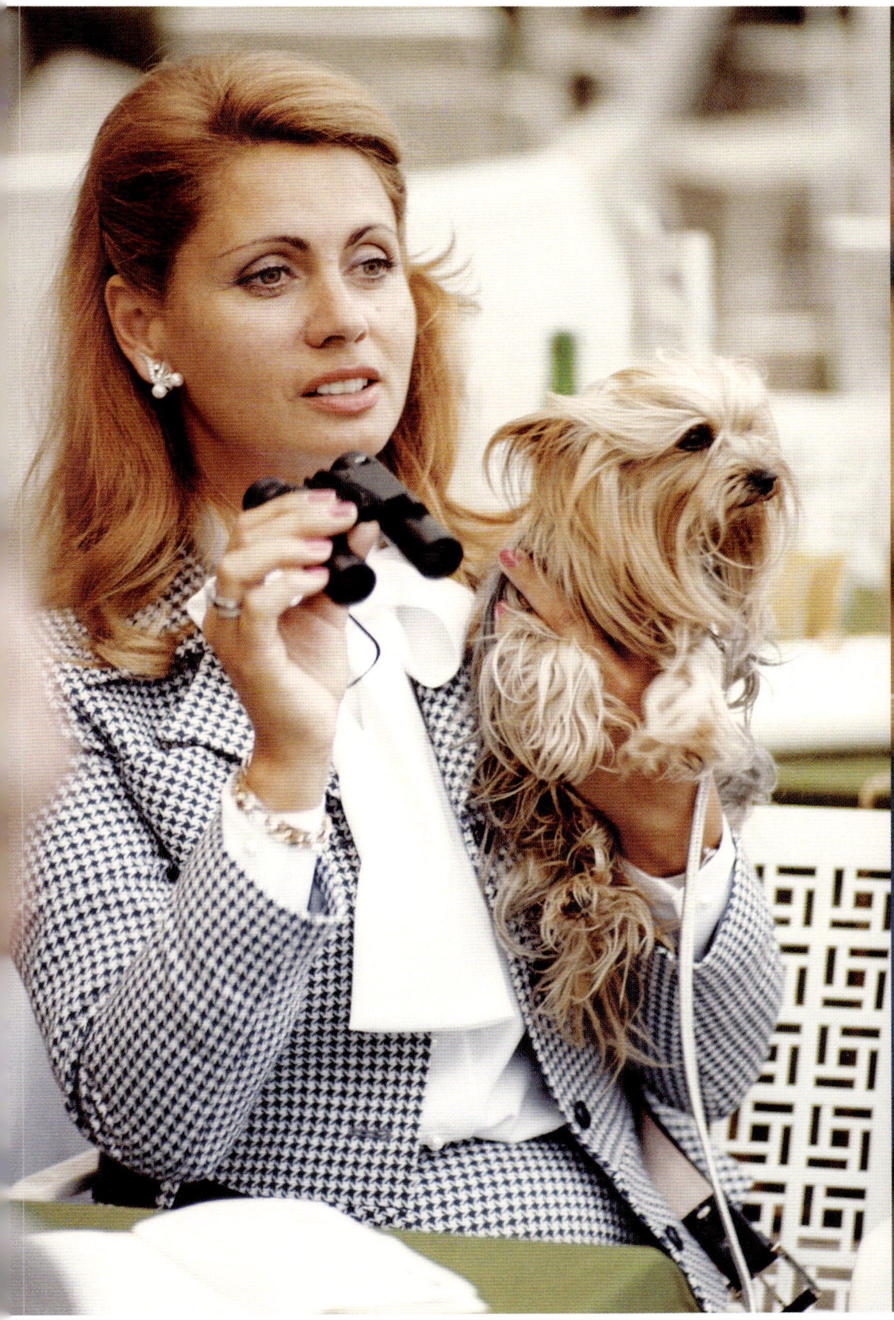

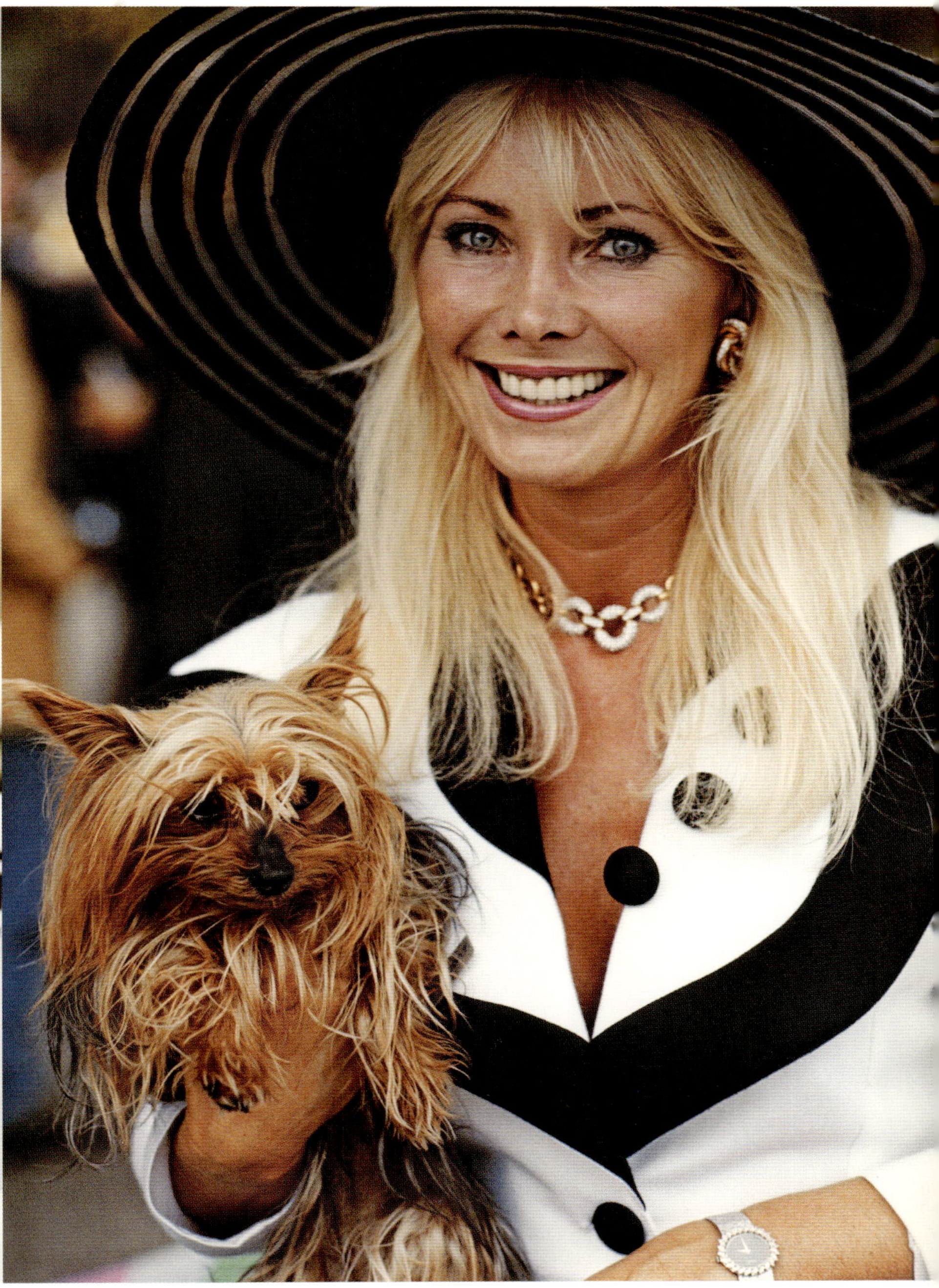

above left Margot Münchow with her dog, Cosy Point, at the races, Baden-Baden, 1978. Münchow, whose stage name was Margot Eskens, was a singer who also appeared in numerous television shows and films, selling more than forty million records and CDs throughout her singing career.

above right Gisela Baronin von Stein, Baden-Baden, 1990. The Munich native came to the fairy-tale village of Baden-Baden, nestled in Germany's Black Forest, as much for the vibrant social life as for the thermal mineral springs. She is pictured with her Yorkshire terrier, Sweetie.

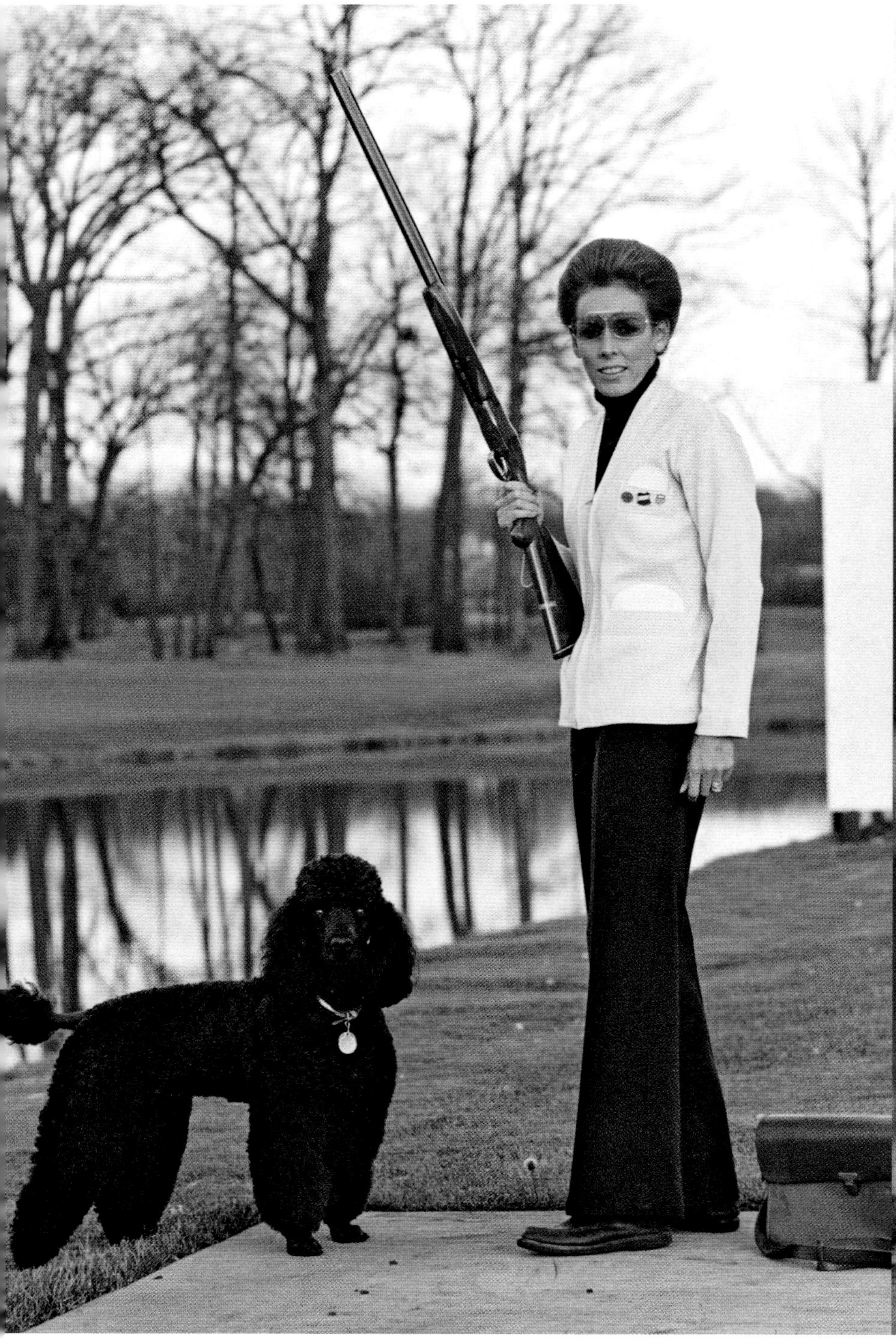
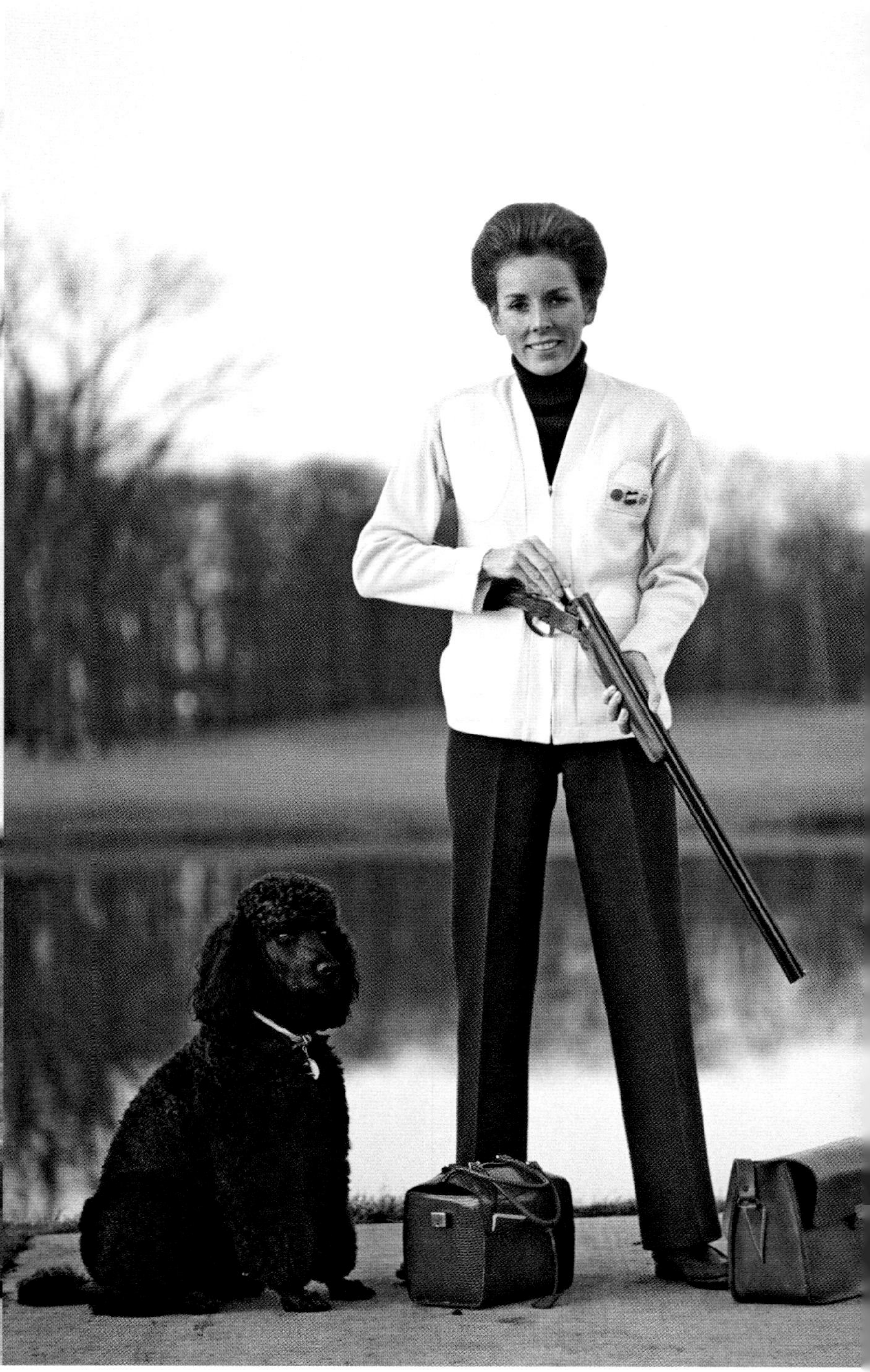

above Diane Palmer, Lake Forest, Illinois, circa 1958. Palmer spent most of her life in pursuit of sporting excellence. She broke records in almost every sport she tried, including skeet and trap shooting, sailboat racing, and golf. She was an alternate on the 1966 Olympic shooting team and was inducted into the Skeet Shooting Hall of Fame in Savannah, Georgia.

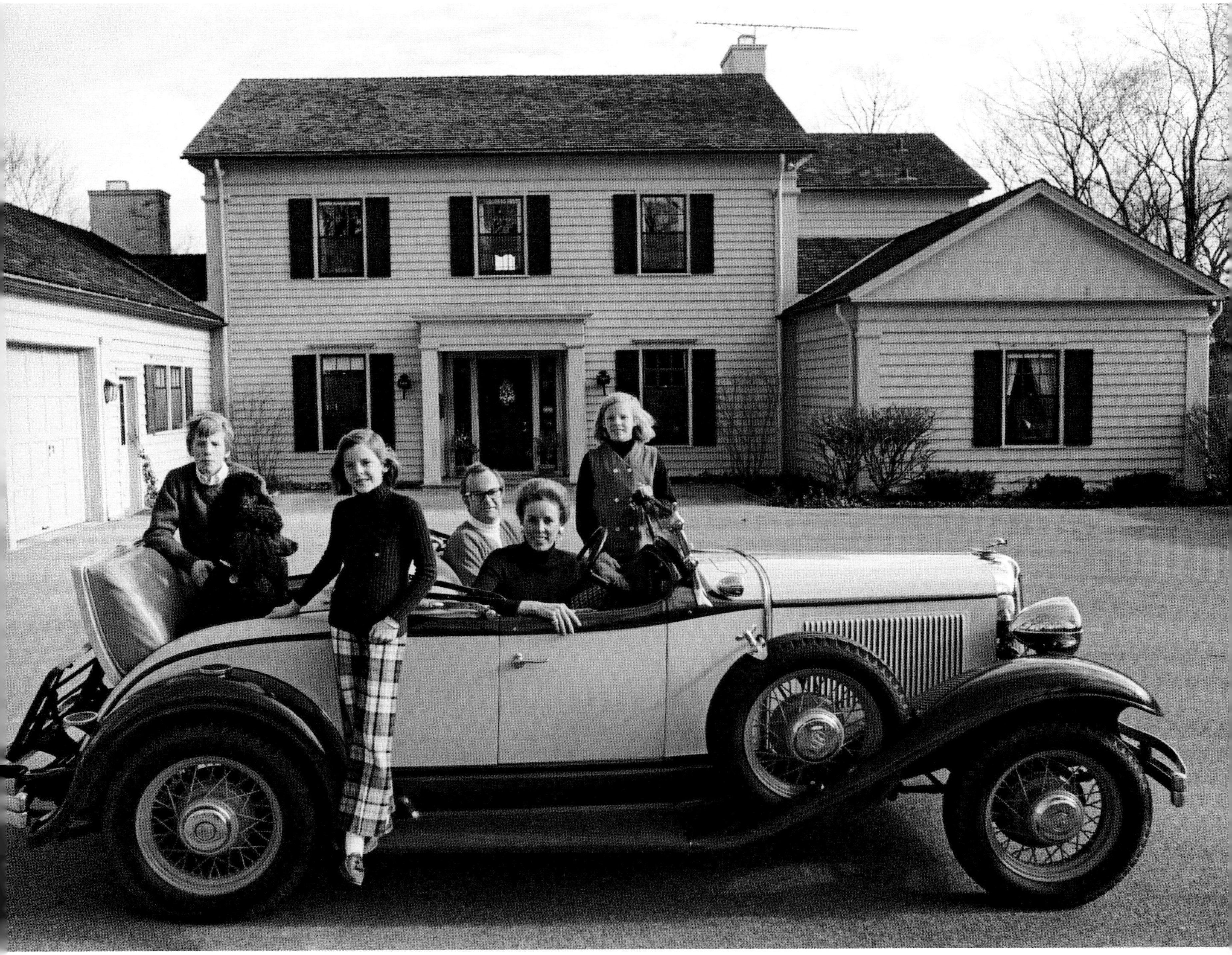

above Diane and Potter Palmer and family, Lake Forest, Illinois, circa 1958. Potter Palmer was the grandson of Potter Palmer, founder of Chicago's famed Palmer House Hotel, and Bertha Honoré Palmer, a wealthy Chicago socialite and entrepreneur.

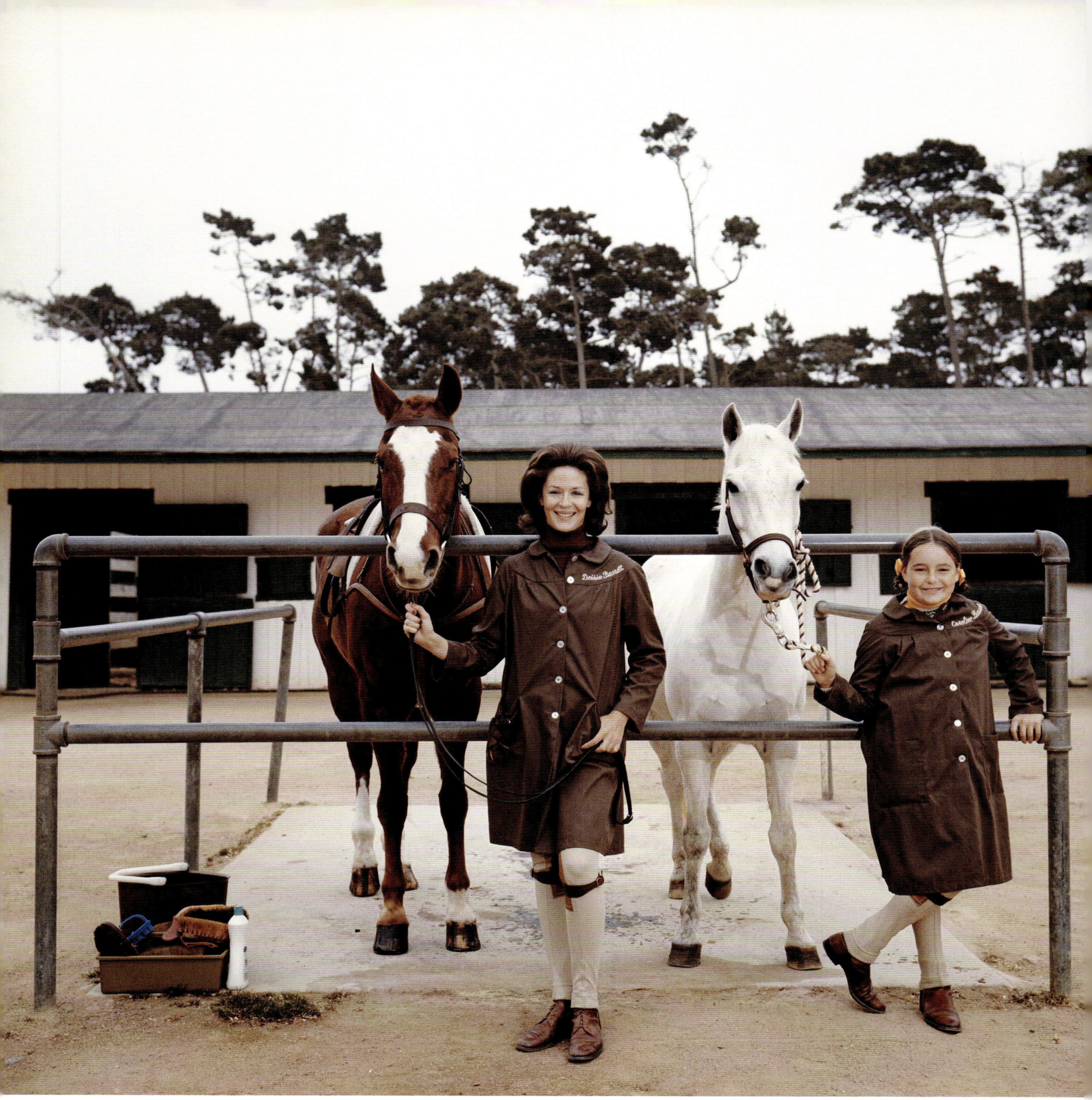

above Dobbie Coleman Bassett, daughter of the Duchess of Manchester, at the stables with her daughter, Caroline, Pebble Beach, California, 1976. Their daylong rides often took them past the wind-blown dunes and countless small coves of Pebble Beach.

opposite Anne Anka with her daughters (left to right) Alicia, Anthea, Alexandra, and Amanda, Pebble Beach, California, 1976. Born in Poland and reared in Sweden, Anka is of English, Lebanese, French, Dutch, and Greek ancestry. She was an Eileen Ford model and

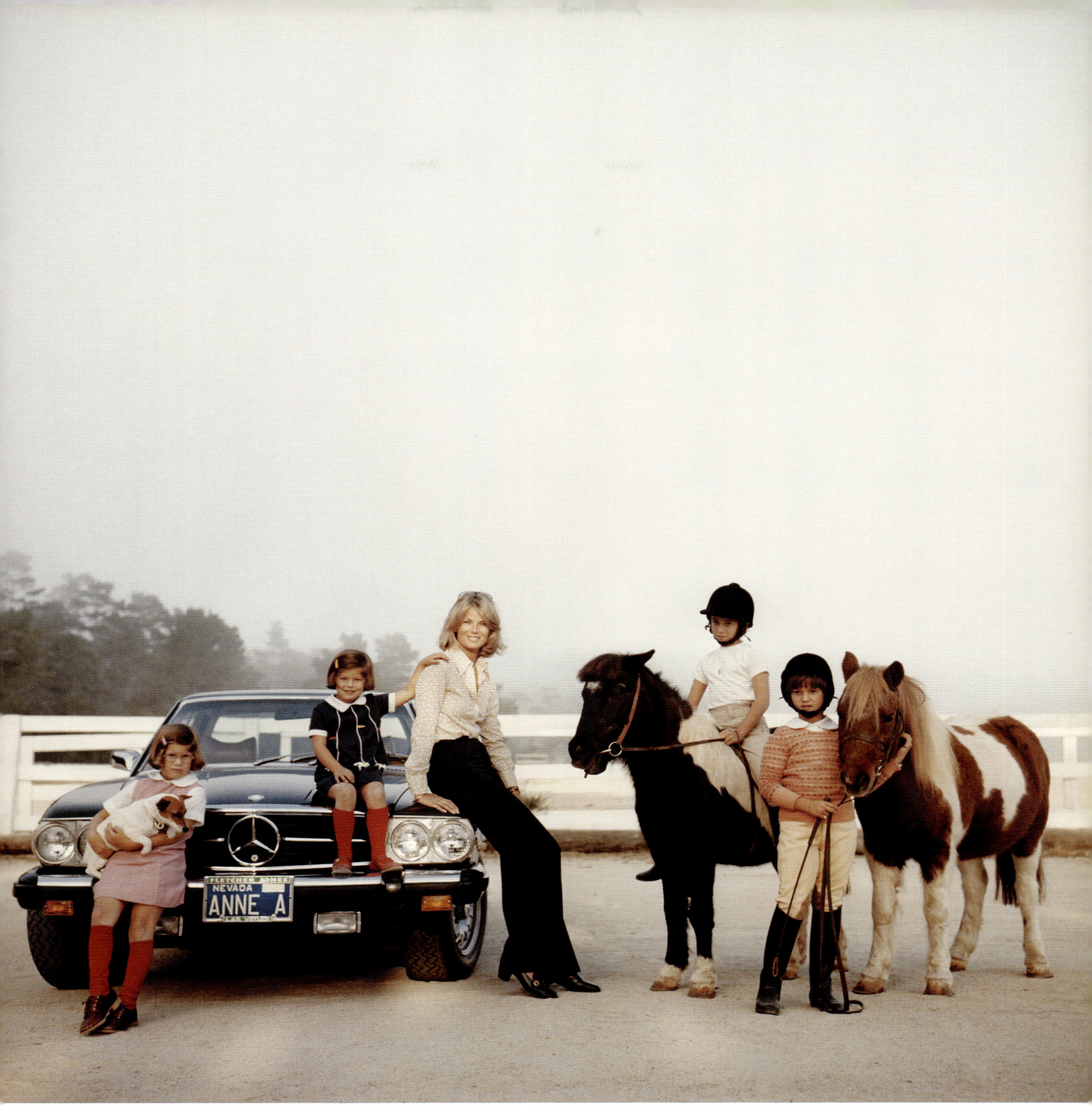

actress who married the Canadian singer Paul Anka. A passionate art collector, she has a tendency toward artistic patronage that hails from her colorful father, Count Charles de Zogheb, a Lebanese diplomat.

following spread Members of the Hunter Hill Pony Club gather for the weekly lesson taught every Thursday by Nancy King, Castle Pines, Colorado, 1990. King (in carriage), with her husband, Paul, owned the thousand-acre Happy Canyon Arabian Farm, adjacent to Castle Pines.

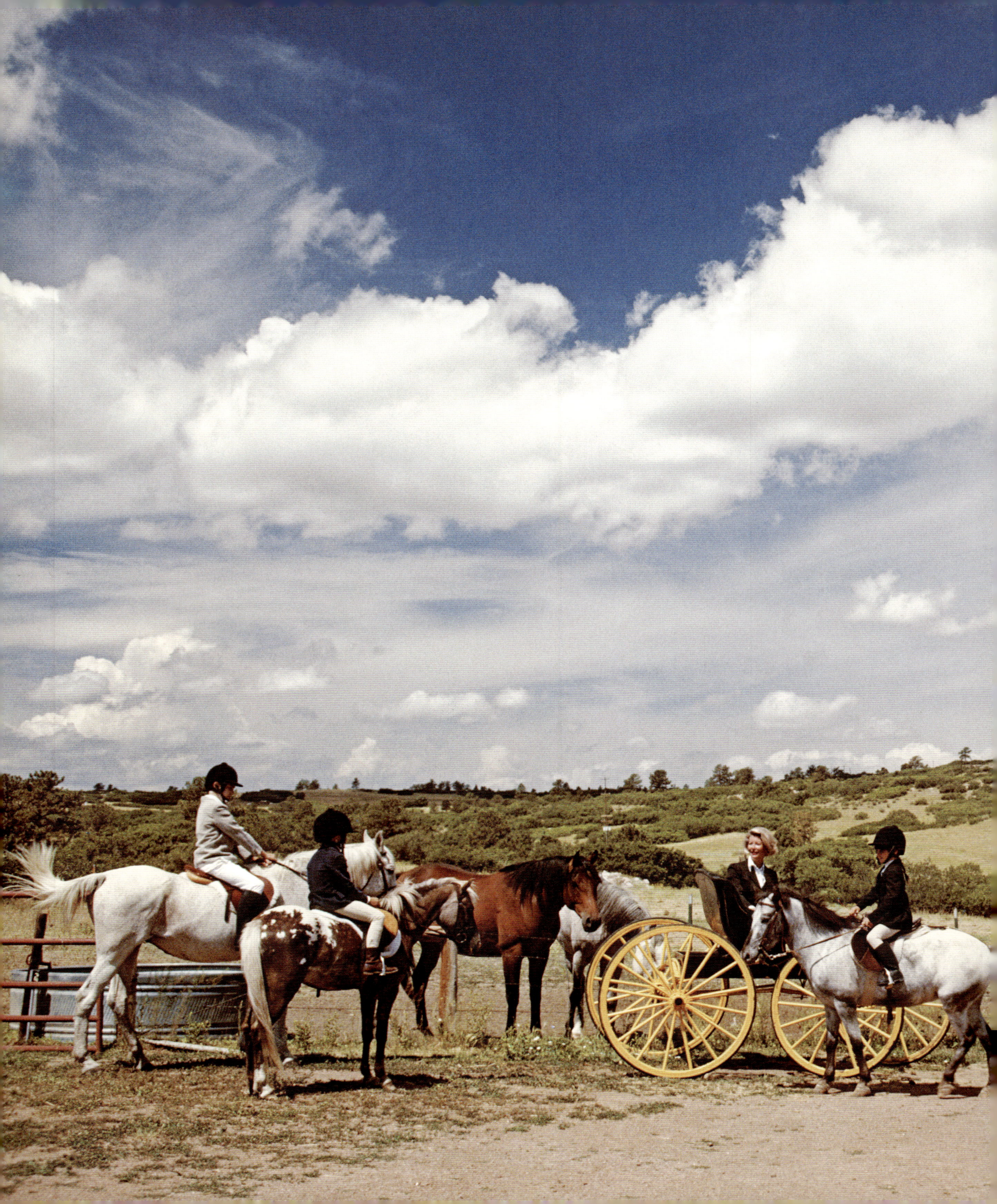

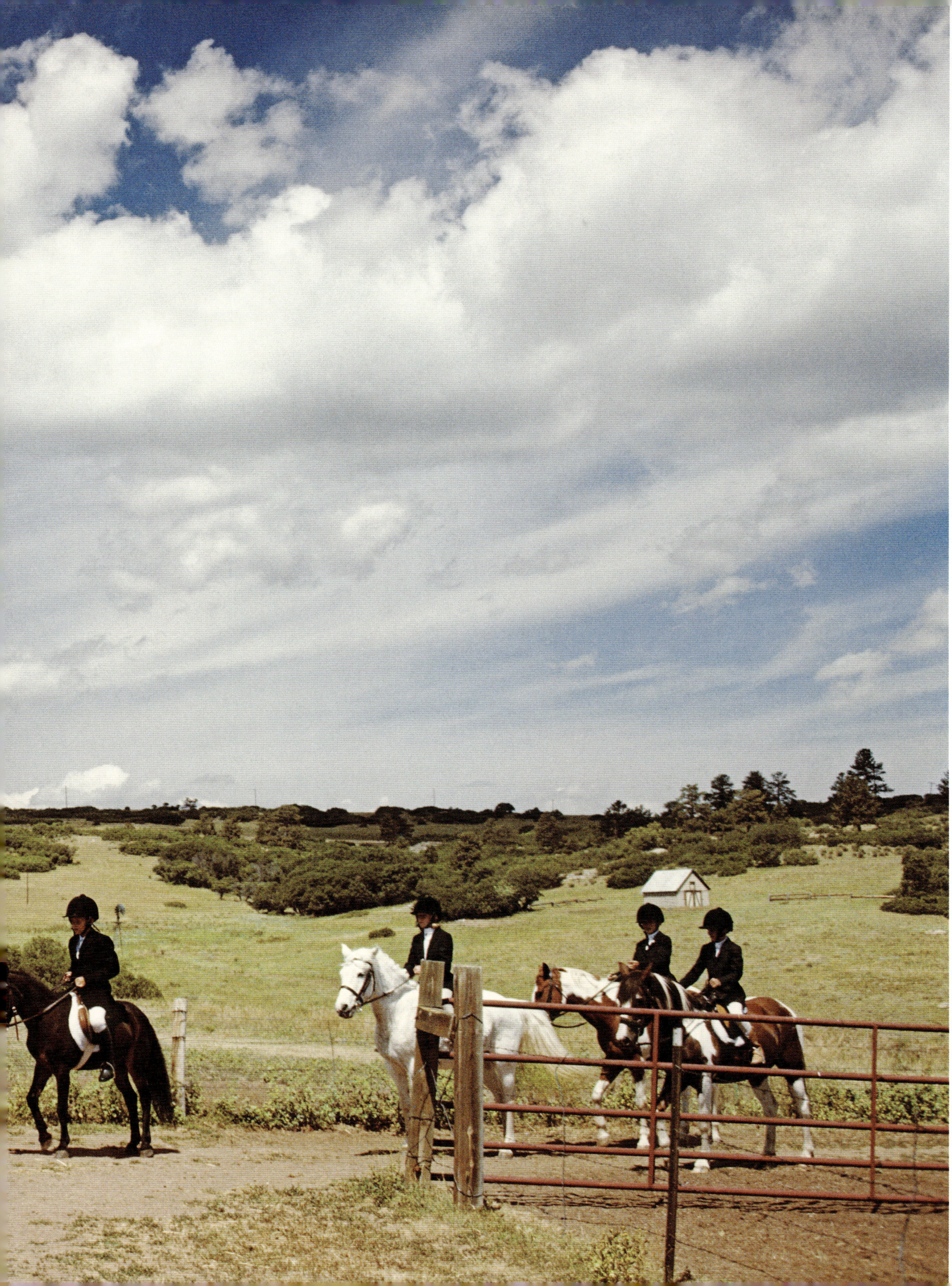

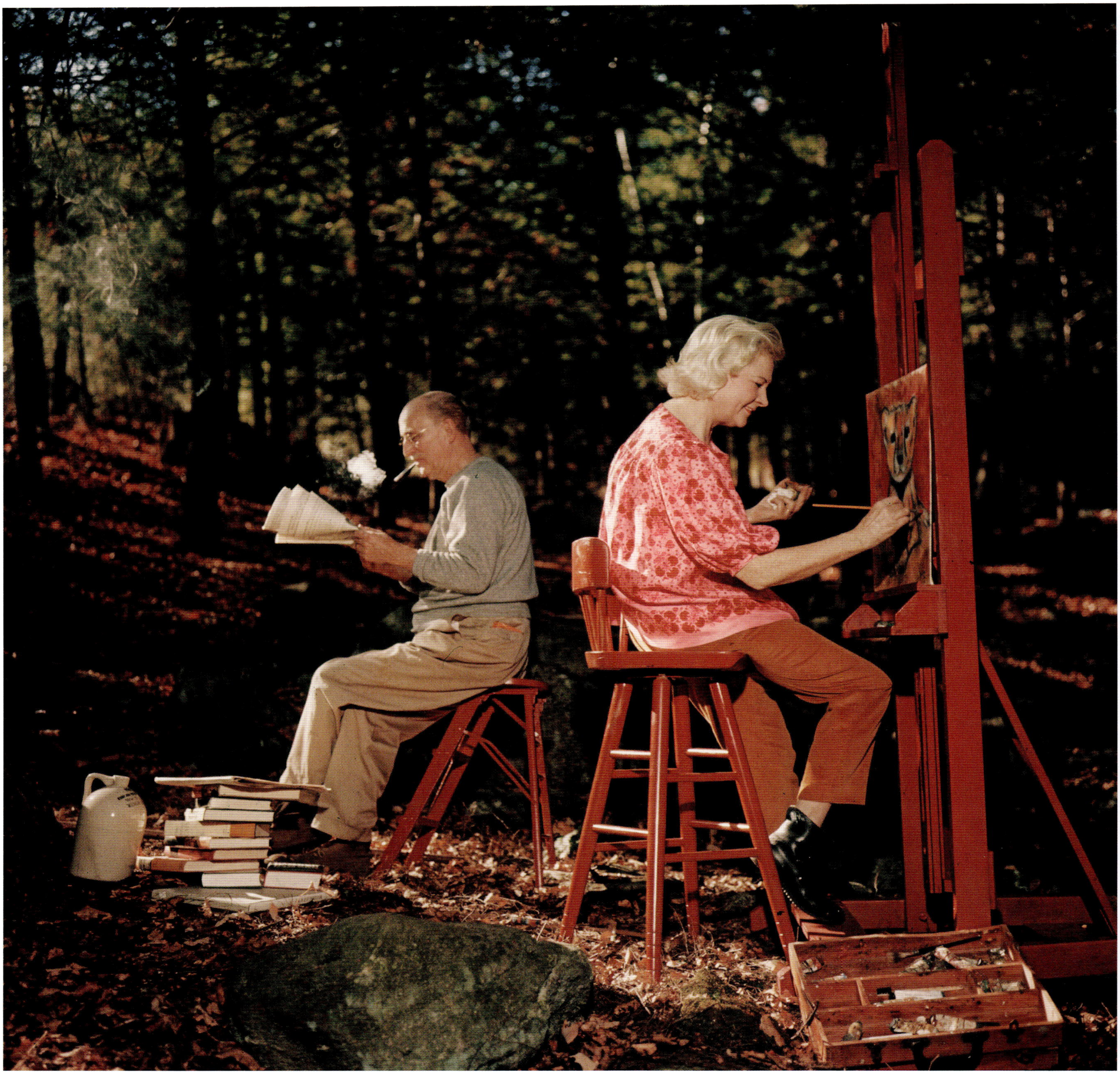

above Ed and Pegeen Fitzgerald at their home in Kent, Connecticut, 1963. *The Fitzgeralds, Book Talk, Back Talk and Small Talk* was the radio show that the couple conducted for forty-two years, becoming what many thought of as a "radio institution," and pioneering the at-home radio format. Pegeen's signature style was quiet, folksy, and liberal, while Ed's was theatrical, intellectual, and conservative. Not only were their shows unscripted, but their daily preparation consisted of only cursory glances at newspapers and the mail. Their banter, sometimes including comments meant to shock the more conventional of their listeners, was often accompanied by the purring of their many cats. The veteran *New York Times* reporter Francis X. Clines wrote of them in 1979, "There is no easy way to describe what they do. They wool-gather and play off each other. They steep themselves daily in remembrances, using the airwaves as their Proustian bed."

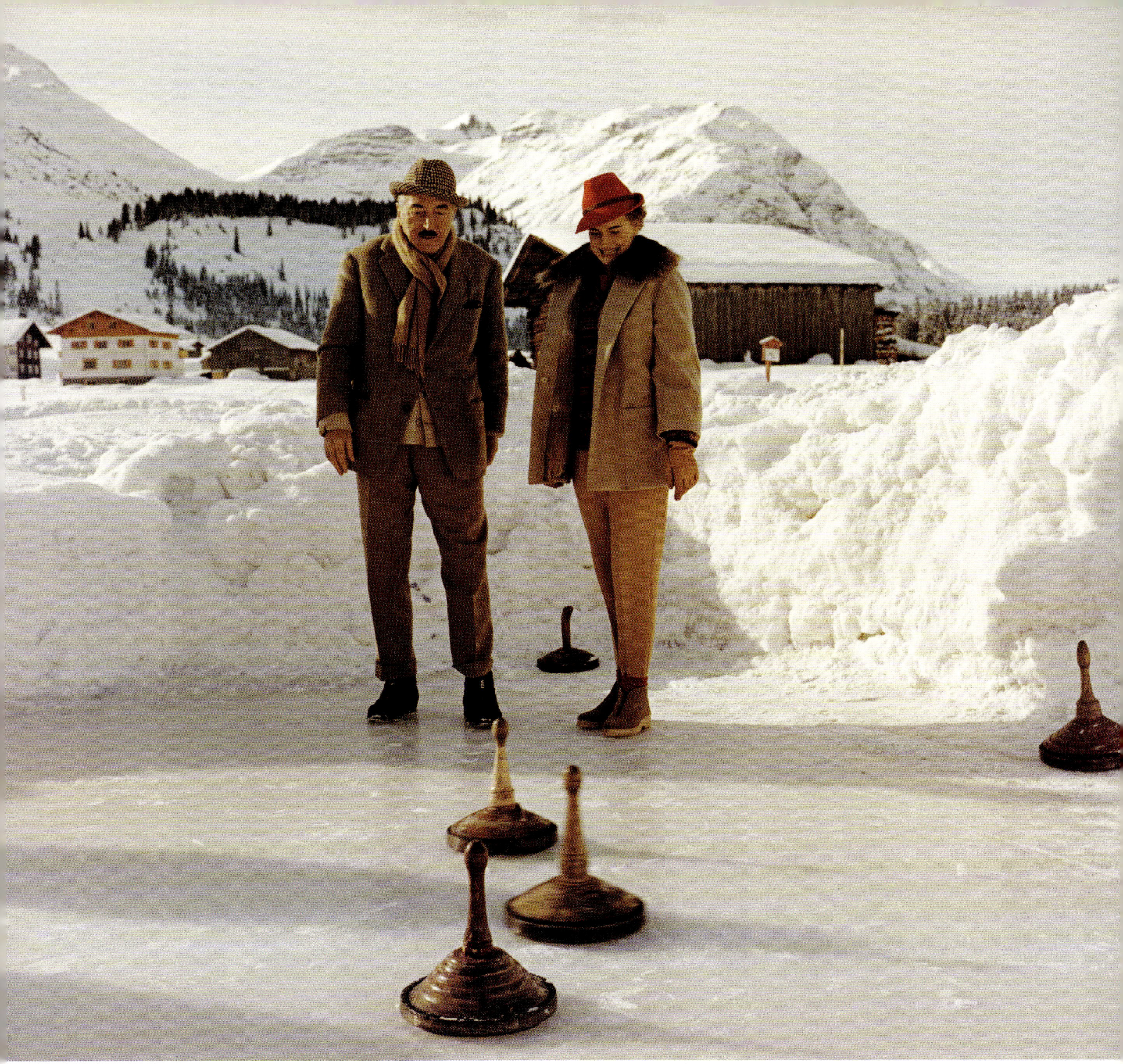

above Heinrich Dite and Leonie Heller try their hand at curling, Lech am Arlberg, Austria, circa 1961. Among the most fashionable ski resorts in Austria, at high season Lech is populated with European royalty, diplomats, and celebrities of both the sporting and the film worlds. Nestled into a sunny mountain pass, the fourteenth-century farming town offers a friendlier, quieter alternative to the glitzy European ski resorts of St. Moritz and Gstaad. Its habitués claim that far more thrill-seeking goes on in Lech by day than by night. For those in search of an activity associated with fewer thrills, Bavarian curling is still a very popular sport.

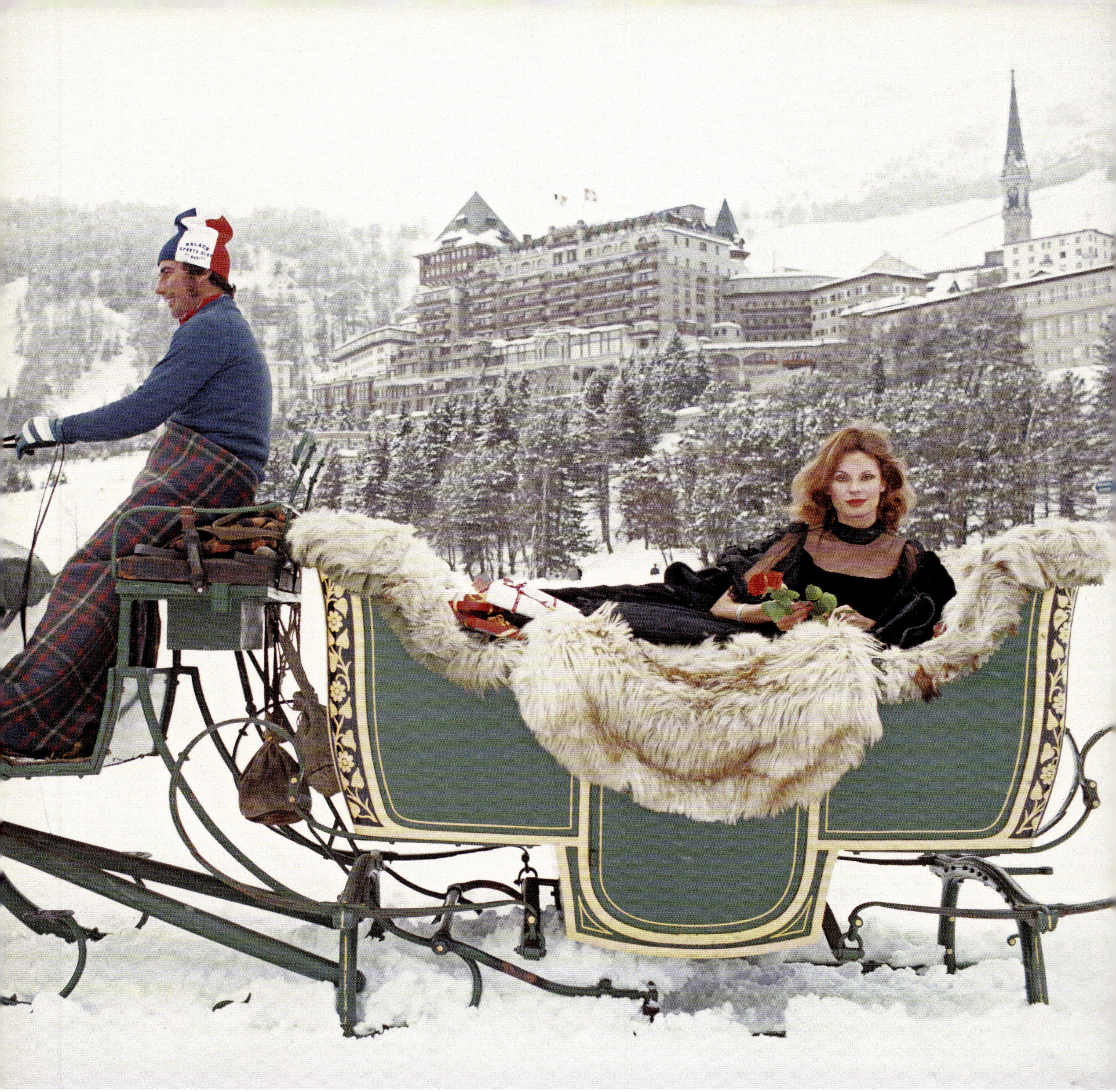

above Karen Kopseng Davis is ferried across a frozen lake with the historic Palace Hotel looming behind, St. Moritz, 1978. An opera singer and Eileen Ford model, she made her operatic debut at La Scala in the 1970s (see also page 47).

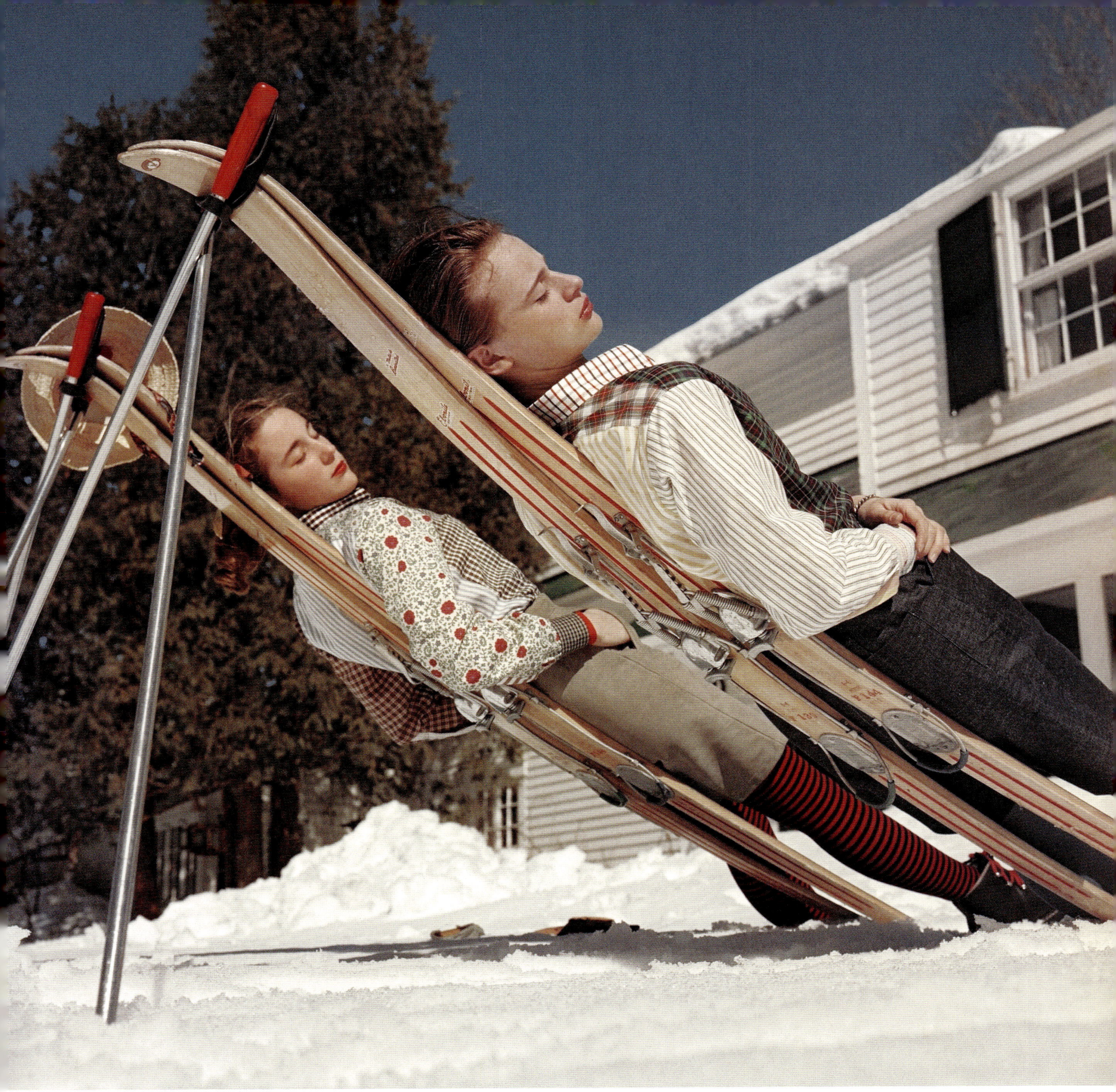

above Skiers bask in the warmth of the winter sun, Cranmore Mountain Resort, North Conway, New Hampshire, 1955.

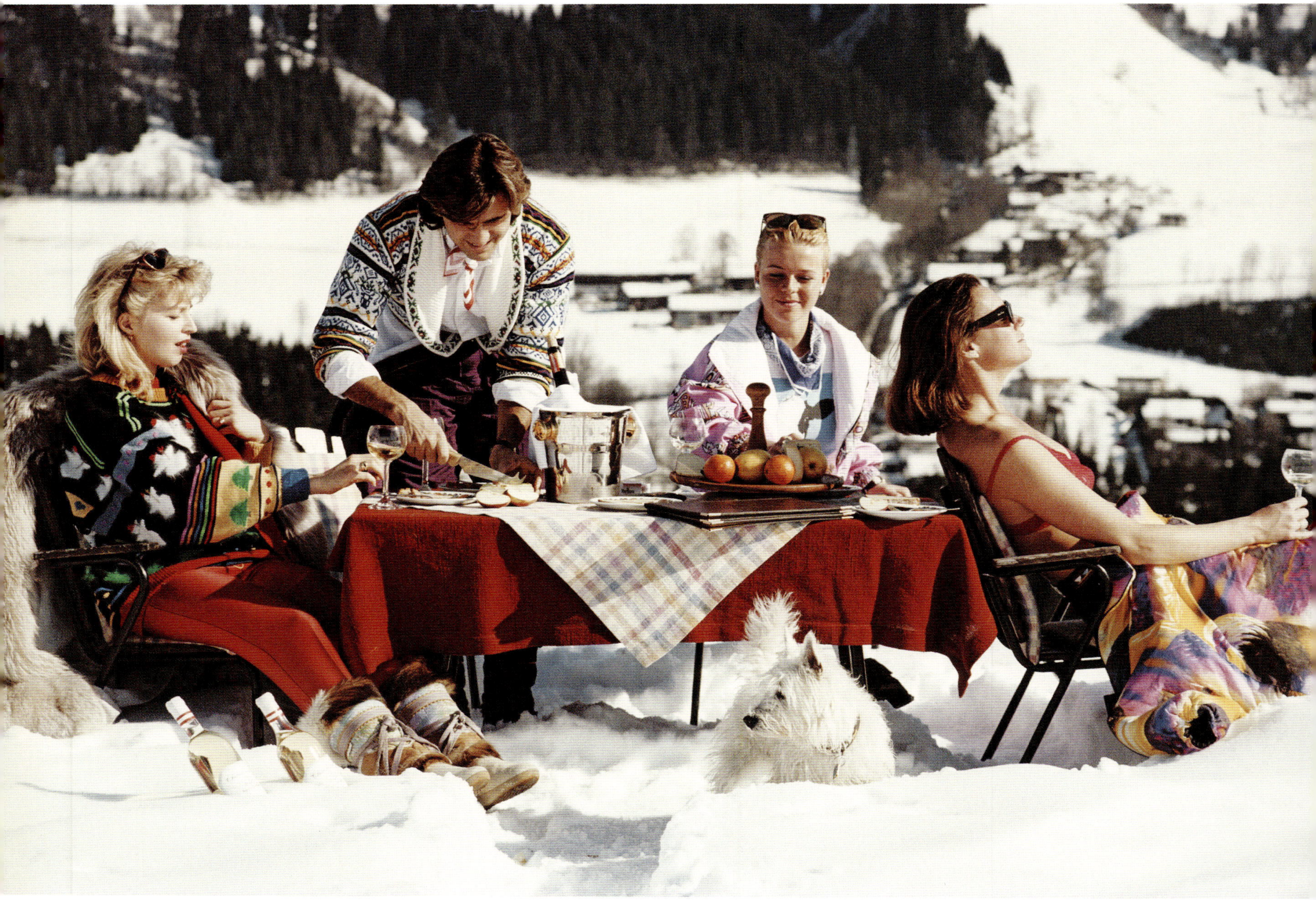

above Uschi Hagsteiner, Manfred Hagsteiner, Kim Schmidl, and Meg O'Neil enjoy a picnic catered slopeside in Kitzbühel, Austria, 1990. The Hagsteiners, longtime Kitzbühel real estate developers, kindled a friendship on the slopes with Meg O'Neil, a writer working on assignment with Slim in Austria.

opposite Relaxing in a sun trap at high altitudes is frequently known to diminish the urge to get back on the slopes, Gstaad, 1963.

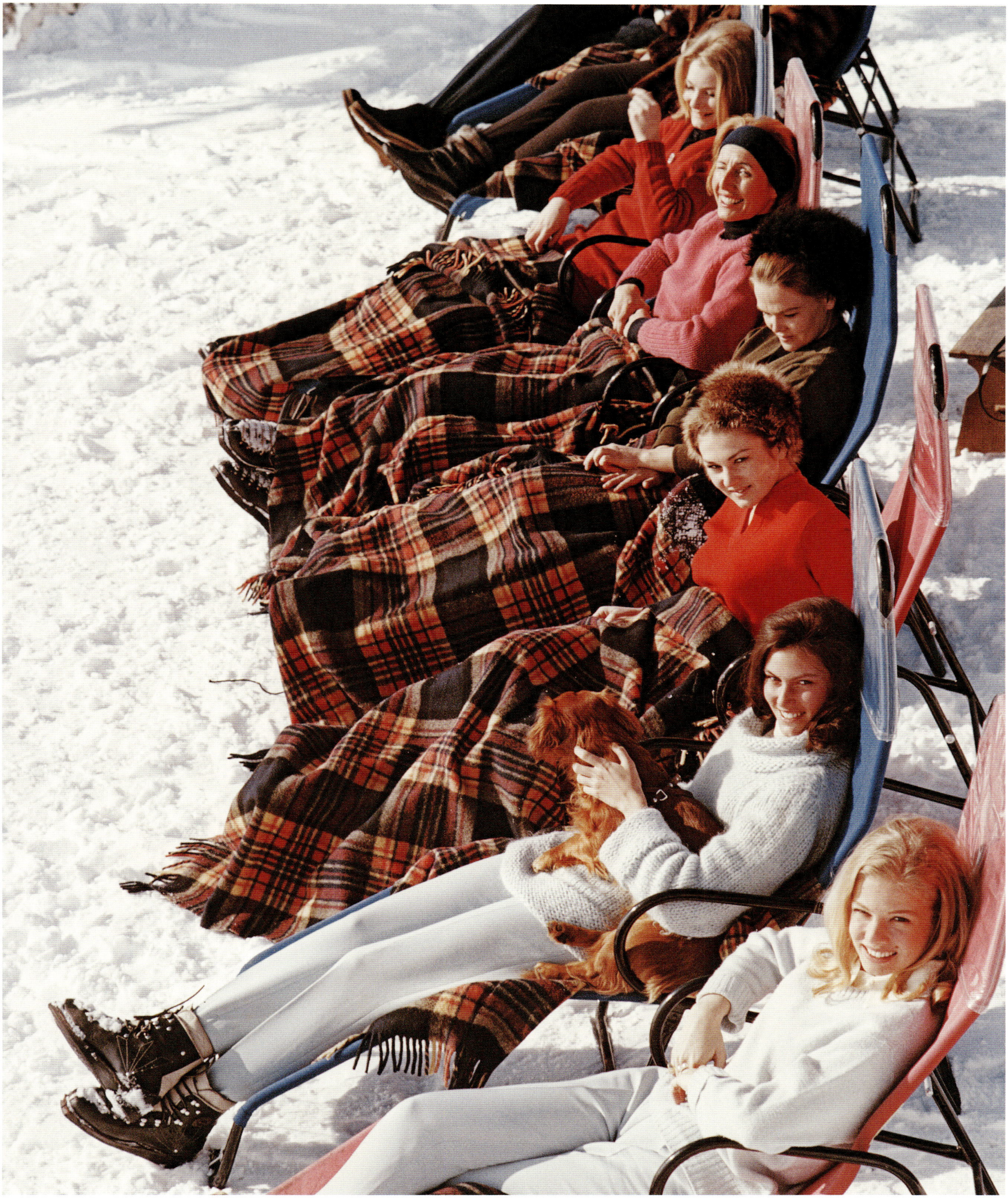

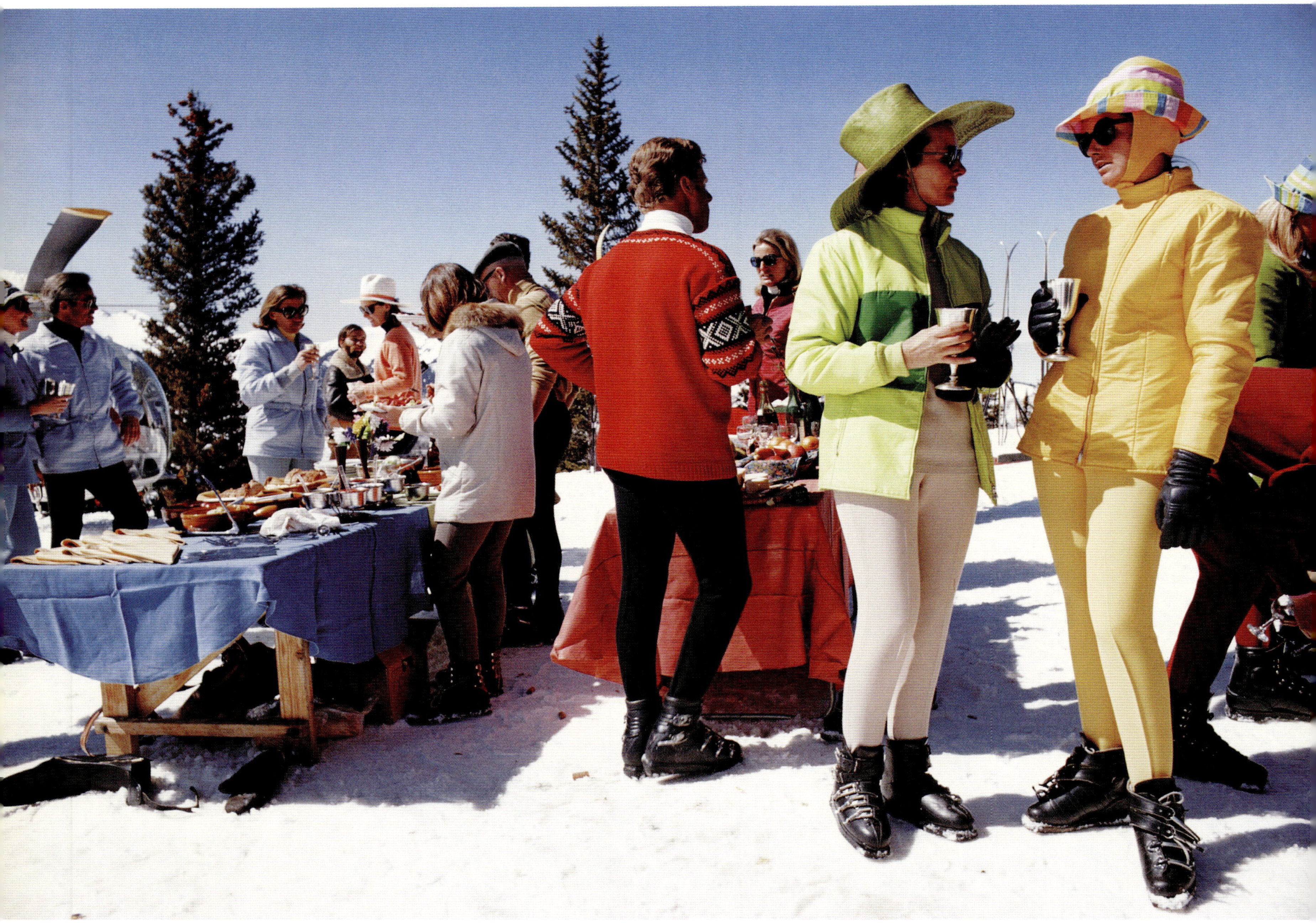

above A mid-slope break for drinks and lunch, Snowmass Village, Colorado, 1968.

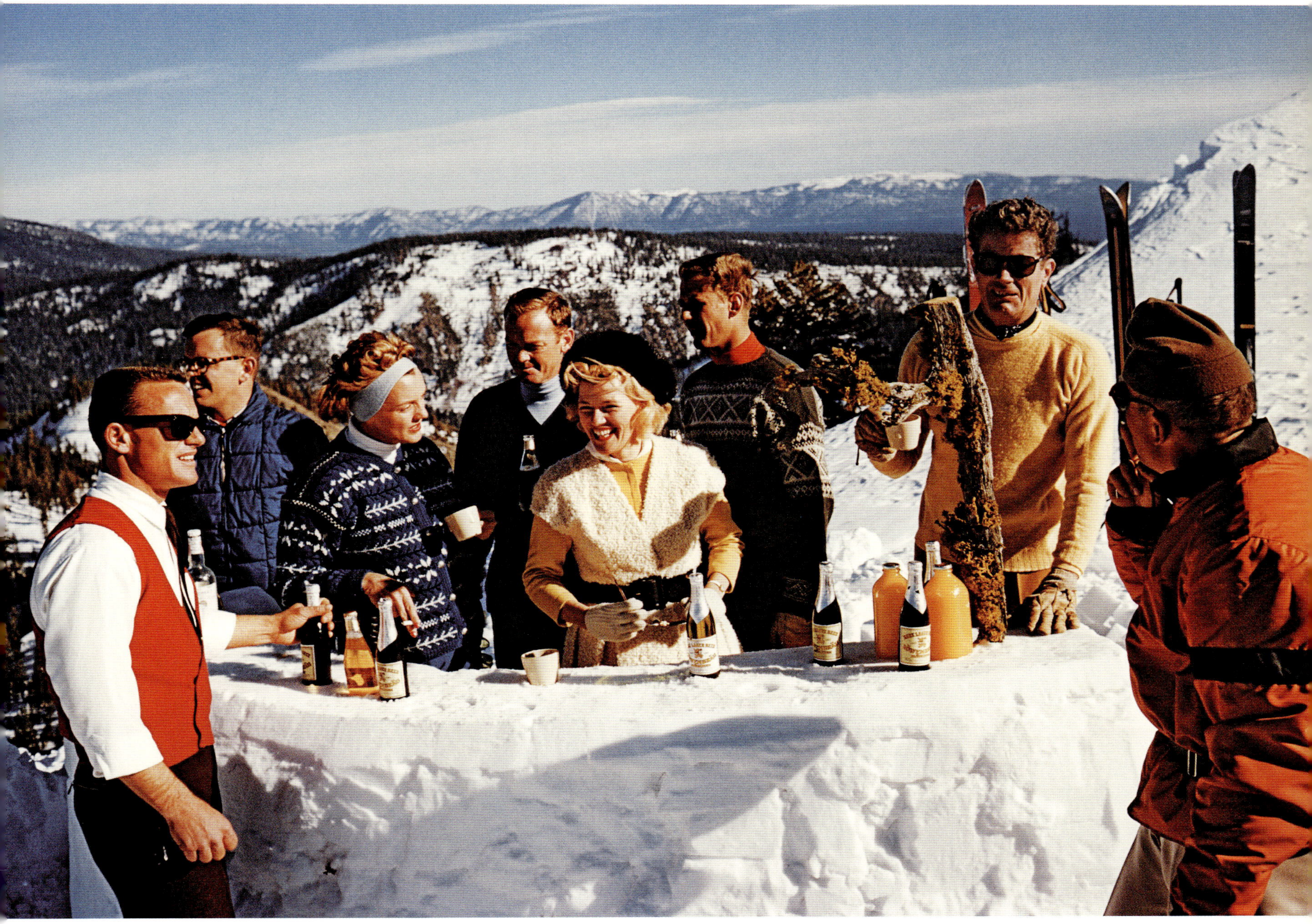

above A party of skiers adjourns for drinks at a snowbar on top of peak KT-22, Squaw Valley, California, 1961. Squaw Valley lays claim to being the pioneer ski region of the United States. Located west of Lake Tahoe in the Sierra Nevada, it was here that organized skiing began in America, as California gold miners donned wooden skis and began to compete with one another. By the 1870s, amateur skiers were racing down the slopes at speeds approaching one hundred miles an hour.

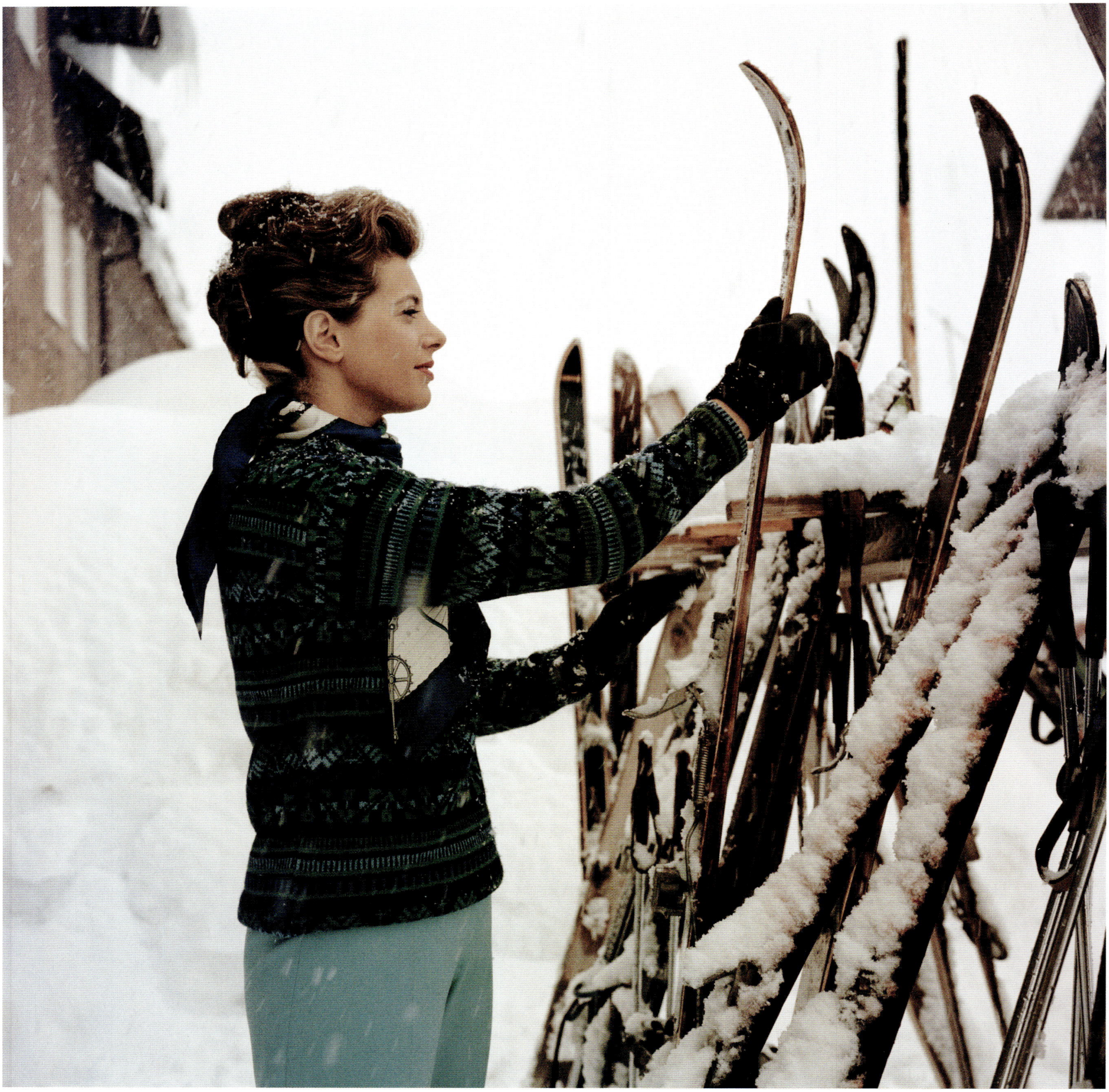

above Princess Luciana Pignatelli on a skiing holiday in Lech am Arlberg, Austria, 1961.

opposite Princess Lucy Ruspoli, Lech am Arlberg, Austria, 1979. The Lexington, Kentucky, native Lucy Young grew up in the horse world—her father having turned his considerable talents to thoroughbred racing after making a fortune on a humble commodity: the peanut. From a very different realm, her husband, Prince Mario Ruspoli, was born into an old and noble Italian family whose roots in Florence date to the thirteenth century. The two wed in 1978 and chose Lech for their first winter foray (see also page 78).

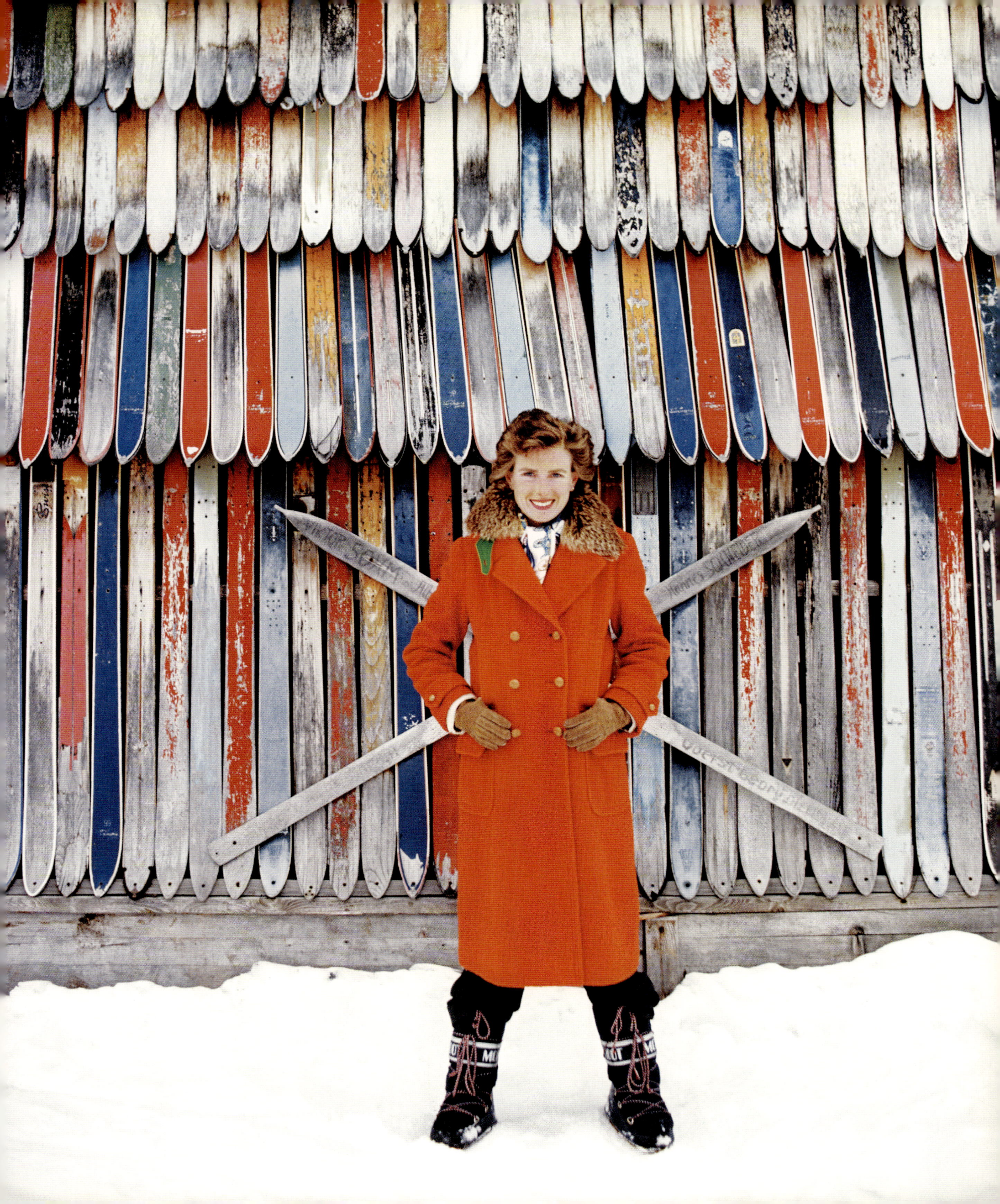

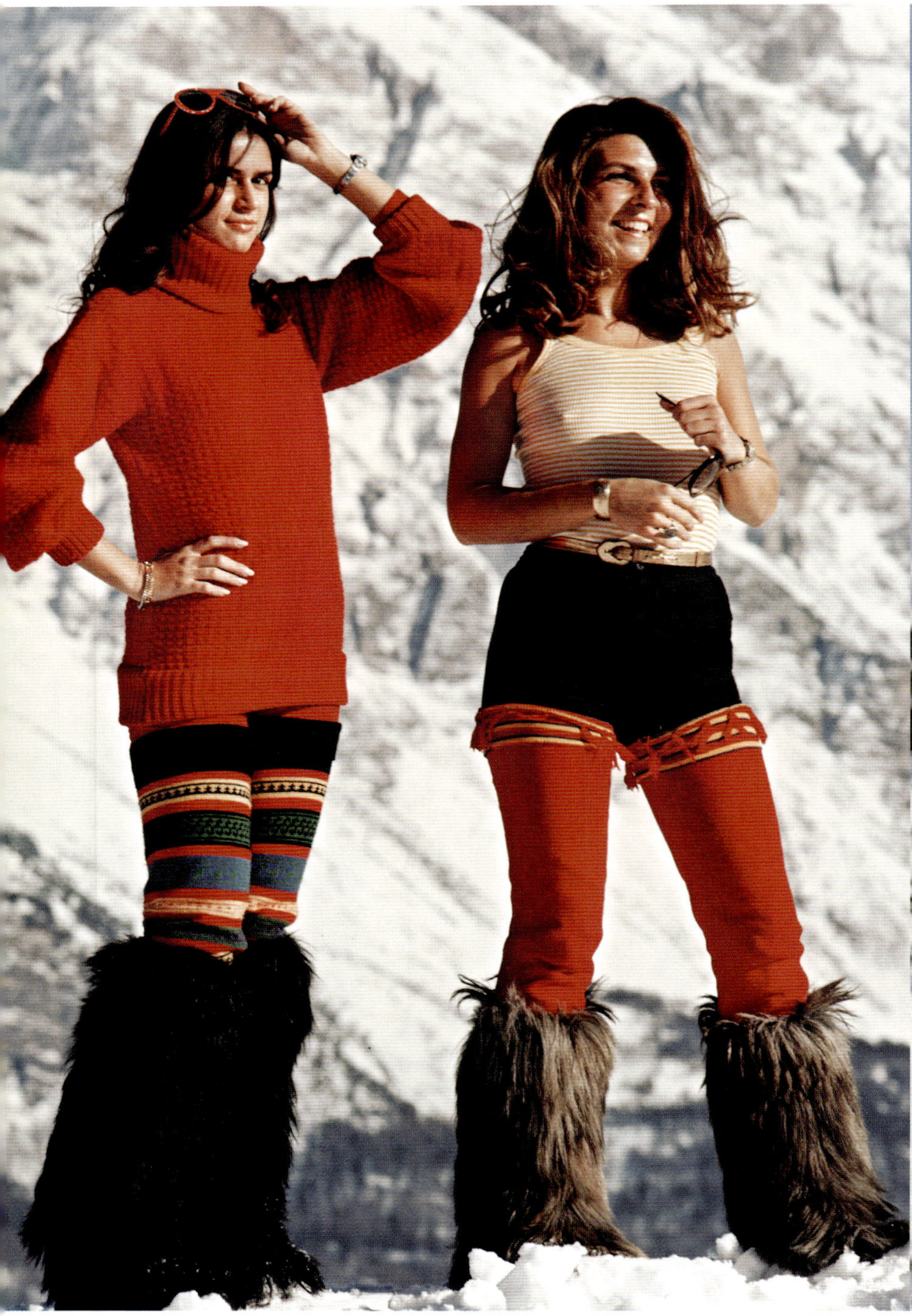

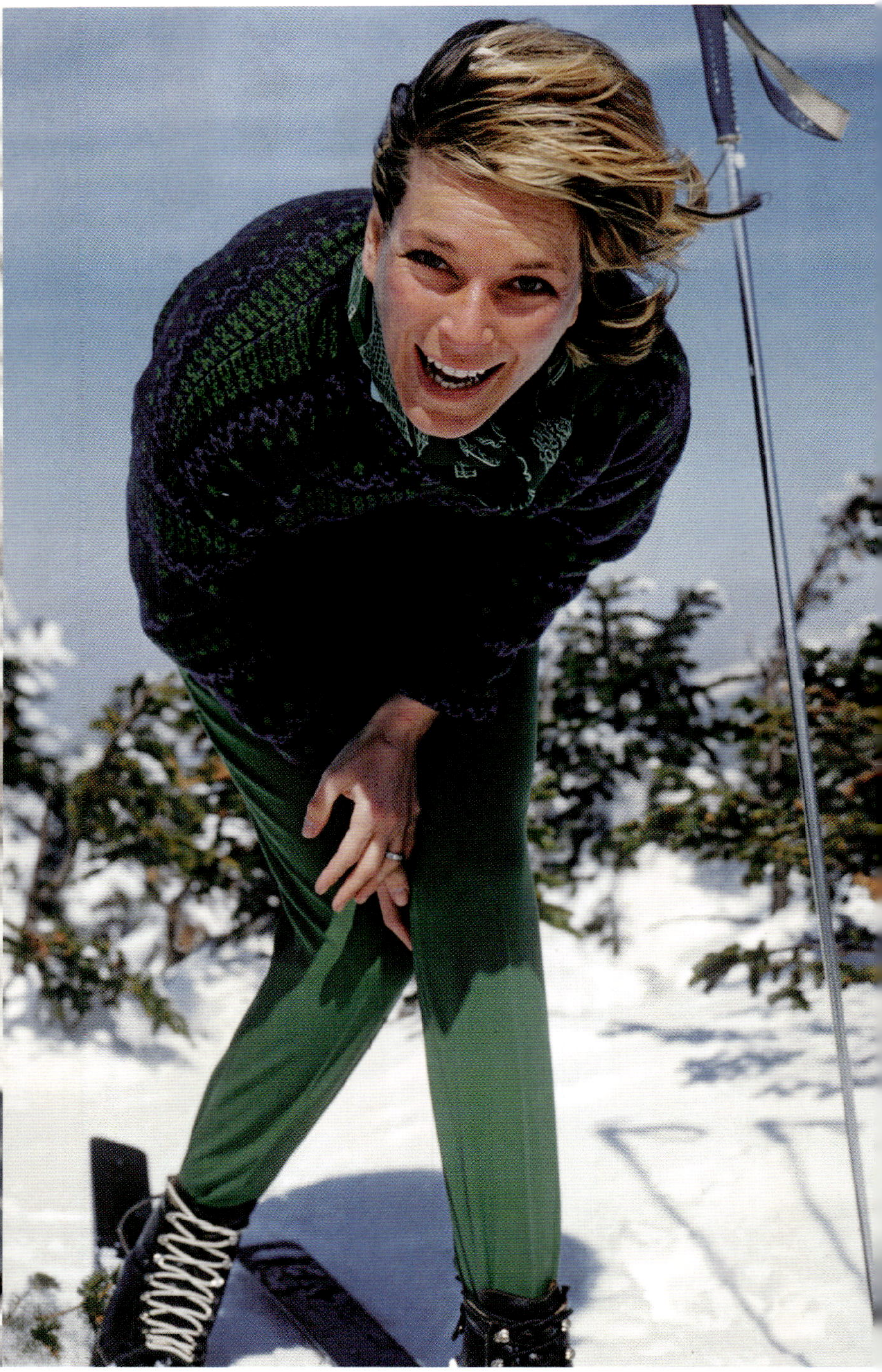

above left Après-ski enthusiasts Manuela Boraomanero and Emanuela Beghelli at the Italian ski resort Cortina d'Ampezzo, 1976.

above right Nan Kempner on the ski slopes at Sugarbush Resort, Warren, Vermont, 1960. Kempner was a New York socialite, famous for charity fund-raising and for her devotion to fashion. Born to a wealthy family in San Francisco, she was reportedly advised by her father, "You'll never make it on your face, so you'd better be interesting." Interesting she was. Known for her self-deprecating sense of humor and her slim-as-a-celery-stalk figure, she was a fixture at top social gatherings all over the world. What she loved best was buying, wearing, and collecting clothes. She amassed the largest private collection in her day of haute couture clothing, including dozens of pieces by Mainbocher, Yves Saint Laurent, and Bill Blass. She was often quoted for the memorable quip, "I tell people all the time I want to be buried naked. I know there will be a store where I'm going."

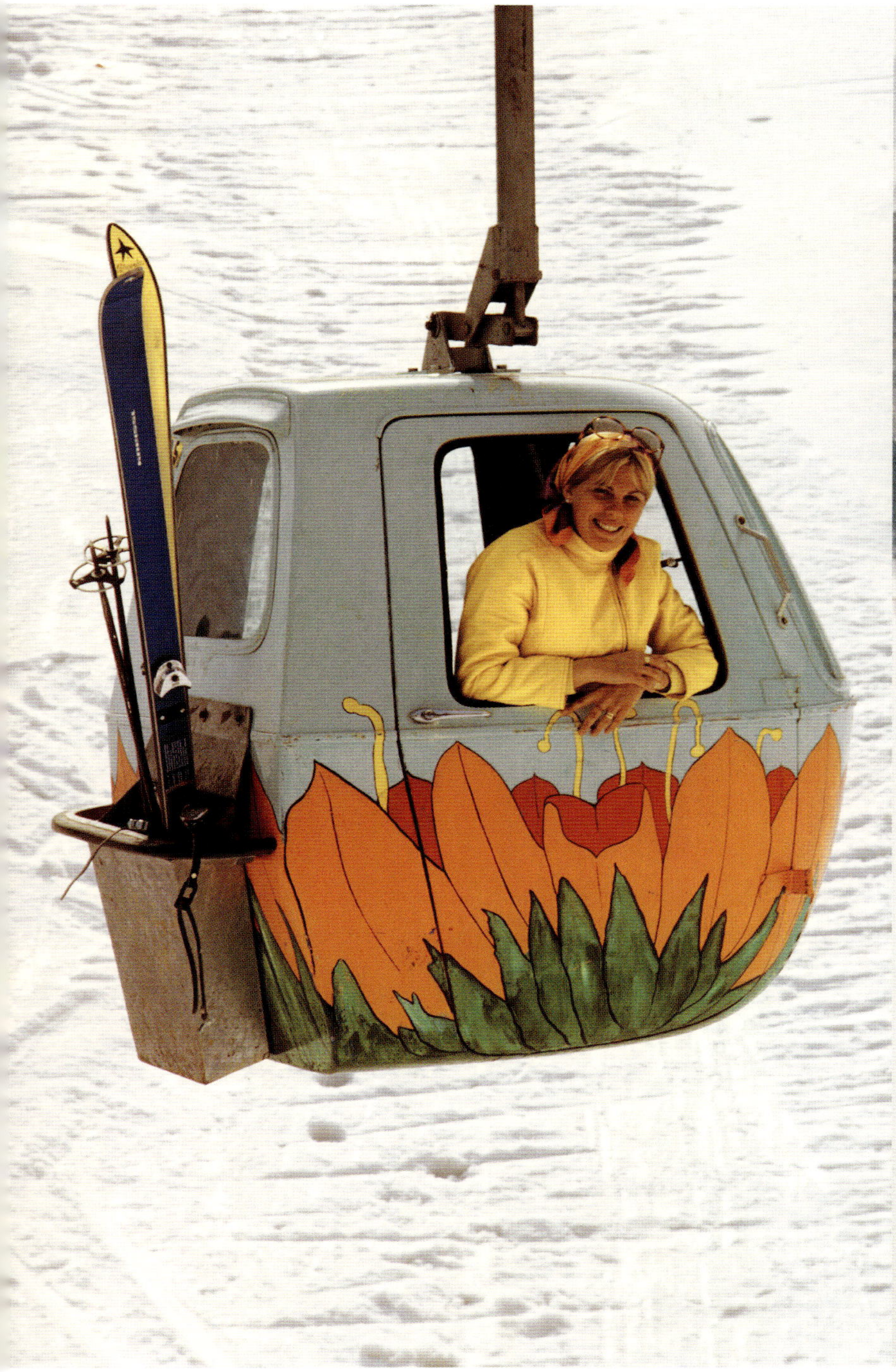

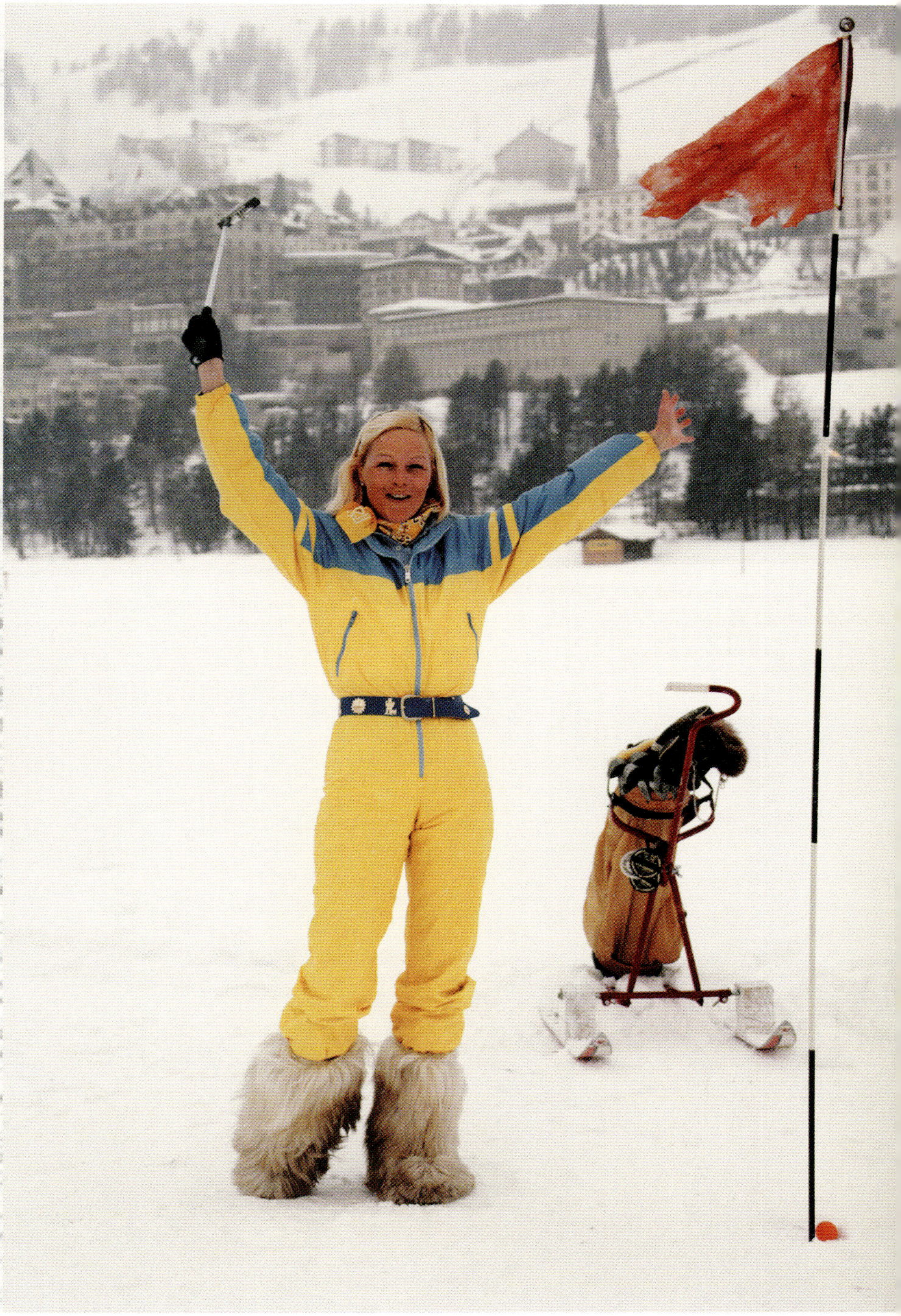

above left A skier at the window of a cable car at the Sugarbush Resort, Warren, Vermont, circa 1960. In his first book, *A Wonderful Time*, Slim wrote: "The big problem for a magazine photographer on a skiing assignment is that all slopes look pretty much alike. To solve this, you have to try for different backgrounds. Over the past twenty years I must have visited Sugarbush a dozen times. It was one of the first resorts to install the colorful gondola lift and had perhaps the first discotheque in America, the Ski Club Ten, a small, very simple, but very nice private club at the foot of the slopes where you could have lunch or après-ski drinks."

above right Didi Fenton celebrates a hole in one on the frozen, snow-covered lake, St. Moritz, 1983. Slim did more stories on this Swiss ski resort than perhaps any other in Europe. Each time he arrived in town, he looked for new ways to report on the famous town's allures. There were always plenty of interesting and glamorous people to photograph on the slopes. The more difficult task was finding activities to photograph beyond skiing and basking on sun-splashed terraces. When his pal Fenton mentioned that she practiced golf on the frozen Lake St. Moritz, he knew he'd found a fresh idea for a shot. Fenton and her husband, Oscar S. Schafer, who is chairman of the New York Philharmonic, have been sponsoring the orchestra's free parks concerts since 2007.

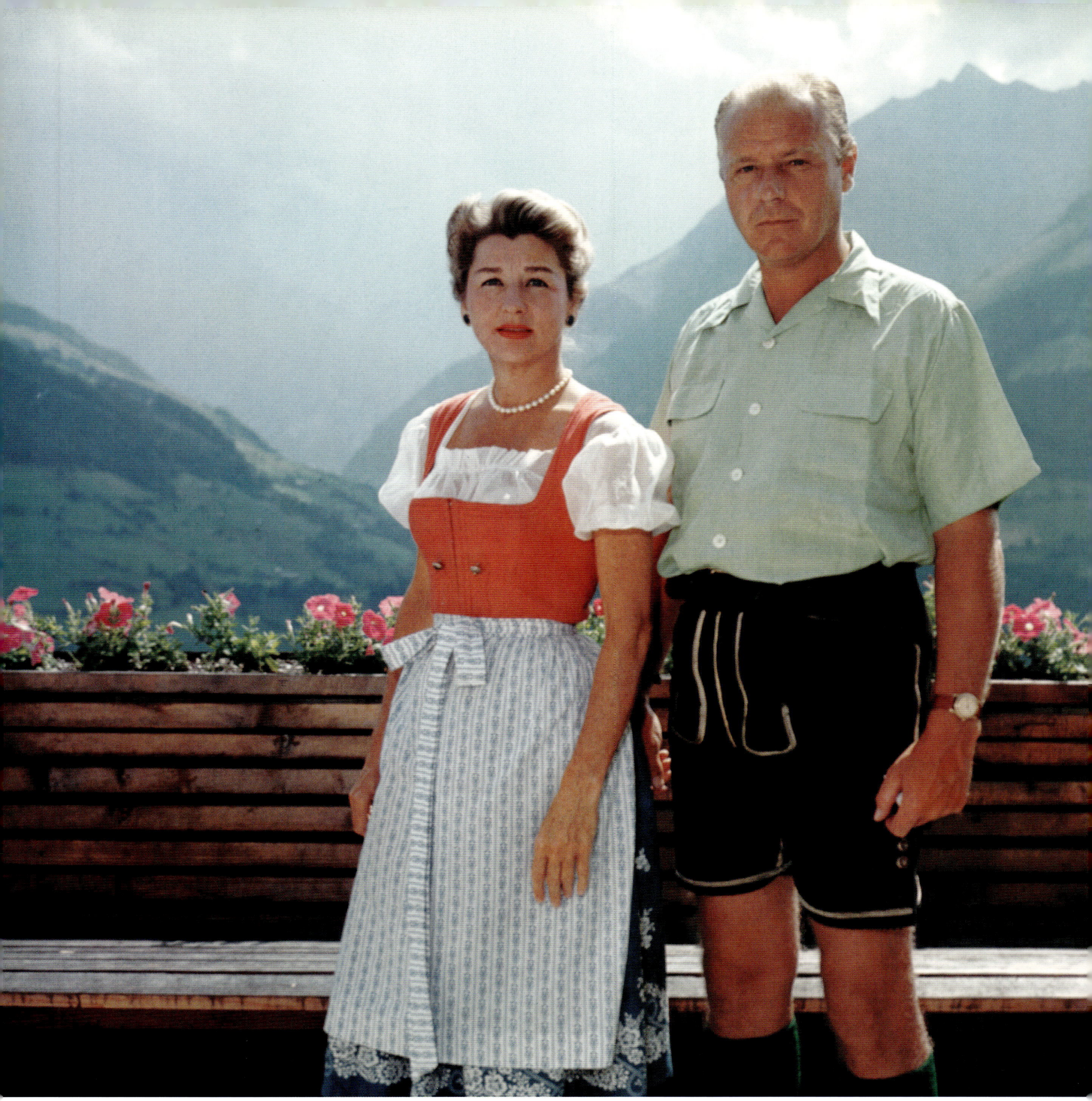

above Prince and Princess Alexander von Hohenlohe-Waldenburg-Schillingfurst in Tyrolean dress, high in the Austrian Alps, 1958. "I could have been a queen but I settled for being a princess," the vivacious and witty Honeychile Wilder is said to have quipped shortly after her marriage to Prince Hohenlohe. Her not-so-veiled reference was to a previous dalliance she'd reportedly had with King Farouk of Egypt. The spirited showgirl from Georgia, known around the world as "Honeychile," is said to have been the inspiration behind the Ian Fleming character Honeychile Rider in the novel

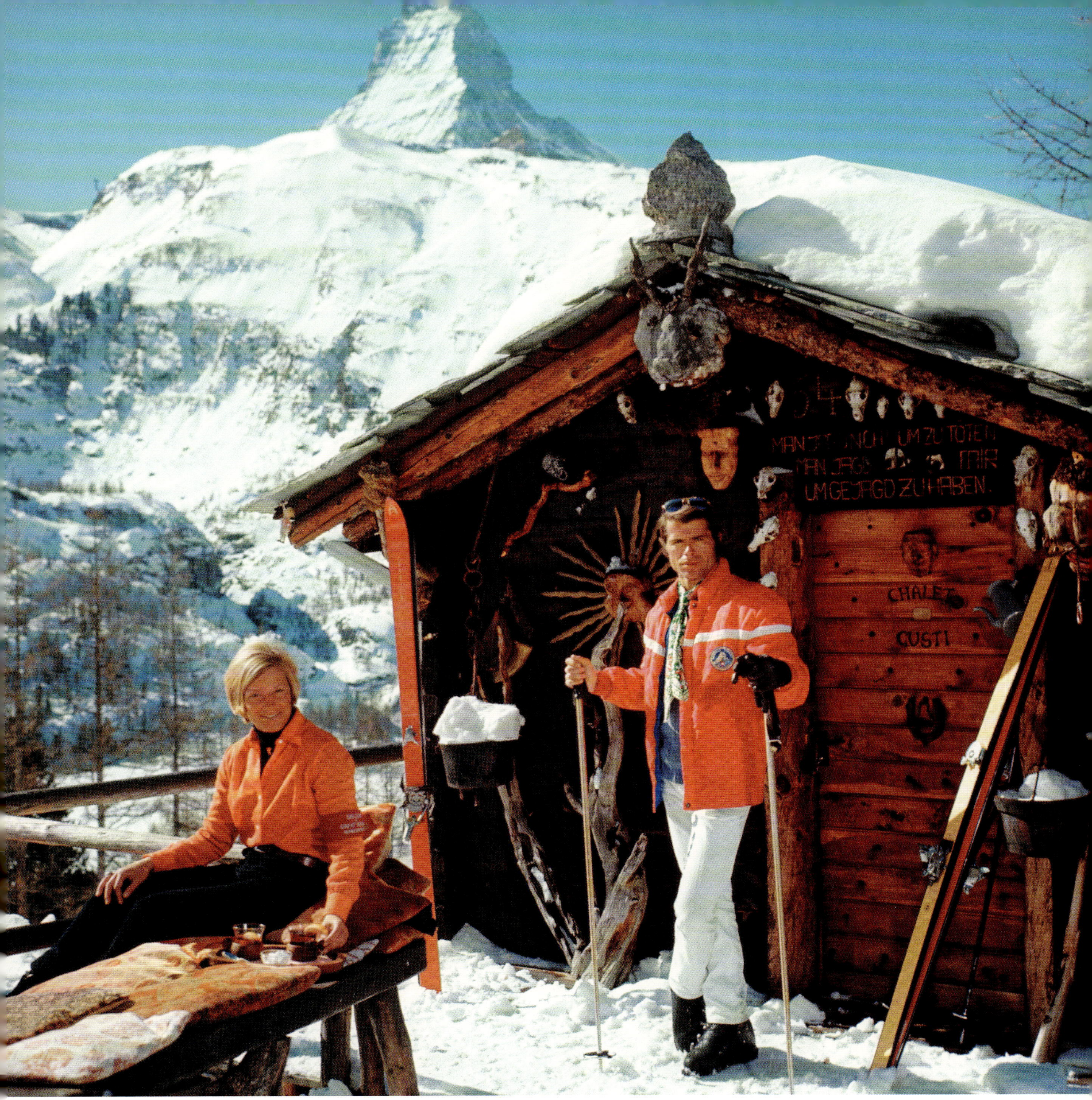

Dr. No (renamed Honey Ryder in the film). Despite her wild and willful ways, her marriage to Prince Hohenlohe—it was her third and his second—held. They spent most of their thirty years of marriage as the favored center of their social set, traveling to their various homes around the world (see also page 207).

above Skiers outside the Chalet Costi, Zermatt, 1968.

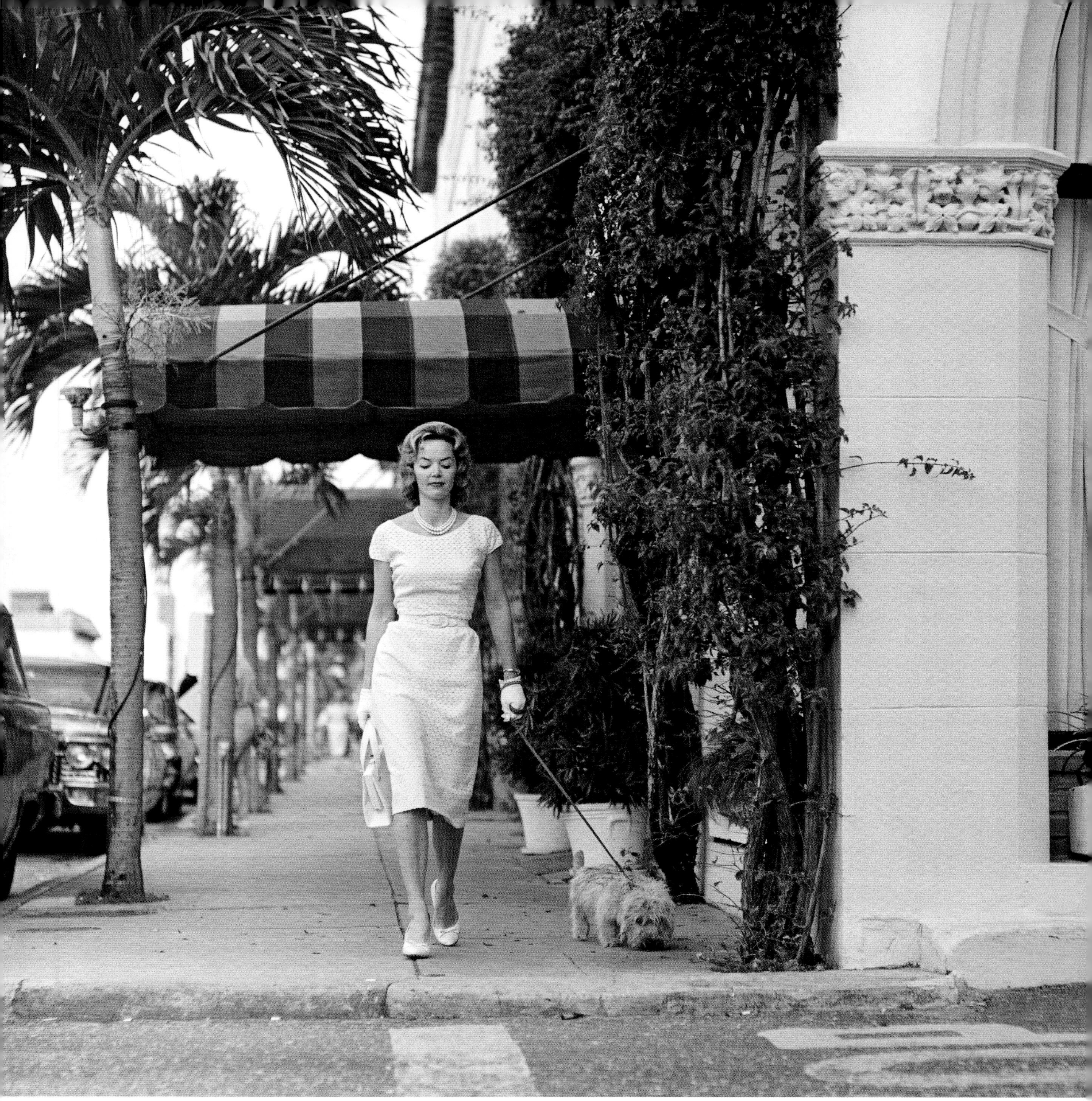

above Jane Dudley walks her Dandie Dinmont Terrier "Tiger" on Worth Avenue, Palm Beach, circa 1955. When southern belle Jane Anderson married Guilford Dudley Jr., the shy and patrician insurance executive from Nashville, they began their reign as one of the South's great power couples, regarded by some as Nashville royalty. Just before he was appointed the ambassador to Denmark in 1969 under the Nixon administration, she founded the Swan Ball, which celebrated its fiftieth anniversary in 2012, and remains one of the grandest of all southern social affairs.

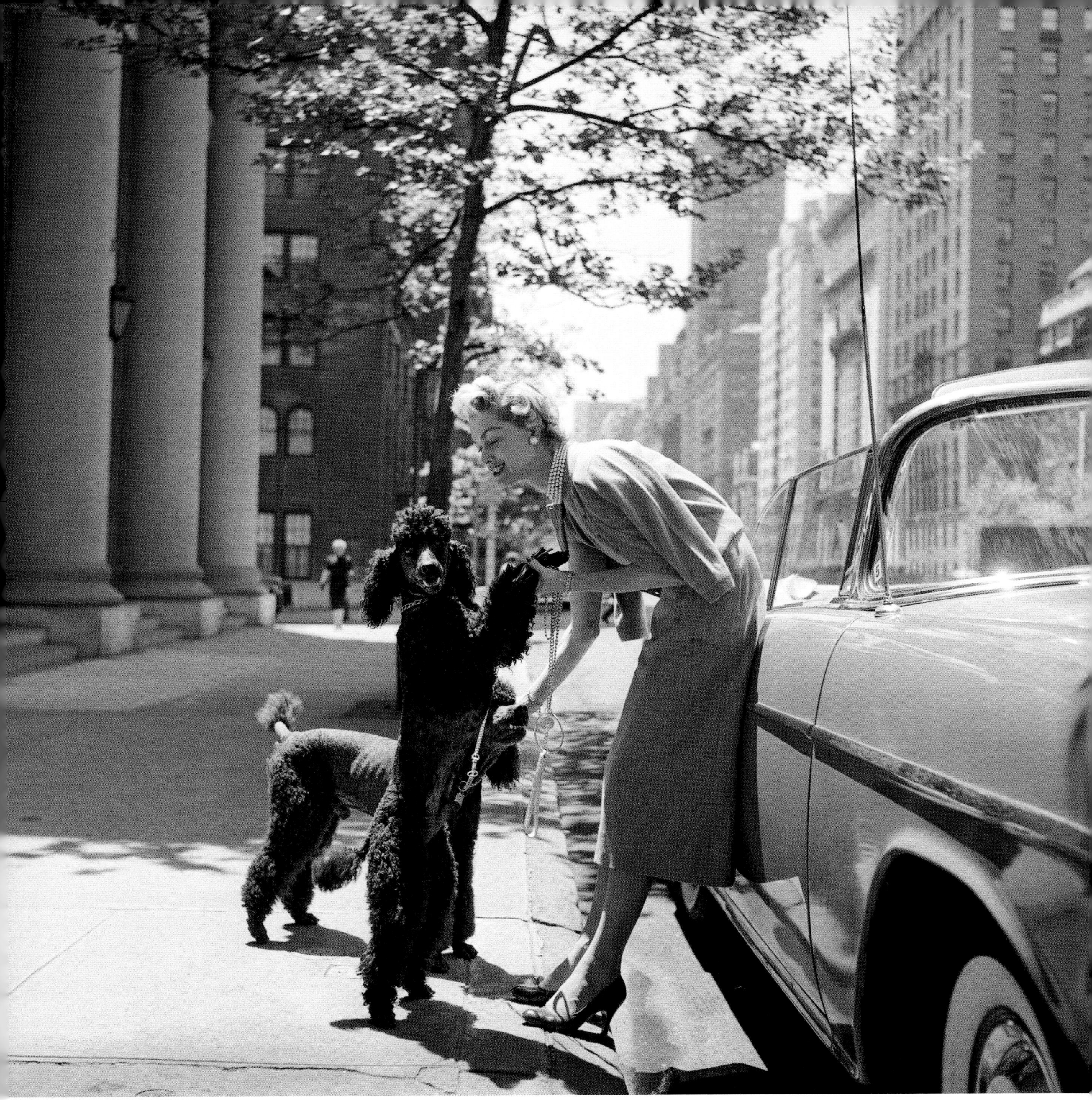

above Model with black standard poodles, Park Avenue, New York, 1954. Slim took this photo for a story on Park Avenue for *Holiday* magazine. The tone of the story typified the erudite, witty tone that the formidable travel magazine was known for. The article carried an amusing subtitle: "Here is the frank, brilliantly engaging story of Manhattan's Golden Miles—the romanticized, glamorized, scandalized, one and only Park Avenue. Is it really the citadel of Manhattan Society or just the street 'where bad girls walk good dogs'?"

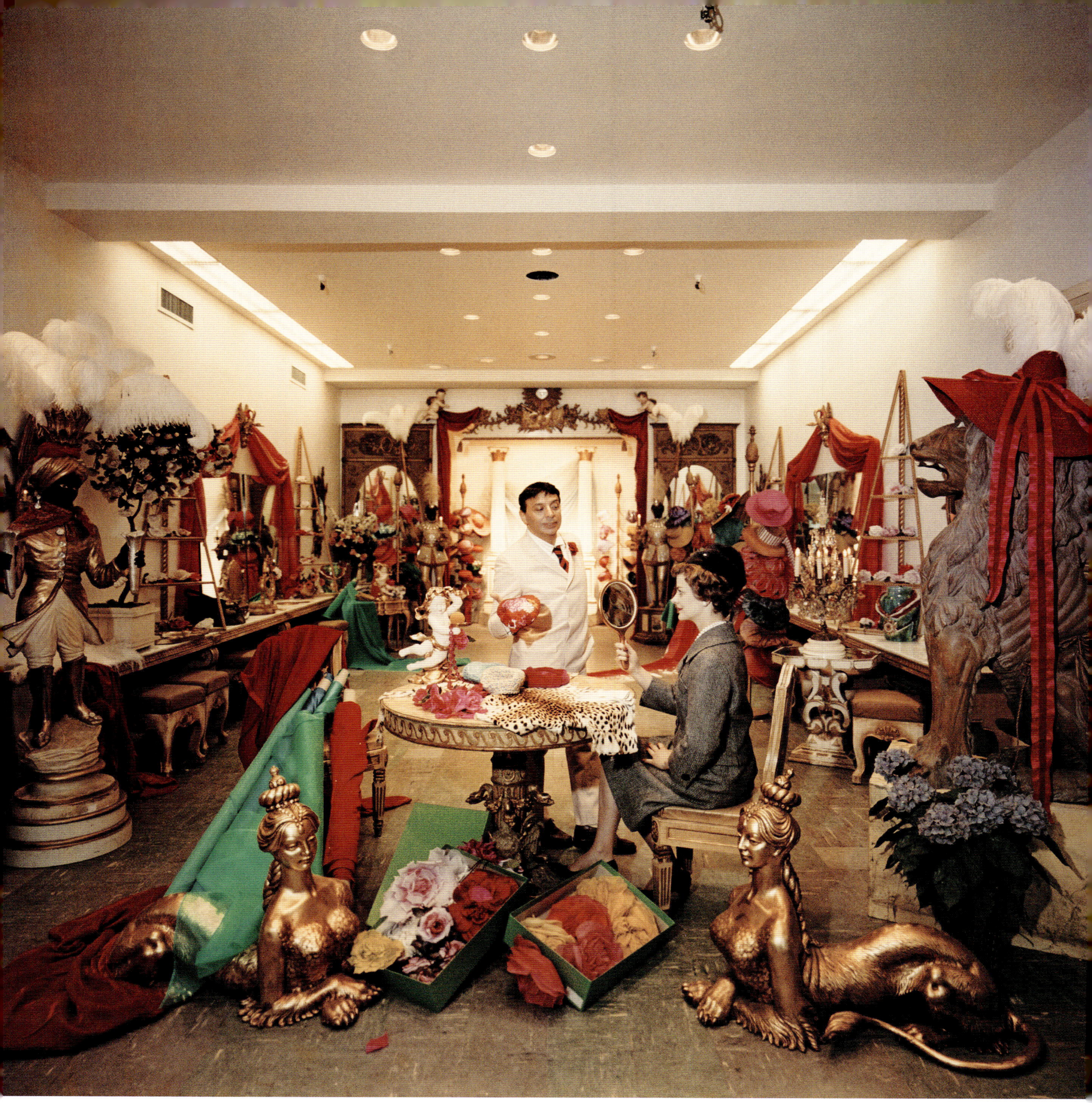

above As a socialite and a *Vogue* editor, Denise Lawson-Johnston is doubly compelled to consider the offerings of couturier-milliner John P. John, known as "the King of the Hatters," in his white and gold salon on West Fifty-Seventh Street, New York, circa 1960. He roamed the world searching for materials, styles, and objets d'art worthy of his discerning customers. His advertising tagline beckoned, "Stroll with me through my garden and fashion your own incredibly beautiful bouquet."

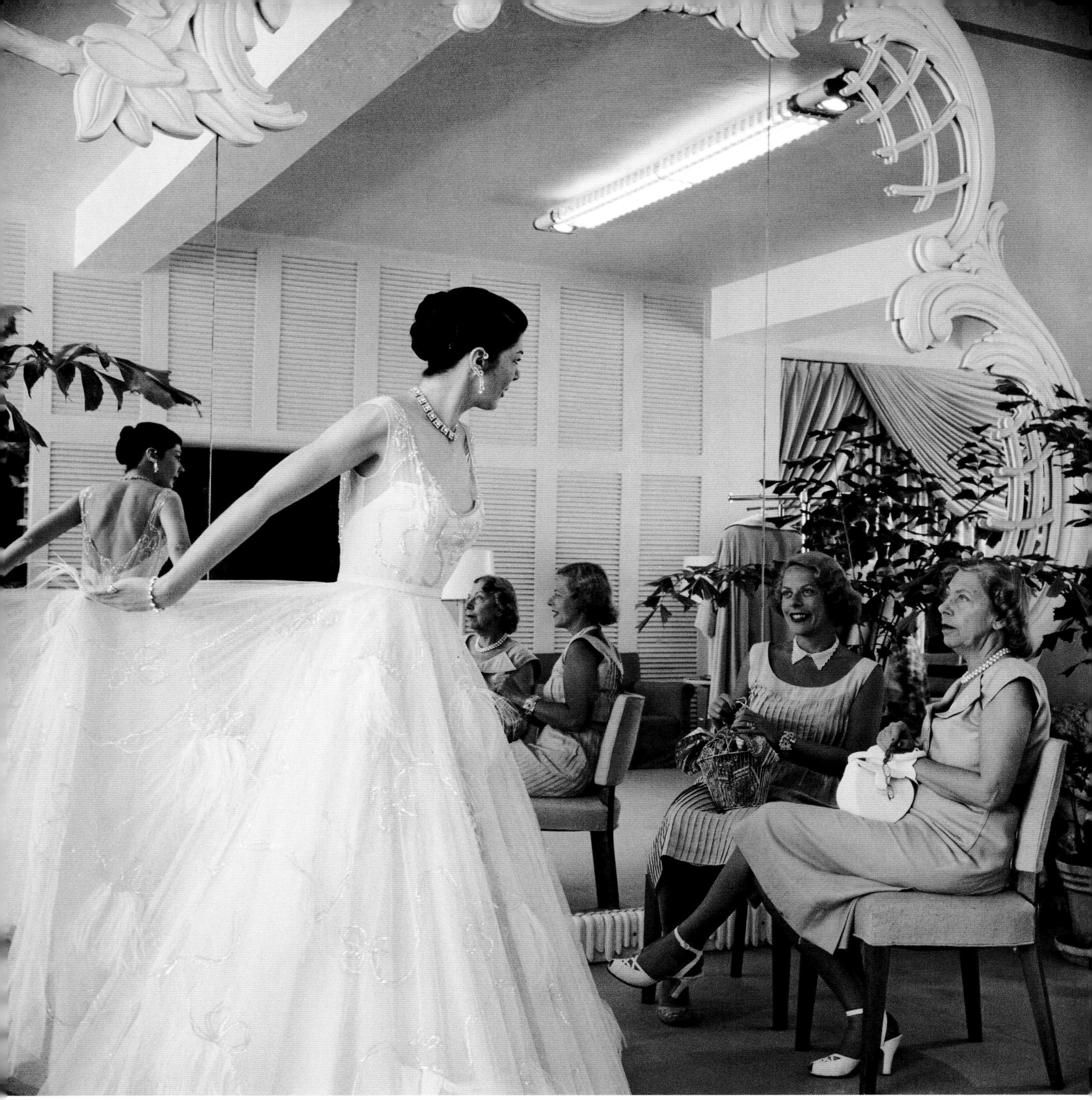

above Mrs. T. R. Potter (left) and Mrs. Edward Magnus at a Saks Fifth Avenue fashion show, Worth Avenue, Palm Beach, circa 1955.

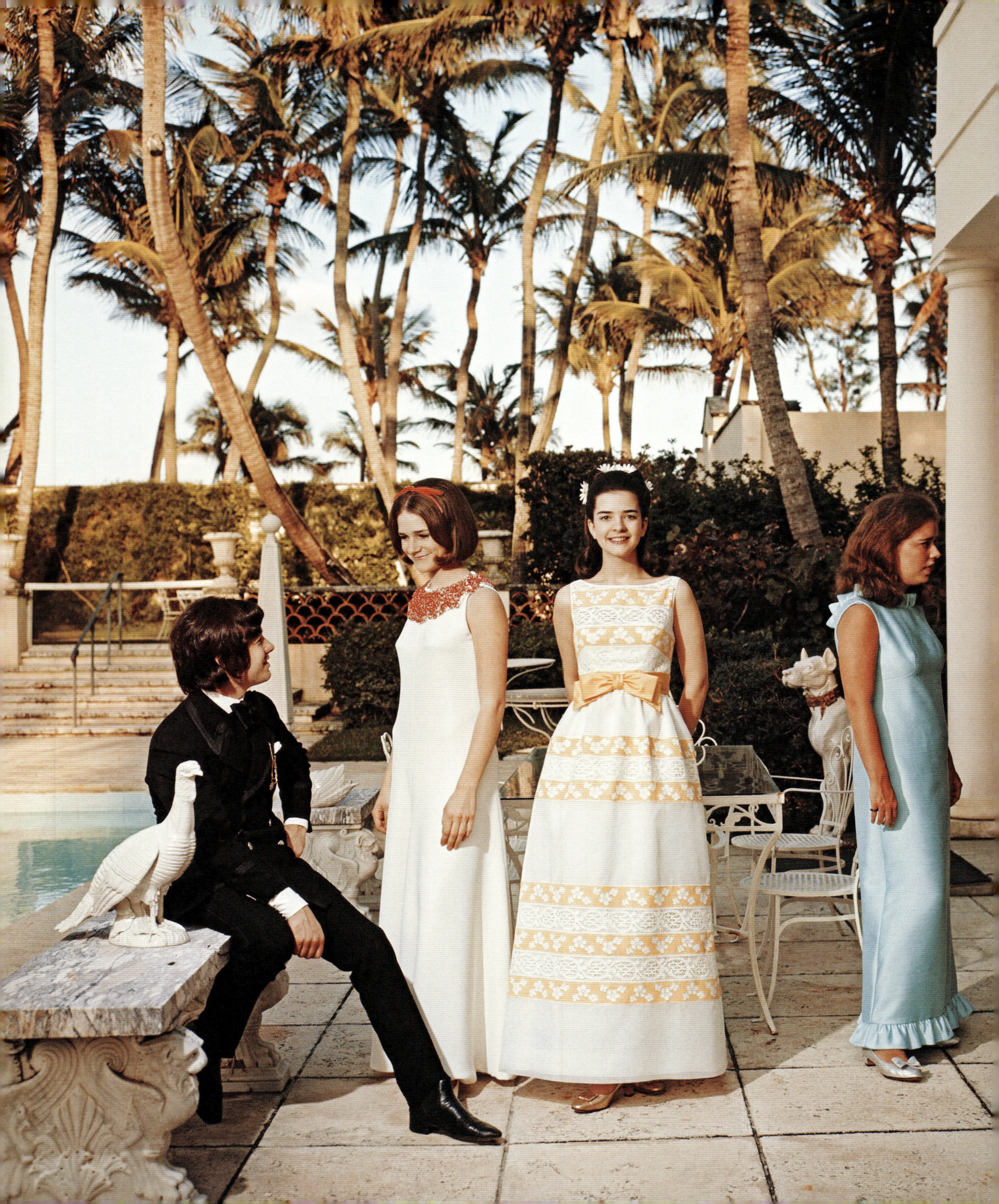

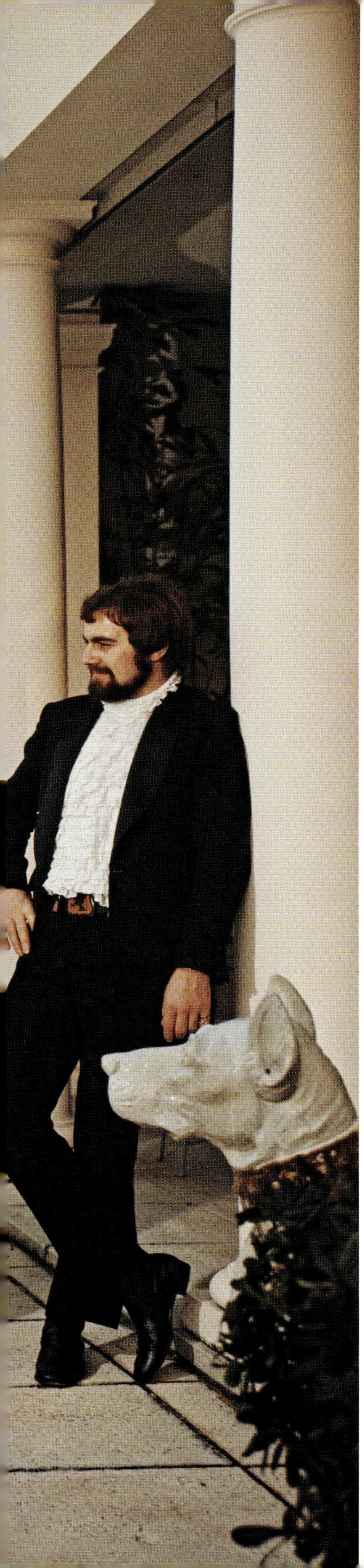

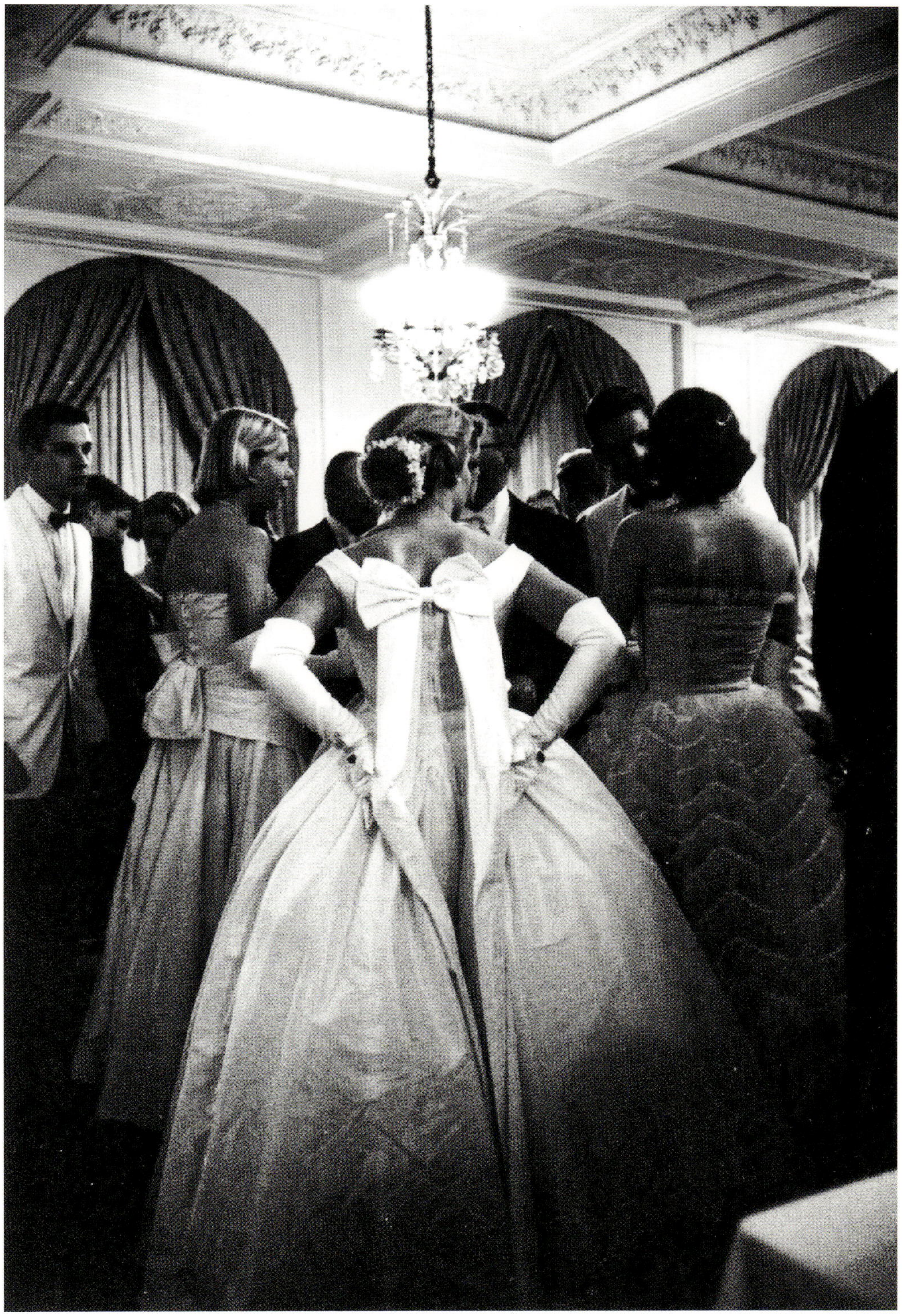

opposite Debutantes, Palm Beach, 1968.

above The season's debs and their escorts prepare to perform at a debutante ball, Copley Plaza Hotel, Boston, 1958.

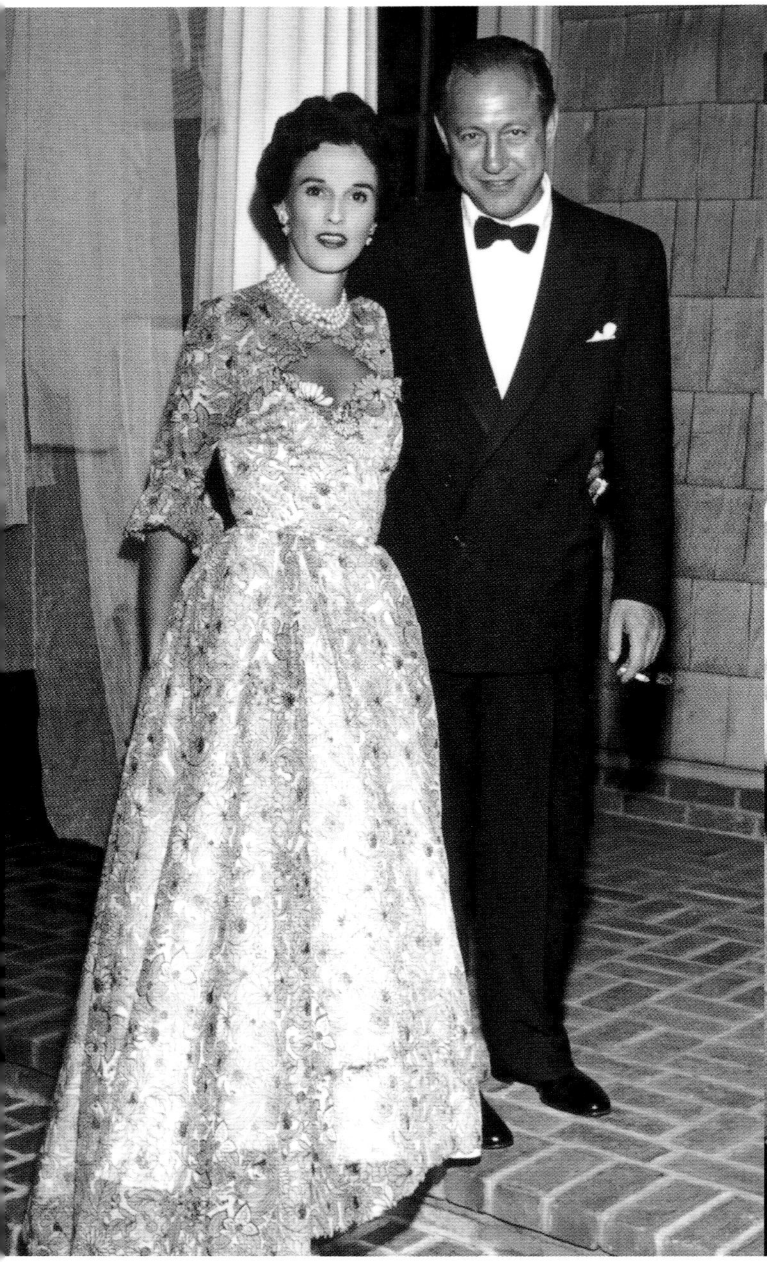

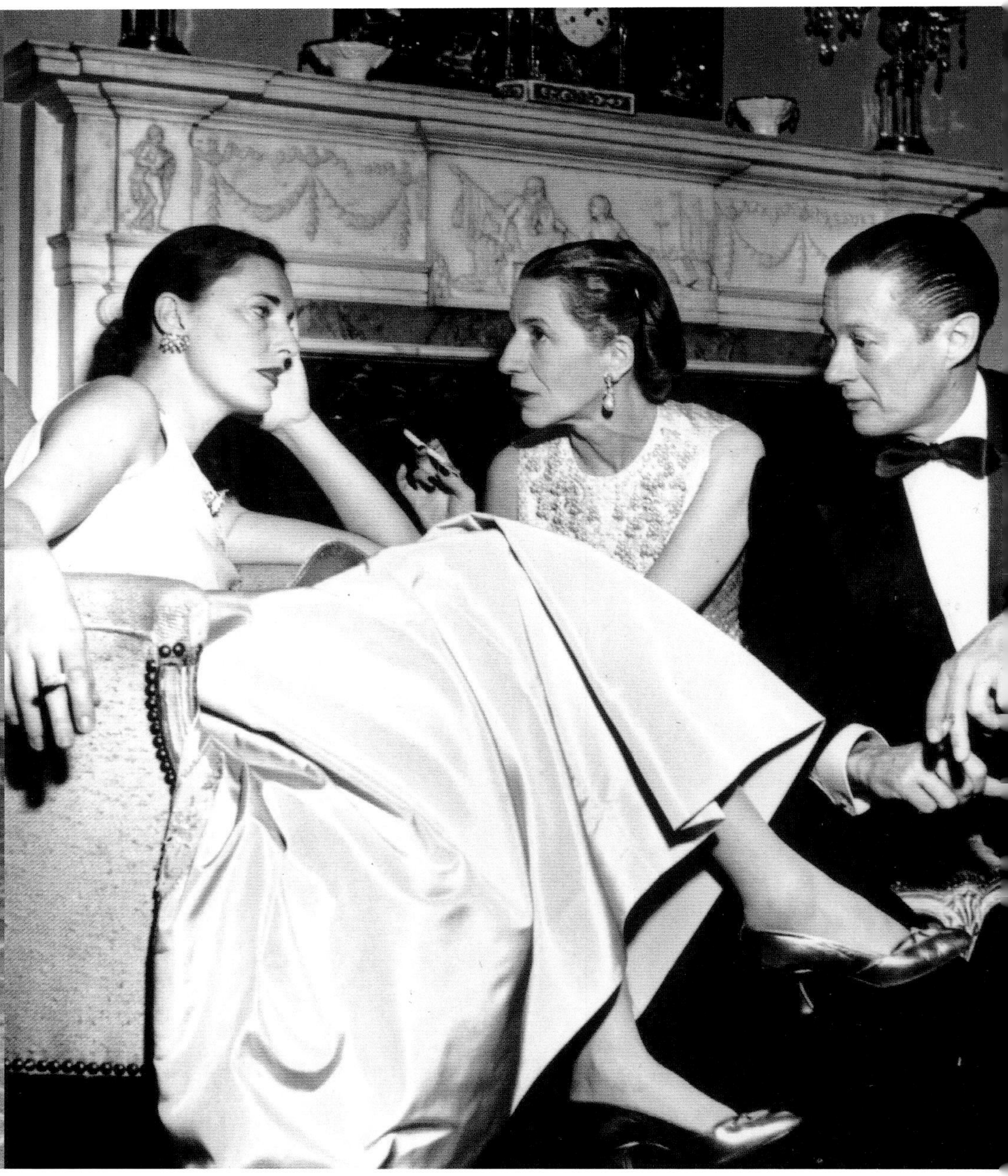

above left William S. Paley, chairman of CBS, and his wife Babe (see also page 36) at the going-away party for her niece Sara Roosevelt, Manhasset, New York, circa 1952. The party was held at Greentree, the four-hundred-acre Long Island estate of Sara's parents, Jock Whitney and Betsey Roosevelt Whitney.

above right Slim Hawks (left) chatting with the *Vogue* editor Diana Vreeland and her husband, Reed, at Kitty Miller's New Year's Eve party on Park Avenue, New York, 1952. Slim Hawks was a California girl who struck it big in Hollywood and Broadway circles, becoming a socialite and fashion icon of the 1950s and 1960s. Married first to the legendary director Howard Hawks and then to the theatrical producer Leland Hayward, Hawks may have been admired—but Vreeland was worshipped. Imitated and adulated—and at times excoriated—Vreeland was the American original who headed *Harper's Bazaar* magazine for

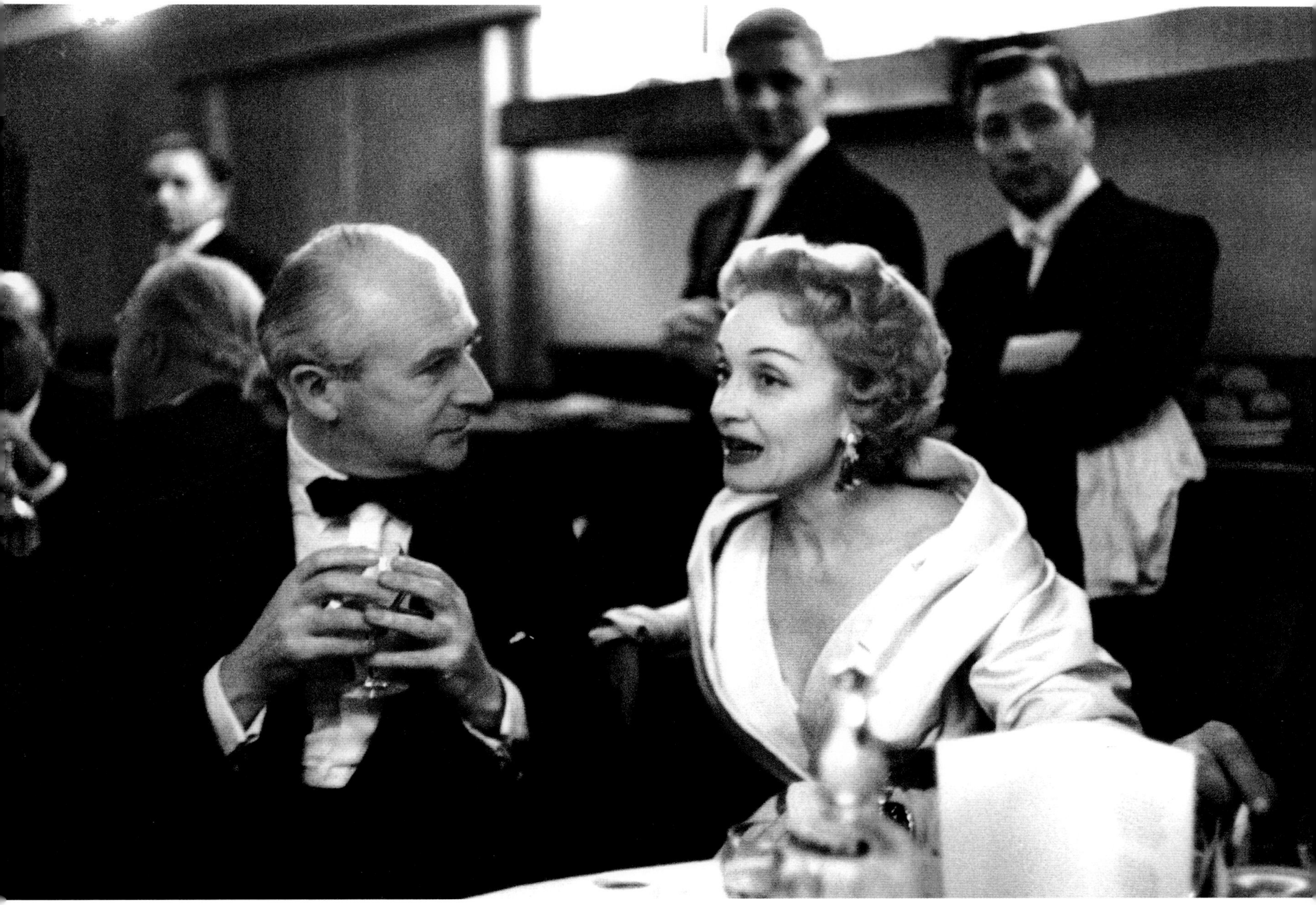

twenty-three years and *Vogue* magazine for nine years. Her admirers called her "the High Priestess of Fashion," "the Archpresbyter of Elegance," and "the Vicaress of Style." Though imperious and unpredictable, she could never have been accused of vacillating. Her definition of originality went something like this: "The energy of imagination, deliberation, and invention, which fall into a natural rhythm totally one's own, maintained by innate discipline and a keen sense of pleasure—these are the ingredients of style. And all who have it share one thing: originality."

above Cecil Beaton—the celebrated costume and set designer, fashion photographer, and diarist—and film star Marlene Dietrich in conversation at Lord Camrose's election-day party at the Savoy Hotel, London, 1955.

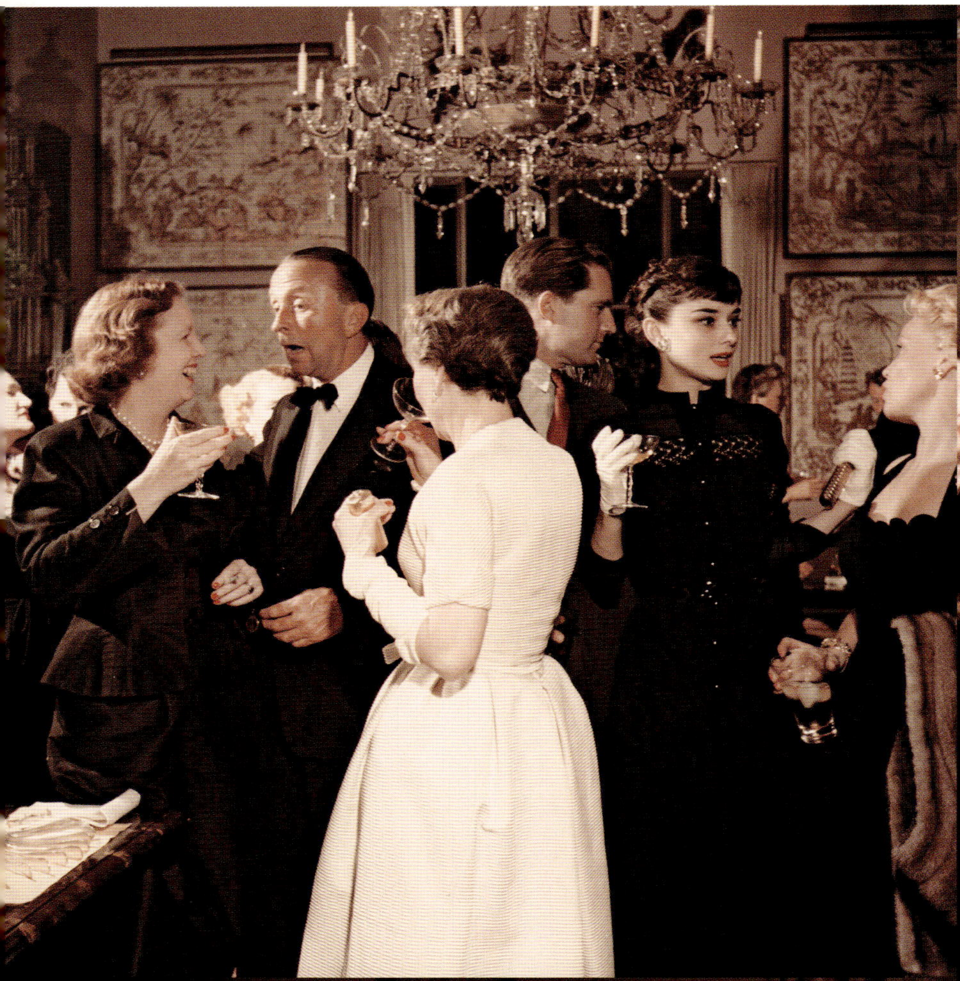
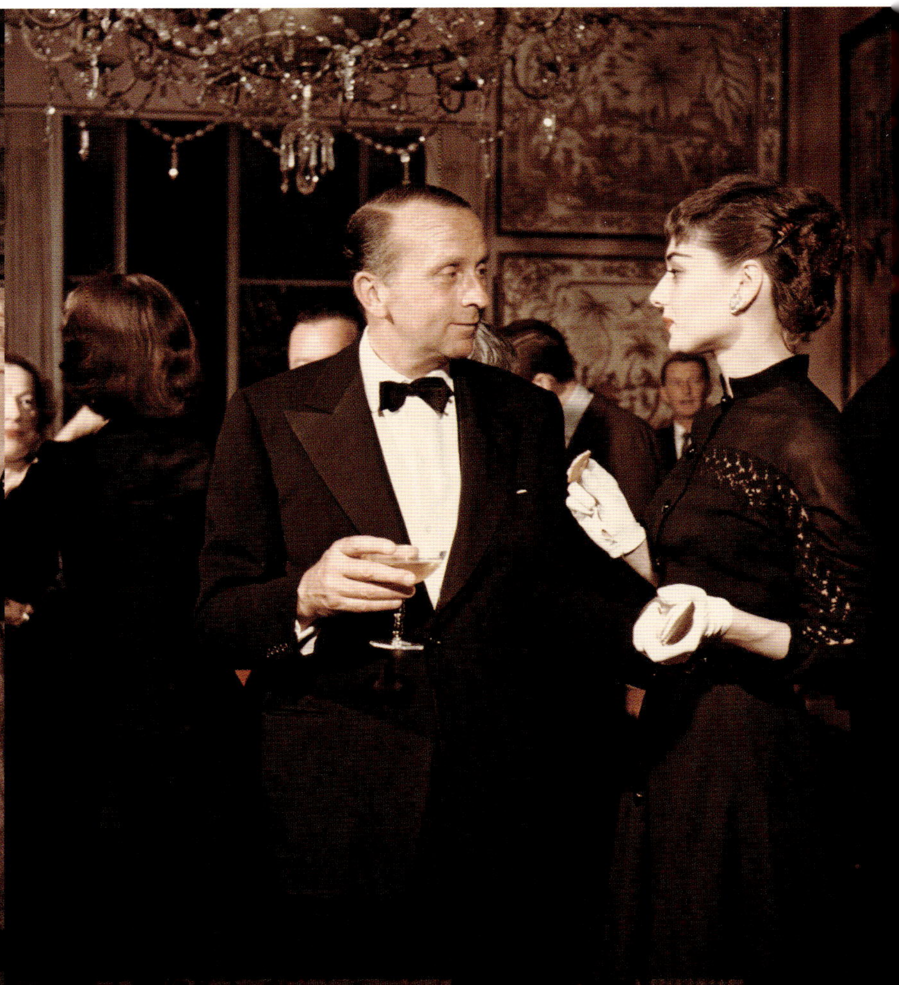
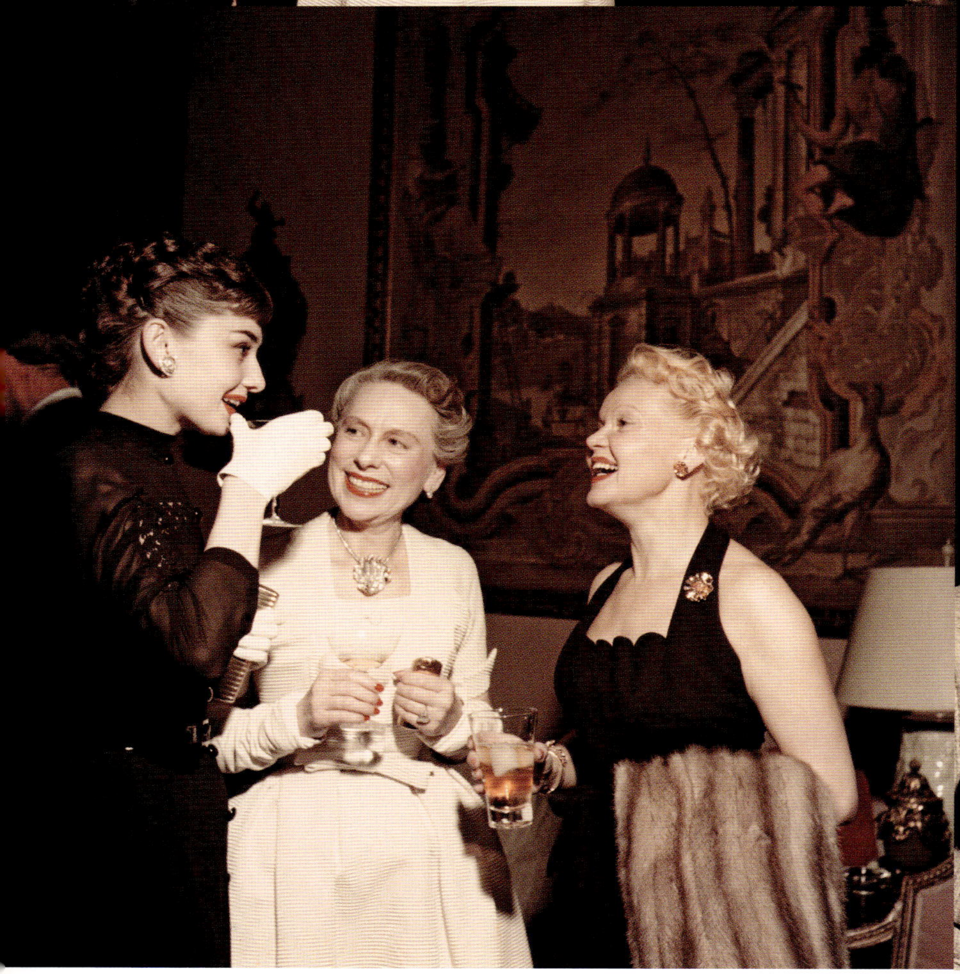
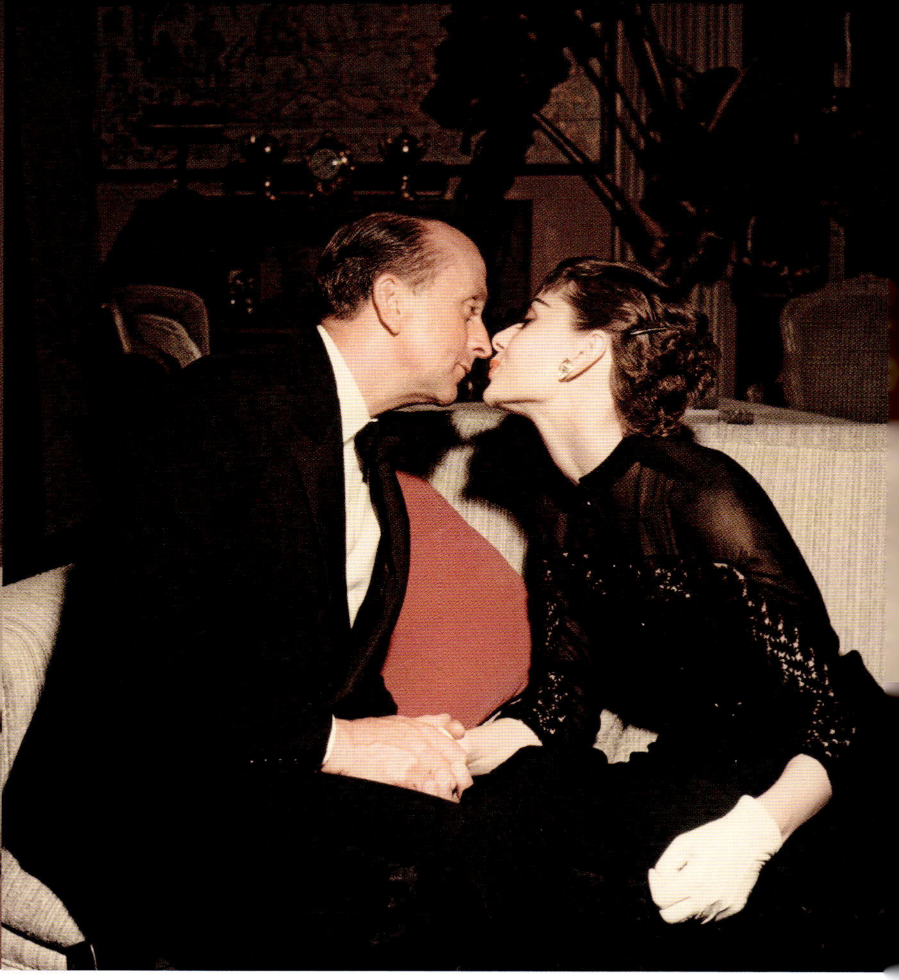

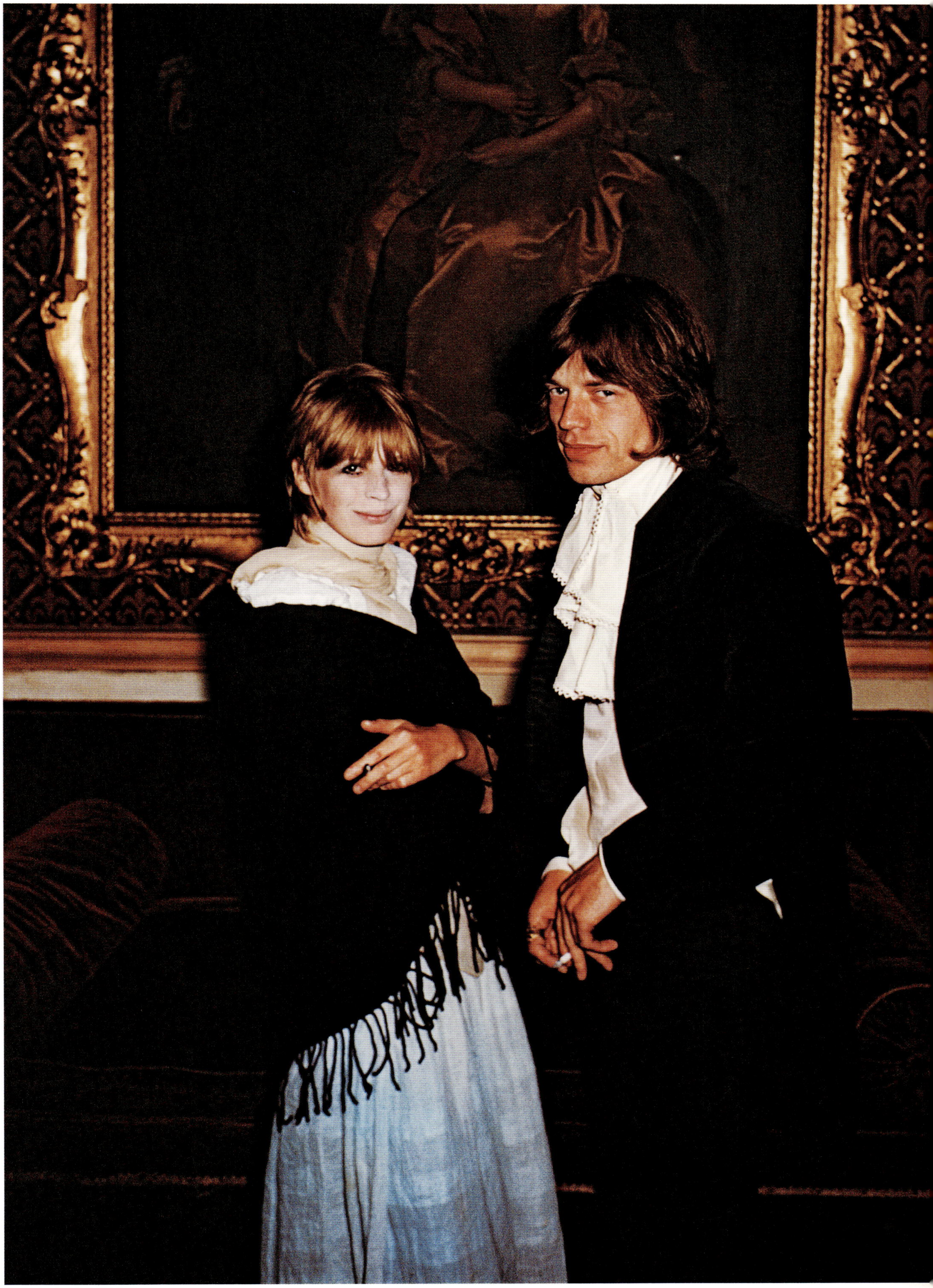

opposite "I love people who make me laugh. I honestly think it's the thing I like most, to laugh. It cures a multitude of ills." So mused Audrey Hepburn, pictured here with socialite Whitney Warren and others at a party in San Francisco, where she was appearing in a production of the play *Ondine*, circa 1960.

right Singer Marianne Faithfull and Mick Jagger at Leixlip Castle, County Kildare, Ireland, 1968. Faithfull and Jagger had attended an open-air performance by the Chieftains before a banquet at the castle—the Georgian estate of the Honorable Desmond Guinness, conservationist and author. Afterward, they attended the Edinburgh music festival.

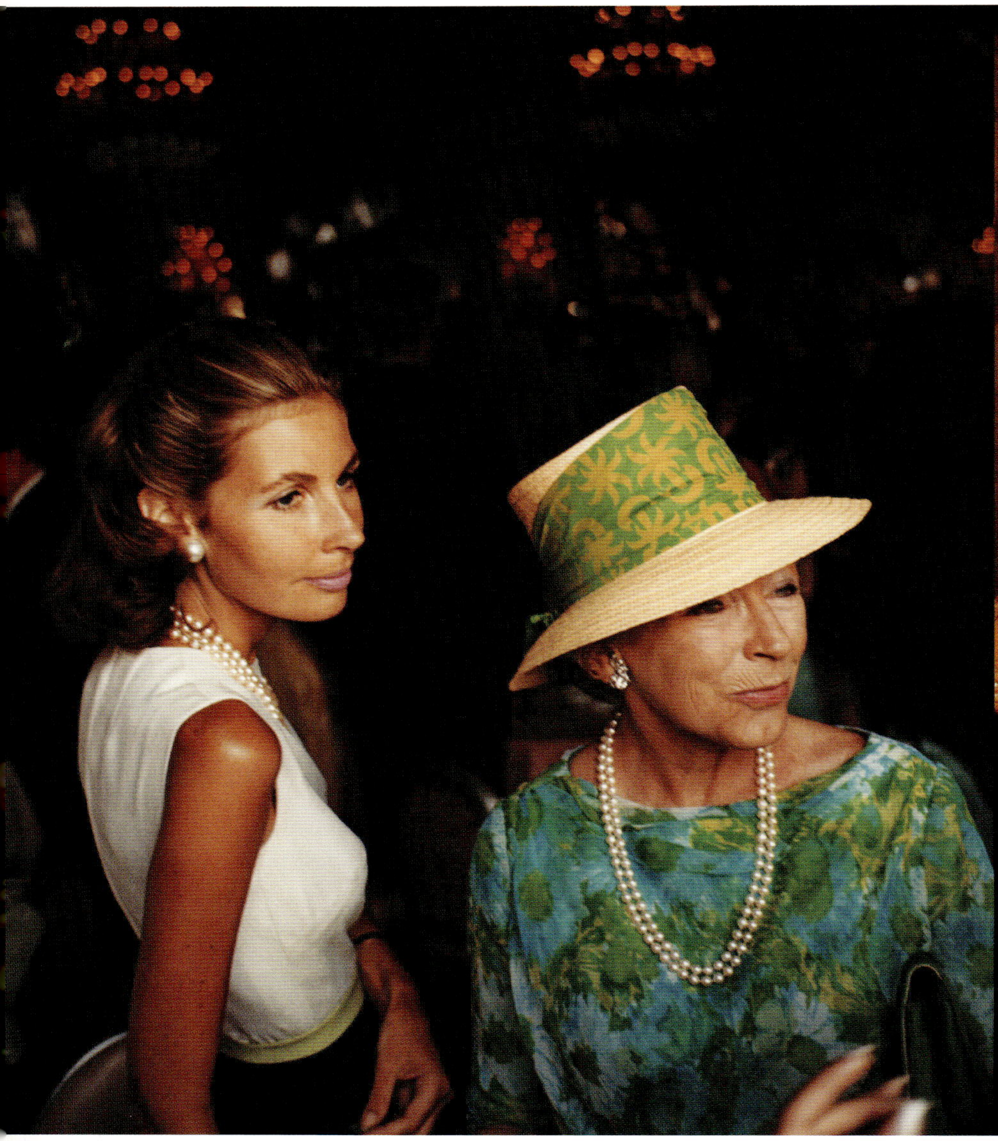

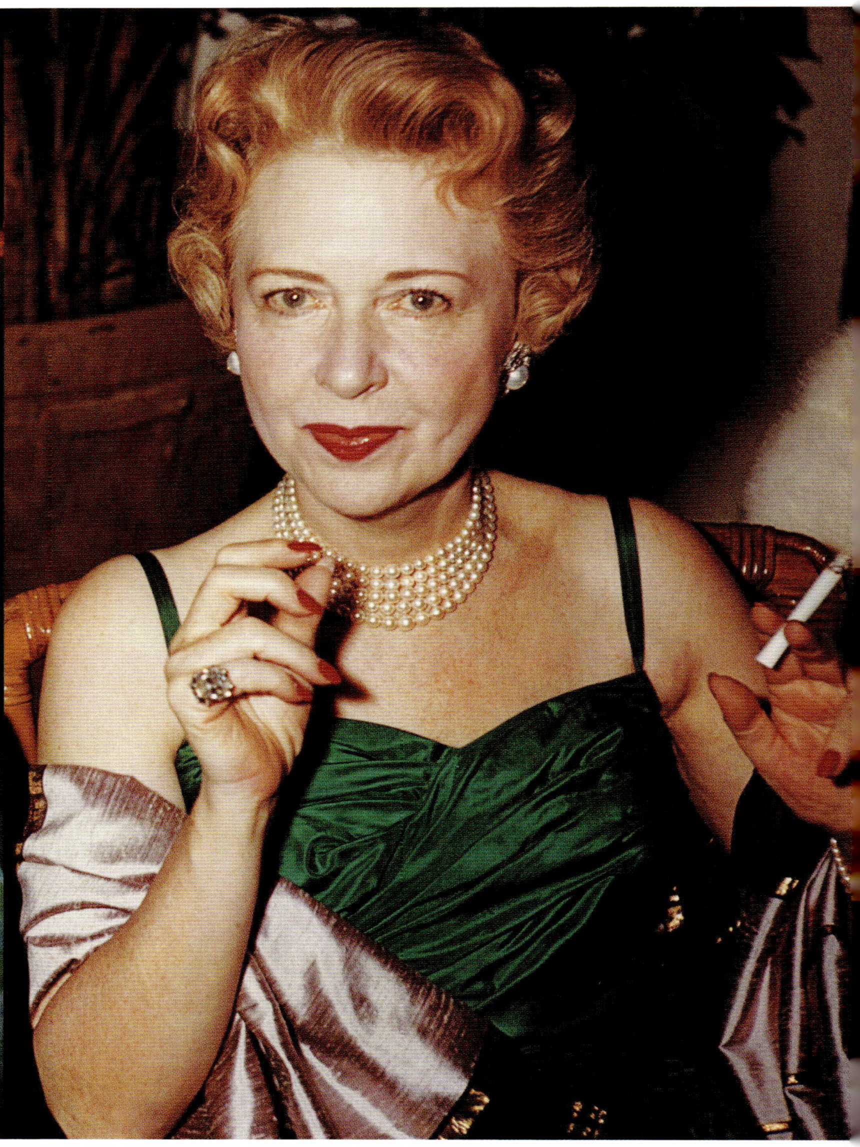

above left Jean Harvey Vanderbilt and Mary Hemingway at the wedding reception of Cheray and Peter Duchin, held at the St. Regis Hotel, New York, 1965.

above right Dolly O'Brien, Palm Beach, 1955. She was considered one of the great femmes fatales of her era, with marriages to silk manufacturer Louis Marshall Heminway, yeast heir Julius Fleischmann, polo player Jay O'Brien, and finally—after reportedly turning down Clark Gable—Count Jose Dorelis. Slim simply called her "the fabulous Dolly O'Brien."

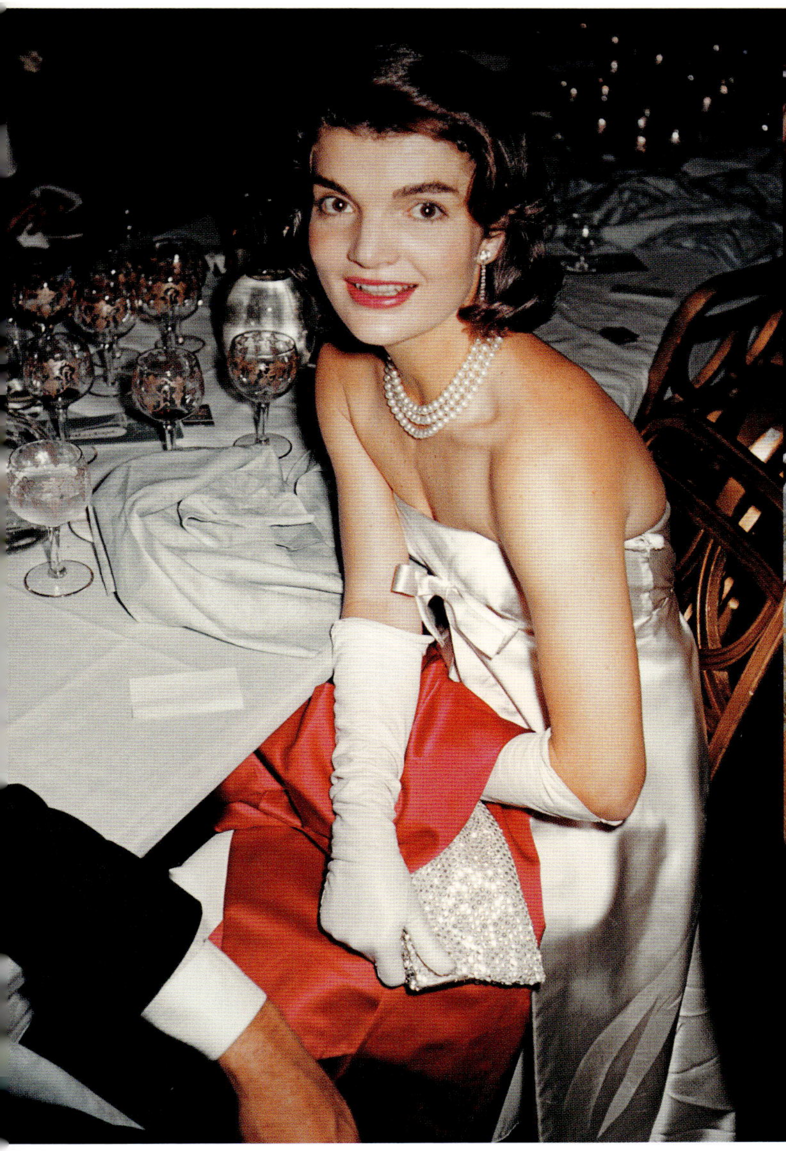

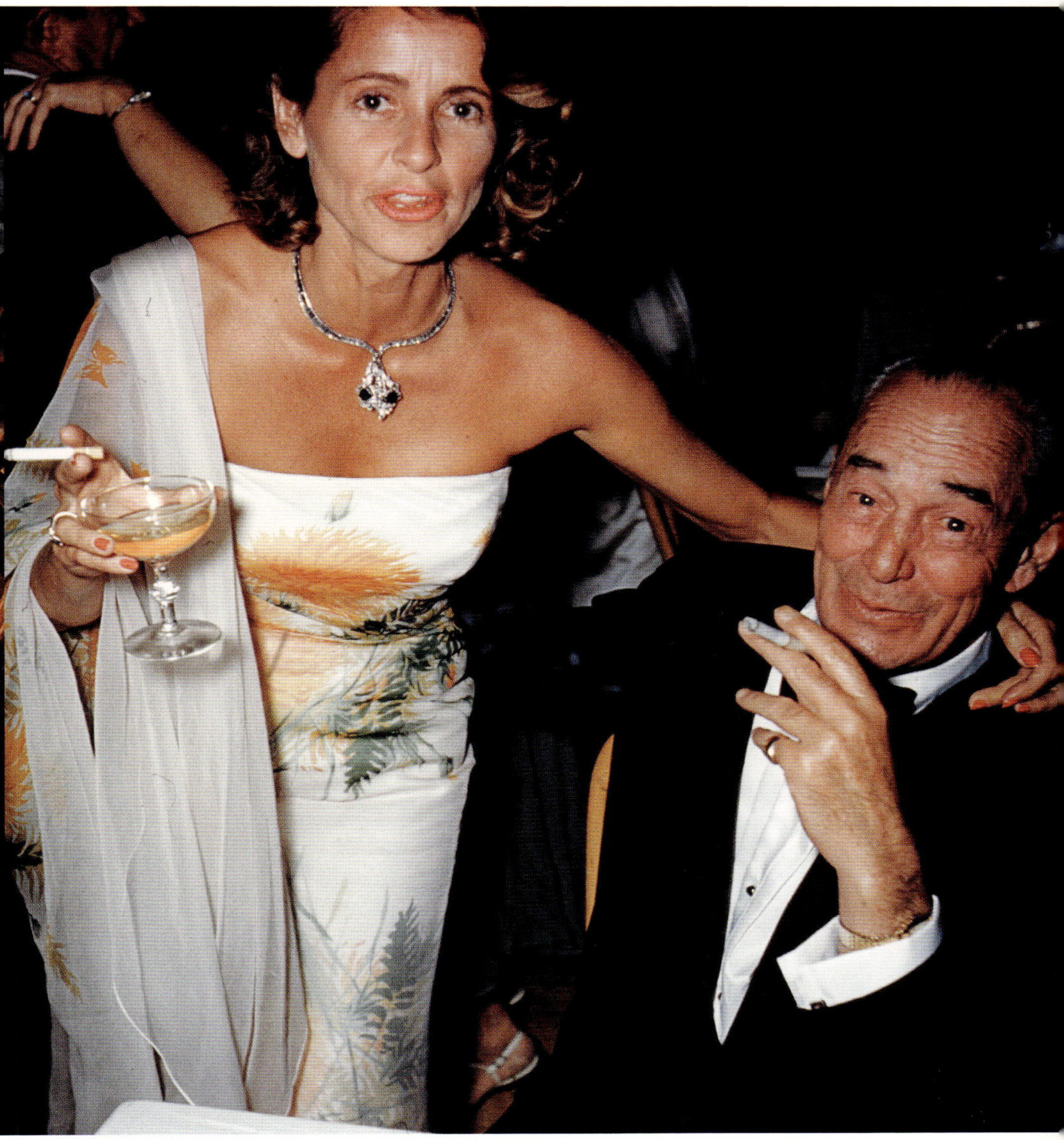

above left Jacqueline Kennedy, wife of Senator John F. Kennedy, at the April in Paris Ball, New York, 1959. In his first book, *A Wonderful Time*, Slim captioned this photo of Jackie Kennedy: "In the Waldorf's Grand Ballroom, I ran into the young senator from Massachusetts and his wife, whom I'd already met. I was up on a balcony at the time, scouting for an overall shot. Later I joined him at his table, where I got a shot of Jackie, looking very pretty. Jack asked where I'd been and whom I'd been photographing. Jackie was, as always, interested in the mechanics of the camera and the strobe light."

above right Mrs. Leverett Saltonstall Shaw (see also pages 179 and 191), wife of Senator Saltonstall, with Milton "Doc" Holden at a party in Palm Beach, 1959. The Saltonstalls and the Shaws were Boston Brahmin families with roots extending back to the *Mayflower*. Boston Brahmins typically played an integral role in the East Coast establishment—they were most often wealthy, politically influential, and extremely discreet about their mores and lifestyles. Doc Holden was a perennial Palm Beach bachelor, a notably agreeable man of a certain age who was known for his omnipresence as a social fixture in Palm Beach and Southampton, as well as for his moves on the croquet field.

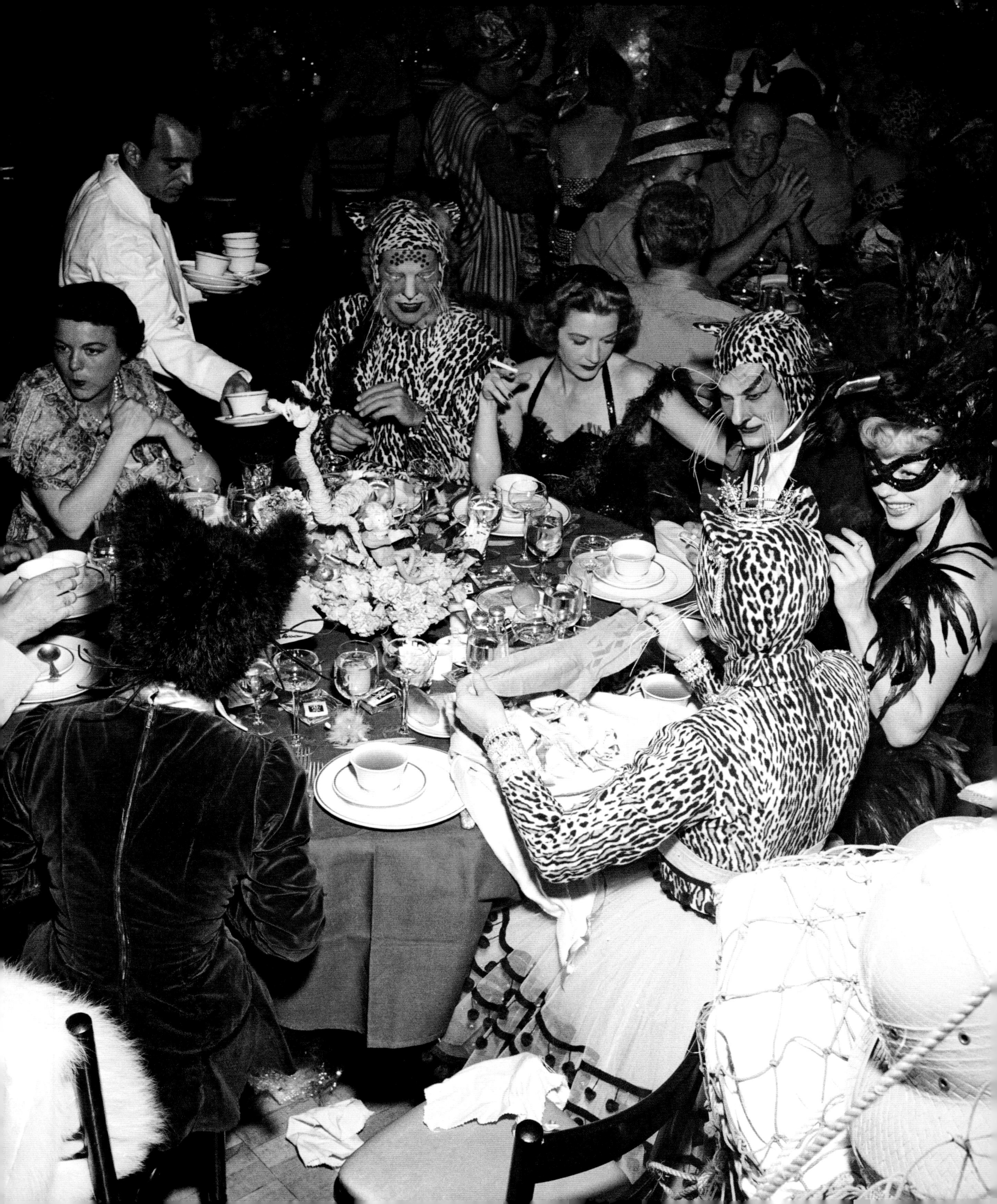

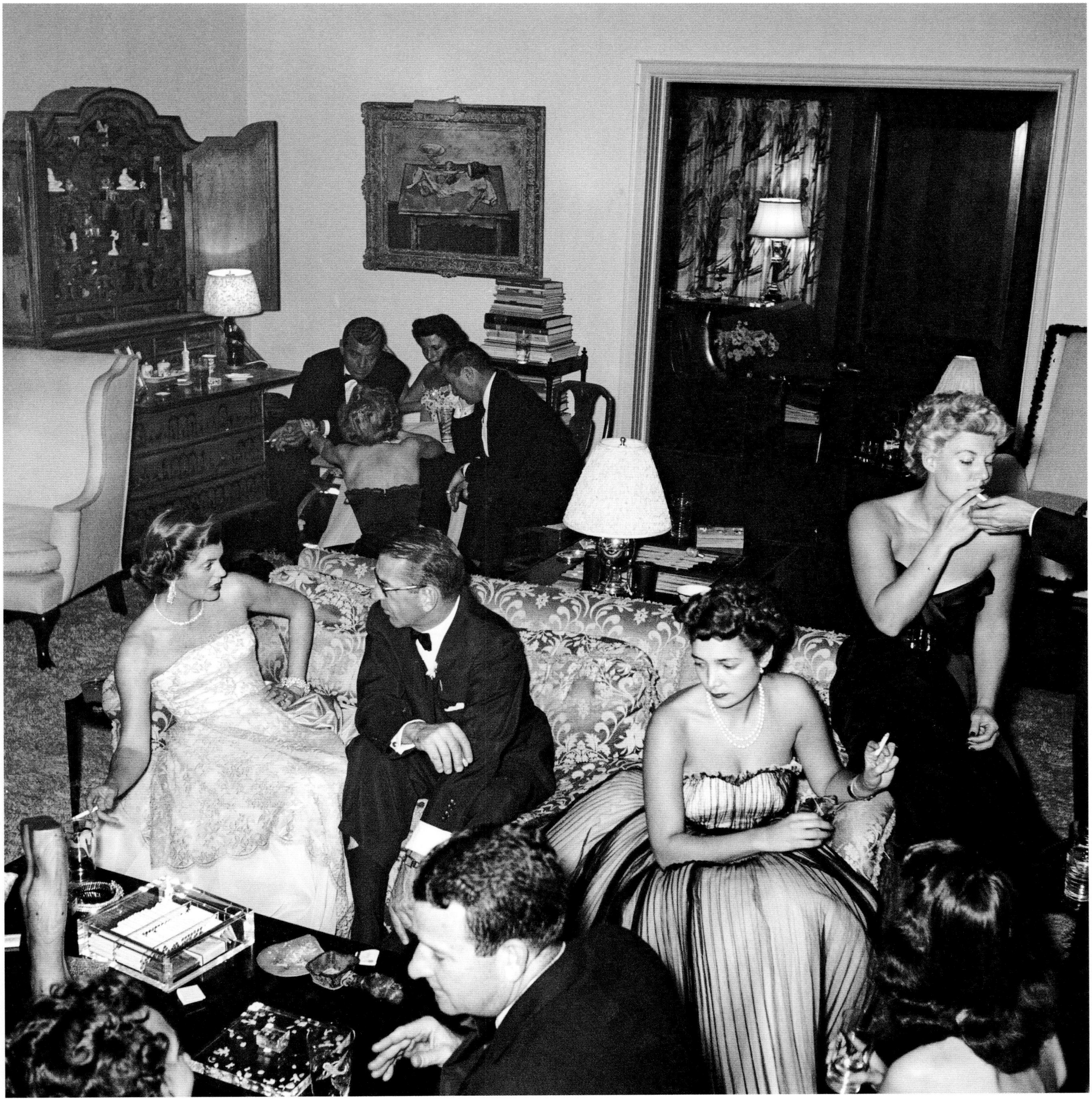

opposite A costume party at Romanoff's in Hollywood, 1950.

above Rocky Cooper (the wife of actor Gary Cooper), Van Herbick, Joy Page (the daughter of Jack Warner), and Ginger Macrae (lighting her cigarette), Beverly Hills, 1952.

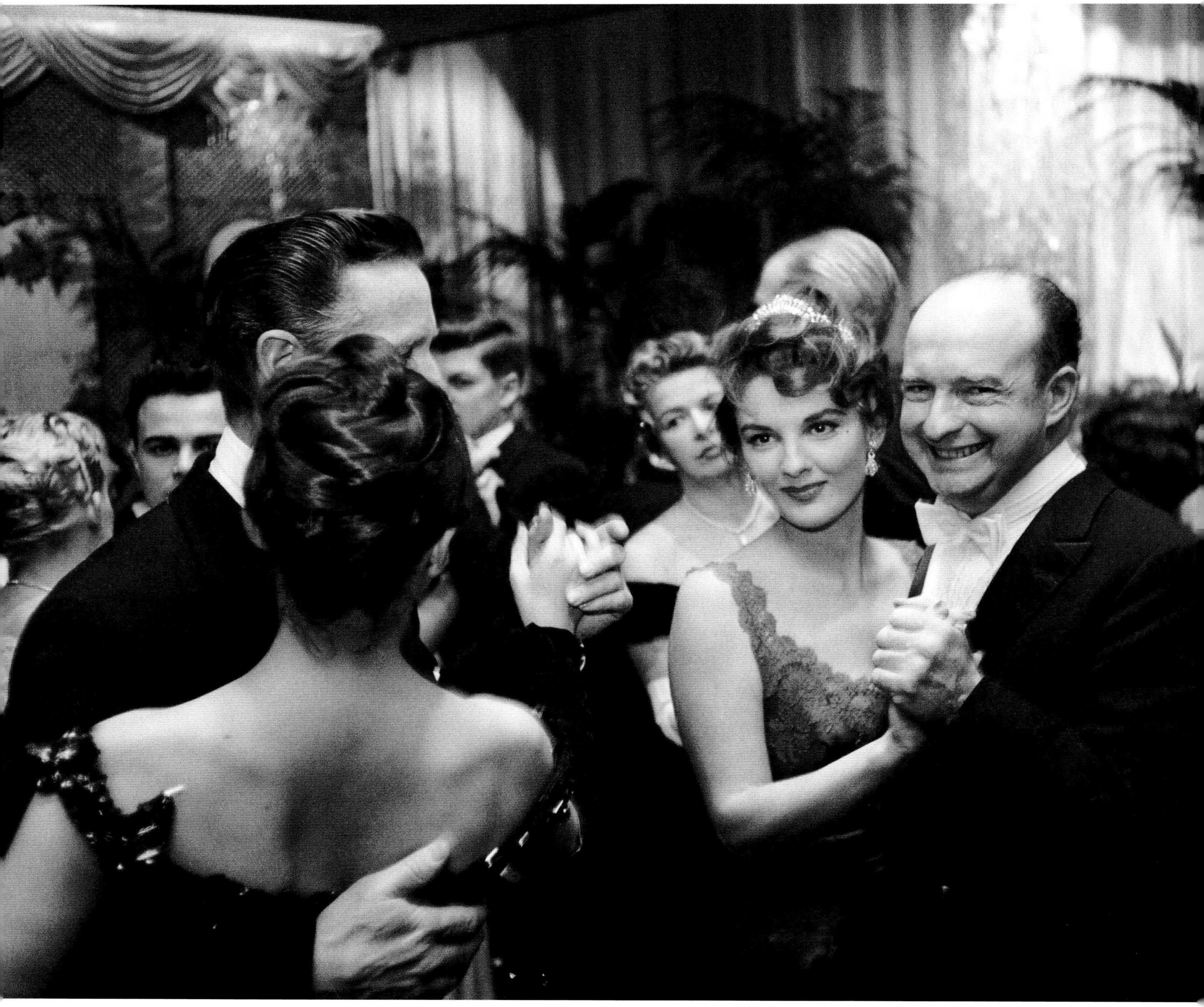

above Guests dancing at a New Year's Eve party given by Mrs. David Daniel Feldman at Romanoff's in Hollywood, 1956.

opposite left The American actor Tyrone Power dances with his new bride, actress Linda Christian, at a wedding party thrown by Countess di Frasso, Rome, 1949. Covering the wedding was one of the highlights of Slim's career. He would go on to photograph individuals of far greater standing or distinction, but for an unworldly young photographer just out of army fatigues and just into a fledgling career, this experience made an impression on him that he spoke about his entire life. Power and Christian were popular matinee idols, and Slim's assignment was to follow the couple around Rome in the days leading up to their church wedding at Santa Francesca Romana.

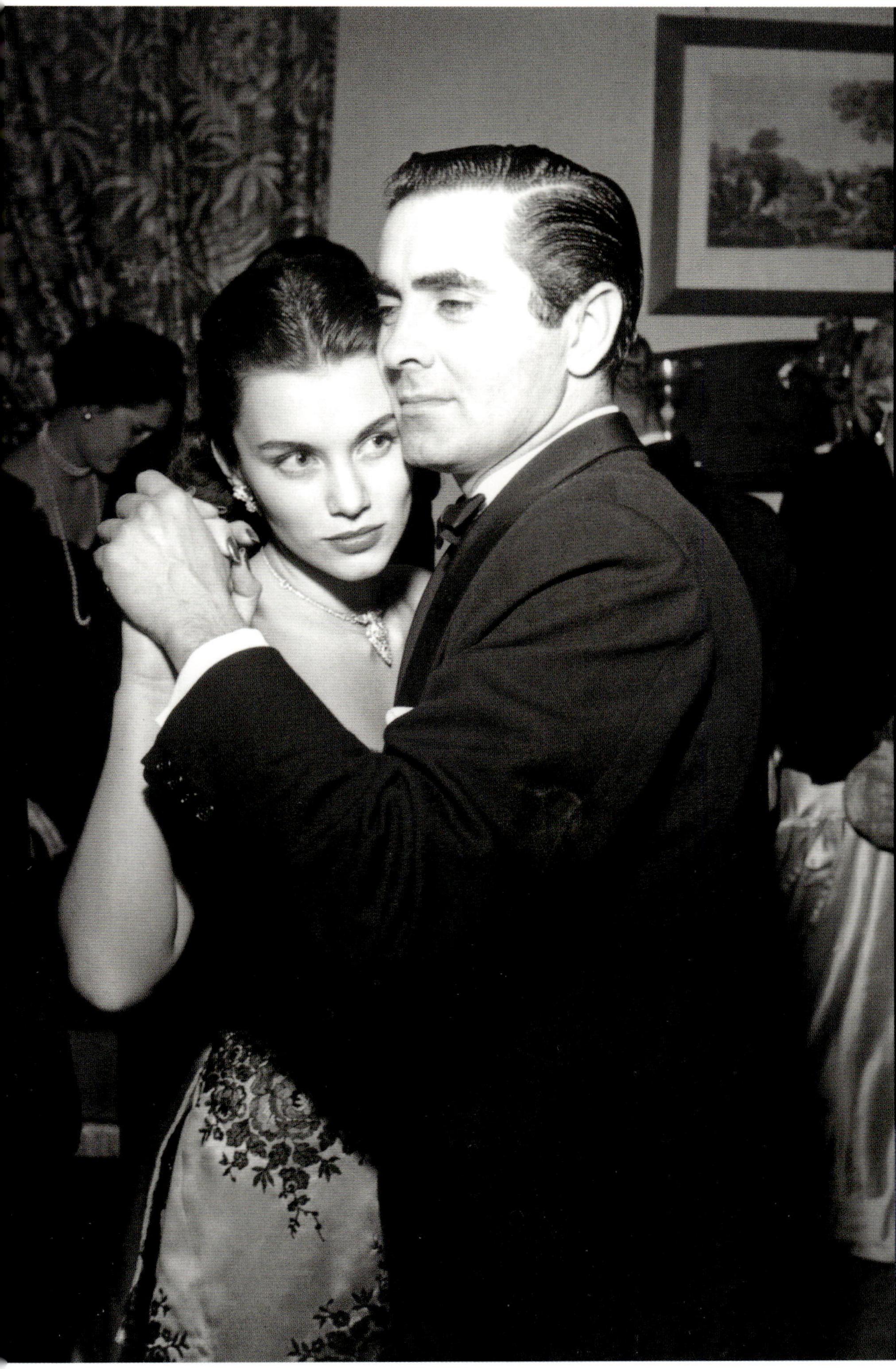

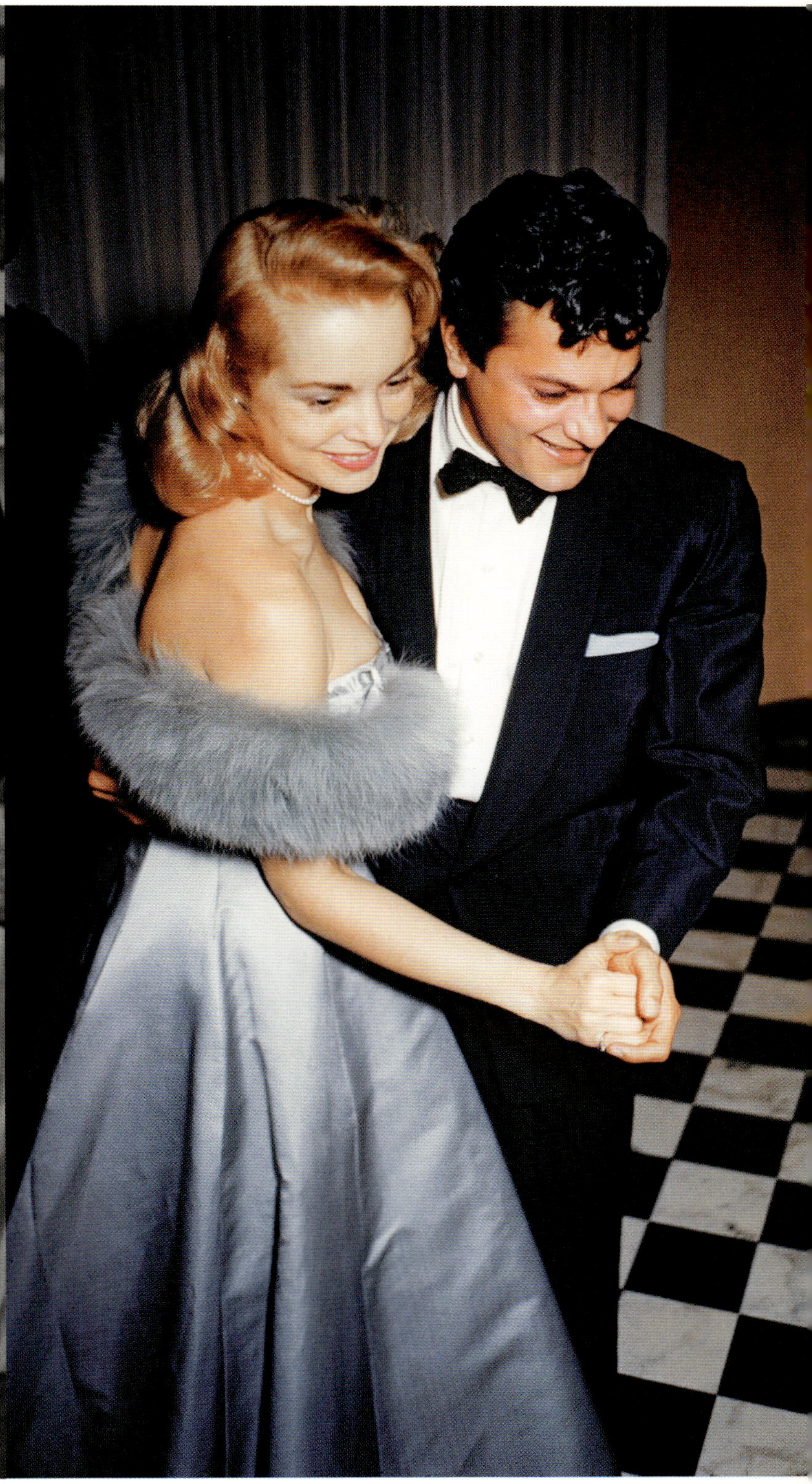

above right Film stars Tony Curtis and his first wife, Janet Leigh, enjoying a dance at a party held at actor James Mason's home in Beverly Hills, 1954. For a period they were both Hollywood idols, starring in five films together while married. Her most famous role was in Alfred Hitchcock's *Psycho*, in which she played the ill-fated showering secretary Marion Crane, on the lam for stealing money from her boss so that she could run away with her boyfriend. She received a Golden Globe award for Best Supporting Actress and an Academy Award nomination for her performance.

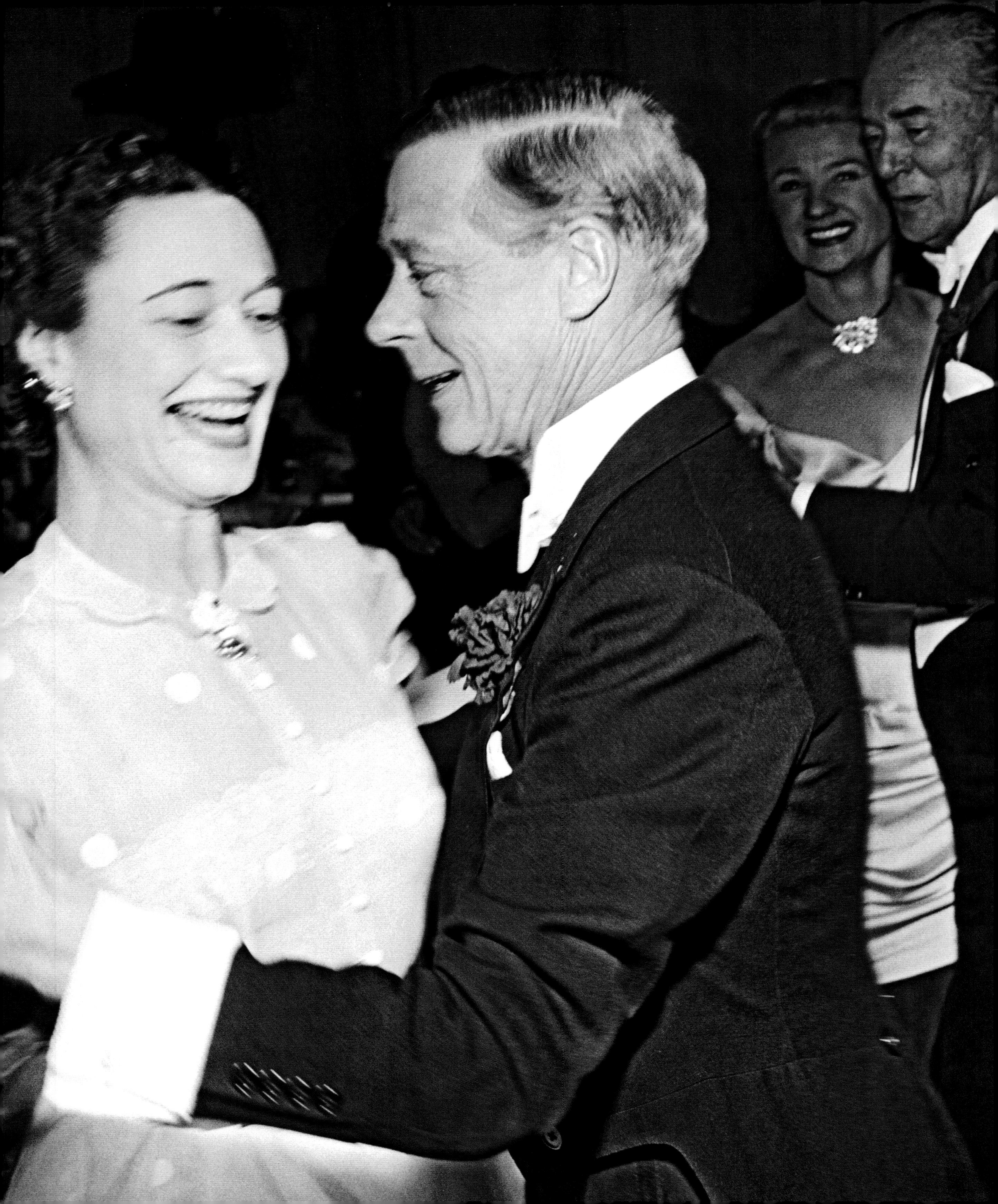

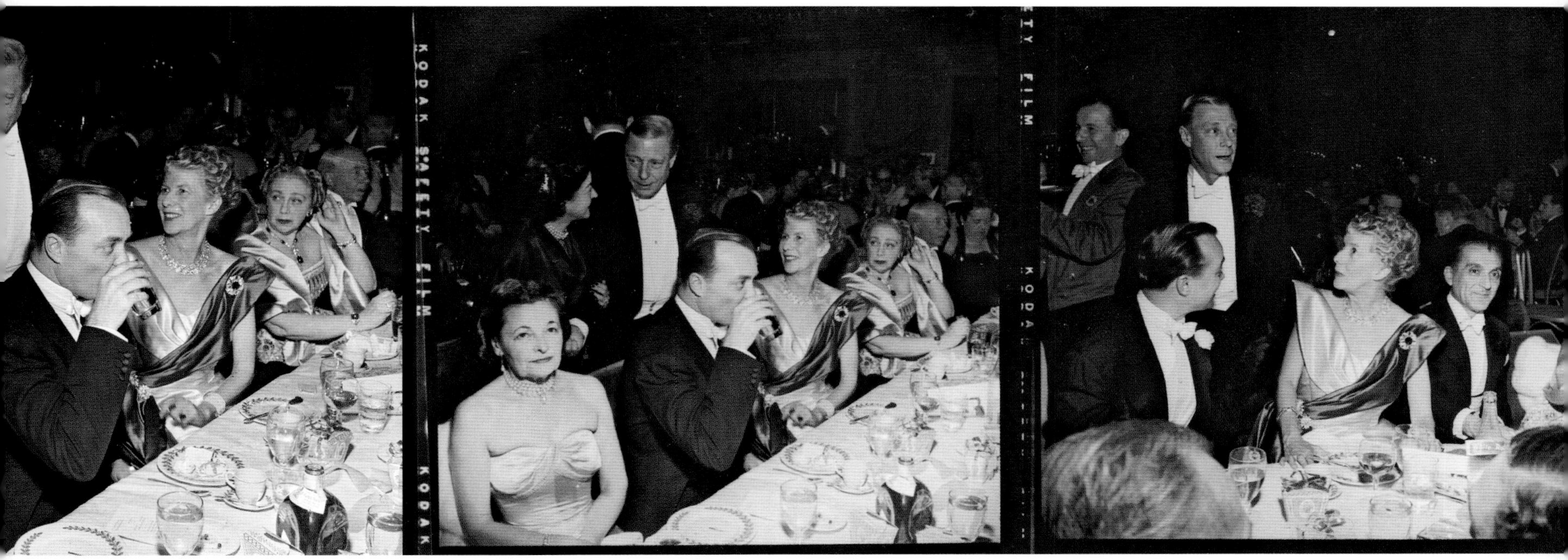

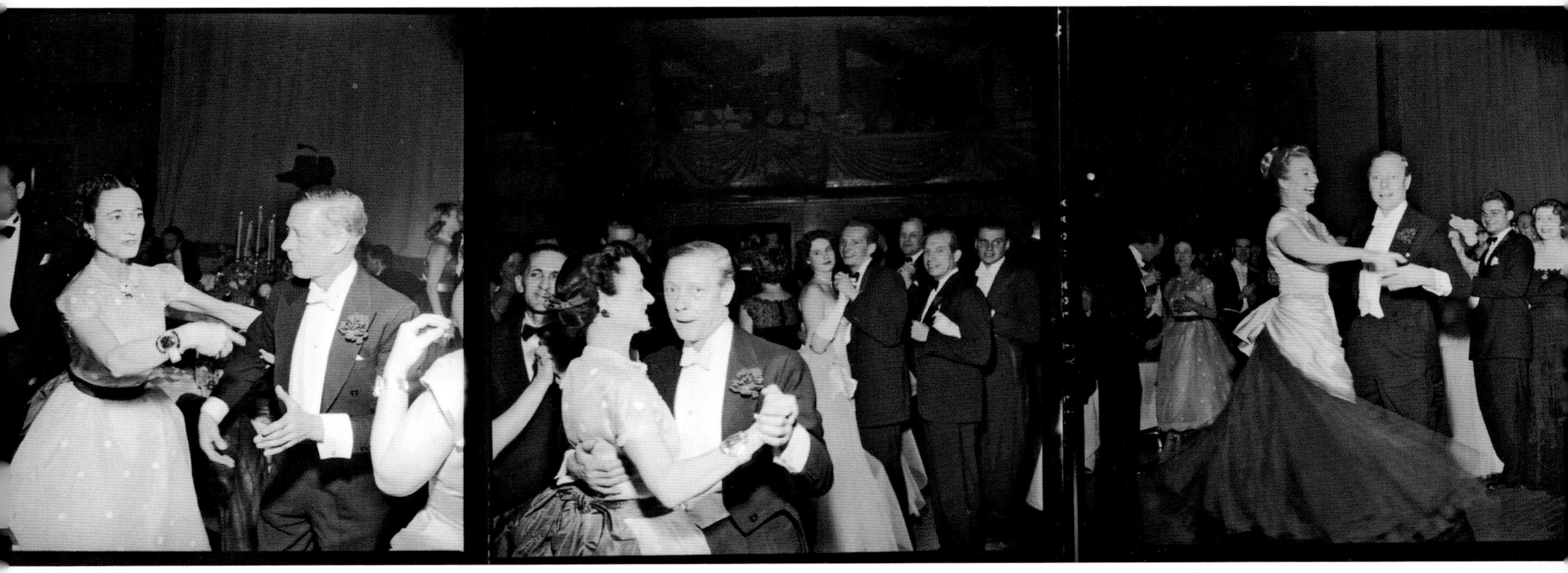

opposite and above The Duke and Duchess of Windsor—he was King Edward VIII until he gave up his throne for the woman he loved—dancing at a party given in their honor at the Waldorf-Astoria Hotel, Park Avenue, New York, 1953. Outtakes from the party (above) capture the festive atmosphere. The image opposite of the duke and duchess dancing has become one of Slim's most sought-after photos. Behind them, dancing cheek to cheek, are Constance Carpenter and Milton "Doc" Holden.

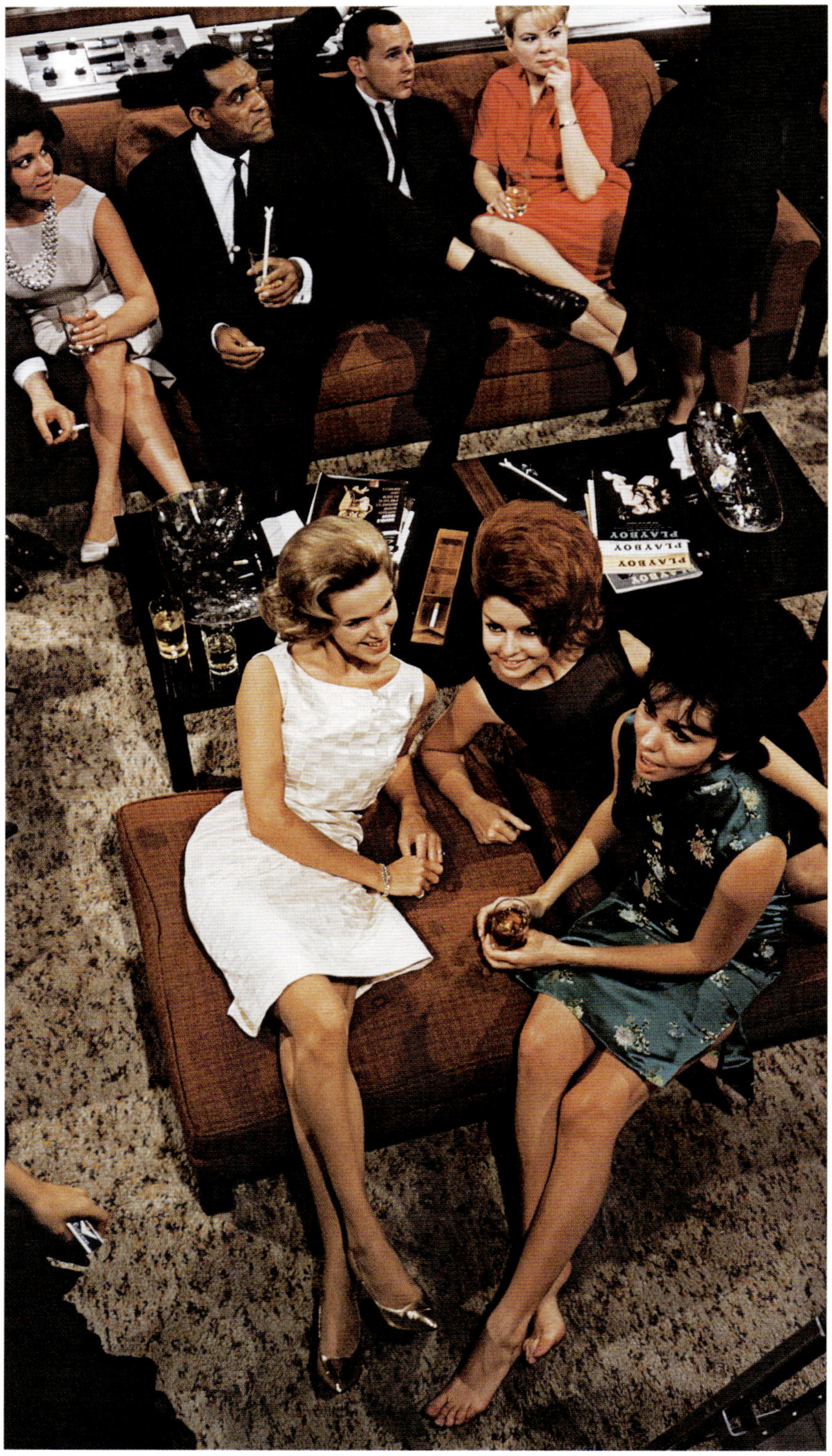

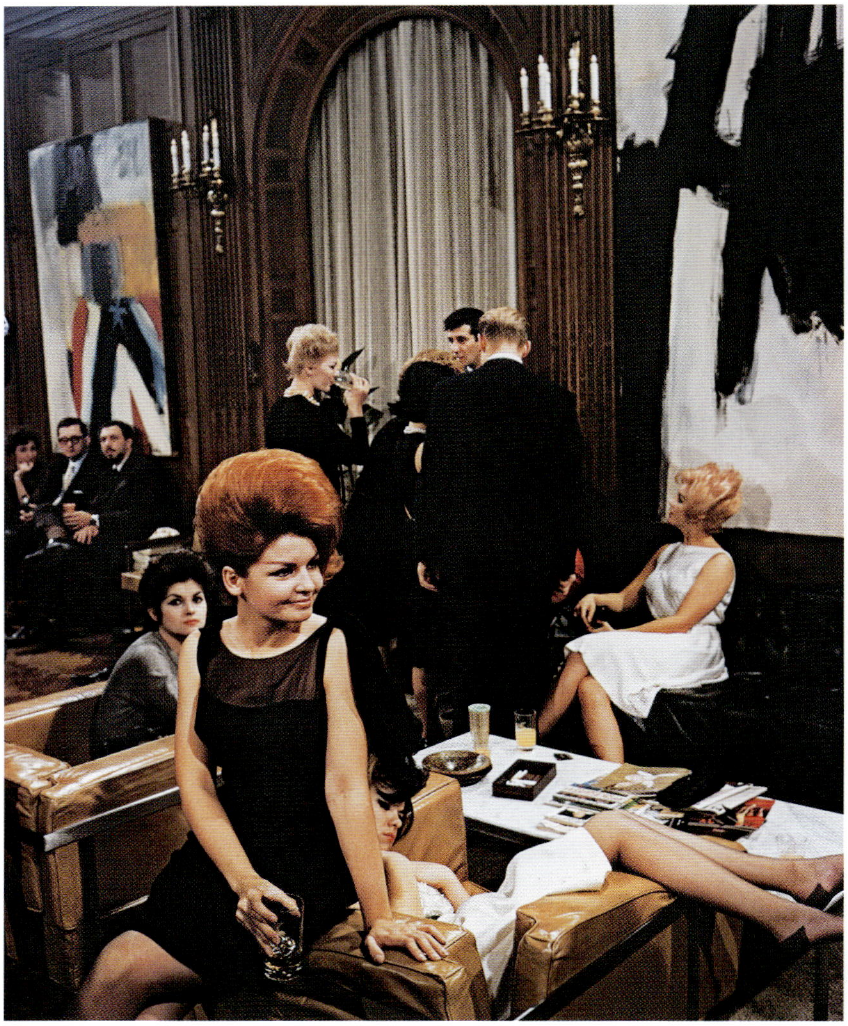

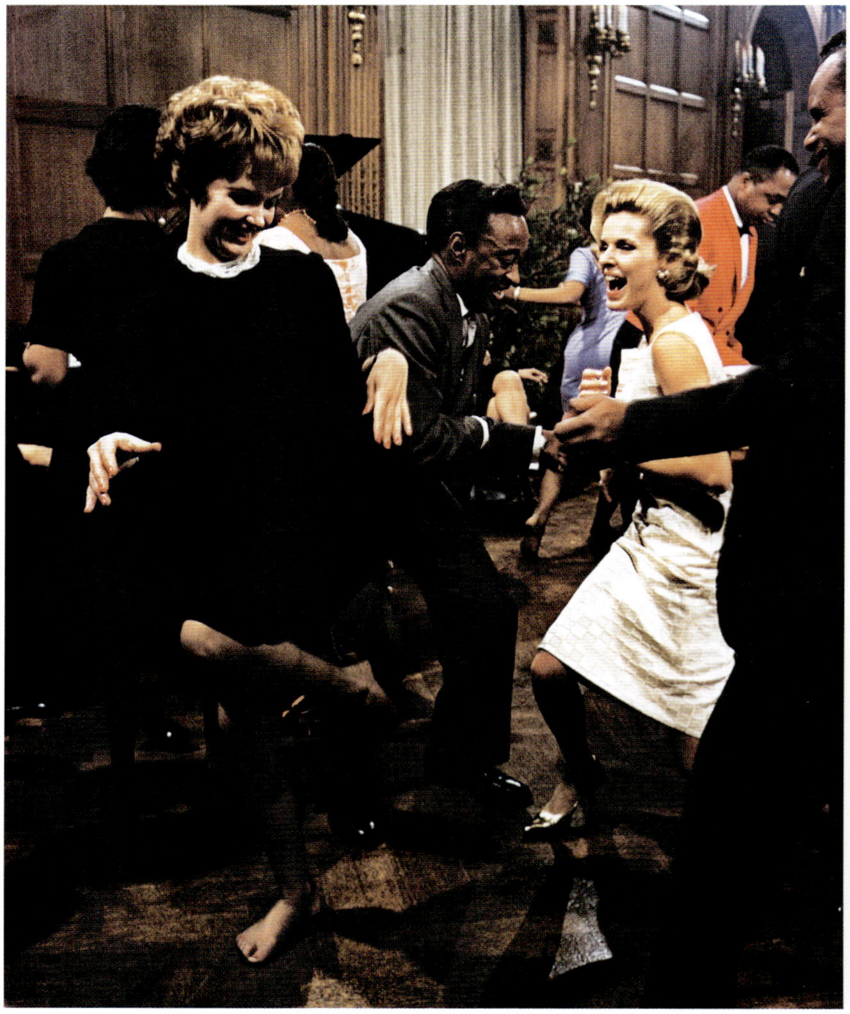

above and opposite In 1961 Slim did a story on the young Hugh Hefner and the social scene at his Playboy Mansion in Chicago. These are outtakes from this story.

following spread Guests of the American publisher Hugh Hefner (far right) at his Playboy Mansion, Chicago, 1961.

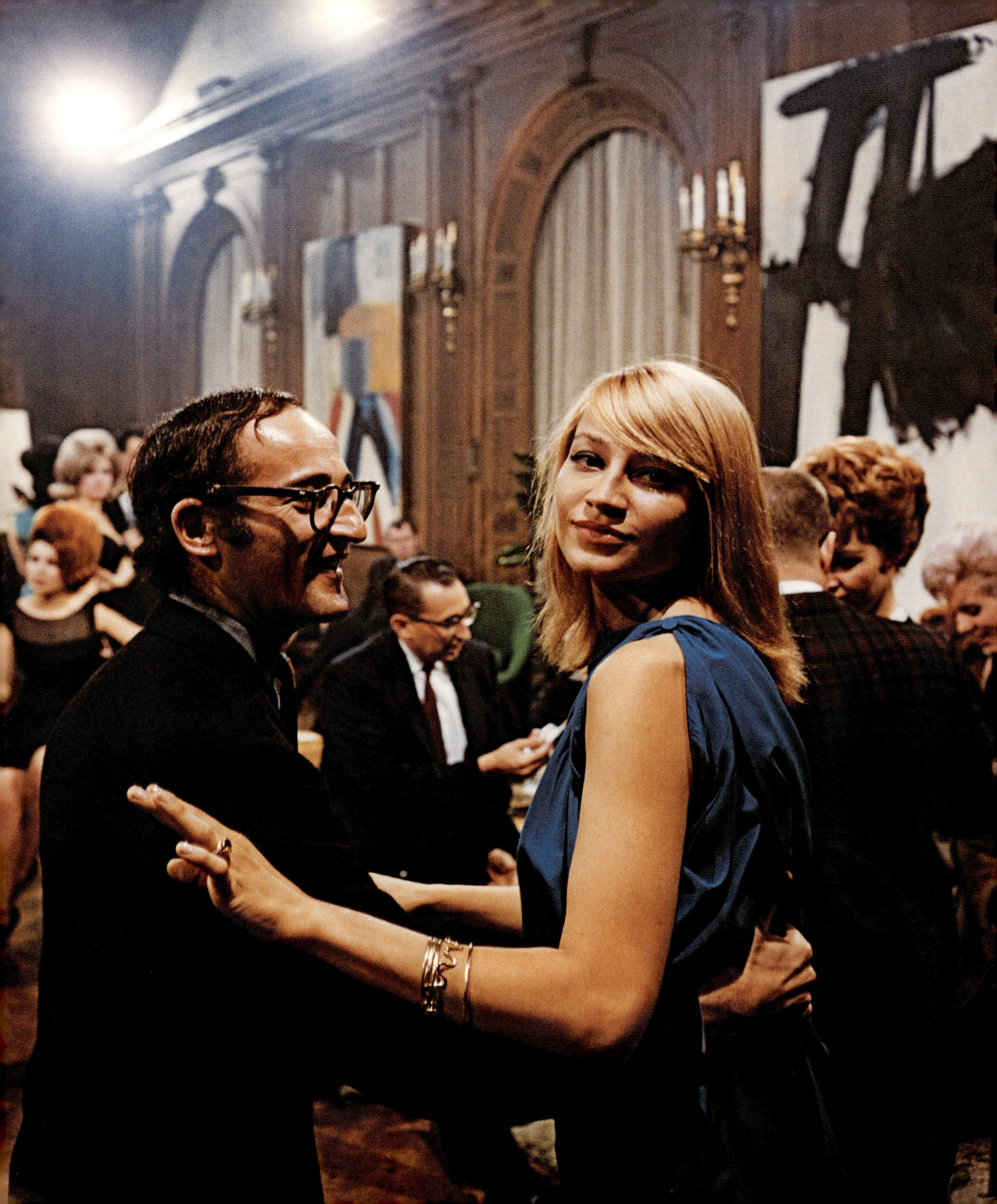

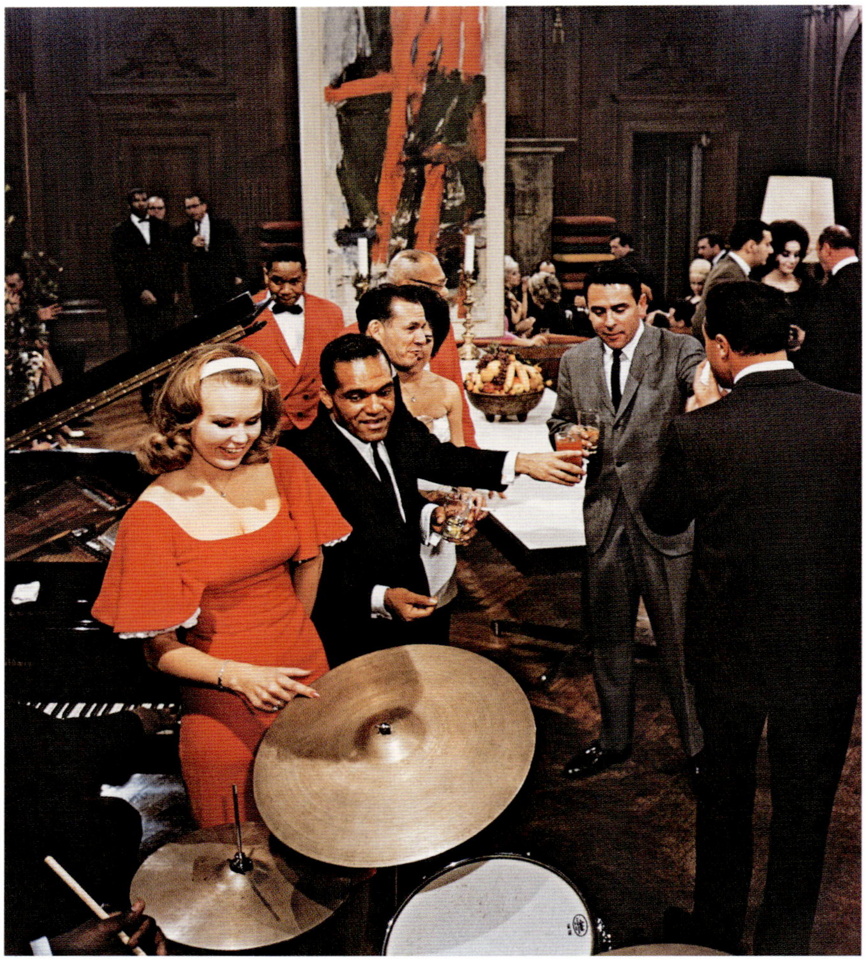

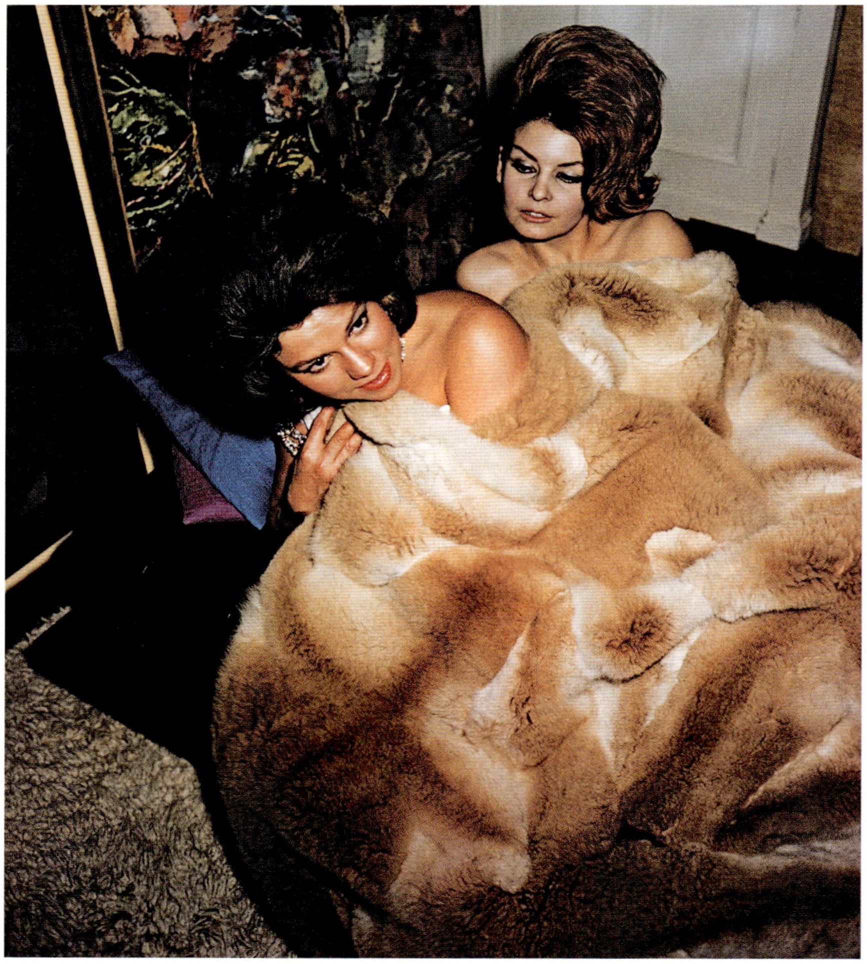

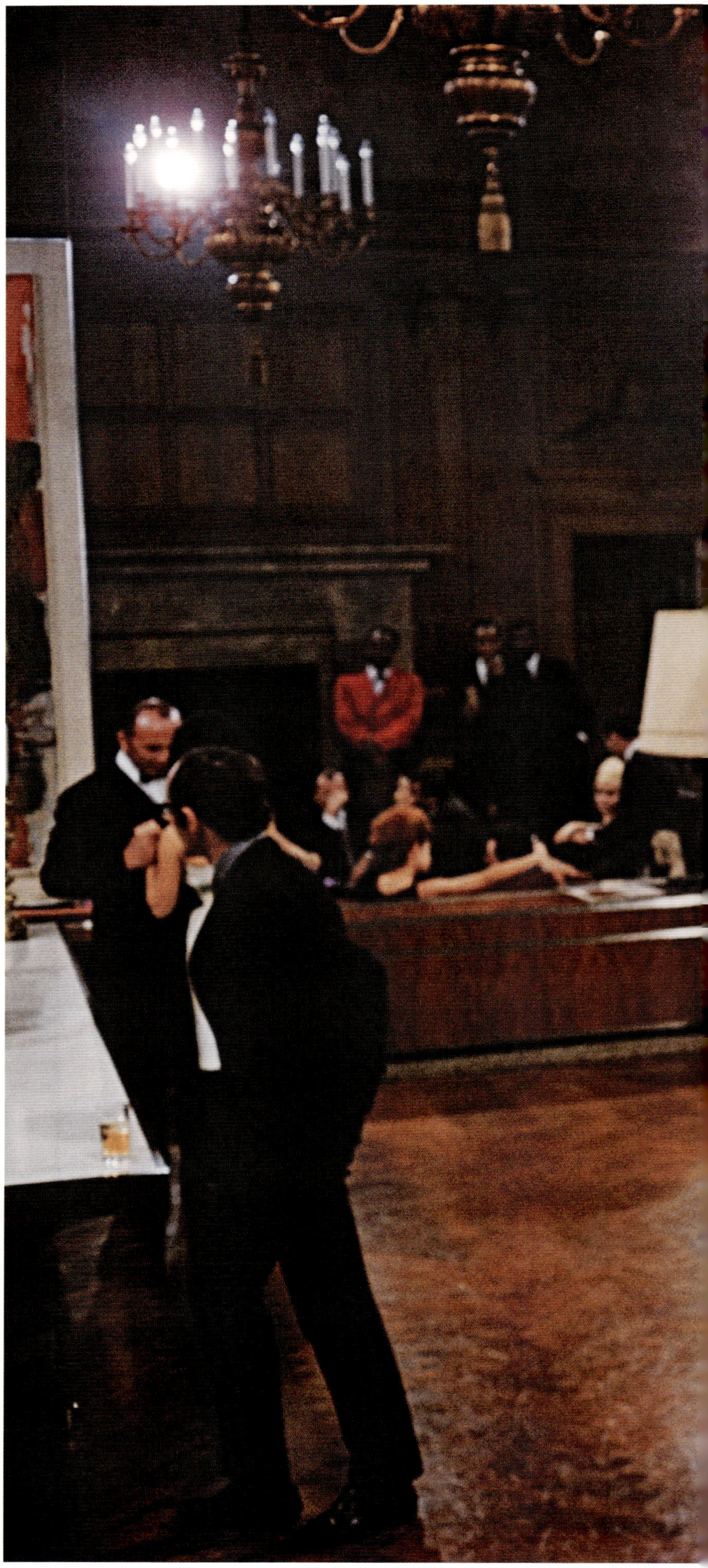

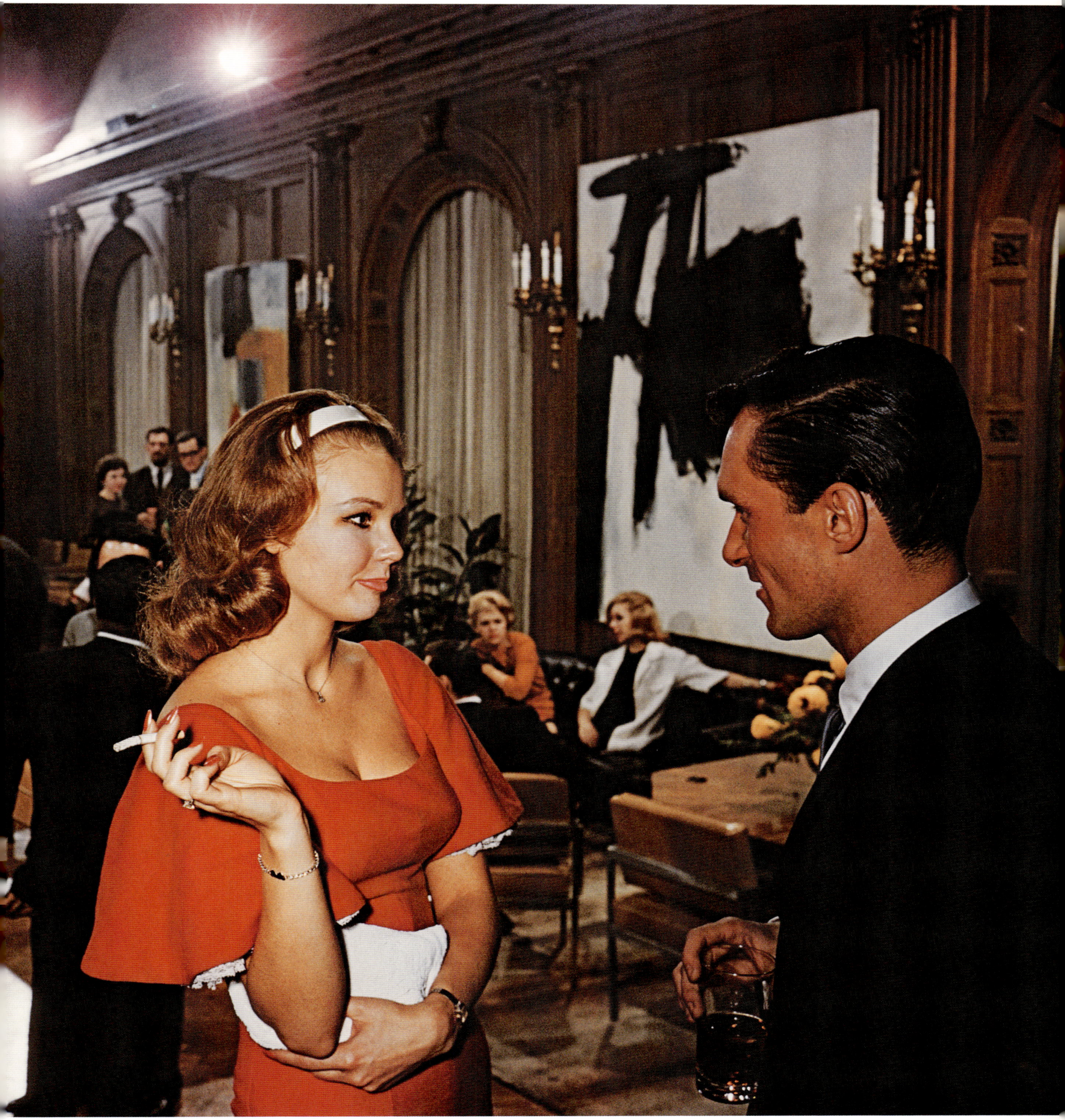

below The English-born actor James Mason (left), restaurateur Michael Romanoff (see page 25), and Mason's first wife, the English actress Pamela Mason, at a party in Beverly Hills, 1954.

opposite Laughter and music ensure the success of this party in San Antonio, 1976.

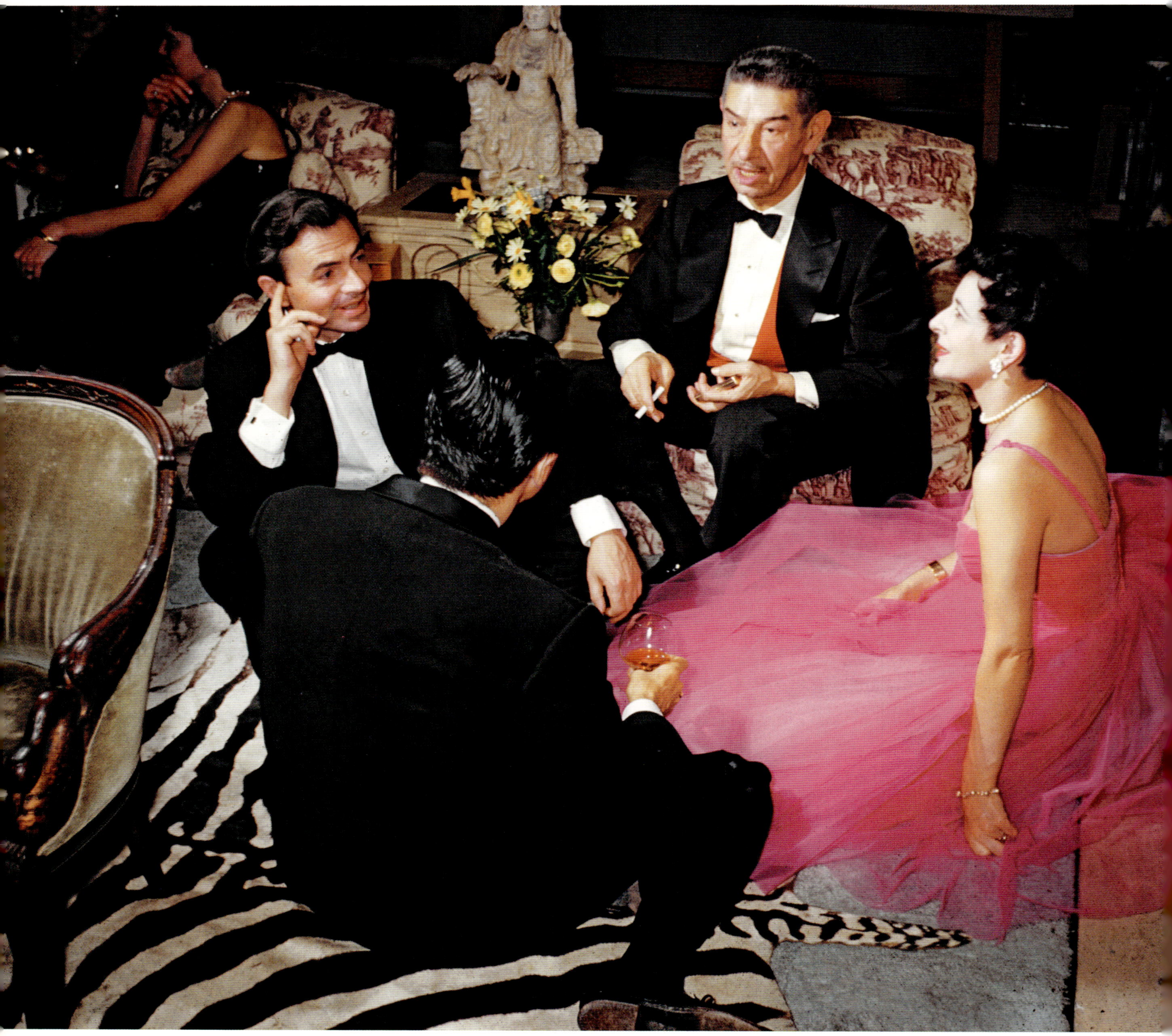

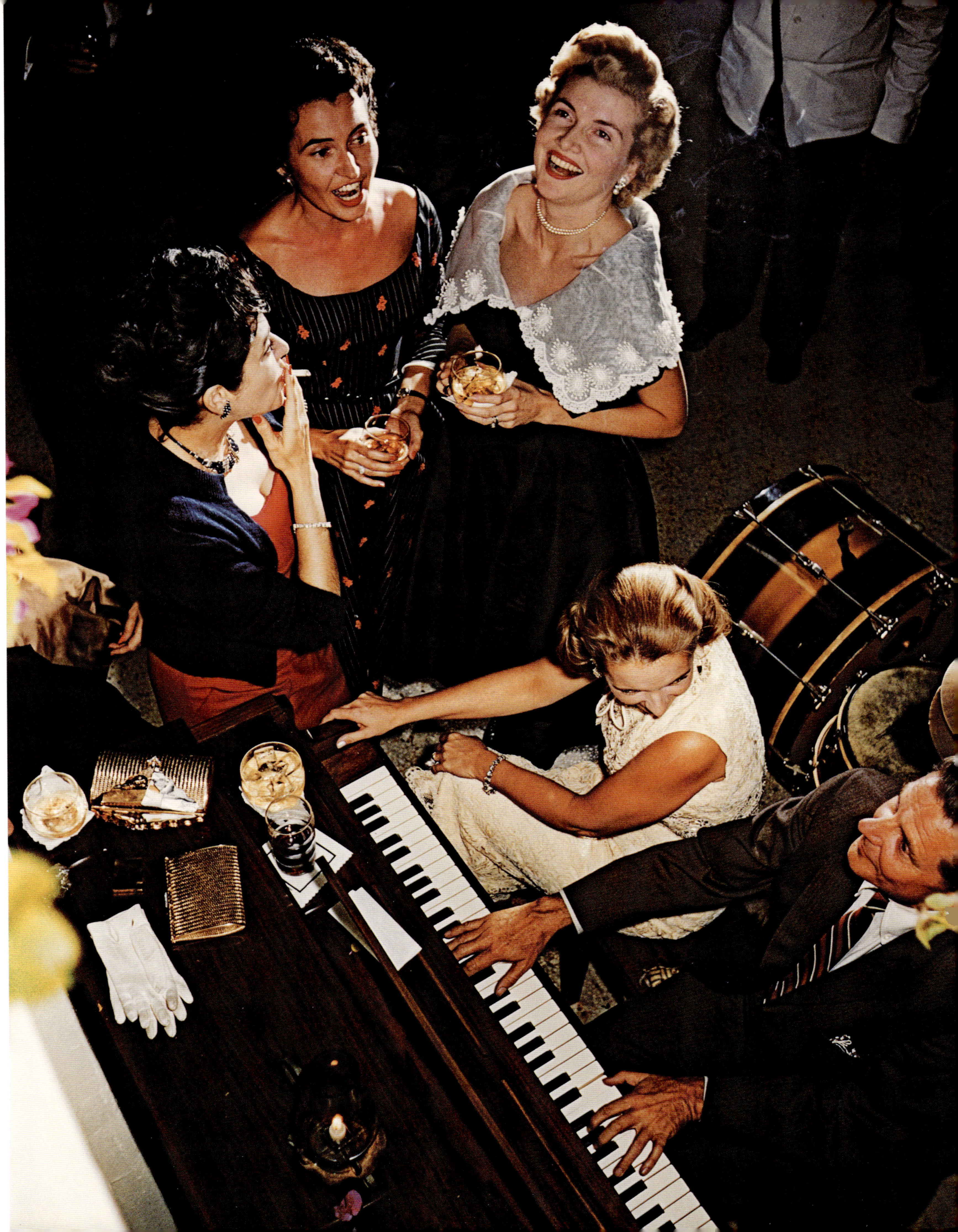

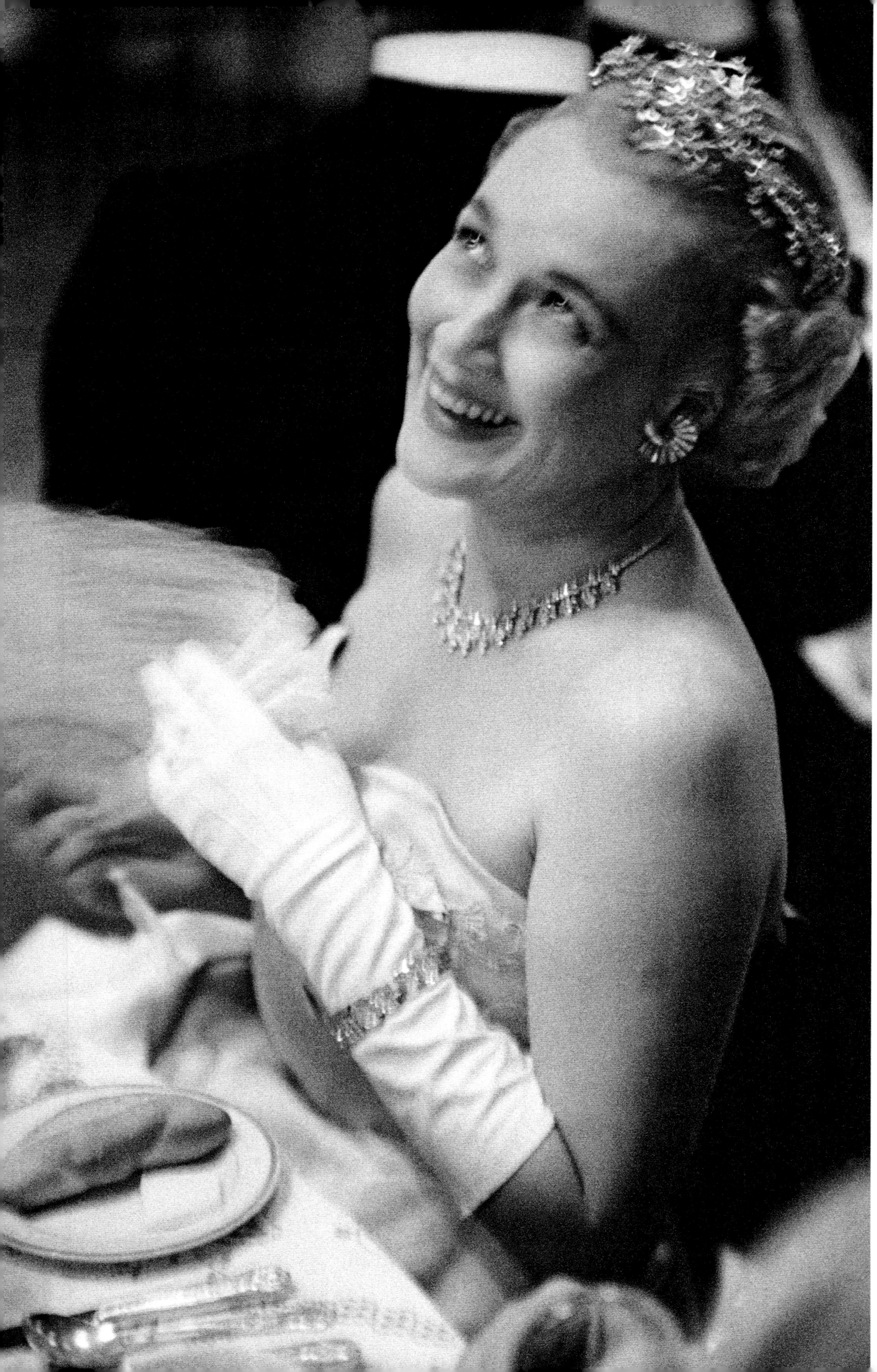

left Kay Spreckels, who became the fifth wife of actor Clark Gable in 1955, at a New Year's Eve party held at Romanoff's in Hollywood, 1956.

opposite The French actress Capucine (see also pages 26–27) at a New Year's Eve party held at Romanoff's in Beverly Hills, 1956.

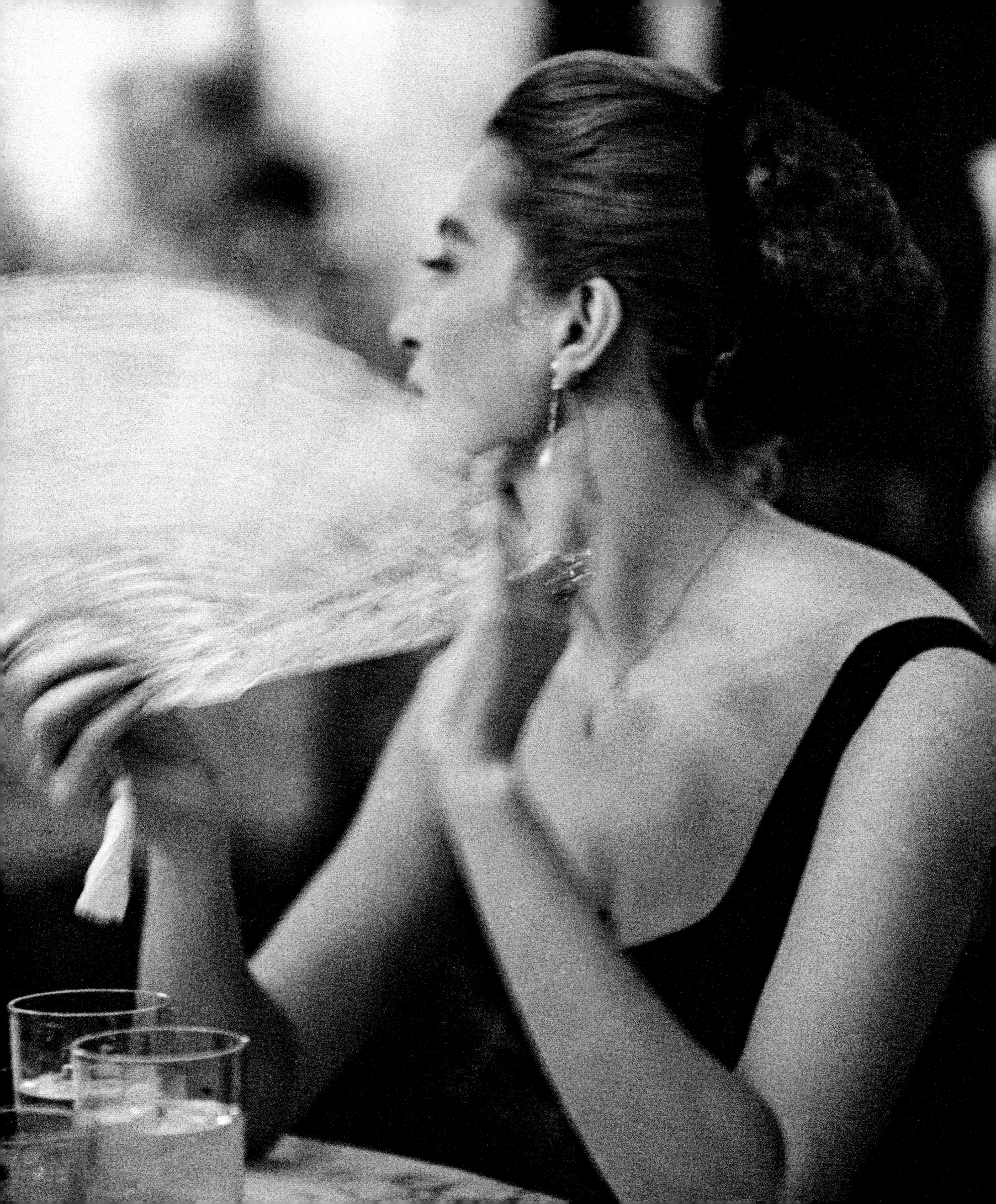

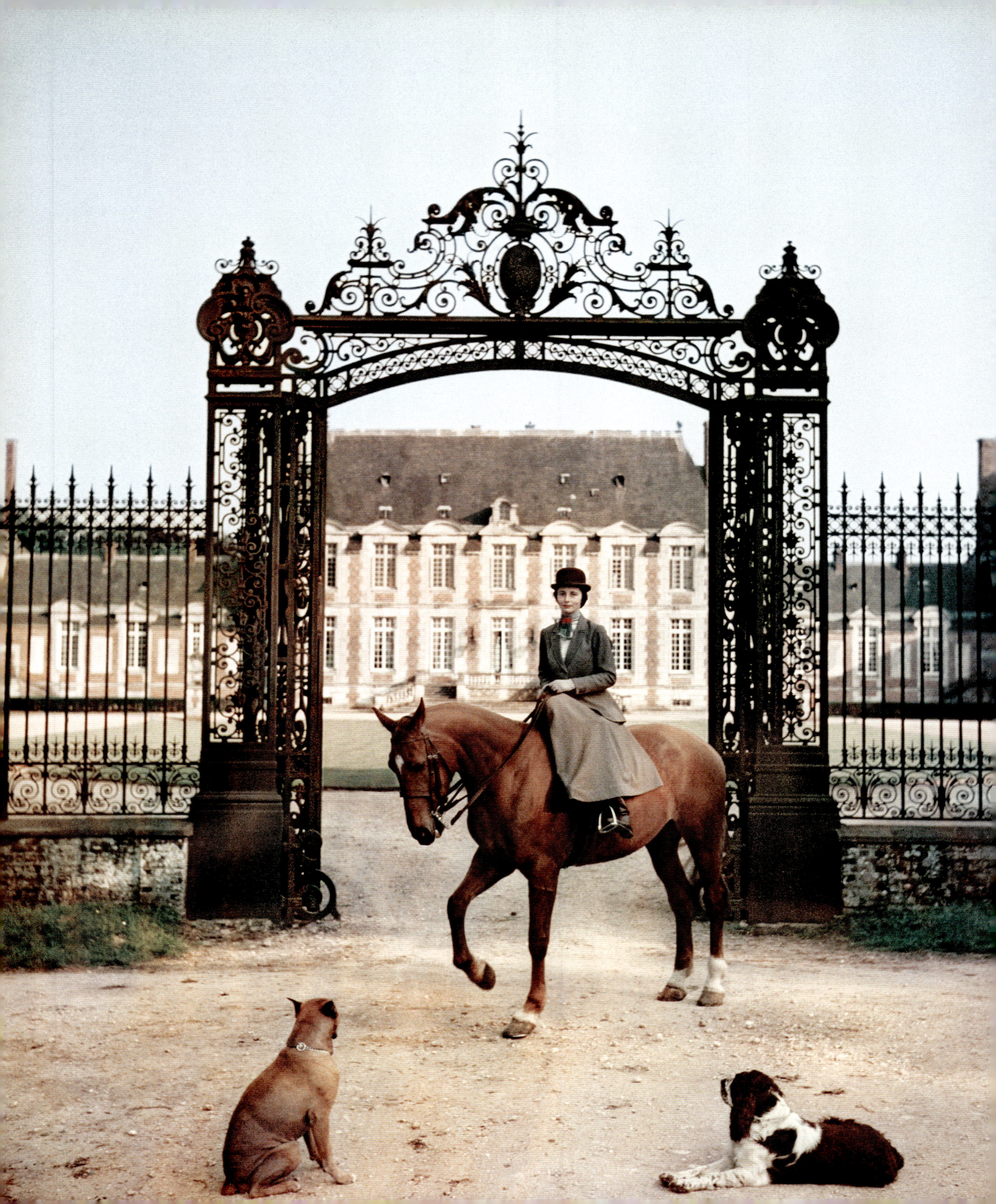

. . . *IN* ATTRACTIVE *PLACES* . . .

Slim's fascinating approach to environmental portraiture is examined in this chapter. He not only tracked down the world's most enchanting women; he then found the most sublime backdrops within their homes—a cloistered garden or an entire room painted in Pompeian-style trompe l'oeil—against which to photograph them. Slim's penchant for spending hours orchestrating these scenes, his minute attention to detail, and his desire to imbue their stories with a stitch or two of his own fairy-tale embroidery make his environmental portraits exceptional.

opposite Laure de La Haye-Jousselin at the gates to her château in Normandy, 1957. Married to Bertrand de La Haye-Jousselin, she was a descendant of the comtesse de Noailles, a French aristocrat and the first lady to Marie Antoinette, who called the countess "Madame Etiquette" for her insistence that no minutia of court etiquette ever be overlooked. Slim waited four days in the village of Saint-Aubin-d'Écrosville to get this shot. Once the scene was set, he not only managed to get the subject to engage with the camera, but got her horse and two dogs to cooperate as well. As Slim's longtime friend and editor Frank Zachary observed, "Slim managed to get the horse to raise his hoof. A real, honest-to-God seventeenth-century portrait." Zachary also said of Slim's work, "Slim's pictures are the work of a consummate artist in the guise of a photo journalist."

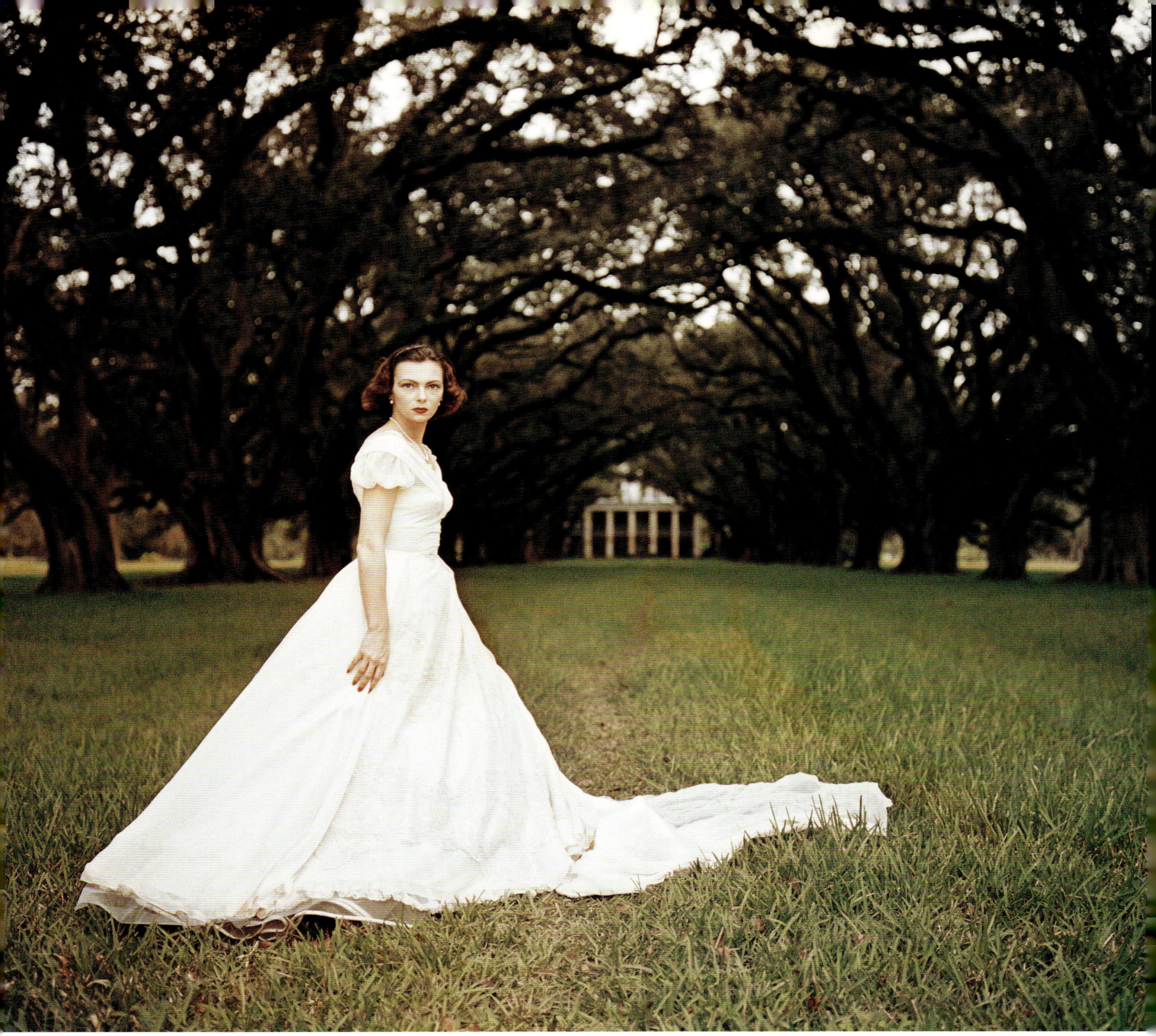

above Mrs. William Ferguson (Margarette Anne Williams), New Orleans, 1957. Slim explained how things unfolded on the day this picture was taken: "It was pouring rain on the morning we had made the appointment, but when I called her, she said that she had set aside the whole day for the shot, so why didn't we drive down and see what happened? That's what we did—drove down in the pouring rain to Oak Alley, which is on the levee below New Orleans. We had picked up a picnic lunch and a bottle of white wine from Brennan's, one of the choice New Orleans restaurants." They sat on the porch, eating cold chicken and cheese and drinking wine while it rained. "It was very pleasant. Finally it stopped raining, Anne changed into her wedding dress, and we went ahead and shot the picture."

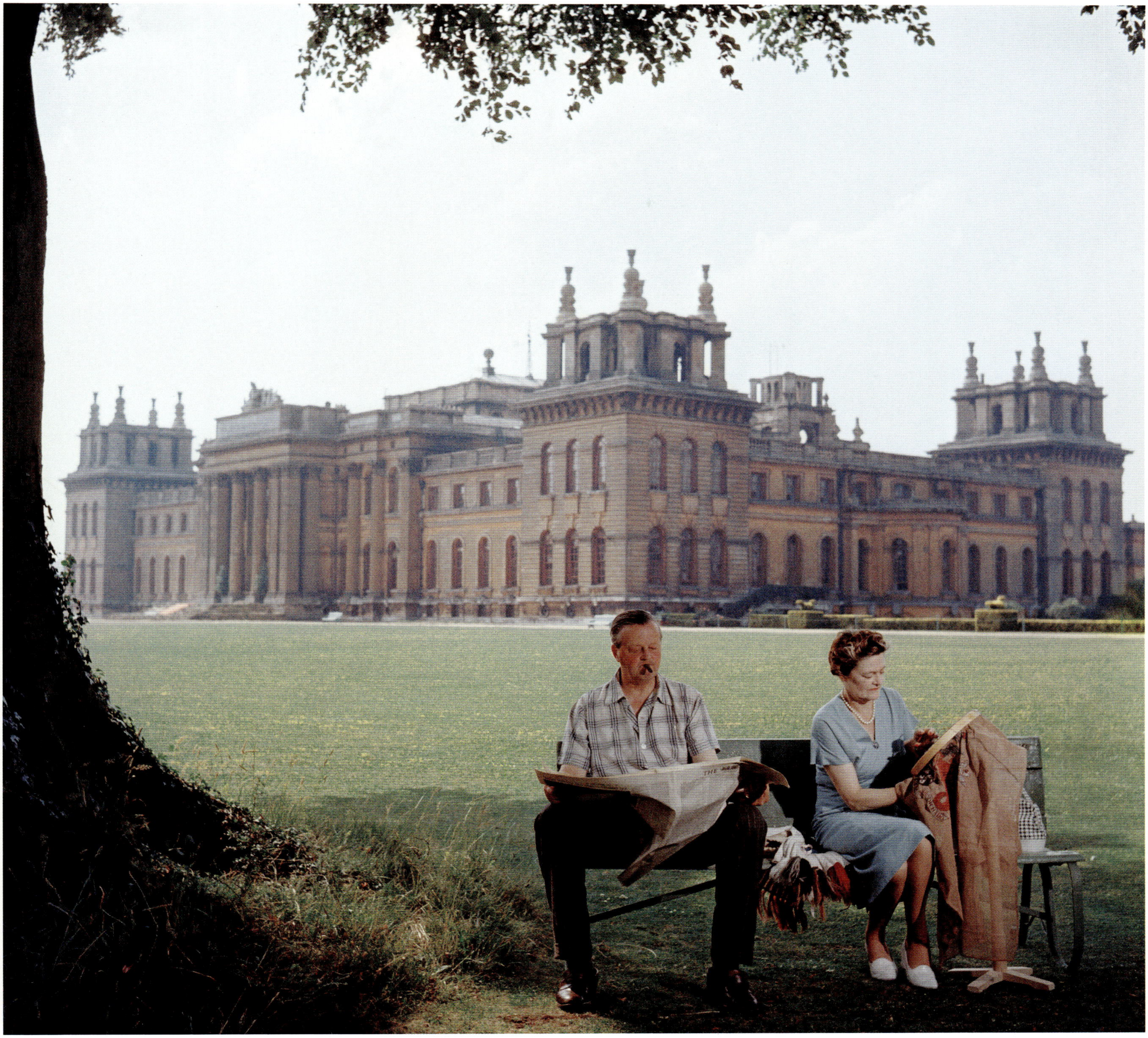

above John Spencer-Churchill, 10th Duke of Marlborough, and his wife Mary relax on the grounds of his ancestral estate, Blenheim Palace, Oxfordshire, England, 1957. She was born Alexandra Mary Cadogan, daughter of Viscount Chelsea, and in 1920 married the duke, elder son of the famously wealthy American railroad heiress Consuelo Vanderbilt. Vanderbilt's arranged marriage to the 9th Duke of Marlborough was said to have been one of the unhappiest in history, but one that saved Blenheim, the family seat since 1722, from ruin while advancing the Vanderbilts' social standing. Upon Mary's marriage to "Bert," as the duke was widely known, Vanderbilt gave her a diamond and pearl tiara and a pearl necklace with a pendant of aquamarines and diamonds. Blenheim is one of the most resplendent and storied palaces—with 187 rooms, three acres of roofs, and eleven thousand acres of surrounding land. It is said to have been spared bombing by the Nazis because Adolf Hitler intended to occupy it himself after his forces invaded England; it's not known whether the mere magnificence of the palace was the lure—or the fact that Winston Churchill had been born there.

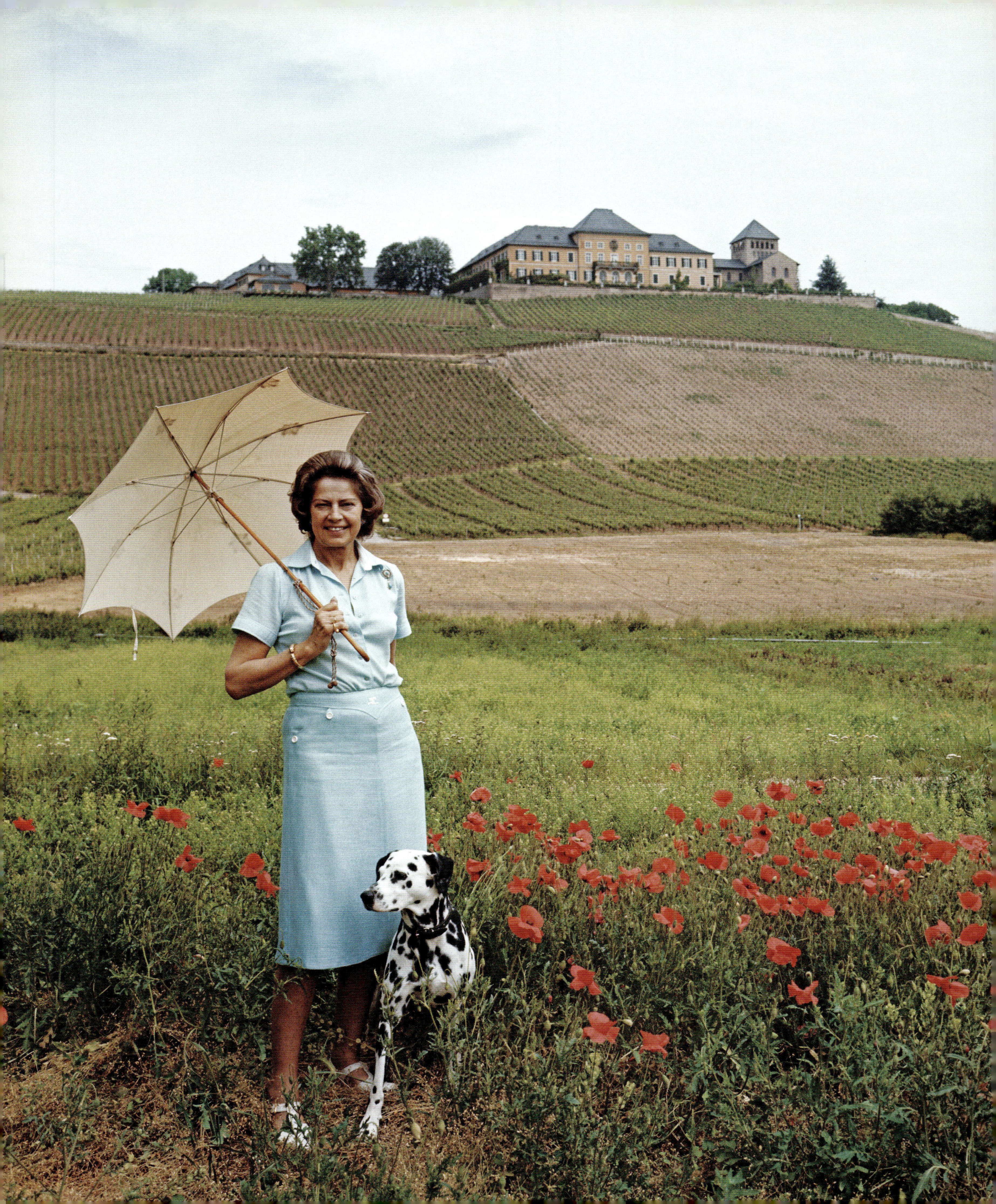

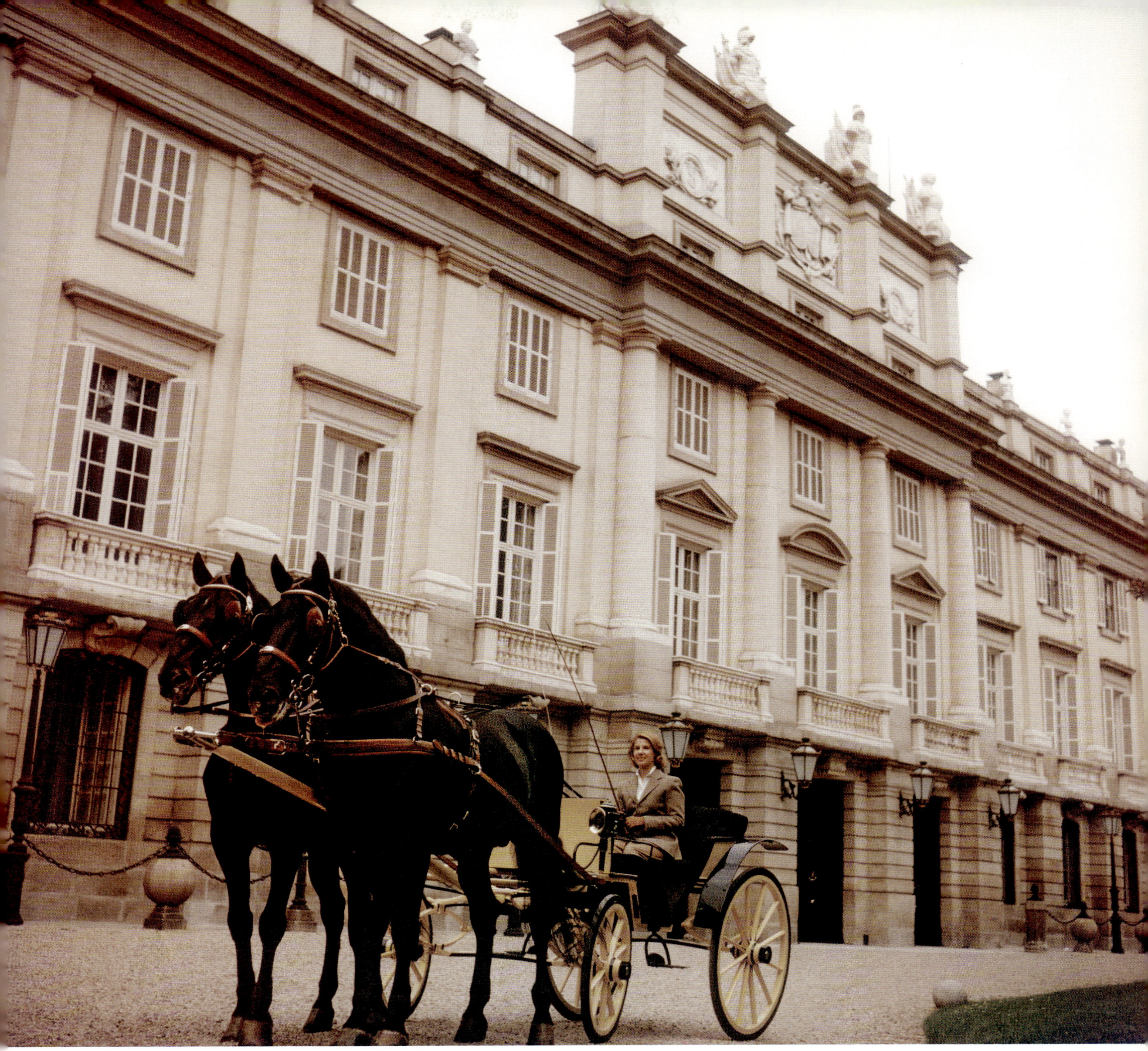

opposite Her Serene Highness Tatiana Fürstin von Metternich-Winneburg at Schloss Johannisberg along the Rhine River in Germany, 1977.

above The Duchess of Alba, head of one of Spain's oldest noble families, outside her home, the Palacio de Liria, Madrid, 1976. With more than forty titles, the duchess was considered to be the most titled aristocrat in the world and the wealthiest woman in Spain. When she married, her husbands (there were three in all) had to give up their names to become the Duke of Alba. Born Doña Maria del Rosario Cayetana Fitz-James Stuart y Silva, the duchess was a famous beauty who reportedly turned down a request as a young woman to be Picasso's muse. She also renounced many royal conventions and spent her life immersed in patronage of the arts. Upon her death in 2014, she was said to have amassed a private collection of masterpieces that rivaled any in Europe, and her children inherited the bulk of her billion-dollar fortune—plus a palace each.

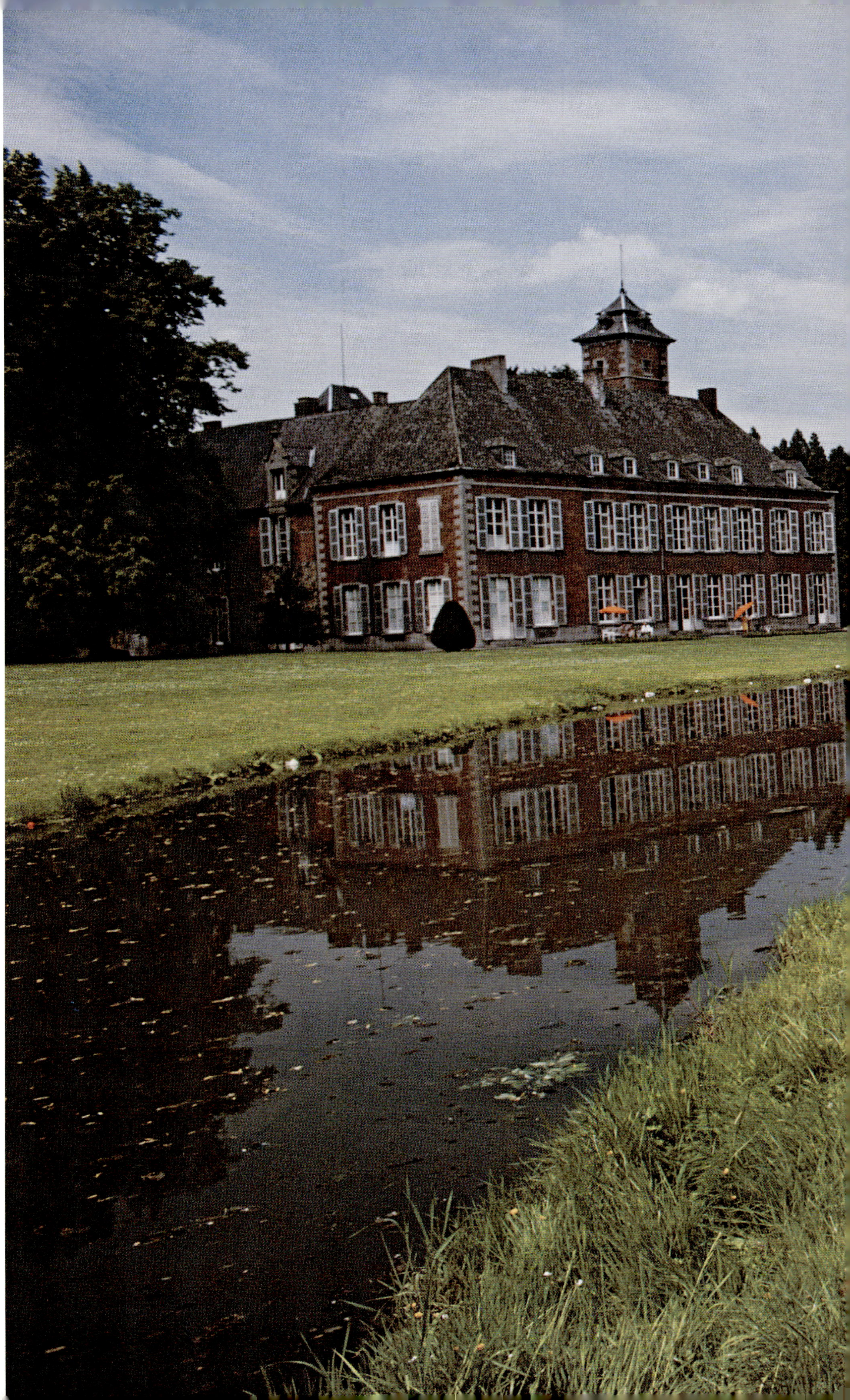

right Christiane de Lichtervelde and children at their home, La Follie, Écaussinnes-d'Enghien, Belgium, 1979. The Lichtervelde family is one of Belgium's oldest noble families. La Follie, the family seat, is a sixteenth-century mansion.

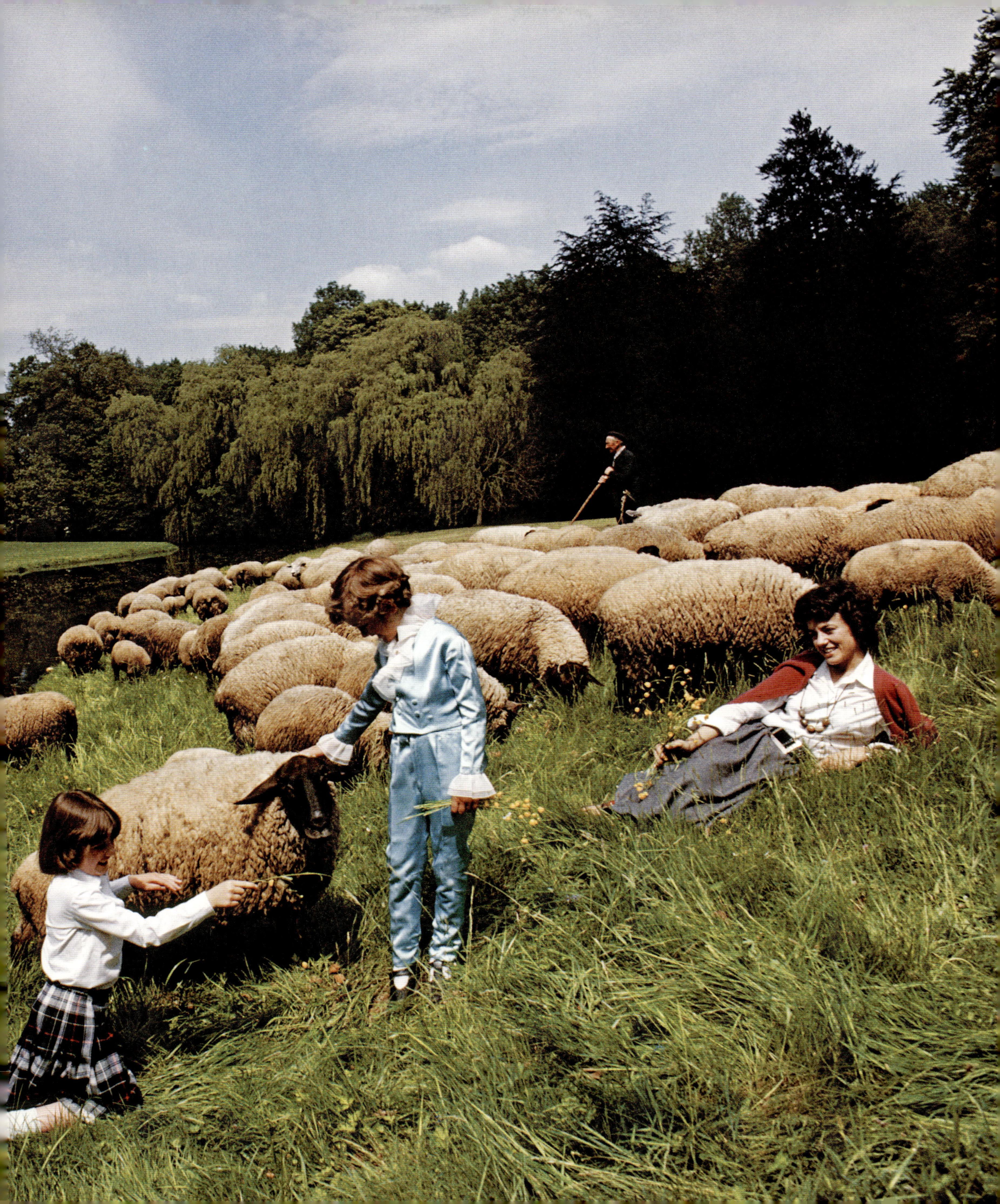

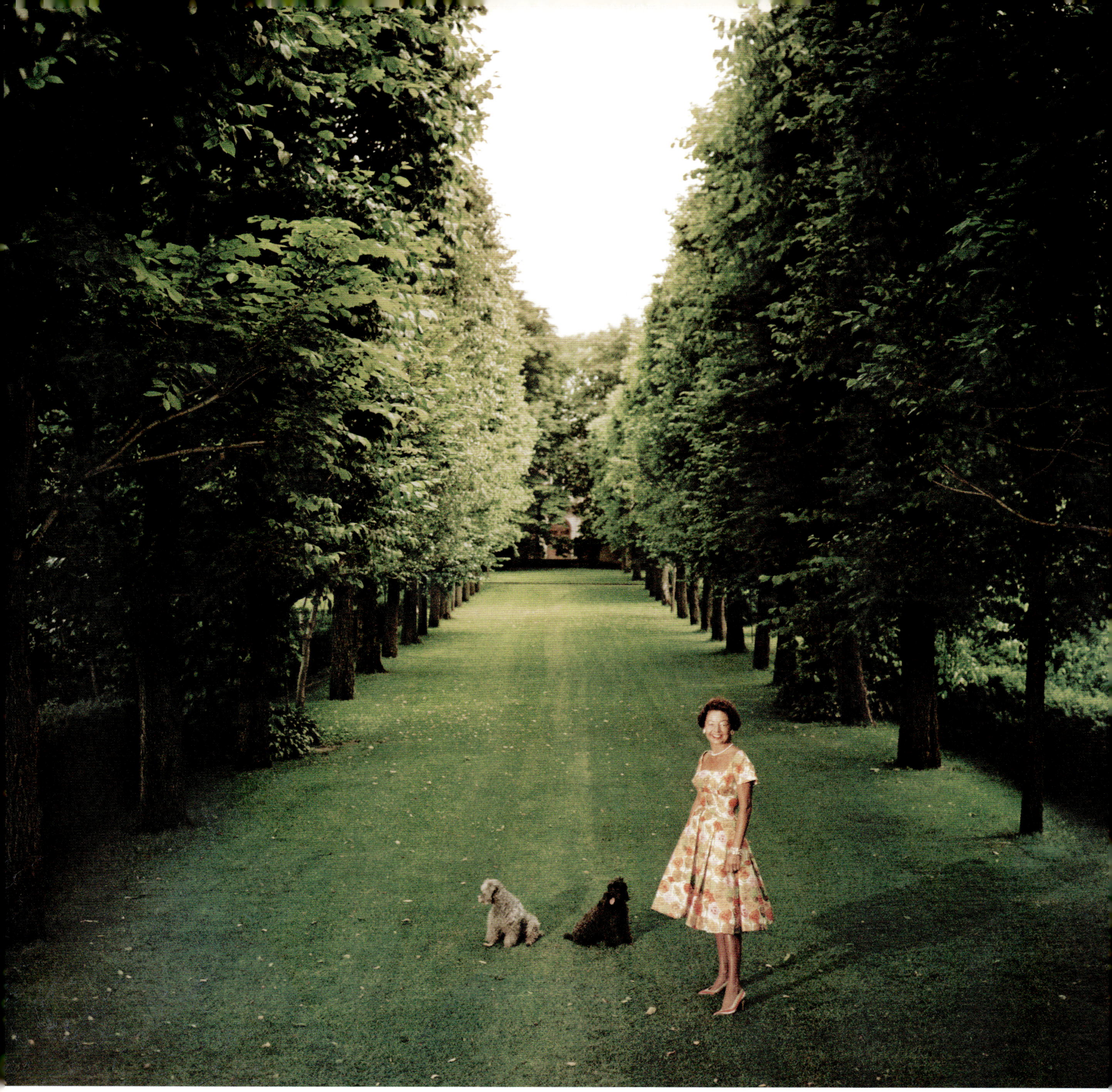

above Mrs. A. Watson Armour, Lake Forest, Illinois, 1960. "We marched to bed, and she usually played a Schubert march . . . so our love of music, it was almost genetic," remembered Whitney Addington of his mother.

She was born Sarah Wood in the Panama Canal Zone to American parents, both opera lovers; her father, a US Army general, took her to her first opera at age eight. She became an accomplished pianist who married

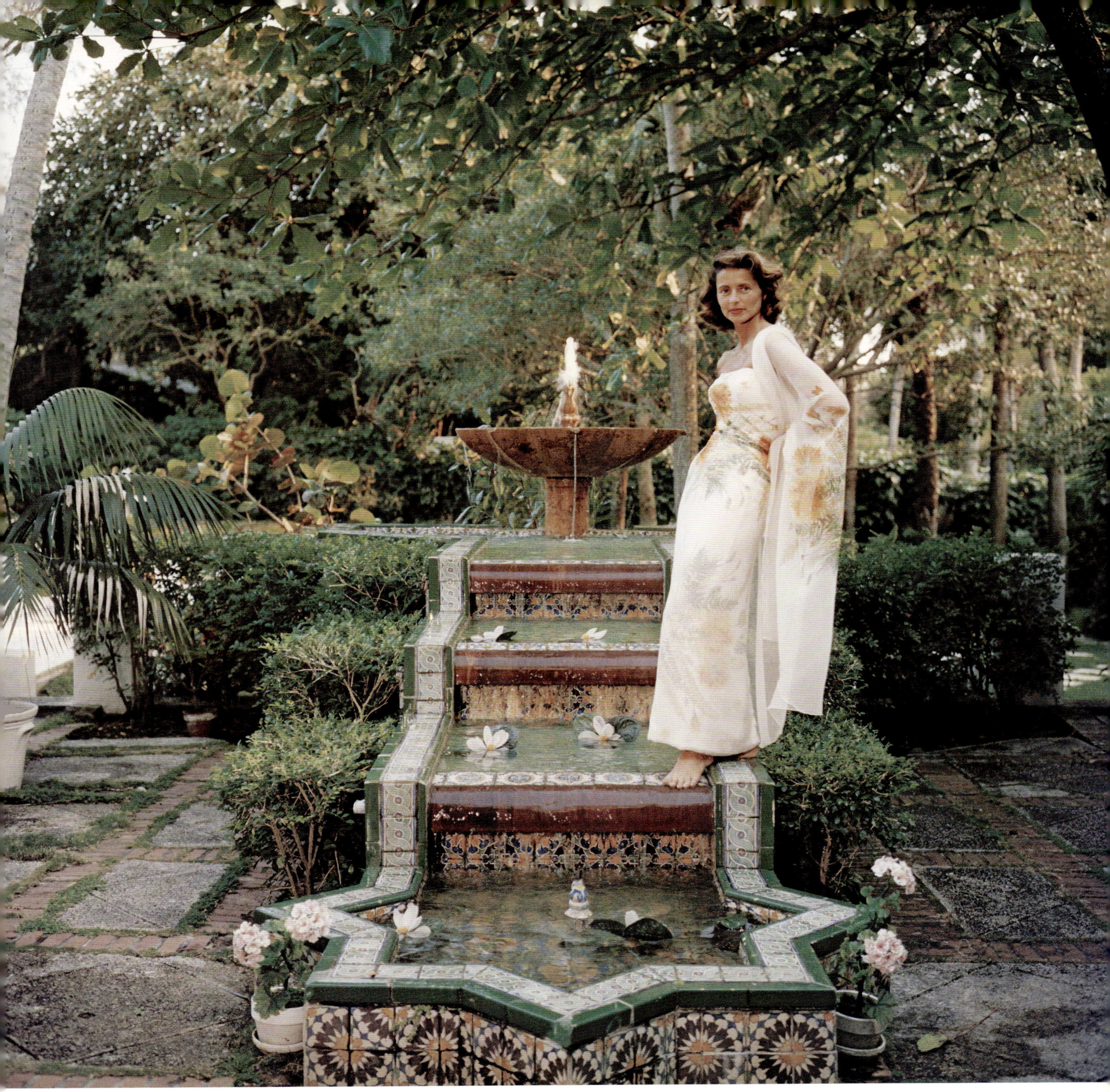

Andrew Watson Armour III, scion of the Armour meatpacking family. As a longtime board member and generous supporter of the Lyric Opera of Chicago, she was renowned for her patronage of the arts in the windy city.

above Mrs. Leverett Saltonstall Shaw, Palm Beach, circa 1950. See also pages 155 and 191.

below Writer and poet Elizabeth Bowen at Bowen's Court, her ancestral home, County Cork, Ireland, 1962. In 1930 she became the only woman to inherit Bowen's Court, where she hosted fellow writers, including Virginia Woolf, Eudora Welty, Carson McCullers, Iris Murdoch, and Veronica Wedgwood. Nevertheless, she thought of herself as solitary and "unrelatable"—one of her most characteristic phrases was "life with the lid on." She gained fame writing stories about life in wartime London, but her skill was particularly on display in her love letters to the Canadian

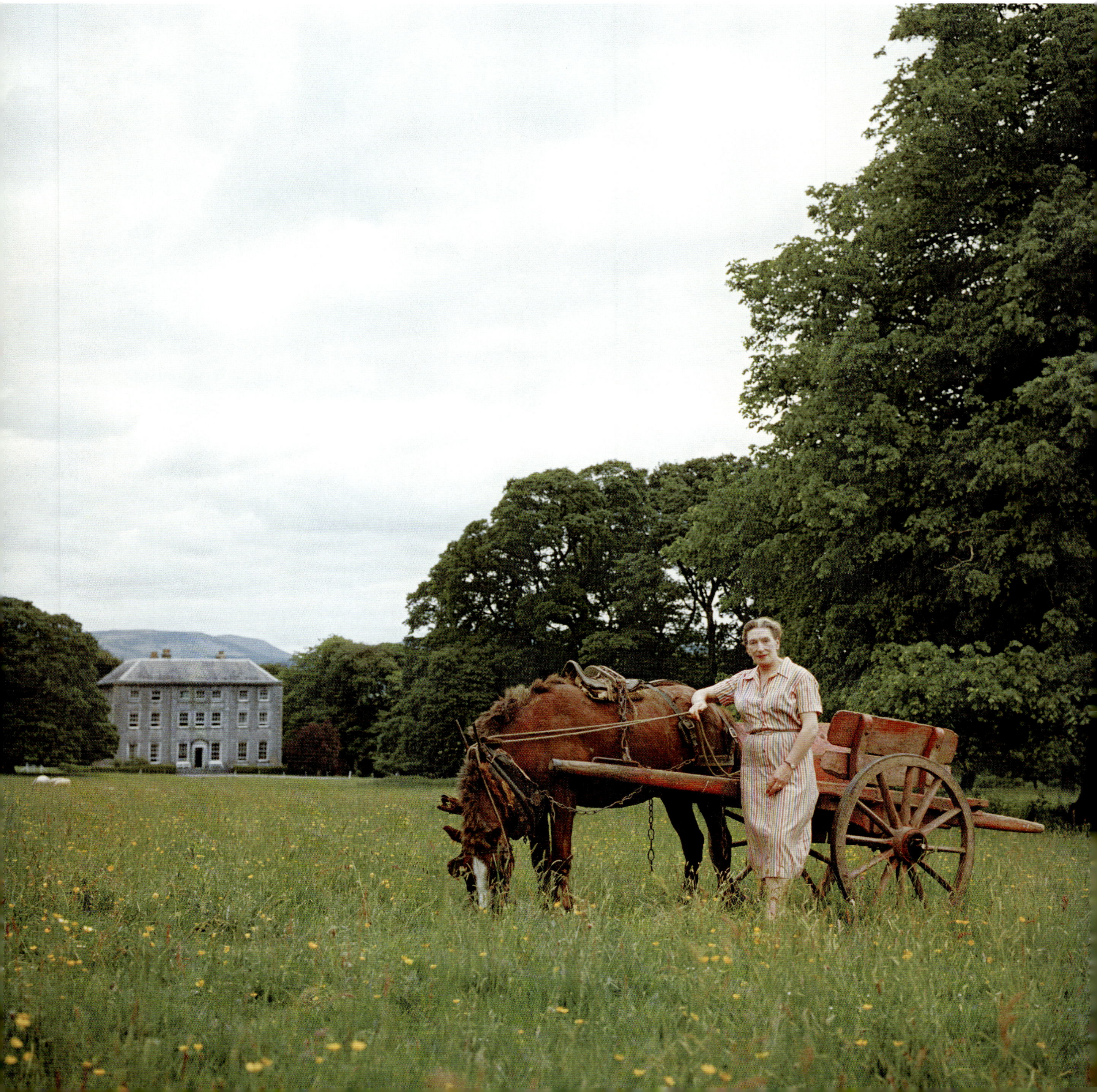

diplomat Charles Ritchie. When they met, she was forty-one and had been married eighteen years; Ritchie was seven years younger and unmarried. Their love affair lasted until her death thirty-two years later.

below Mr. and Mrs. Richard Mason, Kenya, 1955. At an altitude of nine thousand feet and just twenty-five miles from the equator, the Masons' Kenyan wheat farm was home to cattle, sheep, horses, and hounds. Princess Margaret of the United Kingdom once stayed at their highland home.

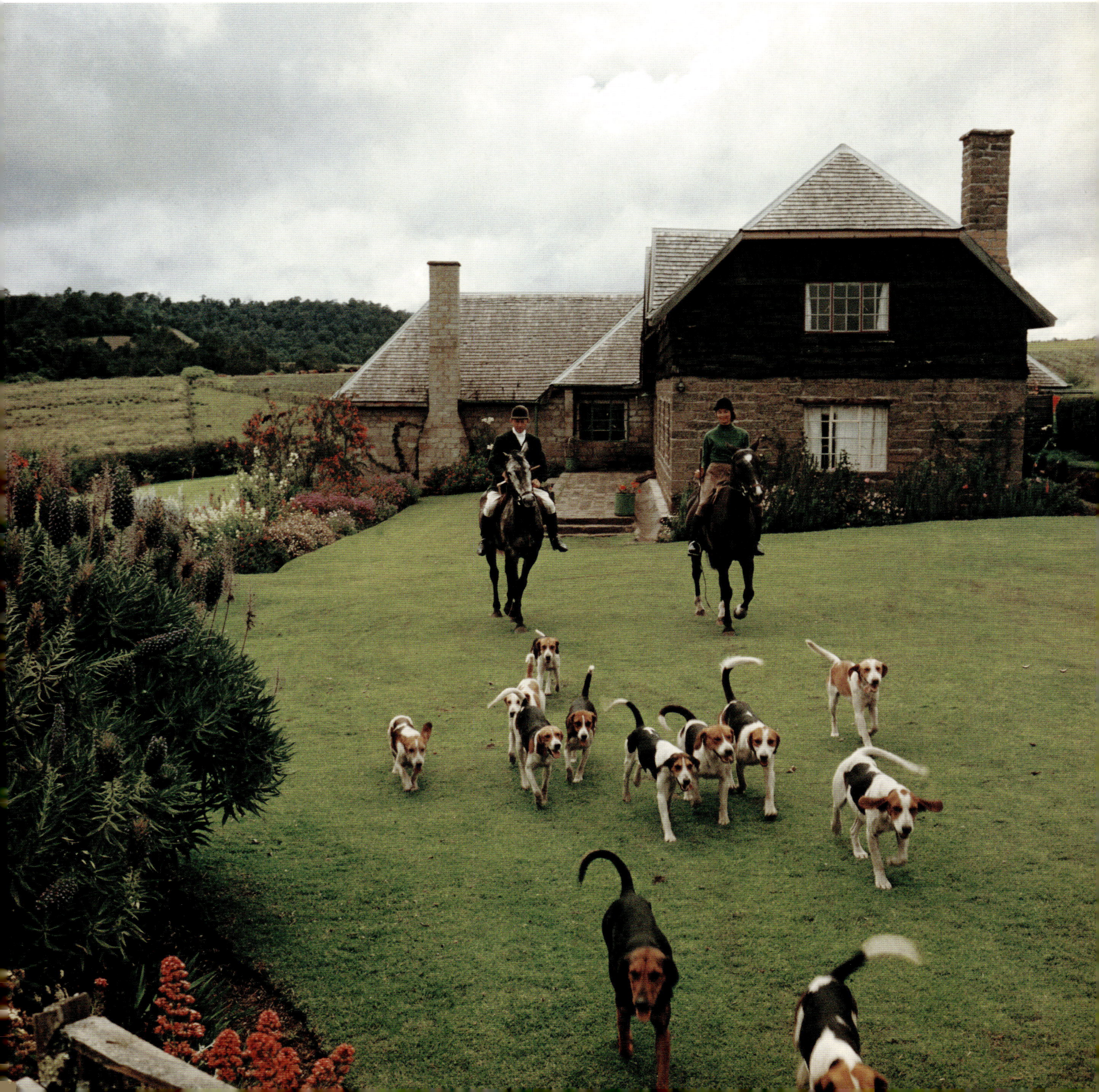

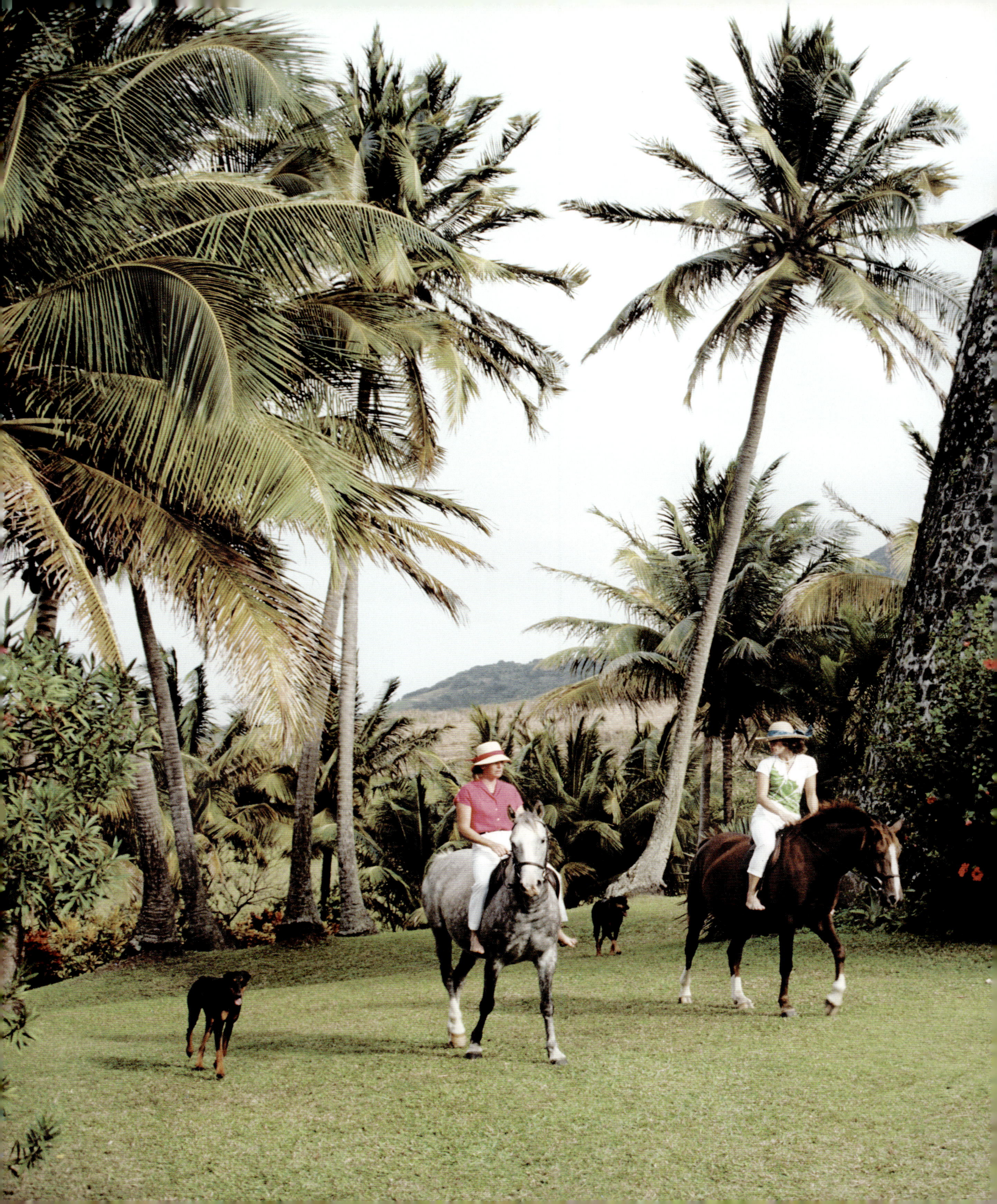

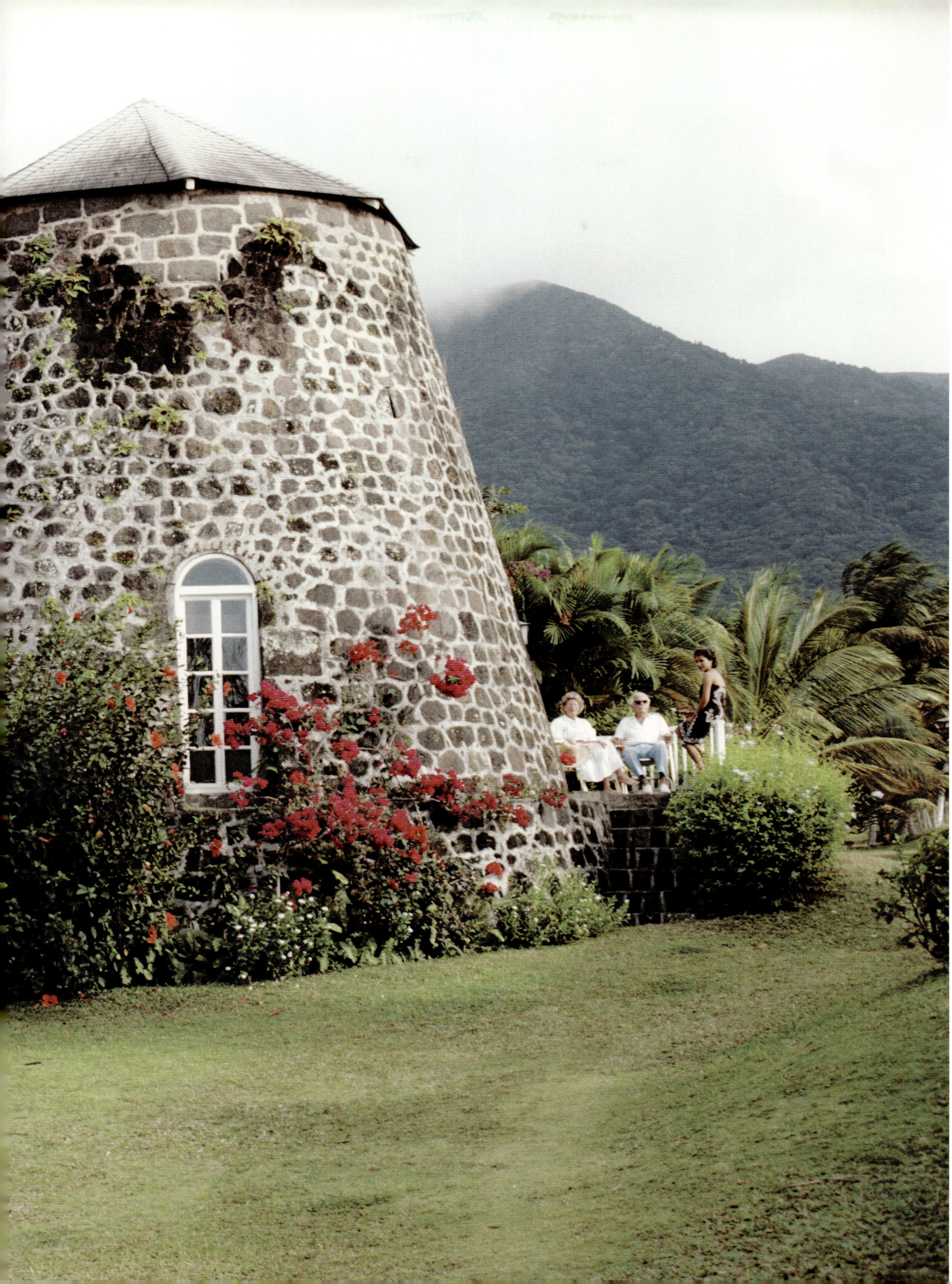

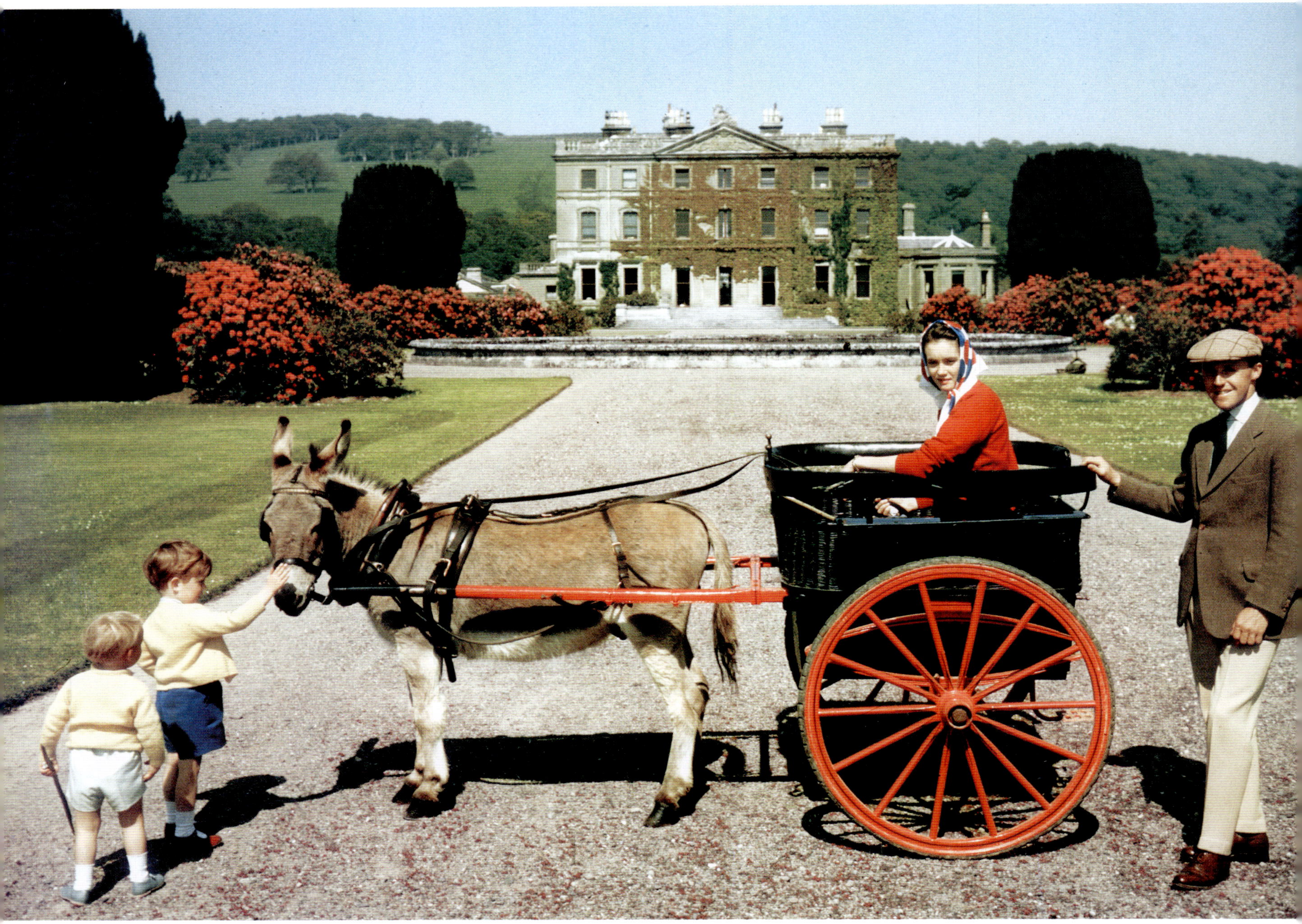

preceding spread Rawlins Plantation, St. Kitts and Nevis, West Indies, 1984. When Philip Walwyn and his wife Frances inherited a seventeenth-century sugarcane plantation from his family, at first they made their home there. They later decided to establish an inn on the property as well, restoring the stone sugar mill and turning it into a honeymoon suite. The Walwyns' inn comprised the best of English country life: gardens, horses, guest cottages, even a grass tennis court. The inn sat at the base of Mount Misery with spectacular views of St. Eustatius and the neighboring French and Dutch islands from its expansive veranda.

above The Marquess and Marchioness of Waterford and their children, the eldest of whom is the Earl of Tyrone, pictured on the grounds of their home, Curraghmore, County Waterford, Ireland, circa 1970. The title held by John Beresford, 8th Marquess of Waterford, is the premier marquessate in the Peerage of Ireland. The marchioness was born Lady Caroline Olein Geraldine Wyndham-Quin, daughter of the 6th Earl of Dunraven and Mount-Earl. Curraghmore castle—the largest private demesne in Ireland, composed of twenty-five hundred acres of formal gardens, woodlands, and fields—is believed to have been erected on this site in the twelfth century.

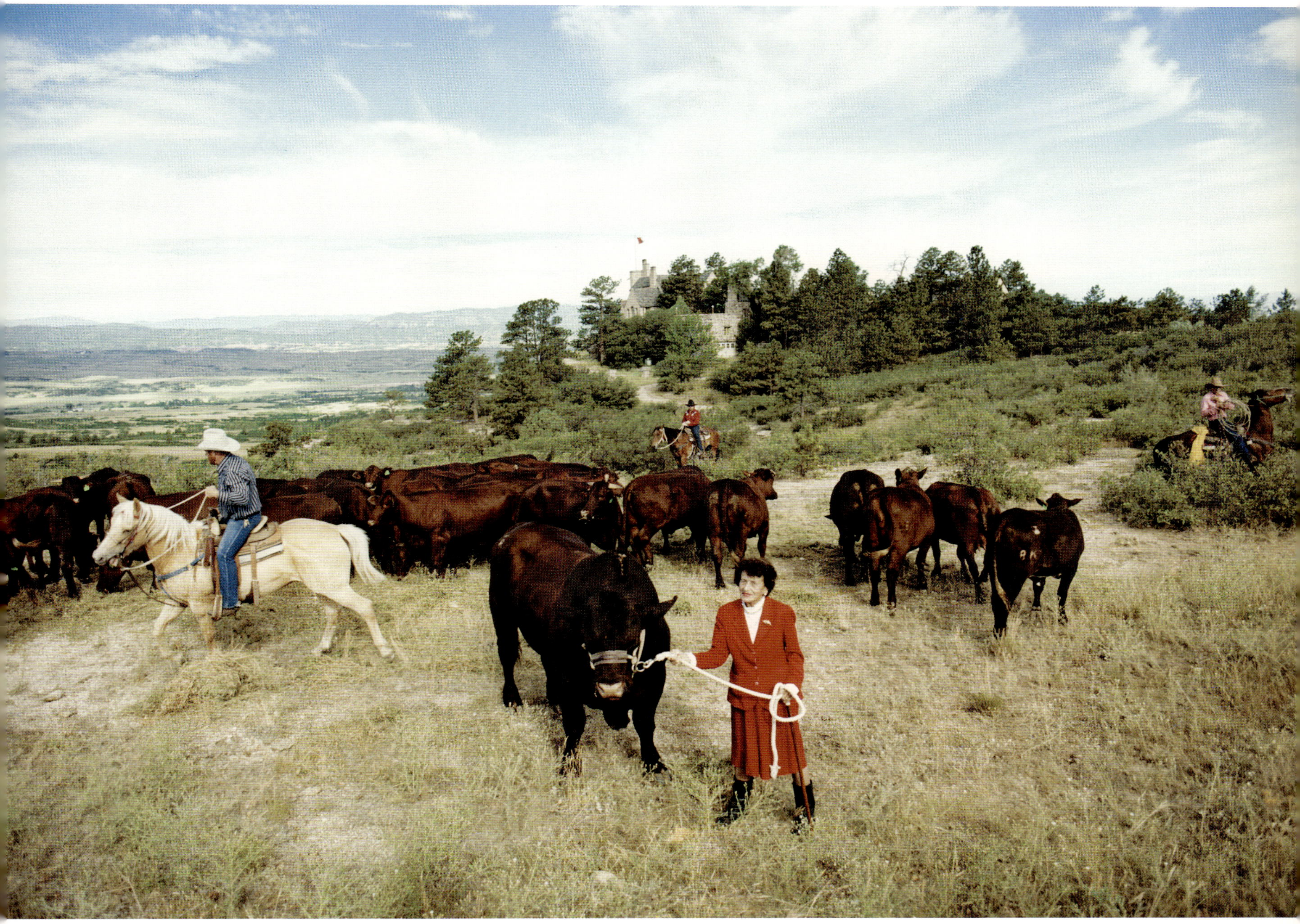

above Tweet Kimball, Castle Pines, Colorado, 1991. Mildred Montague Genevieve Kimball, known to all as "Tweet," began breeding her prized Santa Gertrudis cattle in 1954 on her thirty-four-hundred-acre spread, called Cherokee Ranch, with its vistas of the snow-capped Rockies. She brought the Santa Gertrudis, bred for warmer climes of Texas, to her Colorado ranch against the advice of her critics, who said they would not thrive. She proved them wrong for four decades. Kimball sat on various charitable and environmental boards nationwide and hosted a cadre of European royalty and American dignitaries at her home.

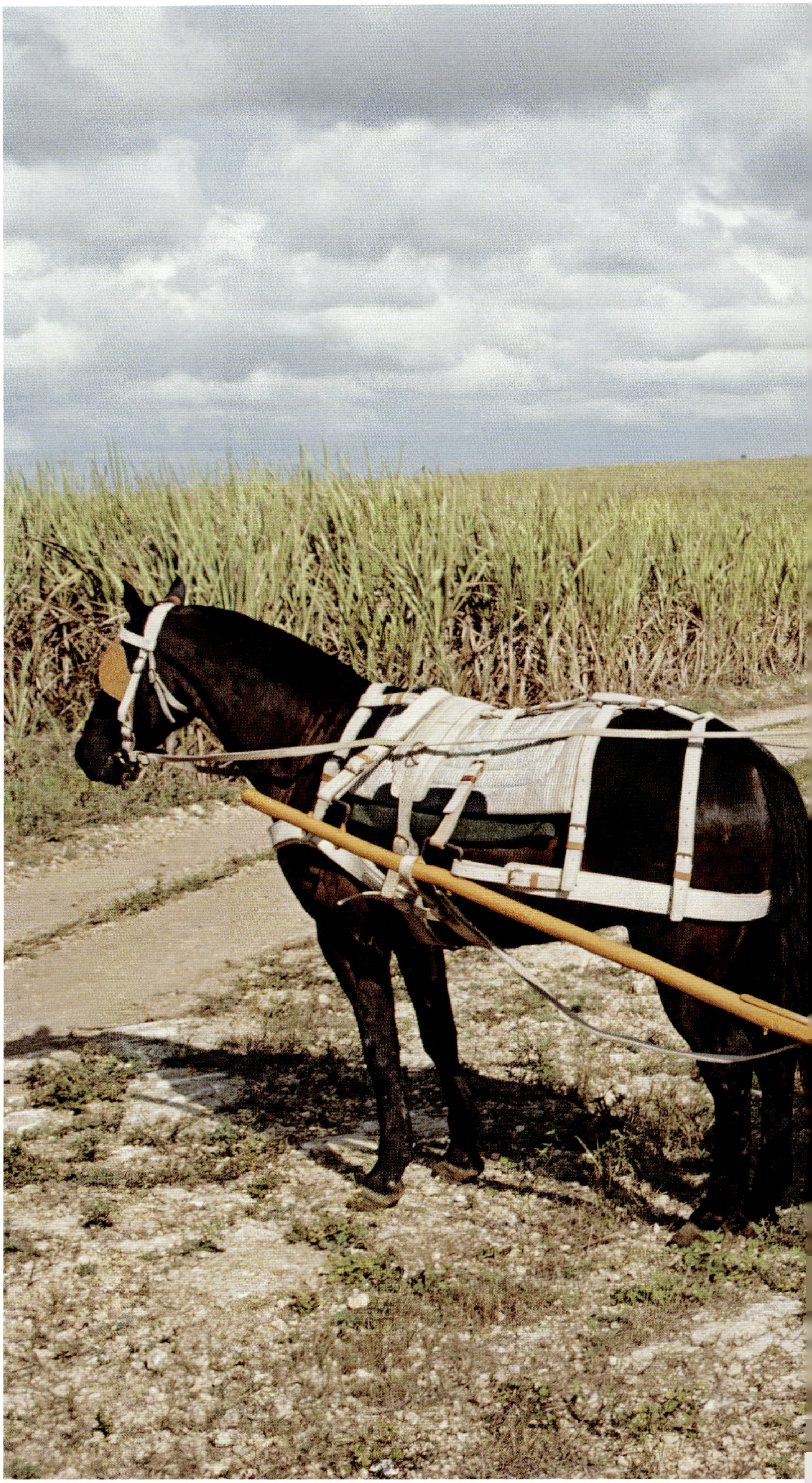

right Emilia (in blue) and Tina (standing) Fanjul, wives of the Cuban sugar barons José and Alfonso Fanjul, respectively, Casa de Campo, Dominican Republic, 1990. The Fanjuls are an unusual American success story—they fled Fidel Castro's Cuba for the United States in 1959 with nothing more than their pedigree as one of Cuba's foremost sugar plantation families. The latter-day sugar barons then rebuilt their fortune in America extending their reach into real estate and philanthropy.

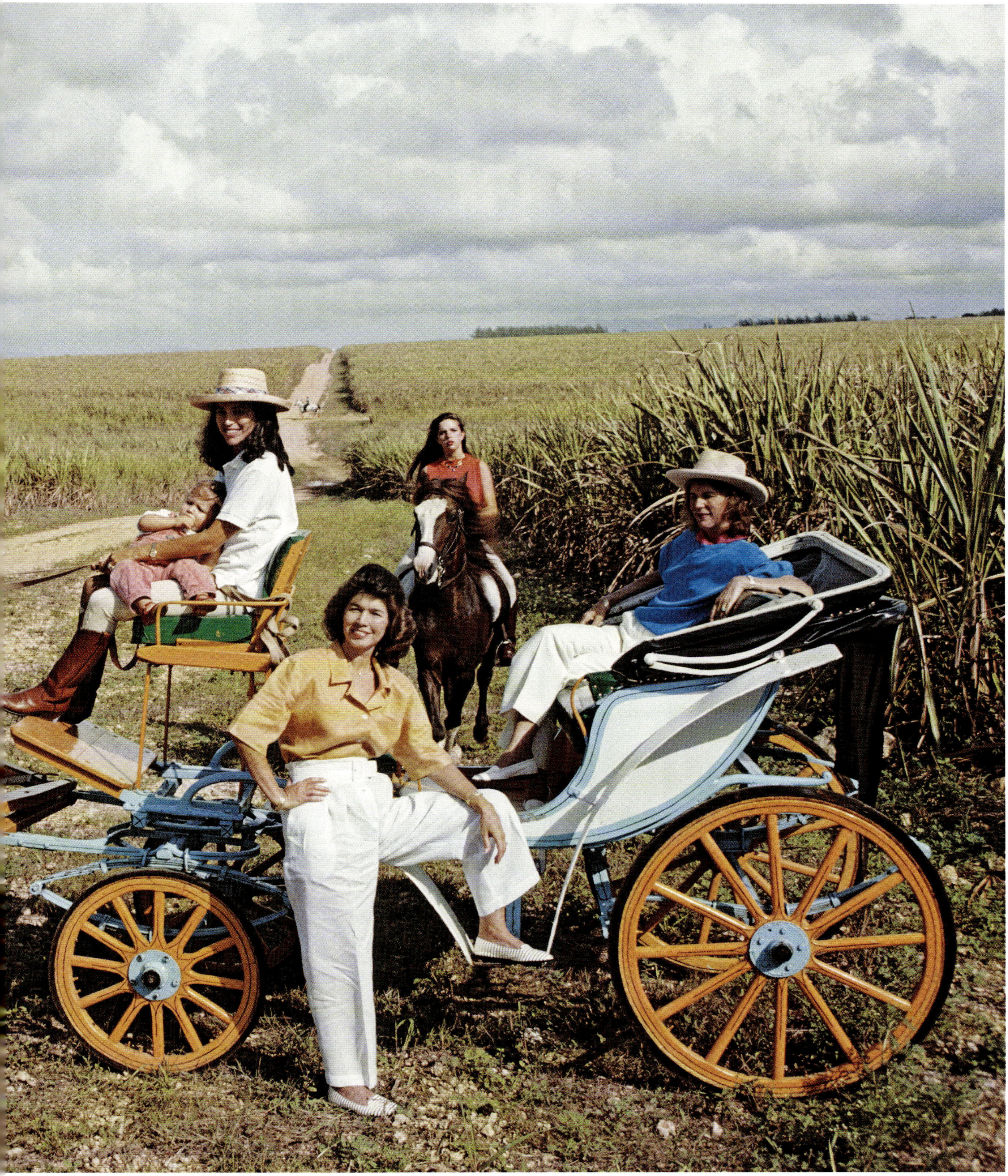

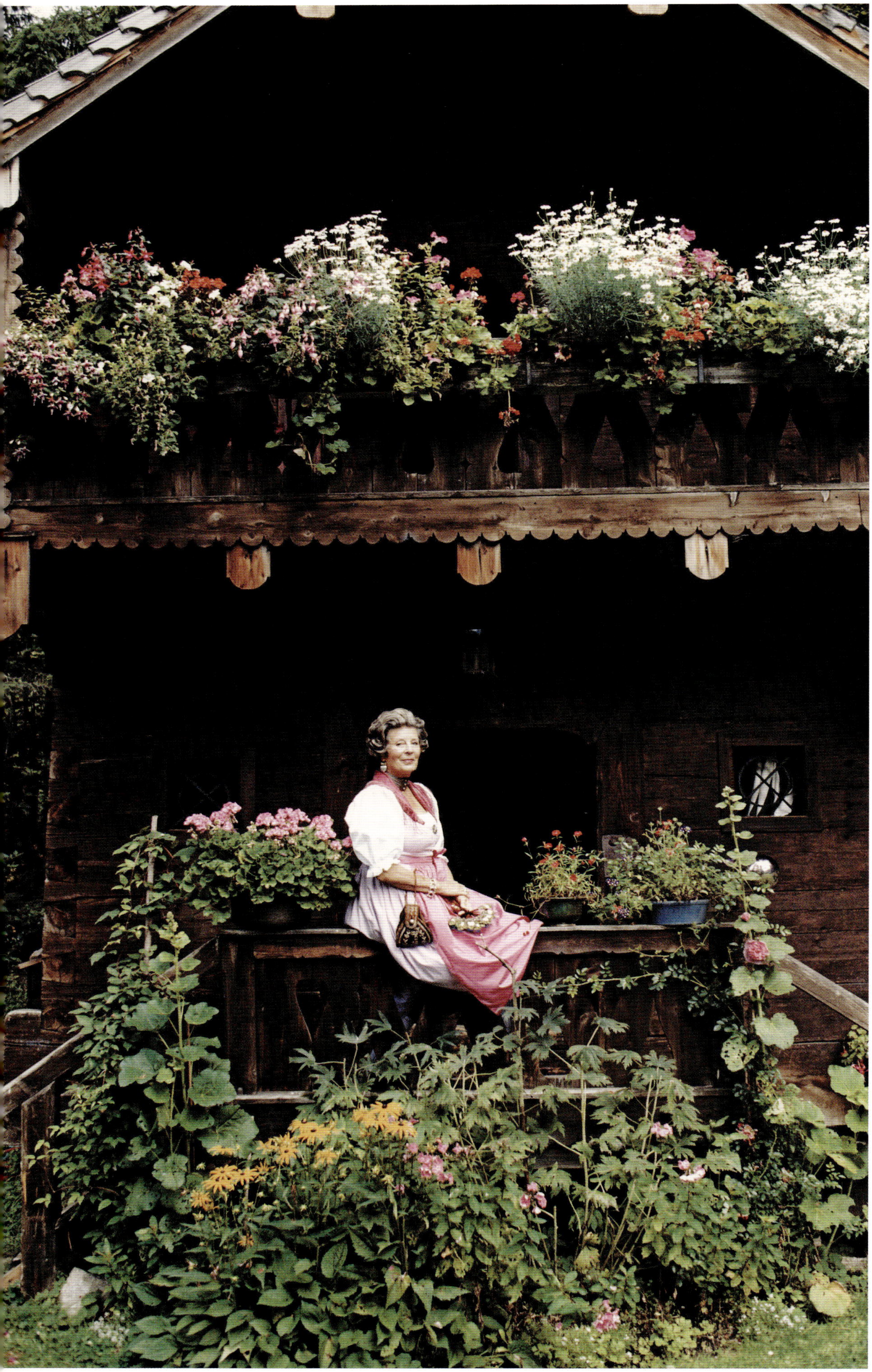

left Princess Marianne Sayn-Wittgenstein-Sayn, known as "Manni," Fuschl, Austria, 1986. Manni Wittgenstein was one of Slim's favorite people—they shared a common interest in photography and knew many of the same people. He used to say that "anybody who is anybody in Europe is a cousin of Manni's." A descendant of the Austrian Mayr Melnhof family on her father's side, Manni was the great-great-great-great-granddaughter of Empress Maria Theresa of Austria, a princess in the House of Habsburg, on her mother's side. During World War II Manni's husband was declared missing in action and then taken prisoner; a decade later he was killed in an automobile accident. Energetic, self-reliant, and generous by nature, she raised their five children by herself, at some point turning her pastime of taking photos at social functions into a vocation. Over the years she became the unofficial goodwill ambassador for Salzburg and for all of Austria. "Mamarazza," the nickname coined for her by Princess Caroline of Monaco, is also the title of her book of photographs depicting a half century in the life of a princess. A number of notable personalities are featured, such as Britain's Queen Mother, Queen Sirikit of Thailand, Margaret Thatcher, President Sukarno of Indonesia, Kurt Waldheim, the Nobel Prize winner Sir Francis Crick, Karl Lagerfeld, Oscar de la Renta, and many more.

opposite Mrs. Joseph Verner Reed, Palm Beach, circa 1960. As arbiter of the very quiet and exclusive Jupiter Island Club in neighboring Hobe Sound, Permelia Reed was therefore long known as "Mrs. Hobe Sound."

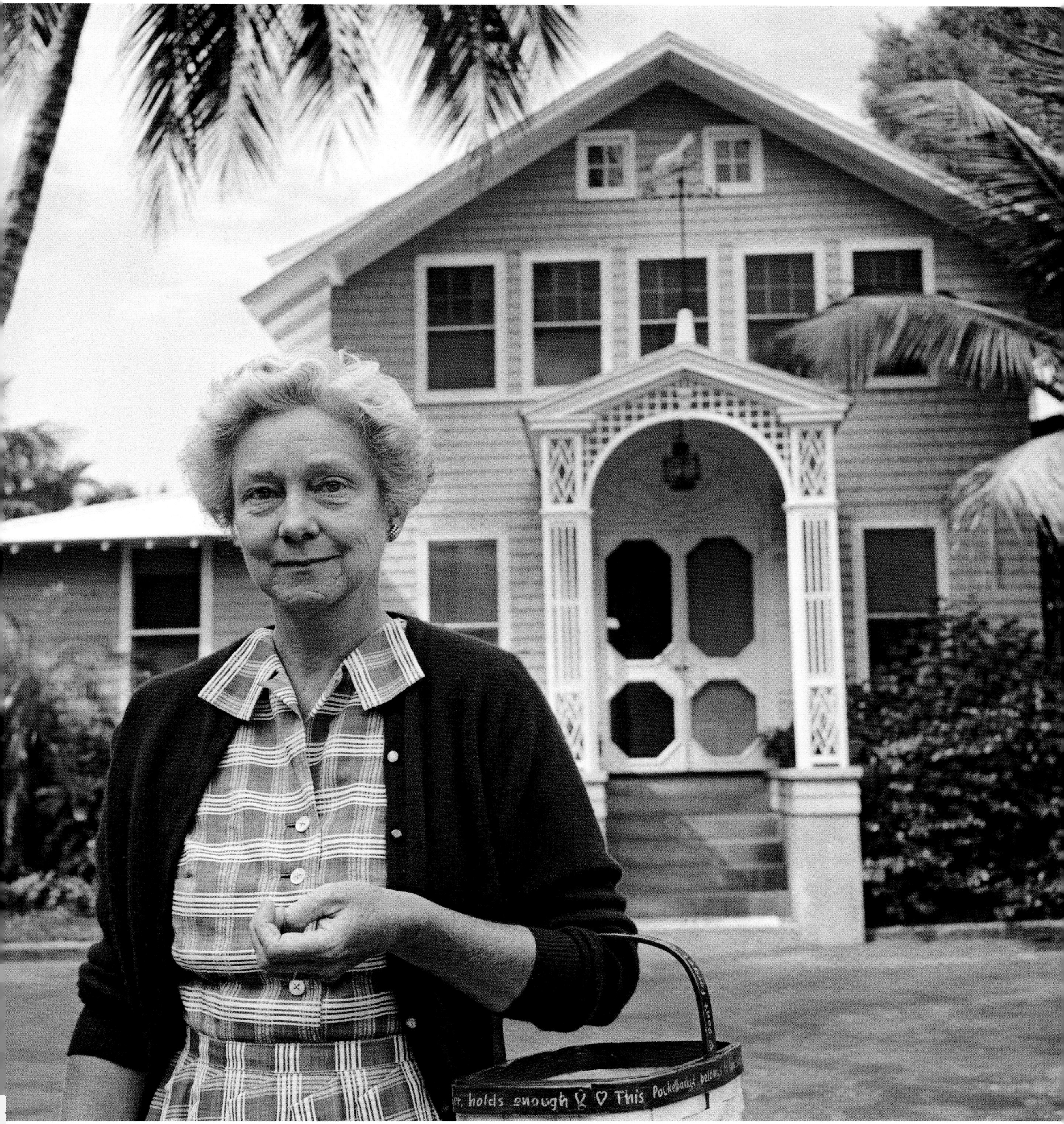
holds enough
This Pocketbasket belongs

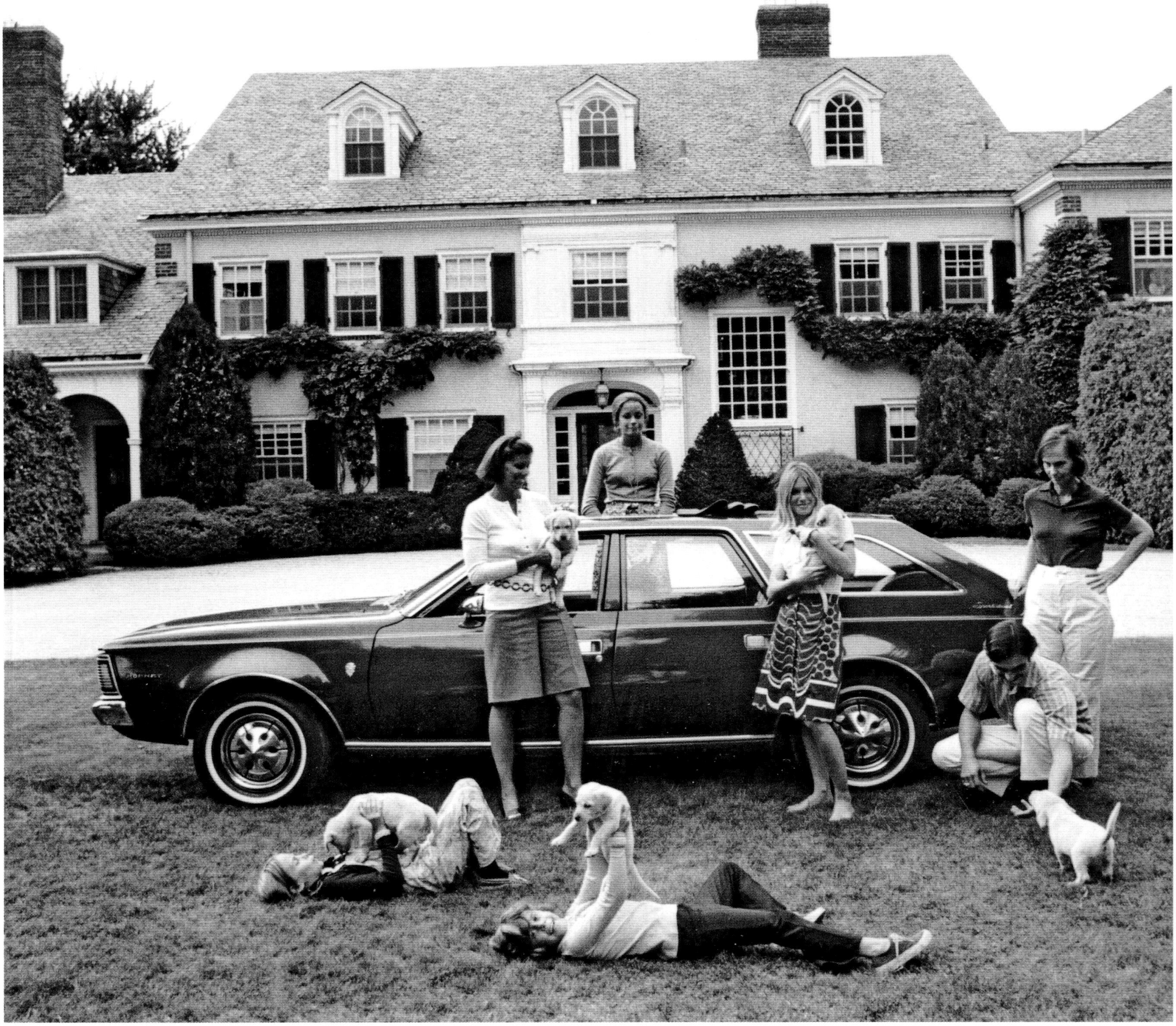

above Mrs. Roy Chapin (the former Sis Baldwin) and family members outside their home, Grosse Pointe, Michigan, circa 1968. Roy Chapin was the head of American Motors in the 1960s, when Grosse Pointe was the favored Detroit suburb for automobile executives to live with their families.

opposite Mrs. Leverett Saltonstall Shaw (see also pages 155 and 179) watches as her children dig for clams at low tide on Black Beach, Massachusetts Bay, circa 1960. Slim wrote of this photo in 1971, "In the warm summer months there is swimming in the brisk waters of Massachusetts Bay from any number of beaches in the area, and you can go clamming and sailing in all but the bitterest of the winter months. In front of my wife's family's house in Manchester is a little sandy cove known as Black Beach, a favorite clamming spot at low tide."

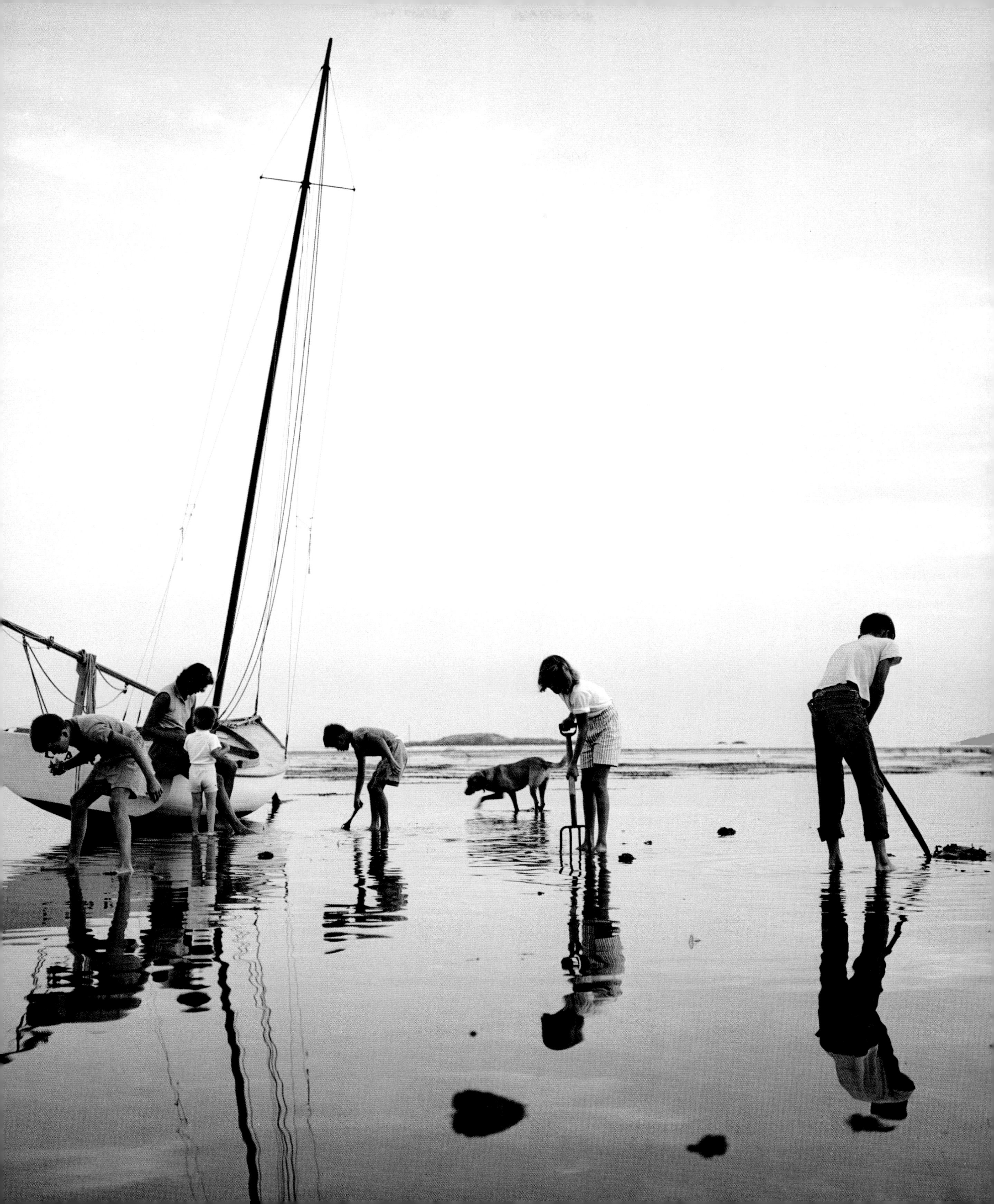

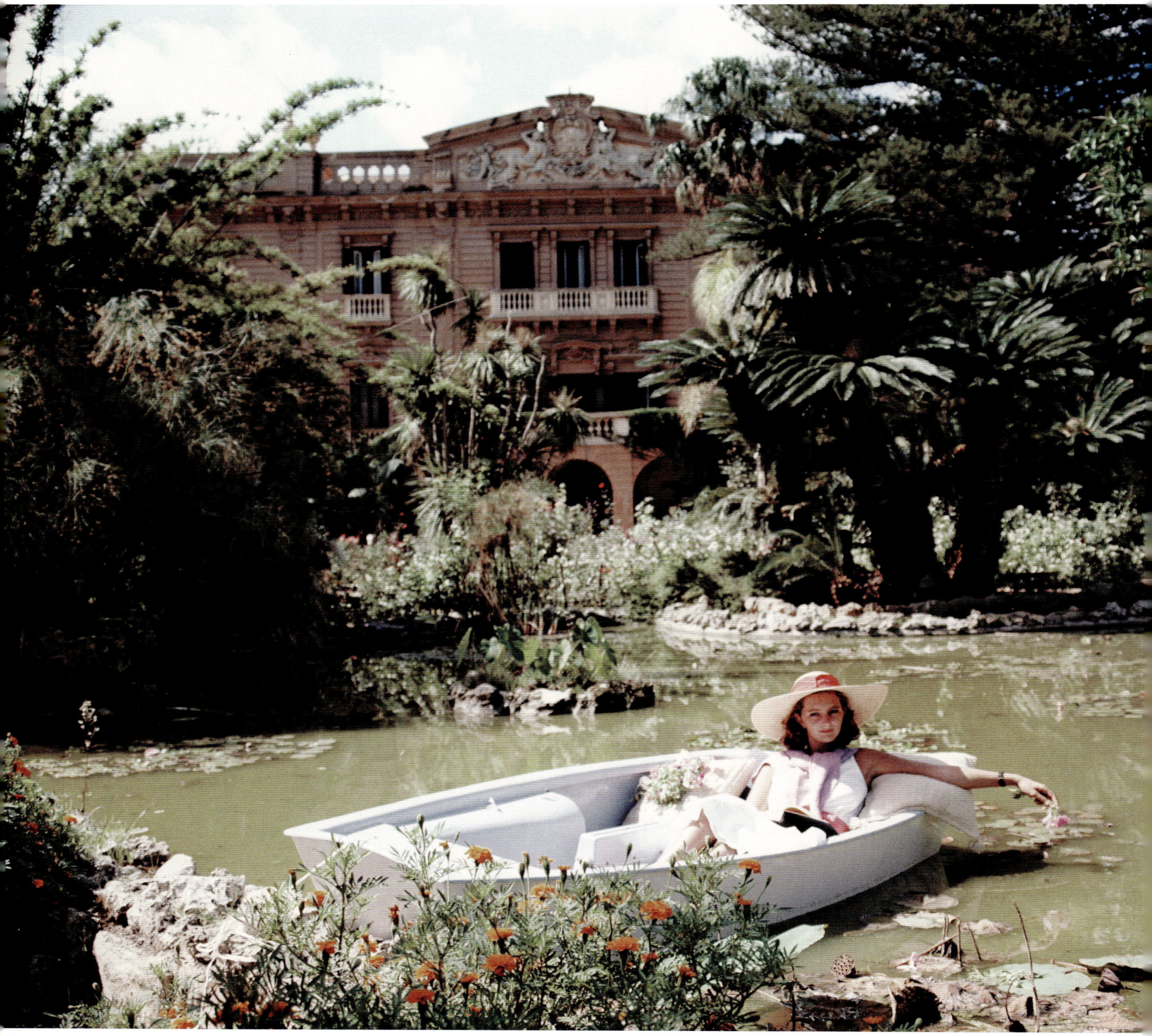

above Donna Fabrizia Lanza di Mazzarino on the grounds of her ancestral Villa Tasca d'Almerita, Sicily, 1984. More than thirty years later, Fabrizia reflected on having had her photo taken by Slim: "It was such a hot day and I'd just come up from swimming in the sea. I was young and against all of the establishment ideas, rather bored with the idea of dressing up and sitting in a boat. No one ever used this boat, and Slim decided to pull it out and have me get into it. Now, thirty years later, I see this photograph in so many different places—my son saw it again just the other day!"

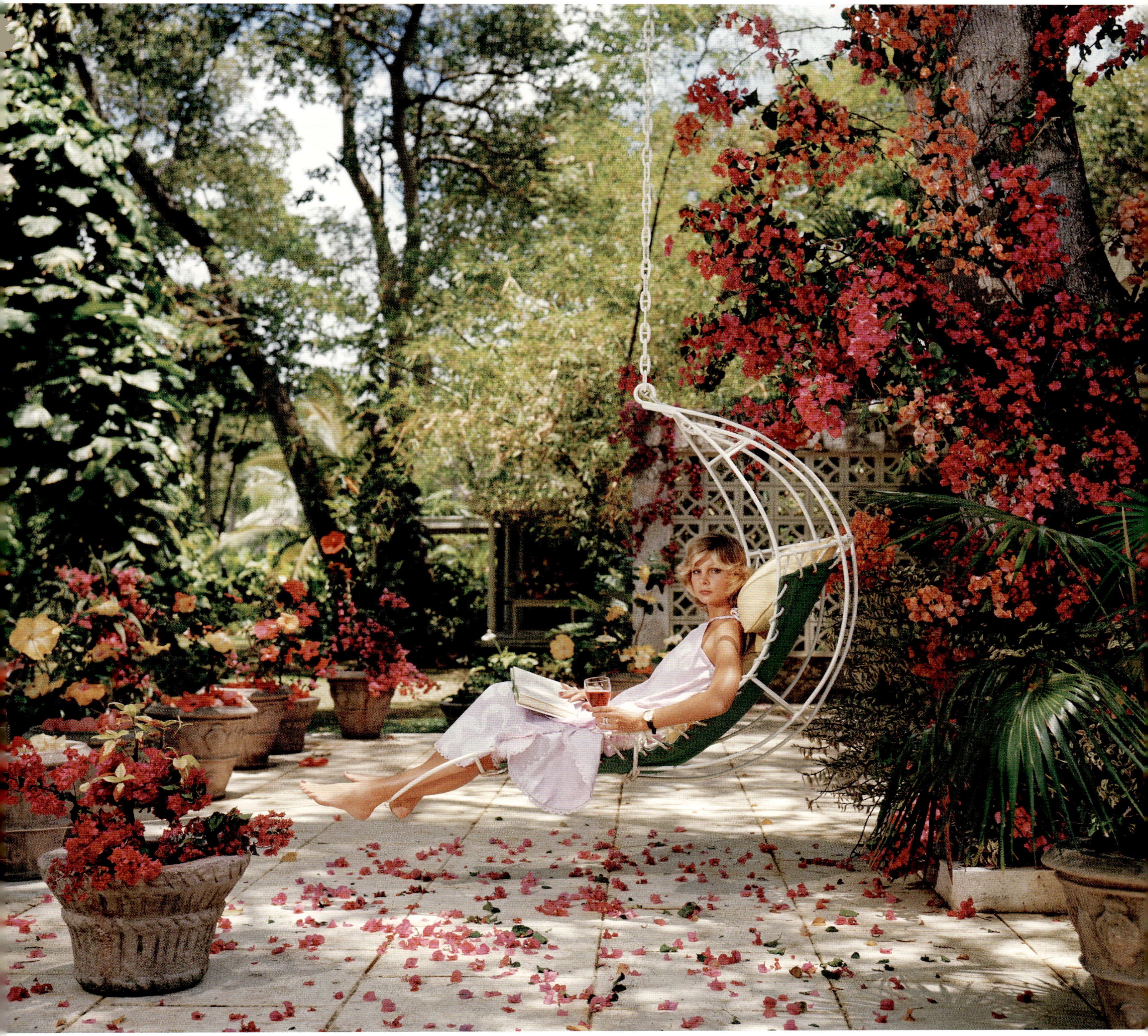

Today she is the head of a world-renowned Sicilian cooking school, Anna Tasca Lanza, started by and named for her late mother and located at the family's Regaleali vineyard.

above Ava Marshall, Barbados, 1976. Her Barbadian family tree dates back to the seventeenth century.

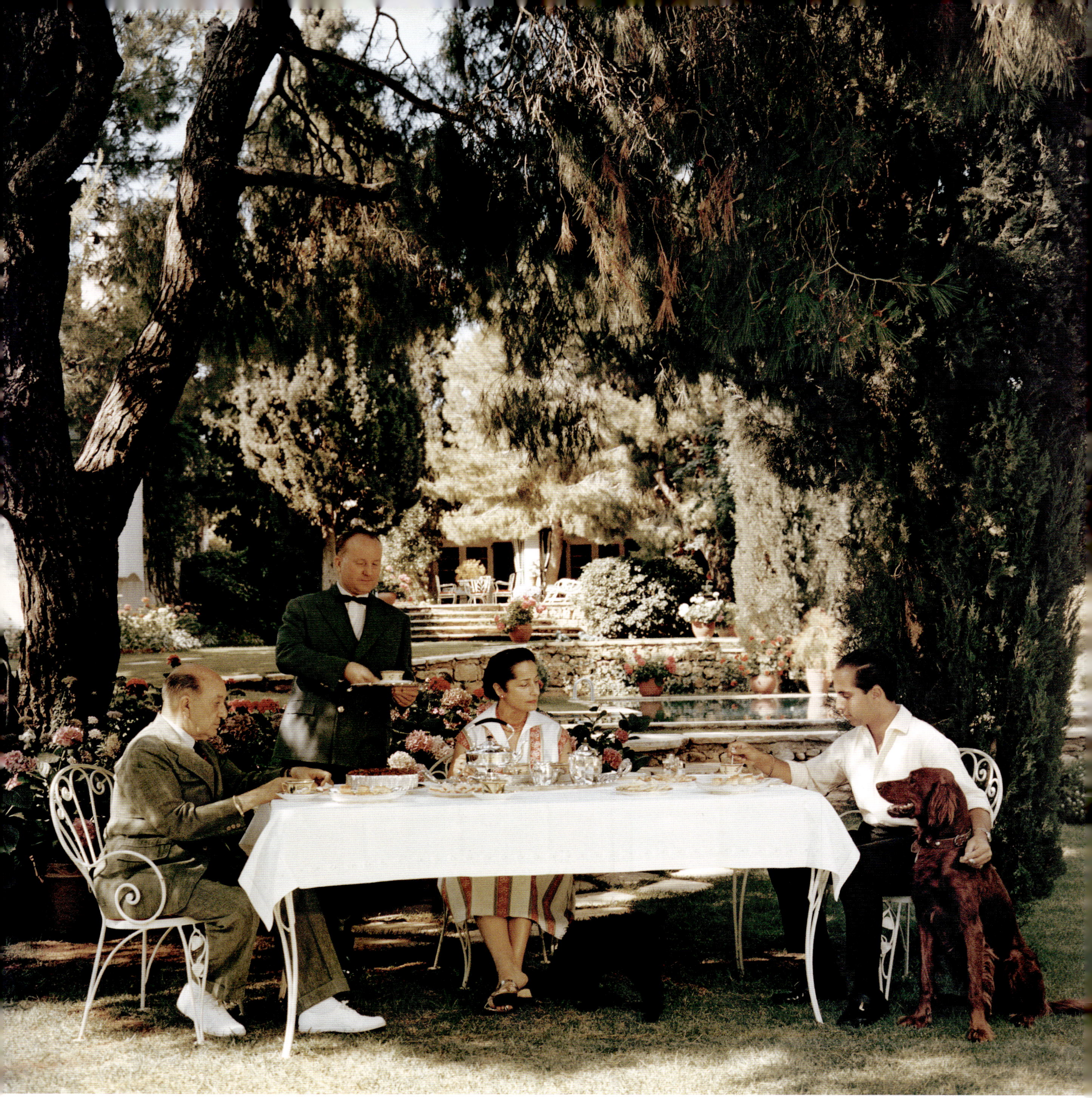

above Admired widely for her horticultural expertise, Madame Levidis designed the spectacular gardens at the home she shared with her husband, Colonel Demitris Levidis, grand marshal of the Greek court, and their son, Athens, 1961.

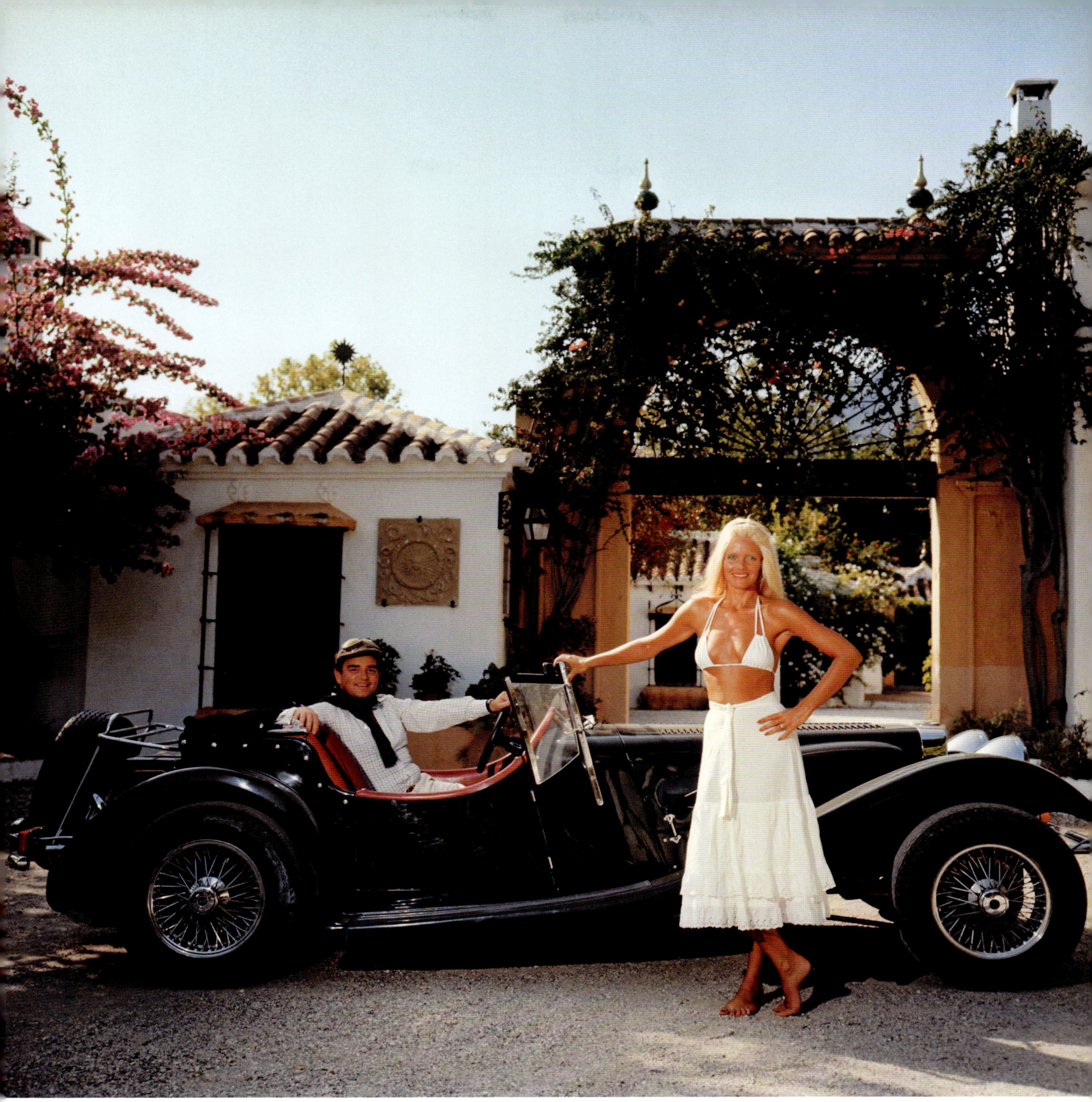

above Countess Gunilla von Bismarck and Count Rudi von Schönburg in Marbella, Spain, 1976. The countess is a descendant of Otto von Bismarck, "the Iron Chancellor," whose German noble family's roots can be traced to the thirteenth century. As for "Count Rudi," as he is known to all, he is the brains and soul of the Marbella Club, one of Spain's most exclusive resorts.

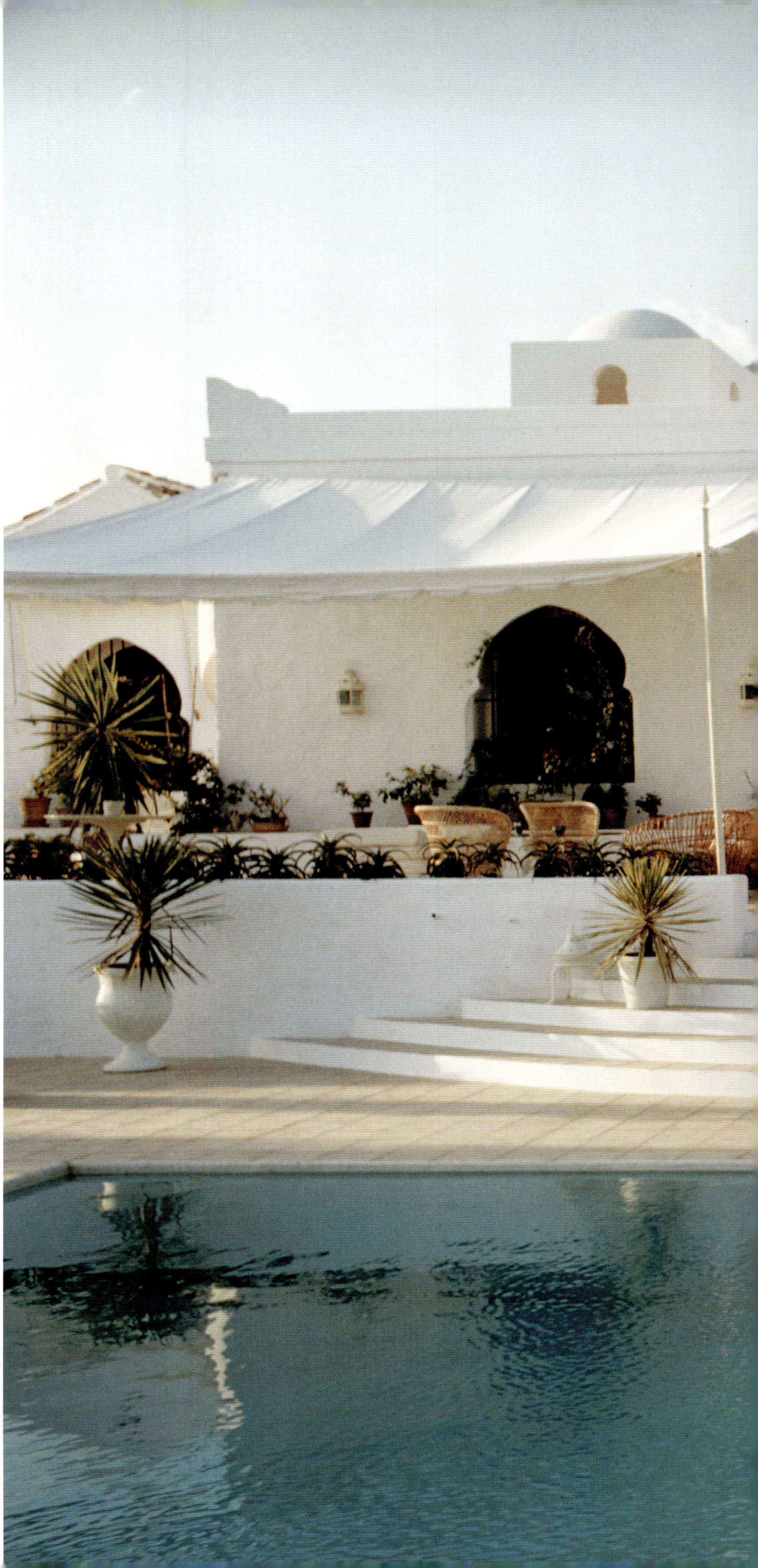

right El Venero, the Moorish villa of Hector and Chico de Ayala in Marbella, Spain, 1971. El Venero is one of Marbella's loveliest villas, lying to the west of the city in a cluster of other impressive villas. The gathering that Slim encountered there was precisely the kind of scene where he excelled. He usually timed his arrival for an hour or two before lunch and milled among the guests, seeking the most attractive and elegant to photograph. If the overall scene was striking enough, as in this case with the Sierra Blanca foothills in the background, he took advantage of its unique tableau and set up an overall shot as well.

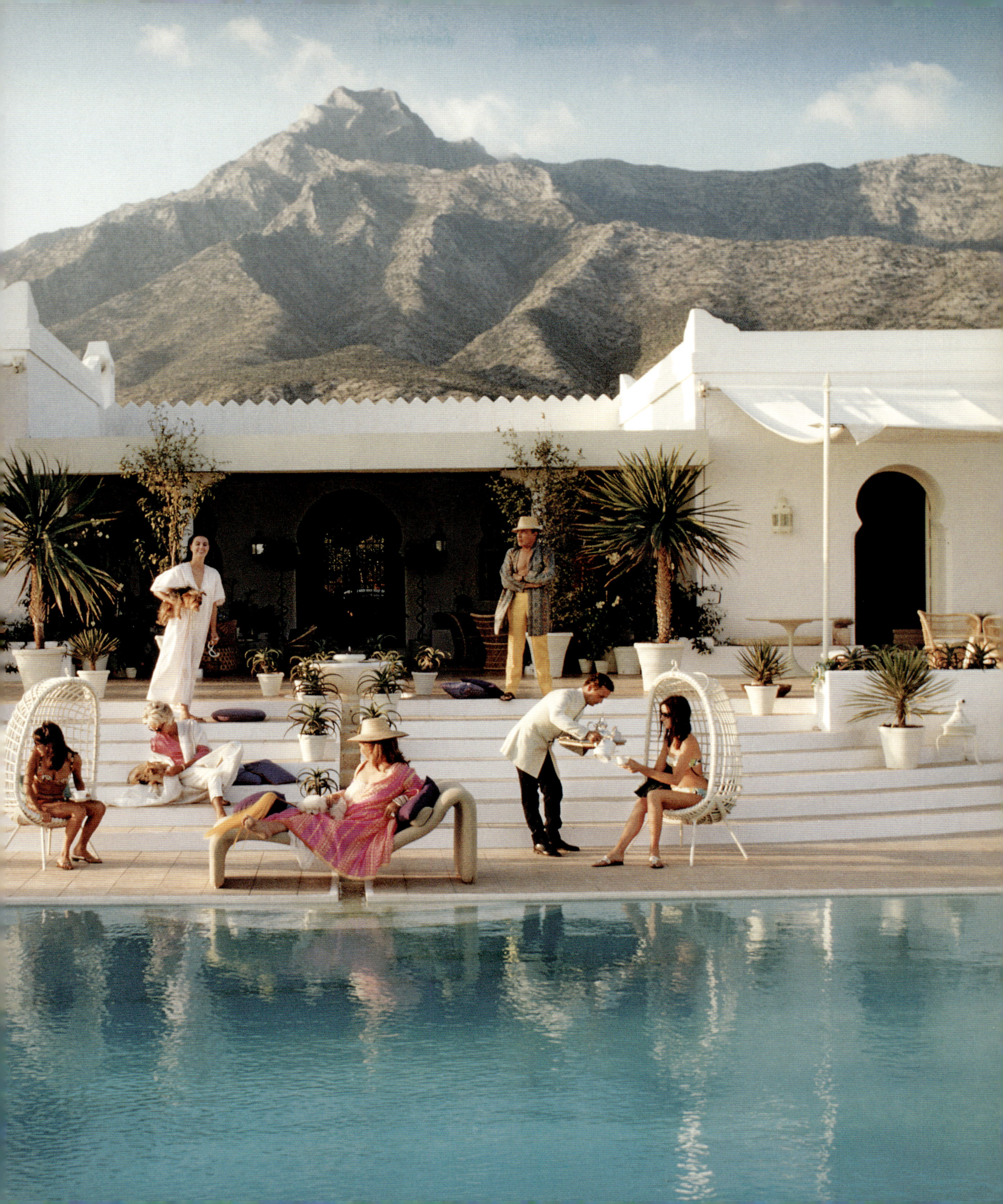

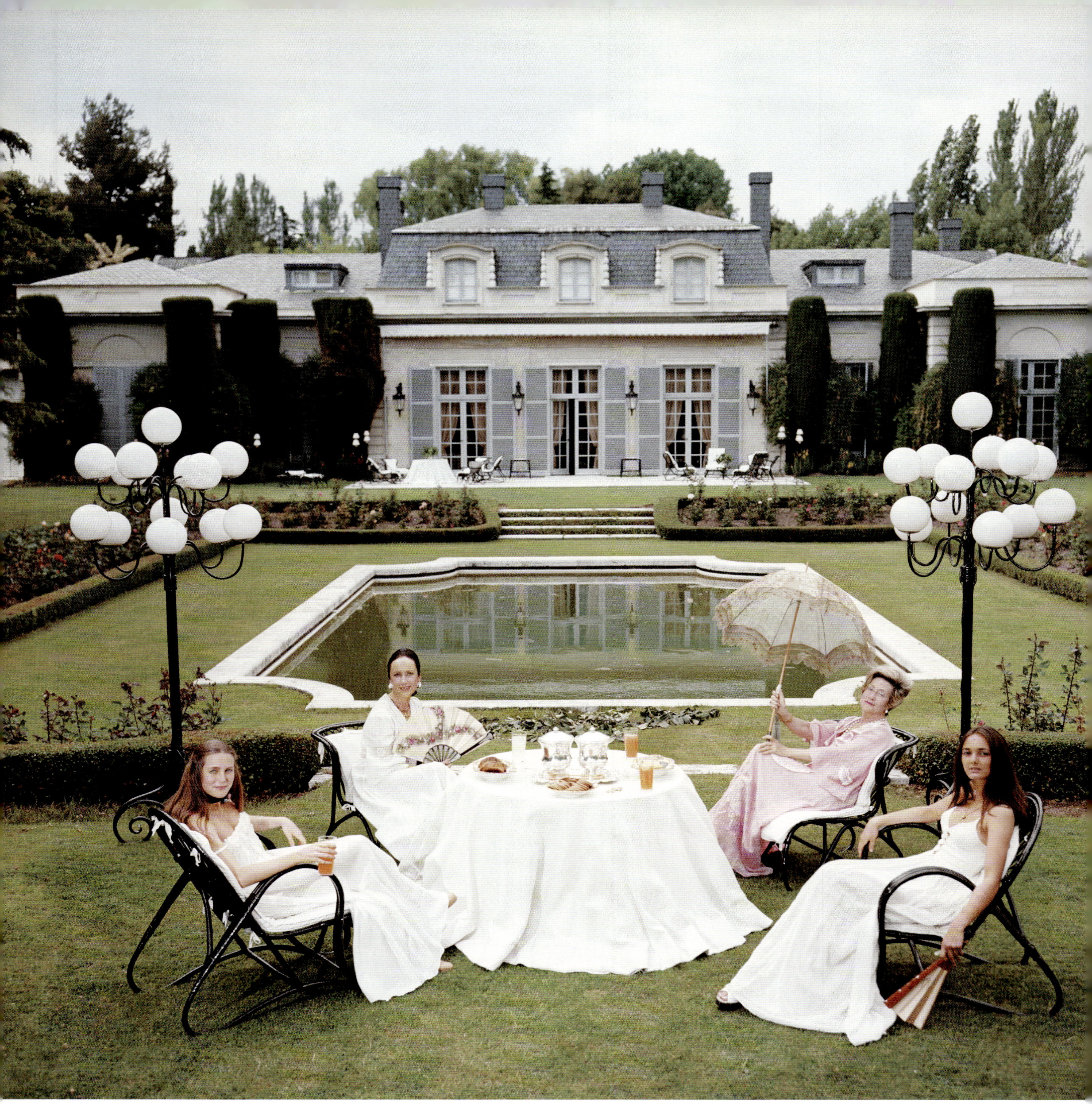

above Eileen Romanones and family in the garden at her home in Spain, 1976.

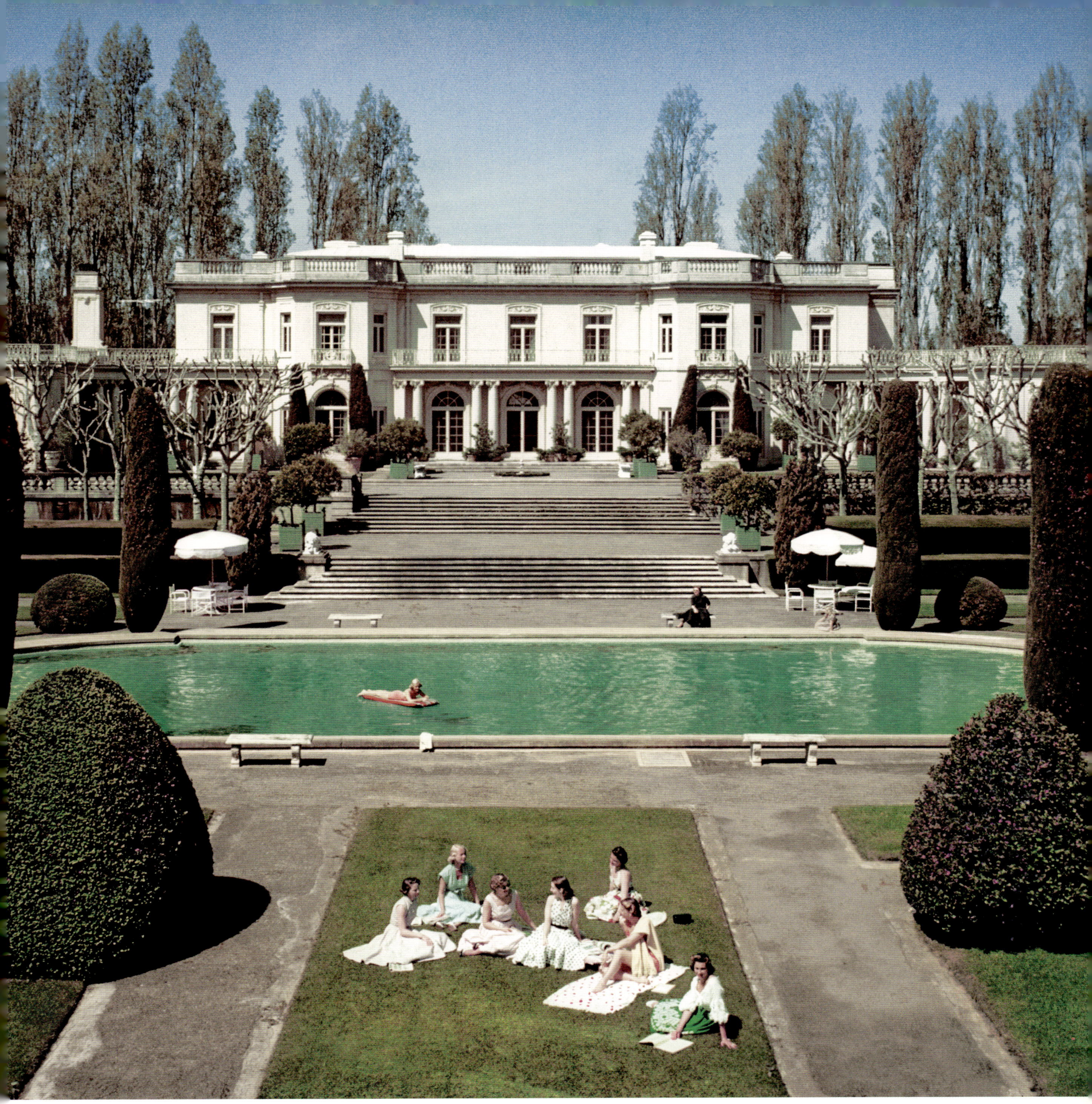

above A gathering on the lawn of the former George Newhall estate, San Francisco, 1960. The house and gardens were modeled on the Petit Trianon at Versailles. The Newhall Land and Farming Company, started in 1883 by the five sons of real estate tycoon Henry Newhall, owned a swath of land that swept from Monterey to Los Angeles. One son, George Newhall, eventually went into farming and real estate development and, in an effort to fund his lavish lifestyle, sold one thirty-eight-thousand-acre piece of land to William Randolph Hearst for one million dollars.

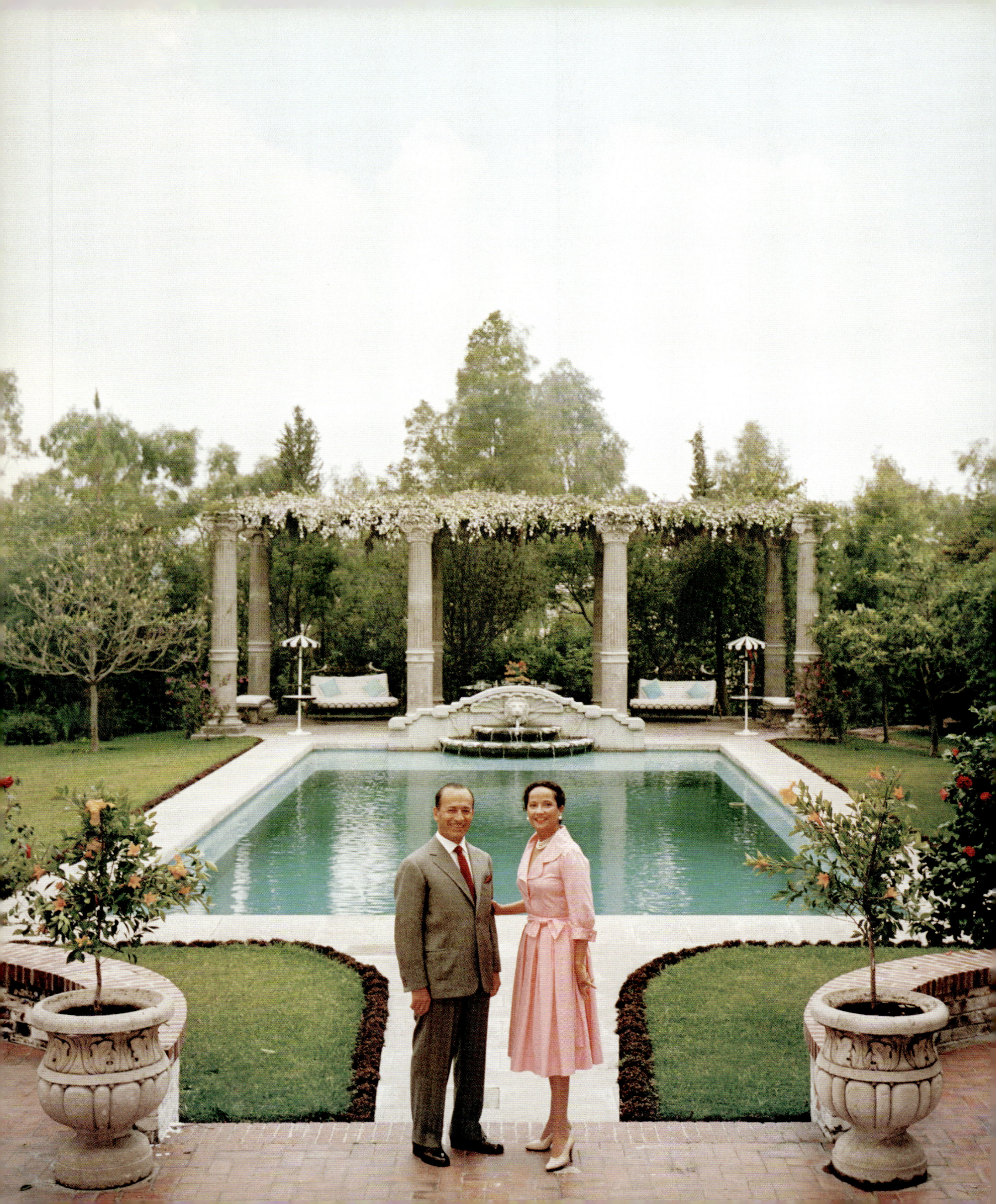

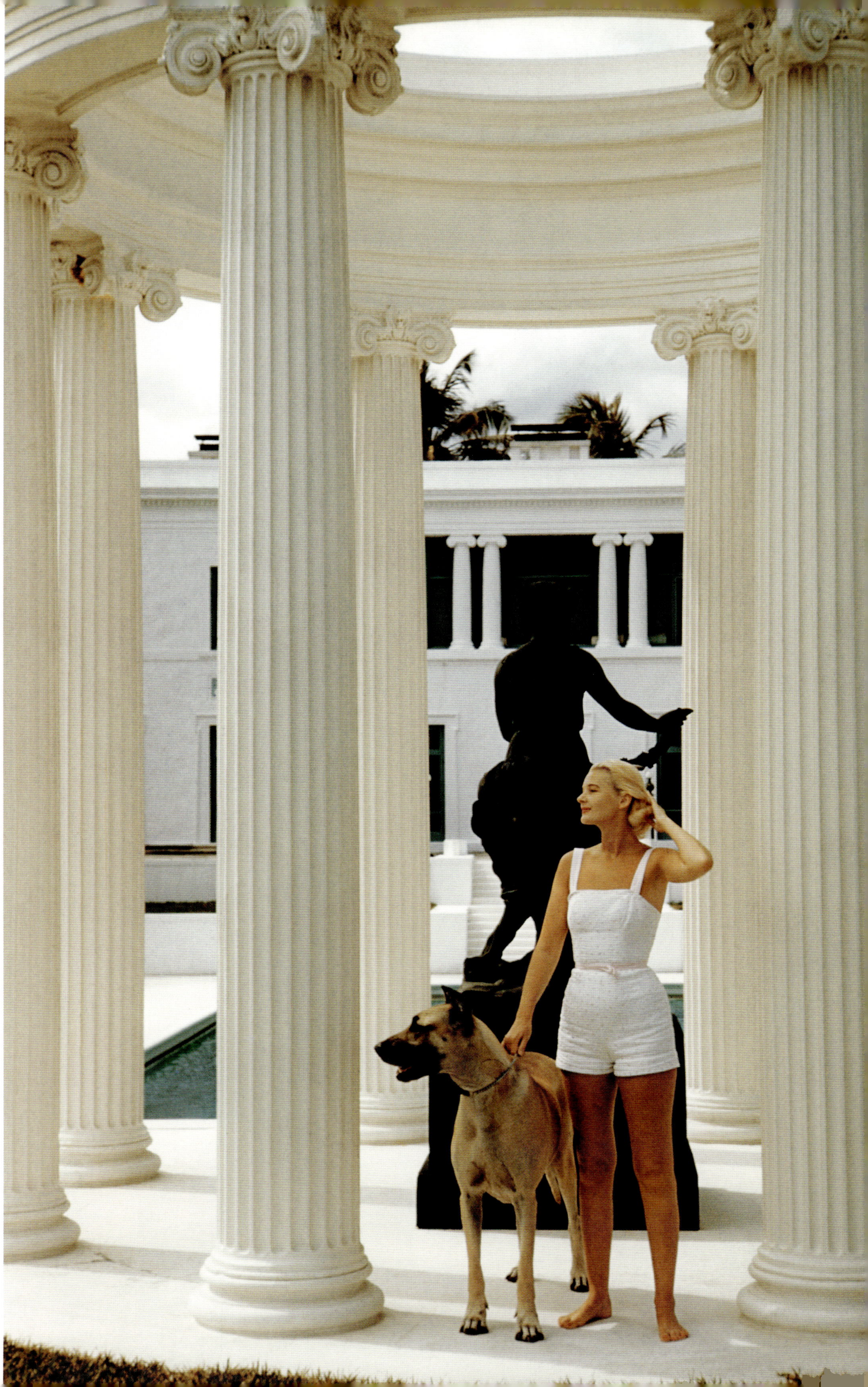

opposite The Indian-born English actress Merle Oberon with her husband, the Italian industrialist Bruno Pagliai, in the garden of their home in Acapulco, 1958. Oberon designed the pool and fountain, and the sculptures were found at Coyoacán, an ancient Aztec village.

right The American socialite C. Z. Guest (see also pages 14 and 54) at her oceanfront estate, Villa Artemis, Palm Beach, 1955. Slim's series of photographs of Guest poolside in Palm Beach in 1955 captured the imagination of a generation and secured her place as the principal archetype for Slim's female photographic subjects. She was without question his favored muse.

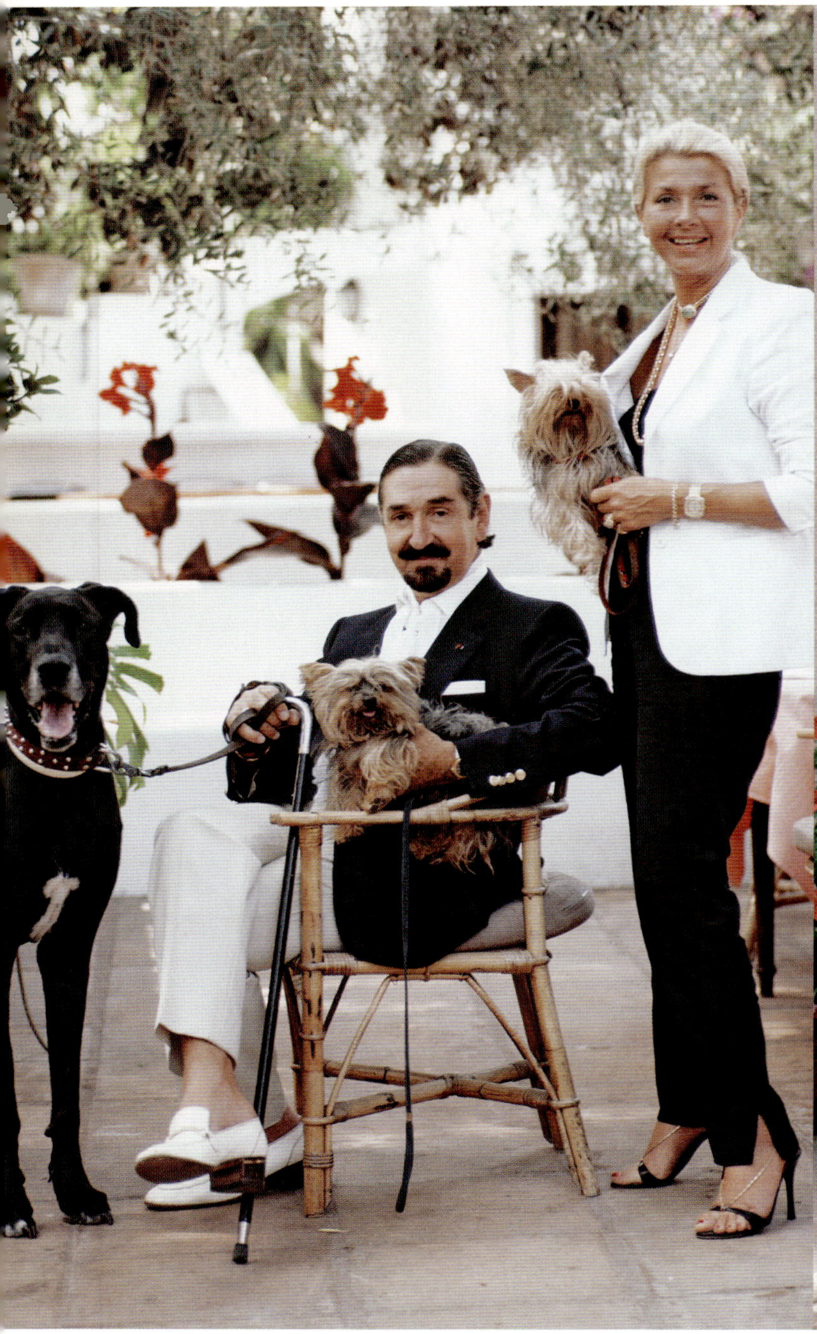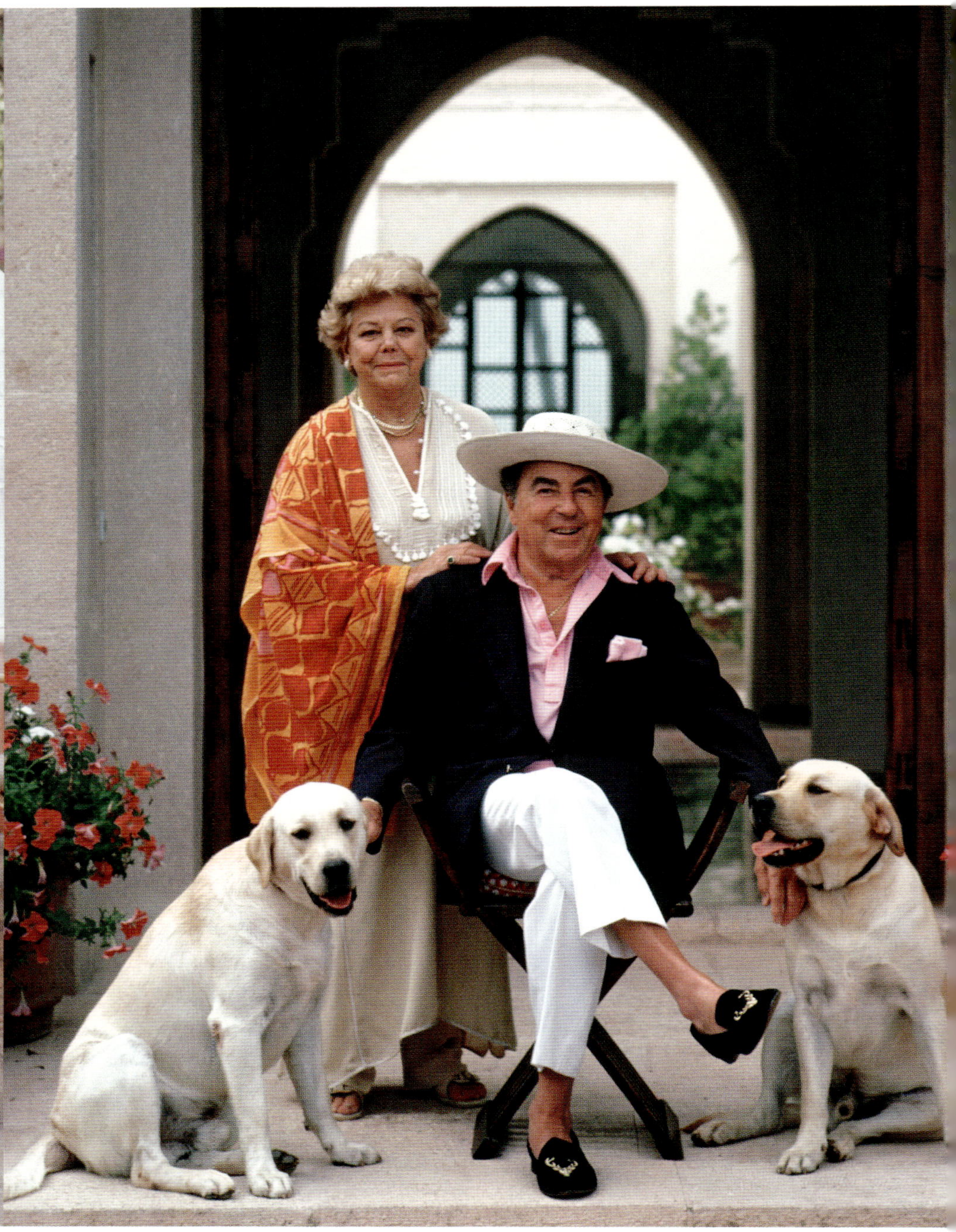

above left Count and Countess Jaime de Mora y Aragon, Marbella, Spain, 1980. He was a wellborn bon vivant from Madrid and the brother of Queen Fabiola of Belgium. The countess was the former Margit Ohlson. Longtime fixtures on the Marbella scene, they were known for their theatrical and stylish bearing. On their farm outside Marbella, they raised Arabian horses and their dogs—Douschka, the Great Dane, and Mini and Chiky, the Yorkshire terriers.

above right Baron and Baroness Hubert and Terry von Pantz at their villa, El Rincón, Marbella, Spain, 1986. Hubert and Terry were two of Slim's closest friends. They had homes all over the world, and Slim always made a point to look them up. He loved to annotate their story this way: "Hubert was an impoverished Austrian baron, and Terry was an heir to the Avon fortune. Their match was made in heaven!" In reality, Hubert von Pantz descended from one of the oldest noble families in Austria, known for controlling the iron mines of Central Europe for five centuries. Terry McConnell was an heir to the Avon beauty products fortune, and together they became two of Europe's most engaging and sought-out hosts. Slim called Terry "the big sister of the international social scene."

opposite Nightclub owner Olivier Coquelin and the Hawaiian beauty Lahaina Kameha in Haiti, 1981.

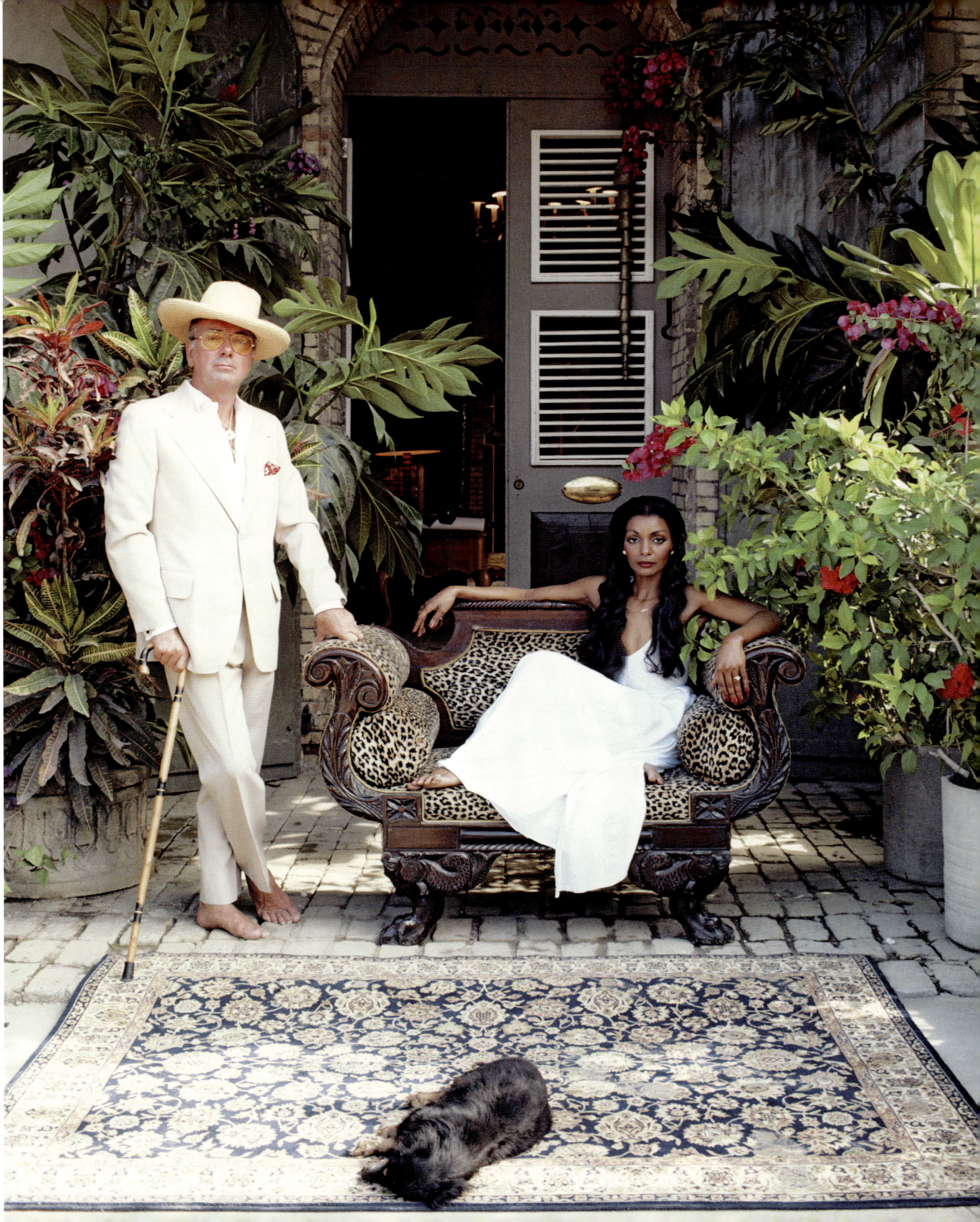

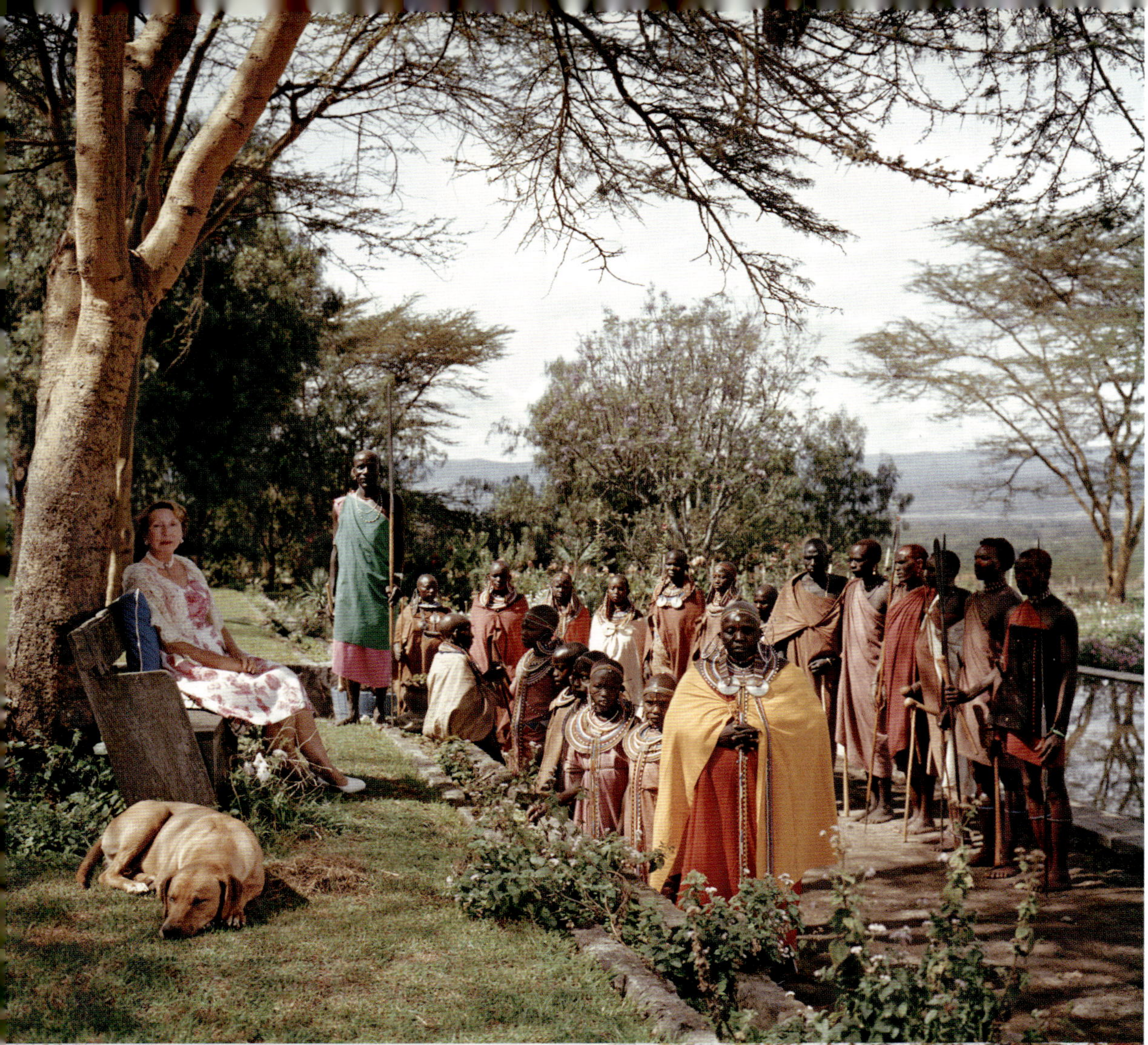

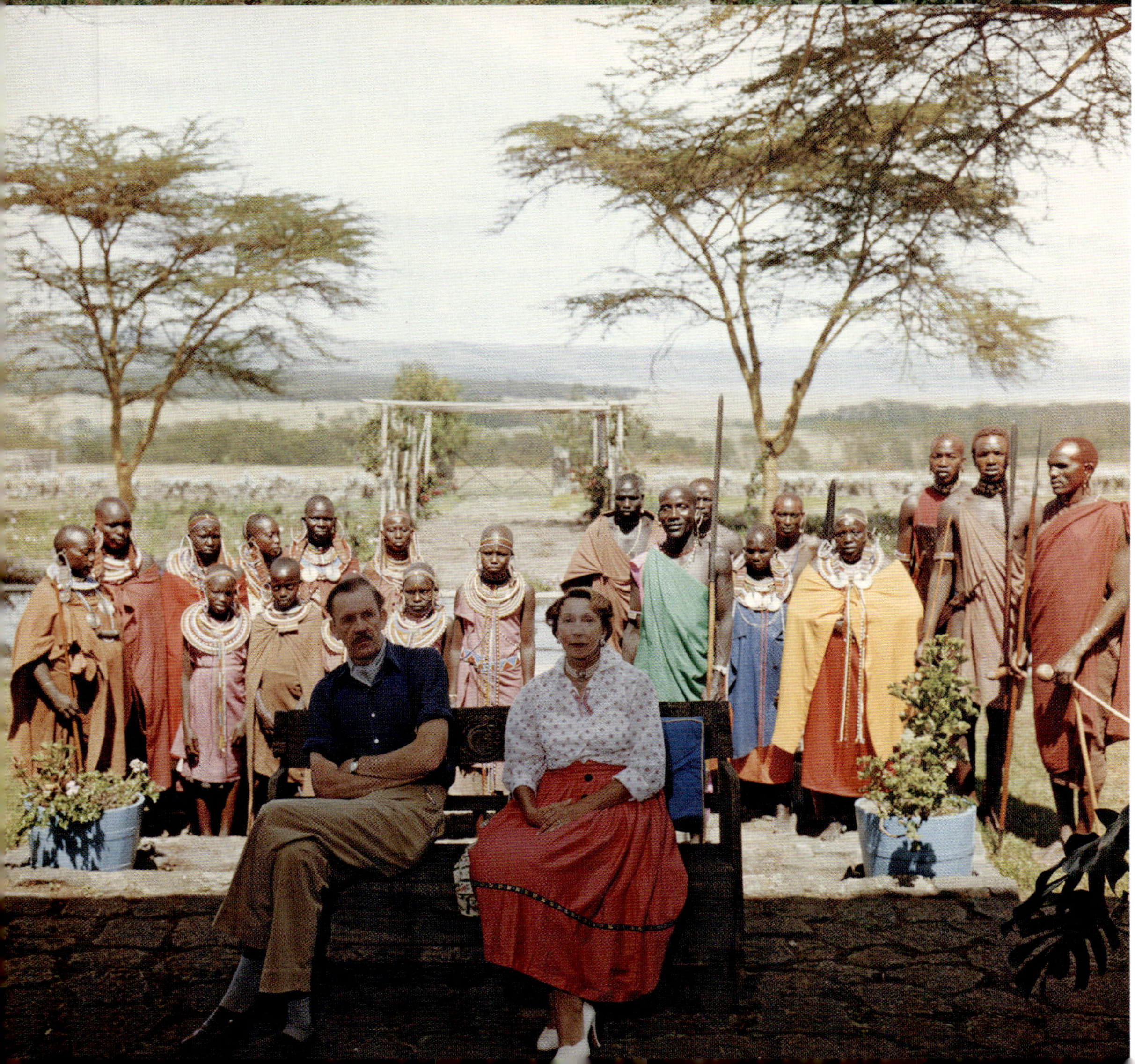

left and opposite Lady Genesta Hamilton and her husband Lord Claud Hamilton, Kenya, circa 1955. "So few friends and so precious they are," wrote Lady Hamilton, referring perhaps to the solitary life of an expatriate in colonial Kenya. Genesta Hamilton grew up in refined social circles in England during World War I. When she and her husband moved to Kenya, they became members of a group of expats led by Lord Delamere, one of the first and most influential English settlers there. Karen Blixen, better known as the writer Isak Dinesen, was a friend as well. Lord and Lady Hamilton designed and built the stately house known as Nderit on Lake Nakuru in Kenya, where they lived. Lady Hamilton's book, *A Stone's Throw*, elegantly chronicles their travels around Kenya and other parts of Africa over the course of six decades.

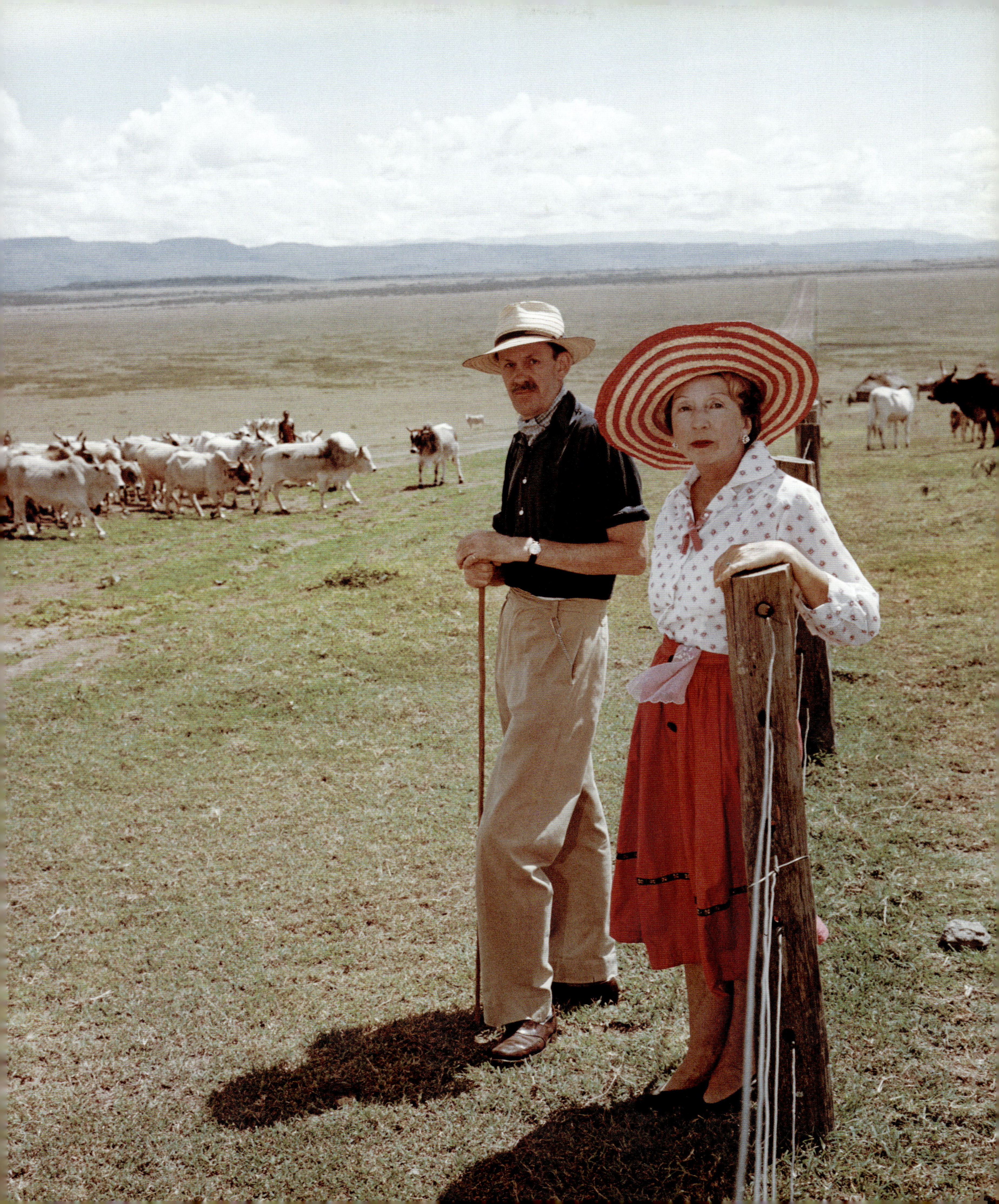

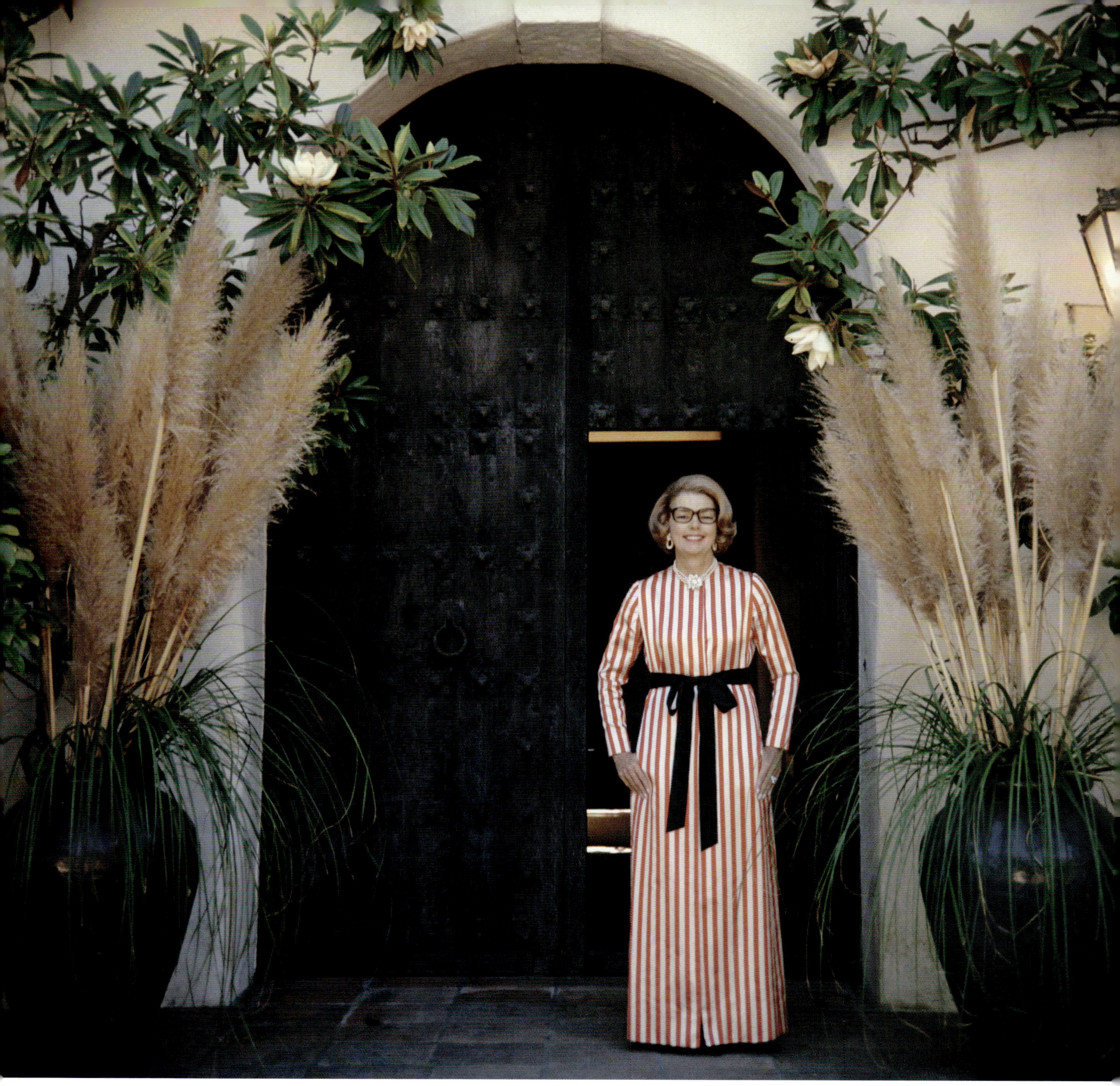

above Mrs. James Hoover of the famous vacuum cleaner family, Pebble Beach, California, 1976. Starting humbly as the Hoover Suction Sweeper Company in the early twentieth century, it experienced phenomenal success, making the brand name Hoover synonymous with vacuuming in the United States and Great Britain.

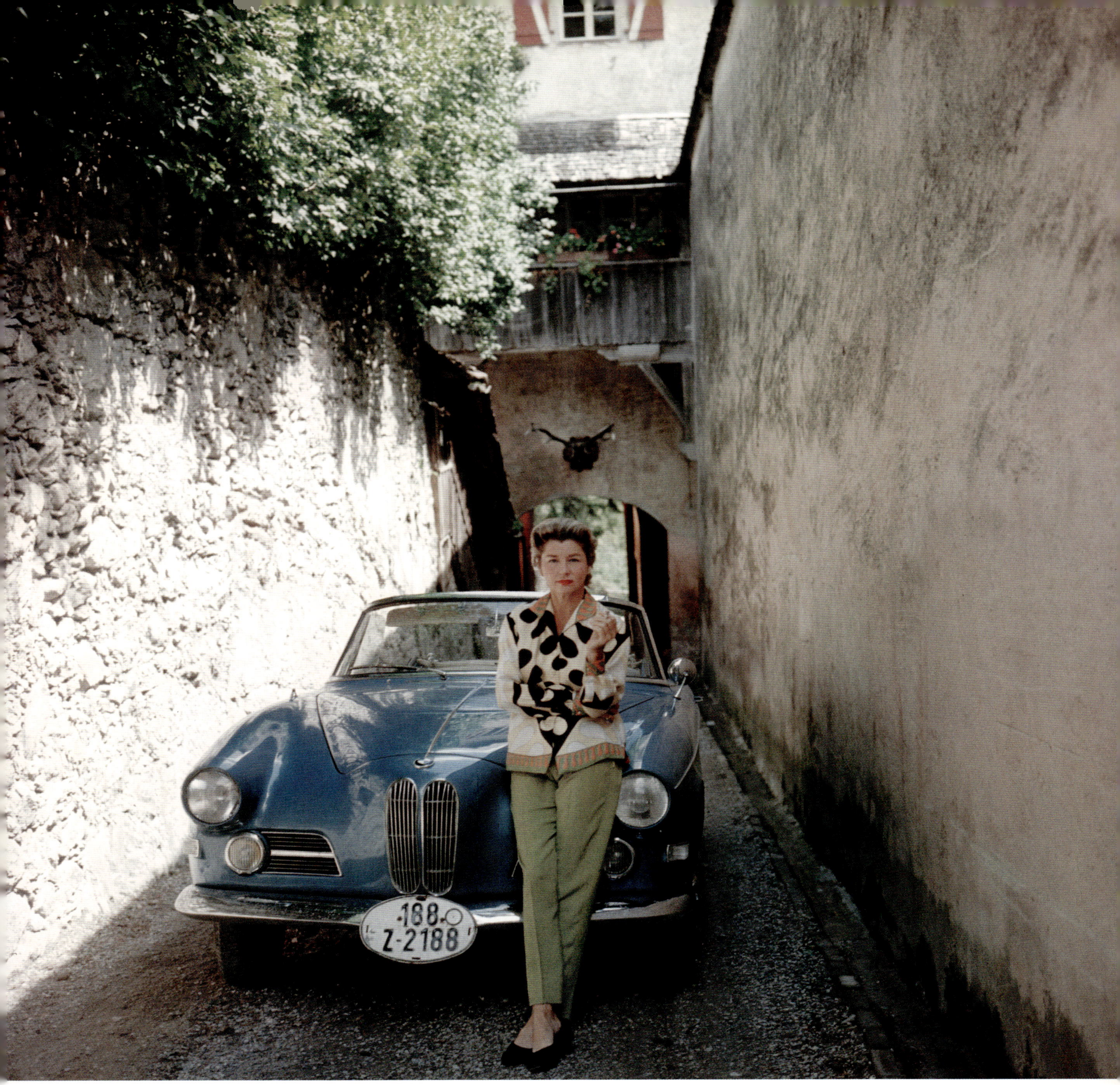

above Princess Honeychile Hohenlohe in Mittersill, Austria, 1958. When Patricia Wilder left her small hometown in Georgia for New York in the 1930s, the Southern belle, who called herself simply "Honeychile," got a job as a showgirl at the Palace Theatre within a day of arriving. Her personal life would prove far more theatrical than her work life, inspiring headlines about her liaisons. Such was her Southern charm that she became a celebrity fixture at the city's many watering holes, including El Morocco, the Stork Club, and the famous former speakeasy the "21" Club. The bartender at "21" even named a drink in her honor—the Honeychile, a whiskey sour made with honey in place of sugar. She finally settled down, marrying Prince Alexander Hohenlohe of Austria (see page 142), and thereafter was known simply as "Princess Honeychile."

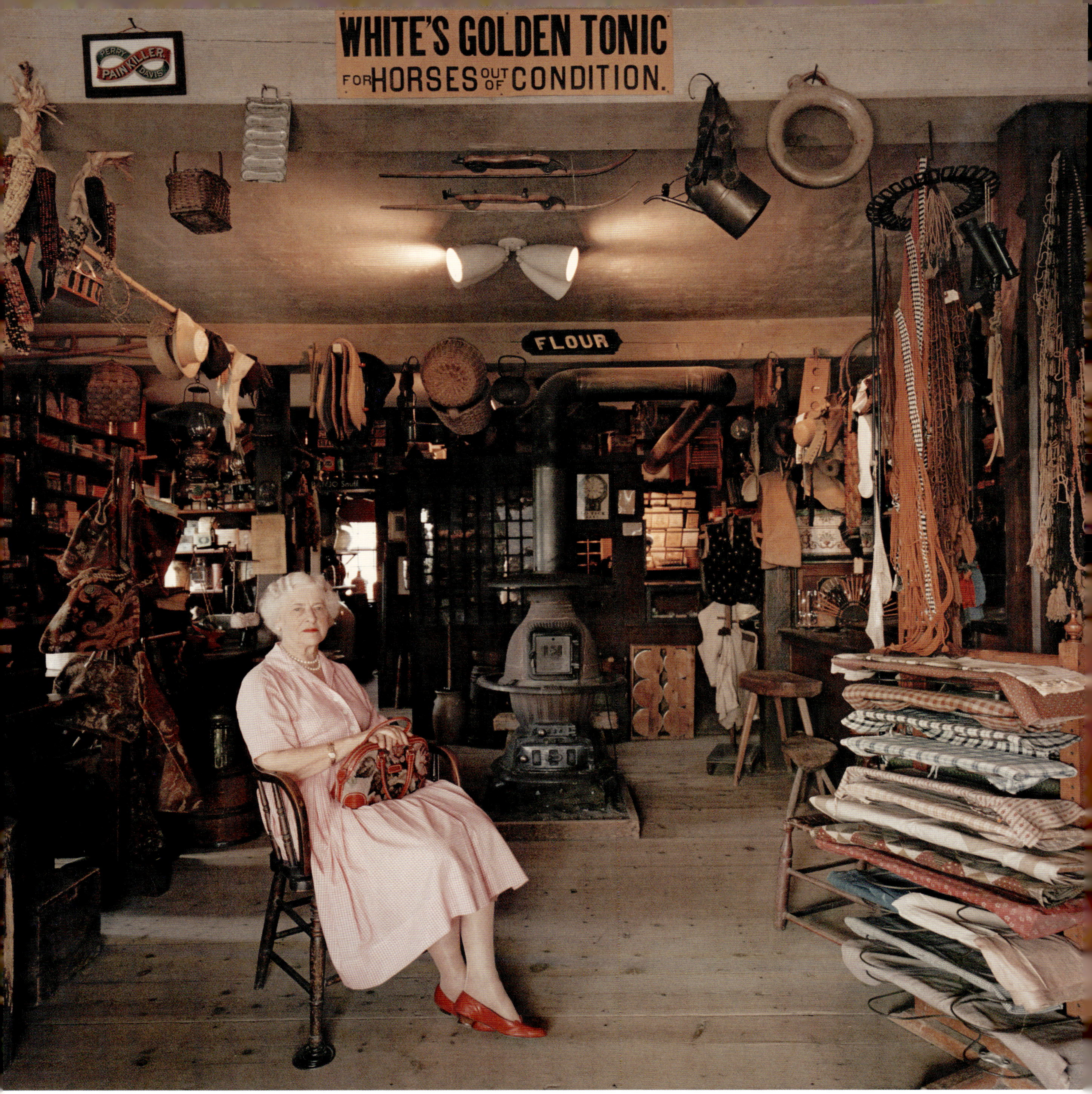

above Mrs. J. Watson Webb in the general store that is part of the Shelburne Museum, which she founded, Shelburne, Vermont, circa 1960. Slim tapped a wonderful vein when he spoke with Mrs. Webb—born Electra Havemeyer—after taking this photo. As he retold the story, "Mrs. Webb, the daughter of the Henry O. Havemeyers, a prominent New York family, was brought up in the presence of one of the great collections of European paintings, much of it now at the Metropolitan Museum of Art. In an article in *Art in America,* she quoted her mother's reaction to her

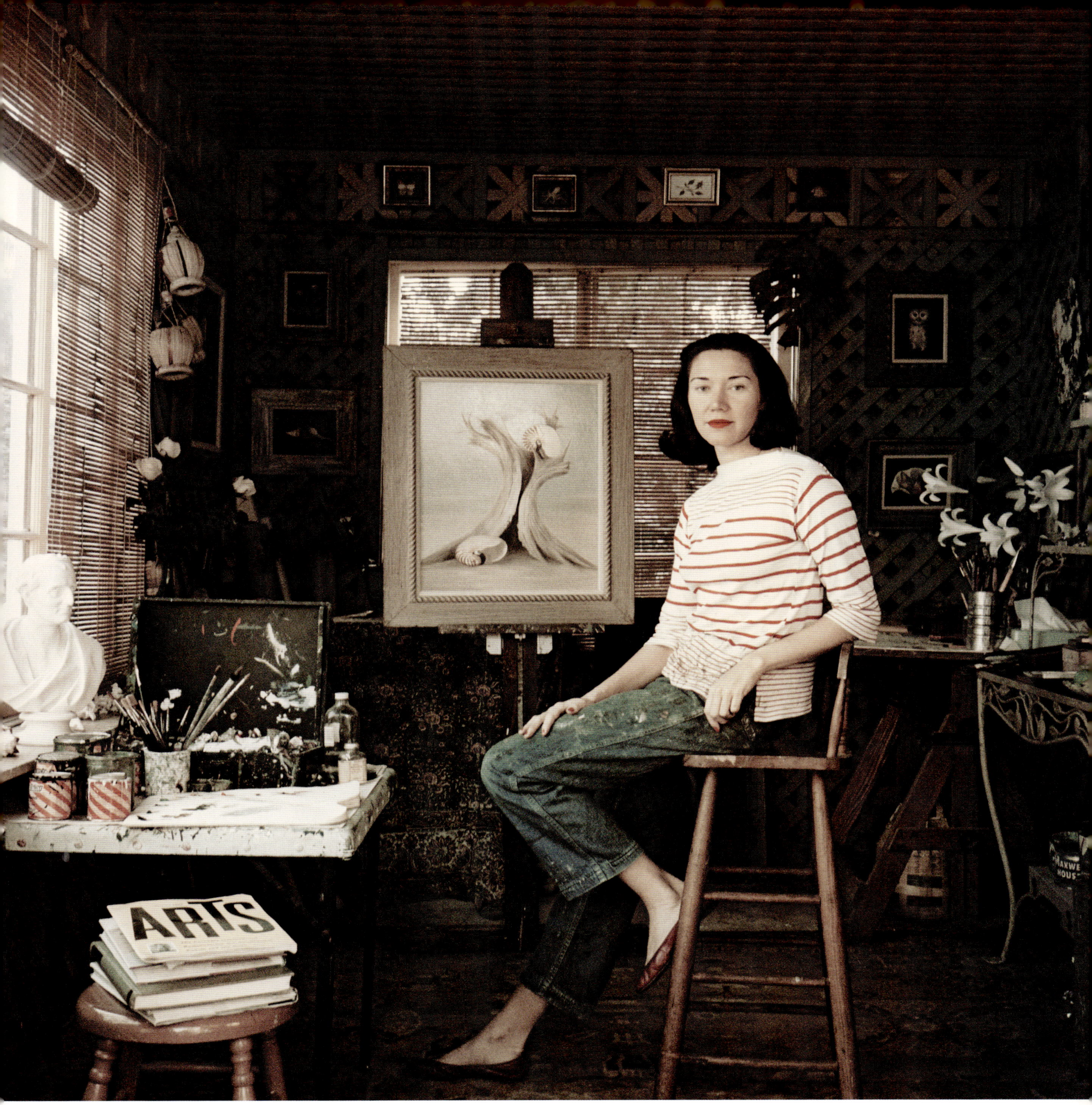

interest in things American: 'How can you, who have been brought up with Rembrandts and Manets, collect and live with such American trash?' 'Obviously my mother did not consider my eagles, cigar store Indians, and primitive furniture art at all.'"

above Tish Massie Widener, a miniaturist and member of an old local family, in her studio, Palm Beach, 1960.

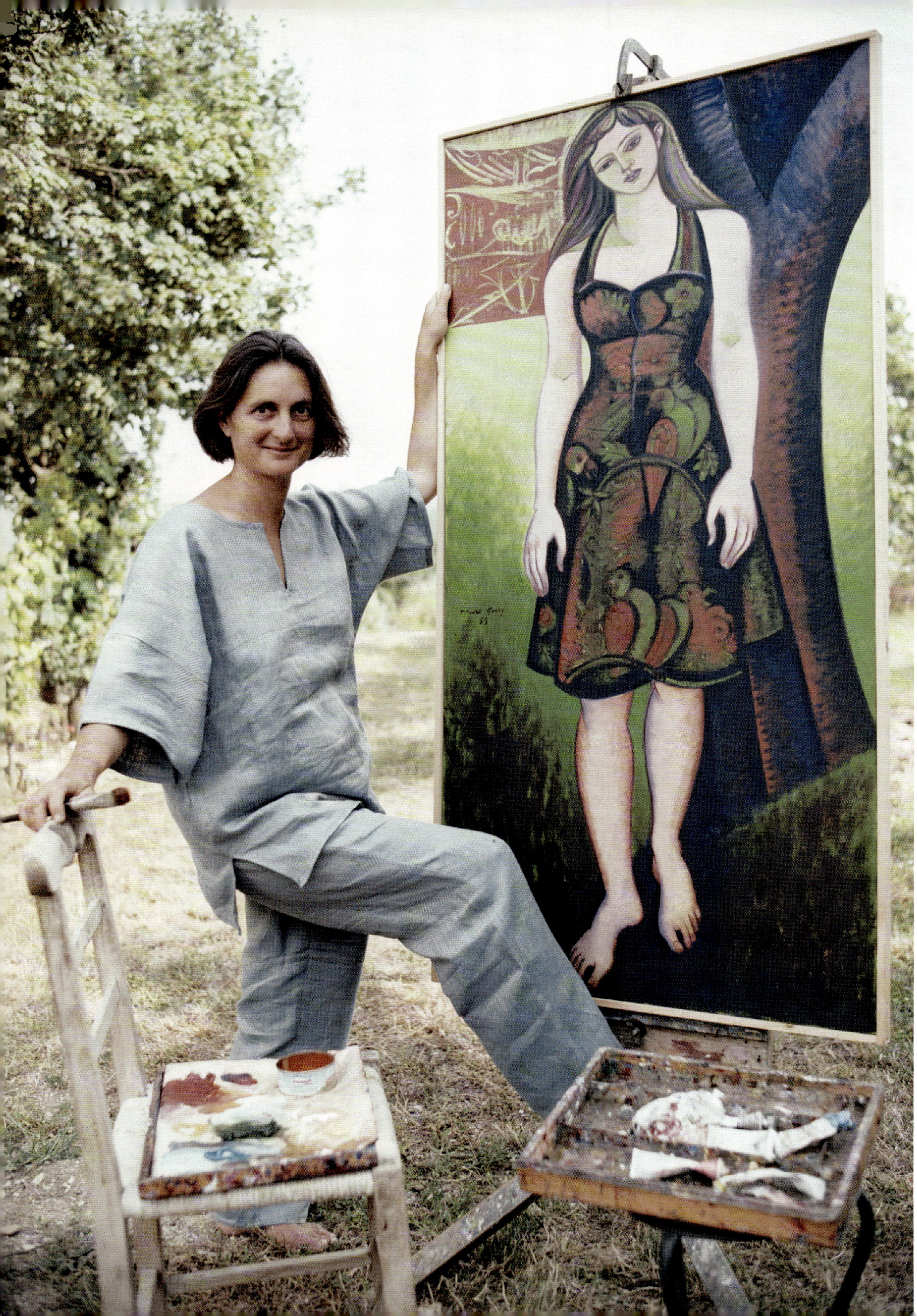

opposite Maro Gorky beside one of her paintings in Tuscany, Italy, 1991. She is the daughter of artist Arshile Gorky and wife of Matthew Spender, son of the British poet Stephen Spender.

right Mercedes Herrera de Benacerraf at her sumptuous Spanish-style villa, Quinta Mercedes, Formentor, Spain, 1987. A native of Caracas, she summered in Formentor most of her life.

following spread Art collector and socialite Peggy Guggenheim, the definitive American in Venice, at her Palazzo Venier dei Leoni, Venice, 1978. The palace houses her private art collection, including Picasso's *On the Beach* (left), as well as the Peggy Guggenheim Collection, which is open to the public. Located on the Grand Canal, it is one of the city's most visited attractions. She was born Marguerite Guggenheim. Her mother, Florette Seligman, was a member of New York's Jewish old guard, and her father, Benjamin Guggenheim, was the son of a peddler—and was regarded by high society as an upstart despite a fortune he'd made in copper. She characterized her childhood in the strict Jewish upper class as "excessively unhappy" in her autobiography *Out of This Century: Confessions of an Art Addict*. Her first job as a young woman was at an avant-garde bookstore, and this kindled her lifelong interest in bohemian lifestyles and the Surrealists. This led to great friendships, collaborations, and patronage to such artists as Man Ray, Constantin Brancusi, Marcel Duchamp, and Wassily Kandinsky.

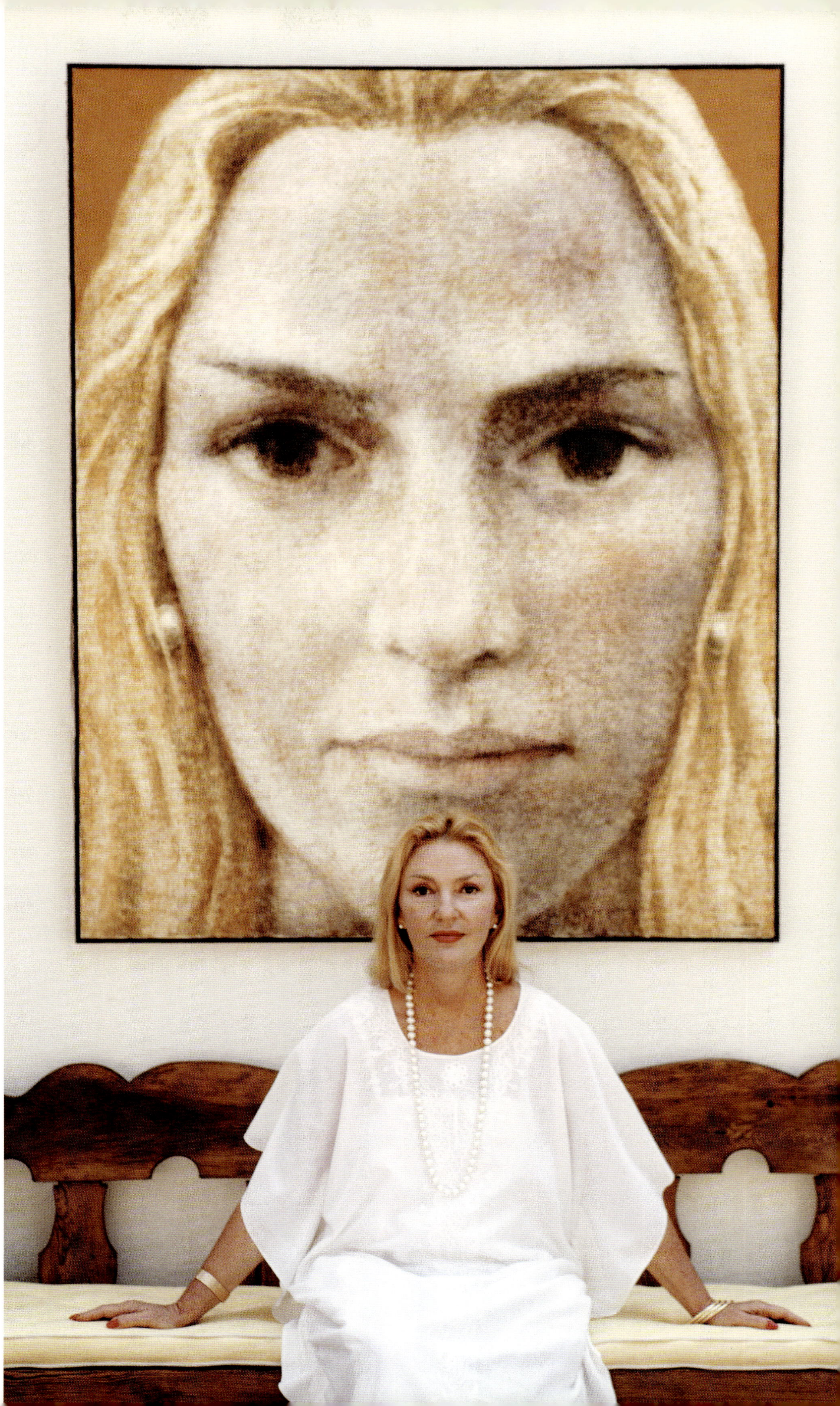

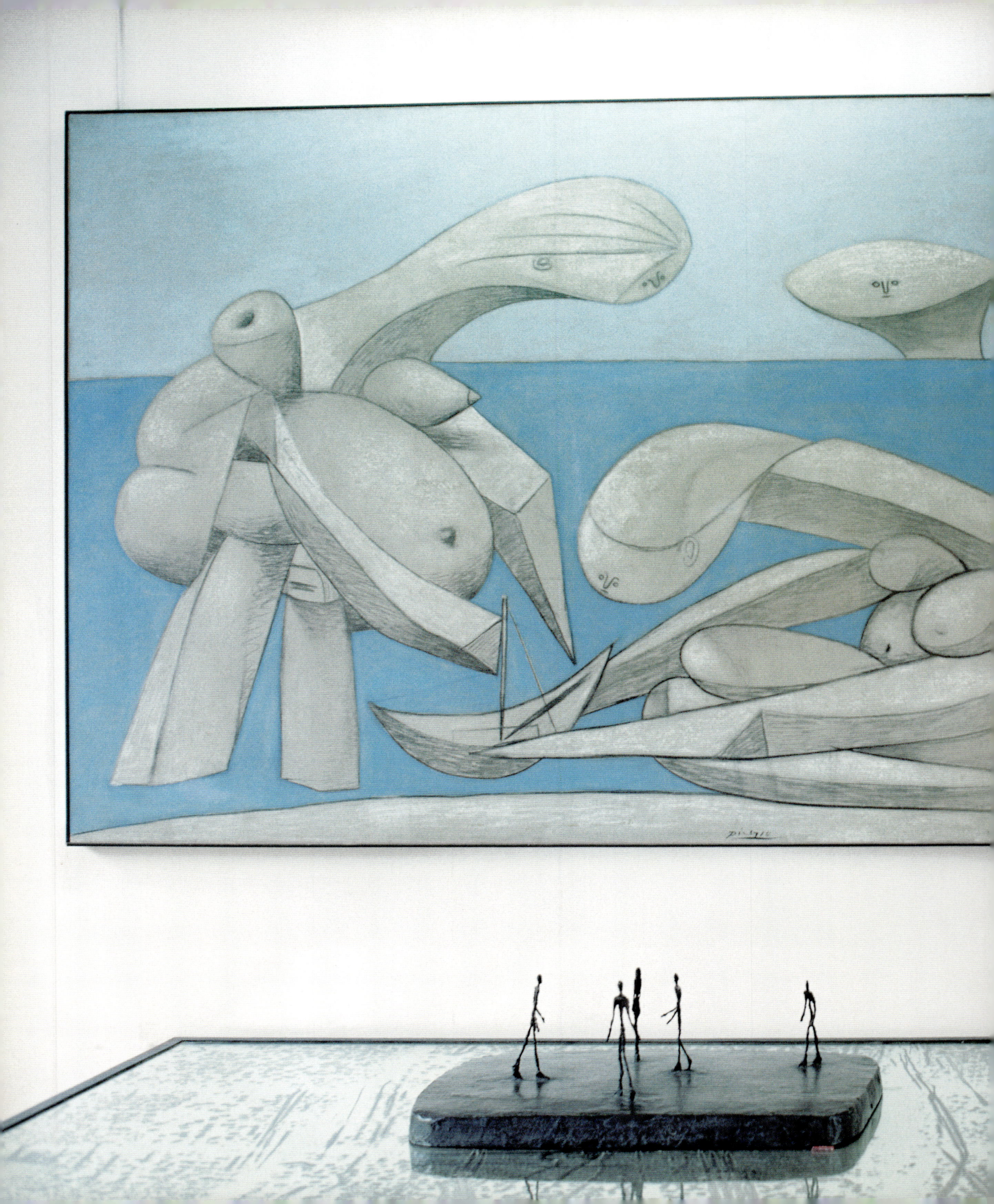

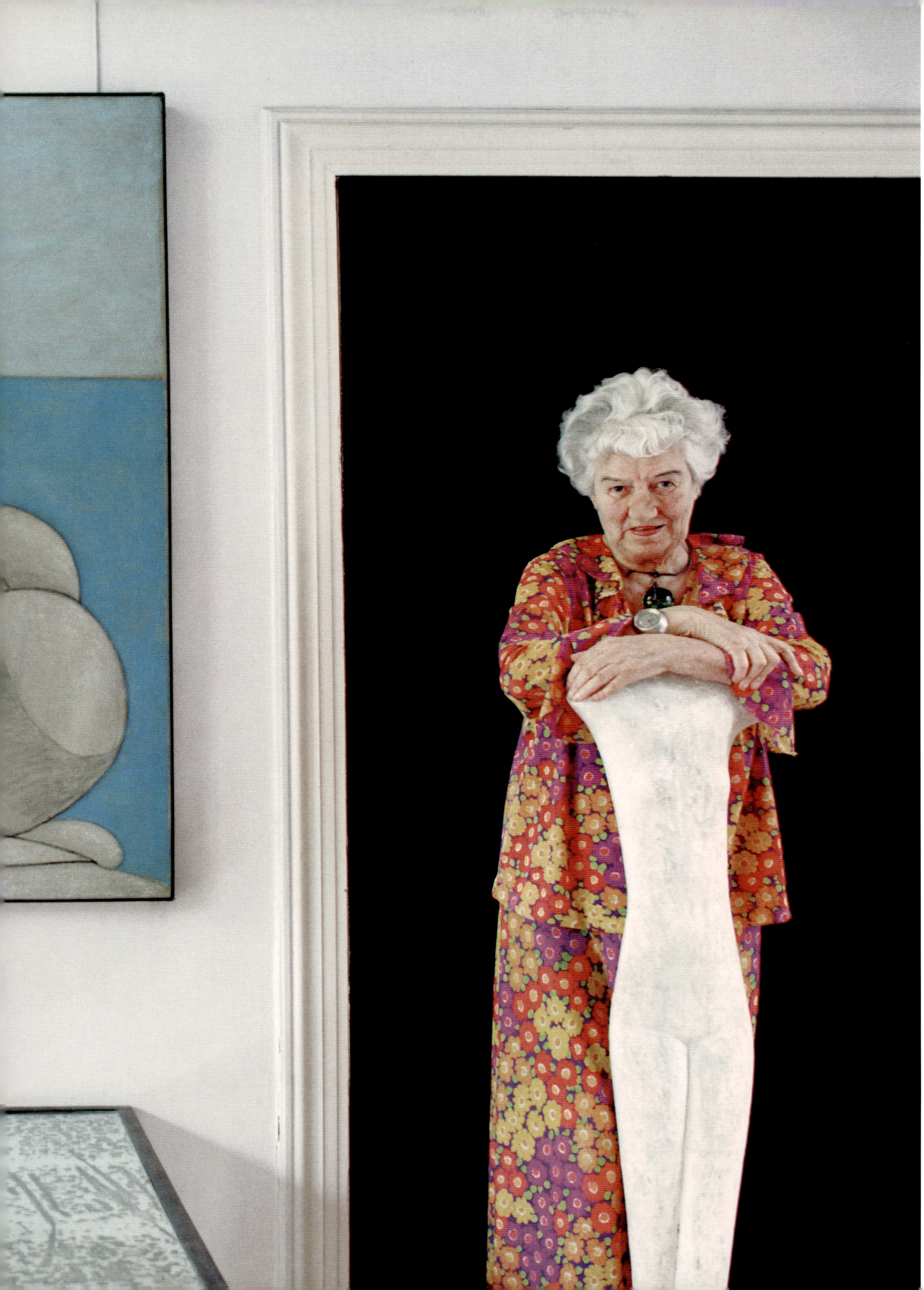

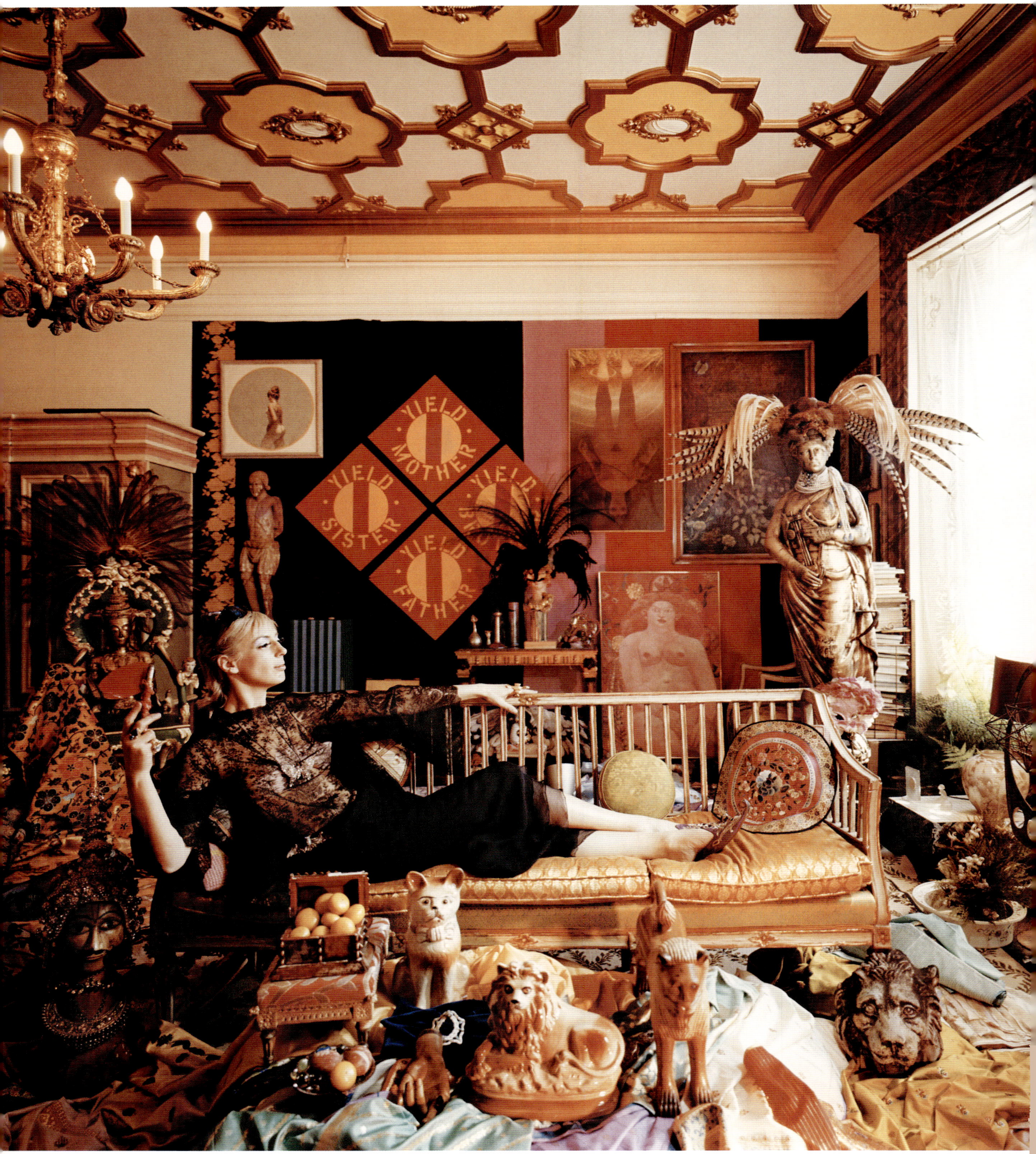
YIELD MOTHER
YIELD SISTER
YIELD FATHER

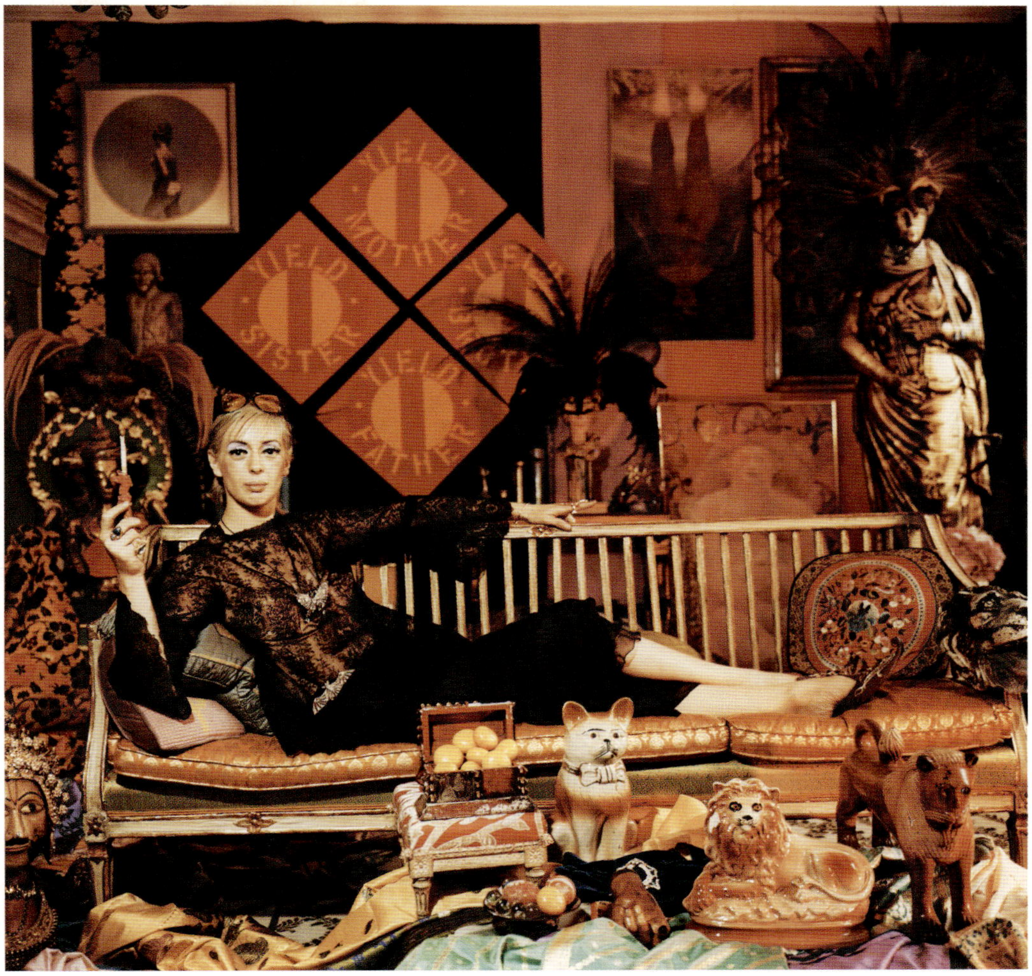

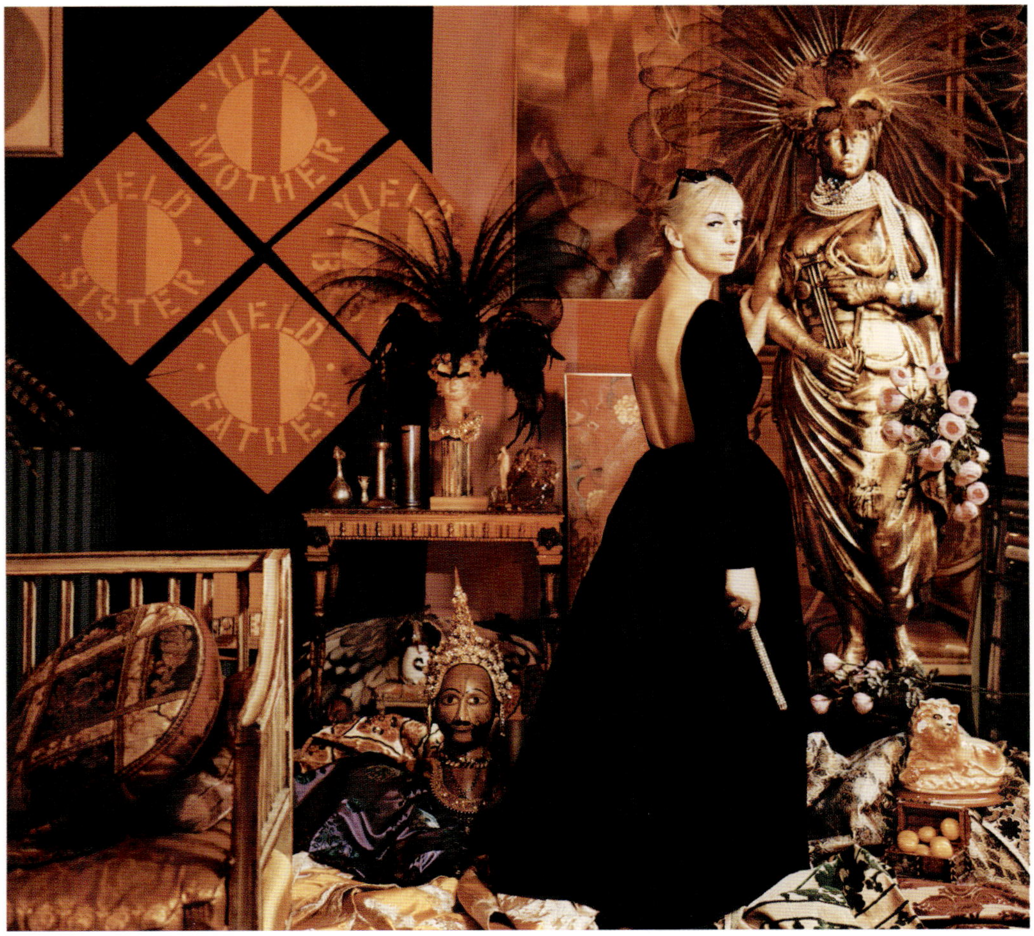

opposite and right Joan "Tiger" Morse at home in her A La Carte shop, New York, 1964. Morse was a New York socialite and gal pal of Andy Warhol who found her calling as a fashion designer of all things mod and psychedelic. She ran this boutique out of her New York apartment as well as a Madison Avenue boutique called Teeny Weeny with her friend Diana Dew. She is widely credited with the invention of illuminated minidresses, often made from silver Mylar but always with pulsing lights powered by battery packs worn hidden at the waist. As a regular at Warhol's Factory with Ultra Violet, Ondine, and others, she favored such fashion accessories as feathered headdresses, thigh-high brocade boots, rhinestone sunglasses, and the de rigueur 1960s white lipstick.

following spread left Donatella Flick at the Blue Safari Club on Manda Island, Lamu Archipelago, Kenya, 1987. Born Princess Donatella Missikoff, she earned a philosophy degree from the University of Rome and was an Olympic gymnast. The princess married Gert Rudolph "Muck" Flick (not to be confused with his brother Friedrich Christian "Mick" Flick), scion of one of Germany's wealthiest industrial dynasties. She is the founder of the Donatella Flick Conducting Competition, which boasts Prince Charles as one of its principal patrons.

following spread right Mary Lau Toda on her private island in the Philippines, 1973.

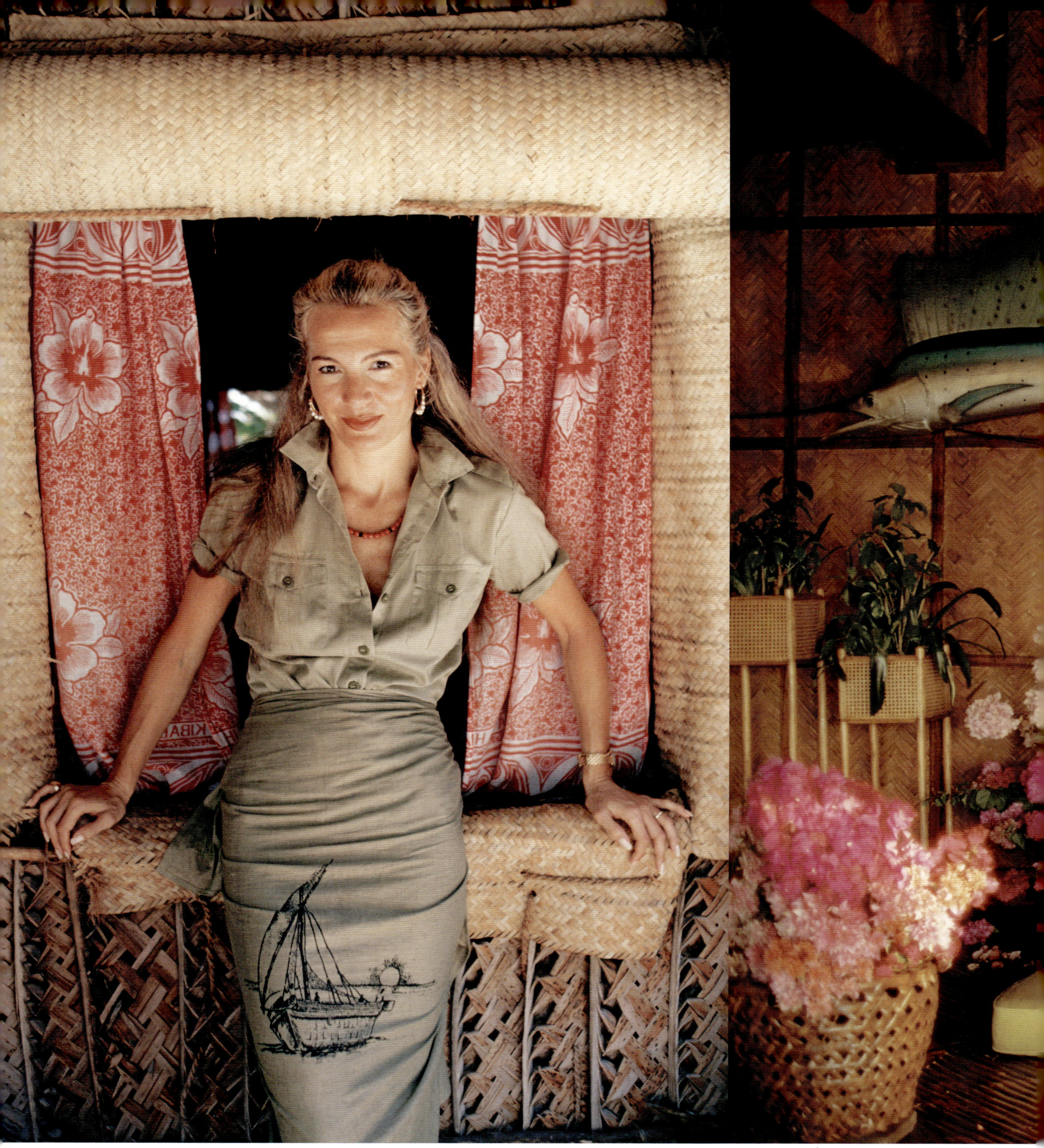

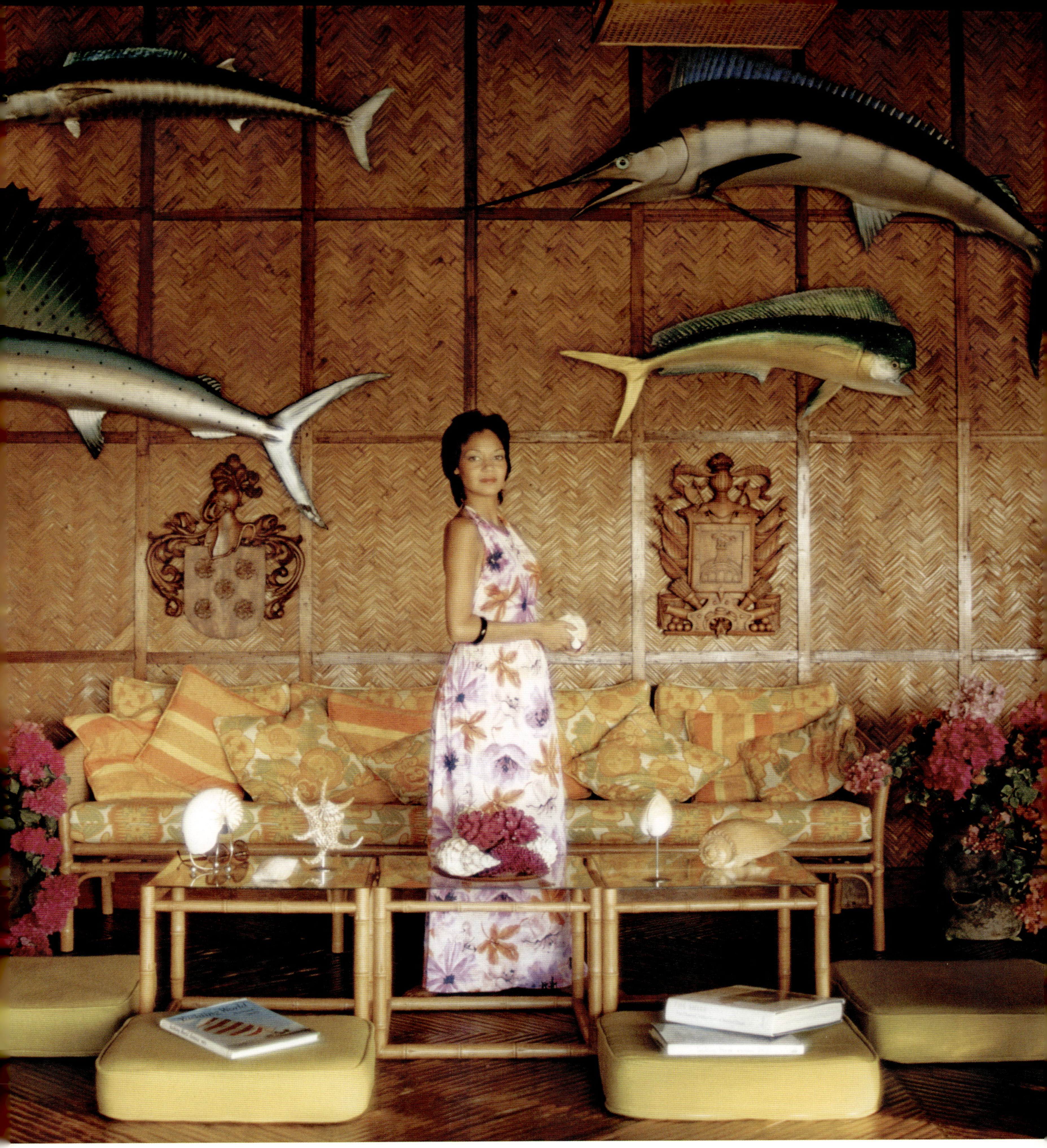

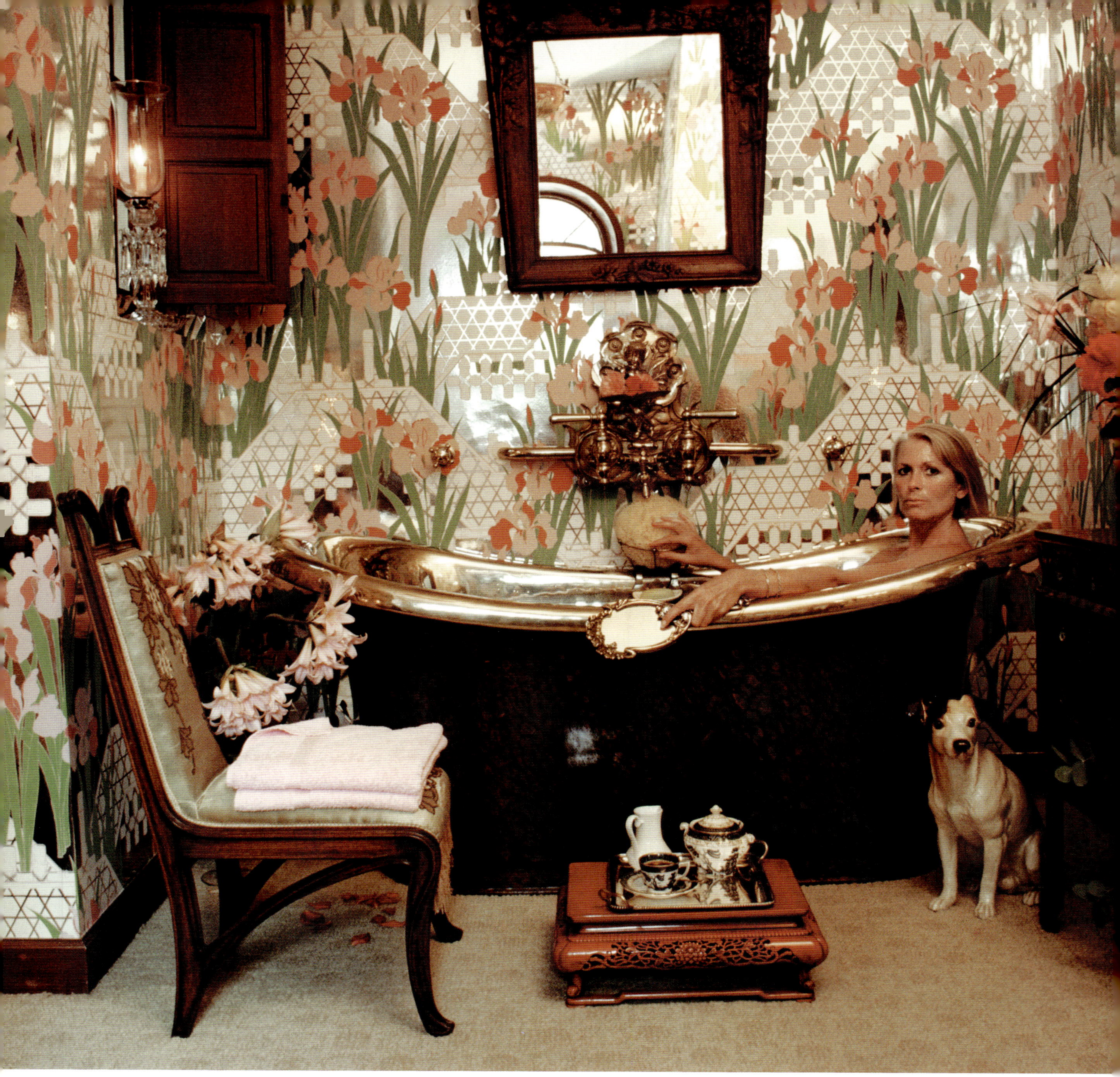

above Joyce Pallardy relaxes at Villa Macopa, the home of Mrs. André Hammel, Saint-Tropez, 1977. The Belle Epoque bath came from the home of Mrs. Hammel's grandmother: Château d'Aubiry, an official French historical monument.

opposite Countess Anna Laetitia Pecci-Blunt, Rome, 1960. The countess, known as "Mimi," built her private theater, La Cometa, as an addition to her palace in the late 1950s. Despite being the grandniece of Pope Leo XIII, she and her husband produced plays here written by some of the most provocative playwrights of the time, such as Tennessee Williams and Eugène Ionesco. She is famously quoted telling the story of her

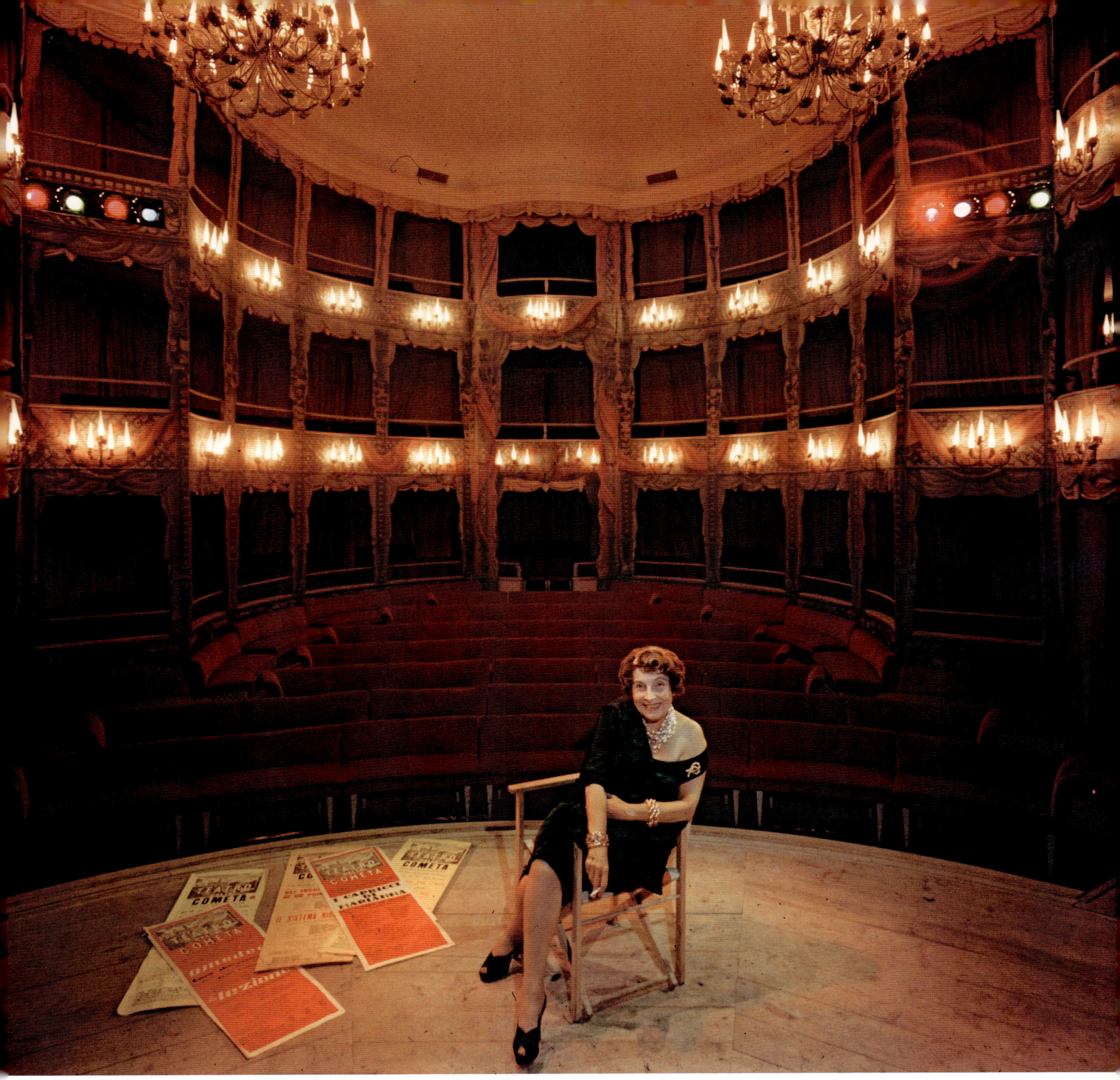

much-anticipated birth: "The pope, of course, would have been pleased if his nephew had a son. My father had to tell him I was a girl. 'Are you sure?' the pope asked. 'Oh yes,' said my father." The pope nonetheless presided at her first communion and supervised her education, even tutoring her for quizzes. When she married an American named Cecil Blunt, the pope created for both of them what was then an unusual married name, splicing their surnames together into Pecci-Blunt. Her artistic patronage and philanthropy were honored in 1960 with a Medaglia d'Oro per L'arte e la Cultura by the Italian government, and in 1964 she was awarded the Légion d'Honneur by the French government for her encouragement of cross-cultural exchange.

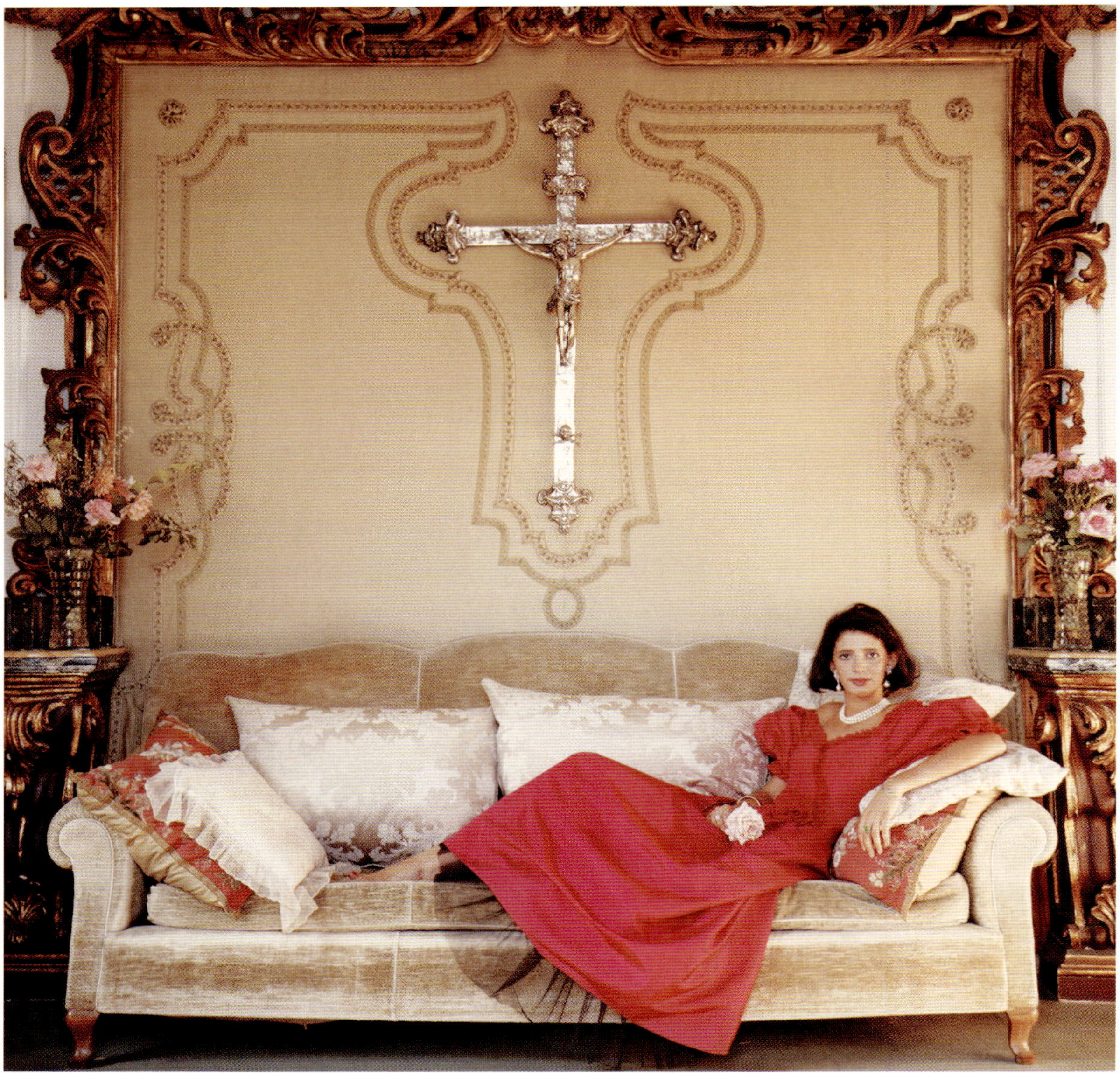

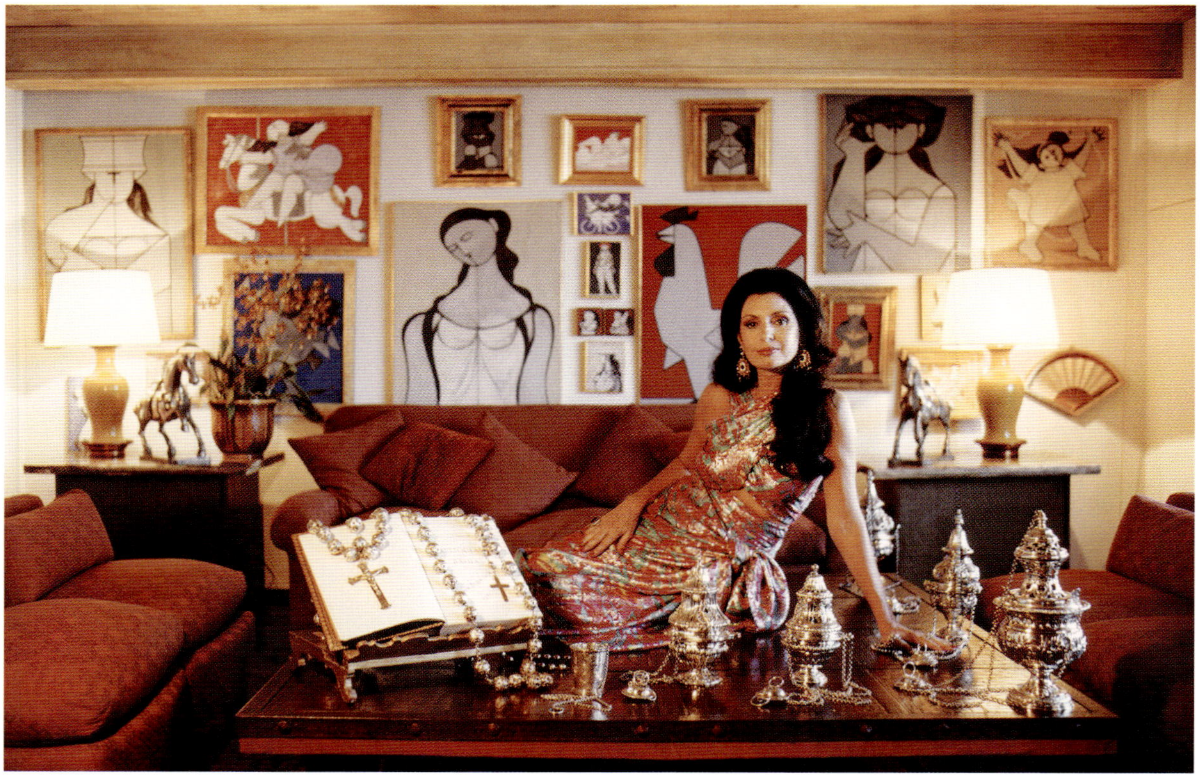

above left Laura Cibrario, Naples, 1985. Recalling the day nearly three decades ago when Slim happened to take her picture, Cibrario said: "I was at my grandmother's house (Villa Leonetti) only by chance because I was in Naples for a ball. . . . I was very young—a teenager—and was very pleased and excited to be photographed, but I was very shy. I brought out the pink dress—the one I planned to wear to the ball. He told me to think of beautiful things with my eyes. I think I looked a little sad in the photo but I wasn't sad at all. In fact, I still remember to this day that I felt, lying there on my grandmother's sofa in a ball gown with my bare feet, for the first time, very grown up, like a woman instead of a girl." Today, Laura Cibrario Franzan is a specialist in the restoration of seventeenth-century paintings and frescoes and is an adviser to the American Academy in Rome.

below left Carmen Mayrink-Veiga, Rio de Janeiro, 1986. Carmen and her husband Antonio were regulars on the Gstaad, Paris, and New York social circuit and were widely thought of as the most fashionable South Americans of their era. Home base was their luxuriously appointed apartment in Rio, a jewel box of artwork and objets d'art collected on travels around the world. Photographed by numerous fashion photographers such as Richard Avedon and Francesco Scavullo, Carmen was also a favorite subject of Slim's—not solely for her command of fashion, but as much for her intrinsic sense of style and glamour and her great confidence and wit.

opposite Nancy Borland, Pebble Beach, California, 1976. She was the daughter of Samuel F. B. Morse, who developed Pebble Beach in 1916; a branch of her family tree included Samuel Morse, inventor of the telegraph.

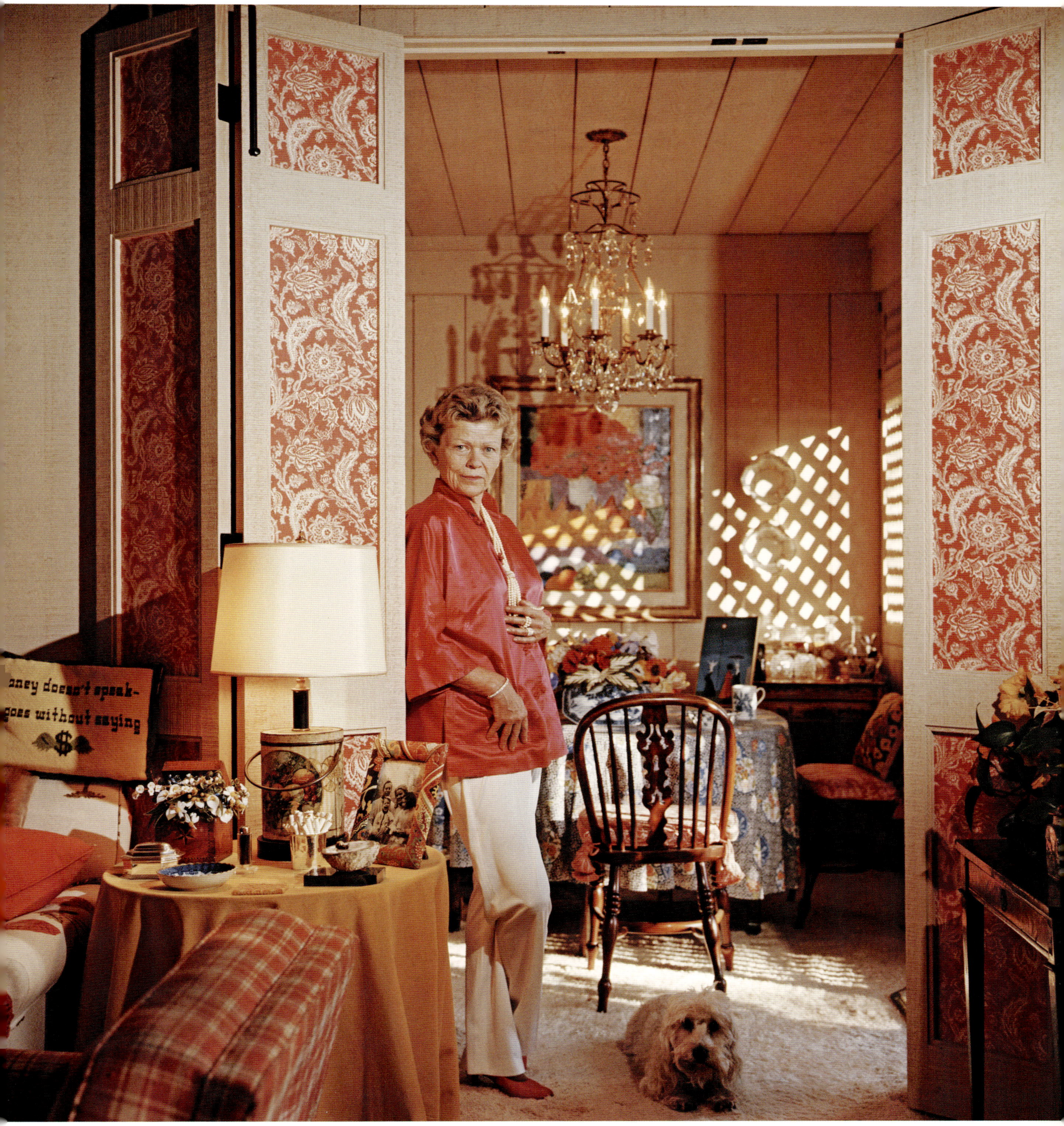
oney doesn't speak-
goes without saying

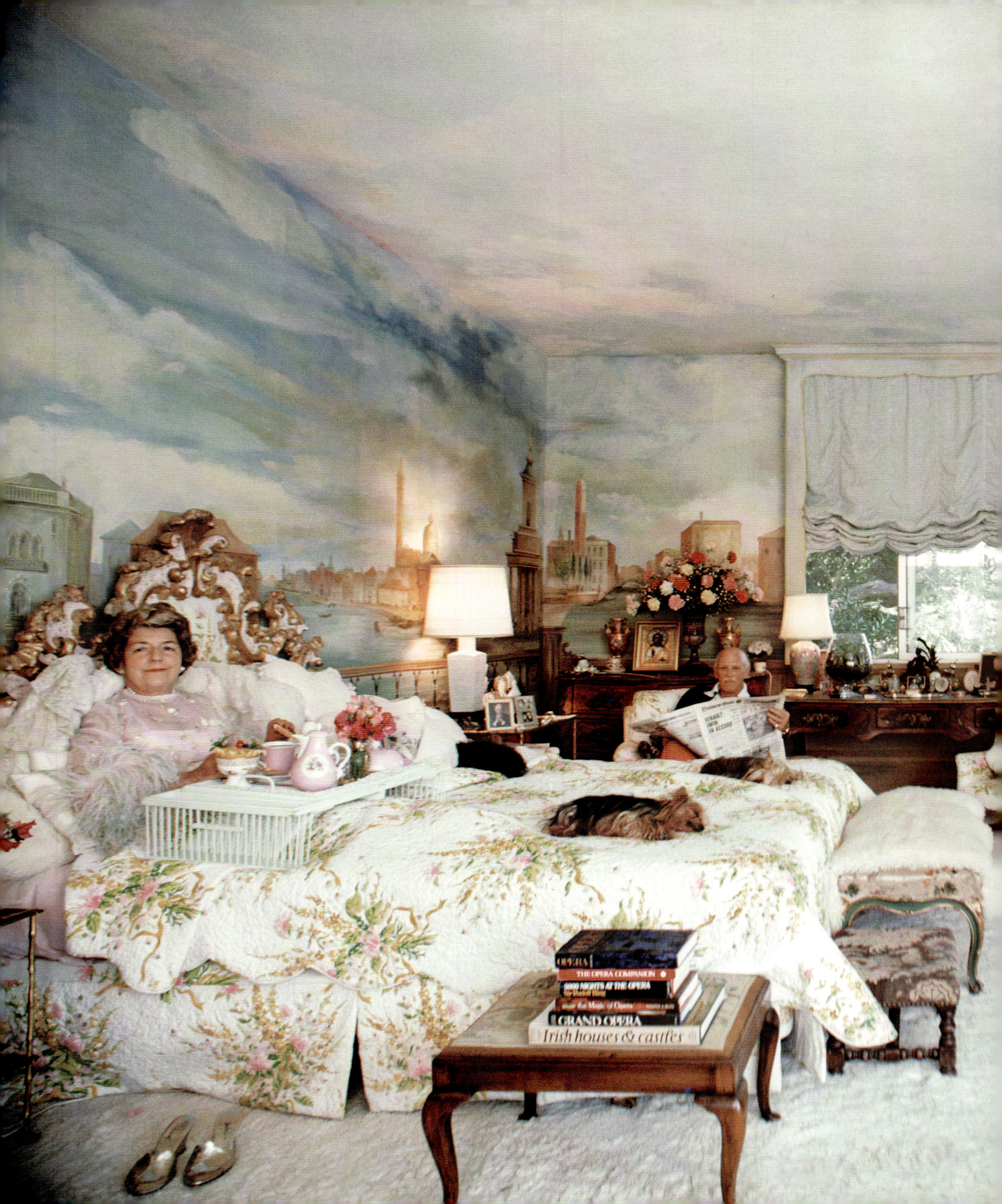
OPERA
THE OPERA COMPANION
NIGHTS AT THE OPERA
GRAND OPERA
Irish houses & castles

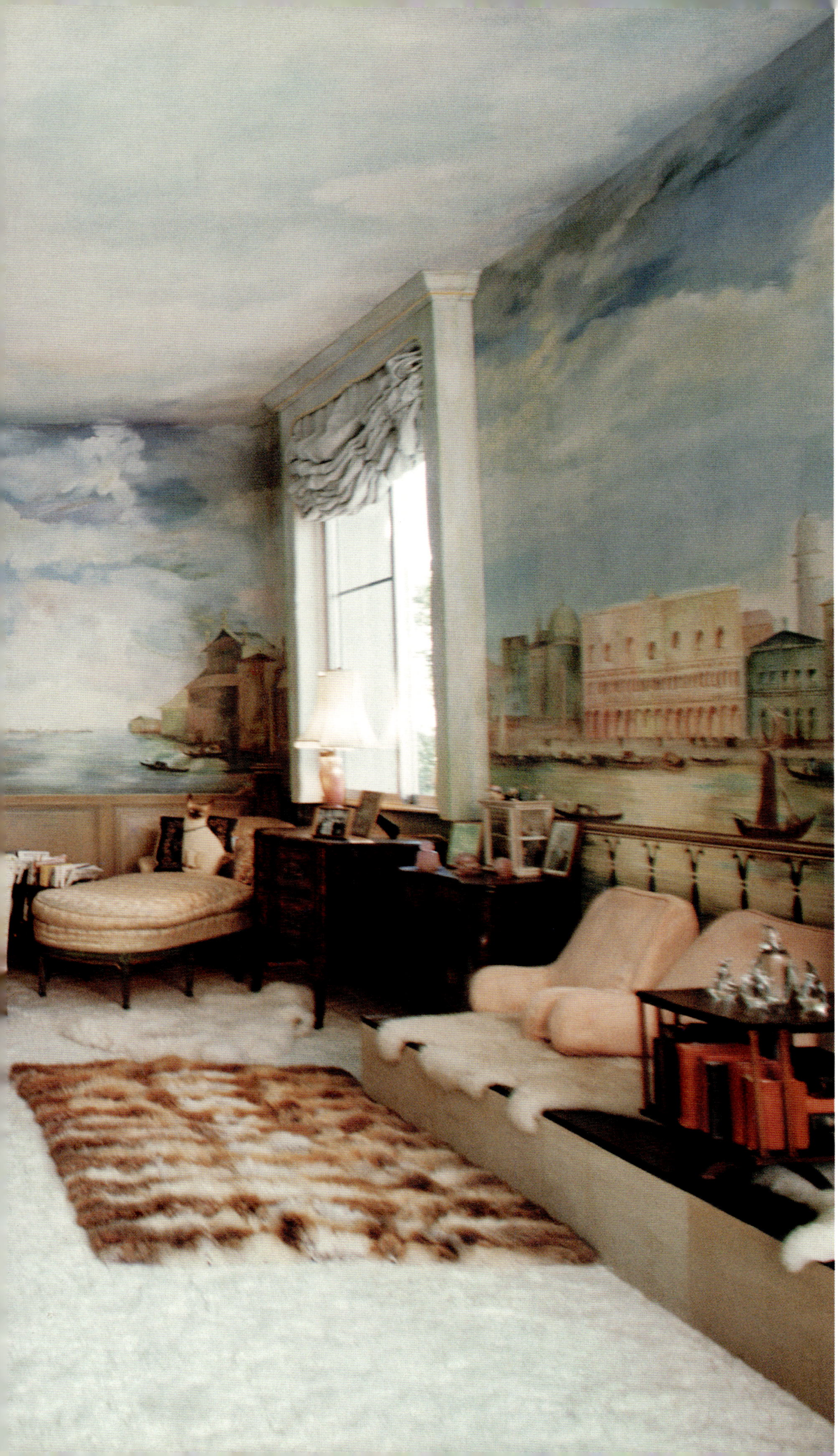

left Mr. and Mrs. Alexander Saunderson in the bedroom of their home in Montecito, an opulent residential enclave of Santa Barbara, 1976. Louise Saunderson, a Newport native, was the granddaughter of socialite Lulu Vanderbilt. The English artist John Sander traveled to Montecito to paint a trompe l'oeil view of Venice, as seen from the Gritti Palace, on their bedroom walls.

below Painter and sculptor Wendy Vanderbilt Lehman, Palm Beach, 1964. Although she never studied art formally, the genes were strong—she is the grandniece of Gertrude Vanderbilt Whitney, the founder of the Whitney Museum of American Art in New York. Her paintings and sculptures are owned by the National Gallery of Art in Washington, D.C., as well as ten other museums. Wendy remembers that while she was growing up, Slim would stop by whenever he was in Palm Beach doing a story: "He came over to the house one day to see my parents, and he asked if he could photograph me. They got me all dressed up and I was so embarrassed. I was around fifteen and at that awkward young stage. Mummy was a great beauty and I was always scowling. He said to my mother, 'Oh, Mollie, in a few years she's going to be such a beauty.' Those were the days when we women were

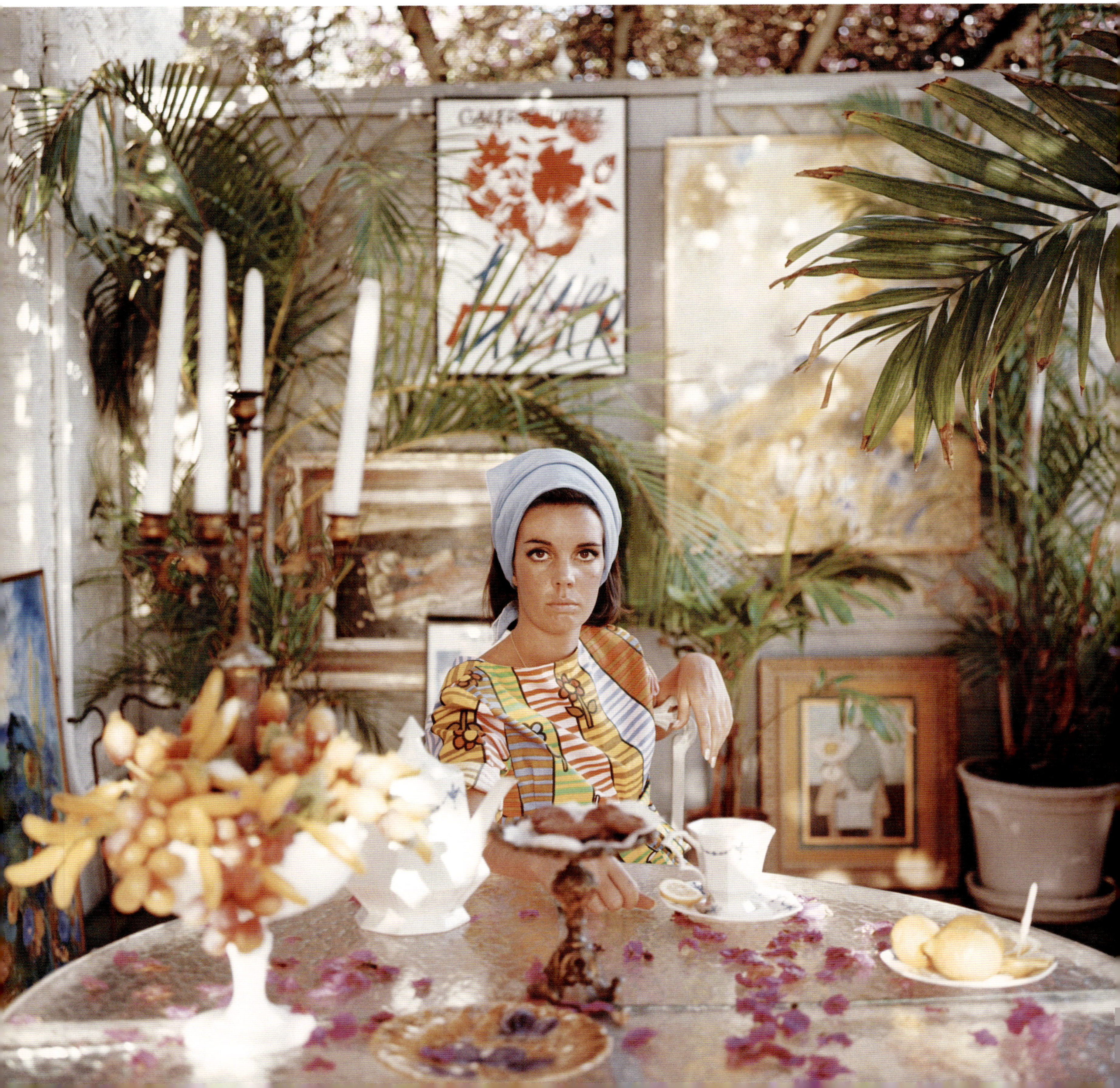

only as lovable as we were pretty. Then the next time he came around and photographed me, he'd say, 'Oh, Mollie, she's going to be such a beauty.' But somehow it wasn't happening! And over the years it became a great joke between me and Slim wherever I ran into him in the world. For years we kidded about it."

below Princess Caroline of Monaco with her dog Tiffany, Monte Carlo, 1977. Slim was very proud of his long friendship with Princess Grace of Monaco, the former Hollywood star Grace Kelly. He was particularly proud when Grace suggested that Caroline work with him, that she'd have trusted him enough to send her daughter traveling around the world with him.

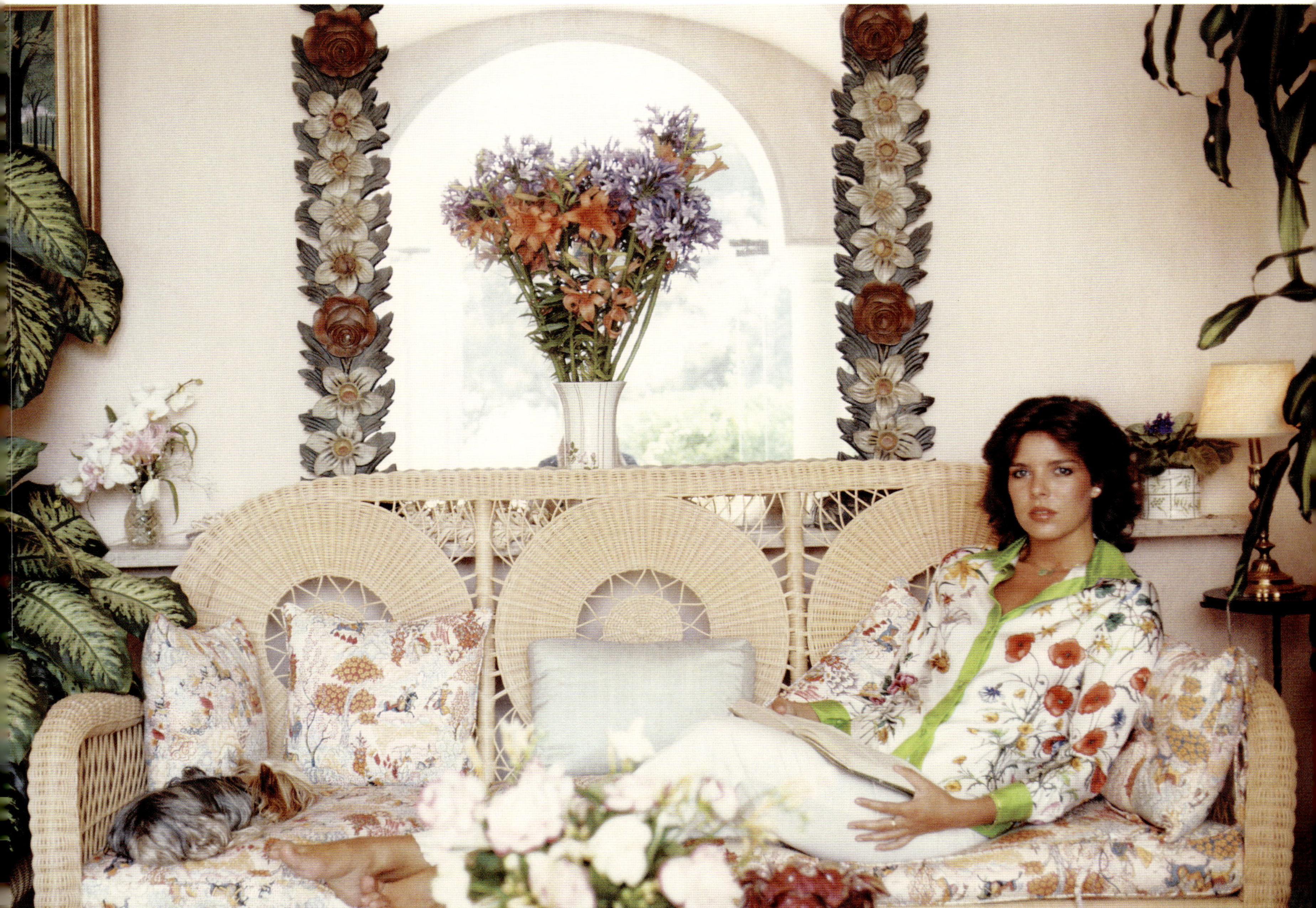

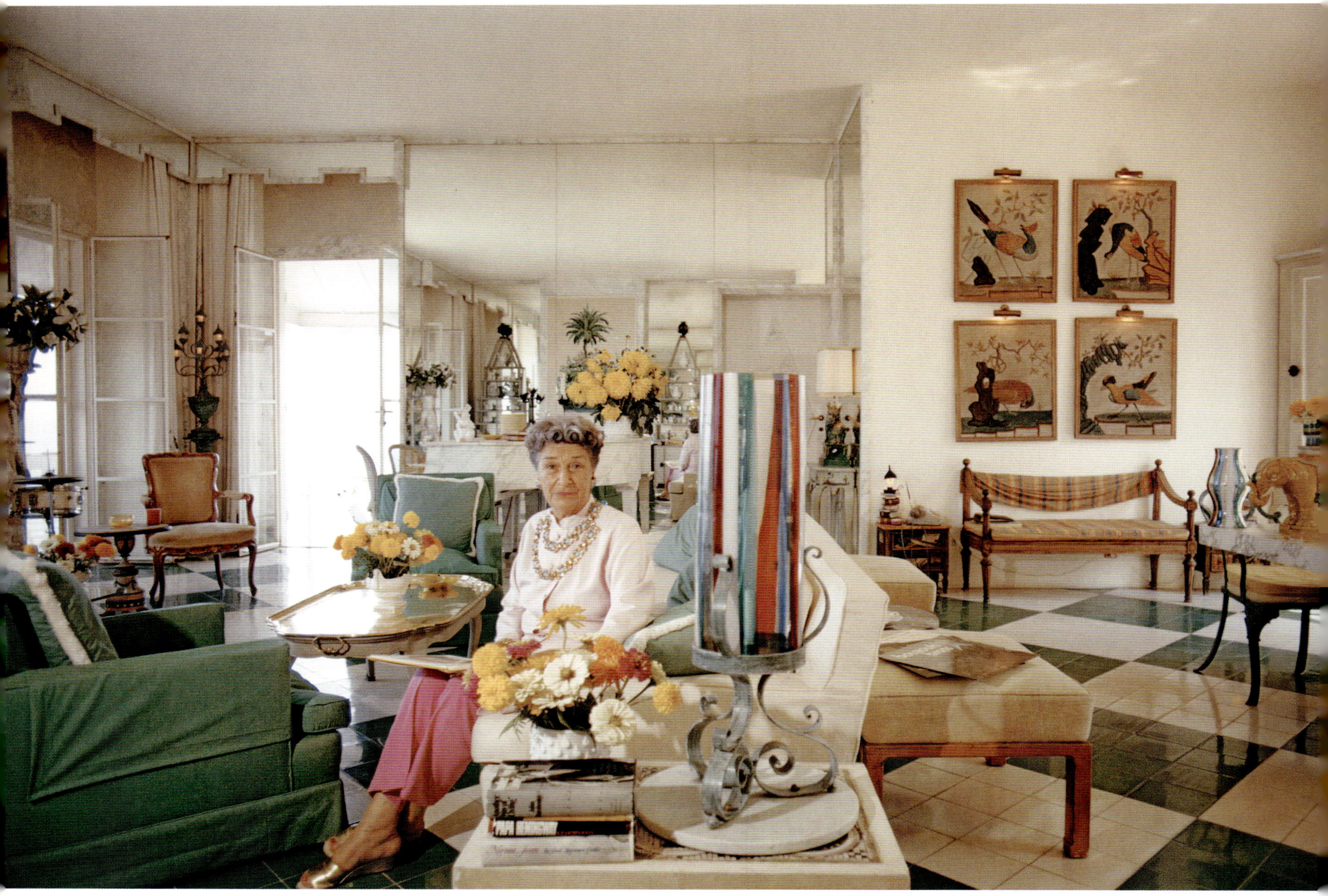

above Countess Lili Gerini at Santa Liberata, the Gerini villa, Porto Ercole, Italy, 1973.

opposite Contessa Giuppi Pietromarchi poses in the garden room at La Ferriera, her family's villa in Capalbio, Italy, 1987.

following spread left The Spanish beauty Gloria Andión against a backdrop of hunting trophies adorning the walls of Castle Židlochovice, Moravia, Czechoslovakia, 1982. Near the present-day Austrian and Slovak borders, the castle dates to the fourteenth century, when it was built along the amber trade path connecting the Mediterranean and Baltic coasts.

following spread right Marion B. "Joe" Carstairs in the museum on her private island, Whale Cay, Bahamas, 1964. Carstairs was born in London in 1900 to the Standard Oil heiress Frances Bostwick and Captain Albert Carstairs. She led an unconventional life, sporting tattoos on both arms, often dressing as a man, and exhibiting a lifelong love of cars, motorboats, speed, and adventure. During World War I she drove ambulances in France

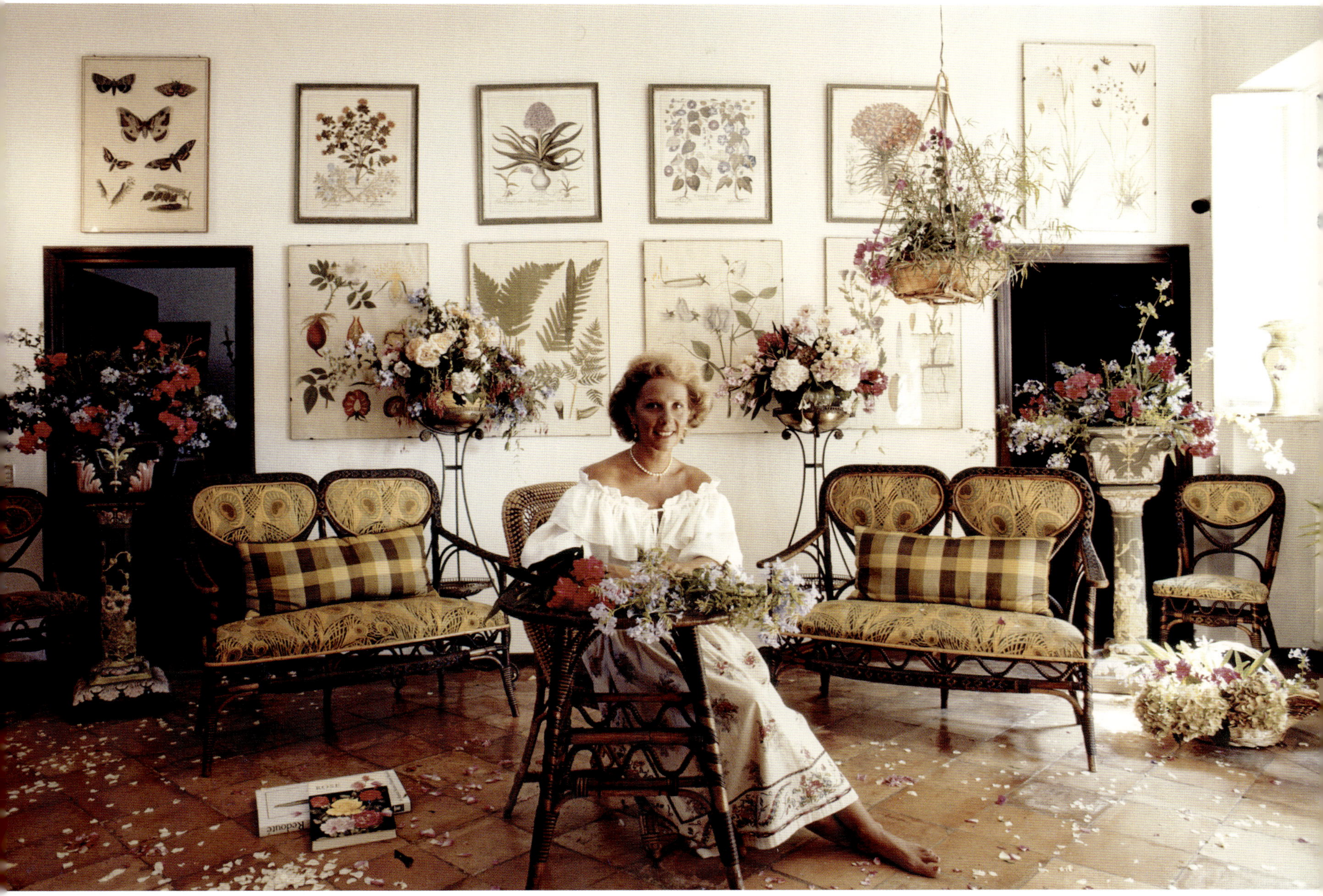

for the American Red Cross, and after the war she started a chauffeur and mechanic service in London that featured a staff of women only. In Paris she entertained Dolly Wilde, Oscar Wilde's niece and fellow ambulance driver, as well as Greta Garbo, Marlene Dietrich, and Tallulah Bankhead. In 1934 she was dubbed "the fastest female speedboat racer in the world" and "the fastest woman on water" by the press. After buying Whale Cay in the Bahamas, she constructed a Great House, where she entertained such guests as Dietrich and the Duke and Duchess of Windsor. She also built a lighthouse, school, church, power plant, radio station, and cannery, and then she acquired the neighboring islands of Bird Cay, Cat Cay, Devil's Cay, and Hoffman's Cay. In his book *A Wonderful Time*, Slim described her this way: "One of the outstanding people in the Berry Islands is Miss Marion B. Carstairs, erect as a marine drill sergeant, who owns and rules her island domain, little Whale Cay, with the cool authority of the absolute monarch. People had told me she would be hostile, but when I contacted her by radiophone and told her I was doing a story, she couldn't have been nicer. She just likes being left alone to do what she wants."

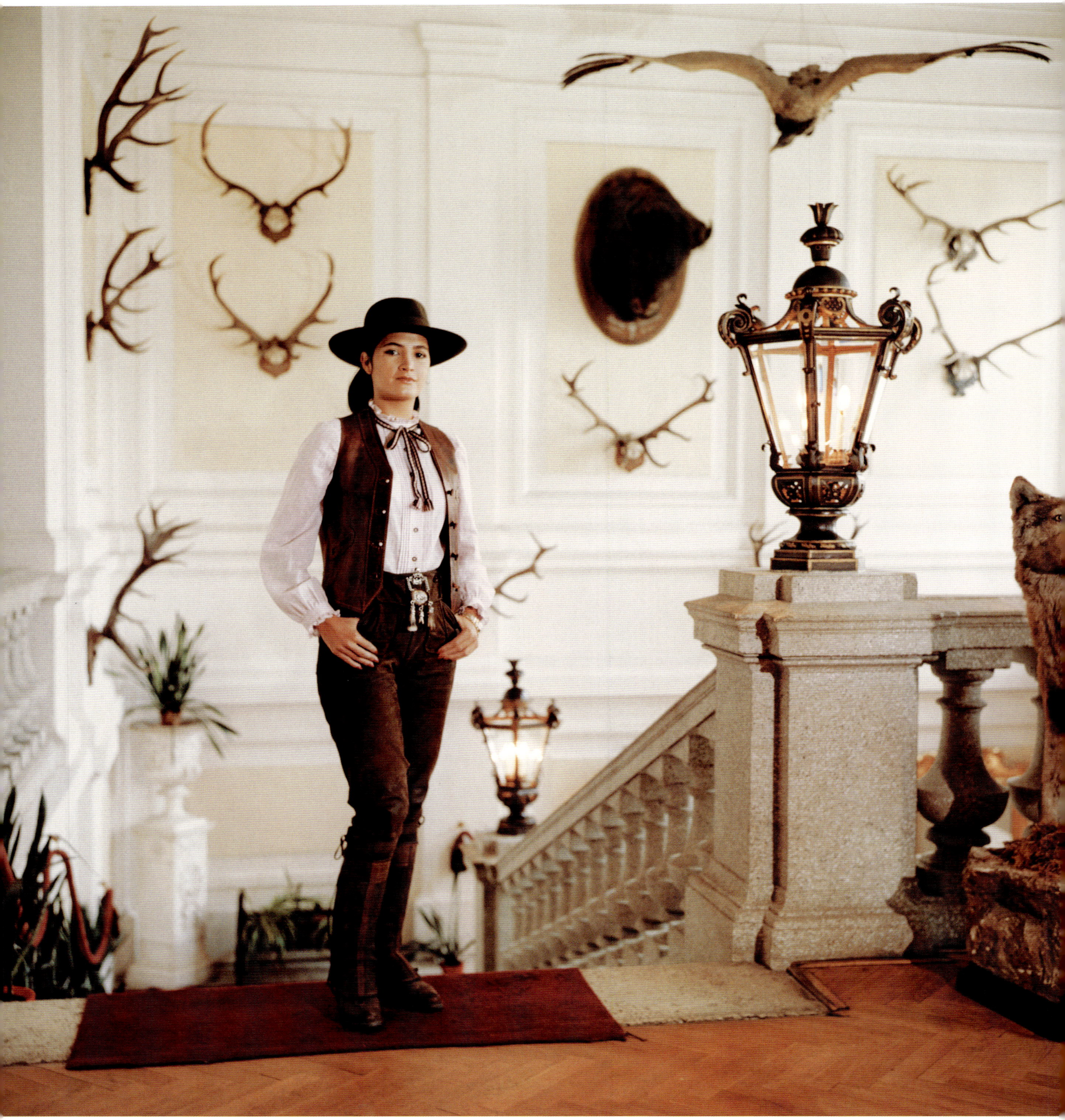

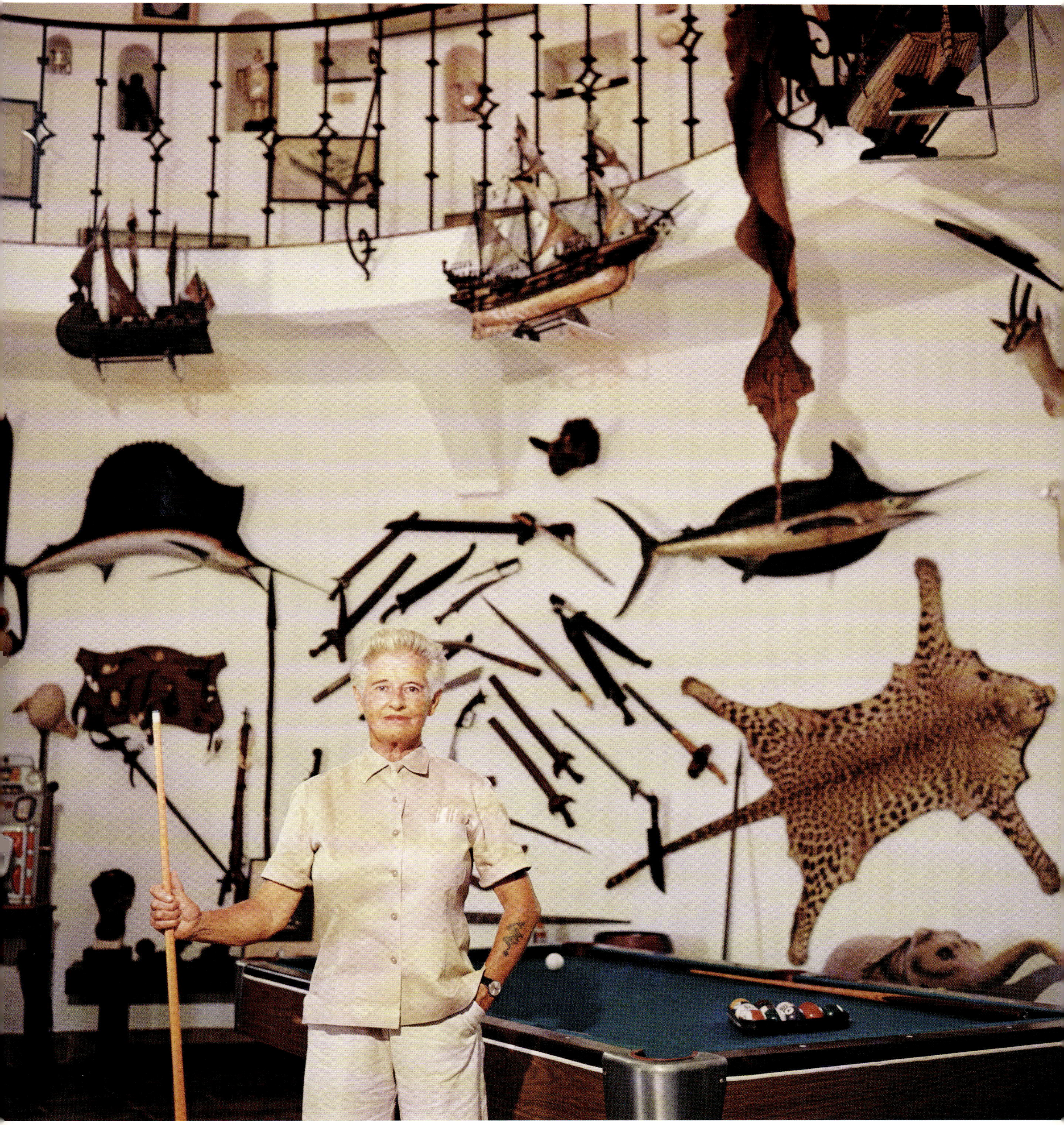

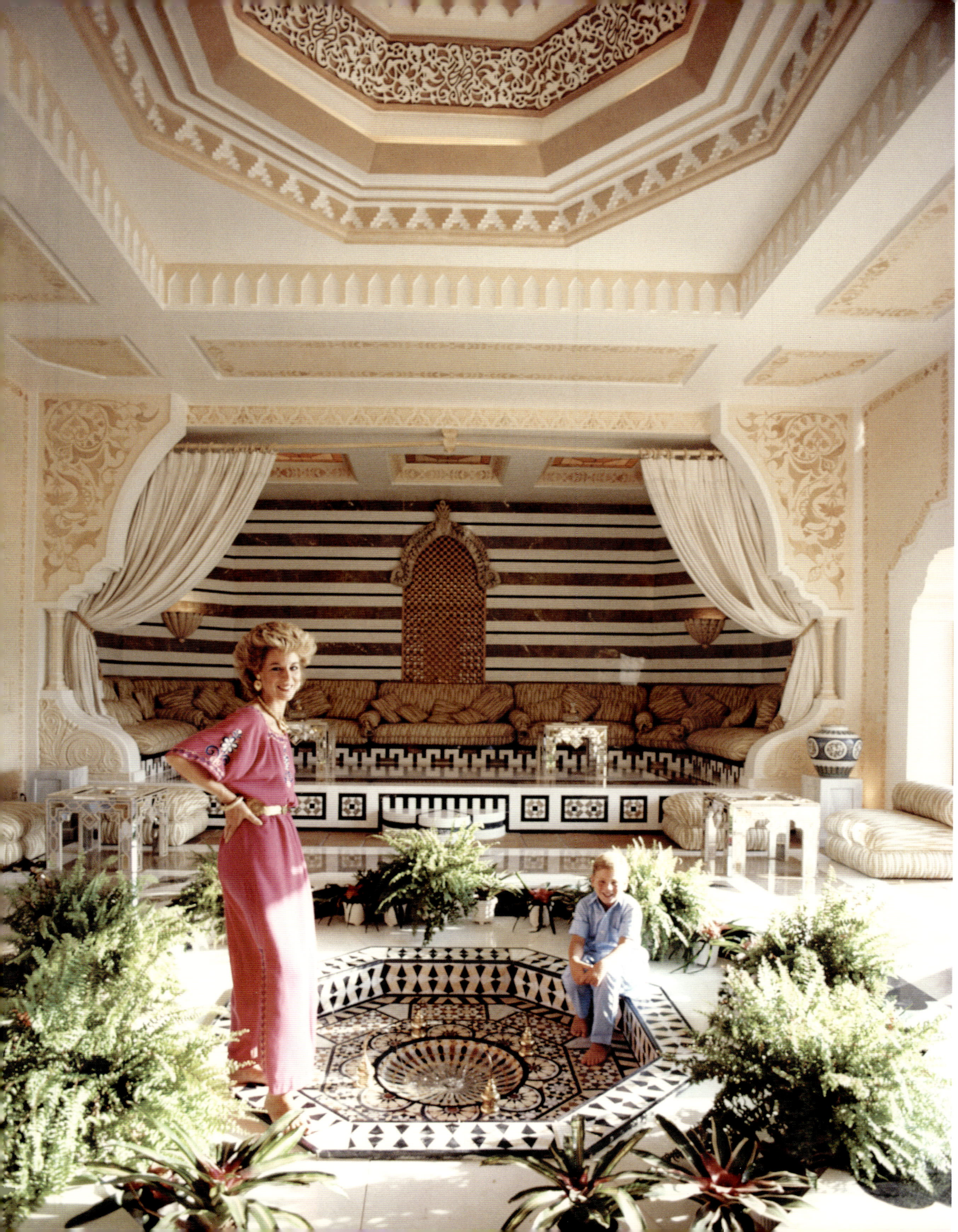

opposite Rosemary Said, wife of the Syrian–Saudi Arabian financier Wafic Said, and their son Khaled, Marbella, Spain, 1983.

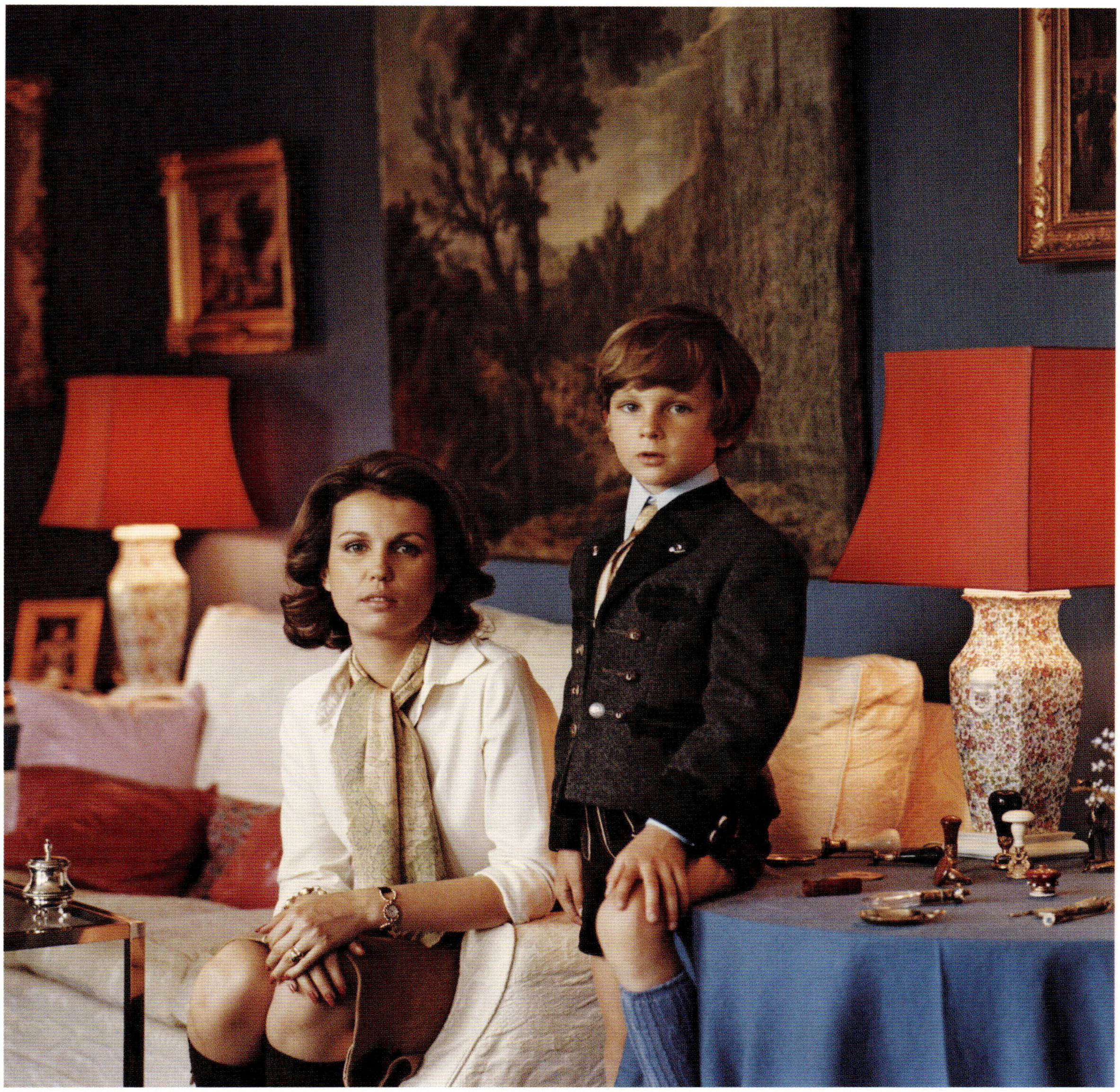

above right Her Serene Highness Gabriela, Fürstin zu Sayn-Wittgenstein-Sayn with her six-year-old son, Heinrich, Koblenz, Germany, 1978. An entrepreneur and philanthropist, the princess established a butterfly garden at the family seat, Sayn Palace, in 1987.

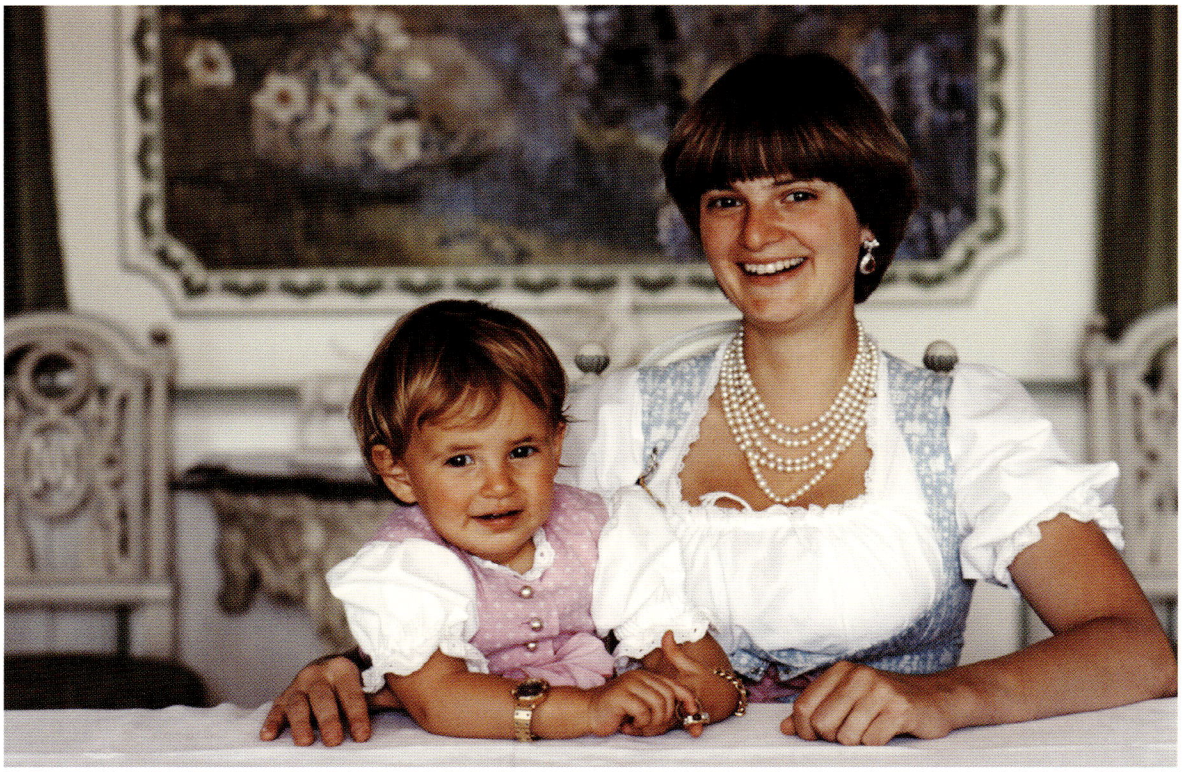

below right Gloria, Princess of Thurn und Taxis and Princess Elisabeth, Regensburg, Germany, 1983. This photo was taken the day after the christening of the princess's newborn son, His Serene Highness Albert II, 12th Prince of Thurn und Taxis. Slim and I were invited to the christening as the only members of the American press because of Slim's long friendship with the infant's father, Johannes, 11th Prince of Thurn und Taxis. The venerated Thurn und Taxis family dates back to twelfth-century Lombardy. Hours after this portrait was finished, there was a knock on my door—we were staying in a small schloss on the grounds of their Regensburg palace. The elderly butler said there was someone to see me. I looked outside and saw a huge Harley-Davidson with a helmeted rider dressed head to toe in black leather. It was Princess Gloria. "Come for a ride through the Bavarian countryside," she beckoned. I graciously declined and she roared off. After her three children were born, the princess became known around the world for her outrageous antics, rock star–studded parties, and lavish lifestyle, earning the nickname "Princess TNT" in the press. Today she is a passionate philanthropist, activist, and businesswoman, widely credited for reorganizing and expanding the family business holdings after the death of her husband in 1990.

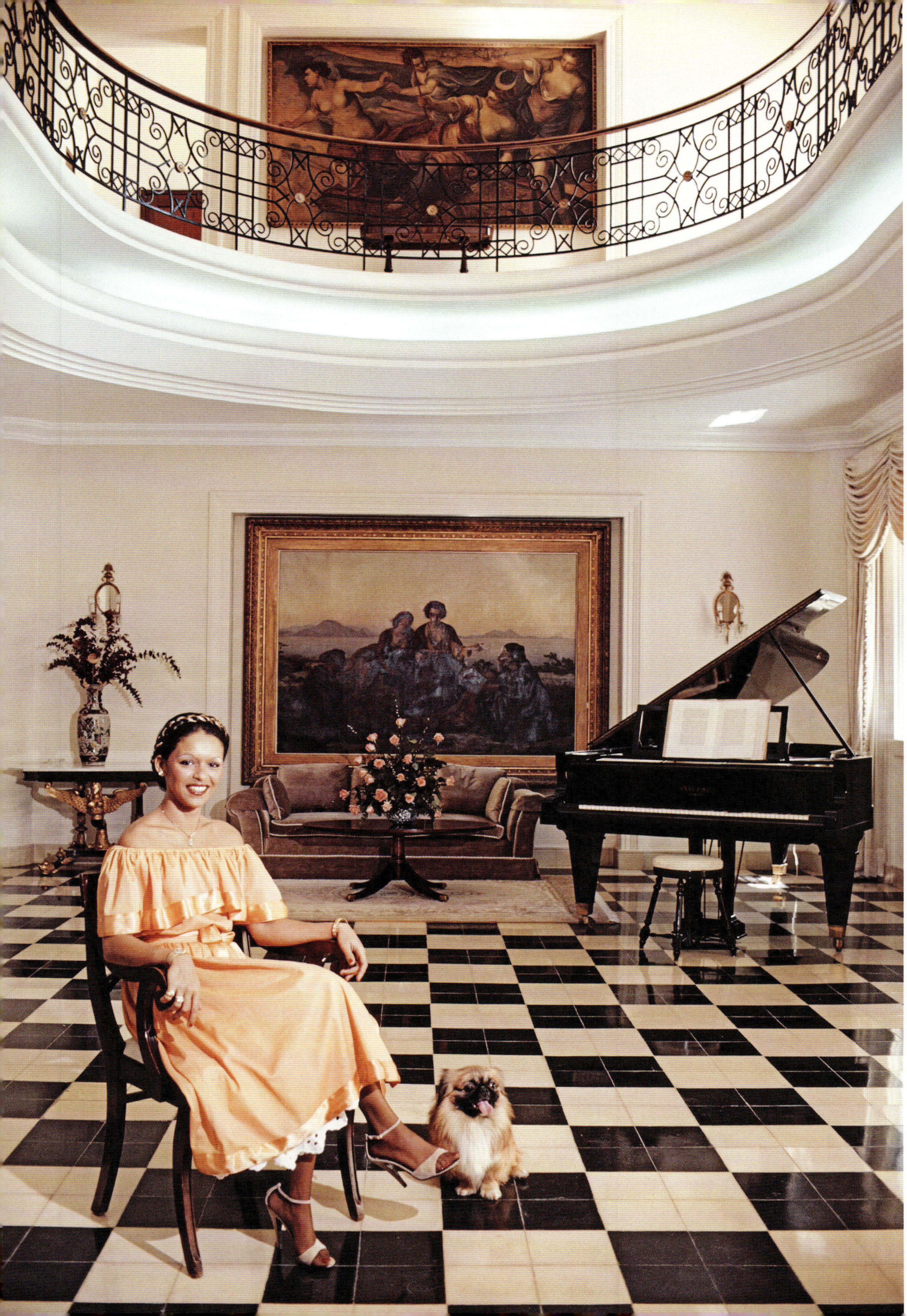

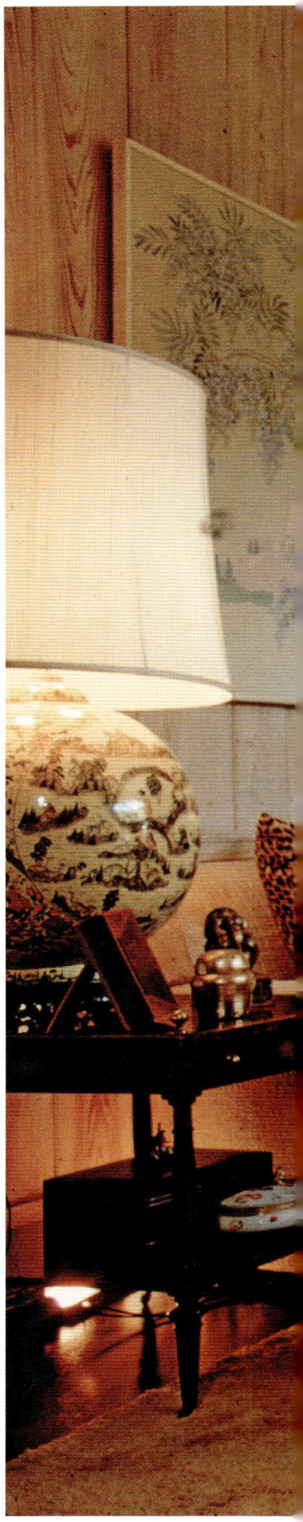

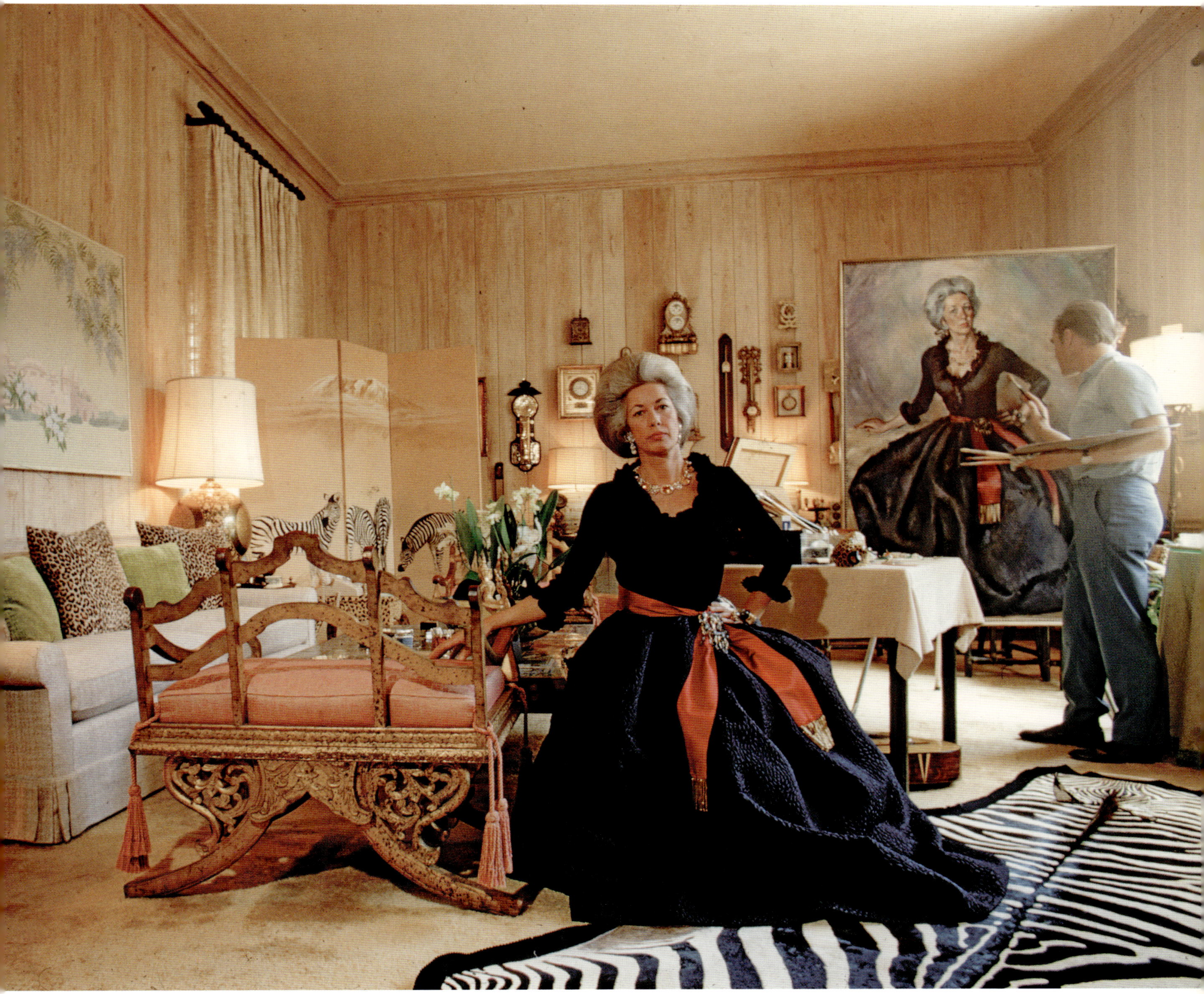

opposite Michèle Bennett, wife of the then president of Haiti, Jean-Claude Duvalier, Haiti, 1981.

above Dysie Davie at home in Palm Beach, 1970. When the exuberant Dysie Davie passed away in 2008, several years after her husband Buddy (E. T. Bedford Davie), her family placed an obituary in the *Palm Beach Post* that read: "Diana Marion Wing Davie, known to all as Dysie, was born in New York City and the date is no one's business. Dysie survived all four of her husbands. Dysie credits this to full-bodied wines, expensive vodka, and dealing with everyday life and people, no matter what you are dealt. Dysie and her last husband of 44 years, Buddy Davie, owned and managed '343 Worth Avenue,' an exquisite custom jewelry and objets d'art emporium. Mrs. Davie, responsible for all custom jewelry designs, was never given full recognition due to Buddy always taking credit for her ideas."

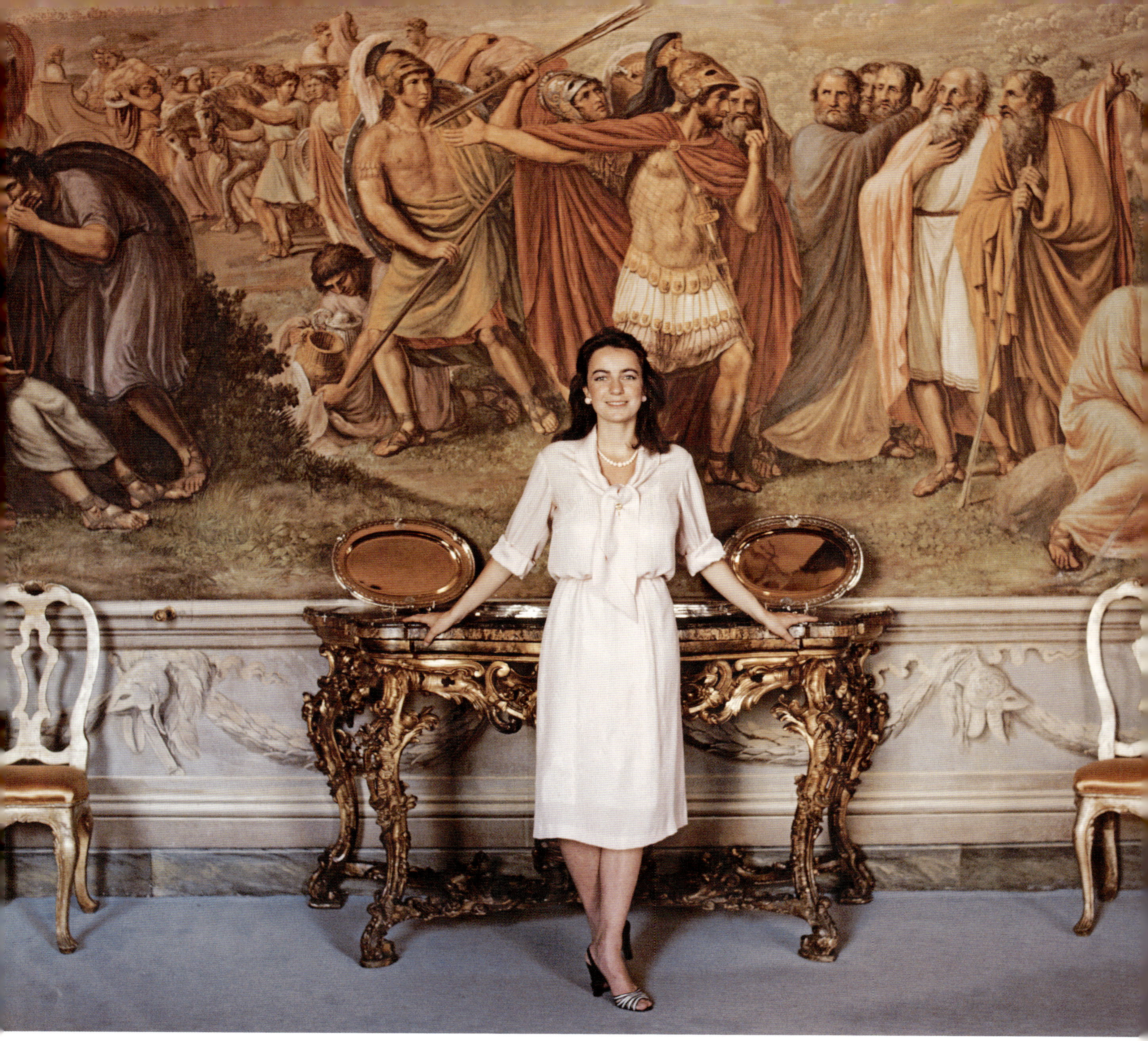

above Laudomia Pucci, Florence, Italy, 1991. A few years before this photo was taken, Laudomia Pucci stepped into the CEO job of the company her ailing father, Emilio Pucci, had started in 1947. His signature brightly colored, kaleidoscopic patterns added a much-needed elegance to the 1960s mod fashion scene. The company was originally sited in Florence at the Palazzo Pucci, a Renaissance palace owned by the family ever since they were advisers to the Medici family in the 1400s. Laudomia Pucci now serves as the brand's image director and deputy chairman, and the company operates out of Granaiolo, the family's one-hundred-fifty-acre country estate south of Florence.

opposite The Duchess of Buccleuch and Queensberry in the hall of Boughton House, Kettering, Northamptonshire, England, 1958. Her husband is the 8th Duke of Buccleuch and the 10th Duke of Queensberry, both peerages created in the seventeenth century. Their lavish and substantial collection of art makes Boughton House—one of their four residences—a kind of private museum, drawing connoisseurs from all corners of the world.

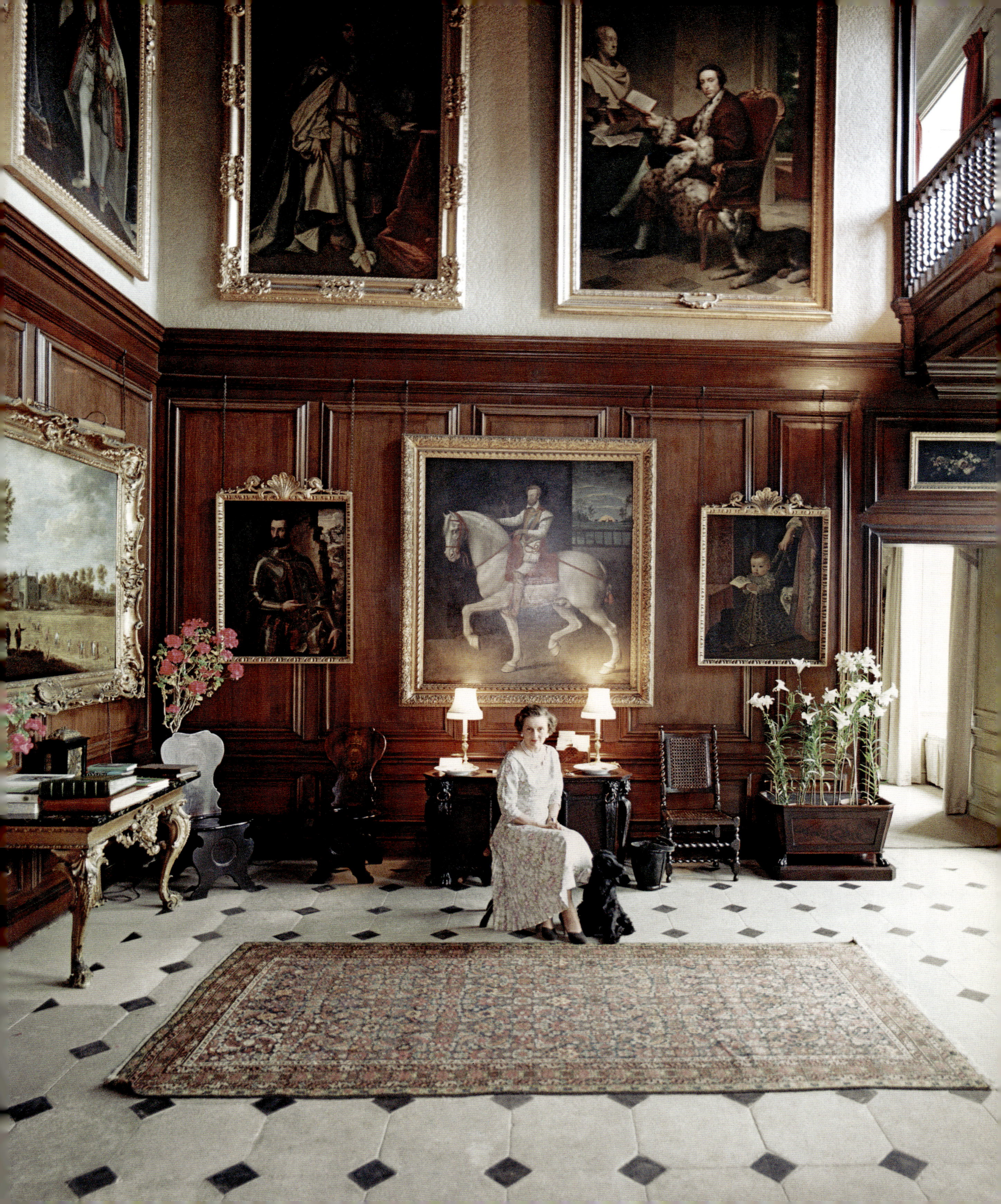

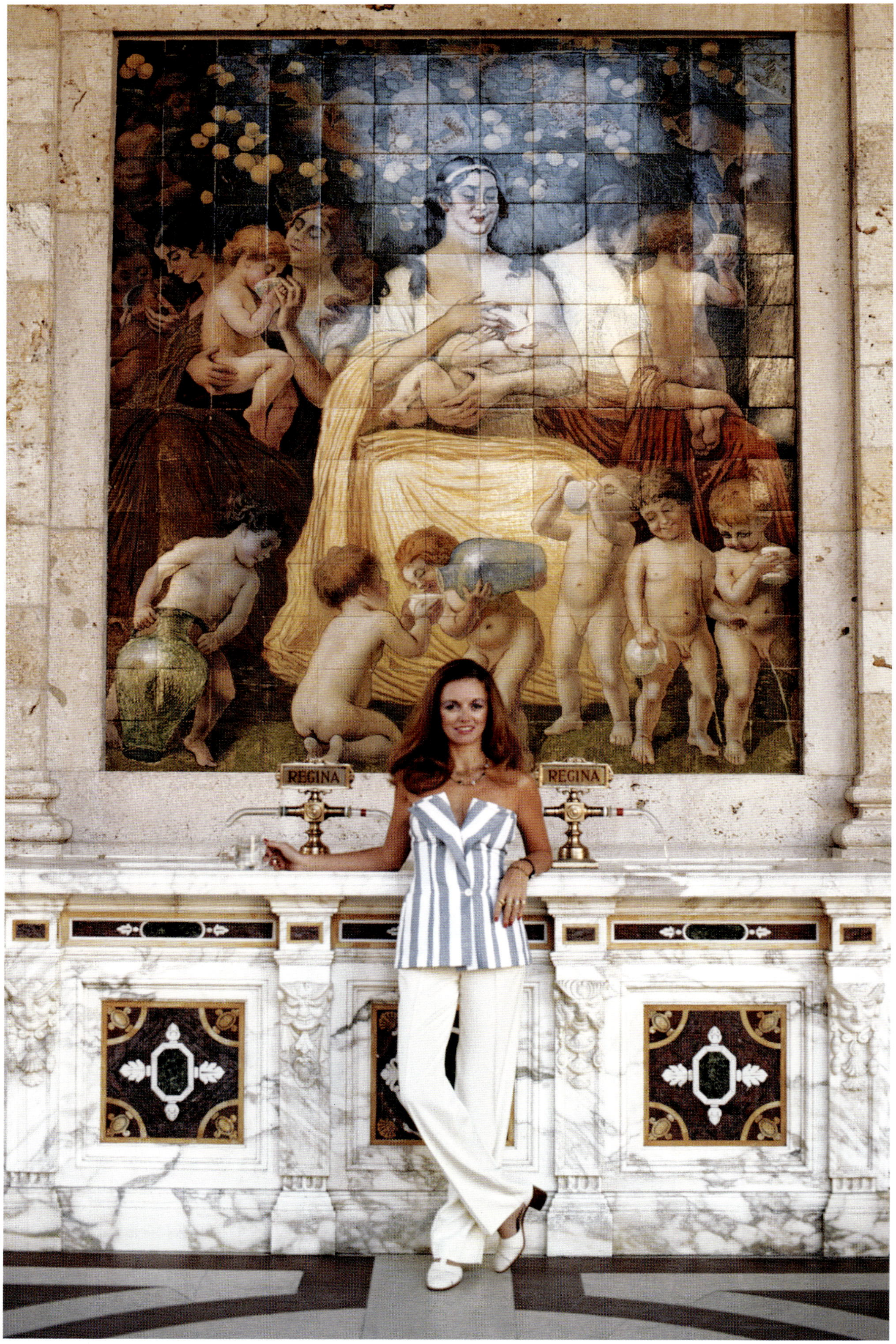

left Marie-Louise Mills Sciò at the Terme Tettuccio in Montecatini, Italy, 1980. The Sciò family home in Rome, where Marie-Louise and her husband Roberto Sciò resided, was always one of the first stops Slim made each time he arrived in Italy. He photographed not only every member of their family, but also frequently at their family hotels, including the fabled Hotel Il Pellicano in Porto Ercole and the seventeenth-century Hotel La Posta Vecchia, outside Rome on the Tyrrhenian Sea, the former home of the American industrialist J. Paul Getty.

opposite Donna Stefanella Vanni Calvello di San Vincenzo in her family's residence, Palazzo Gangi, Palermo, 1984. After arriving for our appointment for this shoot, Stefanella showed us around the eighteenth-century palazzo, which has been compared to Versailles. She led us past the closed doors of a darkened hall. Slim's reliable instincts told him to ask if we could see what was behind the doors. We entered and she threw open several massive shuttered windows. All at once we were standing in a gilded, wood-carved room called the Hall of Mirrors, which had been the focal point of Sicilian Belle Epoque society. I'd never seen anything like it in my life and was fairly certain Slim hadn't either. He knew he had to take the photograph here, but he preferred natural light and rarely traveled with lighting equipment. We searched for every imaginable light source—every shutter thrown open, every chandelier and sconce lighted, even the doors to adjacent rooms opened—to catch every extra ray.

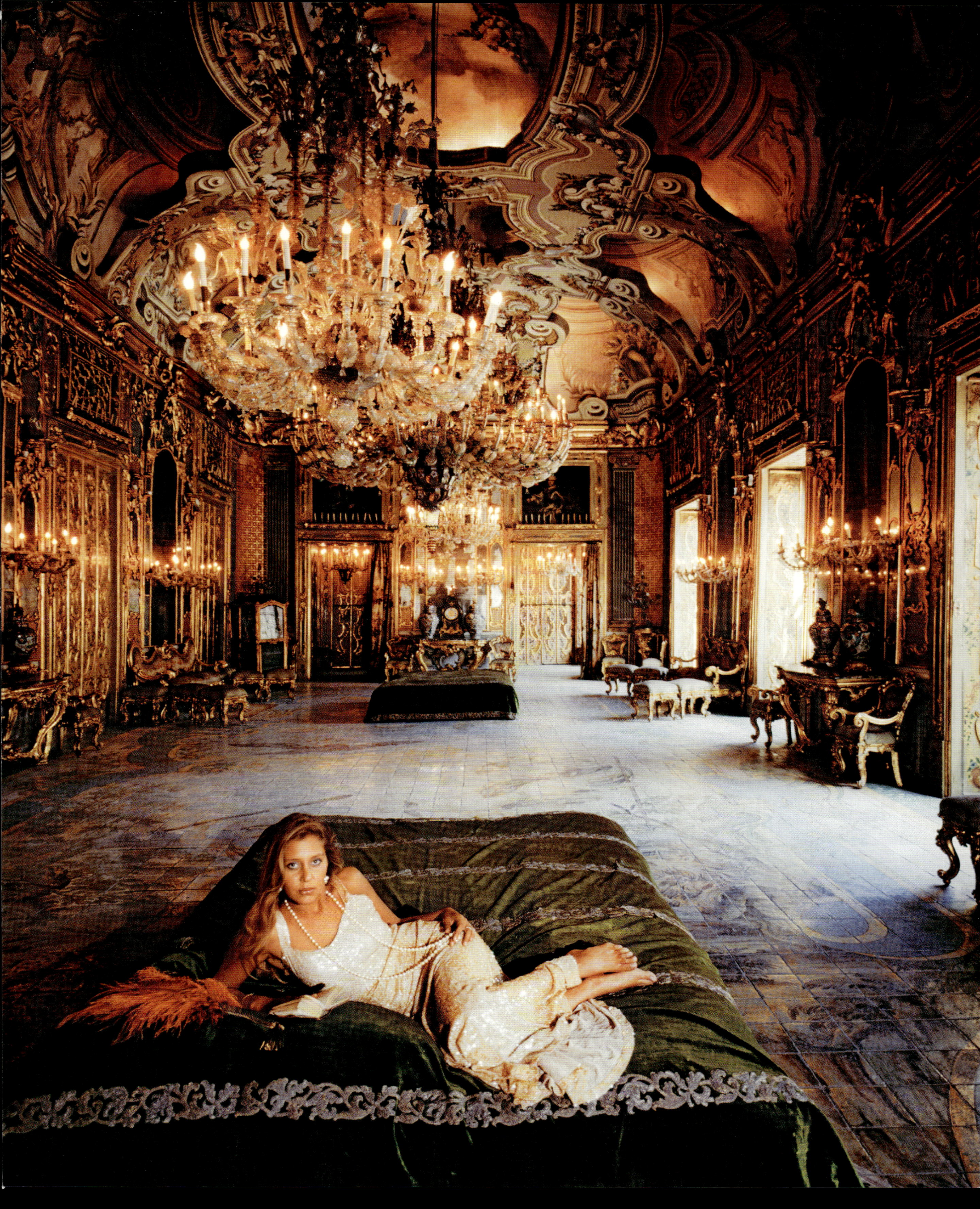

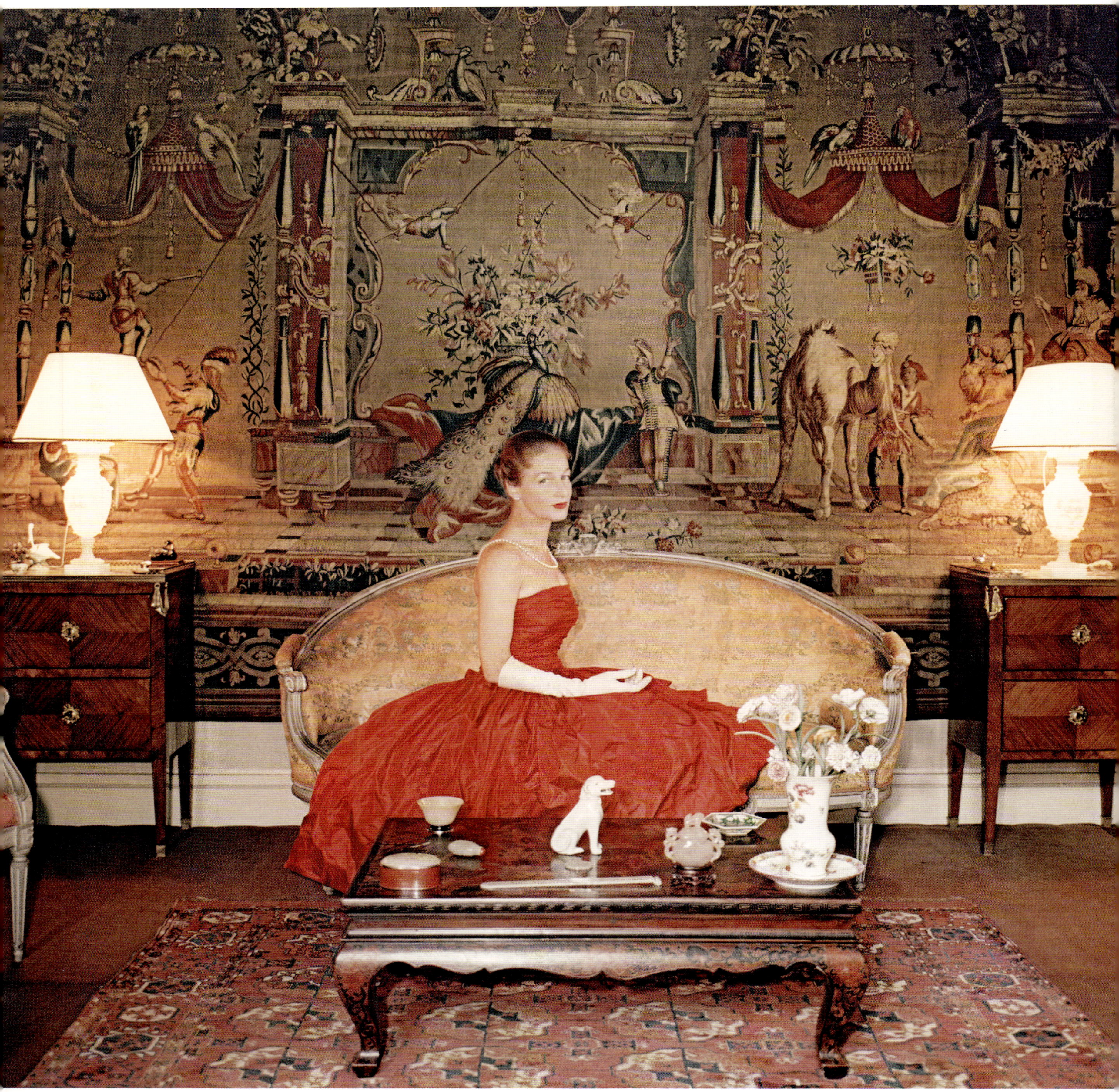

above The Duchess of Montesquieu-Fezensac, Neuilly, France, 1957. The holder of a doctor of medicine degree, the duchess was recognized as one of the most beautiful and well-dressed women in France. In the drawing room of her château in the Parisian suburb of Neuilly is a seventeenth-century Beauvais tapestry and on the Chinese table in the foreground are rare, eighteenth-century Fleurs de Saxe.

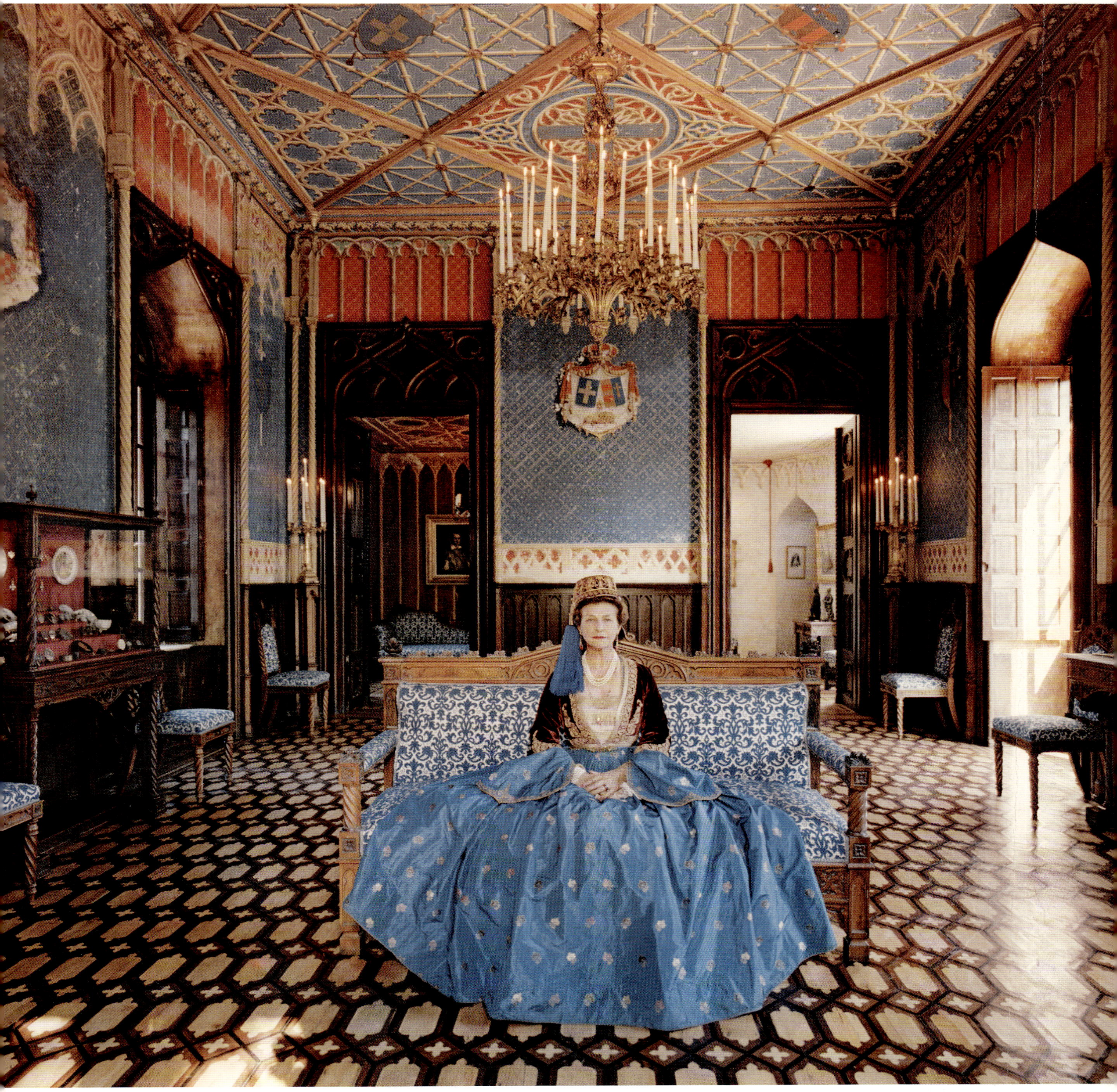

above Madame Jean Serpieri, wearing a gown that belonged to the wife of Otto, the first king of modern Greece, in the ballroom of Tour La Reine, Athens, 1961. Because it has only one distinctive tower, the neo-Gothic castle is called the Queen's Tower—Tour La Reine. It was built for Otto's wife, Queen Amalia, and used as a summer home by the royal family.

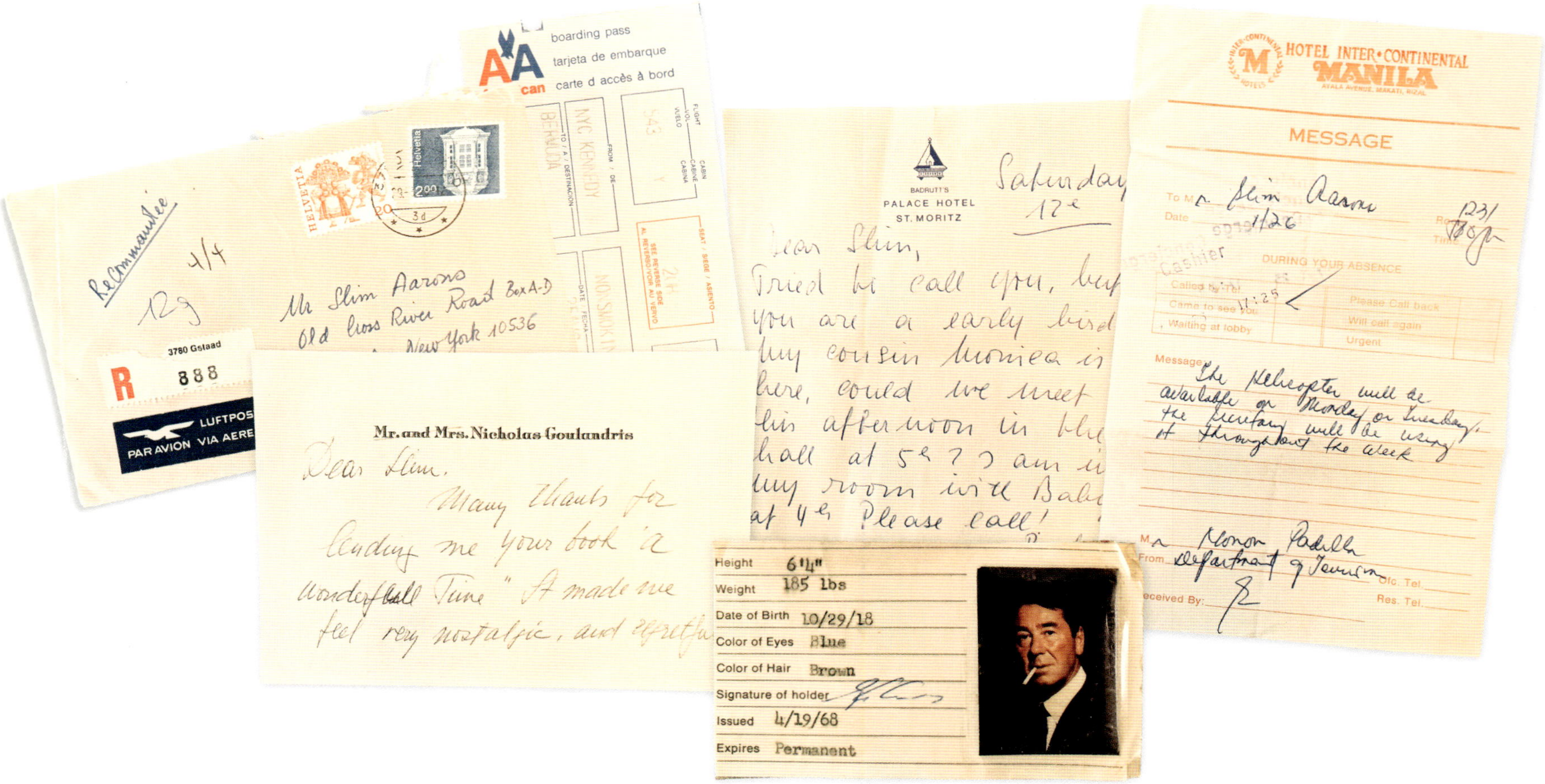

ACKNOWLEDGMENTS

For their professional guidance and encouragement: William Abranowicz, Eric Himmel, Erin Joslyn, Andrea Raisfeld, and Patricia Williams.

For their research and resourcefulness: At Getty Images—Scott Rosen, Allen Stephens, Caroline Theakstone, Brian Doherty, and Alex Timms. At Abrams—Laura Dozier, for keeping all of the balls in the air and keeping us on track, Sarah Gifford, whose flexibility and enthusiasm was unflagging, and Gabby Fisher for her good judgement and tenacity.

For their contributions: Mary Aarons, Janet Carlson, Laura Cibrario, Olimpia Gaetani, Maria Janis, Wendy Vanderbilt Lehman, Kathryn Livingston, Michele Mazzolla, Marie Louise Mills, and Gloria Sidnam.

Special thanks to Eric Rachlis and Andrea Danese for trusting me with the project and to Chris Sweet for paving the way.

And finally, with great fondness, to Slim Aarons, whose good faults always outweighed his bad faults.

above Slim Aarons at his most basic was an old world newspaperman who lived to bring home the story. Among his private papers he left behind a treasure trove of material related to this work. He not only kept every bar tab, letter, passport photo, hotel bill, luggage tag, boarding ticket, and phone message from every story assignment he'd ever been given, he left them all fastidiously archived by year and location. The resulting cache of memorabilia is a visual chronicle of his nearly half-century of life on the road. Pictured here are a few pieces from his files.

Editor: Laura Dozier
Designer: Sarah Gifford
Production Manager: Denise LaCongo
Project Director: Eric Rachlis

Library of Congress Control Number: 2015955625
ISBN: 978-1-4197-2242-4

Printed and bound in China
10 9 8 7 6 5 4 3

Abrams books are available at special discounts when purchased in quantity for premiums and promotions as well as fundraising or educational use. Special editions can also be created to specification. For details, contact specialsales@abramsbooks.com or the address below.

ABRAMS
The Art of Books
115 West 18th Street
New York, NY 10011
abramsbooks.com